CasebookConnect.com

REGISTER NOW to access the Study Center for:

- Hundreds of practice questions
- Selections from popular study aids
- Progress trackers to save you time
- Tutorial videos

Combine this wealth of resources with an **enhanced ebook** and **outlining tool** and you will **SUCCEED** in law school

Use this unique code to connect your casebook today

Go to www.casebookconnect.com and redeem your access code to get started.

PLEASE NOTE: Each access code can only be used once. This access code will expire one year after the discontinuation of the corresponding print title and must be redeemed before then. CCH reserves the right to discontinue this program at any time for any business reason. For further details, please see the Casebook Connect End User License Agreement.

PIN9111149081   28899

PROPERTY

ASPEN CASEBOOK SERIES

PROPERTY

CASES, PROBLEMS, AND SKILLS

CHRISTINE A. KLEIN

Chesterfield Smith Professor of Law
University of Florida Levin College of Law

Published by Wolters Kluwer in New York.

Wolters Kluwer Legal & Regulatory Solutions U.S. serves customers worldwide with CCH, Aspen Publishers, and Kluwer Law International products. (www.WKLegaledu.com)

To contact Customer Service, e-mail customer.service@wolterskluwer.com, call 1-800-234-1660, fax 1-800-901-9075, or mail correspondence to:

Wolters Kluwer
Attn: Order Department
PO Box 990
Frederick, MD 21705

Printed in the United States of America.

2 3 4 5 6 7 8 9 0

ISBN 978-1-4548-6803-3

Library of Congress Cataloging-in-Publication Data

Names: Klein, Christine A., 1956- author.
Title: Property : cases, problems, and skills / Christine A. Klein, Chesterfield Smith
    Professor of Law, University of Florida Levin College of Law.
Description: New York: Wolters Kluwer, 2016. | Series: Aspen coursebook series
Identifiers: LCCN 2016001706 | ISBN 9781454868033
Subjects: LCSH: Property—United States. | LCGFT: Casebooks.
Classification: LCC KF560 .K58 2016 | DDC 346.7304—dc23
LC record available at http://lccn.loc.gov/2016001706

About Wolters Kluwer Legal & Regulatory Solutions U.S.

Wolters Kluwer Legal & Regulatory Solutions U.S. delivers expert content and solutions in the areas of law, corporate compliance, health compliance, reimbursement, and legal education. Its practical solutions help customers successfully navigate the demands of a changing environment to drive their daily activities, enhance decision quality and inspire confident outcomes.

Serving customers worldwide, its legal and regulatory solutions portfolio includes products under the Aspen Publishers, CCH Incorporated, Kluwer Law International, ftwilliam.com and MediRegs names. They are regarded as exceptional and trusted resources for general legal and practice-specific knowledge, compliance and risk management, dynamic workflow solutions, and expert commentary.

For Mark, with love

SUMMARY OF CONTENTS

CONTENTS

Welcome to the study of property law. I hope that you enjoy using this book as much as I enjoyed writing it. Property involves more than the ownership of things by people. Instead, it involves a rich tapestry of *human relationships* with respect to things. As a reminder of this relational nature of property, the text moves outward from a consideration of the rights of individual owners (Part One), to the overlapping rights and duties of multiple owners of shared property (Part Two), to the process of transferring property from one owner to another (Part Three), to the accommodation of private rights and the public interest through contractual, common law, statutory, and constitutional law provisions (Part Four).

The text raises four recurrent themes to highlight tensions inherent in property law and to encourage students to think more broadly about property as a unified discipline: (1) a bundle of sticks vs. a web of interests (suggesting the tension between individual rights and the public interest); (2) the importance of place (highlighting the tension between property as a market commodity and as a place capable of fostering personhood and community interactions); (3) "just passing through" (raising the issue of "dead hand control"); and (4) "a changing world" (addressing the tension between traditional, stable property principles and changing social and physical landscapes).

Pedagogical Features

This text offers a number of innovative features designed to make the study of property law fresh and engaging. All are contained in the printed text for easy access.

"A Place to Start" text boxes and follow-up problems: As an entry point to complex doctrines, *A Place to Start* text boxes give an overview of legal rules as a reference that should be consulted often. Most boxes invite students to "dig deeper" by highlighting ambiguity and subtleties that deserve further consideration. By providing an overview of the law upfront, the text equips students with the framework necessary to maximize their understanding of the case law

that follows, and allows instructors to move through basic doctrines quickly and focus on more nuanced questions. Subsequent *Test Your Understanding* problems provide an opportunity for students to tease out additional detail through self-directed learning, or a reservoir of problems that the class can work through together.

Reading guide: Each case is preceded by a reading guide to help students place the cases into the broader context of the chapter.

Beyond the black letter discussion problems: Each chapter features an emerging contemporary challenge that will impact and potentially reshape property law. Topics include the sharing economy, cybersquatting, mobile apps for city parking, climate change, real estate bubbles, drones, urban agriculture, and others.

Sample documents: The text contains numerous property documents and focused questions that encourage students to study those documents carefully. Examples include a lease, a contract for the purchase of real estate, a general warranty deed, and an easement agreement.

Chapter reviews: Each chapter offers students a variety of review problems (both multiple-choice and essay) with answers supplied in the casebook Appendix.

Statutory practice: Statutes, uniform state laws, and Restatement sections are judiciously reproduced in stand-alone sections, rather than scattered in snippets throughout the chapter. Such excerpts show students the interplay between common law and statutory law, and provide opportunities to develop the skill of close statutory reading and interpretation. Selections include the Fair Housing Act, the Uniform Partition of Heirs Property Act, The Restatement (Second) of Torts, Nuisance, and others. In addition, each chapter review contains a "Bringing It Home" section that suggests important topics of state statutory law that students might want to research for their home jurisdictions (including guidance about the skill of statutory research).

Visual learning: The text features dozens of two-color photographs, timelines, figures, and other visual aids to facilitate learning. Each chapter opens with a map showing the location where each of the chapter's cases took place. This serves as a visual geographic table of contents, and also as a reminder that property disputes can be heavily influenced by the places where they arose (majority or minority jurisdiction? private property or public shop? newly discovered continent or outer space?).

Skills exercises: Each chapter includes a skills exercise that provides a group exercise that can be completed in one class session or less. Skills include the following:

Category	Skill	Chapter
Legal analysis	Fact-based argument	1
	Precedent-based argument	1
	Policy-based argument	2 (conditional gifts) 10 (common interest communities)
	Statutory analysis	2 (finders and canons of construction) 6 (statutes and regulations) 6 (Outer Space Treaty)
Client-related skills	Interviewing and counseling	4 (interests v. position) 5 (tenants in common) 7 (purchase offers) 8 (constructive notice) 11 (interests v. position) 13 (discovery plan)
Drafting documents	Savings clauses	3 (rule against perpetuities)
	Lease	4
	Tenants in common agreement	5
	Tenant estoppel statements	8
	Easement agreement	9
	Zoning regulations	12 (statement of purpose)
Negotiation	Tenants in common agreement	5 (BATNA)
	Easement agreement	9

I welcome the comments and suggestions of adopters, and can be reached at kleinc@law.ufl.edu.

Christine A. Klein
Gainesville
February 2016

ACKNOWLEDGMENTS

I would like to thank my student assistants for their meticulous research and infectious enthusiasm—Maggie Howell, Susan Johns, Tiffany M. Miles, and Madonna M. Snowden, all of the University of Florida Levin College of Law class of 2016. I am grateful to Aspen Publishers/Wolters Kluwer for their support of this book, as well as three editions of the Natural Resources Law casebook I wrote with co-authors Fred Cheever and Bret Birdsong. In particular, Carol McGeehan provided encouragement, vision, and friendship, and John Devins offered unwavering support over the years. I am also grateful to Troy Froebe and his team at The Froebe Group for producing this book, with special thanks to developmental editor Kathy Langone and design coordinator Sarah Hains. Thanks also to Meri Keithley and her team at Keithley & Associates, Inc. for their design of the numerous figures that grace this text. Generous research grants from the University of Florida and from the University of Florida Levin College of Law made this book possible. And as always, my deepest appreciation goes to my husband, Mark Ely.

Additionally, I acknowledge the permissions kindly granted to reproduce excerpts from, or illustrations of, the materials indicated below.

American Law Institute, Restatement (Second) of Torts, Nuisance (1979), Chapter 40; § 821D, § 821D Comment b, § 821F, § 822, § 825, § 826, § 827, § 828; Restatement (Second) of Contracts (1981), § 129. Copyright © 1979, 1981 The American Law Institute. Reprinted by permission.

Applegate, Aaron, "Norfolk Sea Level Rise Takes Shine Off Waterfront Homes," The Virginian-Pilot, Sept. 28, 2014. Copyright © 2014 The Virginian-Pilot. Reprinted by permission.

Bandholtz, F. J., "Albert Lea, Minnesota" (1908), photograph. Courtesy of the Library of Congress.

Batson, Bill, "Nyack Sketch Log: A Legally Haunted House," illustration. Copyright © 2014 Bill Batson. Reprinted by permission.

Branas, Javier, "AT&T Park," photograph. Copyright © 2005 Javier Branas. Reprinted by permission.

Breuer, Marcel / American Society of Landscape Architects, "Design for Office Tower Atop Grand Central Terminal," illustration. Copyright © 1968 Marcel Breuer. Reprinted by permission.

Bucco-Lechat, Clément, "WMCH Drone" (2013), photograph. Courtesy of Wikimedia Commons.

Carroll, James C., "Mammoth Cave Railroad, No. 3," photograph. Courtesy of the James C. Carroll Collection via the National Park Service.

CDA's World History Wiki, "Feudalism in Europe," illustration. Courtesy of CDA's World History Wiki.

Center of the American West, "Atlas of the New West," illustration. Copyright © 1997 Center of the American West. Reprinted by permission.

Detroit Publishing Company, "Hotel Crossman, Thousand Islands" (c. 1901). Courtesy of the Library of Congress.

Detroit Publishing Company, "Illinois Central Railway Depot, Chicago, IL" (1900), photograph. Courtesy of the Library of Congress.

Eiler, Lyntha Scott, "The Electric Shovel 'Big John'" (1995), photograph. Courtesy of the Library of Congress.

Francis, Nancy, "The Shelley House, 4600 Labadie Avenue" (2008), photograph. Courtesy of Wikimedia Commons.

Greene, C. O., "Historic Building on Edisto Island, Charleston County, S.C." (1940), photograph. Courtesy of the Library of Congress.

Hardin, Gareth, "The Tragedy of the Commons," 162 Science 1243 (1968). Copyright © 1968 The American Association for the Advancement of Science. Reprinted by permission.

Klein, Christine A., "The Home at #4 Kingsbury Place," photograph. Copyright © 2015 Christine A. Klein. Reprinted by permission.

Klein, Christine A., "Main Street Pier and Sky Tower," photograph. Copyright © 2015 Christine A. Klein. Reprinted by permission.

Knox County Public Library, "Deitch's Department Store Lingerie and Undergarments' Staff," photograph. Copyright © Knox County Public Library. Reprinted by permission.

National Cancer Institute, "Chimney Sweeps," illustration. Courtesy of the National Cancer Institute.

The Nature Conservancy, "Submerged Lands," illustration. Copyright © The Nature Conservancy. Reprinted by permission.

Oppenheimer, David, "Isle of Palms, Charleston Harbor Resort," photograph. Copyright © 2013 David Oppenheimer, Performance Impressions, LLC. Reprinted by permission.

Ostrom, Elinor. Governing the Commons: The Evolution of Institutions for Collective Action. Copyright © 1990 Cambridge University Press. Reprinted by permission.

Pennsylvania Department of Environmental Protection, "Pennsylvania House Damaged by Subsidence," photograph. Courtesy of the Pennsylvania Department of Environmental Protection.

Platt, Spencer, "The Home of Susette Kelo, June 27, 2005," photograph. Copyright © 2005 Spencer Platt / Staff / Getty Images. Reprinted by permission.

Schiele, Egon, "Artist Gustav Klimt in a Light Blue Smock" (1913), drawing. Courtesy of Wikimedia Commons.

Shepherd, Thomas H., "An Early View of the Great Globe Without the Galleries" (1850), illustration. Courtesy of Wikimedia Commons.

Stephens, H. L., "African American Slave Reaching Freedom" (c. 1863), illustration. Courtesy of the Library of Congress.

Tennessee Association of Realtors, Transaction Desk, "Purchase and Sale Agreement." Copyright © Tennessee Association of Realtors. Reprinted by permission.

Titus, Simmons & Titus, "Residence of W. S. Streator, No. 807 Euclid Avenue, Cleveland, Ohio" (1873), illustration. Courtesy of Wikimedia Commons.

Uniform Law Commission, Uniform Partition of Heirs Property Act. Copyright © 2010 the National Conference of Commissioners on Uniform State Laws. Reprinted by permission.

United States Department of Agriculture, "Uncle Sam Says, Garden to Cut Food Costs" (c. 1917), illustration. Courtesy of the National Archives.

United States Department of Housing and Urban Development, "Pruitt-Igoe Collapses, With the St. Louis Arch in the Background" (1972), photograph. Courtesy of Wikimedia Commons.

Van Vechten, Carl, "Portrait of Dr. Albert C. Barnes, Barnes Foundation" (1940), photograph. Courtesy of the Library of Congress.

Wolf, Michael Allan, "The Ambler Property," photograph. Copyright © Michael Allan Wolf. Reprinted by permission.

PROPERTY

PART ONE

PROPERTY, POSSESSION, AND TRANSFERABILITY

Introduction to Property

A. What Can Be Owned?
B. What Does Ownership Mean?
C. Beyond the Black Letter: The Rise of the Sharing Economy
D. Skills Practice: Common Law Analysis
E. Chapter Review

Chapter 1–Cases

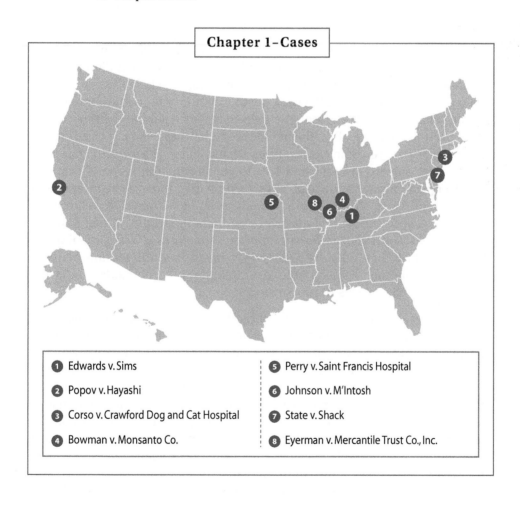

1. Edwards v. Sims
2. Popov v. Hayashi
3. Corso v. Crawford Dog and Cat Hospital
4. Bowman v. Monsanto Co.

5. Perry v. Saint Francis Hospital
6. Johnson v. M'Intosh
7. State v. Shack
8. Eyerman v. Mercantile Trust Co., Inc.

Welcome to the study of property law. Even before law school, you probably had experience with a number of property issues: renting an apartment, buying a car, giving and receiving gifts, owning a pet, perhaps even buying real estate. But beyond these common experiences lurk many subtle premises you might not have thought about. For example, all property must have an owner—not just now, but in perpetuity. This course will give you an opportunity to test your preconceived notions about property, and to refine, modify, and deepen them.

Modern theory accepts the notion that property is a human construct that is created, enforced, and defined by human laws. Those laws, in turn, reflect a rich tapestry of sometimes conflicting norms and aspirations—property rights should be stable; vested expectations should be protected; owners should be free to exercise their rights or transfer them to others; the public interest should be protected; the law should be fair and equitable. It is no small task for property law to accommodate all of these goals. Likewise, it is no small task to understand property law as it struggles to do so, and sometimes falls short. Four recurrent themes will guide our study:

A bundle of sticks or a web of interests?   Generations of property students have compared property rights to a bundle of sticks (or a bundle of rights). Depending on the type of property, those sticks might include the right to possession, the right to use (and the right *not* to use), the right to transfer to others (by gift, sale, will, or inheritance), the right to destroy, and the right to exclude others from the property. But, the bundle metaphor has been criticized from a variety of perspectives. Some have suggested that it limits its focus too narrowly to individual property owners, and fails to capture the full scope of property and its impact on society. Instead, perhaps property more closely resembles a web of interests that should be envisioned "as an interconnected web of relationships between people and an object, and among people." Craig Anthony (Tony) Arnold, *The Reconstitution of Property: Property as a Web of Interests*, 26 Harvard Envtl. L. Rev. 281, 364 (2002). We will explore the tension between these competing metaphors, as the law attempts to accommodate both the private and public aspects of property.

The importance of place: After a brief introduction to tangible personal property (things) and intangible personal property (such as copyrights, patents, trademarks, and contract rights), this text will focus primarily on *real property*—land. In some cases, land represents a fungible commodity—like books or widgets—that is important to its owner primarily because of its market value. In many other cases, however, land derives significant value because of the *place* where it is located. As every real estate agent knows, the location of property affects its market value. Beyond that, people often care deeply about a particular piece of property because of its location—such as the place where they raised their family, or the community in which they are rooted. Place also matters in settling disputes. For example, a valuable home-run baseball in a stadium might be awarded to the person who first caught it, whereas the same baseball found on someone's front lawn might be awarded to the landowner (even if unaware of the baseball's presence) rather than to the first passerby who found it. And, as we will see, property law is primarily state law, and can vary significantly from place to place. To remind you of these multiple roles of place and to provide you with a pictoral table of contents, each chapter opens with a map of the cases contained in that chapter.

Just passing through: Every piece of property will have a succession of owners throughout perpetuity. If you own property today, but a past owner purported to place a permanent restriction on it—"I give this property to Amanda and her successors to be used for restaurant purposes only"—should you be bound by that restriction, and risk losing the property (or paying damages) if you use the property for some other purpose? Looking forward, should you and your neighbors be allowed to place binding restrictions on all future lot owners in your subdivision—such as the condition that the land should be used for residential purposes only—even if the city changes the zoning in the neighborhood at some point in the future? As we will see, this question of so-called "dead hand control" asks how property can accommodate the desires of both present and future generations.

A changing world: Property law values stability and predictability, and yet it must respond to evolving conditions. For example, how can landlord-tenant law—mired in feudal history, with its outdated focus on status and certain privileges—reflect the modern reality of urban tenants? Beyond social change, the law must respond to changing physical conditions. For example, if a river serves as the boundary between two tracts of land, what happens if the river's course changes dramatically? Or, what happens to the boundaries of coastal properties if they become inundated by rising sea levels? Throughout this course, be sure to notice such changing circumstances and the law's response to them.

As you embark on your study of property law, keep these broad themes in mind. Further, consider a preliminary question—why does the law recognize property rights at all? We will return to this foundational question in Chapter 6, after you have had a chance to see the benefits and challenges of property ownership in a wide variety of contexts. For now, you might like to preview Chapter 6.A's brief overview of property's supporting rationales.

A. WHAT CAN BE OWNED?

Before you came to law school, you probably thought of property as the ownership of *things* by *people*. But the legal concept of property is *relational.* That is, "property" is not the thing itself, but a set of rights and duties *among people* with respect to things. This concept reflects the tension between the individual and the community—both of which are critical to property law.

Let's begin by considering the types of things that can be owned—land and personal property (both tangible and intangible). As you read the materials that follow, observe whether the law treats different types of property differently, and think about whether (and how) the nature of the *thing* owned should matter.

1. Real Property

> **Note to students:** This book frequently introduces new topics with *A Place to Start* boxes. This feature gives you an overview of doctrine and terminology to help you grapple deeply with the cases and materials that follow. As such, it is simply a starting point for your study and a reference to which you should return frequently. The final *Digging Deeper* note in most boxes suggests areas of ambiguity that you will encounter. Be sure to challenge yourself to uncover additional subtleties as you refine and deepen your understanding of the topic.

Real property refers to rights in land and the *fixtures* attached to it, such as a structure or a furnace affixed to that structure. The land (and its fixtures) itself is referred to as *real estate* or *realty*. As a place to start, take note of the physical extent of real property and legal actions available to protect possessory rights in real property, as explained in the following text box.

A Place to Start | **Real Property**

- *Physical extent of property:* The determination of property boundaries is no simple thing, and gives rise to some wonderfully intricate doctrines:
  - *The ad coelum doctrine:* An old doctrine provides, *cujus est solum, ejus est usque ad infernos*—"to whomsoever the soil belongs, he owns also to the sky above and to the depths below." Today, this doctrine is not taken literally. Scientific advances allow us to better understand the mysteries of the earth (including subsurface mineral deposits and groundwater), and technological advances allow us to make greater use of places beneath and above the earth (as through mining and air travel).
  - *Severing the parcel:* State law generally allows surface landowners to convey separately the subsurface estate, such as mineral rights between specified depths (*see Brown v. Lober*, Chapter 7) or air rights up to a specified height or altitude (*see Penn Central Transportation Co. v. City of New York*, Chapter 13).
  - *Boundary lines:* Property boundaries can be marked by systems including *metes and bounds* descriptions ("from the old red maple tree, then west 25 feet along Spring Creek . . .") and the *Government Survey System* developed by Thomas Jefferson ("the W1/2 of the NE1/4 of Section 10, Township 5 South, Range 10 West of the principal meridian"). Sometimes, a river or stream can mark a boundary. If the watercourse changes gradually (*accretion*), then title migrates with the watercourse, but if it changes abruptly (*avulsion*), then the property boundaries remain unchanged.

■ *Legal actions for wrongful interference with possessory rights in real property:*

■ *Trespass:* An action for damages for wrongful interference with possessory rights to land (Chapter 11).

■ *Ejectment:* An action to recover possession of land wrongfully withheld.

DIGGING DEEPER: *Why* does the law recognize ownership of land? If more than one party claims the same property, what principles can courts use to resolve competing claims?

Edwards v. Sims

24 S.W.2d 619 (Ky. Ct. App. 1929)

Reading Guide

The primary issue in this phase of a long-running dispute is whether a court can require an underground cave survey, contrary to the wishes of one of the overlying landowners. For our purposes, however, the related questions are more interesting—who owns Great Onyx Cave, and why? This was a novel question for the court, and even today, there continues to be very little case law on the subject of the lower boundary of property.

The federal government's attempt to condemn title to Great Onyx Cave (and numerous other caves in the area) for incorporation into Mammoth Cave National Park precipitated this phase of the litigation. In Chapter 13, we will study the power of *eminent domain*, which allows federal, state, and local governments to condemn private property for public use in appropriate cases, provided they pay just compensation. Overall, condemnations resemble forced sales from landowners to the government.

STANLEY, J.

["Plaintiff L. P. Edwards discovered a cave under land belonging to him and his wife, Sally Edwards. The entrance to the cave is on the Edwards land. Edwards named it the 'Great Onyx Cave,' no doubt because of the rock crystal formations within it which are known as onyx. This cave is located in the cavernous area of Kentucky, and is only about three miles distant from the world-famous Mammoth Cave. Its proximity to Mammoth Cave, which for many years has had an international reputation as an underground wonder, as well as its beautiful formations, led Edwards to embark upon a program of advertising and exploitation for the purpose of bringing visitors to his cave. . . . The authorities in charge of the development of the Mammoth Cave area as a national park undertook to secure the Great Onyx Cave through condemnation proceedings, and in that suit the value of the cave was fixed by a jury at $396,000. In April, 1928, F. P. Lee, an adjoining landowner, filed this suit against

Edwards and the heirs of Sally Edwards, claiming that a portion of the cave was under his land, and praying for damages, for an accounting of the profits which resulted from the operation of the cave, and for an injunction prohibiting Edwards and his associates from further trespassing upon or exhibiting any part of the cave under Lee's land. At the inception of this litigation, Lee undertook to procure a survey of the cave in order that it might be determined what portion of it was on his land. The chancellor ordered that a survey be made, and Edwards prosecuted an appeal from that order to this court. [seeking] . . . a writ of prohibition against the circuit judge, the Honorable N.P. Sims, to prevent the carrying out of the order of survey."][1]

In *Cox v. Colossal Cavern Co.*, 276 S.W. 540 (Ky. Ct. App. 1925), the subject of cave rights was considered, and this court held there may be a severance of the estate in the property, that is, that one may own the surface and another the cave rights, the conditions being quite similar to but not exactly like those of mineral lands. But there is no such severance involved in this case, as it appears that the defendants are the owners of the land and have in it an absolute right.

Cujus est solum, ejus est usque ad coelum ad infernos (to whomsoever the soil belongs, he owns also to the sky and to the depths), is an old maxim and rule. It is that the owner of realty, unless there has been a division of the estate, is entitled to the free and unfettered control of his own land above, upon, and beneath the surface. So whatever is in a direct line between the surface of the land and the center of the earth belongs to the owner of the surface. . . .

With this doctrine of ownership in mind, we approach the question as to whether a court of equity has a transcendent power to invade that right through its agents for the purpose of ascertaining the truth of a matter before it, which fact thus disclosed will determine certainly whether or not the owner is trespassing upon his neighbor's property. . . . It seems to the court . . . that there can be little differentiation, so far as the matter now before us is concerned, between caves and mines. And as declared in 40 C.J. 947: "A court of equity, however, has the inherent power, independent of statute, to compel a mine owner to permit an inspection of his works at the suit of a party who can show reasonable ground for suspicion that his lands are being trespassed upon through them. . . ."

. . . [T]he controversy can be quickly and accurately settled by surveying the cave. . . . If the survey shows the Great Onyx Cave extends under the lands of

---

1. [This factual summary is taken from a later phase of the litigation, *Edwards v. Lee's Administrator*, 96 S.W.2d 1028, 1028-30 (Ky. Ct. App. 1936) (summarizing the facts of *Edwards v. Sims*). Do you understand why plaintiff Edwards is suing Chancellor Sims, when his real quarrel is with his neighbor F.P. Lee? After the government's condemnation proceedings revealed the sizable value of the cave that Edwards had developed and promoted, neighbor Lee apparently wanted to get a piece of the action. By seeking to block the survey ordered by Chancellor Sims at Lee's request, Edwards likely hoped to thwart Lee's efforts to share in the profits from the cave operation, or from a potential condemnation award if the government acquired the cave.—Eds.]

[Lee] . . . , [the Edwards] should be glad to know this fact and should be just as glad to cease trespassing upon [Lee's] lands, if they are in fact doing so. The peculiar nature of these conditions, it seems to us, makes it imperative and necessary in the administration of justice that the survey should have been ordered and should be made. . . .

LOGAN, J., dissenting.

. . . I must dissent from the majority opinion, confessing that I may not be able to show, by any legal precedent, that the opinion is wrong, yet having an abiding faith in my own judgment that it is wrong. . . .

It sounds well in the majority opinion to tritely say that he who owns the surface of real estate, without reservation, owns from the center of the earth to the outmost sentinel of the solar system. The age-old statement, adhered to in the majority opinion as the law, in truth and fact, is not true now and never has been. . . .

A cave or cavern should belong absolutely to him who owns its entrance, and this ownership should extend even to its utmost reaches if he has explored and connected these reaches with the entrance. When the surface owner has discovered a cave and prepared it for purposes of exhibition, no one ought to be allowed to disturb him in his dominion over that which he has conquered and subjected to his uses.

It is well enough to hang to our theories and ideas, but when there is an effort to apply old principles to present-day conditions, and they will not fit, then it becomes necessary for a readjustment, and principles and facts as they exist in this age must be made conformable. . . . Man had no dominion over the air until recently, and, prior to his conquering the air, no one had any occasion to question the claim of the surface owner that the air above him was subject to his dominion. . . .

Shall a man be allowed to stop airplanes flying above his land because he owns the surface? He cannot subject the atmosphere through which they fly to his profit or pleasure; therefore, so long as airplanes do not injure him, or interfere with the use of his property, he should be helpless to prevent their flying above his dominion. . . .

If he who owns the surface does not own and control the atmosphere above him, he does not own and control vacuity beneath the surface. . . .

. . . Edwards owns this cave through right of discovery, exploration, development, advertising, exhibition, and conquest. Men fought their way through the eternal darkness, into the mysterious and abysmal depths of the bowels of a groaning world to discover the theretofore unseen splendors of unknown natural scenic wonders. . . . They let themselves down by flimsy ropes into pits that seemed bottomless; they clung to scanty handholds as they skirted the brinks of precipices while the flickering flare of their flaming flambeaux disclosed no bottom to the yawning gulf beneath them; they waded through rushing torrents, not knowing what awaited them on the farther side; . . . they wounded their bodies on stalagmites and stalactites and other curious and weird formations; they found chambers, star-studded and filled with scintillating light reflected by a phantasmagoria revealing fancied phantoms. . . . Through days, weeks, months, and years—ever linking chamber with chamber, disclosing an underground land of enchantment, they continued their explorations; through the years they toiled connecting these wonders with the outside world through the entrance on the land of Edwards which he had discovered. . . .

. . . The cave was [Edwards'] because he had made it what it was, and without what he had done it was nothing of value. The value is not in the black vacuum that the uninitiated call a cave. That which Edwards owns is something intangible and indefinable. It is his vision translated into a reality.

. . . Then came the "surface men" crying, "I think this cave may run under my lands." They do not know they only "guess," but they seek to discover the secrets of Edwards so that they may harass him and take from him that which he has made his own. They have come to a court of equity and have asked that Edwards be forced to open his doors and his ways to them so that they may go in and despoil him. . . . What may be the result if they stop his ways? They destroy the cave, because those who visit it are they who give it value, and none will visit it when the ways are barred so that it may not be exhibited as a whole.

It may be that the law is as stated in the majority opinion of the court, but equity, according to my judgment, should not destroy that which belongs to one man when he at whose behest the destruction is visited, although with some legal right, is not benefited thereby. Any ruling by a court which brings great and irreparable injury to a party is erroneous. . . .

Notes

1. *Who owns Great Onyx Cave?—the rule:* The majority and the dissent each cite to a different rule to determine the *ownership* of the cave (as distinct from the issue of whether a court-ordered surveyor may *trespass*, contrary to the cave owner's wishes). What rule does the majority cite, and what rationale supports its application? Conversely, what rule does the dissent favor, and what rationale supports it? Under the dissent's view, if Edwards had done nothing to discover or develop the cave, would he still own it in its entirety? In general, it is said that rules should be clear and straightforward. Does this case cause you to question that statement? What concerns other than clarity might be important?

2. *John Locke's labor theory:* The influential English philosopher John Locke (1632-1704) posited that title to previously unowned common land could be acquired through *labor*:

> As much land as a man tills, plants, improves, cultivates, and can use the product of, so much is his property. He by his labour does, as it were, inclose it from the

common. . . . God and his reason commanded him to subdue the earth, *i.e.* improve it for the benefit of life, and therein lay out something upon it that was his own, his labour. He that in obedience to this command of God, subdued, tilled and sowed any part of it, thereby annexed to it something that was his property, which another had no title to, nor could without injury take from him.

John Locke, Two Treatises of Government, Book II, Ch. V, § 32 (1690). Can you identify where the dissent draws from similar principles in the above case?

Locke's theory has captured the popular and legal imagination. Be sure to look for other potential applications of his theory throughout this course. But before you buy into it wholesale, consider a critique from a legal outsider, ecologist Dr. Carl Safina:

> But what if the labor harms the land? Land stays, after all, and men pass. Does a man really own a thousand-year-old tree because he has just cut it down, or is he a thief who has severed history and taken a little of the future? Locke believed ownership is justified as long as it doesn't violate the liberty of others to also get "as much and as good." This is possible only as long as there are thousand-year-old trees enough for all, land enough for all—still imaginable in Locke's sparsely populated time. Times change.

Carl Safina, The View from Lazy Point: A Natural Year in an Unnatural World 51-52 (2011). Do you agree with Safina, agree with Locke, or take some other position? Why?

3. *The* ad coelum *doctrine today:* The advent of air travel forced the courts to rethink the uppermost boundary of title to land. *See United States v. Causby*, 328 U.S. 256, 266-67 (1946) ("The airplane is part of the modern environment of life. . . . The airspace, apart from the immediate reaches above the land, is part of the public domain. We need not determine at this time what those precise limits are."). But the law governing the lower boundary of surface property rights remains less developed. At least two circumstances, however, promise to force courts to take a closer look at the issue. First, to combat climate change, there is a growing interest in "carbon capture and sequestration"—which involves capturing carbon dioxide emissions from power plants and injecting them into deep underground geologic formations for long-term storage. *See* Alexandra B. Klass & Elizabeth J. Wilson, *Climate Change, Carbon Sequestration, and Property Rights*, 2010 U. Ill L. Rev. 363 (2010) (exploring, among other topics, questions relating to ownership of subsurface pore space). Second, there has been increased use of the hydraulic fracturing mining technique, which injects fluids underground at high pressure to break apart oil- and gas-bearing rock formations; as a consequence, fluids, oil, and gas can migrate beneath neighboring properties. *See* Troy A. Rule, *Property Rights and Modern Energy*, 20 Geo. Mason L. Rev. 803 (2013).

4. *The place—the Great Onyx Cave:* This opinion represents just one phase of the Great Onyx Cave dispute, which involved about a dozen years of litigation. That dispute, in turn, was part of the great "Kentucky cave

wars" that led to the creation of Mammoth Cave National Park in 1941. Mammoth is the world's longest known cave system by far, according to the National Park Service. It began forming about 10 million years ago, and includes about 400 miles of mapped and surveyed cave passages. The disputed portion was about 360 feet below the surface of the earth.

Mammoth Cave Railroad, No. 3, which transported visitors to the Mammoth Cave Hotel
Source: James C. Carroll collection via National Park Service

As the National Park Service explains,

By 1920, a war had broken out in the Kentucky Cave Country—a war of economics. . . . Mammoth Cave, by this time a century-old tourist attraction, had demonstrated the profit to be had in tourism. That other cave owners would seek to share that profit was inevitable, and the competition grew rancorous. Colossal Cave, Long Cave, Short's Cave, Great Onyx Cave, Indian Cave, Salts Cave and Crystal Cave all vied for the attention of passing motorists bound for the world-famous Mammoth, and strange signs began to sprout by the roadside, reading, "Do not be confused—no one has the right to stop you on this road." Agents from the various caves began intercepting cars on the road, and conversations such as this were not uncommon:

Excuse me sir—What did you stop me for?

Pardon, sir, but are you headed for the Mammoth Cave?

Well, yes, not that it's any of your business.

Oh, it's a good thing I caught you sir. Mammoth Cave has been flooded clear to the ceiling by the rain last week. There's no way in.

You don't say! And here I've driven all this way.

Well! You don't have to be disappointed, sir! Colossal Cave is just up the road, a little past Mammoth Cave, high and dry! I've even got a couple of tickets on me I could sell you. . . .

Mammoth Cave, of course, had not been flooded.

National Park Service, *Mammoth Cave: Cave Wars. See also* David Kem, *The Kentucky Cave Wars* (www.lulu.com 2014, visited Aug. 1, 2015); Bruce Ziff, *The Great Onyx Cave Cases—A Micro-History*, 40 N. Kentucky L. Rev. 1 (2013).

Problems

Note to students: In many of the post-case "Problems" sections in this book, a citation to case law will appear at the end of the problem. Such citations are for the curious only, and you should not feel compelled to look up the cases (unless your professor specifies otherwise, of course). Each problem will provide sufficient facts for you to answer the questions posed, or at least to set out a range of possible responses and supporting rationales.

For each problem below, answer the following questions: (a) How would the case be decided under the rule of *Edwards v. Sims*? (b) Is that a good result? and, (c) If not, can the facts be distinguished from those of *Edwards* to compel a different result?

1. *How high?* The Causby family owned 2.8 acres near an airport outside of Greensboro, North Carolina. They lived on the land, and also used it as a commercial chicken farm. The federal government leased the airport beginning June 1, 1942 (during World War II). The army and navy conducted frequent and regular flights over the Causby property. Such flights passed only 83 feet above the ground (which was 67 feet above the house, 63 feet above the barn, and 18 feet above the highest tree). At times, the military planes came so close to the tops of the family's trees as to blow the old leaves off. The noise was startling and at night the glare from the planes brightly lit up the property. Hundreds of chickens died as they flew into walls from fright, and the Causbys were forced to give up their commercial operation. In addition, the family was frequently deprived of sleep and became nervous and frightened. The Causbys sued the United States, claiming they owned the airspace above their property, that the government had taken that airspace from them, and that the government should provide just compensation for their loss. *See generally United States v. Causby*, 328 U.S. 256 (1946).

2. *How deep?* James B. Gardner and Amanda Woodbury owned a ranch in South Park, Colorado (yes, the setting of the long-running adult animated sit-com *South Park*). They obtained a water right under Colorado law, which allowed them to store water beneath about 115 square miles of land, including beneath their neighbors' property. Through wells on the Gardner/Woodbury

ranch, clean water would be injected at low pressure into the underlying "aquifer"—a subsurface formation that naturally stores water in the spaces between sand, gravel, silt, clay, and rock. Such "artificial recharge" projects—on a smaller scale—are not uncommon in the arid west, and are designed to make water available for use throughout the year, independent of surface precipitation. The neighbors brought a lawsuit against Gardner and Woodbury, claiming that the defendants would be trespassing onto their subsurface estate and must compensate them. *See generally Park County v. Park County Sportsmen's Ranch, LLP*, 45 P.3d 693 (Colo. 2002).

2. Tangible Personal Property

Tangible personal property (also referred to as *personalty* or *chattels*) refers to rights in movable things. It can also include living things such as cats, dogs, and in some cases, wild animals that have been captured.

A Place to Start | Tangible Personal Property

- *Fugitive resources:* Things that move under their own force (such as wild animals) are called *fugitive resources.* Before capture, they are considered unowned, and are generally under the control of the state. Natural resources such as water, oil, and natural gas are sometimes treated as fugitive resources, although they move under the force of gravity rather than under their own force.

- *Rule of capture:* The first person that *captures* fugitive resources can become their owner—such as a hunter, with a valid hunting license, who kills a deer. But beware—"capture" is a term of art that is not as simple as it sounds. Some fugitive natural resources are subject to the rule of capture, but also tend to be heavily regulated under state and federal statutes.

- *Legal actions relating to personal property:*
  - *Conversion:* Conversion is an intentional and wrongful exercise of dominion over the chattels of another, giving rise to an action for damages (usually measured by the value of the property).
  - *Trover:* An action for damages against one who has wrongfully interfered with the possessory rights of another, or who has wrongfully converted goods to his or her own use.
  - *Replevin:* An action for the recovery of possession of chattels wrongfully taken or detained.

DIGGING DEEPER: Why should *capture* establish title in relevant cases, and what does "capture" mean? Does ambiguity in the definition serve any useful purpose?

Popov v. Hayashi

2002 WL 31833731, (Cal. Super. Ct. Dec. 18, 2002)

Reading Guide

Who owns baseballs that are hit into the stands? Millions of dollars can be at stake, as in the case of record-breaking home-run balls. This case turns on the meaning of "possession." What does it mean to "possess" a flying baseball in the midst of an unruly crowd?

McCARTHY, J.

In 1927, Babe Ruth hit sixty home runs. That record stood for thirty four years until Roger Maris broke it in 1961 with sixty one home runs. Mark McGwire hit seventy in 1998. On October 7, 2001, at PacBell Park in San Francisco, Barry Bonds hit number seventy three. That accomplishment set a record which, in all probability, will remain unbroken for years into the future. . . .

The ball that found itself at the receiving end of Mr. Bond's bat garnered some of that attention. Baseball fans in general, and especially people at the game, understood the importance of the ball. It was worth a great deal of money[2] and whoever caught it would bask, for a brief period of time, in the reflected fame of Mr. Bonds.

With that in mind, many people who attended the game came prepared for the possibility that a record setting ball would be hit in their direction. Among this group were plaintiff Alex Popov and defendant Patrick Hayashi. They were unacquainted at the time. Both men brought baseball gloves, which they anticipated using if the ball came within their reach.

They, along with a number of others, positioned themselves in the arcade section of the ballpark. . . .

Barry Bonds came to bat in the first inning. With nobody on base and a full count, Bonds swung at a slow knuckleball. He connected. The ball sailed over the right-field fence and into the arcade.

Josh Keppel, a cameraman who was positioned in the arcade, captured the event on videotape. . . .

In addition to the Keppel tape, seventeen percipient witnesses testified as to what they saw after the ball came into the stands. . . .

The factual findings in this case are the result of an analysis of the testimony of all the witnesses as well as a detailed review of the Keppel tape. Those findings are as follows:

---

2. [FN 1] It has been suggested that the ball might sell for something in excess of $1,000,000.

When the seventy-third home run ball went into the arcade, it landed in the upper portion of the webbing of a softball glove worn by Alex Popov. While the glove stopped the trajectory of the ball, it is not at all clear that the ball was secure. Popov had to reach for the ball and in doing so, may have lost his balance.

Even as the ball was going into his glove, a crowd of people began to engulf Mr. Popov. He was tackled and thrown to the ground while still in the process of attempting to complete the catch. . . .

Eventually, Mr. Popov was buried face down on the ground under several layers of people. At one point he had trouble breathing. Mr. Popov was grabbed, hit and kicked. People reached underneath him in the area of his glove. . . .

The videotape clearly establishes that this was an out of control mob, engaged in violent, illegal behavior. . . .

Mr. Popov intended at all times to establish and maintain possession of the ball. At some point the ball left his glove and ended up on the ground. It is impossible to establish the exact point in time that this occurred or what caused it to occur.

Mr. Hayashi was standing near Mr. Popov when the ball came into the stands. He, like Mr. Popov, was involuntarily forced to the ground. He committed no wrongful act. While on the ground he saw the loose ball. He picked it up, rose to his feet and put it in his pocket. . . .

Mr. Hayashi kept the ball hidden. He asked Mr. Keppel to point the camera at him. . . . Finally after someone else in the crowd asked Mr. Keppel to point the camera at Mr. Hayashi, Mr. Keppel complied. It was only at that point that Mr. Hayashi held the ball in the air for others to see. . . .

Mr. Popov eventually got up from the ground. . . . When he saw that Mr. Hayashi had the ball he expressed relief and grabbed for it. Mr. Hayashi pulled the ball away. Security guards then took Mr. Hayashi to a secure area of the stadium.

It is important to point out what the evidence did not and could not show. Neither the camera nor the percipient witnesses were able to establish whether Mr. Popov retained control of the ball as he descended into the crowd. . . .

Plaintiff has pled causes of actions for conversion, . . . injunctive relief and constructive trust. . . .

Conversion is the wrongful exercise of dominion over the personal property of another. . . . If a person entitled to possession of personal property demands its return, the unjustified refusal to give the property back is conversion.

The act constituting conversion must be intentionally done. There is no requirement, however, that the defendant know that the property belongs to another or that the defendant intends to dispossess the true owner of its use and enjoyment. . . .

Conversion does not exist, however, unless the baseball rightfully belongs to Mr. Popov. One who has neither title nor possession, nor any right to possession, cannot sue for conversion. The deciding question in this case then, is whether Mr. Popov achieved possession or the right to possession as he attempted to catch and hold on to the ball.

The parties have agreed to a starting point for the legal analysis. Prior to the time the ball was hit, it was possessed and owned by Major League Baseball. At the time it was hit it became intentionally abandoned property. The first person who came in possession of the ball became its new owner.

The parties fundamentally disagree about the definition of possession. In order to assist the court in resolving this disagreement, four distinguished law professors participated in a forum to discuss the legal definition of possession. The professors also disagreed.

... Although the term possession appears repeatedly throughout the law, its definition varies depending on the context in which it is used. Various courts have condemned the term as vague and meaningless. ...

While there is a degree of ambiguity built into the term possession, such ambiguity exists for a purpose. Courts are often called upon to resolve conflicting claims of possession in the context of commercial disputes. A stable economic environment requires rules of conduct which are understandable and consistent with the fundamental customs and practices of the industry they regulate. ... Because each industry has different customs and practices, a single definition of possession cannot be applied to different industries without creating havoc. ...

Professor Roger Bernhardt has recognized that "[p]ossession requires both physical control over the item and an intent to control it or exclude others from it. . . ."

Professor Brown argues that "[t]he orthodox view of possession regards it as a union of the two elements of the physical relation of the possessor to the thing, and of intent. This physical relation is the actual power over the thing in question, the ability to hold and make use of it. . . . There must also be manifested an intent to control it." . . .

We start with the observation that possession is a process which culminates in an event. The event is the moment in time that possession is achieved. . . .

... Mr. Popov has clearly evidenced an intent to possess the baseball and has communicated that intent to the world. The question is whether he did enough to reduce the ball to his exclusive dominion and control. Were his acts sufficient to create a legally cognizable interest in the ball?

... Professor Brian Gray[] suggests the following definition [hereinafter referred to as Gray's Rule]: "A person who catches a baseball that enters the stands is its owner. A ball is caught if the person has achieved complete control of the ball at the point in time that the momentum of the ball and the momentum of the fan while attempting to catch the ball ceases. A baseball, which is dislodged by incidental contact with an inanimate object or another person, before momentum has ceased, is not possessed. Incidental contact with another person is contact that is not intended by the other person. The first person to pick up a loose ball and secure it becomes its possessor." . . .

Professors Finkelman and Bernhardt have correctly pointed out that some cases recognize possession even before absolute dominion and control is achieved. Those cases require the actor to be actively and ably engaged in efforts to establish complete control. Moreover, such efforts must be significant and they must be reasonably calculated to result in unequivocal dominion and control at some point in the near future.

This rule is applied in cases involving the hunting or fishing of wild animals or the salvage of sunken vessels. The hunting and fishing cases recognize that a mortally wounded animal may run for a distance before falling. The hunter acquires possession upon the act of wounding the animal not the eventual capture. . . .

These rules are contextual in nature. . . . Moreover, they are influenced by the custom and practice of each industry. The reason that absolute dominion and control is not required to establish possession in the cases cited by Mr. Popov is that such a rule would be unworkable and unreasonable. The "nature and situation" of the property at issue does not immediately lend itself to unequivocal dominion and control. It is impossible to wrap ones arms around a whale, a fleeing fox or a sunken ship. . . .

The opposite is true of a baseball hit into the stands of a stadium. Not only is it physically possible for a person to acquire unequivocal dominion and control of an abandoned baseball, but fans generally expect a claimant to have accomplished as much. The custom and practice of the stands creates a reasonable expectation that a person will achieve full control of a ball before claiming possession. There is no reason for the legal rule to be inconsistent with that expectation. Therefore Gray's Rule is adopted as the definition of possession in this case.

The central tenant of Gray's Rule is that the actor must retain control of the ball after incidental contact with people and things. Mr. Popov has not established by a preponderance of the evidence that he would have retained control of the ball after all momentum ceased and after any incidental contact with people or objects. Consequently, he did not achieve full possession.

That finding, however, does not resolve the case. The reason we do not know whether Mr. Popov would have retained control of the ball is not because of incidental contact. It is because he was attacked. His efforts to establish possession were interrupted by the collective assault of a band of wrongdoers.

A decision which ignored that fact would endorse the actions of the crowd by not repudiating them. Judicial rulings, particularly in cases that receive media attention, affect the way people conduct themselves. This case demands vindication of an important principle. We are a nation governed by law, not by brute force. . . .

. . . [T]he court adopts the following rule. Where an actor undertakes significant but incomplete steps to achieve possession of a piece of abandoned personal property and the effort is interrupted by the unlawful acts of others, the actor has a legally cognizable pre-possessory interest in the property. That pre-possessory interest constitutes a qualified right to possession which can support a cause of action for conversion.

Possession can be likened to a journey down a path. Mr. Popov began his journey unimpeded. He was fast approaching a fork in the road. A turn in one direction would lead to possession of the ball—he would complete the catch. A turn in the other direction would result in a failure to achieve possession—he would drop the ball. Our problem is that before Mr. Popov got to the point where the road forked, he was set upon by a gang of bandits, who dislodged the ball from his grasp. . . .

[This] . . . does not, however, address the interests of Mr. Hayashi. The court is required to balance the interests of all parties.

Mr. Hayashi was not a wrongdoer. He was a victim of the same bandits that attacked Mr. Popov. The difference is that he was able to extract himself from their assault and move to the side of the road. It was there that he discovered the loose ball. When he picked up and put it in his pocket he attained unequivocal dominion and control. . . .

On the other hand, while Mr. Hayashi appears on the surface to have done everything necessary to claim full possession of the ball, the ball itself is encumbered by the qualified pre-possessory interest of Mr. Popov. At the time Mr. Hayashi came into possession of the ball, it had, in effect, a cloud on its title.

An award of the ball to Mr. Popov would be unfair to Mr. Hayashi. It would be premised on the assumption that Mr. Popov would have caught the ball. That assumption is not supported by the facts. An award of the ball to Mr. Hayashi would unfairly penalize Mr. Popov. It would be based on the assumption that Mr. Popov would have dropped the ball. That conclusion is also unsupported by the facts.

Both men have a superior claim to the ball as against all the world. Each man has a claim of equal dignity as to the other. We are, therefore, left with something of a dilemma.

Thankfully, there is a middle ground.

The concept of equitable division was fully explored in a law review article authored by Professor R.H. Helmholz in the December 1983 edition of the Fordham Law Review. . . .

There is no reason . . . that the same remedy cannot be applied in a case such as this, where issues of property, tort and equity intersect. . . .

. . . The court therefore declares that both plaintiff and defendant have an equal and undivided interest in the ball. Plaintiff's cause of action for conversion is sustained only as to his equal and undivided interest. In order to effectuate this ruling, the ball must be sold and the proceeds divided equally between the parties. . . .

Notes

1. *Rules and ambiguity:*   Articulate precisely the rules of possession considered by the court—the Bernhardt rule, the Brown rule, and Gray's rule. What rule did the court adopt? What is ambiguous about the definition of possession, and why did the court embrace such ambiguity? Notice the court's mention of custom. As here, where the appropriate legal rule is not clear, courts sometimes look to the customs of the relevant community (major league baseball and its fans). Can you think of any reasons why courts might be influenced by custom?

2. *Possession and ownership:*   What is the relationship between possession and ownership? In *Popov*, the court concluded that the baseball had been abandoned by Major League Baseball. Therefore, the court confronted a challenge fairly unique in modern society: determining the *very first owner* of the baseball for the purpose of establishing a new chain of title. Today, most property already has an owner and it is rare for courts to engage in determinations of this nature.

The court considered which claimant had acquired *first possession* of the abandoned baseball. First possession might offer a practical basis for sorting out competing claims, but *why* should society recognize it as a basis for awarding title to previously unowned things? According to one possible rationale, qualifying acts of first possession are an important form of communication that provides notice to the world that the first possessor intends to appropriate the property as its own. But why does communication matter? Professor Carol Rose considers this issue in a seminal article on possession:

> Why, then, is it so important that property owners make and keep their communications clear? Economists have an answer: clear titles facilitate trade and minimize resource-wasting conflict. If I am careless about who comes on to a corner of my property, I invite others to make mistakes and to waste their labor on improvements to what I have allowed them to think is theirs. I thus invite a free-for-all over my ambiguously held claims, and I encourage contention, insecurity, and litigation—all of which waste everyone's time and energy and may result in overuse or underuse of resources. But if I keep my property claims clear, others will know that they should deal with me directly if they want to use my property. We can bargain rather than fight; through trade, all items will come to rest in the hands of those who value them most. If property lines are clear, then, anyone who can make better use of my property than I can will buy or rent it from me and turn the property to his better use. In short, we will all be richer when property claims are unequivocal, because that unequivocal status enables property to be traded and used at its highest value.

Carol M. Rose, *Possession as the Origin of Property*, 52 U. Chi. L. Rev. 73, 81-82 (1985). Is first possession a valid basis for ownership? Are there other important policies that courts should consider when sorting out claims of title? Keep these question in mind as we confront competing claims of title throughout this course.

3. *People and things:*   Is this case about the relationship between plaintiff Alex Popov and the baseball, about the relationship between the plaintiff and defendant Patrick Hayashi, or about something else? Does either the bundle of sticks metaphor or the web of interests metaphor apply? Why?

4. *The place—the arcade of San Francisco's AT&T Park:*   In 2006, Pacific Bell Park ("PacBell Park") was renamed AT&T Park. In *Popov*, the parties agreed that the baseball league abandoned any baseballs hit into the stands. But why is that so? In football or basketball, fans generally return balls that leave the area of play. Why should different rules apply to different sports? As an alternative to abandonment, could the court have found that the baseball league made a gift of the errant ball to the fan that first possessed it? Or instead, could the court have found that as a matter of contract, the ticket to a baseball game gives fans the right to baseballs that enter the stands?

AT&T Park. The Arcade where the Bonds baseball was caught is the shallow seating area between right field and San Francisco Bay.
Photo by Javier Branas (2005)

5. *More to the story:*   After this case, the baseball was sold at auction in Times Square, New York, for $450,000. Hayashi reportedly said, "After legal fees, I guess it will be a wash." Ira Berkow, *Baseball: 73rd Home Run Ball Sells for $450,000*, New York Times, June 26, 2003.

As for Barry Bonds, he later became enmeshed in a controversy concerning performance-enhancing steroids. In 2002, the Internal Revenue Service initiated an investigation into a San Francisco laboratory suspected of distributing steroids to Bonds and other professional athletes, and of laundering the proceeds from the sale of those drugs. In 2003, under a grant of immunity, Bonds testified before a grand jury and denied that he had knowingly used steroids provided by the suspect laboratory. Bonds continued to play for the San Francisco Giants through 2007, when his contract was not renewed. Subsequently, Bonds was convicted of obstruction of justice (in connection with the grand jury's investigation), but the conviction was later reversed. *United States v. Bonds*, 784 F.3d 582 (9th Cir. 2015).

For more on property rights in baseballs, *see* Gideon Parchomovsky, Peter Siegelman & Steve Thei, *Of Equal Wrongs and Half Rights*, 82 N.Y.U. L. Rev. 738 (2007) (arguing that in a limited set of cases, an equal division entitlement promotes both efficiency and fairness); and Steven Semeraro, *An Essay on Property Rights in Milestone Home Run Baseballs*, 56 SMU L. Rev. 2281 (2003) (arguing that considerations of judicial economy and public safety weigh in favor of awarding superior rights in milestone home-run baseballs to the home team or the batter, rather than the fan that caught it).

Problems

For each of the factual scenarios below, answer these questions: (a) Under the rule in *Popov*, who should be recognized as the owner of the property? (b) Does the *Popov* rule produce a good result under each scenario below? (c) If not, can you *distinguish* the facts of *Popov*? That is, explain how the two sets of facts are meaningfully distinct, such that the same rule should not govern both cases. Keep in mind the *Popov* court's statement that rules of possession are "contextual in nature" and that the rules are "influenced by the custom and practice of each industry."

1. *Possessing a fox:*   A fox was running wild on an uninhabited "waste land"—a tract of land not owned by anyone. A wealthy sportsman, with his dogs and hounds, was in full pursuit of the fox, with a reasonable prospect of its capture. A farmer swooped in, killed the fox, and carried it off. Both parties agreed that a fox is a "wild and noxious beast" whose "depredations on farmers and on barn yards" are well known. Assume that under local custom, title would go to the hunter who had been in "hot pursuit." The hunter sued the farmer for damages. *See Pierson v. Post*, 3 Cai. R. 175 (N.Y. Sup. 1805). *See generally* Bethany R. Berger, *It's Not About the Fox: The Untold History of Pierson v. Post*, 55 Duke L.J. 1089 (2006).

2. *Possessing a whale:*   A fisherman from Provincetown, Massachusetts, pursued a fin-back whale in an open fishing vessel, and then shot and killed the whale with a bomb lance that contained a mark that could be traced back to

the fisherman. When so killed, some whales float out to sea and are never recovered, but many whales wash up on shore. This particular whale floated 17 miles to shore, where Ellis found it. Ellis sold the whale, and the fisherman sued Ellis to recover its value (an individual whale can yield an average of 20 barrels of oil). Assume that under local custom, title would go to those who killed the whale, but those fishermen would give a "finder's fee" to any person on shore who found the whale and notified them of its location. *See Ghen v. Rich*, 8 F. 159 (D. Mass. 1881).

The next case looks at another type of tangible property. But unlike a home-run baseball, this property is (or was) alive.

Corso v. Crawford Dog and Cat Hospital, Inc.

415 N.Y.S.2d 182 (N.Y. Civ. Ct. 1979)

Reading Guide

Should the law regard pets as personal property or as something more? Did the plaintiff in this case own the 15-year-old poodle (either before or after death)? How, if at all, does that determination affect the outcome of this case?

FRIEDMAN, J.

... On or about January 28, 1978, the plaintiff [Kay Corso] brought her 15 year old poodle into the defendant's premises for treatment. After examining the dog, the defendant recommended euthanasia and shortly thereafter the dog was put to death. The plaintiff and the defendant agreed that the dog's body would be turned over to Bide-A-Wee, an organization that would arrange a funeral for the dog. The plaintiff alleged that the defendant wrongfully disposed of her dog, failed to turn over the remains of the dog to the plaintiff for the funeral. The plaintiff had arranged for an elaborate funeral for the dog including a head stone, an epitaph, and attendance by plaintiff's two sisters and a friend. A casket was delivered to the funeral which, upon opening the casket, instead of the dog's body, the plaintiff found the body of a dead cat. ...

The question before the court now is two-fold. (1) Is it an actionable tort that was committed? (2) If there is an actionable tort, is the plaintiff entitled to damages beyond the market value of the dog?

Before answering these questions the court must first decide whether a pet such as a dog is only an item of personal property as prior cases have held. This court now overrules prior precedent and holds that a pet is not just a thing, but occupies a special place somewhere in between a person and a piece of personal property.

As in the case where a human body is withheld, the wrongful withholding or, as here, the destruction of the dog's body, gives rise to an actionable tort.

In ruling that a pet such as a dog is not just a thing I believe the plaintiff is entitled to damages beyond the market value of the dog. A pet is not an inanimate thing that just receives affection—it also returns it. I find that plaintiff Ms. Corso did suffer shock, mental anguish and despondency due to the wrongful destruction and loss of the dog's body.

She had an elaborate funeral scheduled and planned to visit the grave in the years to come. She was deprived of this right.

This decision is not to be construed to include an award for the loss of a family heirloom which would also cause great mental anguish. An heirloom, while it might be the source of good feelings, is merely an inanimate object and is not capable of returning love and affection. It does not respond to human stimulation; it has no brain capable of displaying emotion, which in turn causes a human response. Losing the right to memorialize a pet rock, or a pet tree or losing a family picture album is not actionable. But a dog, that is something else. To say it is a piece of personal property and no more is a repudiation of our humaneness. This I cannot accept.

Accordingly, the court finds the sum of $700 to be reasonable compensation for the loss suffered by the plaintiff.

Note

A changing world—living property: Should the law continue to classify animals as property? For example, should the law treat your pet more like a child or more like your property casebook? And if the law continues to treat pets as property, would it be desirable (or even possible) to award them legal rights, and if so, what rights?

One scholar argues that that the classification of at least some animals as mere personal property no longer reflects society's values and norms. Instead, Professor David Favre asserts that the traditional three categories of property (real property, tangible personal property, and intangible personal property) should be expanded to include a fourth category—living property. He explains,

> Animals already have a modest variety of legal rights. . . . To make a more coherent package of all the animal-related public policy issues, it will be useful to acknowledge the existence of a fourth category of property, living property. Once this new category is separated out from other property, a focused scholarly consideration of the issues will result in a new list of legal rights for at least some of these animals. . . .

> At this point in history, the non-human animals of our Earth are not our brothers, nor our equals, but like our children. They have interests of their own that deserve to be nurtured and protected from human harm, both in the consideration of ethical acts and the laws that we humans implement on their behalf.

David Favre, *Living Property: A New Status for Animals Within the Legal System*, 93 Marquette L. Rev. 1021, 1071 (2010). Others argue that animals should not be considered property, and that humans should cease keeping, owning, and using pets. *See* Gary L. Francione, *Animals—Property or Persons?*, in Animal Rights: Current Debates and New Directions 108, 134 (Cass R. Sunstein & Martha C. Nussbaum eds., 2004) ("We should care for domestic animals presently alive, but we should bring no more into existence"), cited in Favre, at 1023 n.3.

3. Intangible Personal Property

The category of intangible personal property is broad and expanding. It can include such things as intellectual property (IP), contract rights, goodwill, and assets with economic value (stocks, bonds, bank accounts, debts, and the like). More recently, new personal property rights have emerged, such as a person's "right of publicity" (prohibiting without permission the commercial use of another's name, face, or persona).

Intellectual property is perhaps the most prominent type of intangible personal property. In general, the common law provides very little protection against copying, but the Constitution authorizes Congress to grant limited monopolies over certain types of intellectual property:

> The Congress shall have power . . . to promote the progress of science and useful arts, by securing for limited times to authors and inventors the exclusive right to their respective writings and discoveries.

U.S. Constitution, art. I, § 8, cl. 8.

A Place to Start | **Intangible Personal Property**

- *Copyright:* The federal Copyright Act protects eight types of works, including literary (which may encompass computer programs), musical, dramatic, and architectural works. Protected works must satisfy additional statutory standards of *originality* and *fixation* into a tangible medium. Protection generally lasts for the life of the author plus 70 years (although renewal of pre-1978 copyrights might extend the protected period).

- *Patent:* Under the federal Patent Act, "Whoever invents or discovers any new and useful process, machine, manufacture, or composition of matter, or any new and useful improvement thereof, may obtain a patent therefor." 35 U.S.C. § 101. Patentable subject matter must satisfy additional statutory requirements of *novelty*, *utility*, *non-obviousness*, and *enablement*. Patents, which usually have a term of 20 years, grant to the holder "the right to exclude others from making, using, offering for sale, or selling the invention throughout the United States or importing the invention into the United States." 35 U.S.C. § 154(a)(1).

- *Trademark:* A trademark is a word, name, symbol, or device that identifies and distinguishes the sources of goods from other sources (the closely related *service mark* identifies and distinguishes the source of a service). Common examples include McDonald's double arches, Apple Inc.'s logo of an apple with a missing bite, and Nike's slogan "Just do it." The common law of unfair competition protects trademarks. The federal Lanham Act supplements the common law by providing for the registration and protection of marks, provided the holder satisfies the statutory elements of *distinctiveness, non-functionality,* and *first use in trade.*

DIGGING DEEPER: Does *first possession* (and the rule of capture) play a role in determining ownership of intellectual property? Notice that the constitutional treatment of IP rights highlights the tension between individual rights and the public interest. For example, how can Congress simultaneously promote creative activity, stimulate competition, and ensure that important ideas and information are easily and affordably available to the public?

Bowman v. Monsanto Co.

133 S. Ct. 1761 (2013)

Reading Guide

The law of intellectual property must account for rapid scientific and technological advances. Are the general rules of real and personal property helpful for resolving disputes over the ownership and use of intellectual property? Conversely, does IP law offer any lessons to real and personal property doctrines?

KAGAN, J., for a unanimous Court.

Under the doctrine of patent exhaustion, the authorized sale of a patented article gives the purchaser, or any subsequent owner, a right to use or resell that article. Such a sale, however, does not allow the purchaser to make new copies of the patented invention. The question in this case is whether a farmer who buys patented seeds may reproduce them through planting and harvesting without the patent holder's permission. We hold that he may not.

Respondent Monsanto invented a genetic modification that enables soybean plants to survive exposure to glyphosate, the active ingredient in many herbicides (including Monsanto's own Roundup). Monsanto markets soybean seed containing this altered genetic material as Roundup Ready seed. Farmers planting that seed can use a glyphosate-based herbicide to kill weeds without damaging their crops. Two patents issued to Monsanto cover various aspects of its Roundup Ready technology, including a seed incorporating the genetic alteration.

Monsanto sells, and allows other companies to sell, Roundup Ready soybean seeds to growers who assent to a special licensing agreement. That agreement permits a grower to plant the purchased seeds in one (and only one) season. He can then consume the resulting crop or sell it as a commodity, usually to a grain elevator or agricultural processor. But under the agreement, the farmer may not save any of the harvested soybeans for replanting, nor may he supply them to anyone else for that purpose. These restrictions reflect the ease of producing new generations of Roundup Ready seed. Because glyphosate resistance comes from the seed's genetic material, that trait is passed on from the planted seed to the harvested soybeans: Indeed, a single Roundup Ready seed can grow a plant containing dozens of genetically identical beans, each of which, if replanted, can grow another such plant—and so on and so on. The agreement's terms prevent the farmer from co-opting that process to produce his own Roundup Ready seeds, forcing him instead to buy from Monsanto each season.

Petitioner Vernon Bowman is a farmer in Indiana who, it is fair to say, appreciates Roundup Ready soybean seed. He purchased Roundup Ready each year, from a company affiliated with Monsanto, for his first crop of the season. In accord with the agreement just described, he used all of that seed for planting, and sold his entire crop to a grain elevator (which typically would resell it to an agricultural processor for human or animal consumption).

Bowman, however, devised a less orthodox approach for his second crop of each season. Because he thought such late-season planting "risky," he did not want to pay the premium price that Monsanto charges for Roundup Ready seed. He therefore went to a grain elevator; purchased "commodity soybeans" intended for human or animal consumption; and planted them in his fields. Those soybeans came from prior harvests of other local farmers. And because most of those farmers also used Roundup Ready seed, Bowman could anticipate that many of the purchased soybeans would contain Monsanto's patented technology. When he applied a glyphosate-based herbicide to his fields, he confirmed that this was so; a significant proportion of the new plants survived the treatment, and produced in their turn a new crop of soybeans with the Roundup Ready trait. Bowman saved seed from that crop to use in his late-season planting the next year—and then the next, and the next, until he had harvested eight crops in that way....

After discovering this practice, Monsanto sued Bowman for infringing its patents on Roundup Ready seed. Bowman raised patent exhaustion as a defense, arguing that Monsanto could not control his use of the soybeans because they were the subject of a prior authorized sale (from local farmers to the grain elevator). The District Court rejected that argument, and awarded damages to Monsanto of $84,456. The Federal Circuit affirmed....

The doctrine of patent exhaustion limits a patentee's right to control what others can do with an article embodying or containing an invention.[3] Under the doctrine, "the initial authorized sale of a patented item terminates all patent

---

3. [FN 2] The Patent Act grants a patentee the "right to exclude others from making, using, offering for sale, or selling the invention." 35 U.S.C. § 154(a)(1)....

rights to that item." *Quanta Computer, Inc. v. LG Electronics, Inc.*, 553 U.S. 617, 625 (2008). And by "exhaust[ing] the [patentee's] monopoly" in that item, the sale confers on the purchaser, or any subsequent owner, "the right to use [or] sell" the thing as he sees fit. *United States v. Univis Lens Co.*, 316 U.S. 241, 249-250 (1942). We have explained the basis for the doctrine as follows: "[T]he purpose of the patent law is fulfilled with respect to any particular article when the patentee has received his reward . . . by the sale of the article"; once that "purpose is realized the patent law affords no basis for restraining the use and enjoyment of the thing sold." *Id.* at 251.

Consistent with that rationale, the doctrine restricts a patentee's rights only as to the "particular article" sold, *ibid.*; it leaves untouched the patentee's ability to prevent a buyer from making new copies of the patented item. . . . Rather, "a second creation" of the patented item "call[s] the monopoly, conferred by the patent grant, into play for a second time." *Aro Mfg. Co. v. Convertible Top Replacement Co.*, 365 U.S. 336, 346 (1961). That is because the patent holder has "received his reward" only for the actual article sold, and not for subsequent recreations of it. *Univis*, 316 U.S., at 251. If the purchaser of that article could make and sell endless copies, the patent would effectively protect the invention for just a single sale. . . .

Unfortunately for Bowman, that principle decides this case against him. Under the patent exhaustion doctrine, Bowman could resell the patented soybeans he purchased from the grain elevator; so too he could consume the beans himself or feed them to his animals. Monsanto, although the patent holder, would have no business interfering in those uses of Roundup Ready beans. But the exhaustion doctrine does not enable Bowman to make *additional* patented soybeans without Monsanto's permission (either express or implied). And that is precisely what Bowman did. He took the soybeans he purchased home; planted them in his fields at the time he thought best; applied glyphosate to kill weeds (as well as any soy plants lacking the Roundup Ready trait); and finally harvested more (many more) beans than he started with. That is how "to 'make' a new product," to use Bowman's words, when the original product is a seed. . . .

Were the matter otherwise, Monsanto's patent would provide scant benefit. After inventing the Roundup Ready trait, Monsanto would, to be sure, "receiv[e] [its] reward" for the first seeds it sells. But in short order, other seed companies could reproduce the product and market it to growers, thus depriving Monsanto of its monopoly. And farmers themselves need only buy the seed once, whether from Monsanto, a competitor, or (as here) a grain elevator. The grower could multiply his initial purchase, and then multiply that new creation, *ad infinitum*—each time profiting from the patented seed without compensating its inventor. . . . The exhaustion doctrine is limited to the "particular item" sold to avoid just such a mismatch between invention and reward. . . .

Bowman principally argues that exhaustion should apply here because seeds are meant to be planted. The exhaustion doctrine, he reminds us, typically prevents a patentee from controlling the use of a patented product following an authorized sale. And in planting Roundup Ready seeds, Bowman continues, he is merely using them in the normal way farmers do. Bowman thus concludes that allowing Monsanto to interfere with that use would "cre-at[e] an impermissible exception to the exhaustion doctrine" for patented seeds and other "self-replicating technologies."

But it is really Bowman who is asking for an unprecedented exception—to what he concedes is the "well settled" rule that "the exhaustion doctrine does not extend to the right to 'make' a new product." ... That is because, once again, if simple copying were a protected use, a patent would plummet in value after the first sale of the first item containing the invention. The undiluted patent monopoly, it might be said, would extend not for 20 years (as the Patent Act promises), but for only one transaction. And that would result in less incentive for innovation than Congress wanted. ...

Nor do we think that rule will prevent farmers from making appropriate use of the Roundup Ready seed they buy. Bowman himself stands in a peculiarly poor position to assert such a claim. ...

Still, Bowman has another seeds-are-special argument: that soybeans naturally "self-replicate or 'sprout' unless stored in a controlled manner," and thus "it was the planted soybean, not Bowman" himself, that made replicas of Monsanto's patented invention. But we think that blame-the-bean defense tough to credit. Bowman was not a passive observer of his soybeans' multiplication; or put another way, the seeds he purchased (miraculous though they might be in other respects) did not spontaneously create eight successive soybean crops. ... In all this, the bean surely figured. But it was Bowman, and not the bean, who controlled the reproduction (unto the eighth generation) of Monsanto's patented invention.

Our holding today is limited—addressing the situation before us, rather than every one involving a self-replicating product. We recognize that such inventions are becoming ever more prevalent, complex, and diverse. In another case, the article's self-replication might occur outside the purchaser's control. Or it might be a necessary but incidental step in using the item for another purpose. ... In the case at hand, Bowman planted Monsanto's patented soybeans solely to make and market replicas of them, thus depriving the company of the reward patent law provides for the sale of each article. Patent exhaustion provides no haven for that conduct. We accordingly affirm the judgment of the Court of Appeals for the Federal Circuit.

Note

Overlapping property rights: Monsanto sued farmer Vernon Bowman for patent infringement. Identify precisely Monsanto's property right in the soybean seeds planted on Mr. Bowman's farm; identify precisely Bowman's property right in those same seeds. How does the Court (and Congress) reconcile these two competing rights? What policies does the Court seek to advance through its resolution of this dispute?

Problems

1. *The right to exclude—blowing in the wind?*   Between 1997 and 2010, Monsanto brought some 144 patent infringement suits for unauthorized use of its Roundup Ready seeds against farmers who replanted saved seeds, or who planted Roundup Ready seeds without authorization.

But unlike farmer Vernon Bowman, some farmers do not want to plant Monsanto's seeds—in fact, they would like to keep the seeds away from their property. Given the rapidly increasing use of Monsanto's genetically modified seeds by conventional farmers, many organic farmers and organic seed growers worry that their crops will inevitably become contaminated by Monsanto's transgenic (genetically altered) seed. Further, organic growers contend that they have been forced to forgo altogether the growing of certain crops, including corn, cotton, canola, sugar beets, soybeans, and alfalfa, because over 85-90% of such crops grown in the United States contain Monsanto's genetically altered seeds. As a result, the organic growers claim they cannot satisfy the requirements of their organic certification without costly precautions, including seed testing and the creation of buffer zones between their farms and those of neighbors growing modified crops.

Assume you represent the organic growers. Make an argument on their behalf against Monsanto for trespass. Alternatively, assume you represent Monsanto. Make an argument against the organic growers for patent infringement. As a matter of policy, how should the competing interests of Monsanto and organic farmers be resolved? *See generally Organic Seed Growers and Trade Assoc. v. Monsanto Co.*, 718 F.3d 1350 (Fed. Cir. 2013), *cert. denied*, 134 S. Ct. 901 (2014).

2. *Patenting life:* In 1972, microbiologist Ananda Chakrabarty filed an application to patent a human-created, genetically engineered bacterium. Chakrabarty's micro-organism was able to break down crude oil, thus making it potentially useful for oil spill cleanups. The new bacterium has markedly different characteristics from any found in nature, but it is a live organism. Recall the scope of patentable subject matter under the federal Patent Act: "Whoever invents or discovers any new and useful process, machine, manufacture, or composition of matter, or any new and useful improvement thereof, may obtain a patent therefor, subject to the conditions and requirements of this title." Under the language of the statute, can Chakrabarty patent this bacterium? As a matter of public policy, should he be allowed to do so? *See Diamond v. Chakrabarty*, 447 U.S. 303 (1980).

B. WHAT DOES OWNERSHIP MEAN?

Society's understanding of property changes over time. For now, let's begin with an often-quoted statement by William Blackstone (1723-1780), who defined property as "that sole and despotic dominion which one man claims and exercises over the external things of the world, in total exclusion of the right of any other individual in the universe." 2 Commentaries on the Laws of England (1765-1769). Perhaps Blackstone's statement was hyperbolic, but his single-minded focus on the rights of individuals with respect to things is an important starting point against which the law reacted. You can think of this as an "ownership" model or an "*in rem* rights" model (focusing on the rights in a particular thing that are binding on all others).

Sometime later, the "bundle of rights" metaphor developed; it is often attributed to the work of Yale law professor Wesley Newcomb Hohfeld (1879-1918). The phrase itself was probably first used in 1888, in a treatise on eminent domain: "The dullest individual among the people knows and understands that his property in anything is a bundle of rights." John Lewis, A Treatise on the Law of Eminent Domain in the United States 57 (1888). In 1936, Justice Benjamin Cardozo adopted the metaphor, asserting "The privilege of use is only one attribute, among many, of the bundle of privileges that make up property or ownership. A state is at liberty, if it pleases, to tax them all collectively, or to separate the faggots [sticks] and lay the charge distributively." *Henneford v. Silas Mason Co.*, 300 U.S. 577, 582 (1936).

A Place to Start | **Rights, Limitations, and Duties**

- *Property rights:* Ownership generally includes some or all of the following rights:
  - The right to possession
  - The right to use (including the right of nonuse)
  - The right to transfer to others during life by sale or gift, or at death by will or inheritance
  - The right to destroy
  - The right to exclude others

- *Limitations on rights:* Property rights can be limited (as well as protected) by constitutional, statutory, or common law. For example, nuisance is a common law limitation that prevents owners from using their property in an unreasonable or unlawful manner that interferes with others' reasonable use and enjoyment of their property. *See* Chapter 11.

- *Duties:* Property rights can also entail some affirmative duties. For example, owners of rental property are generally required to maintain their property in "habitable" condition for the benefit of their tenants. *See* Chapter 4.

DIGGING DEEPER: As you read the remaining materials in this chapter, think about whether the *bundle of sticks*, the *web of interests*, or some other metaphor best expresses the nature of property rights.

Despite its longevity, the bundle of rights metaphor has received its share of criticism from a variety of viewpoints. Some argue that that it is misguided to regard property as simply a bundle of rights because that view dignifies "any distribution of rights and privileges among persons with respect to things . . . with the (almost meaningless) label 'property.'" Thomas W. Merrill & Henry E. Smith, *What Happened to Property in Law and Economics?*, 111 Yale L.J. 357, 359 (2001). They argue instead for "an explicit recognition of the in rem dimension of property":

> . . . [F]ar from being a quaint aspect of the Roman or feudal past, the in rem character of property and its consequences are vital to an understanding of property as a legal and economic institution. Because core property rights attach to persons only through the intermediary of some thing, they have an impersonality and generality that is absent from rights and privileges that attach to persons directly. When we encounter a thing that is marked in the conventional manner as being owned, we know that we are subject to certain negative duties of abstention with respect to that thing—not to enter upon it, not to use it, not to take it, etc. And we know all this without having any idea who the owner of the thing actually is. In effect, these universal duties are broadcast to the world from the thing itself.

Other critiques of the bundle metaphor challenge its focus on the individual in isolation from others:

> The common conception of property as protection of individual control over valued resources is both intuitively and legally powerful. . . . However, internal tensions within this conception and the inevitable impacts of one person's property rights on others make it inadequate as the sole basis for resolving property conflicts. . . . For [that] task, we must look to the underlying human values that property serves and the social relationships it shapes and reflects. . . . Values promoted by property include life and human flourishing, the protection of physical security, the ability to acquire knowledge and make choices, and the freedom to live one's life on one's own terms. They also include wealth, happiness, and other aspects of individual and social well-being.

Gregory S. Alexander, Eduardo M. Peñalver, Joseph William Singer & Laura S. Underkuffler, *A Statement of Progressive Property*, 94 Cornell L. Rev. 743 (2009).

For each case in this section, consider whether the court's analysis is consistent with the ownership model, the bundle model, the relational/web model, or some other perspective. Note especially the particular right, limitation, or duty at issue. Together, what do these cases tell us about the modern conception of property and of ownership?

Perry v. Saint Francis Hospital & Medical Center, Inc.

886 F. Supp. 1551 (D. Kan. 1995)

Reading Guide

◆ *Property, contracts, and torts:* This case illustrates the interplay of property, tort, and contract law—which we will see throughout the course. For example, landlord-tenant agreements (Chapter 4) raise both property and contract issues, and the law of nuisance (Chapter 11) involves both property and tort law.

◆ *Statutory law:* As this case shows, property law is not solely a matter of state common law. Instead, federal and state *statutes* and local *ordinances* are also part of property law.

CROW, J.

Death is unique. It is unlike aught else in its certainty and its incidents. A corpse in some respects is the strangest thing on earth. A man who but yesterday breathed, and thought, and walked among us has passed away. Something has gone. The body is left still and cold, and is all that is visible to mortal eye of the man we knew. Around it cling love and memory. Beyond it may reach hope. It must be laid away. And the law—that rule of action which touches all human things—must touch also this thing of death. *Louisville & N.R. Co. v. Wilson,* 51 S.E. 24 (1905).

This is a tissue donation case in which the plaintiffs [Kenneth Perry's widow, Mary Ann Perry, and Kenneth's adult children] allege the defendants took from the deceased Kenneth Perry's body more tissue than what the plaintiff's had agreed to donate. . . .

For purposes of [defendant Saint Francis Hospital's motion for summary judgment] only, the court considers the following facts to be uncontroverted.

1. On January 28, 1992, Kenneth Perry suffered a heart attack at his home and was transported by ambulance to the defendant St. Francis Hospital. . . . [H]e was pronounced dead shortly after arriving at St. Francis. . . .

4. Nancy McDonald, a night shift staff nurse . . . , visited the plaintiffs in the waiting room and discussed before all the plaintiffs the matter of tissue donations. Nurse McDonald explained that Kenneth's death prevented an organ donation but that a donation of his body for research or a tissue donation of bone, skins and corneas remained as possible options. Saying they were opposed to disfiguring Kenneth's body because that is not what Kenneth would have wanted, the plaintiffs initially responded, "No" to Nurse McDonald's question about donations. Nurse McDonald then explained the procedure for

donating the corneas in which they were just "peeled off" without removing the eyes from the dead body.

5. Nurse McDonald then left the waiting room while the plaintiffs discussed whether Kenneth would have wanted to donate his corneas. The plaintiffs decided the donation would have been acceptable to Kenneth as the procedure simply involved "peeling them off."

6. When Nurse McDonald returned, the plaintiffs told her of their decision to donate Kenneth's corneas. Nurse McDonald then asked again about a skin or bone donation and explained that only sections of bones could be taken. The plaintiffs again said they were opposed to such a donation. One of Kenneth's sons adamantly said that his father's body was not going to be taken apart. Nurse McDonald then began discussing a bone marrow donation and explained a procedure involving a needle and syringe without any disfigurement. Nurse McDonald again left the waiting room while the family discussed a bone marrow donation.

7. Nurse McDonald returned a short time later with a consent form for tissue donation. The plaintiffs informed her of their consent to donate only the corneas and the bone marrow. . . . The [consent] form had been completed with lines drawn through the "yes" column opposite all the separately listed body parts for donation. Mary Ann Perry modified the consent form by separately checking the "no" boxes opposite each named body part except for the boxes opposite "eyes" and "bone" in which she wrote "yes" in the "yes" boxes. Mary Ann Perry asked Nurse McDonald why the form just said "bone" when all that was being donated was bone marrow. Nurse McDonald assured Mary that those doing the surgical procedure would understand that bone marrow and not the bones were to be removed. Mary Ann Perry . . . then executed the consent form.

8. Nurse McDonald's recollection of these events and conversations differs significantly from the plaintiffs. She recalls asking the family first whether Kenneth had ever signed his driver's license indicating organ donation or discussed donation with Mary Ann Perry. The family said this had not been discussed. Nurse McDonald remembers explaining the procedure for cutting the skin, removing the larger bones, and replacing the bones with rods or forms. She also recalls telling them that the entire eye is removed and replaced with a form. She said that these procedures kept the donations from causing a change that could be noticeable during an open casket funeral. . . .

11. A retrieval team employed by the American Red Cross actually harvested the bone tissue from Kenneth's body. They cut the skin and removed "[t]he upper section of the arm, femur whole right and left, tibia whole right and left, fibula whole right and left, and iliac crest right and left." They replaced the bones with wooden dowels and gauze cloth and sutured the skin.

12. Mary Ann Perry first learned that bones were removed from Kenneth's body when a representative with the funeral home told her to bring heavy clothing for the body to cover the bones that had been removed. She did not learn that the eyes had been removed until after this lawsuit. . . .

Tort of Outrage

Kansas recognizes the tort of intentional infliction of emotional distress or outrage. . . .

Accepting the plaintiffs' testimony, the court believes a reasonable person looking at this situation could exclaim, "Outrageous!" Nurse McDonald's conduct could be said to have exploited a position of trust and respect gained from an emotionally vulnerable family. . . . St. Francis is not entitled to summary judgment on the intentional infliction of emotional distress claim.

Breach of Contract

. . . In their briefs, the plaintiffs outline their understanding of this alleged contract:

> In the present case the subject matter of the contracts is the corneas and bone marrow of Kenneth Perry. There was an offer made by Nurse McDonald on behalf of defendant St. Francis and the undisclosed principal, defendant Red Cross, to the Perrys after some negotiation. The "offer" was that the family of Kenneth Perry would donate tissue of Kenneth Perry. The plaintiffs accepted the offer as orally conveyed to them by Nurse McDonald that they could donate the corneas of Kenneth Perry and Kenneth Perry's bone marrow. . . . The consideration of the contracts [was] the corneas and bone marrow of Kenneth Perry. . . .

The plaintiffs' breach of contract claim is an effort to force a square peg into a round hole. In their designated deposition testimony, the Perrys do not describe the consent form as functioning anything like a contract. . . . The court rejects the plaintiffs' attempts to construct an enforceable contract from these facts.

Mary Ann Perry does not establish that her property right in Kenneth's body includes a right to convey it for consideration. As the court previously held, Kansas law considers Mary Ann Perry to be the exclusive owner of a quasi-property right in the body, namely, the right to possess it for the limited purposes of preserving and burying it. Kansas common law on this matter is no different from the position universally held by other states which recognizes no property right, commercial or material, in the corpse itself but only a right of possession in order to dispose of the corpse appropriately. This "dubious property right to the body . . . cannot be conveyed, can be used only for the one purpose of burial, and not only has no pecuniary value but is a source of liability for funeral expenses." W. Prosser, *The Law of Torts,* 43-44 (2d ed. 1955). . . .

A contract approach to organ and tissue donation is not reconcilable with societal beliefs and values on this subject. The Uniform Anatomical Gift Act embodies "a commitment to the belief that organs should be given as a gift, either to a specific individual or to society at large." *Developments in the Law— Medical Technology and the Law,* 103 Harv. L. Rev. 1519, 1622 (1990). The same is reflected in federal law at 42 U.S.C. § 274e, which prohibits the "transfer [of] any human organ[4] for valuable consideration for use in human transplantation" but permits reasonable payments for the costs associated with organ procurement and use. 42 U.S.C. § 274e(a). For whatever reason, whether it be metaphysical, religious, or philosophical, society presently rejects the commercialization of human organs and tissues and tolerates only an altruistic system of voluntary donation. Because society accepts the exchange of human body parts only when based on a gift model, courts should be reluctant to recognize a cause of action that contravenes this fundamental public philosophy. . . .

It is therefore ordered that St. Francis' motion for summary judgment is granted on the plaintiffs' breach of contract claim and is denied in all other respects.

Notes

1. *Ownership of what?*   Exactly what property right do the Perrys claim? The court defines their interest as a "quasi property right"—what does that mean? One commentator places the court's imprecision into a broader context:

> There are only a few "things" that challenge our neat bifurcation of people and property. Primarily, these "things" are products of the human body that have been divorced from a living person and are not themselves alive, such as organs, cells, and unviable fetuses. The biological matter that remains after a human being dies is one such "thing" that exists in limbo between people and property. Like the material it governs, the law of human remains does not fit neatly into any pre-existing area of law. It is distinct and unique.

Tanya D. Marsh, *Selected Excerpts from The Law of Human Remains* 1-2 (2015), http://ssrn.com/abstract=2646184 (visited Sept. 10, 2015). Professor Marsh concludes, "The collective failure of legislatures, courts, attorneys, and scholars to carefully consider the law of human remains has resulted in an often disjointed and ad hoc collection of doctrines and statutes." *Id.*

2. *Transferability:*   To what extent do the plaintiffs claim they have the right to transfer (or alienate) the claimed property? Does the court agree? While Kenneth Perry was still alive, did he have the right to sell or give away his tissue and organs?

---

4. [FN 9] Congress defined "human organ" to include: "kidney, liver, heart, lung, pancreas, bone marrow, cornea, eye, bone, and skin or any subpart thereof and any other human organ . . . specified by the Secretary of Health and Human Services by regulation." 42 U.S.C. § 274e(c)(1). A violation of § 274e carries a maximum sentence of five-years imprisonment and a $50,000 fine.

Problems

1. *The sale of organs:*   As the court explains, federal law forbids the sale of "human organs" 42 U.S.C. § 274e. Look closely at the statutory definition of "human organ" (reproduced in the court's footnote 9) and determine whether federal law permits each of the following actions: (a) selling one's own blood plasma, sperm, eggs, or hair; (b) participating in clinical medical trials for payment; and, (c) the practice of surrogacy (whereby a woman carries a baby to term on behalf of others, resulting from an embryo conceived by others implanted in her womb).

State law may be relevant, too. For example, many states have adopted some version of the Uniform Anatomical Gift Act. This act is but one of many drafted by the Uniform Law Commission, which describes itself as a nonprofit, nonpartisan association that "has served the states and their citizens by drafting state laws on subjects on which uniformity across the states is desirable and practicable." *See* http://www.uniformlaws.org (visited Sept. 7, 2015); U.S. Dept. of Health & Human Services, *State Organ Donation Legislation,* http://www.organdonor.gov (visited Aug. 1, 2015) (follow link to legislation). We will examine several other uniform laws later in this course.

2. *A stolen spleen?*   John Moore underwent treatment for hairy-cell leukemia at UCLA Medical Center. His physicians recommended removal of his spleen to slow the progress of his life-threatening disease and Moore agreed. After the splenectomy, Moore returned to the Medical Center several times for what he understood to be medically beneficial post-operative care. During those visits, physicians withdrew additional tissue samples, including blood, skin, and bone marrow aspirate. Unknown to Moore, his physicians were using his samples for medical research of potentially vast market value. About five years after Moore's surgery, his doctor established a cell line from Moore's T-lymphocytes and applied for a patent on the cell line. The proteins produced by the cell line had an estimated market value of three billion dollars, with the share of the doctors and the Medical Center reaching perhaps into the millions of dollars. Moore sued the physicians and the Medical Center, alleging that (a) the defendants' failure to disclose the extent of their research and economic interests in his cells before obtaining his consent to extract them breached the defendants' fiduciary duty to Moore for failure to obtain his informed consent, and (b) the defendants' unauthorized use of Moore's cells constituted conversion—a tort that protects against interference with possessory and ownership interests in personal property. How should the court decide this case? Did Moore have a property interest in his cells *before* they were removed from his body? *After*? *See Moore v. Regents of the University of California,* 793 P.2d 479 (Cal. 1990), *cert. denied,* 499 U.S. 936 (1991).

Perry v. St. Francis Hospital raised questions of the transferability of human tissue and organs, by gift and by sale. We will next consider issues related to the transferability of land.

Johnson v. M'Intosh

21 U.S. (8 Wheat.) 543 (1823)

Reading Guide

Who is the *very first owner* of land? Before the United States existed as a nation, who owned the land that would eventually be encompassed within its borders? Should title be recognized in the Native American tribes already present on the continent (and in those to whom they conveyed their land), or in the European explorers who came to its shores (and if so, in which European nation)? Before you read this case, reflect for a moment on the immense consequences that follow from such questions of title.

MARSHALL, C.J.

[This was an action of ejectment brought by plaintiffs Thomas Johnson, Jr. of Annapolis, Maryland, and others, for lands in the state and district of Illinois, purportedly purchased from the Illinois and Piankeshaw tribes for upwards of $31,000. In 1818, the United States conveyed to the defendant, William M'Intosh, 11,560 acres within the state of Illinois and contained within the tracts purportedly granted and conveyed to the plaintiffs. Defendant M'Intosh entered these lands under his patent from the United States, and acquired possession of them before the institution of this suit.]

The plaintiffs in this cause claim the land . . . under two grants, purporting to be made, the first in 1773, and the last in 1775, by the chiefs of certain Indian tribes, constituting the Illinois and the Piankeshaw nations; and the question is, whether this title can be recognised in the Courts of the United States?

The facts, as stated in the case agreed, show the authority of the chiefs who executed this conveyance, so far as it could be given by their own people; and likewise show, that the particular tribes for whom these chiefs acted were in rightful possession of the land they sold. The inquiry, therefore, is, in a great measure, confined to the power of Indians to give, and of private individuals to receive, a title which can be sustained in the Courts of this country.

As the right of society, to prescribe those rules by which property may be acquired and preserved is not, and cannot be drawn into question; as the title to lands, especially, is and must be admitted to depend entirely on the law of the nation in which they lie; it will be necessary, in pursuing this inquiry, to examine, not singly those principles of abstract justice, which the Creator of all things has impressed on the mind of his creature man, and which are admitted to regulate, in a great degree, the rights of civilized nations, whose perfect independence is acknowledged; but those principles also which our own government has adopted in the particular case, and given us as the rule for our decision.

On the discovery of this immense continent, the great nations of Europe were eager to appropriate to themselves so much of it as they could respectively acquire. Its vast extent offered an ample field to the ambition and enterprise of all; and the character and religion of its inhabitants afforded an apology for considering them as a people over whom the superior genius of Europe might claim an ascendency. The potentates of the old world found no difficulty in convincing themselves that they made ample compensation to the inhabitants of the new, by bestowing on them civilization and Christianity, in exchange for unlimited independence. But, as they were all in pursuit of nearly the same object, it was necessary, in order to avoid conflicting settlements, and consequent war with each other, to establish a principle, which all should acknowledge as the law by which the right of acquisition, which they all asserted, should be regulated as between themselves. This principle was, that discovery gave title to the government by whose subjects, or by whose authority, it was made, against all other European governments, which title might be consummated by possession. . . .

Those relations which were to exist between the discoverer and the natives, were to be regulated by themselves. The rights thus acquired being exclusive, no other power could interpose between them.

In the establishment of these relations, the rights of the original inhabitants were, in no instance, entirely disregarded; but were necessarily, to a considerable extent, impaired. They were admitted to be the rightful occupants of the soil, with a legal as well as just claim to retain possession of it, and to use it according to their own discretion; but their rights to complete sovereignty, as independent nations, were necessarily diminished, and their power to dispose of the soil at their own will, to whomsoever they pleased, was denied by the original fundamental principle, that discovery gave exclusive title to those who made it.

While the different nations of Europe respected the right of the natives, as occupants, they asserted the ultimate dominion to be in themselves; and claimed and exercised, as a consequence of this ultimate dominion, a power to grant the soil, while yet in possession of the natives. These grants have been understood by all, to convey a title to the grantees, subject only to the Indian right of occupancy. . . .

No one of the powers of Europe gave its full assent to this principle, more unequivocally than England. The documents upon this subject are ample and complete. So early as the year 1496, her monarch granted a commission to the Cabots, to discover countries then unknown to *Christian people*, and to take possession of them in the name of the king of England. Two years afterwards, Cabot proceeded on this voyage, and discovered the continent of North America, along which he sailed as far south as Virginia. To this discovery the English trace their title. . . .

Thus has our whole country been granted by the crown while in the occupation of the Indians. These grants purport to convey the soil as well as the right of dominion to the grantees. . . .

Thus, all the nations of Europe, who have acquired territory on this continent, have asserted in themselves, and have recognised in others, the exclusive right of the discoverer to appropriate the lands occupied by the Indians. Have the American States rejected or adopted this principle? . . .

Virginia, particularly, within whose chartered limits the land in controversy lay, passed an act, in the year 1779, declaring her "exclusive right of pre-emption from the Indians, of all the lands within the limits of her own chartered territory, and that no person or persons whatsoever, have, or ever had, a right to purchase any lands within the same, from any Indian nation, except only persons duly authorized to make such purchase; formerly for the use and benefit of the colony, and lately for the Commonwealth."[5] The act then proceeds to annul all deeds made by Indians to individuals, for the private use of the purchasers. . . .

The United States, then, have unequivocally acceded to that great and broad rule by which its civilized inhabitants now hold this country. They hold, and assert in themselves, the title by which it was acquired. They maintain, as all others have maintained, that discovery gave an exclusive right to extinguish the Indian title of occupancy, either by purchase or by conquest; and gave also a right to such a degree of sovereignty, as the circumstances of the people would allow them to exercise. . . .

. . . All our institutions recognise the absolute title of the crown, subject only to the Indian right of occupancy, and recognise the absolute title of the crown to extinguish that right. This is incompatible with an absolute and complete title in the Indians.

We will not enter into the controversy, whether agriculturists, merchants, and manufacturers, have a right, on abstract principles, to expel hunters from the territory they possess, or to contract their limits. Conquest gives a title which the Courts of the conqueror cannot deny, whatever the private and

---

5. [FN (e)] This statute is as follows:

An act for declaring and asserting the rights of this Commonwealth, concerning purchasing lands from Indian natives. To remove and prevent all doubt concerning purchases of lands from the Indian natives, Be it declared by the General Assembly, that this Commonwealth hath the exclusive right of pre-emption from the Indians, of all the lands within the limits of its own chartered territory, as described by the act and constitution of government, in the year 1776. That no person or persons whatsoever, have, or ever had, a right to purchase any lands within the same, from any Indian nation, except only persons duly authorized to make such purchases on the public account. . . .

And be it further declared and enacted, That every purchase of lands heretofore made, by, or on behalf of, the crown of England or Great Britain, from any Indian nation or nations, within the before mentioned limits, doth and ought to enure for ever, to and for the use and benefit of this Commonwealth, and to or for no other use or purpose whatsoever; and that all sales and deeds which have been, or shall be made by any Indian or Indians, or by any Indian nation or nations, for lands within the said limits, to or for the separate use of any person or persons whatsoever shall be, and the same are, hereby declared utterly void and of no effect.

speculative opinions of individuals may be, respecting the original justice of the claim which has been successfully asserted. The British government, which was then our government, and whose rights have passed to the United States, asserted title to all the lands occupied by Indians, within the chartered limits of the British colonies. It asserted also a limited sovereignty over them, and the exclusive right of extinguishing the title which occupancy gave to them. These claims have been maintained and established as far west as the river Mississippi, by the sword. The title to a vast portion of the lands we now hold, originates in them. It is not for the Courts of this country to question the validity of this title, or to sustain one which is incompatible with it.

Although we do not mean to engage in the defence of those principles which Europeans have applied to Indian title, they may, we think, find some excuse, if not justification, in the character and habits of the people whose rights have been wrested from them. . . .

But the tribes of Indians inhabiting this country were fierce savages, whose occupation was war, and whose subsistence was drawn chiefly from the forest. To leave them in possession of their country, was to leave the country a wilderness; to govern them as a distinct people, was impossible, because they were as brave and as high spirited as they were fierce, and were ready to repel by arms every attempt on their independence.

What was the inevitable consequence of this state of things? The Europeans were under the necessity either of abandoning the country, and relinquishing their pompous claims to it, or of enforcing those claims by the sword, and by the adoption of principles adapted to the condition of a people with whom it was impossible to mix, and who could not be governed as a distinct society, or of remaining in their neighbourhood, and exposing themselves and their families to the perpetual hazard of being massacred.

Frequent and bloody wars, in which the whites were not always the aggressors, unavoidably ensued. European policy, numbers, and skill, prevailed. As the white population advanced, that of the Indians necessarily receded. . . .

That law which regulates, and ought to regulate in general, the relations between the conqueror and conquered, was incapable of application to a people under such circumstances. The resort to some new and different rule, better adapted to the actual state of things, was unavoidable. Every rule which can be suggested will be found to be attended with great difficulty.

However extravagant the pretension of converting the discovery of an inhabited country into conquest may appear; if the principle has been asserted in the first instance, and afterwards sustained; if a country has been acquired and held under it; if the property of the great mass of the community originates in it, it becomes the law of the land, and cannot be questioned. So, too, with respect to the concomitant principle, that the Indian inhabitants are to be considered merely as occupants, to be protected, indeed, while in peace, in the possession of their lands, but to be deemed incapable of transferring the absolute title to others. However this restriction may be opposed to natural right, and to the usages of civilized nations, yet, if it be indispensable to that system under which the country has been settled, and be adapted to the actual condition of the two people, it may, perhaps, be supported by reason, and certainly cannot be rejected by Courts of justice. . . .

This opinion conforms precisely to the principle which has been supposed to be recognised by all European governments, from the first settlement of America. The absolute ultimate title has been considered as acquired by discovery, subject only to the Indian title of occupancy, which title the discoverers possessed the exclusive right of acquiring. Such a right is no more incompatible with a seisin in fee, than a lease for years, and might as effectually bar an ejectment. . . .

After bestowing on this subject a degree of attention which was more required by the magnitude of the interest in litigation, and the able and elaborate arguments of the bar, than by its intrinsic difficulty, the Court is decidedly of opinion, that the plaintiffs do not exhibit a title which can be sustained in the Courts of the United States; and that there is no error in the judgment which was rendered against them in the District Court of Illinois. Judgment affirmed, with costs.

Notes

1. *The discovery doctrine:* Before plaintiff Johnson and defendant M'Intosh acquired their claims to the disputed land, who owned it—the United States or the occupying Native American tribes? Carefully articulate the discovery rule. Did it purport to resolve title conflicts between the tribes and the first European explorers, or did it answer a different question? What rationale supports the discovery rule, despite the Chief Justice's description of it as an extravagant "pretension"?

2. *First possession:* Chief Justice Marshall said that the tribes were in "rightful possession" of the land they purportedly sold to plaintiff Johnson, and that "the rights of the original inhabitants were, in no instance, entirely disregarded." What does that mean? Does it mean that the tribes owned the land? Why or why not?

3. *The missing stick:* Read carefully the text of the statute excerpted in the Court's footnote (e). What impact did this have on the tribes' ability to sell or give away their lands? What do you suppose was its underlying rationale? Such statutes are sometimes referred to as *Trade and Intercourse Acts.* Recall the sticks included in the typical bundle of rights. What sticks were missing from the tribes' bundle (if indeed, they possessed a bundle at all)?

4. *Property without an owner:* In a modern society, examples of property without an owner are rare. Still, we have encountered a few such situations. In some cases, *creation* confers title. In *Bowman v. Monsanto,* for example,

patent law awarded certain property rights to Monsanto because it had invented a genetically modified soybean plant. In other cases, *first possession* (or, the closely related idea of *first capture*) confers title. For example, in *Popov v. Hayashi*, the court used the concept of possession to determine the owner of a home-run baseball. (Do you recall why the disputed baseball was considered *unowned* in the first case?) Does the rule of *Johnson v. M'Intosh* follow from the idea of first possession? In this context, what qualifies as "possession"?

5. *Patents and chains of title:*   We have already seen that "patent" refers to a certain type of intellectual property. In this case, the court uses "patent" in a different context: When the United States conveyed title to its property under a variety of laws encouraging settlement (such as the Homestead Acts), it gave a *patent* to the new owner, which functions much like a deed from the federal government. When we study real estate transactions (Chapters 7 and 8), we will see that it is important for sellers to have a clear chain of title linking together all former owners of the property. In theory, sellers should trace their chains of title all the way back to the parcel's original governmental holder. Here, what is Johnson's chain of title? What is M'Intosh's chain of title? Which chain is superior?

6. *More to the story—domestic dependent nations:*   Through a series of opinions decided by Chief Justice Marshall, the Supreme Court recognized Native American tribes as *sovereign nations* located within the borders of the United States. But unlike other sovereigns (such as European nations), these sovereigns were treated as *dependent* on the guardianship of the United States. The purposes of this guardianship were both noble (to protect the tribes from overreaching and sharp dealing by states and individuals that would cheat them of their property) and ignoble (flowing from demeaning perceptions of the tribes, such as Justice Marshall's description of the prevailing characterization of them as "fierce savages"). *See Worster v. Georgia*, 31 U.S. (6 Pet.) 515 (1832); *Cherokee Nation v. Georgia*, 30 U.S. (5 Pet.) 1 (1831). *See also* Christine A. Klein, *Treaties of Conquest: Property Rights, Indian Treaties, and the Treaty of Guadalupe Hidalgo*, 26 New Mexico L. Rev. 201 (1996); Felix S. Cohen, *Original Indian Title*, 32 Minn. L. Rev. 28 (1947). To this day, the United States has a trust relationship with the tribes. *See* U.S. Dept. of the Interior, Indian Affairs, *What We Do* (explaining that the "United States has a unique legal and political relationship with the Indian tribes and Alaska Native entities as provided by the Constitution of the United States, treaties, court decisions and Federal statutes"), http://www.indianaffairs.gov (visited Sept. 7, 2015).

7. *Modern ramifications:*   In 1970, three tribes of the Oneida Indians in New York brought suit against Oneida and Madison Counties in New York. They alleged that their ancestors had conveyed 100,000 acres to the state under a 1795 agreement that violated the Trade and Intercourse Act of 1793,

and thus that the transaction was void. The Oneidas were one of the six nations of the Iroquois, who were quite powerful in the northeast at the time of the American Revolution. From time immemorial to shortly after the Revolution, the Oneidas inhabited what is now central New York State. Their aboriginal land was approximately six million acres, extending from the Pennsylvania border to the St. Lawrence River, and from the shores of Lake Ontario to the western foothills of the Adirondack Mountains. The Oneidas actively supported the colonists in the Revolution. After the war, the United States recognized the importance of the Oneidas' role and in the Treaty of Fort Stanwix (1784) the government promised that the Oneidas would be secure "in the possession of the lands on which they are settled." During this period, New York State came under increasingly heavy pressure to open the Oneidas' land for settlement. Consequently, in 1788, the State entered into a "treaty" with the tribes, under which it purchased the vast majority of the Oneidas' land. The Oneidas retained a reservation of about 300,000 acres. In the 1970 lawsuit, the Oneidas sought damages representing the fair rental value of that part of the land presently owned and occupied by the counties. The case reached the U.S. Supreme Court.

Under *Johnson v. M'Intosh*, should the tribes recover for a violation of their possessory rights dating back some 180 years? *See Oneida Cnty. v. Oneida Nation*, 470 U.S. 226 (1985) (holding Indian tribes could maintain an action based on federal common law, and that the action was not barred by limitations, laches, or other such doctrines); *New York v. Jewell*, 2014 WL 841764 (N.D.N.Y., Mar. 4, 2014) (approving settlement agreement); *Sweeping Oneida Indian-New York Settlement Ratified by Federal Court*, Syracuse.com, Mar. 4, 2014 (visited Sept. 7, 2015) (describing settlement that provides, among other things, for the tribes to receive 13,000 acres of land in trust, with provisions to add an additional 12,000 acres of land).

8. *Too many property interests—fractionation:*   Through a complicated series of federal policies, some tribal reservations—lands held by the tribe as a whole—were divided into allotments to individual tribal members. In part, the allotment policy was designed to break up large reservations and to encourage individual Indian landowners to assimilate into the prevailing European-American culture. But, if the owner of a single allotment died without a will, that piece of property would pass to numerous heirs together as co-owners (such as to all of the decedent's children). Over time, a single piece of land could have so many co-owners that it became difficult, if not impossible, for all owners to agree as to how the land should be used. We will see in Chapter 5 (on concurrent ownership) that such problems of excessively divided ownership are not limited to Native Americans.

In a reversal of policy toward the tribes, the federal government is now trying to help Native Americans reassemble their individual parcels into larger tracts of land owned by the tribe as a whole. Do you see how it is much easier to divide land into separately owned parcels than it is to reassemble land into single ownership?

As the Department of the Interior describes the land buy-back program:

What is fractionation? Why is it an issue?

Fractionation refers to divided ownership of Indian lands and is the result of land parcels (allotments) passing to numerous heirs over generations. The land itself is not physically divided; rather, the heirs of an original allottee own undivided interests in the allotment. Many allotments now have hundreds and even thousands of individual owners. Divided ownership makes it difficult, if not impossible, to use the land for any beneficial purpose because consent from at least 50 percent of the owners must first be obtained. As a result, fractionated allotments often lie idle rather than being utilized for agricultural, recreational, cultural, commercial, or even residential purposes. Even when consent can be obtained to lease an allotment, highly divided ownership often results in individual owners receiving only nominal lease returns. Approximately 64 percent of Indian landowners earn $25 or less in annual income from their fractional interests in allotments. There are approximately 150 reservations with fractionated tracts of land with more than 245,000 unique individual owners.

What is the Land Buy-Back Program for Tribal Nations?

The Secretary of the Interior established the Land Buy-Back Program for Tribal Nations to give individual landowners an opportunity to help address the problem of fractionation. The Program has $1.9 billion available to purchase fractional interests in trust or restricted land from willing sellers at fair market value within a 10-year period. Individuals who choose to sell their interests receive payments directly into their Individual Indian Money accounts. Consolidated interests are then immediately restored to tribal trust ownership for uses benefiting the reservation community and tribal members.

U.S. Dept. of the Interior, *Land Buy-Back Program for Tribal Nations, Appendix A: Frequently Asked Questions*, http://www.doi.gov//buybackprogram/index.cfm (visited Apr. 19, 2015).

State v. Shack

277 A.2d 369 (N.J. 1971)

Reading Guide

We began this section with William Blackstone's assertion that owners hold their property "in total exclusion of the right of any other individual in the universe." Can such a sweeping statement really be true? Using the web of interests metaphor, can you think of any situations in which the right to exclude must be limited to accommodate the rights of others? This case takes up that question.

WEINTRAUB, C.J.

Defendants entered upon private property to aid migrant farmworkers employed and housed there. Having refused to depart upon the demand of the owner, defendants were charged with violating N.J.S.A. 2A:170-31 which provides that "(a)ny person who trespasses on any lands . . . after being forbidden so to trespass by the owner . . . is a disorderly person and shall be punished by a fine of not more than $50." . . .

Complainant, Tedesco, a farmer, employs migrant workers for his seasonal needs. As part of their compensation, these workers are housed at a camp on his property.

Defendant Tejeras is a field worker for the Farm Workers Division of the Southwest Citizens Organization for Poverty Elimination, known by the acronym SCOPE, a nonprofit corporation funded by the Office of Economic Opportunity pursuant to an act of Congress. The role of SCOPE includes providing for the "health services of the migrant farm worker."

Defendant Shack is a staff attorney with the Farm Workers Division of Camden Regional Legal Services, Inc., known as "CRLS," also a nonprofit corporation funded by the Office of Economic Opportunity pursuant to an act of Congress. The mission of CRLS includes legal advice and representation for these workers.

Differences had developed between Tedesco and these defendants prior to the events which led to the trespass charges now before us. Hence when defendant Tejeras wanted to go upon Tedesco's farm to find a migrant worker who needed medical aid for the removal of 28 sutures, he called upon defendant Shack for his help with respect to the legalities involved. Shack, too, had a mission to perform on Tedesco's farm; he wanted to discuss a legal problem with another migrant worker there employed and housed. Defendants arranged to go to the farm together. Shack carried literature to inform the migrant farmworkers of the assistance available to them under federal statutes, but no mention seems to have been made of that literature when Shack was later confronted by Tedesco.

Defendants entered upon Tedesco's property and as they neared the camp site where the farmworkers were housed, they were confronted by Tedesco who inquired of their purpose. Tejeras and Shack stated their missions. In response, Tedesco offered to find the injured worker, and as to the worker who needed legal advice, Tedesco also offered to locate the man but insisted that the consultation would have to take place in Tedesco's office and in his presence. Defendants declined, saying they had the right to see the men in the privacy of their living quarters and without Tedesco's supervision. Tedesco thereupon summoned a State Trooper who, however, refused to remove defendants except upon Tedesco's written complaint. Tedesco then executed the formal complaints charging violations of the trespass statute. . . .

The constitutionality of the trespass statute, as applied here, is challenged on several scores. . . .

We think it unnecessary to explore [its] validity. The reason is that we are satisfied that under our State law the ownership of real property does not include the right to bar access to governmental services available to migrant workers and hence there was no trespass within the meaning of the penal statute. . . .

Property rights serve human values. They are recognized to that end, and are limited by it. Title to real property cannot include dominion over the destiny of persons the owner permits to come upon the premises. Their well-being must remain the paramount concern of a system of law. Indeed the needs of the occupants may be so imperative and their strength so weak, that the law will deny the occupants the power to contract away what is deemed essential to their health, welfare, or dignity.

Here we are concerned with a highly disadvantaged segment of our society. We are told that every year farmworkers and their families numbering more than one million leave their home areas to fill the seasonal demand for farm labor in the United States. . . .

The migrant farmworkers are a community within but apart from the local scene. They are rootless and isolated. Although the need for their labors is evident, they are unorganized and without economic or political power. It is their plight alone that summoned government to their aid. In response, Congress provided under Title III-B of the Economic Opportunity Act of 1964 for "assistance for migrant and other seasonally employed farmworkers and their families." . . .

These ends would not be gained if the intended beneficiaries could be insulated from efforts to reach them. It is in this framework that we must decide whether the camp operator's rights in his lands may stand between the migrant workers and those who would aid them. The key to that aid is communication. Since the migrant workers are outside the mainstream of the communities in which they are housed and are unaware of their rights and opportunities and of the services available to them, they can be reached only by positive efforts tailored to that end. . . .

A man's right in his real property of course is not absolute. It was a maxim of the common law that one should so use his property as not to injure the rights of others: "Sic Utere Tuo ut Alienum Non Laedas." Although hardly a precise solvent of actual controversies, the maxim does express the inevitable proposition that rights are relative and there must be an accommodation when they meet. Hence it has long been true that necessity, private or public, may justify entry upon the lands of another. For a catalogue of such situations, see Prosser, Torts (3d ed. 1964) § 24.

The subject is not static. As pointed out in 5 Powell, Real Property § 745, while society will protect the owner in his permissible interests in land, yet,

> [s]uch an owner must expect to find the absoluteness of his property rights curtailed by the organs of society, for the promotion of the best interests of others

for whom these organs also operate as protective agencies. The necessity for such curtailments is greater in a modern industrialized and urbanized society than it was in the relatively simple American society of fifty, 100, or 200 years ago. The current balance between individualism and dominance of the social interest depends not only upon political and social ideologies, but also upon the physical and social facts of the time and place under discussion.

Professor Powell added in § 746:

As one looks back along the historic road traversed by the law of land in England and in America, one sees a change from the viewpoint that he who owns may do as he pleases with what he owns, to a position which hesitatingly embodies an ingredient of stewardship; which grudgingly, but steadily, broadens the recognized scope of social interests in the utilization of things. . . .

The argument in this case understandably included the question whether the migrant worker should be deemed to be a tenant and thus entitled to the tenant's right to receive visitors, or whether his residence on the employer's property should be deemed to be merely incidental and in aid of his employment, and hence to involve no possessory interest in the realty. . . .

We see no profit in trying to decide upon a conventional category and then forcing the present subject into it. That approach would be artificial and distorting. The quest is for a fair adjustment of the competing needs of the parties, in the light of the realities of the relationship between the migrant worker and the operator of the housing facility.

Thus approaching the case, we find it unthinkable that the farmer-employer can assert a right to isolate the migrant worker in any respect significant for the worker's well-being. The farmer, of course, is entitled to pursue his farming activities without interference, and this defendants readily concede. But we see no legitimate need for a right in the farmer to deny the worker the opportunity for aid available from federal, State, or local services, or from recognized charitable groups seeking to assist him. Hence representatives of these agencies and organizations may enter upon the premises to seek out the worker at his living quarters. So, too, the migrant worker must be allowed to receive visitors there of his own choice, so long as there is no behavior hurtful to others, and members of the press may not be denied reasonable access to workers who do not object to seeing them.

It is not our purpose to open the employer's premises to the general public if in fact the employer himself has not done so. We do not say, for example, that solicitors or peddlers of all kinds may enter on their own. . . .

And we are mindful of the employer's interest in his own and in his employees' security. Hence he may reasonably require a visitor to identify himself, and also to state his general purpose if the migrant worker has not already informed him that the visitor is expected. But the employer may not deny the worker his privacy or interfere with his opportunity to live with dignity and to enjoy associations customary among our citizens. These rights are too fundamental to be denied on the basis of an interest in real property and too fragile to be left to the unequal bargaining strength of the parties.

It follows that defendants here invaded no possessory right of the farmer-employer. Their conduct was therefore beyond the reach of the trespass statute. The judgments are accordingly reversed and the matters remanded to the County Court with directions to enter judgments of acquittal.

Notes

1. *Overlapping rights in the same property:* What rights does farmer Tedesco have in the farm? Are there any limitations on those rights? What is the source of those limitations? Now, think about the farmworkers. Do they have property (or other) rights in the farm? How did the court accommodate those two sets of rights and interests? What does it tell you about the qualified nature of the right to exclude?

2. *Limits on the right to exclude:* Throughout this course, we will see many other examples showing that property rights are not absolute. With respect to the right to exclude, can you think of any other factors that might limit its exercise? Does the court's discussion of the human values served by property rights help you answer that question?

3. *The trespassing mobile home:* Steenberg Homes was delivering a mobile home to its purchasers, and the easiest route was across the snow-covered field of neighbors Harvey and Lois Jacque. The only alternative delivery route was a curvy, private road covered in seven feet of snow—a potentially dangerous route that would require Steenberg to set up rollers to maneuver the home around the curves. Steenberg asked the Jacques several times whether the company could move the home across their field, or if it could pay for the right to do so. The Jacques adamantly refused, saying that it was not a question of money, and that Steenberg should "follow the road, that is what the road is for." The assistant manager told his employees, "I don't give a ___ what [Mr. Jacque] said, just get the home in there any way you can." The employees used a bobcat to cut a path through the Jacques' snow-covered field, and hauled the mobile home across the Jacques' property. The Jacques sued for intentional trespass, and the jury awarded $1 in nominal damages and $100,000 in punitive damages. The Wisconsin Supreme Court ultimately concluded that an award of damages, even if nominal, could sustain an award of punitive damages. *See Jacque v. Steenberg Homes, Inc.*, 563 N.W.2d 154 (Wis. 1997).

What accounts for the different outcomes in *State v. Shack* and *Steenberg Homes*? List as many distinguishing facts as you can. Then, describe any policies that might support the distinction. Do you think each case was correctly decided, and why (or why not)? Together, what do the two cases suggest about the scope of the right to exclude?

Eyerman v. Mercantile Trust Co.

524 S.W.2d 210 (Mo. Ct. App. 1975)

| **Reading Guide** |

We have examined numerous aspects of property ownership, including the rights to possess, transfer, and exclude—and potential limitations of those rights. The last case of this chapter invites you to think about the extent to which owners have a right to destroy their property.

RENDLEN, J.

Plaintiffs appeal from denial of their petition seeking injunction to prevent demolition of a house at #4 Kingsbury Place in the City of St. Louis. The action is brought by individual neighboring property owners and certain trustees for the Kingsbury Place Subdivision. We reverse.

Louise Woodruff Johnston, owner of the property in question, died January 14, 1973, and by her will directed the executor "... to cause our home at 4 Kingsbury Place ... to be razed and to sell the land upon which it is located ... and to transfer the proceeds of the sale ... to the residue of my estate." Plaintiffs assert that razing the home will adversely affect their property rights, violate the terms of the subdivision trust indenture for Kingsbury Place, produce an actionable private nuisance and is contrary to public policy.

The area involved is a "private place" established in 1902 by trust indenture which provides that Kingsbury Place and Kingsbury Terrace will be so maintained, improved, protected and managed as to be desirable for private residences. The trustees are empowered to protect and preserve Kingsbury Place from encroachment, trespass, nuisance or injury, and it is "the intention of these presents, forming a general scheme of improving and maintaining said property as desirable residence property of the highest class." The covenants run with the land and the indenture empowers lot owners or the trustees to bring suit to enforce them.

Except for one vacant lot, the subdivision is occupied by handsome, spacious two and three-story homes, and all must be used exclusively as private residences. The indenture generally regulates location, costs and similar features for any structures in the subdivision, and limits construction of subsidiary structures except those that may beautify the property, for example, private stables, flower houses, conservatories, play houses or buildings of similar character.

On trial the temporary restraining order was dissolved and all issues found against the plaintiffs. . . .

Whether #4 Kingsbury Place should be razed is an issue of public policy involving individual property rights and the community at large. The plaintiffs have pleaded and proved facts sufficient to show a personal, legally protectible interest.

Demolition of the dwelling will result in an unwarranted loss to this estate, the plaintiffs and the public. The uncontradicted testimony was that the current value of the house and land is $40,000.00; yet the estate could expect no more than $5,000.00 for the empty lot, less the cost of demolition at $4,350.00, making a grand loss of $39,350.33 if the unexplained and capricious direction to the executor is effected. Only $650.00 of the $40,000.00 asset would remain.

Kingsbury Place is an area of high architectural significance, representing excellence in urban space utilization. Razing the home will depreciate adjoining property values by an estimated $10,000.00 and effect corresponding losses for other neighborhood homes. The cost of constructing a house of comparable size and architectural exquisiteness would approach $200,000.00.

The importance of this house to its neighborhood and the community is reflected in the action of the St. Louis Commission on Landmarks and Urban Design designating Kingsbury Place as a landmark of the City of St. Louis. This designation, under consideration prior to the institution of this suit, points up the aesthetic and historical qualities of the area and assists in stabilizing Central West End St. Louis. It was testified by the Landmarks Commission chairman that the private place concept, once unique to St. Louis, fosters higher home maintenance standards and is among the most effective methods for stabilizing otherwise deteriorating neighborhoods. The executive director of Heritage St. Louis, an organization operating to preserve the architecture of the city, testified to the importance of preserving Kingsbury Place intact:

> The reason[] for making Kingsbury Place a landmark is that it is a definite piece of urban design and architecture. It starts out with monumental gates on Union. There is a long corridor of space, furnished with a parkway in the center, with houses on either side of the street. . . . The existence of this piece of architecture depends on the continuity of . . . both sides. Breaks in this continuity would be as holes in this wall, and would detract from the urban design qualities of the streets. And the richness of the street is this belt of green lot on either side, with rich tapestry of the individual houses along the sides. Many of these houses are landmarks in themselves, but they add up to much more . . . I would say Kingsbury Place, as a whole, with its design, with its important houses . . . is a most significant piece of urban design by any standard.

To remove #4 Kingsbury from the street was described as having the effect of a missing front tooth. The space created would permit direct access to Kingsbury Place from the adjacent alley, increasing the likelihood the lot will be subject to uses detrimental to the health, safety and beauty of the neighborhood. The mere possibility that a future owner might build a new home with the inherent architectural significance of the present dwelling offers little support to sustain the condition for destruction.

. . . It becomes apparent that no individual, group of individuals, nor the community generally benefits from the senseless destruction of the house; instead, all are harmed and only the caprice of the dead testatrix is served. Destruction of the house harms the neighbors, detrimentally affects the community, causes monetary loss in excess of $39,000.00 to the estate and is without benefit to the dead woman. No reason, good or bad, is suggested by the will or record for the eccentric condition. This is not a living person who seeks to exercise a right to reshape or dispose of her property; instead, it is an attempt by will to confer the power to destroy upon an executor who is given no other interest in the property. To allow an executor to exercise such power stemming from apparent whim and caprice of the testatrix contravenes public policy.

The Missouri Supreme Court held in *McClintock v. Guinotte*, 204 S.W. 806 (1918) that the taking of property by inheritance or will is not an absolute or natural right but one created by the laws of the sovereign power. The court points out the state "may foreclose the right absolutely, or it may grant the right upon conditions precedent. . . ." Further, this power of the state is one of inherent sovereignty which allows the state to "say what becomes of the property of a person, when death forecloses his right to control it." *Id.* at 808, 809. While living, a person may manage, use or dispose of his money or property with fewer restraints than a decedent by will. One is generally restrained from wasteful expenditure or destructive inclinations by the natural desire to enjoy his property or to accumulate it during his lifetime. Such considerations however have not tempered the extravagance or eccentricity of the testamentary disposition here on which there is no check except the courts. . . .

In the early English case of *Egerton v. Brownlow*, 10 Eng.Rep. 359, 417, it is stated: "The owner of an estate may himself do many things which he could not (by a condition) compel his successor to do. One example is sufficient. He may leave his land uncultivated, but he cannot by a condition compel his successor to do so. The law does not interfere with the owner and compel him to cultivate his land, (though it may be for the public good that land should be cultivated) so far the law respects ownership; but when, by a condition, he attempts to compel his successor to do what is against the public good, the law steps in and pronounces the condition void and allows the devisee to enjoy the estate free from the condition." . . .

Although public policy may evade precise, objective definition, it is evident from the authorities cited that this senseless destruction serving no apparent good purpose is to be held in disfavor. A well-ordered society cannot tolerate the waste and destruction of resources when such acts directly affect important interests of other members of that society. It is clear that property owners in the neighborhood of #4 Kingsbury, the St. Louis Community as a whole and the beneficiaries of testatrix's estate will be severely injured should the provisions of the will be followed. No benefits are present to balance against this injury and we hold that to allow the condition in the will would be in violation of the public policy of this state.

Having thus decided, we do not reach the plaintiffs' contentions regarding enforcement of the restrictions in the Kingsbury Place trust indenture and actionable private nuisance, though these contentions may have merit.[6] The judgment is reversed and the cause remanded to the Circuit Court to enter judgment as prayed. . . .

CLEMENS, J., dissenting.

. . . The simple issue in this case is whether the trial court erred by refusing to enjoin a trustee from carrying out an explicit testamentary directive. In an emotional opinion, the majority assumes a psychic knowledge of the testatrix' reasons for directing her home be razed; her testamentary disposition is characterized as "capricious," "unwarranted," "senseless," and "eccentric." But the record is utterly silent as to her motives.

The majority's reversal of the trial court here spawns bizarre and legally untenable results. By its decision, the court officiously confers a "benefit" upon testamentary beneficiaries who have never litigated or protested against the razing. The majority opinion further proclaims that public policy demands we enjoin the razing of this private residence in order to prevent land misuse in the City of St. Louis. But the City, like the beneficiaries, is not a party to this lawsuit. The fact is the majority's holding is based upon wispy, self-proclaimed public policy grounds that were only vaguely pleaded, were not in evidence, and were only sketchily briefed by the plaintiffs. . . .

The majority opinion goes far beyond the public-policy argument briefed by plaintiffs. I[t] suggests the court may declare certain land uses, which are not illegal, to be in violation of the City's public policy. And the majority so finds although the City itself is not a litigant claiming injury to its interests. The majority's public-policy conclusions are based not upon evidence in the lower court, but upon incidents which may have happened thereafter. . . .

As much as our aesthetic sympathies might lie with neighbors near a house to be razed, those sympathies should not so interfere with our considered legal judgment as to create a questionable legal precedent. Mrs. Johnston had the right

---

6. [FN 5] The dissenting opinion suggests this case be decided under the general rule that an owner has exclusive control and the right to untrammeled use of real property, citing *Reutner v. Vouga*, 367 S.W.2d 34 (Mo. App. 1963), *City of Fredericktown v. Osborn*, 429 S.W.2d 17 (Mo. App. 1968), and *Gibbs v. Cass*, 431 S.W.2d 662 (Mo. App. 1968). Although Maxims of this sort are attractive in their simplicity, standing alone they seldom suffice in a complex case. None of the cited cases pertains to the qualified right of testatrix to impose, post mortem, a condition upon her executor requiring an unexplained destruction of estate property; instead, they involve, respectively, surface water, use of property for commercial purposes and restrictive covenants as to subdivision lot sizes. Each acknowledges the principle of an owner's "free use" as the starting point but all recognize competing interests of the community and other owners of great importance. Accordingly, the general principle of "free and untrammeled" use is markedly narrowed, supporting in each case a result opposite that urged by the dissent in the case at bar.

during her lifetime to have her house razed, and I find nothing which precludes her right to order her executor to raze the house upon her death. It is clear that "the law favors the free and untrammeled use of real property." *Gibbs v. Cass*, 431 S.W.2d 662 (Mo. App. 1968). This applies to testamentary dispositions. An owner has exclusive control over the use of his property subject only to the limitation that such use may not substantially impair another's right to peaceably enjoy his property. Plaintiffs have not shown that such impairment will arise from the mere presence of another vacant lot on Kingsbury Place. . . .

Notes

1. *The right to destroy:*   The majority and dissent disagree as to the scope of Louise Woodruff Johnston's property right to order her home destroyed, particularly after her death. What policies support each judge's view? According to each, what does it mean to "own" property? There is an emerging rich literature on the right (or lack thereof) to destroy one's property. *See, e.g.*, Lior Jacob Strahilevitz, *The Right to Destroy*, 114 Yale L.J. 781 (2005); Joseph L. Sax, Playing Darts with a Rembrandt: Public and Private Rights in Cultural Treasures (1999). Going further, is there an affirmative duty for owners to maintain their property or to refrain from waste, at least under certain conditions? *See* Michael Pappas, *Anti-Waste*, 56 Ariz. L. Rev. (2014); Nadav Shoked, *The Duty to Maintain*, 64 Duke L.J. 437 (2014); Lee Anne Fennell, *Forcings*, 114 Columbia L. Rev. 1297 (2014).

2. *Just passing through—a capricious testatrix:*   While Louise Woodruff Johnston was alive, would she be permitted to tear down her home? How, if at all, does it matter that she is now deceased? How should the law accommodate the desires of both the living and the dead?

3. *Beyond policy—nuisance and running covenants:*   The court based its decision on public policy considerations, and did not reach issues involving nuisance and restrictions in the Kingsbury Place trust indenture. As we will see in Chapter 11, nuisance law allows landowners to enjoin others from using their own property in a manner that unreasonably interferes with the first landowners' use and enjoyment of their land. Suppose you represent the plaintiffs in this case. What arguments would you make that the razing of #4 Kingsbury Place would unreasonably interfere with your clients' use and enjoyment of their property? For now, notice that the defendant's action need not be illegal, but simply cause an unreasonable interference.

In their third argument, the plaintiffs relied on the trust indenture. This is an agreement among the landowners in Kingsbury Place Subdivision to voluntarily place certain restrictions on their property, which they intended to "run with the land" and bind all future lot owners. We will study such arrangements in Chapter 10. For now, look at the court's description of the restrictions. Can you make an argument on behalf of the plaintiffs that razing the house at #4 Kingsbury Place would violate those restrictions?

4. *The place:*   Today, Kingsbury Place continues to be an upscale neighborhood of large, well-kept homes. The house at #4 is still standing, and there is no evidence of "missing front teeth" elsewhere along the street.

The home at #4 Kingsbury Place
Photo by Christine A. Klein (2015)

C. BEYOND THE BLACK LETTER: THE RISE OF THE SHARING ECONOMY

Your first-year property course is about ownership of real and personal property. But, some have begun to ask the paradigm-shifting question—*is owning overrated?* To be sure, the American dream of homeownership and the desire to own nice and useful things is unlikely to go away any time soon. But, the question is worth thinking about before you immerse yourself in the study of property law and ownership.

In the sharing economy, people transform their underused assets into cash. Often, this sharing is a peer-to-peer transaction facilitated by the Internet, but there can be an intermediary that connects owners with people who want something. The adjective "sharing" is somewhat misleading for this new business model because money changes hands, but it is nevertheless used to evoke the familiar idea of borrowing a cup of sugar from a neighbor, or lending a truck to a friend who is moving. A related idea is the rental economy, in which people choose to rent things, rather than to own them. *The Home Depot* for example, rents power tools that might be too expensive for an occasional user to purchase.

Airbnb—an early and perhaps familiar example of the sharing economy—offers for rent what it describes as "unique places to stay from local hosts in 190+ countries" that "create a sense of belonging around the world." But many other things and services can be the subject of the sharing economy too, including cars, music, tents, designer dresses, surfboards, and dog sitting services. The impact is significant and growing, with an estimated 19% of the total adult population in the United States having participated in at least one transaction in the sharing economy. *Airbnb*, for example, connects hosts with an average of 425,000 guests per night, which is almost 22% greater than *Hilton Worldwide*'s reach. *See* PricewaterhouseCoopers LLP, *The Sharing Economy: Consumer Intelligence Series* (2015), pwc.com/CISsharing (visited Apr. 20, 2015).

Discussion Questions

1. *Why sharing?*   Have you participated in the sharing economy, either as an owner or as a renter? What are the advantages of this new model? What are its limitations, as compared to traditional ownership? How do the ownership and sharing models compare in terms of the rights of possession, use, transferability, destruction, and exclusion? *See* Kellen Zale, *Sharing Property*, Colo. L. Rev. (2016) (developing conceptual framework and taxonomy of sharing as foundation for future discussion of the sharing economy).

2. *Challenges for the law:*   Does the sharing economy raise any challenge for the law in general, and property law in particular? How can the law facilitate the sharing economy, and should it? With respect to housing, the federal government subsidizes homeownership, as through an income tax deduction for mortgage interest. Should it continue to provide such a benefit for homeowners, as opposed to renters?

3. *Learning from the sharing economy:*   As you read the chapters that follow, keep in mind the sharing economy and look for insights that it offers about the nature of property and ownership. For example, think about what it reveals about the tension between the individual and the community, a fundamental issue at the core of many traditional property doctrines, including nuisance (Chapter 11), zoning (Chapter 12), and eminent domain (Chapter 13).

D. SKILLS PRACTICE: COMMON LAW ANALYSIS

There are three basic types of common law analysis used by attorneys on behalf of their clients, and by judges to decide cases: (a) fact-based analysis,

(b) precedent-based analysis, and (c) policy-based analysis. We will consider the first two types here. In Chapter 2, we will take up the third category, and will also turn our attention to the analysis of statutes—laws enacted by state and federal legislatures. In practice, the various types of analysis (and accompanying arguments) can overlap, but it is easier to develop your skills by studying each mode of analysis separately.

A Place to Start | Common Law Analysis

- *Fact-based analysis:* If it is clear which legal rule applies to a particular situation, then the attorneys and the court will likely focus on *applying the law to the facts of the case.* That is, for *each* element of the rule, the parties will analyze whether the record contains sufficient facts to demonstrate satisfaction of that element.

  - *Rule:* First, carefully articulate the relevant rule. Judicial opinions often contain several partial statements of the same rule, and it will take a close reading of the text to determine its full contours.

  - *Facts:* Clearly list the facts that support each element of the rule. Be sure to include even basic facts, rather than assume the decisionmaker is familiar with them. If the same fact satisfies more than one element of the rule, then repeat the fact (or provide a cross-reference to it) in the appropriate place(s) in your discussion.

  - *Example:* The relevant rule provides, "To qualify for a merit-based scholarship at West Dakota Law School, applicants must show that they are West Dakota residents and that they are in the top 20% of their class." In her scholarship application, Amber asserts, (a) She is a West Dakota resident, as demonstrated by her possession of a current West Dakota driver's license, which is only issued to state residents; and (b) She is in the top 20% of her class because her class rank is 20 out of 200 (top 10%), as documented by her attached transcript.

- *Precedent-based analysis:* If the applicable rule is not clear, then each party will likely articulate a rule from a prior judicial opinion (preferably from the same jurisdiction) that is favorable to its position.

  - *Analogizing to precedent:* The attorney will seek to convince the court that the two situations are *analogous*—that is, that the current situation is so similar (if not identical) to the facts in the precedential case that the same rule should apply to both situations.

  - *Distinguishing precedent:* Conversely, each attorney will seek to demonstrate that the precedent offered by the opposing party is *distinguishable* and should not be applied to the current dispute. To do so, the attorney will list as many facts as possible that are meaningfully different from those in the cited precedent.

- *Policy-based analysis:* To be considered in Chapter 2.

Tasks

1. *The nature of the decision:*   Review the cases in this chapter. Determine whether each was decided primarily on the basis of fact-based analysis, precedent-based analysis, or something else.

2. *Argument critique:*   Choose one case in this chapter to critique—choose an example that clearly contains either fact-based or precedent-based reasoning. Then, perform the following tasks: (a) Clearly state one argument made by either the plaintiff or the defendant (you may have to reason backward from the court's holding and piece together the party's likely argument); (b) Critique the effectiveness of that argument, noting its strengths and its weaknesses; and (c) Restate the argument more effectively in your own words.

E. CHAPTER REVIEW

1. Practice Question[7]

Note to students: There is a review at the end of each chapter, with sample answers appearing in the Appendix to this book. Please understand that the reviews are *not* intended to be comprehensive and do not purport to address all important topics covered in the chapter. Instead, they are offered simply to give you practice in the skill of *synthesizing* the law contained in the chapter and applying it to new factual scenarios.

Sunken treasure: The *African Queen* grounded on a shoal nine miles off the coast of Ocean City, Maryland. The bow section split from the stern and floated approximately two miles away. The owners abandoned the vessel, and never returned. A man named Warner found the vessel's stern section, and spent several days aboard examining it. Upon returning to shore he published a legal notice in a local newspaper asserting his right of sole and exclusive possession of the vessel, but he did not return to the vessel nor undertake any salvage operations. Along came Deir and Little, who completed an expensive salvage effort by raising the stern section and towing it into Norfolk under adverse conditions. Following their initial visit, Deir and Little remained continuously aboard the vessel. Later, Warner asserted a claim to the salvage profits against Deir and Little; in response, Deir and Little asked the court to declare them the true and lawful owners of the ship's stern section.

You represent the plaintiff Warner. Assume that *Popov v. Hayashi* is the most relevant precedent in your jurisdiction. What arguments would you make on Warner's behalf that he is entitled to the salvage profits? Be sure to

---

7. Answers appear in the Appendix to this casebook.

discuss whether the facts of *Popov v. Hayashi* are *analogous* to or *distinguishable* from the facts of your case.

2. Bringing It Home

Note to students: Each chapter ends with a *Bringing It Home* section that asks you to research various topics covered by your state's body of statutory law. Please notice that your goal should *not* be to identify and memorize the specific law of your jurisdiction (in fact, it is unlikely that even your professor could cite to all relevant provisions without first conducting some research). Instead, these exercises offer you an opportunity for self-directed development of the skills of statutory research and comprehension.

Research tip: Most states post their compiled statutes online, and make them accessible to all without charge. To find the appropriate website, try typing into your search engine, *yourstate.gov* (as in, NewYork.gov or California .gov), and then looking for links to *legislative* or *statutory* materials. Alternatively, you can use Westlaw, LexisNexis, or another legal database to research statutory materials. No matter what database you use, it is often helpful to begin by looking at the statute's table of contents. This forces you to think logically about how property concepts are interrelated, and to make reasonable assumptions about the broader topic under which your narrow issue will be categorized. If you simply type random search terms into the database, you risk using the wrong key words and failing to find relevant materials.

Research your state's statutory law, and find its relevant provisions on the following topics:

1. *Pets as personal property:*   Because animal companions are uniformly treated as personal property, their owners may be subject to liability for the actions of their pets. Does your state impose liability on dog owners? Under what circumstances?

2. *Organ donation:*   Most states have adopted the Uniform Anatomical Gift Act of 2006—is your state one of them? Go to the website of The National Conference of Commissioners on Uniform State Laws, Uniform Law Commission, then search for the proper act (because all uniform acts begin with the word "uniform," you would search under the second word of the legislative title, "anatomical"). A map will appear, showing adoptions by state. Skim through the Act itself, which is also available on that website. How would you describe its general approach and purpose?

Gifts, Finders, and Adverse Possession

A. Gifts
B. Finders
C. Adverse Possession
D. Beyond the Black Letter: Cybersquatting
E. Skills Practice: Common Law and Statutory Analysis
F. Chapter Review

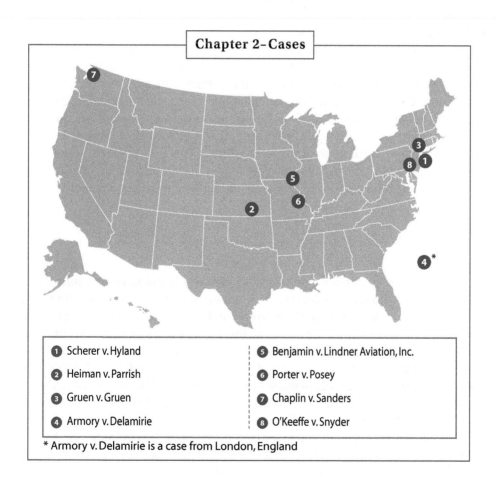

Chapter 2–Cases

① Scherer v. Hyland   ⑤ Benjamin v. Lindner Aviation, Inc.

② Heiman v. Parrish   ⑥ Porter v. Posey

③ Gruen v. Gruen   ⑦ Chaplin v. Sanders

④ Armory v. Delamirie   ⑧ O'Keeffe v. Snyder

* Armory v. Delamirie is a case from London, England

Chapter 1 introduced you to the basic idea of property, and also gave you a glimpse of the importance of first possession in resolving competing claims to property. Further, the chapter introduced the notion that owners should have the right to freely transfer their property to others, a right that was withheld from the Native American tribe in *Johnson v. M'Intosh*, in part because the Court determined they did not fully own the lands they possessed, but instead had a mere right of occupancy.

In this chapter, we will take a closer look at *possession*. As you saw *Johnson v. M'Intosh*, "possession" is a malleable notion. There, only qualifying acts of first possession were deemed sufficient to confer original title to previously un-owned lands. Likewise, *Popov v. Hayashi* explored the nuances of possession, and the consequences that may follow. Although possession is not synonymous with ownership, it is a critical benchmark against which courts often measure competing claims of title. As you ponder the materials in this chapter, you will likely agree with the U.S. Supreme Court that "there is no word more ambiguous in its meaning than possession." *National Safe Deposit Co. v. Stead*, 232 U.S. 58, 67 (1914). And yet, there are few words more important in property law.

We will also look more deeply at the idea of *transferability* (also called *alienability*). Through the act of transfer, owners can give or sell their property to others, which is an important stick in the property bundle. According to an often-quoted maxim, "restraints on alienation are disfavored" in the law. Beyond voluntary transfers, the law sometimes recognizes *involuntary* transfers from one party to another. As we will see, the law of adverse possession provides for certain involuntary transfers, without the first owner's consent or (sometimes) actual knowledge. As you read this chapter, think about what policies are promoted by voluntary and involuntary transfers, respectively.

A. GIFTS

Gifts are present, irrevocable transfers between living persons—*inter vivos* conveyances—without consideration or compensation. They are subject to three requirements: (1) intent, (2) delivery, and (3) acceptance by the recipient (the *donee*). The apparent simplicity of these three requirements can be misleading. Suppose, for example, that a seriously ill donor wants to make a gift in contemplation of death. Can that qualify as an inter vivos gift, or is it subject to the more rigorous safeguards of wills? Our focus here will be on gifts of personal property (also known as *chattels*), saving our study of real estate transfers (with and without consideration) for Chapter 7.

The following *A Place to Start* box introduces the gift requirements. As you read through them, pay special attention to the role of *possession*. Which of the requirements incorporates the notion of possession?

A Place to Start | Inter Vivos Gifts

- **Intent:** The donor must intend to make a present, irrevocable, and absolute transfer of an interest in property.

  - **Present effect:** The property *right* must vest immediately, although the donee might not be entitled to *possession* until some future time. For example, a donor might convey a life estate in certain real property to Anna, and a remainder interest to Baird. Both Anna and Baird hold a present property right, with Anna taking possession now, and Baird taking possession in the future upon Anna's death. *See* Chapter 3 (present estates and future interests).

  - **Future effect:** In contrast, transfers made by will are not inter vivos gifts because they do not take effect until the death of the testator, and remain revocable until that time.

  - **Conditional gifts:** As an exception to the requirement of a present and irrevocable transfer, the law recognizes conditional gifts in some circumstances. For example, gifts *causa mortis* are conditional gifts made in contemplation of the donor's imminent death. Such gifts are generally revocable during the donor's lifetime, but they become irrevocable upon the donor's death if the donor dies from the anticipated cause, and if the donor is survived by the donee.

- **Delivery:** The donor must make a manual, constructive, or symbolic delivery of the gifted property.

  - **Manual delivery:** The donor turns over dominion and control of the property to the donee. This is the preferred method of delivery, unless manual delivery is unreasonable due to the nature of the property or other circumstances.

  - **Constructive delivery:** The donor must transfer something that gives the donee access to the property and control over it. For example, the donor may turn over the key to a locked drawer or safe deposit box that holds the property.

  - **Symbolic delivery:** The donor must transfer something that represents the property, such as a written instrument (a deed to real property, for example).

- **Acceptance:** Although donees might conceivably refuse gifts under some circumstances, acceptance is usually presumed if the property is valuable or beneficial to the donee.

DIGGING DEEPER: Why do you think the law imposes these three requirements? What purposes might each one serve?

The second requirement—delivery—has been the focus of considerable attention. According to one 1926 commentator, this requirement serves the pragmatic function of making the donor feel the "wrench of delivery," which "makes vivid and concrete to the donor the significance of the act performed," provides "unequivocal evidence" of the gift to witnesses, and provides "prima facie evidence" of the gift to the donee. Philip Mechem, *The Requirement of Delivery in Gifts of Chattels and of Choses in Action Evidenced by Commercial Instruments*, 21 Ill. L. Rev. 341, 354 (1926). More recently, however, some have questioned the importance of delivery:

> The uncertainty remaining with respect to gifts, despite centuries of judicial experience, is directly traceable to the troublesome element of delivery, and reflects in large measure the fact that the growth of the decisional law on this topic has been seriously hampered by inertia, an undue concentration on formal requirements and an inordinate fear of fraudulent claims.

Powell on Real Property §§ 85.21(2)(b) & 2(c) (Michael Allan Wolf, gen. ed. 2015). The treatise argues for a change in the law to "benefit the layman-donor by freeing him from the traps for the unsuspecting that now exist in the delivery maze." As you learn more about gifts, consider whether you agree that delivery's importance has been exaggerated, or whether it continues to serve a valid function. What does the law's stubborn focus on delivery reveal about possession as a bedrock principle of property law?

Scherer v. Hyland

380 A.2d 698 (N.J. 1977)

Reading Guide

- ◆ *Intent and delivery:* The following case focuses on the requirements of intent and delivery. As you read it, notice how those two requirements are interrelated.
- ◆ *Conditional gifts:* The dispute below involves one type of *conditional* gift—the gift causa mortis. In such cases, courts typically make an exception to the requirement of a present and irrevocable transfer—why do you think that is so?

SIMONS, J.

Defendant, the Administrator ad litem of the Estate of Catherine Wagner, appeals from an Appellate Division decision, one judge dissenting, affirming a summary judgment by the trial court holding that Ms. Wagner had made a valid gift causa mortis of a check to plaintiff. We affirm.

The facts are not in dispute. Catherine Wagner and the plaintiff, Robert Scherer, lived together for approximately fifteen years prior to Ms. Wagner's death in January 1974. In 1970, the decedent and plaintiff were involved in an automobile accident in which decedent suffered facial wounds and a broken hip. Because of the hip injury, decedent's physical mobility was substantially impaired. She was forced to give up her job and to restrict her activities. After the accident, plaintiff cared for her and assumed the sole financial responsibility for maintaining their household. During the weeks preceding her death, Ms. Wagner was acutely depressed. On one occasion, she attempted suicide by slashing her wrists. On January 23, 1974, she committed suicide by jumping from the roof of the apartment building in which they lived.

On the morning of the day of her death, Ms. Wagner received a check for $17,400 drawn by a Pennsylvania attorney who had represented her in a claim arising out of the automobile accident. The check represented settlement of the claim. Plaintiff telephoned Ms. Wagner at around 11:30 a.m. that day and was told that the check had arrived. Plaintiff noticed nothing unusual in Ms. Wagner's voice. At about 3:20 p.m., decedent left the apartment building and jumped to her death. The police, as part of their investigation of the suicide, asked the building superintendent to admit them to the apartment. On the kitchen table they found the check, endorsed in blank, and two notes handwritten by the decedent. In one, she described her depression over her physical condition, expressed her love for Scherer, and asked him to forgive her "for taking the easy way out." In the other, she indicated that she "bequeathed" to plaintiff all of her possessions, including "the check for $17,400.00." . . .

Under our wills statute it is clear that Ms. Wagner's note bequeathing all her possessions to Mr. Scherer cannot take effect as a testamentary disposition. A donatio causa mortis has been traditionally defined as a gift of personal property made by a party in expectation of death, then imminent, subject to the condition that the donor die as anticipated. Establishment of the gift has uniformly called for proof of delivery.

The primary issue here is whether Ms. Wagner's acts of endorsing the settlement check, placing it on the kitchen table in the apartment she shared with Scherer, next to a writing clearly evidencing her intent to transfer the check to Scherer, and abandoning the apartment with a clear expectation of imminent death constituted delivery sufficient to sustain a gift causa mortis of the check. Defendant, relying on the principles established in *Foster v. Reiss,* 112 A.2d 553 (N.J. 1955), argues that there was no delivery because the donor did not unequivocally relinquish control of the check before her death. Central to this argument is the contention that suicide, the perceived peril, was one which decedent herself created and one which was completely within her control. According to this contention, the donor at any time before she jumped from the apartment roof could have changed her mind, re-entered the apartment, and reclaimed the check. Defendant therefore reasons that decedent did not make an effective transfer of the check during her lifetime, as is required for a valid gift causa mortis.

The majority and dissenting opinions in *Foster v. Reiss* contain thorough analyses of the evolution of the delivery requirement of the gift causa mortis. *See also* Mechem, *The Requirement of Delivery in Gifts of Chattels and of Choses in Action Evidenced by Commercial Instruments,* 21 Ill. L. Rev. 341, 457, 568 (1926). . . .

There is general agreement that the major purpose of the delivery requirement is evidentiary. Proof of delivery reduces the possibility that the evidence of intent has been fabricated or that a mere donative impulse, not consummated by action, has been mistaken for a completed gift. Since "these gifts come into question only after death has closed the lips of the donor," the delivery requirement provides a substantial safeguard against fraud and perjury. *See Keepers v. Fidelity Title and Deposit Co.*, 28 A. 585 (N.J. 1893). In *Foster*, the majority concluded that these policies could best be fulfilled by a strict rule requiring actual manual tradition of the subject-matter of the gift except in a very narrow class of cases where "there can be no actual delivery" or where "the situation is incompatible with the performance of such ceremony." Justice Jacobs, in his dissenting opinion . . . questioned the reasonableness of requiring direct physical delivery in cases where donative intent is "freely and clearly expressed in a written instrument." He observed that a more flexible approach to the delivery requirement had been taken by other jurisdictions and quoted approvingly from *Devol v. Dye*, 24 N.E. 246, (Ind. Sup. Ct. 1890). That case stated:

> (G)ifts causa mortis are not to be held contrary to public policy, nor do they rest under the disfavor of the law, when the facts are clearly and satisfactorily shown which make it appear that they were freely and intelligently made. . . . [E]ach case must be determined upon its own peculiar facts and circumstances. The rule requiring delivery, either actual or symbolical, must be maintained, but its application is to be militated and applied according to the relative importance of the subject of the gift and the condition of the donor. The intention of a donor in peril of death, when clearly ascertained and fairly consummated within the meaning of well-established rules, is not to be thwarted by a narrow and illiberal construction of what may have been intended for and deemed by him a sufficient delivery. . . .

In essence, this approach takes into account the purposes served by the requirement of delivery in determining whether that requirement has been met. It would find a constructive delivery adequate to support the gift when the evidence of donative intent is concrete and undisputed, when there is every indication that the donor intended to make a present transfer of the subject-matter of the gift, and when the steps taken by the donor to effect such a transfer must have been deemed by the donor as sufficient to pass the donor's interest to the donee. We are persuaded that this approach, which does not minimize the need for evidentiary safeguards to prevent frauds upon the estates of the deceased, reflects the realities which attend transfers of this kind.

In this case, the evidence of decedent's intent to transfer the check to Robert Scherer is concrete, unequivocal, and undisputed. The circumstances definitely rule out any possibility of fraud. The sole question, then, is whether the steps taken by the decedent, independent of her writing of the suicide notes, were sufficient to support a finding that she effected a lifetime transfer of the check to Scherer. We think that they were. First, the act of endorsing a check represents, in common experience and understanding, the only act needed (short of actual delivery) to render a check negotiable. The significance of such an act is universally understood. . . . Second, we note that the only person other than the decedent who had routine access to the apartment was Robert Scherer. Indeed, the apartment was leased in his name. It is clear that Ms. Wagner before leaving the apartment placed the check in a place where Scherer could not fail to see it and fully expected that he would take actual possession of the check when he entered. And, although Ms. Wagner's subsequent suicide does not itself constitute a component of the delivery of this gift, it does provide persuasive evidence that when Ms. Wagner locked the door of the apartment she did so with no expectation of returning. When we consider her state of mind as it must have been upon leaving the apartment, her surrender of possession at that moment was complete. We find, therefore, that when she left the apartment she completed a constructive delivery of the check to Robert Scherer. In light of her resolve to take her own life and of her obvious desire not to be deterred from that purpose, Ms. Wagner's failure manually to transfer the check to Scherer is understandable. She clearly did all that she could do or thought necessary to do to surrender the check. Her donative intent has been conclusively demonstrated by independent evidence. The law should effectuate that intent rather than indulge in nice distinctions which would thwart her purpose. Upon these facts, we find that the constructive delivery she made was adequate to support a gift causa mortis.

. . . While it is true that a gift causa mortis is made by the donor with a view to impending death, death is no less impending because of a resolve to commit suicide. Nor does that fixed purpose constitute any lesser or less imminent peril than does a ravaging disease. Indeed, given the despair sufficient to end it all, the peril attendant upon contemplated suicide may reasonably be viewed as even more imminent than that accompanying many illnesses which prove ultimately to be fatal. . . . We also observe that an argument that the donor of a causa mortis gift might have changed his or her mind loses much of its force when one recalls that a causa mortis gift, by definition, can be revoked at any time before the donor dies and is automatically revoked if the donor recovers.

Finally, defendant asserts that this gift must fail because there was no acceptance prior to the donor's death. Although the issue of acceptance is rarely litigated, the authority that does exist indicates that, given a valid delivery, acceptance will be implied if the gift is unconditional and beneficial to the donee. The presumption of acceptance may apply even if the donee does not learn of the gift until after the donor's death. A donee cannot be expected to accept or reject a gift until he learns of it and unless a gift is rejected when the donee is informed of it the presumption of acceptance is not defeated. Here the gift was clearly beneficial to Scherer, and he has always expressed his acceptance.

Judgment affirmed.

Notes

1. *Intent:*   Carefully articulate the condition attached to the gift in this case. Why does the law recognize conditional gifts, particularly in the context of impending death? Could not a will serve the purpose just as well, or even better? Can you think of any other types of gifts worthy of conditional gift treatment?

2. *Delivery:*   What type of delivery did Catherine purport to make in this case, and in what ways did it potentially fall short of an effective delivery? If Catherine had not endorsed the check, would there have been a delivery? Keeping in mind the purposes of the delivery requirement, what safeguards should courts impose? Should those safeguards be relaxed in cases of attempted gifts causa mortis, or in other types of cases?

3. *Preview—testamentary gifts by will:*   What is the difference between an inter vivos gift and a testamentary gift (by will)? Why do you think the law is careful to separate the two, even in cases of gifts causa mortis that will not take effect until the donor's death?

Problem

Joint and survivorship bank accounts—arguing the facts: Joseph Gladowski opened a joint savings account in the name of himself and his adult daughter, Ann Mazuran, as joint tenants with the right of survivorship. Both Joseph and Ann signed the bank signature card, which stated that either party could withdraw funds from the account, and that upon the death of Joseph or Ann, the survivor would be the sole owner of the account. On the same day, Joseph executed a will naming Ann executrix and authorizing her upon his death to divide his estate in equal shares to his seven named children. The initial deposit in the bank account was $217, and subsequent deposits by Joseph (and none by Ann) increased the balance to $16,226. Joseph fell ill and Ann cared for him. She transacted business on his behalf when he was physically unable to do so, and made withdrawals from the joint account for Joseph's expenses. Upon Joseph's death, Ann claimed that Joseph had made an inter vivos gift of the funds to her. Joseph's surviving children brought a challenge, claiming that the bank account funds were part of Joseph's estate that should be divided equally among all the children.

The evidence demonstrated that when the bank account was opened, Joseph intended that at the time of his death the money would be divided equally among his children. But according to Ann, he changed his mind about six years later after he became ill, and after the other children failed to visit or help in caring for him. At that time, Joseph reportedly told Ann that he wanted her to have everything.

Recall our consideration of fact-based analysis in the Skills Practice exercise in Chapter 1. Assume you represent Ann in the litigation. What fact-based arguments would you make on her behalf? What arguments do you anticipate Joseph's children will make? *See In re Gladowski's Estate*, 396 A.2d 631 (Pa. 1979). We will learn about joint tenancies with the right of survivorship in Chapter 5.

Heiman v. Parrish

942 P.2d 631 (Kan. 1997)

Reading Guide

◆ *Engagement rings:* The court below wrestles with the issue of whether an engagement ring should be treated as a *conditional* gift. What consequences follow from the classification of a gift as conditional, as opposed to irrevocable?

◆ *Skills practice—policy-based arguments:* This case forms the basis of the skills practice exercise in section E. You might wish to preview the brief discussion of policy-based arguments in that section before you read this case.

McFarland, C.J.

The issue before us concerns the ownership of an engagement ring after the engagement was terminated. . . .

The parties stipulate to the following facts:

1. The issue to be determined is the ownership of an engagement ring.
2. The plaintiff purchased the engagement ring.
3. The ring was given to defendant as an engagement ring in contemplation of marriage between the parties.
4. The plaintiff is the party who ended the relationship.
5. Neither party stipulates to whose fault caused the relationship to terminate. . . .

. . . Additional uncontroverted facts are that the ring was purchased in August 1994 for $9,033. Plaintiff terminated the engagement in October 1995. Defendant refused to return the ring, and this action was filed April 3, 1996. For the sake of simplicity, plaintiff will henceforth be referred as Jerod and defendant will be referred to as Heather. . . .

The issues may be summarized as follows. Was the engagement ring a conditional gift given in contemplation of marriage? If this question is answered affirmatively, then, upon termination of the engagement, should ownership of the ring be determined on a fault or no-fault basis? These are issues of first impression in Kansas.

Conditional Gift

Heather argues that the gift of an engagement ring should be gauged by the same standards as for any other inter vivos gift, and that, once delivery and acceptance have occurred, the gift is irrevocable. She contends Kansas does not recognize conditional gifts.

Jerod argues that an engagement ring is inherently a conditional gift, as it is given in contemplation of marriage. If the wedding does not occur, the ring should be returned to its donor.

To establish a gift inter vivos there must be (a) an intention to make a gift; (b) a delivery by the donor to the donee; and (c) an acceptance by the donee. The gift must be absolute and irrevocable. . . .

While there is a paucity of Kansas law on gifts in contemplation of marriage in general, and engagement rings in particular, courts in many other states have wrestled with the issues arising therefrom. Most courts recognize that engagement rings occupy a rather unique niche in our society. One court characterized the engagement ring as follows:

> The ring is employed in rites of courtship and marriage in many cultures, primitive and sophisticated; in widely dispersed regions of the earth; persisting through the centuries, in fact millennia. In our culture, the ring is generally placed on one of the fingers, in others it may be attached to other positions of the anatomy, at intermediate points from the top of the head to the tip of the toes. It is a universal symbol of deep seated sexual and social ramifications, a seminal area of research for behavioral scientists. Is it any wonder that it presents such complicated problems for mere lawyers?

Brown v. Thomas, 379 N.W.2d 868 (Wis. Ct. App. 1985).

By tradition and the mores of our society, an engagement ring is the symbol of the parties' mutual promises to marry. It is unlike any other gift given or exchanged by lovers. The single sentence "She returned his ring" illustrates this. These four words, standing alone, paint the picture of mutual promises to wed, a ring being given and received to symbolize these promises, and the intended bride reneging on her promise and so advising the would-be groom by returning the ring. No like picture is engendered by the phrase "She returned his bracelet." . . .

In the absence of a contrary expression of intent, it is logical that engagement rings should be considered, by their very nature, conditional gifts given in contemplation of marriage. Once it is established the ring is an engagement ring, it is a conditional gift. . . .

In the action herein, the parties stipulated that the object in dispute is an engagement ring given in contemplation of marriage. We conclude the district court correctly held that it was a conditional gift.

Fault or No Fault . . .

Generally, with regard to who is entitled to the engagement ring once the engagement has been broken, courts have taken two divergent paths. One rule states that when an engagement has been unjustifiably broken by the donor, the donor shall not recover the ring. However, if the engagement is broken by mutual agreement or, unjustifiably by the donee, the ring should be returned to the donor. This is the fault-based line of cases. The other rule, the so-called "modern trend," holds that as an engagement ring is an inherently conditional gift, once the engagement has been broken the ring should be returned to the donor. Thus, the question of who broke the engagement and why, or who was "at fault," is irrelevant. This is the no-fault line of cases. . . .

Justification for the fault-based rule was picturesquely stated in *Pavlicic v. Vogtsberger*, 136 A.2d 127 (Pa. 1957), as follows:

> A gift given by a man to a woman on condition that she embark on the sea of matrimony with him is no different from a gift based on the condition that the donee sail on any other sea. If, after receiving the provisional gift, the donee refuses to leave the harbor—if the anchor of contractual performance sticks in the sands of irresolution and procrastination—the gift must be restored to the donor.

Presumably, if the donor of the ring was the party refusing to leave the pier, the Pennsylvania court would rule the donee was entitled to the ring.

Mate v. Abrahams, 62 A.2d 754 (N.J. County Ct. 1948), applied the fault-based rule, stating:

> On principle, an engagement ring is given, not alone as a symbol of the status of the two persons as engaged, the one to the other, but as a symbol or token of their pledge and agreement to marry. As such pledge or gift, the condition is implied that if both parties abandon the projected marriage, the sole cause of the gift, it should be returned. Similarly, if the woman, who has received the ring in token of her promise, unjustifiably breaks her promise, it should be returned.
>
> When the converse situation occurs, and the giver of the ring, betokening his promise, violates his word, it would seem that a similar result should follow, *i.e.,* he should lose, not gain, rights to the ring. In addition, had he not broken his promise, the marriage would follow, and the ring would become the wife's absolutely. The man could not then recover the ring. . . . No man should take advantage of his own wrong. Of course, were the breaking of the engagement to be justifiable, there would be no violation of the agreement legally, and a different result might follow. . . .

We turn now to the no-fault line of cases. . . . Likening a broken engagement to a broken marriage, the court [in *Vigil v. Haber*, 888 P.2d 455 (N.M. 1994)] noted that no-fault divorce is the modern approach to a broken marriage. Thus, the court believed, a no-fault approach to a broken engagement was equally appropriate. Following the lead of Iowa, New Jersey, New York, and Wisconsin, the court held that when the condition precedent of marriage fails, an engagement gift must be returned. . . .

The same result was reached in *Aronow v. Silver*, 538 A.2d 851 (N.J. Super. 1987). Although "[t]he majority rule in this country concerning the disposition of engagement rings is a fault rule: the party who unjustifiably breaks the engagement loses the ring," the *Aronow* court believed the majority rule to be "sexist and archaic":

> . . . In ancient Rome the rule was fault. When the woman broke the engagement, however, she was required not only to return the ring, but also its value, as a penalty. No penalty attached when the breach was the man's. In England, women were oppressed by the rigidly stratified social order of the day. They worked as servants or, if not of the servant class, were dependent on their relatives. The fact that men were in short supply, marriage above one's station rare and travel difficult abbreviated betrothal prospects for women. Marriages were arranged. Women's lifetime choices were limited to a marriage or a nunnery. Spinsterhood was a centuries-long personal tragedy. Men, because it was a man's world, were much more likely than women to break engagements. When one did, he left behind a woman of tainted reputation and ruined prospects. The law, in a *de minimis* gesture, gave her the engagement ring, as a consolation prize. When the man was jilted, a seldom thing, justice required the ring's return to him. Thus, the rule of life was the rule of law—both saw women as inferiors. . . .

> What fact justifies the breaking of an engagement? The absence of a sense of humor? Differing musical tastes? Differing political views? The painfully-learned fact is that marriages are made on earth, not in heaven. They must be approached with intelligent care and should not happen without a decent assurance of success. When either party lacks that assurance, for whatever reason, the engagement should be broken. No justification is needed. Either party may act. Fault, impossible to fix, does not count. . . .

After careful consideration, we conclude the no-fault line of cases is persuasive. . . .

The granting of the divorce decree in Kansas, and the division of marital property, are generally thought to be based on a no-fault determination. . . .

The engagement period is one where each party should be free to reexamine his or her commitment to the other and be sure he or she desires the commitment of marriage to the other. If the promise to wed were rashly or improvidently made, public policy would be better served if the engagement promise to wed would be broken rather than the marriage vows.

The ring which was given on the promise of a future marriage and is the symbol of the parties' commitment to each other and their life together is, after the engagement is broken, a symbol of failed promises and hopes, hardly a treasured keepsake for its formerly betrothed wearer. Broken engagements engender hurt pride, anger, and wounded egos. They do not ordinarily present the major questions of changes in lifestyles, standards of living, etc., that broken marriages involve. Yet the legislature has applied the no-fault principle to divorces on the grounds of public policy. It is difficult to see how the public policies involving divorce and the division of marital property are best served by no-fault principles, but broken engagements should require a fault-based determination as to ownership of the engagement ring. Litigating fault for a broken engagement would do little but intensify the hurt feelings and delay the parties' being able to get on with their lives.

We conclude that fault is ordinarily not relevant to the question of who should have ownership and possession of an engagement ring after the engagement is broken. Ordinarily, the ring should be returned to the donor, regardless of fault. [W]e recognize there may be extremely gross and rare situations where fault might be appropriately considered. No such rare situation has been suggested to be involved herein.

The district court did not err in awarding the ring to Jerod after concluding fault was irrelevant. The judgment is affirmed.

MARQUARDT, J., dissenting. . . .

The courts throughout our country seem to have difficulty in deciding which legal theory applies to ownership of an engagement ring when the engagement is broken. Is the engagement ring a gift or is it used as consideration for the promise to be engaged? If it is a gift, why is it not a completed gift? If it is a conditional gift, what makes it conditional? May a court infer a condition on a gift that was intended to be given and was delivered and accepted? If the ring is consideration for a contract, why not apply breach of contract rules? . . .

We get into legal contortions when we adopt the majority's view that "an engagement ring is the symbol of the parties' mutual promises to marry." This statement indicates that the majority views the giving of an engagement ring as consideration for a contract. It is difficult to reconcile contract principles with this statement. If the parties have exchanged mutual promises, the consideration for the woman's promise to marry is the man's promise to marry. Under this analysis, the ring is transferred without consideration and is a gift. The majority then disregards the "mutual promise" statement and finds that an engagement ring is a conditional gift in contemplation of marriage.

A conditional gift is one that is conditioned or qualified, and the title does not vest in the donee. . . . The majority states: "The engagement period is one where each party should be free to reexamine his or her commitment." Although that may not be the way some people view the engagement period, it has no bearing on the ownership of an engagement ring when an engagement is broken. The majority seems to intertwine the commitment to be engaged with the commitment to be married. The law does not ordinarily become involved with engagements; however, public policy mandates that the law be involved in the breakup of marriages. The commitment to be engaged is given at the time of the engagement, while the commitment to be married is given at the wedding ceremony.

Applying the "no fault" concept to the ring does not take into account the many expenditures made by the woman in contemplation of marriage. What is the woman to do when she buys a costly dress that cannot be returned?

In addition, a bride-to-be may make deposits on a place for the ceremony, a caterer, a reception hall, and entertainment; buy items to be used jointly after the marriage; move from one city to another; etc.-all of which are costly and for the most part, nonrefundable. This court's ruling implies that these expenditures are irrelevant. Although Jerod is made whole, there is no attempt to put Heather back to her preengagement position, despite the fact that he breached the engagement agreement. . . .

In the event of a broken engagement, the engagement ring should be considered a completed inter vivos gift. Regardless, Heather is entitled to keep the engagement ring whether this case is analyzed on the principles of gift law, contract law, or equity.

Notes

1. *Issues of first impression:*   This dispute raises two *issues of first impression*. That is, the jurisdiction had no direct precedent on the issues, and the court therefore had to select an appropriate rule to resolve the case. *Policy* considerations often guide courts in such situations.

2. *Conditional gifts:*   The court concluded, "it is logical that engagement rings should be considered, by their very nature, as conditional gifts given in contemplation of marriage." What is the court's rationale for that conclusion? What is the practical consequence of treating the ring as a conditional, rather than irrevocable, gift?

3. *The relevance of fault:*   In Kansas, this was a case of first impression. Do you think the court reached the right result? The matter is far from settled. Although the predominant view is that engagement rings are conditional gifts, there is very little case law on whether fault should matter in determining who keeps the ring after the couple terminates the engagement. Herbert Hovenkamp et al., The Law of Property: An Introductory Survey § 3.4 (6th ed. 2014).

4. *A changing world—toward gender equality:*   When evaluating the gift status of engagement rings, some courts express concern about gender inequality. In *Aronow* (cited in the principal case), the New Jersey Superior Court rejected the fault rule as "sexist and archaic." The Montana Supreme Court expressed a similar concern, but reached a different conclusion—that conditional gift theory should not be applied to engagement ring cases at all. In *Albinger v. Harris*, 48 P.3d 711 (Mont. 2002), the court explained:

> Article II, Section 4 of the Montana Constitution recognizes and guarantees the individual dignity of each human being without regard to gender. . . .
>
> The Montana Legislature made the social policy decision to relieve courts of the duty of regulating engagements by barring actions for breach of promise. While

not explicitly denying access to the courts on the basis of gender, the "anti-heart balm" statutes closed courtrooms across the nation to female plaintiffs seeking damages for antenuptial pregnancy, ruined reputation, lost love and economic insecurity. During the mid-20th Century, some courts continued to entertain suits in equity for antenuptial property transfers. The jurisprudence that rose upon the implied conditional gift theory, based upon an engagement ring's symbolic associations with marriage, preserved a right of action narrowly tailored for ring givers seeking ring return [and created a bright-line rule of ring return on a no-fault basis that ignores the particular circumstances of a couple's decision not to marry].

Conditional gift theory applied exclusively to engagement ring cases, carves an exception in the state's gift law for the benefit of predominately male plaintiffs. Montana's "anti-heart balm" statute bars all actions sounding in contract law that arise from mutual promise to marry, absent fraud or deceit, and bars all plaintiffs from recovering any share of expenses incurred in planning a canceled wedding. While antenuptial traditions vary by class, ethnicity, age and inclination, women often still assume the bulk of pre-wedding costs, such as non-returnable wedding gowns, moving costs, or non-refundable deposits for caterers, entertainment or reception halls. Consequently, the statutory "anti-heart balm" bar continues to have a disparate impact on women. If this Court were to fashion a special exception for engagement ring actions under gift law theories, we would perpetuate the gender bias attendant upon the Legislature's decision to remove from our courts all actions for breach of antenuptial promises. . . .

To preserve the integrity of our gift law and to avoid additional gender bias, we decline to adopt the theory that an engagement ring is a gift subject to an implied condition of marriage. Judicial imputation of conditional gifting would stake new legal territory in Montana.

The dissenting opinion, in contrast, reasoned that "gender equity has about as much to do with this case as banking law." *Id.* at 722. Does gender bias infect gift law? Is it true, as feared by the *Albinger* court, that women are disparately impacted by breach of marriage cases? If so, how can gift law best respond to that concern?

Gruen v. Gruen

496 N.E.2d 869 (N.Y. App. 1986)

Reading Guide

◆ *Gifts during life, gifts at death:* This case explores the relationship between inter vivos gifts, which become effective during the donor's life, and testamentary gifts (those made by will), which become effective at the donor's death.

◆ *Preview—life estates and remainders:* The court below talks about *life estates* and *remainders*, topics which we will cover in Chapter 3. For now, it is enough to know that property can be shared over time. For example, one person can have the right to present possession throughout his lifetime (a life estate), and then that person's son might have the right to future possession upon the death of the parent (a remainder). Both parties have a present legal *right*, independent of their respective turns at *possession.*

SIMONS, J.

Plaintiff commenced this action seeking a declaration that he is the rightful owner of a painting which he alleges his father, now deceased, gave to him. He concedes that he has never had possession of the painting but asserts that his father made a valid gift of the title in 1963 reserving a life estate for himself. His father retained possession of the painting until he died in 1980. Defendant, plaintiff's stepmother, has the painting now and has refused plaintiff's requests that she turn it over to him. She contends that the purported gift was testamentary in nature and invalid insofar as the formalities of a will were not met or, alternatively, that a donor may not make a valid inter vivos gift of a chattel and retain a life estate with a complete right of possession. . . . The Appellate Division held that a valid gift may be made reserving a life estate and, finding the elements of a gift established in this case, it reversed and remitted the matter for a determination of value. That determination has now been made and defendant appeals directly to this court . . . from the subsequent final judgment entered in Supreme Court awarding plaintiff $2,500,000 in damages representing the value of the painting, plus interest. We now affirm.

The subject of the dispute is a work entitled "Schloss Kammer am Attersee II" painted by a noted Austrian modernist, Gustav Klimt. It was purchased by plaintiff's father, Victor Gruen, in 1959 for $8,000. On April 1, 1963 the elder Gruen, a successful architect with offices and residences in both New York City and Los Angeles during most of the time involved in this action, wrote a letter to plaintiff, then an undergraduate student at Harvard, stating that he was giving him the Klimt painting for his birthday but that he wished to retain the possession of it for his lifetime. This letter is not in evidence, apparently because plaintiff destroyed it on instructions from his father. Two other letters were received, however, one dated May 22, 1963 and the other April 1, 1963. Both had been dictated by Victor Gruen and sent together to plaintiff on or about May 22, 1963. The letter dated May 22, 1963 reads as follows:

Dear Michael:

I wrote you at the time of your birthday about the gift of the painting by Klimt.

Now my lawyer tells me that because of the existing tax laws, it was wrong to mention in that letter that I want to use the painting as long as I live. Though

I still want to use it, this should not appear in the letter. I am enclosing, therefore, a new letter and I ask you to send the old one back to me so that it can be destroyed.

I know this is all very silly, but the lawyer and our accountant insist that they must have in their possession copies of a letter which will serve the purpose of making it possible for you, once I die, to get this picture without having to pay inheritance taxes on it.

Love,

s/Victor

Enclosed with this letter was a substitute gift letter, dated April 1, 1963, which stated:

Dear Michael:

The 21st birthday, being an important event in life, should be celebrated accordingly. I therefore wish to give you as a present the oil painting by Gustav Klimt of Schloss Kammer which now hangs in the New York living room. You know that Lazette and I bought it some 5 or 6 years ago, and you always told us how much you liked it.

Happy birthday again.

Love,

s/Victor

Plaintiff never took possession of the painting nor did he seek to do so. Except for a brief period between 1964 and 1965 when it was on loan to art exhibits and when restoration work was performed on it, the painting remained in his father's possession. Following Victor's death plaintiff requested possession of the Klimt painting and when defendant refused, he commenced this action.

The issues framed for appeal are whether a valid inter vivos gift of a chattel may be made where the donor has reserved a life estate in the chattel and the donee never has had physical possession of it before the donor's death and, if it may, which factual findings on the elements of a valid inter vivos gift more nearly comport with the weight of the evidence in this case, those of Special Term or those of the Appellate Division. The latter issue requires application of two general rules. First, to make a valid inter vivos gift there must exist the intent on the part of the donor to make a present transfer; delivery of the gift, either actual or constructive to the donee; and acceptance by the donee. Second, the proponent of a gift has the burden of proving each of these elements by clear and convincing evidence.

Donative Intent

There is an important distinction between the intent with which an inter vivos gift is made and the intent to make a gift by will. An inter vivos gift requires that the donor intend to make an irrevocable present transfer of ownership; if the intention is to make a testamentary disposition effective only after death, the gift is invalid unless made by will.

Defendant contends that the trial court was correct in finding that Victor did not intend to transfer any present interest in the painting to plaintiff in 1963 but only expressed an intention that plaintiff was to get the painting upon his death. The evidence is all but conclusive, however, that Victor intended to transfer ownership of the painting to plaintiff in 1963 but to retain a life estate in it and that he did, therefore, effectively transfer a remainder interest in the painting to plaintiff at that time. Although the original letter was not in evidence, testimony of its contents was received along with the substitute gift letter and its covering letter dated May 22, 1963. The three letters should be considered together as a single instrument and when they are they unambiguously establish that Victor Gruen intended to make a present gift of title to the painting at that time. But there was other evidence for after 1963 Victor made several statements orally and in writing indicating that he had previously given plaintiff the painting and that plaintiff owned it. Victor Gruen retained possession of the property, insured it, allowed others to exhibit it and made necessary repairs to it but those acts are not inconsistent with his retention of a life estate. Furthermore, whatever probative value could be attached to his statement that he had bequeathed the painting to his heirs, made 16 years later when he prepared an export license application so that he could take the painting out of Austria, is negated by the overwhelming evidence that he intended a present transfer of title in 1963. Victor's failure to file a gift tax return on the transaction was partially explained by allegedly erroneous legal advice he received, and while that omission sometimes may indicate that the donor had no intention of making a present gift, it does not necessarily do so and it is not dispositive in this case. . . .

Defendant recognizes that a valid inter vivos gift of a remainder interest can be made not only of real property but also of such intangibles as stocks and bonds. . . . That being so, it is difficult to perceive any legal basis for the distinction she urges which would permit gifts of remainder interests in those properties but not of remainder interests in chattels such as the Klimt painting here. . . . Insofar as some of our cases purport to require that the donor intend to transfer both title and possession immediately to have a valid inter vivos gift, they state the rule too broadly and confuse the effectiveness of a gift with the transfer of the possession of the subject of that gift. The correct test is "whether the maker intended the [gift] to have *no effect* until after the maker's death, or whether he intended it to transfer *some present interest*." As long as the evidence establishes an intent to make a present and irrevocable transfer of title or the right of ownership, there is a present transfer of some interest and the gift is effective immediately. . . .

Defendant suggests that allowing a donor to make a present gift of a remainder with the reservation of a life estate will lead courts to effectuate otherwise invalid testamentary dispositions of property. The two have entirely different characteristics, however, which make them distinguishable. Once the gift is made it is irrevocable and the donor is limited to the rights of a life tenant not an owner. Moreover, with the gift of a remainder title vests immediately in the donee and any possession is postponed until the donor's death whereas under a will neither title nor possession vests immediately. Finally, the postponement of enjoyment of the gift is produced by the express terms of the gift not by the nature of the instrument as it is with a will.

Delivery

In order to have a valid inter vivos gift, there must be a delivery of the gift, either by a physical delivery of the subject of the gift or a constructive or symbolic delivery such as by an instrument of gift, sufficient to divest the donor of dominion and control over the property. As the statement of the rule suggests, the requirement of delivery is not rigid or inflexible, but is to be applied in light of its purpose to avoid mistakes by donors and fraudulent claims by donees. Accordingly, what is sufficient to constitute delivery "must be tailored to suit the circumstances of the case." *Matter of Szabo,* 176 N.E.2d 395 (N.Y. 1961). The rule requires that "[t]he delivery necessary to consummate a gift must be as perfect as the nature of the property and the circumstances and surroundings of the parties will reasonably permit." *Id.*

Defendant contends that when a tangible piece of personal property such as a painting is the subject of a gift, physical delivery of the painting itself is the best form of delivery and should be required. Here, of course, we have only delivery of Victor Gruen's letters which serve as instruments of gift. Defendant's statement of the rule as applied may be generally true, but it ignores the fact that what Victor Gruen gave plaintiff was not all rights to the Klimt painting, but only title to it with no right of possession until his death. Under these circumstances, it would be illogical for the law to require the donor to part with possession of the painting when that is exactly what he intends to retain.

Nor is there any reason to require a donor making a gift of a remainder interest in a chattel to physically deliver the chattel into the donee's hands only to have the donee redeliver it to the donor. As the facts of this case demonstrate, such a requirement could impose practical burdens on the parties to the gift while serving the delivery requirement poorly. Thus, in order to accomplish this type of delivery the parties would have been required to travel to New York for the symbolic transfer and redelivery of the Klimt painting which was hanging on the wall of Victor Gruen's Manhattan apartment. Defendant suggests that such a requirement would be stronger evidence of a completed gift, but in the absence of witnesses to the event or any written confirmation of the gift it would provide less protection against fraudulent claims than have the written instruments of gift delivered in this case.

Acceptance

Acceptance by the donee is essential to the validity of an inter vivos gift, but when a gift is of value to the donee, as it is here, the law will presume an acceptance on his part. Plaintiff did not rely on this presumption alone but also presented clear and convincing proof of his acceptance of a remainder interest in the Klimt painting by evidence that he had made several contemporaneous statements acknowledging the gift to his friends and associates, even showing some of them his father's gift letter, and that he had retained both letters for over 17 years to verify the gift after his father died. Defendant relied exclusively on affidavits filed by plaintiff in a matrimonial action with his former wife, in which plaintiff failed to list his interest in the painting as an asset. These affidavits were made over 10 years after acceptance was complete. . . . We agree with the Appellate Division that interpretation of the affidavit was too speculative to support a finding of rejection and overcome the substantial showing of acceptance by plaintiff.

Notes

1. *Intent:*   Did Victor intend to make a present irrevocable transfer of ownership of the painting to his son, or did he intend to make a testamentary gift of the property, effective upon his death? In either case, Michael would not have the right to possession of the painting until his father's death. As a practical matter, what difference does it make whether this was an inter vivos gift or a testamentary gift?

2. *Delivery:*   By what method did Victor purport to deliver the gift to his son, and did the court find delivery to be effective? Instead, if Victor had intended to give Michael full ownership (and immediate possession) of the painting, would the purported delivery have been effective? Should the two situations be treated the same or differently? In the cases of real property and intangible personal property (such as stocks and bonds), New York already recognized remainder interests, which would not become possessory until some future point. Should tangible personal property (such as artwork) be treated in the same way? Why or why not?

3. *Practice pointer—tax considerations:*   If Victor Gruen wanted to enjoy the painting during his life and then pass it on to his son upon his death, why didn't he just convey the painting to Michael by will? As suggested by the reference to Victor's attorney, tax considerations may have played a role in his decision. *See* Suzanne Tucker Plybon & Jeremy T. Ware, *Longer Lives and Greater Wealth: Solutions to the Gifting Dilemma*, Estate Planning (Oct. 2008).

4. *The places—Austria, New York, and California:*   Victor Gruen was born in Vienna, Austria in 1903. His family enjoyed vacationing in the Lake District outside of Salzburg, Austria. While staying at Lake Attersee with his son,

Michael, and with his second wife, Victor met hotel maid Kemija, who would later become his *fourth* wife and the defendant in *Gruen v. Gruen.* Lake Attersee was the focus of a series of five works by Austrian artist Gustav Klimt (1862-1918). The disputed painting depicts a castle on Lake Attersee, which Klimt reportedly painted while housed in a boat shed, peering across the lake at the castle through binoculars and telescope. Victor founded the highly successful architectural firm Victor Gruen Associates, with offices in Los Angeles, New York, and Washington, D.C. Among other things, he became known for developing the concept of the enclosed suburban shopping mall, which he envisioned as a cultural and civic town center. *See Gustav Klimt Museum,* http://www.klimt.com (visited Oct. 23, 2015).

Artist Gustav Klimt in a light blue smock, drawing by Egon Schiele, 1913
Source: Public domain via Wikimedia Commons

Place played a prominent role in the litigation. As a preliminary matter, the court had to decide whether to apply the law of New York—the location of Victor's apartment and the painting—or the law of California—the legal domicile of Victor and Michael, and the place where the gift letters were written. The trial court applied New York law and delivered a resounding defeat to Michael, based on some archaic cases on delivery and acceptance. On appeal, the court reversed. It gave scant attention to the choice of law question and interpreted both New York and California law as favorable to Michael. *See* Susan F. French, *Gruen v. Gruen: A Tale of Two Stories*, in Property Stories (Gerald Korngold & Andrew P. Morriss, eds., 2d ed. 2009).

B. FINDERS

Our study of gifts focused on the voluntary transfer of title to personal property according to the *intent* of the owner. In contrast, finders law involves the transfer of possessory rights (but not title) by unknown owners who part *unintentionally* with their property. In resolving competing claims to the property by the first finder and subsequent possessors, the law's overarching goal is to reunite owners with their property. Thus, the shadow of the true owner hovers in the background of any finders dispute, even though the true owner is unknown, and therefore unnamed in the litigation.

Because it is not possible to identify the true owner in many cases, the law relies on the concept of *relativity of title*. Suppose, for example, that after the true owner parted with an item of personal property, it was picked up by a finder, who then sold it to a buyer, who then lost the item, only to have it found by a second finder. All claim the property (except for the true owner who remains unknown). Applying the concept of relativity of title, a court would award the property to the claimant who has *relatively better* title than all the others—even though none of them can claim to be the actual owner. That person will be entitled to maintain possession, generally until the time the true owner shows up (if ever). As you study the materials in this section, think about what the notion of relativity of title reveals about the relationship between possession and ownership.

As explained in the following *A Place to Start* box, the common law has established purportedly clear rules to resolve competing possessory claims, depending on whether the property has been *lost, mislaid, abandoned,* or qualifies as *treasure trove.* But are those rules really as clear as they first appear to be? If true owners are unknown, how can courts determine the circumstances under which they parted with their property?

A Place to Start | Finders Law

- *Bailments:* A bailment is the rightful possession of goods by one who is not the true owner, as when a person (the bailor) delivers clothing to a dry cleaning establishment (the bailee) for laundering. The bailee owes a duty of care to the bailor. Finders (and owners of the places where property is found) are *involuntary bailees* of the true owner.

- *Property categories:* The common law separates found personal property into four categories:

  - *Lost property:* Lost property is that which the true owner parts with unintentionally and involuntarily, such as a necklace that comes unclasped and falls off unnoticed. The finder has a better right to the property than all but the true owner.

  - *Mislaid property:* Mislaid property is that which the true owner places somewhere intentionally, but then leaves behind unintentionally, such as a purse that is tucked beneath a chair in a restaurant and then forgotten and left behind. The common law awards the property to the owner of the premises on which the property is found (the "locus in quo"), with the landowner acting as bailee for the true owner.

  - *Abandoned property:* Abandoned property is that to which the true owner intends to relinquish all right of possession and title. The finder has a better right than all, *including* the former owner.

  - *Treasure trove:* Treasure trove refers to money, coins, gold, silver, or bullion (bars or ingots of precious metal), long ago hidden in the ground or in a secret place, the true owner of which is unknown. Under the common law in the United States, the finder has a better right than all, including the former owner (although under English common law, treasure trove reverted—*escheated*—to the crown).

- *Causes of action:* Causes of action concerning found personal property include:

  - *Replevin:* An action to recover possession of personal property. The analogous action to recover possession of real property is *ejectment* (recall *Johnson v. M'Intosh* from Chapter 1).

  - *Trover:* An action to recover damages for the wrongful detention of goods. The analogous action to recover damages in the context of land is *trespass.*

DIGGING DEEPER: Suppose the true owner never appears. At some point in time, should the law extinguish the true owner's title, and recognize full title in the person holding *relatively better title* than all but the true owner? We will return to this question in *O'Keeffe v. Snyder* (section C).

In ambiguous cases, courts examine a number of factors. First, as suggested above, they try to determine the likely circumstances under which the *true owner* parted with the item. Did the owner lose the property, mislay it, abandon it, or hide it in the ground for later recovery? Why should that matter? Hint: recall the overarching goal of finders law.

Next, courts will consider *the place* where the item was found. Was it found on someone's private property under the landowner's control (rather than open to the public as a shop, restaurant, or the like)? If so, courts might say that the owner of the premises (the "locus in quo") has better title than the actual finder because the landowner has "constructive" possession of everything on the premises, and is therefore the first "finder." This would be true even if the landowner is unaware that lost, mislaid, abandoned, or treasure trove items are on the premises. In addition, true owners might retrace their steps to the place where they parted with their property, so awarding possession to the owner of the locus in quo might facilitate the property's return to the owner.

Finally, courts will delve more deeply into the *finder's* circumstances. Was the finder an employee or agent of the owner of the locus in quo? If so, then finders might have little claim to the property under the theory that they act for the benefit of their employer or principal. Was the finder a trespasser? If so, then the finder might be similarly disfavored because the law does not want to reward trespassers. Or perhaps the finder was an honest person who made diligent, but unsuccessful, efforts to find the true owner. Under what rationale could a court award found property to such a person?

After courts consider all of these factors, are the four common law rules of finders really so clear after all?

Test Your Understanding

Note to students: From time to time, this book will introduce new terminology, rules, or concepts in *A Place to Start* boxes, followed by questions that provide an opportunity for self-directed learning. You are not expected to have a full command of the subject matter after such a brief introduction to it. Instead, this feature is designed as a starting point so that you can dig deeper in your case reading and during class discussions. As you try to apply the new concepts to specific factual circumstances, take note of any ambiguities or questions that occur to you. Then, look for answers to those questions (or at least insights about how to approach those questions) as you read the remaining material in the chapter.

In each of the following situations, (a) determine how a court will likely classify the property (lost, mislaid, abandoned, or treasure trove) and why; (b) articulate the appropriate common law rule for that type of property; (c) identify any areas of ambiguity or additional factors that a court might consider; and (d) suggest a tentative resolution to the competing claims to the found item.

1. *The wallet in the barber shop:* A customer found a wallet in a barber shop. When the owner of the shop asked where it had been found, the customer

replied that the wallet had been lying on a table. Who should be awarded possession of the wallet—the customer or the shop owner? *See McAvoy v. Medina*, 93 Mass. 548 (1866). Assume instead that the customer asserted that the wallet had been found lying on the floor beneath the table. Who should be awarded possession of the wallet? *See Bridges v. Hawkesworth*, 7 Eng. Law & Eq. R. 424.

2. *The watch on the lawn:*   Someone dropped a valuable watch on your front lawn without your knowledge. A passing jogger found the watch. Who has a better claim to the watch—you or the jogger? Assume instead that the jogger found the watch on the public sidewalk in front of your house. Who has a better claim—you or the jogger? Finally, assume that after the jogger found the watch on your front lawn, she put it in her pocket. Later, the watch slipped out through a hole in the pocket and was found by a second jogger. Who has better title—you, the first jogger, or the second jogger?

3. *The money in the hotel:*   Mrs. Laura Jackson worked at the Arthur Hotel in Portland, Oregon. While cleaning one of the guest rooms, Mrs. Jackson found $800 in cash concealed under the paper lining of a dresser drawer. She removed the bills and delivered them immediately to the hotel manager so that they could be returned to the true owner, if such owner could be found. The hotel owner, Karl Steinberg, made an unsuccessful effort to discover the owner of the bills by writing each person who had occupied that particular room during the past six weeks. Mrs. Jackson then demanded the return of the money, and Mr. Steinberg refused. Who has a better claim to the money—Mrs. Jackson or Mr. Steinberg? *See Jackson v. Steinberg*, 200 P.2d 376 (Or. 1948).

4. *The golden driveway:*   Jann Wenner, co-founder and publisher of *Rolling Stone* magazine, hired an asphalt paving company to construct a driveway on his property in Idaho. While digging up soil to lay the driveway, a company employee found a glass jar buried in the ground. The jar was full of gold coins carefully wrapped in paper. Who has better title to the coins—Mr. Wenner, the paving company, or the employee? *See Corliss v. Wenner*, 34 P.3d 1100 (Idaho App. 2001).

Armory v. Delamirie

King's Bench, 1 Strange 505 (1722)

> **Reading Guide**
>
> After you read this brief case, recite the rule of *Armory*. Does it resolve the "test your understanding" problems above? Can you add one word to the rule, consistent with the court's holding, to expand its usefulness? Are there still cases your amended rule cannot resolve?

Finder of a jewel may maintain trover.

The plaintiff being a chimney sweeper's boy found a jewel and carried it to the defendant's shop (who was a goldsmith) to know what it was, and delivered it into the hands of the apprentice, who under pretence of weighing it, took out the stones, and calling to the master to let him know it came to three halfpence, the master offered the boy the money, who refused to take it, and insisted to have the thing again; whereupon the apprentice delivered him back the socket without the stones. And now in trover against the master these points were ruled:

1. That the finder of a jewel, though he does not by such finding acquire an absolute property or ownership, yet he has such a property as will enable him to keep it against all but the rightful owner, and consequently may maintain trover.

2. That the action well lay against the master, who gives a credit to his apprentice, and is answerable for his neglect.

3. As to the value of the jewel several of the trade were examined to prove what a jewel of the finest water that would fit the socket would be worth; and the Chief Justice directed the jury, that unless the defendant did produce the jewel, and shew it not to be of the finest water, they should presume the strongest against him, and make the value of the best jewels the measure of their damages: which they accordingly did.

Note

The place—chimney sweeps in 18th century England: Ash and soot accumulate in chimneys, making them a serious fire hazard. Before the invention of scrubbing machines, chimney sweeps manually performed this task. The job was perilous. As early as 1770, English surgeon Sir Percivall Pott identified chimney sweeps as susceptible to occupational cancer as a result of inhaling coal dust, soot, and smoke. Children (both boys and girls) were ideal for the job—their small size allowed them to crawl inside chimneys as narrow as 18 inches. But often, children became stuck in chimneys or fell to their deaths, and cruel masters reportedly lit fires below to encourage sweeps to work more quickly. The Dickensonian character Oliver Twist is believed to be modeled after a "climbing boy" who was sold at the age of six to a London chimney sweep. In 1840, Parliament adopted the Chimney Sweepers and Chimneys Regulation Act, making it unlawful to apprentice chimney sweepers under the age of 16, or to compel or allow young people under the age of 21 to clean chimneys. Still, the practice continued until the Chimney Sweepers Act of 1875 imposed strict supervision and registration requirements. Given the powerlessness of child laborers during the period when *Armory* was decided, it is indeed noteworthy that the sweep prevailed against famed silversmith Paul de Lamerie, who has been described as "the greatest silversmith working in

England in the 18th century." *See* Annabel Venning, *Britain's Child Slaves*, DailyMail, Sept. 17, 2010, reviewing Jane Humphries, Childhood and Child Labour in the British Industrial Revolution (Cambridge Univ. Press 2010); Victoria and Albert Museum (London), *Silver Objects by Paul de Lamerie*, http://www.vam.ac.uk/content/articles/s/paul-de-lamerie-objects/ (visited Mar. 28, 2015).

Chimney Sweeps, 18th century drawing
Source: National Cancer Institute AV-8000-0620

Problem

Finder, thief: We know that the goldsmith (or at least, his apprentice) was a scoundrel, but we know very little about the chimney sweep and the circumstances under which he came into possession of the jewel. It is possible that the sweep was also a thief—perhaps he found the jewel inside the house and pocketed it without the homeowner's notice. In addition, we could imagine an alternative version of the facts under which the second claimant might be a good faith finder (for example, if the jewel slipped out of the chimney sweep's pocket on the way to the goldsmith's shop).

With two claimants other than the true owner, four logical possibilities suggest themselves. In each situation, who should prevail in a lawsuit by the first party against the second? Assume that the true owner is unknown or unaware that anything is amiss. What role does relativity of title play in your responses?

- Finder 1 *v.* Finder 2
- Finder *v.* Thief
- Thief *v.* Finder
- Thief 1 *v.* Thief 2

Benjamin v. Lindner Aviation, Inc.

534 N.W.2d 400 (Iowa 1995)

Reading Guide

◆ *Surprise inside an airplane wing:* In the case below, appellant Benjamin found $18,000 wrapped in aluminum foil packets, which had been stuffed inside an airplane wing and left there for up to 35 years. Can you imagine any plausible explanation to account for those facts?

◆ *Skills practice:* Although heavily rooted in the common law, finders law is often modified by state statute. The careful attorney will be mindful of the potential interplay of these two bodies of law. The Iowa finders statute discussed in this case is the subject of the skills practice exercise in section E, below.

Ternus, J.

Appellant, Heath Benjamin, found over $18,000 in currency inside the wing of an airplane. At the time of this discovery, appellee, State Central Bank, owned the plane and it was being serviced by appellee, Lindner Aviation, Inc. All three parties claimed the money as against the true owner. After a bench trial, the district court held that the currency was mislaid property and belonged to the owner of the plane. The court awarded a finder's fee to

Benjamin. Benjamin appealed and Lindner Aviation and State Central Bank cross-appealed. We reverse on the bank's cross-appeal and otherwise affirm the judgment of the district court.

Background Facts and Proceedings

In April of 1992, State Central Bank became the owner of an airplane when the bank repossessed it from its prior owner who had defaulted on a loan. In August of that year, the bank took the plane to Lindner Aviation for a routine annual inspection. Benjamin worked for Lindner Aviation and did the inspection.

As part of the inspection, Benjamin removed panels from the underside of the wings. Although these panels were to be removed annually as part of the routine inspection, a couple of the screws holding the panel on the left wing were so rusty that Benjamin had to use a drill to remove them. Benjamin testified that the panel probably had not been removed for several years.

Inside the left wing Benjamin discovered two packets approximately four inches high and wrapped in aluminum foil. He removed the packets from the wing and took off the foil wrapping. Inside the foil was paper currency, tied in string and wrapped in handkerchiefs. The currency was predominately twenty-dollar bills with mint dates before the 1960s, primarily in the 1950s. The money smelled musty.

Benjamin took one packet to his jeep and then reported what he had found to his supervisor, offering to divide the money with him. However, the supervisor reported the discovery to the owner of Lindner Aviation, William Engle. Engle insisted that they contact the authorities and he called the Department of Criminal Investigation. The money was eventually turned over to the Keokuk police department.

Two days later, Benjamin filed an affidavit with the county auditor claiming that he was the finder of the currency under the provisions of Iowa Code chapter 644 (1991). Lindner Aviation and the bank also filed claims to the money. The notices required by chapter 644 were published and posted. No one came forward within twelve months claiming to be the true owner of the money. [Under the statute,] if [the] true owner does not claim [the] property within twelve months, the right to the property vests in the finder. . . .

Does Chapter 644 Supersede the Common Law Classifications of Found Property?

Benjamin argues that chapter 644 governs the rights of finders of property and abrogates the common law distinctions between types of found property. As he points out, lost property statutes are intended "to encourage and facilitate the return of property to the true owner, and then to reward a finder for his honesty if the property remains unclaimed." *Paset v. Old Orchard Bank & Trust*

Co., 378 N.E.2d 1264, 1268 (Ill. 1978). These goals, Benjamin argues, can best be achieved by applying such statutes to all types of found property. . . .[1]

Although a few courts have adopted an expansive view of lost property statutes, we think Iowa law is to the contrary. . . . As recently as 1991, we stated that "[t]he rights of finders of property vary according to the characterization of the property found." *Ritz v. Selma United Methodist Church,* 467 N.W.2d 266, 268 (Iowa 1991). We went on to define and apply the common law classifications of found property in deciding the rights of the parties. As our prior cases show, we have continued to use the common law distinctions between classes of found property despite the legislature's enactment of chapter 644 and its predecessors.

The legislature has had many opportunities . . . to amend the statute so that it clearly applies to all types of found property. However, it has not done so. When the legislature leaves a statute unchanged after the Supreme Court has interpreted it, we presume the legislature has acquiesced in our interpretation. Therefore, we presume here that the legislature approves of our application of chapter 644 to lost property only. . . .

In summary, chapter 644 applies only if the property discovered can be categorized as "lost" property as that term is defined under the common law. Thus, the trial court correctly looked to the common law classifications of found property to decide who had the right to the money discovered here.

Classification of Found Property

Under the common law, there are four categories of found property: (1) abandoned property, (2) lost property, (3) mislaid property, and (4) treasure trove. The rights of a finder of property depend on how the found property is classified.

Abandoned property. Property is abandoned when the owner no longer wants to possess it. Abandonment is shown by proof that the owner intends to abandon the property and has voluntarily relinquished all right, title and interest in the property. Abandoned property belongs to the finder of the property against all others, including the former owner.

Lost property. Property is lost when the owner unintentionally and involuntarily parts with its possession and does not know where it is. Stolen property found by someone who did not participate in the theft is lost property. Under chapter 644, lost property becomes the property of the finder once the statutory procedures are followed and the owner makes no claim within twelve months.

Mislaid property. Mislaid property is voluntarily put in a certain place by the owner who then overlooks or forgets where the property is. It differs from lost property in that the owner voluntarily and intentionally places mislaid property

---

1. [FN3] Iowa's lost property statute was adopted in 1851 at Iowa's constitutional convention. It had earlier appeared in Revised Statutes of the Territory of Iowa ch. 158 (1843).

in the location where it is eventually found by another. In contrast, property is not considered lost unless the owner parts with it involuntarily.

The finder of mislaid property acquires no rights to the property. The right of possession of mislaid property belongs to the owner of the premises upon which the property is found, as against all persons other than the true owner.

Treasure trove. Treasure trove consists of coins or currency concealed by the owner. It includes an element of antiquity. To be classified as treasure trove, the property must have been hidden or concealed for such a length of time that the owner is probably dead or undiscoverable. Treasure trove belongs to the finder as against all but the true owner.

Is There Substantial Evidence to Support the Trial Court's Finding That the Money Found by Benjamin Was Mislaid?

We think there was substantial evidence to find that the currency discovered by Benjamin was mislaid property. In the *Eldridge* case, we examined the location where the money was found as a factor in determining whether the money was lost property. *Eldridge v. Herman,* 291 N.W.2d 319 (Iowa 1980). Similarly, in *Ritz,* we considered the manner in which the money had been secreted in deciding that it had not been abandoned.

The place where Benjamin found the money and the manner in which it was hidden are also important here. The bills were carefully tied and wrapped and then concealed in a location that was accessible only by removing screws and a panel. These circumstances support an inference that the money was placed there intentionally. This inference supports the conclusion that the money was mislaid. *Jackson v. Steinberg,* 200 P.2d 376, 378 (Or. 1948) (fact that $800 in currency was found concealed beneath the paper lining of a dresser indicates that money was intentionally concealed with intention of reclaiming it; therefore, property was mislaid, not lost).

The same facts that support the trial court's conclusion that the money was mislaid prevent us from ruling as a matter of law that the property was lost. Property is not considered lost unless considering the place where and the conditions under which the property is found, there is an inference that the property was left there unintentionally. *See Sovern v. Yoran,* 20 P. 100 (Or. 1888) (holding that coins found in a jar under a wooden floor of a barn were not lost property because the circumstances showed that the money was hidden there intentionally). Contrary to Benjamin's position the circumstances here do not support a conclusion that the money was placed in the wing of the airplane unintentionally. Additionally, as the trial court concluded, there was no evidence suggesting that the money was placed in the wing by someone other than the owner of the money and that its location was unknown to the owner. For these reasons, we reject Benjamin's argument that the trial court was obligated to find that the currency Benjamin discovered was lost property.

We also reject Benjamin's assertion that as a matter of law this money was abandoned property. Both logic and common sense suggest that it is unlikely someone would voluntarily part with over $18,000 with the intention of terminating his ownership. The location where this money was found is much more consistent with the conclusion that the owner of the property was placing the money there for safekeeping. *See Ritz,* 467 N.W.2d at 269 (property not abandoned where money was buried in jars and tin cans, indicating a desire by the owner to preserve it). We will not presume that an owner has abandoned his property when his conduct is consistent with a continued claim to the property. Therefore, we cannot rule that the district court erred in failing to find that the currency discovered by Benjamin was abandoned property.

Finally, we also conclude that the trial court was not obligated to decide that this money was treasure trove. Based on the dates of the currency, the money was no older than thirty-five years. The mint dates, the musty odor and the rusty condition of a few of the panel screws indicate that the money may have been hidden for some time. However, there was no evidence of the age of the airplane or the date of its last inspection. These facts may have shown that the money was concealed for a much shorter period of time.

Moreover, it is also significant that the airplane had a well-documented ownership history. The record reveals that there were only two owners of the plane prior to the bank. One was the person from whom the bank repossessed the plane; the other was the original purchaser of the plane when it was manufactured. Nevertheless, there is no indication that Benjamin or any other party attempted to locate and notify the prior owners of the plane, which could very possibly have led to the identification of the true owner of the money. Under these circumstances, we cannot say as a matter of law that the money meets the antiquity requirement or that it is probable that the owner of the money is not discoverable.

We think the district court had substantial evidence to support its finding that the money found by Benjamin was mislaid. The circumstances of its concealment and the location where it was found support inferences that the owner intentionally placed the money there and intended to retain ownership. We are bound by this factual finding.

Is the Airplane or the Hangar the "Premises" Where the Money Was Discovered?

Because the money discovered by Benjamin was properly found to be mislaid property, it belongs to the owner of the premises where it was found. Mislaid property is entrusted to the owner of the premises where it is found rather than the finder of the property because it is assumed that the true owner may eventually recall where he has placed his property and return there to reclaim it.

We think that the premises where the money was found is the airplane, not Lindner Aviation's hangar where the airplane happened to be parked when the money was discovered. The policy behind giving ownership of mislaid property to the owner of the premises where the property was mislaid supports this conclusion. If the true owner of the money attempts to locate it, he would initially look for the plane; it is unlikely he would begin his search by contacting businesses where the airplane might have been inspected. Therefore, we affirm the trial court's judgment that the bank, as the owner of the plane, has the right to possession of the property as against all but the true owner.

Is Benjamin Entitled to a Finder's Fee?

Benjamin claims that if he is not entitled to the money, he should be paid a ten percent finder's fee under section 644.13. The problem with this claim is that only the finder of "*lost* goods, money, bank notes, and other things" is rewarded with a finder's fee under chapter Because the property found by Benjamin was mislaid property, not lost property, section 644.13 does not apply here. The trial court erred in awarding Benjamin a finder's fee. . . .

SNELL, HARRIS, and ANDRAESEN, JJ., dissenting [omitted].

Notes

1. *Common law categories:* Why does the common law distinguish between lost property, mislaid property, abandoned property, and treasure trove? Did the court's classification of the $18,000 in currency discovered by appellant Heath Benjamin advance those purposes? Do you agree with the court's characterization of the currency?

2. *The interplay of common law and statutory law:* According to the court, what is the relationship between Iowa Chapter 644 and the state's common law of finders? How, if at all, did the statute change the result that the common law alone would have reached? Do you agree with the court's analysis and conclusion? Three justices joined in a dissent in which they vigorously disagreed with the majority. Can you imagine what arguments they made?

3. *Evaluating the common law of finders:* In an ironic summary of finders law, one commentator wrote:

> The "ownership" rights of those who find and take possession of lost goods is a favorite introductory subject for first-year law students studying property law. The precise source and nature of this pedagogic appeal are somewhat enigmatic, but they are probably related to the fact that finders' rights have traditionally been creatures of judicial decision, that the decisions and their underlying policy motivations are often in profound conflict, and that they derive directly from experiences in everyday life. Thus for generations new law students have struggled with the seemingly irreconcilable inconsistencies of the classic finders'

cases, learning useful skills of case analysis, but left unenlightened as to the [application of the] prevailing rules of law to ultimate solutions.

2-13 Thomson on Real Property, Thomas Editions § 13.04. How would you respond to that critique? Does the common law of finders represent a coherent body of law? Do statutes offer more promise, either alone or in combination with the common law? If so, what does *Benjamin* tell us about the importance of clarity in statutory drafting?

C. ADVERSE POSSESSION

Adverse possession may strike you as a strange, perhaps unjustifiable, doctrine. And yet, it has been recognized in Anglo-American law as far back as the thirteenth century. Under the doctrine, a trespasser can gain title to the land of another, provided that the trespasser continuously satisfies requirements designed to give the record owner notice of the adverse occupation and ample opportunity to bring an action to eject the trespasser. The expiration of the applicable statute of limitations bars the true owner's right to assert title in a judicial action. As a practical matter, this barring of the remedy serves also to extinguish the true owner's title and to vest a *new title* in the possessor. As one treatise notes, the doctrine "provides a rare instance in which original title may arise in a mature society." William B. Stoebuck & Dale A. Whitman, The Law of Property § 11.7 (3d ed. 2000). This title relates back to the date of the claimant's adverse entry—that is, the time at which the trespasser simultaneously satisfied all the required elements of adverse possession. *See Konantz v. Stein*, 167 N.W.2d 1, 4 (Minn. 1969).

To confirm this putative title, the claimant can bring an action to quiet title. If successful, the judicial opinion can be recorded just like a deed, thereby providing "marketable" and "record" title (considered further in Chapters 7 and 8). Generally, but not universally, adverse possession cannot be asserted against local, state, or federal government property. Many modern jurisdictions have adopted adverse possession statutes, making adverse possession law—like finders law—a mix of common law and statutory law. *See generally* Powell on Real Property § 91.01 (Michael Allan Wolf, gen. ed. 2015).

Why would the law legalize such "theft" by trespassers? As Justice Oliver Wendell Holmes asserted,

> I should suggest that the foundation of the acquisition of rights by lapse of time is to be looked for in the position of the person who gains them, not in that of the loser. . . . [T]he connection is further back than the first recorded history. It is in the nature of man's mind. A thing which you have enjoyed and used as your own for a long time, whether property or an opinion, takes root in your being and cannot be torn away without your resenting the act and trying to defend yourself,

however you came by it. The law can ask no better justification than the deepest instincts of man. . . .

Oliver Wendell Holmes, *The Path of the Law*, 10 Harv. L. Rev. 457, 476-77 (1897). Pragmatic concerns also underlie the doctrine. As one treatise writer explains,

> Adverse possession serves the social policy of not disturbing what has become the status quo. Thus, where a person has adversely possessed land for such a long period that the community effectively recognizes the possessor as owner, the costs of wresting the land from the possessor at the request of the true owner (who sat on his or her rights) may be too great.

Powell on Real Property § 91.0[4] (Michael Allan Wolf, gen. ed. 2015). As you read the cases in this section, think of additional rationales that support (or reject) the adverse possession doctrine. The following *A Place to Start* box introduces you to the basic elements of adverse possession.

A Place to Start | **Adverse Possession**

- **Elements:** Although requirements vary by state, the following elements are typical. Each must be satisfied continuously throughout the limitations period, or the statute will begin to run anew.

  - **Actual possession:** The claimant must actually use or possess the land in the same manner as would the true owner. Marking boundaries or enclosing the property strengthens the claimant's position. In the case of undeveloped lands in their natural (or in a wild) state, courts sometimes interpret fairly limited actions such as hunting, brush clearing, and wood gathering as constituting actual possession.

  - **Continuous possession for the statutory period:** The possession must continue without significant interruption. Seasonal or occasional use may be enough, if consistent with the nature of the property (such as seasonal use of vacant land or vacation property).

  - **Exclusive possession:** The possessor must exclude, rather than share with, the true owner. Others must also be excluded, at least to the extent that a true owner would exclude them. Some courts will tolerate occasional use by others (including the true owner), provided the possessor is acting as the owner of the property.

  - **Hostile possession:** The claimant's possession must be without the permission of the true owner throughout the limitations period. In some jurisdictions, the payment of taxes by the trespasser is a supporting or required element of proving hostility.

  - **Open and notorious possession:** The claimant's possession must be sufficiently visible such that the true owner knows of the trespass, or at least would have such knowledge upon reasonable inspection.

■ *Alternative doctrines and miscellaneous points*:

■ *Remedy—the innocent improver doctrine:* If a *good faith* possessor makes improvements to the owner's land (as by building a garage or driveway) but is unable to satisfy the elements of adverse possession, to prevent unjust enrichment some courts will compel the owner to pay fair compensation to the possessor before title to the improvement will be quieted in the owner.

■ *Alternatives to adverse possession—agreement, acquiescence, estoppel:* When the boundary between neighboring properties is uncertain or in dispute and the neighbors come to an *agreement* (often oral) fixing its location, or *acquiesce* in a specific boundary line, many courts will uphold the redefined boundary as the true boundary if it has been observed for a sufficient period of time. Alternatively, an owner may be *estopped* from denying a boundary line if that owner erroneously represented the line as true and the neighboring landowner acted in detrimental reliance on the erroneous representation, as by building improvements on the first owner's land. These three doctrines overlap, and courts often conflate their elements. But notice that these doctrines are distinct from adverse possession: the required time period is not necessarily the same as the limitation period for adverse possession, and the elements of adverse possession are irrelevant.

DIGGING DEEPER: Why should trespassers be able to gain good title, provided they satisfy the elements of adverse possession? What purpose does each element serve in justifying such a doctrine?

Actual possession: Sometimes, a trespasser enters under *color of title*—that is, the trespasser has a deed or other document that purports to convey title, but does not actually do so because of some technical or other defect that is not apparent on the document's face. In many such cases, the document makes the trespasser's claim stronger. In addition, some courts will credit a trespasser with satisfying the "actual possession" requirement for the entire acreage covered by the document, not just the portion of the property that the trespasser actually possesses. For example, suppose a deed purports to give Daniel title to a 100-acre wooded property, but the deed has a non-obvious defect. Daniel goes into possession of only one acre of the property, which has been cleared of vegetation and contains a home and garage. If he remains on the property long enough and satisfies all other elements of adverse possession, then a court will likely award him title to all 100 acres at the end of the statutory period. Under a legal fiction, the court will say that Daniel has been in *constructive possession* of all 100 acres. Notice that this is simply an exception to the actual possession requirement and applies only to a small subset of cases—those in which the possessor enters under color of title.

The statute of limitations and disabilities: All states will extend the statute of limitations if the true owner is under a *disability.* That is, some circumstances give owners an excuse for "sleeping on their rights" and failing to take action to eject trespassers—including such things as minority (the owner is under the age of 21, or other age of "majority" recognized in the jurisdiction), legal incompetence, or imprisonment. Generally, the disability must be in place *at the time the trespasser entered,* and any disabilities that arise later do not give the owner an excuse for failing to take action. To provide relief, disability statutes might (1) suspend the running of the statute of limitations for as long as the owner suffers from the disability; (2) postpone the start of the limitations period until after the disability has been removed, and then give the owner the entire statutory period to take action against the trespasser; or (3) give the owner an additional grace period after the normal statute of limitations has expired to eject the trespasser.

For example, assume that a jurisdiction recognizes 21 as the age of majority, and that it has an applicable 10-year statute of limitations, with the following disability provision:

> If a person entitled to commence an action is under a disability because of infancy, mental incompetence, or incarceration at the time the cause of action accrues, the time within which the action must be commenced shall be extended for up to 10 years after the disability ceases or the person under the disability dies, whichever event first occurs. The time within which the action must be commenced shall not be extended by this provision beyond 20 years after the cause of action accrues.

Olivia, who was born in 1994, owned a parcel of land in 2005 at the time Andrew entered and took possession adversely and openly. Soon after Andrew's entry, Olivia was injured in an automobile accident, which rendered her mentally incompetent. In what year could Andrew acquire title by adverse possession to Olivia's property? Answer: 2025.

Adverse Possession Timeline

Figure 1

Notice that Olivia was under a disability (minority) at the time the cause of action accrued in 2005 (when Andrew entered adversely). The subsequent disability of mental incompetence is irrelevant because this statute, like most, requires that relevant disabilities be in place "at the time the cause of action accrues." Olivia's disability was removed in 2015, when she turned 21 (the age of majority). Under the statute, she has an additional 10 years—until the year 2025—to bring an action in ejectment against Andrew. The statute does not allow the period to be extended *beyond* 2025 (which would be "beyond 20 years after the cause of action accrues" in 2005 with Andrew's entry), but that does not matter here, because the 10-year extension expires in 2025.

Assume instead that Olivia had been rendered mentally incompetent in 2004 and that she remained so until 2024, at which time she recovered and her disability was removed. (Continue to assume that Olivia had been born in 1994.) In what year could Andrew acquire title by adverse possession?

Exclusivity, hostility, open and notorious possession: We will take a closer look at the remaining elements of adverse possession in the three cases that follow.

Porter v. Posey

592 S.W.2d 844 (Mo. App. 1979)

Reading Guide
This case provides a good introduction to the elements of adverse possession. In particular, notice what is required to demonstrate *exclusive* possession of another's property.

SATZ, J.

Defendants, who held record title to .18 acres of land located in Franklin County, Missouri, appeal from a judgment which quieted title to this land in plaintiffs. We affirm.

Defendants, Donald E. Posey and Edna Posey, purchased land from an Elsie Mae Kapp in October, 1975. The .18 acres in dispute lies within the property described in the deed conveying Ms. Kapp's property to defendants. Ms. Kapp had obtained title to her property as an inheritance from the estate of Ola Everson, and Ms. Kapp held the land only briefly before selling it to defendants. There is no indication how long Ms. Everson held the property.

In July, 1976, about 9 months after defendants had purchased their property, plaintiffs, Eugene Porter and Grace Porter, purchased land which adjoined and bordered defendants' land on the east and south. Plaintiffs purchased their property from the Engelmeyers, the parents of plaintiff Grace Porter. The deed from the Engelmeyers to plaintiffs described property which the Engelmeyers had acquired in three parcels, in a period between June, 1955, and January, 1956, but this deed did not contain a description of the disputed .18 acres.

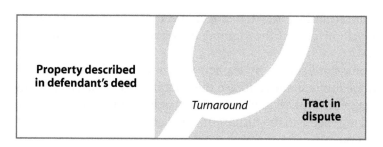

**Property described in deed
from the Engelmeyers to plaintiffs**

For clarity, we set out a sketch of all these parcels of land, in particular, the .18 acres of land in dispute.

Soon after the Engelmeyers had acquired the noted three parcels of land, they proceeded to clear the tract in dispute with a bulldozer and, as reflected in the sketch, they built and graveled a turnaround roadway on this tract. The Engelmeyers maintained and used the turnaround and the land surrounding it until 1976, when they transferred their property to plaintiffs. The Engelmeyers used the area immediately adjacent to the turnaround as a means of access to their property and, also, as a site for volleyball games and overflow parking. The Engelmeyers believed they owned the turnaround and the land upon which it was built.

During the Engelmeyers' tenure on the tract in question, motorists occasionally used the turnaround to go back onto the highway. However, there is no evidence that defendants' predecessors in title used this land in any way. Moreover, the record is silent as to who paid the taxes on the .18 acre tract prior to 1976, when defendants began paying these taxes. Mrs. Engelmeyer believed all along that their tax assessment included the .18 acre tract in question.

Sometime prior to their purchase of land . . . in October, 1975, defendants had this property surveyed and discovered the turnaround was within the property lines described in their deed. Sometime later, apparently in the summer of 1976, although the time was not clearly established at trial, the father of defendant Donald Posey threatened Mr. Engelmeyer with a shotgun and told him to get off the land in dispute. Whether this threat or other facts led plaintiffs to discover the tract in dispute was not within the land described in the Engelmeyers' deed, plaintiffs did discover this omission just prior to their purchase of the land from the Engelmeyers. Plaintiff Eugene Porter sought the advice of an attorney, who assured him that this omission in the Engelmeyers' deed would have no bearing on the transfer. Thus, according to plaintiff Eugene Porter, at the time he and his wife purchased the Engelmeyers' land in July, 1976, he was aware that the .18 acres in question was not described in the deed, but he did believe it was a part of the land he was purchasing.

In addition, according to Mrs. Engelmeyer, the Engelmeyers believed they owned the .18 acres and they intended to transfer all the land they owned to plaintiffs.

. . . [T]he record shows, by explicit testimony and by inference, that plaintiffs continued to maintain and use the tract in dispute just as the Engelmeyers did. Subsequently, on September 4, 1976, defendant Donald Posey installed a cable blocking access to the turnaround, which precipitated the initiation of the present action. . . .

Plaintiffs' claim of title . . . is that the Engelmeyers acquired title by adverse possession and, that under Missouri law, the Engelmeyers may and did transfer their title to the disputed tract without a written conveyance describing the tract. According to plaintiffs, this transfer was accomplished simply by the intention of the Engelmeyers to transfer the title so acquired to plaintiffs and by plaintiffs receiving or taking possession of the land from the Engelmeyers.

In response to plaintiffs' claim, defendants contend that (1) the Engelmeyers did not acquire title to the .18 acre tract by adverse possession and (2) that even if the Engelmeyers did so acquire title, they did not transfer their "rights" or title so acquired to the plaintiffs. We do not agree with defendants. . . .

In order for the trial court to have vested title in plaintiffs on the present record, it must have found that title first vested in the Engelmeyers by adverse possession. Thus, implicit in the court's ultimate decision is a finding that the Engelmeyers occupied the tract in dispute intending to possess it as their own, or, more specifically, that the Engelmeyers occupied or used the tract and their occupation or use of the tract was (1) actual (2) open and notorious (3) hostile (4) exclusive and (5) continuous for ten years. Defendants limit their attack on these implicit findings to an attack on the open and notorious, hostile and exclusive elements of the Engelmeyers' adverse possession.

. . . The determination of openness and notoriety centers on whether the particular acts in question are acts of ownership and are sufficient to give the existing owner notice of the claim being made. Thus, the element of open and notorious [possession] is satisfied by a showing that the occupancy or possession manifested a claim of ownership and was conspicuous, widely recognized and commonly known.

In the instant case, the Engelmeyers entered the disputed tract with a bulldozer, cleared the land, built the turnaround, then maintained it and the land surrounding it. The family also played volleyball and parked on this land. In addition, a neighbor testified that he believed the Engelmeyers to be the owners of this tract of land because they were the only ones who maintained it and used it with any regularity for a period of 18 years. Changing the physical structure of the land by clearing it, building a turnaround and then using and maintaining the turnaround and the land surrounding the turnaround was sufficient evidence to support the court's finding that the Engelmeyers' acts were acts of ownership, sufficient to give the then existing owner notice of this claim and were commonly known so as to constitute open and notorious occupancy or possession. . . .

Defendants next argue that the Engelmeyers' use and possession was not hostile. Hostility of possession does not imply ill will or acrimony. Moreover, to prove hostility, an expressed declaration of hostility need not be made. Hostile possession is simply an assertion of ownership adverse to that of the true owner and all others; *i.e.,* "the claimant must occupy the land with the intent to possess it as his own and not in subservience to a recognized, superior claim of another." *Teson v. Vasquez,* 561 S.W.2d 119, 127 (Mo. App. 1977). Thus, as with other elements of adverse possession, the element of hostility is founded upon the intent with which the claimant held possession and, since the elements of adverse possession are not mutually exclusive, acts which are open and notorious, supporting a claim of ownership, may and often do logically satisfy the element that the claim be hostile.

In the present case, as we have previously noted, there was sufficient evidence for the trial court to find that the Engelmeyers, occupied and used the disputed tract with the intent to possess it as their own and, thus, clearly their use and occupancy was hostile. In addition, we note that defendants failed to adduce any evidence to support a conclusion that the Engelmeyers' use of this tract was permissive. . . .

Defendants' next attack on adverse possession is that the Engelmeyers' possession was not exclusive because others occasionally used the turnaround and, thus, defendants contend, plaintiffs' evidence, at best, merely established a common easement by prescription. . . .

[P]ossession or use is exclusive when the claimant occupies or uses the land for his own use and not for that of another. The present record reveals that the Engelmeyers built the turnaround believing it to be on their property. The fact that travelers occasionally also used this roadway to turn around does not imply nor indicate that the Engelmeyers' [possession was not exclusive]. Indeed, even occasional use of disputed property by the record owner will not of itself negate the exclusive use by an adverse claimant, if the record owner's knowledge or notice of the adverse claim is not otherwise altered. For these reasons, defendants' argument against exclusivity is not persuasive. . . .

These elements having been satisfied, the Engelmeyers' adverse possession extinguished the title to the tract held by defendants' predecessors in title and vested independent title to the tract in the Engelmeyers. This title could only be divested in the same manner as other title. There is no evidence that the Engelmeyers transferred their title to someone other than plaintiffs, nor is there any evidence that defendants or their predecessors in title reacquired ownership of the disputed tract by adverse possession.

The remaining question, then, is whether the Engelmeyers properly transferred title to plaintiffs. As noted, the principle urged by plaintiffs to support the Engelmeyers' transfer of title to plaintiffs, in effect, permits title to property acquired by adverse possession to be transferred without a written conveyance, and simply requires the title owner to intend to transfer the property so acquired and the transferee to receive or take possession of that property. In addition, this principle implicitly permits a person acquiring title by adverse possession to convey it to another without having title quieted in him prior to the conveyance; and it also permits an oral conveyance of title which seemingly violates the requirement that land may only be conveyed by a written instrument. Moreover, facially, the principle parallels and is similar to the doctrine of "tacking" which permits an adverse possessor, in possession of land for less than the prescriptive period, to add his period of possession to that of a prior adverse possessor in order to establish a continuous possession for the requisite prescriptive period. . . .

In the present case, Mrs. Engelmeyers' unrefuted testimony was that she and her husband intended to convey the disputed tract to plaintiffs. Moreover, this was plaintiffs' understanding, and the fact that plaintiff Eugene Porter sought legal advice to carry out that intention merely enforces the weight to be given to Mrs. Engelmeyers' testimony. Further, there was sufficient explicit testimony and inferential evidence for the trial court to find that, after the transfer, plaintiffs took possession of the disputed tract. Thus, the Engelmeyers transferred their title to the disputed tract to plaintiffs.

Defendants rely on *Riebold v. Smith*, 150 S.W.2d 599 (Mo. App. 1941) for their contention that the Engelmeyers' and plaintiffs' acknowledgment of record title in another, in effect, was recognition of superior title in another and that this recognition precluded plaintiffs' "right to tack." . . . Here plaintiffs are not claiming title by tacking their possession on to their predecessors' possession to establish the proper cumulative period of adverse possession. Rather, as noted, plaintiffs claim title was acquired by their predecessors, the Engelmeyers, who subsequently transferred title to plaintiffs. Moreover, in the present case, there was no need for the court to determine either the Engelmeyers' or plaintiffs' intent by inference. Their intent was explicitly stated and unrefuted. The Engelmeyers intended to convey the tract in dispute and plaintiffs intended to receive it. Admittedly, upon learning of defendants' claim of ownership, plaintiffs sought the advice of an attorney to determine how the disputed tract should be transferred. Without commenting on the validity or propriety of that attorney's advice, plaintiffs' request was based upon a belief that the Engelmeyers owned the disputed tract, and, as noted, the Engelmeyers' belief was no different. Plaintiffs' request for legal advice sensibly followed from their explicitly stated belief that the Engelmeyers owned the tract in dispute and, thus, in its worst light, plaintiffs' request was no more than an implicit acknowledgment of their explicitly stated belief. Sensibly construed, plaintiffs' request was merely an attempt on their part to settle the dispute without court action and, thus, their request would not extinguish the Engelmeyers' title nor divest them of that title and would not preclude them from transferring their title to plaintiffs.

The judgment of the trial court is affirmed.

Notes

1. *The elements of adverse possession:*   What are the elements of adverse possession in Missouri? Has each element been satisfied here? Carefully articulate the facts supporting each element, noting that the same evidence may support more than one legal requirement. At what point did the Porters learn that they were trespassing on their neighbors' property? Did their awareness of the trespass matter?

2. *Exclusive possession:* The requirement of exclusivity focuses on whether the trespasser has excluded the *true owner* of the property, and otherwise occupies the land as would an owner. What evidence did the Porters present on this issue? Was it sufficient to satisfy the exclusivity element?

3. *Open and notorious possession:*   What types of activities did the Porters (and the Engelmeyers before them) undertake on the Poseys' land? Was it enough to alert the Poseys that they were in danger of losing a portion of their property to their neighbors? Be sure to notice that the trespasser has no obligation to provide actual notice to the true owner. Rather, true owners have the responsibility of diligently policing their property, and those who "sleep on their rights" risk failing to notice that an adverse possessor has taken over the property. In some jurisdictions, information appearing in the public records—such as the payment of property taxes by the claimant— provides constructive notice and satisfies the open and notorious requirement.

4. *Continuous possession for the statutory period and tacking:*   The court held that the Engelmeyers had acquired title to the property by adverse possession, and could subsequently transfer their interest to the Porters, even without a written conveyance. As we will see in Chapter 7, in most states the Statute of Frauds requires a written conveyance to transfer an interest in land (subject to certain exceptions). Notice that the Porters brought an action to *quiet title* in themselves. After their success in this litigation, they could record the judicial decree in the county records as a type of deed substitute that gives notice to all others of their good title to the property. We will study the recording system in Chapter 8.

But what would happen if the Engelmeyers had not yet acquired title by 1976—the year in which they sold their interest to the Porters? The doctrine of *tacking* permits a series of claimants to add together their periods of possession, provided there is *privity* among them. Many courts adopt a relaxed view of privity in this context, and only require some sort of *reasonable relationship* among successive possessors. But not all successive possessors can tack their possessory periods together. For example, one who enters property after the prior possessor has *abandoned* it lacks privity with the predecessor, as does one who *ousts* (expels) the predecessor. Likewise, a series of unrelated trespassers cannot tack their period of possession together (the derogatory label "squatter" is sometimes applied to such possessors). If the statute of limitations had not yet expired in 1976, could the Porters tack their period of possession onto that of the Englemeyers to satisfy the statute?

Chaplin v. Sanders

676 P.2d 431 (Wash. 1984)

Reading Guide

Should it matter whether trespassers know that they are using land that does not belong to them, or should the trespasser's mental state be irrelevant?

UTTER, J.

. . . Petitioners Peter and Patricia Sanders, d/b/a Shady Glen Trailer Park, are record title owners of property in Snohomish County. Their property adjoins property owned by respondents Kent and Barbara Chaplin and Kenneth and Hazel Chaplin. The Chaplin property is to the east of the Sanders' property. This action concerns a dispute over a strip of land owned of record by the Chaplins, forming the western portion of their property and bordering the Sanders' eastern boundary line.

In 1957 or 1958, Mr. and Mrs. Hibbard, the Sanders' predecessors in interest, decided to clear their land of woods and overgrowth and set up a trailer park (hereinafter the western parcel). There was no obvious boundary between the western and eastern parcels, so Mr. Hibbard cleared the land up to a deep drainage ditch and opened his park. He, further, installed a road for purposes of ingress and egress to the park.

In 1960, Mr. McMurray, then owner of the eastern parcel, had a survey conducted whereupon he discovered the true boundary. He then informed the Hibbards that their driveway encroached upon his land. Two years later, the Hibbards sold their parcel to the Gilberts. The 1962 Hibbard-Gilbert recorded contract of sale contained the following provision:

> The purchaser here has been advised that the existing blacktop road used by the trailer park encroaches on the adjoining property by approximately 20 feet and purchaser agrees that no claim will be made by him for any ownership of said 20 foot strip of property; and, in the event the owner of the adjoining property should remove blacktop, no claim will be made by the purchaser herein. Purchaser agrees to remove blacktop if requested to do so.

In 1967, the western parcel was sold to a Mr. French, who had no actual notice of the true boundary line. The western parcel changed hands once again before the Sanders purchased it in 1976. None of these subsequent owners were made aware that their road encroached on the eastern parcel; but were informed rather casually that the boundary was the drainage ditch. The Sanders were given actual notice of the contract provision, but purportedly mistook the road to which it referred.

Since its initial development in 1958, there was little change in the use of the western parcel. The road remained in continuous use in connection with the trailer park. The area between the road and the drainage ditch was also used by trailer park residents for parking, storage, garbage removal and picnicking. Grass was mowed up to the drainage ditch and flowers were planted in the area by trailer personnel and tenants. In the spring of 1978, the Sanders installed underground wiring and surface power poles in the area between the roadway and the drainage ditch.

In May of 1978, the Chaplins purchased the still undeveloped eastern parcel without the benefit of a survey. Soon thereafter they contacted an architectural consultant for the purpose of designing commercial buildings for their property. They had a survey conducted for this purpose and discovered the Sanders' encroachments. Despite this evidence, which indicated that the Sanders claimed some interest in the land, the Chaplins secured a rezone to a more intensive commercial classification and instructed the architectural engineers to design buildings for the development based on the true survey line. They then brought this action to quiet title to the disputed portion and sought damages for increased construction costs due to the delay necessitated by this action.

The trial court determined that 1967, the date of acquisition by the Sanders' predecessor Mr. French, was the appropriate time from which to compute the 10-year period necessary to establish adverse possession. It then found that the Sanders had satisfied each element of adverse possession with regard to the road and its 3-foot shoulder (Parcel A), and quieted title in them to this portion. It found that the Sanders had not satisfied their burden of proving open and notorious possession with regard to the property between the roadway and the ditch (Parcel B) and quieted title to this portion in the Chaplins. The trial court then issued a mandatory injunction requiring the Sanders to remove their underground wiring and surface power poles at an estimated cost of $20,000.

The Court of Appeals found that, due to the Sanders' actual notice of McMurray's interest, the requirement of hostility had not been satisfied for either parcel. It therefore reversed the trial court's holding with respect to Parcel A, and remanded the cause with directions to quiet title in the Chaplins.

In order to establish a claim of adverse possession, the possession must be: 1) exclusive, 2) actual and uninterrupted, 3) open and notorious and 4) hostile and under a claim of right made in good faith. The period throughout which these elements must concurrently exist is 10 years. Hostility, as defined by this court, "does not import enmity or ill-will, but rather imports that the claimant is in possession as owner, in contradistinction to holding in recognition of or subordination to the true owner." *King v. Bassindale*, 220 P. 777 (Wash. 1923). We have traditionally treated the hostility and claim of right requirements as one and the same. *Bowden-Gazzam Co. v. Hogan*, 154 P.2d 285 (Wash. 1944).

Although the definition of hostility has remained fairly constant throughout this last century, the import we have attributed to this definition has varied. For example, in *Bassindale* we held that, because the claimant believed the land to be his own and treated it as such, his possession was hostile as to the rest of the world. In contrast, in *Hogan*, we held that an adverse user who appropriated land knowing it was not his own, but who used it as his own for over the statutory period, was entitled to title by adverse possession. Our reasoning was that the claimant's subjective belief as to who owned the land was irrelevant so long as he intended to claim the land as his own. Yet, in dicta, we affirmed the age-old requirement that the claimant neither recognize a superior interest nor claim in bad faith. Our interpretation of this definition was further muddied in *Brown v. Hubbard*, 259 P.2d 391 (Wash. 1953) wherein the claimant had mistakenly included a portion of his neighbor's property when fencing his own land. Although he had openly claimed and used the land as his own for well over the statutory period, we held that he had never formed the requisite hostile intent because he would not have claimed the land as his own had he known it belonged to his neighbor.

Thus, in *Bassindale* we required the claimant to possess a good faith belief that the land possessed was his own, in *Hogan* we deemed the claimant's belief irrelevant and in *Hubbard* we required the claimant to possess the unrighteous intent to deprive the true owner of his land. . . . The resulting confusion necessitates our reexamination of this area of the law and mandates a new approach to the requirement of hostility.

The doctrine of adverse possession was formulated at law for the purpose of, among others, assuring maximum utilization of land, encouraging the rejection of stale claims and, most importantly, quieting titles. Because the doctrine was formulated at law and not at equity, it was originally intended to protect both those who knowingly appropriated the land of others and those who honestly entered and held possession in full belief that the land was their own. Thus, when the original purpose of the adverse possession doctrine is considered, it becomes apparent that the claimant's motive in possessing the land is irrelevant and no inquiry should be made into his guilt or innocence.

Washington is not the only state which looks to the subjective belief and intent of the adverse claimant in determining hostility. However, the requirement has been regarded as unnecessarily confusing by many legal commentators, and has been abandoned by the apparent majority of states.

For these reasons, we are convinced that the dual requirement that the claimant take possession in "good faith" and not recognize another's superior interest does not serve the purpose of the adverse possession doctrine. The "hostility/claim of right" element of adverse possession requires only that the claimant treat the land as his own as against the world throughout the statutory period. The nature of his possession will be determined solely on the basis of the manner in which he treats the property. His subjective belief regarding his true interest in the land and his intent to dispossess or not dispossess another is irrelevant to this determination. Under this analysis, permission to occupy the land, given by the true title owner to the claimant or his predecessors in interest, will still operate to negate the element of hostility. . . .

In the present case, due to the contract language manifesting Hibbard and Gilberts' recognition of McMurray's superior title, the trial court determined that their possession was not hostile to McMurray's interest. Under our holding today the contractual provision is no longer relevant. What is relevant is the objective character of Hibbard's possession and that of his successors in interest. Because the trial court did not make explicit findings regarding the character of the pre-1967 possession, we will look to the 1967-77 period in making our determination.

The trial court found the character of possession to have been hostile for at least a 10-year period. We agree. The Sanders and their predecessors used and maintained the property as though it was their own for over the statutory period. This was sufficient to satisfy the element of hostility.

The Sanders also appeal from the trial court's finding that Parcel B was not possessed in an open and notorious manner.

. . . [T]he requirement of open and notorious [possession] is satisfied if the title holder has actual notice of the adverse use throughout the statutory period. This is consistent with the purpose of the requirement, which is to ensure that the user makes such use of the land that any reasonable person would assume he is the owner. For this reason the owner is held to constructive notice of the possession. When the owner has actual knowledge of the possession, the requirement's purpose has been satisfied.

Here the trial court found that McMurray knew of the Hibbards' encroachments in 1960. He was aware of these encroachments until he sold to the Chaplins in 1978. Although the trial court explicitly found that McMurray knew of the road's encroachment on his land, it did not explicitly so find with regard to the strip running between the roadway and the ditch (Parcel B). Mrs. Hibbard testified at trial that she and her husband consistently maintained and mowed Parcel B. It would have been so maintained in 1960 when Mr. McMurray informed the Hibbards that their road was encroaching on his land. We are compelled to conclude, from this evidence, that McMurray was aware of the Hibbards' use of the strip abutting the roadway. This conclusion is all the more compelling when the disparate condition of McMurray's undeveloped, overgrown property and the cleared, mowed and maintained strip of land separating the roadway and McMurray's land is considered.

Although we could rest our holding that the requirement of open and notorious was satisfied on this alone, we find ample evidence to rest our holding on another ground as well.

In determining what acts are sufficiently open and notorious to manifest to others a claim to land, the character of the land must be considered. "The necessary use and occupancy need only be of the character that a true owner would assert *in view of its nature and location.*" *Krona v. Brett*, 433 P.2d 858 (Wash. 1967).

In the present case the trial court found that, during the relevant statutory period, the western parcel was cleared up to the drainage ditch while the eastern parcel remained vacant and overgrown. The residents of the trailer park mowed the grass in Parcel B and put the parcel to various uses: guest parking, garbage disposal, gardening and picnicking. Some residents used portions of Parcel B as their backyard. The trial court concluded that the contrast between the fully developed parcel west of the drainage ditch and the overgrown, undeveloped parcel east of the drainage ditch was insufficient to put the owners of the eastern parcel on notice of the Sanders' claim of ownership. We disagree.

Accordingly, the case is reversed and remanded with directions to quiet title to the disputed property in the Sanders.

Notes

1. *The elements of adverse possession:*   What are the elements of adverse possession in Washington? How do they differ, if at all, from the requirements in Missouri?

2. *Time period:*   What is the required length of trespass in Washington to acquire title by adverse possession? On remand, to what time period should the court look when evaluating the Sanders' adverse possession claim?

3. *Hostility:*   What is the court's rationale for recognizing title by adverse possession? What mental status *should* be required of adverse users to best advance that purpose? Here, the Gilberts agreed to remove their driveway if requested to do so. Does that satisfy the requirement of hostility? Despite its name, hostility does not require ill will or animus between the parties. The predominant and probably better view is that the claimant's subjective intent should be irrelevant, in part because states of mind are notoriously difficult to prove and prone to manipulation. However, some courts will find the hostility requirement to be satisfied only if claimants act in *good faith* (for example, under the mistaken belief that they own the possessed property, or neighbors who admit that they intended to claim only to the true boundary line). Other courts, somewhat perversely, require possessors to act in *bad faith* (knowingly occupying property they do not own). Over the past few decades, some states have experienced a legislative backlash against adverse possession and have added an explicit good faith requirement. *See, e.g.,* Alaska Stat. § 09.45.052 (2003); Colo. Rev. Stat. § 38-41-101 (2008); and Fla. Stat. § 95.18 (2011).

Sometimes, courts use the phrases "claim of right" or "claim of title" (not to be confused with "color of title," which can give rise to constructive possession) as a substitute for, or amplification of, the hostility requirement. At least one commentator has complained, "because the phrases have no clear fixed meaning and cause much trouble, it would be better if they, and the notions they have spawned, were forgotten." William B. Stoebuck & Dale A. Whitman, The

Law of Property § 11.7 (3d ed. 2000). Did the *Chaplin* court use one of these phrases and, if so, in what context?

4. *Open and notorious possession:* What is the nature of the notice that the Gilberts and successors provided to the true owners? That they and the trailer park residents use the blacktop road, or that the blacktop road encroaches on the McMurray property? As a practical matter, how could property owners such as the McMurrays and Chaplin protect themselves against encroachments by their neighbors?

We have just studied two cases considering how the owners of *real property* can lose title through adverse possession. Should the doctrine apply also to *chattels*? The next case takes up that question.

O'Keeffe v. Snyder

416 A.2d 862 (N.J. 1980)

> ┤ **Reading Guide** ├
>
> Suppose a thief steals a valuable piece of artwork from its owner/creator, and then sells it to an unsuspecting good faith purchaser. As between those two relatively innocent parties—the artist and the good faith purchaser—to whom should a court award the painting? Does the doctrine of adverse possession provide a good answer to that question, or is the doctrine a poor fit for *personal property* (as opposed to the adverse possession of land)?

POLLOCK, J.

This is an appeal from an order of the Appellate Division granting summary judgment to plaintiff, Georgia O'Keeffe, against defendant, Barry Snyder ... for replevin of three small pictures painted by O'Keeffe. In her complaint, filed in March, 1976, O'Keeffe alleged she was the owner of the paintings and that they were stolen from a New York art gallery in 1946. Snyder asserted he was a purchaser for value of the paintings, he had title by adverse possession, and O'Keeffe's action was barred by the expiration of the six-year period of limitations provided by N.J.S.A. 2A:14-1 pertaining to an action in replevin. Snyder impleaded third party defendant, Ulrich A. Frank, from whom Snyder purchased the paintings in 1975 for $35,000. ...

We reverse and remand the matter for a plenary hearing in accordance with this opinion.

I

The record ... is fraught with factual conflict. ...

O'Keeffe contended the paintings were stolen in 1946 from a gallery, An American Place. The gallery was operated by her late husband, the famous photographer Alfred Stieglitz.

. . . In 1946, Stieglitz arranged an exhibit which included an O'Keeffe painting, identified as Cliffs. According to O'Keeffe, one day in March, 1946, she and Stieglitz discovered Cliffs was missing from the wall of the exhibit. O'Keeffe estimates the value of the painting at the time of the alleged theft to have been about $150.

About two weeks later, O'Keeffe noticed that two other paintings, Seaweed and Fragments, were missing from a storage room at An American Place. She did not tell anyone, even Stieglitz, about the missing paintings, since she did not want to upset him. . . .

There was no evidence of a break and entry at An American Place. . . . Neither Stieglitz nor O'Keeffe reported them missing to the New York Police Department or any other law enforcement agency. . . . Similarly, neither O'Keeffe nor Stieglitz advertised the loss of the paintings in Art News or any other publication. Nonetheless, they discussed it with associates in the art world. . . . O'Keeffe does not contend that Frank or Snyder had actual knowledge of the alleged theft.

Stieglitz died in the summer of 1946, and O'Keeffe explains she did not pursue her efforts to locate the paintings because she was settling his estate. . . . Finally, in 1972, O'Keeffe . . . report[ed] the theft to the Art Dealers Association of America, Inc., which maintains for its members a registry of stolen paintings. The record does not indicate whether such a registry existed at the time the paintings disappeared.

In September, 1975, O'Keeffe learned that the paintings were in the Andrew Crispo Gallery in New York. . . . On February 11, 1976, O'Keeffe discovered that Ulrich A. Frank had sold the paintings to Barry Snyder, d/b/a Princeton Gallery of Fine Art. She demanded their return and, following Snyder's refusal, instituted this action for replevin.

Frank traces his possession of the paintings to his father, Dr. Frank, who died in 1968. . . . Frank does not know how his father acquired the paintings, but he recalls seeing them in his father's apartment in New Hampshire as early as 1941-1943, a period that precedes the alleged theft. Consequently, Frank's factual contentions are inconsistent with O'Keeffe's allegation of theft. Until 1965, Dr. Frank occasionally lent the paintings to Ulrich Frank. In 1965, Dr. and Mrs. Frank formally gave the paintings to Ulrich Frank, who kept them in his residences. . . .

Frank claims continuous possession of the paintings through his father for over thirty years and admits selling the paintings to Snyder. . . .

. . . Snyder moved for summary judgment on the theory that O'Keeffe's action was barred by the statute of limitations and title had vested in Frank by adverse possession. For purposes of his motion, Snyder conceded that the paintings had been stolen. . . .

II

. . . The Appellate Division accepted O'Keeffe's contention that the paintings had been stolen. [However,] . . . [t]he factual dispute about the loss of the paintings by O'Keeffe and their acquisition by Frank, as well as the other sub-sequently described factual issues, warrant a remand for a plenary hearing. . . .

III

. . . Our decision begins with the principle that, generally speaking, if the paintings were stolen, the thief acquired no title and could not transfer good title to others regardless of their good faith and ignorance of the theft. Proof of theft would advance O'Keeffe's right to possession of the paintings absent other considerations such as expiration of the statute of limitations. . . .

On this appeal, the critical legal question is when O'Keeffe's cause of action accrued. The fulcrum on which the outcome turns is the statute of limitations in N.J.S.A. 2A:14-1, which provides that an action for replevin of goods or chat-tels must be commenced within six years after the accrual of the cause of action. . . .

Since the alleged theft occurred in New York, a preliminary question is whether the statute of limitations of New York or New Jersey applies. The New York statute has been interpreted so that the statute of limitations on a cause of action for replevin does not begin to run until after refusal upon demand for the return of the goods. Here, O'Keeffe demanded return of the paintings in February, 1976. If the New York statute applied, her action would have been commenced within the period of limitations. . . .

IV

. . . The purpose of a statute of limitations is to "stimulate to activity and punish negligence" and "promote repose by giving security and stability to human affairs." *Wood v. Carpenter,* 101 U.S. 135, 139 (1879). . . .

To avoid harsh results from the mechanical application of the statute, the courts have developed a concept known as the discovery rule. . . .

This Court first announced the discovery rule in *Fernandi v. Strully,* 173 A.2d 277 (N.J. 1961). In *Fernandi,* a wing nut was left in a patient's abdomen following surgery and was not discovered for three years. The majority held that fairness and justice mandated that the statute of limitations should not have commenced running until the plaintiff knew or had reason to know of the presence of the foreign object in her body. The discovery rule has since been extended to other areas of medical malpractice. . . .

[W]e conclude that the discovery rule applies to an action for replevin of a painting under N.J.S.A. 2A:14-1. O'Keeffe's cause of action accrued when she first knew, or reasonably should have known through the exercise of due dili-gence, of the cause of action, including the identity of the possessor of the paintings. . . .

In determining whether O'Keeffe is entitled to the benefit of the discovery rule, the trial court should consider, among others, the following issues: (1) whether O'Keeffe used due diligence to recover the paintings at the time of the alleged theft and thereafter; (2) whether at the time of the alleged theft there was an effective method, other than talking to her colleagues, for O'Keeffe to alert the art world; and (3) whether registering paintings with the Art Dealers Association of America, Inc. or any other organization would put a reasonably prudent purchaser of art on constructive notice that someone other than the possessor was the true owner.

V

The acquisition of title to real and personal property by adverse possession is based on the expiration of a statute of limitations.

To establish title by adverse possession to chattels, the rule of law has been that the possession must be hostile, actual, visible, exclusive, and continuous. *Redmond v. New Jersey Historical Society,* 28 A.2d 189 (E. & A. 1942). . . .

The only other New Jersey case applying adverse possession to chattels is *Joseph v. Lesnevich,* 153 A.2d 349 (App. Div. 1949). . . .

As *Lesnevich* demonstrates, there is an inherent problem with many kinds of personal property that will raise questions whether their possession has been open, visible, and notorious. In *Lesnevich,* the court strained to conclude that in holding bonds as collateral, a credit company satisfied the requirement of open, visible, and notorious possession.

Other problems with the requirement of visible, open, and notorious possession readily come to mind. For example, if jewelry is stolen from a municipality in one county in New Jersey, it is unlikely that the owner would learn that someone is openly wearing that jewelry in another county or even in the same municipality. Open and visible possession of personal property, such as jewelry, may not be sufficient to put the original owner on actual or constructive notice of the identity of the possessor.

The problem is even more acute with works of art. Like many kinds of personal property, works of art are readily moved and easily concealed. O'Keeffe argues that nothing short of public display should be sufficient to alert the true owner and start the statute running. Although there is merit in that contention from the perspective of the original owner, the effect is to impose a heavy burden on the purchasers of paintings who wish to enjoy the paintings in the privacy of their homes. . . .

The problem is serious. According to an affidavit submitted in this matter by the president of the International Foundation for Art Research, there has been an "explosion in art thefts" and there is a "worldwide phenomenon of art theft which has reached epidemic proportions."

The limited record before us provides a brief glimpse into the arcane world of sales of art, where paintings worth vast sums of money sometimes are bought without inquiry about their provenance. There does not appear to be a reasonably available method for an owner of art to record the ownership or theft of paintings. Similarly, there are no reasonable means readily available to a purchaser to ascertain the provenance of a painting. It may be time for the art world to establish a means by which a good faith purchaser may reasonably obtain the provenance of a painting. An efficient registry of original works of art might better serve the interests of artists, owners of art, and bona fide purchasers than the law of adverse possession with all of its uncertainties. Although we cannot mandate the initiation of a registration system, we can develop a rule for the commencement and running of the statute of limitations that is more responsive to the needs of the art world than the doctrine of adverse possession.

We are persuaded that the introduction of equitable considerations through the discovery rule provides a more satisfactory response than the doctrine of adverse possession. The discovery rule shifts the emphasis from the conduct of the possessor to the conduct of the owner. The focus of the inquiry will no longer be whether the possessor has met the tests of adverse possession, but whether the owner has acted with due diligence in pursuing his or her personal property.

For example, under the discovery rule, if an artist diligently seeks the recovery of a lost or stolen painting, but cannot find it or discover the identity of the possessor, the statute of limitations will not begin to run. The rule permits an artist who uses reasonable efforts to report, investigate, and recover a painting to preserve the rights of title and possession. . . .

A purchaser from a private party would be well-advised to inquire whether a work of art has been reported as lost or stolen. However, a bona fide purchaser who purchases in the ordinary course of business a painting entrusted to an art dealer should be able to acquire good title against the true owner. Under the U.C.C. entrusting possession of goods to a merchant who deals in that kind of goods gives the merchant the power to transfer all the rights of the entruster to a buyer in the ordinary course of business. N.J.S.A. 12A:2-403(2). In a transaction under that statute, a merchant may vest good title in the buyer as against the original owner. The interplay between the statute of limitations as modified by the discovery rule and the U.C.C. should encourage good faith purchases from legitimate art dealers and discourage trafficking in stolen art without frustrating an artist's ability to recover stolen art works.

The discovery rule will fulfill the purposes of a statute of limitations and accord greater protection to the innocent owner of personal property whose goods are lost or stolen. Accordingly, we overrule *Redmond v. New Jersey Historical Society, supra,* and *Joseph v. Lesnevich, supra,* to the extent that they hold that the doctrine of adverse possession applies to chattels.

By diligently pursuing their goods, owners may prevent the statute of limitations from running. The meaning of due diligence will vary with the facts of each case, including the nature and value of the personal property. For example, with respect to jewelry of moderate value, it may be sufficient if the owner reports the theft to the police. With respect to art work of greater value, it may be reasonable to expect an owner to do more. In practice, our ruling should contribute to more careful practices concerning the purchase of art.

The considerations are different with real estate, and there is no reason to disturb the application of the doctrine of adverse possession to real estate. Real estate is fixed and cannot be moved or concealed. The owner of real property knows or should know where his property is located and reasonably can be expected to be aware of open, notorious, visible, hostile, continuous acts of possession on it.

Our ruling not only changes the requirements for acquiring title to personal property after an alleged unlawful taking, but also shifts the burden of proof at trial. Under the doctrine of adverse possession, the burden is on the possessor to prove the elements of adverse possession. Under the discovery rule, the burden is on the owner as the one seeking the benefit of the rule to establish facts that would justify deferring the beginning of the period of limitations.

VI

Read literally, the effect of the expiration of the statute of limitations under N.J.S.A. 2A:14-1 is to bar an action such as replevin. The statute does not speak of divesting the original owner of title. By its terms the statute cuts off the remedy, but not the right of title. Nonetheless, the effect of the expiration of the statute of limitations, albeit on the theory of adverse possession, has been not only to bar an action for possession, but also to vest title in the possessor. There is no reason to change that result although the discovery rule has replaced adverse possession. History, reason, and common sense support the conclusion that the expiration of the statute of limitations bars the remedy to recover possession and also vests title in the possessor. . . .

VII

We next consider the effect of transfers of a chattel from one possessor to another during the period of limitation under the discovery rule. . . . Subsequent transfers of the chattel are part of the continuous dispossession of the chattel from the original owner. The important point is not that there has been a substitution of possessors, but that there has been a continuous dispossession of the former owner. . . .

The majority and better view is to permit tacking, the accumulation of consecutive periods of possession by parties in privity with each other. . . .

Treating subsequent transfers as separate acts of conversion could lead to absurd results. As explained by Dean Ames:

> The decisions in the case of chattels are few. As a matter of principle, it is submitted this rule of tacking is as applicable to chattels as to land. A denial of the right to tack would, furthermore, lead to this result. If a converter were to sell the chattel, five years after its conversion, to one ignorant of the seller's tort, the

disposed owner's right to recover the chattel from the purchaser would continue five years longer than his right to recover from the converter would have lasted if there had been no sale. In other words, an innocent purchaser from a wrong-doer would be in a worse position than the wrong-doer himself, a conclusion as shocking in point of justice as it would be anomalous in law.

Ames, *The Disseisin of Chattels,* 3 Harv. L. Rev. 313, 323 (1890). . . .

SULLIVAN, J., dissenting [omitted].

HANDLER, J., dissenting.

The Court today rules that if a work of art has been stolen from an artist, the artist's right to recover his or her work from a subsequent possessor would be barred by the statute of limitations if the action were not brought within six years after the original theft. This can happen even though the artist may have been totally innocent and wholly ignorant of the identity of the thief or of any intervening receivers or possessors of the stolen art. The Court would grudgingly grant some measure of relief from this horrendous result and allow the artist to bring suit provided he or she can sustain the burden of proving "due diligence" in earlier attempting to retrieve the stolen artwork. No similar duty of diligence or vigilance, however, is placed upon the subsequent receiver or possessor, who, innocently or not, has actually trafficked in the stolen art. Despite ritualistic disavowals, the Court's holding does little to discourage art thievery. Rather, by making it relatively more easy for the receiver or possessor of an artwork with a "checkered background" to gain security and title than for the artist or true owner to reacquire it, it seems as though the Court surely will stimulate and legitimatize art thievery. . . .

Notes

1. *Adverse possession of chattels:* What are the elements of adverse possession in New Jersey? Applying the law to the facts of this case, construct the fact-based argument that Barry Snyder would make in support of his claim. Be sure to consider the doctrine of tacking. If he prevails, will he then have good title to the paintings? Does it make sense to extend the doctrine of adverse possession from land to chattels? Think about the purposes of adverse possession, including the rationales of Justice Holmes and *Powell on Real Property* excerpted at the beginning of section C. Do either of those rationales help you decide whether the doctrine is a good fit for personal property? As early as the 19th century, some American courts applied adverse possession to personal property, but by the middle of the 20th century, courts began to reverse course again. *See* Michael Allan Wolf, *Conservation Easements and the "Term Creep" Problem*, 33 Utah Envtl. L. Rev. 101, 106-07 (2013) (citing cases). *O'Keeffe* is a

leading case demonstrating the move away from adverse possession of chattels and the application of an alternative doctrine—here, the discovery rule.

2. *Statutes of limitation and adverse possession compared:*   What is the relationship between statutes of limitation—as applied here—and the doctrine of adverse possession? Pay particular attention to the burdens of proof. Which would likely be more favorable to the true owner of goods, such as Georgia O'Keeffe? Further, think about the two modifications to the statute of limitations that the court considered: the discovery rule and the demand rule (as followed in New York). Again, which would true owner O'Keeffe likely prefer? Use the timeline presented in Figure 2 to help you answer these questions.

Adverse Possession Timeline

Figure 2

Overall, what is the practical impact of the court's decision? In an omitted portion of the case, dissenting Justice Handler complained, "The majority has in this case gone well beyond a simple and understandable desire for quietude in litigation. It has actually placed the entire burden of proof as to the absence of comparative fault upon the original owner-artist, albeit in the sheep's clothing of the discovery rule." 416 A.2d at 878-79. Do you agree? Which doctrine do you favor—adverse possession or the statute of limitations? And if the latter, do you favor the discovery rule or the demand rule, and why? *See generally* Patricia Youngblood Reyhan, *A Chaotic Palette: Conflict of Laws in Litigation Between Original Owners and Good-Faith Purchasers of Stolen Art*, 50 Duke L.J. 955 (2001).

3. *Thieves and bona fide purchasers:*   The court suggests that Barry Snyder is a *bona fide purchaser*—that is, one who takes property in good faith (*bona fide*) and without notice that there is a problem with the title, and who also pays value for the property (*purchaser*). Notice the court's statement, "generally speaking, if the paintings were stolen, the thief acquired no title and could not transfer good title to others regardless of their good faith and ignorance of the theft. Proof of theft would advance O'Keeffe's right to possession of the paintings *absent other considerations* such as expiration of the statute of limitations" (emphasis added). In other words, after enough time, O'Keeffe would be barred from asserting a claim to her property, which would have the practical result of giving good title to the thief or to a subsequent possessor (good faith or not).

But, in some limited cases, a bona fide purchaser can acquire good title immediately from a thief, without waiting for the statute of limitations to expire.

As referenced by the court, the "entrusting" provision of the Uniform Commercial Code (U.C.C.) calls for such a result if (a) the true owner "entrusts" her property to "a merchant that deals in goods of that kind" (here, artwork), and (b) if the merchant subsequently sells to a "buyer in the ordinary course of business" (which is defined as "a person that buys goods in good faith, without knowledge that the sale violates the rights of another person in the goods, and in the ordinary course from a person, other than a pawnbroker, in the business of selling goods of that kind. . . .") U.C.C. §§ 2-403(2) & (3). Why would the U.C.C. take that position? As between two relatively blameless parties, the owner's decision to deliver her goods to that particular merchant helped to create the impression that the merchant had good title to convey. The owner is therefore estopped from asserting against the bona fide purchaser the dealer's lack of good title.

D. BEYOND THE BLACK LETTER: CYBERSQUATTING

Our study of adverse possession has taken us from real property to tangible personal property such as artwork. Can the doctrine be stretched yet further—to the context of *intangible* personal property, including trademarks? The notion of "cybersquatting" suggests that such a thing might be possible. As you recall, the unflattering label *squatter* is sometimes applied to bad-faith possessors of real property, and particularly to short-term trespassers. But, what does it mean to "squat" in cyberspace against a trademark owner? Recall from Chapter 1 that trademarks are words, names, symbols, or devices that identify and distinguish the sources of goods from other sources. According to the Coalition Against Domain Name Abuse (CADNA),

> Cybersquatting is the bad-faith registration and use of a domain name that would be considered confusingly similar to an existing trademark, for example . . . AppleProducts.com. Whereas "apple" can be a generic term, here it is clearly used in reference to Apple, Inc. Cybersquatters often conduct a variety of illegal and illicit practices: they can deliver malware, sell counterfeit goods, host phishing schemes, steal identities, and make money from deceptive advertising ruses. They also often use highly sophisticated automated programs to acquire Internet domain names on a massive scale, which means they exploit Internet users on a massive scale.

CADNA, *What is the Problem?*, http://cadna.org/what-is-cybersquatting/ (visited Sept. 10, 2015). Cybersquatters typically register domain names (for a very modest fee) that are confusingly similar to the names of prominent companies, and then hold onto those names until they can sell them back to the companies at a profit. Corporate victims of cybersquatting include such giants as Panasonic, Hertz, and Avon.

Cybersquatting can cause considerable damage because it leads unsuspecting consumers to websites that they believe are hosted by reputable companies.

Consequences include theft of personal information, credit card fraud, sale of counterfeit goods, cybercrimes, and infection of personal computers with "malware." Cybersquatters register thousands of deceptive domain names each year, at an estimated annual cost to the global economy of hundreds of billions of dollars.

In 1999, Congress passed the Anticybersquatting Consumer Protection Act, which created a cause of action for owners of protected marks against one who "registers, traffics in, or uses a domain name that . . . is identical or confusingly similar to that mark" in a "bad faith intent to profit from that mark." 15 U.S.C. § 1125(d)(1)(A).

Discussion Questions

1. *What is it?*   One court has described cybersquatting as "the internet version of an unlawful land grab" because cybersquatters "register well-known brand names as Internet domain names in order to force the rightful owners of the marks to come forward and pay for the right to engage in electronic commerce under their own name." *Interstellar Starship Services, Ltd. v. Epix, Inc.*, 304 F.3d 936, 946 (9th Cir. 2002). Is cybersquatting analogous to adverse possession, or is it something else? If cybersquatters have possession of a domain name long enough and satisfy all the other elements of adverse possession, should they be able to claim confusingly similar domain names against unsuspecting victims that sleep on their rights? Does it matter that cybersquatters pay for their deceptive domain names (albeit, for a modest fee)? Should cybersquatters be prosecuted, or are they simply astute business-people who seize opportunities as they arise?

2. *Adverse possession of copyright?*   Copyrights—another type of intangible personal property—protect literary, musical, dramatic, architectural, and other original works. Can copyright infringers acquire title to the original work by adverse possession? At least one court has held that they can. *Gee v. CBS, Inc.*, 471 F. Supp. 600 (E.D. Pa. 1979), *aff'd*, 612 F.2d 572 (3d Cir. 1979). For more on this intriguing topic, *see* Matthew W. Daus, *The Adverse Possession of Copyright*, 13 Loy. L.A. Ent. L. Rev. 45 (1992).

E. SKILLS PRACTICE: COMMON LAW AND STATUTORY ANALYSIS

In Chapter 1, we practiced two types of common law analysis: (1) fact-based arguments, and (2) precedent-based arguments. Here, we will take up yet a third type of common law argument—those that are based on policy. In the second part of this skills practice section, we will turn our attention to the analysis of statutory law.

1. Common Law Analysis—Policy-Based Arguments

According to an old aphorism, policy is the argument of last resort: "If you don't have the law, argue the facts; if you don't have the facts, argue the law; if you have neither facts nor the law, then argue policy."[2] But in the hands of a skilled advocate, policy can provide a powerful complement to the other bases of argument. In fact, the various types of argument are often intertwined, with policy playing a decisive role. Judges, too, rely on policy. For example, when facing issues of first impression or other situations where the court can choose from among several alternative standards, judges often turn to policy to help them decide what the relevant rule ought to be. As a place to start, consider the following model for effective policy arguments:

A Place to Start | **Common Law Analysis: Policy-Based Arguments**

A strong policy argument generally takes the form, "If the court adopts position X, the result will promote policy Y *because.* . . ."

- *Articulate your position:* Clearly set forth the rule or outcome that you would like the court to adopt on behalf of your client.

- *Predict positive outcomes:* What are the broader ramifications of your position, beyond the facts of your case? What types of benefits will it promote? Benefits fall into a number of categories, including the following:

  - *Support for the judicial system:* Does your position support or improve the efficiency and fairness of the courts? For example, by rejecting your opponent's claim, a court might avoid the "slippery slope" of an overwhelming number of similar claims for relief.

  - *Respect for separation of powers:* Does your position show deference to the most capable and appropriate branch of government as decisionmaker under the facts of the case? For example, one party might argue that the courts are better suited to resolving the issue at hand, whereas the other party might argue that the issue should be decided by the legislature.

  - *Promotion of economic efficiency:* Does your position promote economic efficiency?

  - *Promotion of the public interest:* Does your position advance desirable social goals, values, or policies?

- *Provide authority supporting your prediction:* Be sure to provide authority for your prediction that if the court adopts position X, then desirable consequence Y will follow. Sources of authority include publications, theories, and data from fields such as the following:

---

2. Some versions give policy even shorter shrift by omitting it altogether: "If you have the facts on your side, pound the facts into the table. If you have the law on your side, pound the law into the table. If neither the facts nor the law are on your side, then pound the table."

■ Law

■ Psychology and sociology

■ History

■ Medicine

■ Economics

Tasks

1. *Heiman v. Parrish:*   Review *Heiman v. Parrish* in section A, above. Then, decide whether you will represent plaintiff Jerod or defendant Heather.

2. *Conditional gift?* Should the court regard the engagement ring as a conditional gift? Clearly articulate your client's position, and craft at least two policy arguments in support of that position. What types of authority might support the prediction that your position will promote favorable social policies?

3. *Fault or no-fault?*   If the court regards the ring as a conditional gift, then upon the termination of the engagement, should ownership of the ring be determined on a fault or no-fault basis? State your client's position clearly. Then, make at least two policy arguments in support of that position. As above, be sure to specify what types of authority might support your position.

2. Statutory Analysis—Canons of Construction

In *Benjamin v. Lindner Aviation* (section B, above) the Iowa Supreme Court considered the relationship between the four common law categories of found property and the jurisdiction's "lost property" statute, then appearing as Chapter 644 of the Iowa Code (now renumbered as Chapter 556F). The statute dates back to the mid-19th century and its initial sections address matters perhaps more relevant at the time of the law's enactment rather than in modern times—such as the finding of drifting logs worth more than five dollars. Nevertheless, the fate of some $18,000 turned on the language of that old law.

How should a court, such as the *Benjamin* court, interpret an ambiguous statute? Was Chapter 644 intended to codify the common law or to change it? To answer questions such as these, courts use a variety of interpretive tools—sometimes called *canons of construction*—for determining the meaning of statutes. Here are three canons that might have been useful in interpreting the Iowa statute

| A Place to Start | Statutory Analysis: Selected Canons of Construction |

■ *The expression of one thing implies the exclusion of the other (expressio unius est exclusio alterius):* When a statute explicitly sets forth certain terms (such as "lost property" in the Iowa Code), then a reviewing court might conclude that the legislature meant to exclude other similar terms (such as "mislaid" or "abandoned" property, or "treasure trove"). Alternatively, a court might conclude that the legislature did not consider the precise issue in question, and that the legislature intended for the court to "fill in the gaps" when applying the statute to a range of unforeseen circumstances.

■ *Statutory preambles:* If the statute is clear on its face, then its terms will govern. If it is ambiguous, however, then courts will search for evidence of the intent of the drafters. One such piece of evidence might be found in a statute's preamble or statement of purpose.

■ *The whole act rule:* Courts presume that the various provisions of a statute are designed to work together as a consistent and harmonious whole. Therefore, to determine the meaning of an ambiguous statutory provision, courts might consider how that provision fits into the broader statutory scheme.

Tasks

You are a legislator from Iowa and the chairperson of a committee that has been charged with amending the Iowa Code sections on "lost property" in response to the *Benjamin* opinion. Perform the following tasks:

1. *Review the existing statute:*   Read the statutory excerpt that appears below, taken from the 1989 version of the Iowa Code. Discuss with your committee the amendments that you would like to make to update the law, keeping in mind the canons of construction that future courts will likely use when interpreting your new legislation.

2. *The purpose of the statute:*   What should be the purpose of Chapter 644? (Recall that the appellant, Heath Benjamin, suggested one potential purpose in *Benjamin*.) Draft a brief preamble or statement of purpose to clarify the statutory purpose.

3. *The relationship to the common law:*   Are the code provisions (including the section on compensation for finders) intended to supersede the common law, or to supplement the common law? Do they apply to all categories of found property or only to "lost" property? Draft statutory language to clarify these areas of ambiguity.

4. *Definitions:*   Should the statute contain a definitions section? If so, consider drafting a definition of "premises" in response to *Benjamin*.

Chapter 644—Lost Property

§ 644.1 Taking up vessels, rafts, logs and lumber. If any person shall stop or take up any vessel or watercraft, or any raft of logs, or part thereof, or any logs suitable for making lumber or hewn timber, or sawed lumber, found adrift within the limits or upon the boundaries of this state, of the value of five dollars or upwards, . . . such person, within five days thereafter, . . . shall go before some district judge . . . where such property is found, and make affidavit setting forth the exact description of such property [and] where and when the same was found. . . .

§ 644.6 Lost goods or money. If any person shall find any lost goods, money, bank notes, or other things of any description whatever, of the value of five dollars and over, such person shall inform the owner thereof, if known, and make restitution thereof. . . .

§ 644.7 Where owner unknown. If the owner be unknown, such person shall, within five days after such finding, take such money, bank notes, and a description of any other property before the county auditor . . . where the property was found, and make affidavit of the description thereof [and] the time when and place where the same was found. . . .

§ 644.8 Advertisement. The finder of such lost goods, money, bank notes, or other things, shall forthwith give written notice of the finding of such property. . . . Said notice shall: 1) Be posted at the door of the courthouse in the county in which the property was found . . . ; and 2) In case the property found shall exceed ten dollars in value, the notice shall be published once each week for three consecutive weeks in some newspaper . . . having general circulation in said county. . . .

§ 644.11 Vesting of title. If no person appears to claim and prove ownership to said goods, money, bank notes, or other things within twelve months of the date when proof of said publication and posting is filed in the office of the county auditor, the right to such property shall irrevocably vest in said finder. . . .

§ 644.13 Compensation. As a reward for the taking up of boats and other vessels, and for finding lost goods, money, bank notes, and other things, before restitution of the property . . . shall be made, the finder shall be entitled to ten percent upon the value thereof. . . .

Iowa Code (1989), The Iowa Legislature, *Iowa Code Archive*, https://www.legis.iowa.gov/archives/shelves/code (visited Sept. 6, 2015).

F. CHAPTER REVIEW

1. Practice Questions[3]

   1. *The pocket watch at the farm:*   Baird Brown owns a 1,000-acre farm. As a young man, Farmer Brown grew a variety of crops on his land. Now, however,

---

3. Answers appear in the Appendix to the casebook.

his health is failing and he is no longer able to farm the property. In fact, it has been years since Farmer Brown has even been able to get outside to inspect his property and his fences. As a result, the farm has become overgrown and its natural vegetation has become attractive to wildlife. To generate income, Farmer Brown allows hunters to enter his land for a reasonable fee. On a cold Saturday in January, April Adams made proper arrangements to hunt on Farmer Brown's property. As she was walking along, Adams spotted an old barn ahead, and decided to step inside to get out of the wind. As she got closer, however, Adams noticed that the barn door was sagging off its hinges and would be difficult to open. Undaunted, Adams dragged over a stump from an old stack of firewood to help her climb in through a window on the side of the barn. As she was doing so, she noticed something shiny in the depression where the stump had been resting. Scraping away the dirt with her fingers, Adams found a gold pocket watch.

Later that day, Adams stopped by Farmer Brown's house and showed him the pocket watch. Brown had never seen the watch, but said that he would run a "lost and found" notice in the local newspaper. After six months, no one had responded to the notice, and Farmer Brown took the watch to a jeweler for an appraisal. Upon learning that the watch was an antique valued at $5,000, Brown refused to return the watch to Adams. She promptly filed a lawsuit to compel Brown to return the watch to her.

Carefully state the central issue of the lawsuit *Adams v. Brown*. What arguments should Adams make? What arguments will Brown make in response? Does it make a difference if the common law rules apply or if statutory rules have been enacted to govern the issues?

2. *The neighbor's fence:* Last year, without Nora's permission, her neighbor, Joseph, put up a privacy fence that extends several feet into her yard. Nora wanted to maintain good neighborly relations, so she told Joseph that she didn't object to the fence's placement. Nora knew that Joseph only had a one-car garage and needed the extra space to park his new second car. In addition, she had heard rumors that his company was opening a new facility out of town, so there was a good possibility that Joseph would be selling his house in the near future. She also felt sorry for Joseph, and heard that his job was very stressful and that he had suffered some sort of mental breakdown a little while ago. Advise Nora what action she should take. Your jurisdiction has a 10-year statute of limitations for actions in ejectment.

3. *The bracelet at the coffee shop:* Linda found a valuable bracelet on the sidewalk outside of the local coffee shop. She showed it to the owner of the coffee shop who told her to leave it with him so he could display the item in the hope that its true owner would claim it. Six months later, Linda returned and asked about the bracelet. The shop owner told her that no one had claimed it, and that he had given it to his wife as a birthday present. Linda's rights are best described as:

A. Superior to rights of the true owner, and those of the shop owner and his wife, because the bracelet was lost.

B. Superior to rights of the true owner, but inferior to rights of the shop owner and his wife.

C. Inferior to rights of the true owner, but superior to rights of the shop owner and his wife.

D. Inferior to rights of the true owner, and to those of the shop owner and his wife.

2. Bringing It Home

Research your state's statutory law, and find its relevant provisions, if any, on the following topics:

1. *The law of finders:*   Does your state continue to recognize the four categories of found property recognized at common law? If not, does it supersede the common law in whole, or modify it in part? (Recall that this was one of the dispositive issues in *Benjamin v. Lindner Aviation*). Does the statute impose any reporting, advertising, or other requirements upon finders, or provide for the award of finders fees?

2. *Adverse possession:*   What is your state's limitations period for actions in ejectment? Is the running of the statute delayed in cases of the owner's disability? Substantively, what elements must adverse possessors satisfy? Is there a "claim of right" element—and if so, what precisely does it require? Is the claimant's subjective state of mind (good faith or bad faith) relevant? Are the requirements relaxed if trespassers act under color of title, or if they pay taxes on the property? Does the statutory law clarify whether or not personal property can be acquired by adverse possession? <u>Hint:</u> Your state's adverse possession statute might not be titled as such. If not, look in the table of contents under key words such as *quiet title, limitations of actions, statutes of limitation*, and other similar phrases.

PART TWO

SHARED PROPERTY—CONSECUTIVE AND CONCURRENT POSSESSION

Estates and Future Interests

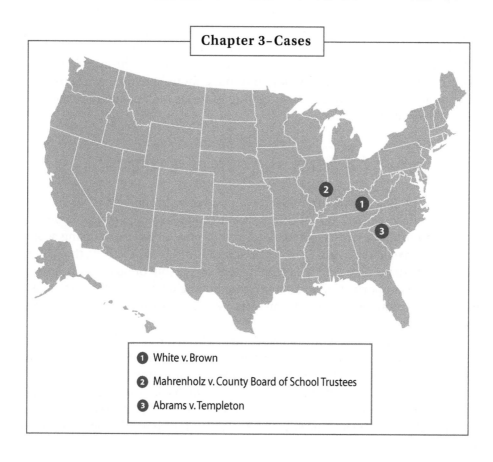

Chapter 3–Cases

❶ White v. Brown

❷ Mahrenholz v. County Board of School Trustees

❸ Abrams v. Templeton

The first two chapters gave you a broad overview of the law of property. In them, we focused primarily on individual ownership at a particular point in time. But, as we will see in Chapters 3 through 6, ownership can be shared across both *time* and *space*. In this chapter, we will study the topic of estates and future interests—an intricate system under which multiple parties *simultaneously* hold legal interests in the same property, but *consecutive* rights of possession. Under a traditional example, a man might leave property to his wife for her life, and then to his children and their heirs forever. In that example, both wife and children presently hold legal interests in the property, but they will take their turns at possession. Likewise, Chapter 4 will examine sharing across time, but in the context of landlord-tenant law. As you probably know from your own experience, both landlord and tenant hold legal rights in the same property: The tenant holds the present right to present possession, and the landlord holds the present right to retake possession at some future point when the lease expires. In Chapters 5 and 6, we will turn our attention to sharing across *space*. First, we will look at so-called concurrent estates and marital interests under which parties share possession of the same property at the *same time*. Finally, Chapter 6 highlights public property and commons property, in which many parties simultaneously share rights of use.

Sharing across time and space offers many benefits. But, as we will see, it also poses significant challenges. As you read Chapters 3 through 6, keep in mind the web of interests metaphor, and think about how the law can respect the complicated and sometimes competing interests held by many parties in a single parcel of land.

A. OVERVIEW OF ESTATES AND FUTURE INTERESTS

At least in theory, property must have an owner throughout all of eternity. We are about to embark on the study of a marvelous system of law known as estates and future interests—*marvelous* in the sense of its breathtaking scope. For every parcel of land, and for every moment throughout eternity, the system endeavors to determine *who* holds the right of ownership or possession, and *for how long*. It is important to understand that no one developed this system as a unified whole. Rather, it evolved slowly in reaction to historical forces over the past millennium.

Property is a subject both old and new. Throughout this course, we will consider a variety of modern applications for property law, including the sharing economy, cybersquatting, outer space mining, and drones. But our focus in this chapter will be backward looking—all the way back to 1066 and the feudal period in England. As unlikely as it seems, the events of that time would continue to influence Anglo-American property law for about the next thousand years.

1. Historical Overview

In 1066, the French noble William the Conqueror and his forces invaded England. William claimed the throne and reigned until his death in 1087. He confiscated all lands held by the Saxon nobles and redistributed them to his relatives and loyal supporters. In fact, he gave almost one quarter of England to only 10 of his staunchest followers.[1] To organize the conquered territory, William imposed a system of feudal landholding in England, adapted from the practices of his homeland. Under that system, the king distributed vast expanses of land through a process known as *infeudation* to the loyal Norman barons who had helped him gain the English throne. In return for the right to possess the land (and the king's protection of that right), the barons pledged loyalty and performed a variety of *feudal services* for the king—including the provision of military aid, the performance of domestic services for the royal household, and the payment of fees that resembled modern rental payments. Importantly, the barons did not themselves hold the lands, but were regarded as *tenants in chief* who "held under" the king and enjoyed the right of *possession* at his pleasure. It is also important to note that the relationship between the king and the tenants in chief was highly personal, as the king relied on their service to protect his claim to the throne. As a result, at least at the start, the land did not pass automatically to the barons' heirs at their death. Instead, the king maintained a personal interest in selecting those who would next take possession of the land and provide the critical feudal services.

For their part, the tenants in chief *subinfeudated* portions of their lands to knights, who held under the barons. In exchange for the right of possession, these tenants would provide military service (thereby satisfying the barons' obligation to the king) or perform other feudal services such as household or agricultural work, or the payment of rents. Similarly, knights would subinfeudate their land, and so on, creating additional layers of sub-tenures. At the bottom of the feudal pyramid were the peasants, who worked the land and paid rents. All of these positions were relational—those in the intermediate levels of the pyramid were the *lords* of those beneath them, and the *tenants* of those above them.

Feudalism distinguished between free and unfree tenures—the precursors of today's *freehold* and *nonfreehold* estates—a distinction that was premised on the nature of the feudal services extracted in exchange for possessory rights in the land. Those holding free tenures enjoyed a special type of possessory right known as *seisin* (pronounced SEE-zin). Under feudalism, then, one's social and economic *status* depended on one's place in this hierarchy of landholding. Even today, the modern system of *estates* hearkens back to the core notion that the right to land is an important determinant of one's wealth and power

---

1. Moynihan's Introduction to the Law of Real Property 2 (Sheldon F. Kurtz ed., 5th ed. 2011).

Feudalism in Europe
Source: CDA's World History Wiki, Licensed under Creative Commons Attribution-ShareAlike 3.0 License

in society. Notably, the feudal structure recognized overlapping rights of numerous parties in the same lands—an attribute that continues with today's system of present estates and future interests.

Over time, the feudal system of property began to develop some of the modern features that we take for granted today. First, the barons and the lords began to loosen their grip on the selection of new tenants upon the death of an existing tenant. Instead, they began to recognize the right of *inheritance*, under which tenants' possessory rights could pass at their death to their heirs, generally upon the payment of a *relief* that resembled the modern inheritance tax. This practice began as a matter of custom in the intermediate levels of the pyramid, but by 1100, even the King (Henry I) recognized the automatic right of inheritance upon payment of the relief. If the deceased tenant (the *decedent*) left no heirs, then the property would *escheat* back to the decedent's lord.

As a second development, tenants gradually gained the right to transfer their land during their lives without the consent of their lords, but generally contingent on the payment of a fine. In 1290, the *Statute Quia Emptores* gave intermediate tenants the right to alienate their lands without paying the fine (but did not relieve tenants in chief to the king of the fine). Quia Emptores also prohibited subinfeudation, thus leading to the collapse of the feudal pyramid.

Finally, as a third modern development, the 1540 *Statute of Wills* gave land-holders the right to *devise* their freehold lands by will. This would effectively preclude any claims by the decedent's heirs. Thus, by 1540, estates in land could be transferred by each of the three methods recognized today—inheritance, inter vivos conveyance, and devise by will.

2. Basic Terminology and Themes

The text box below provides a reference for some important terminology that you will see throughout this chapter.

A Place to Start | **Terminology**

- *Classification of estates:* The owners of present estates and future interests hold *present legal rights* in the property, regardless of when those rights will become possessory, if ever.

  - *Present v. future:* A present estate is one that entitles its owner to immediate possession of the property, whereas the owner of a future interest is not entitled to possession until some future time. Thus, the owner of a present estate has the *present* right to *present* possession, whereas the owner of a future interest has a *present* right to *future* possession.

  - *Freehold v. nonfreehold:* A freehold estate is an interest in land, the owner of which is said to hold *seisin*. A nonfreehold estate is an interest in real property that does not include seisin, and is of interest today primarily in the context of landlord-tenant law (*see* Chapter 4). In feudal times, seisin was a special type of possessory right held by those who owed feudal duties to the lord (or king) under whom they held the land.

  - *The numerus clausus principle:* Under this principle, new types of estates cannot be created. Instead, courts will only recognize estates that fit into established categories, or will interpret ambiguous conveyances as creating one of the recognized types of estates.

- *Transferability of property:* Property can be transferred (or, *alienated*) by the following methods:

  - *Inter vivos conveyance:* An *inter vivos* conveyance is the transfer of land among living persons. In this chapter, we will generally refer to the transferor as *O*, the person who grants a property interest to another.

■ ***Devise:*** A devise is the transfer of property by will. The transferor is known as the *testator* (*T*) and the transferee is known as the *devisee.* Be sure to note that one who takes under a will is *not* described as an "heir" (who is someone who takes when there is no will). The Statute of Wills (1540) gave landholders the right to devise their freehold lands by will. One who dies without a will is said to die *intestate* (pronounced in-TES-tate).

■ ***Inheritance:*** When a person dies intestate, that person's property is distributed according to the state's law of *intestate succession.* Such laws specify how the property should be distributed among *issue* (blood descendants), *ascendants* (parents, grandparents, and so on), and *collaterals* (blood relatives other than issue—such as brothers and sisters, nephews and nieces, uncles and aunts, and cousins). Note carefully that heirs cannot be determined until the moment of death—therefore, a living person has no heirs, but only heirs apparent (those who are likely to be the person's surviving heirs).

Estates and future interests is an enormously complicated subject, which you can study in further detail in upper-level courses on estates and trusts. Our goals in this chapter are quite modest. First, you should become familiar with basic terminology and concepts (introduced in section A). Second, you should be able to look at the language of a conveyance or will and identify by name the types of estates and future interests that it creates (sections B and C). Finally, you should develop some appreciation of the basic tensions inherent in the law of estates, and how they led to the creation of various common law rules designed to promote marketability of real property rights (section D).

This chapter illustrates in sharp relief the casebook theme, "just passing through." As you know, the law seeks to give owners maximum control over their property. But what does that mean when ownership is divided over time? As property passes from one generation to the next, for how long should members of each generation exert "dead hand control" beyond their own lives and into the future? For example, should parents be able to leave property to their children by will, subject to forfeiture if the children violate certain conditions—such as divorcing (or failing to marry) a particular person, practicing (or not practicing) a particular religion, graduating (or not graduating) from a particular law school, or allowing the property to be used (or not used) for a certain purpose? What is the appropriate weight that should be given to the desires of past, present, and future generations? Should it matter whether the conditions are rooted in parental protectionism or some other less supportable instinct? The subject of estates and future interests provides a vehicle for considering these fascinating—yet often unanswerable—questions.

B. PRESENT ESTATES

In this section, we will introduce three present *freehold estates* and also preview the *nonfreehold estates* (which will be covered in more depth in Chapter 4). Then, we will see that the present estates can be made *defeasible* such that they expire earlier than they normally would upon the occurrence of a specified condition or event that is uncertain to occur. Section C will introduce the corresponding types of future interests recognized by law.

Under the *numerus clausus* ("the number is closed") principle analogized from civil law, courts generally will not recognize new types of estates. *See* Thomas W. Merrill and Henry E. Smith, *Optimal Standardization in the Law of Property: The Numerus Clausus Principle*, 110 Yale L.J. 1 (2000) (justifying the standardization of property rights for its ability to reduce the cost of processing information about idiosyncratic rights that might otherwise be created). As a corollary, courts interpret ambiguous conveyances as creating one of the established types of estates. That is, courts will "squeeze" ambiguous conveyances into an existing box. To do so, they will examine the language of the conveyance and apparent intent of the grantor to determine which recognized estate the ambiguous interest most closely resembles. Thus, a careful drafter would be wise to use the "magic words" traditionally used to describe the type of estate the grantor intends to create.

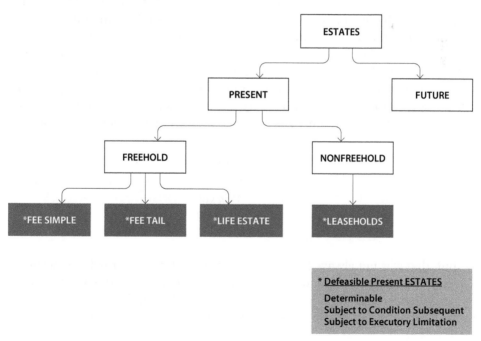

Figure 1

1. The Basic Categories of Present Estates

Since common law times (and continuing today), the law has recognized only four categories of present possessory estates, as highlighted in red in Figure 1. Each estate is described in more detail below.

Fee simple absolute: The fee simple absolute is of potentially infinite duration, and is therefore considered to be the "largest" estate in temporal terms. It will end only if the owner dies intestate (without a will) and also without heirs, in which case it will escheat to the state.[2] Today, the fee simple absolute is freely alienable inter vivos, devisable, and inheritable. If you see the phrase "fee simple," you can presume that it is a shorthand reference to the fee simple absolute, unless it is modified by another term.

> *Example 1.*   *O* conveys, "To *A* and his heirs."

The phrase "To *A*" contains *words of purchase* because they tell us *to whom* the property has been conveyed—to *A*. In this context, "purchase" does not require that *A* paid value for the property, but would also include situations where *A* received the property as a donee (either *A* received a gift from *O* during *O*'s lifetime or through *O*'s will). In contrast, "and his heirs" are *words of limitation* because they tell us *what estate* has passed to *A*—a fee simple absolute. Note carefully that "and his heirs" are not words of purchase. That is, the conveyance gives nothing to *A*'s heirs. If it were otherwise, then *A* would not subsequently be able to convey the land, unless the heirs joined in and agreed to the conveyance. But, that would not be possible because *A*'s heirs cannot be identified until the moment of *A*'s death. Therefore, recognizing a property right in the heirs (under words of purchase) would impose a *restraint on alienation* that would make it virtually impossible for *A* to sell, mortgage, or otherwise dispose of the property. Instead, in modern times, "and his heirs" are merely words that identify the conveyance to *A* as a fee simple absolute.

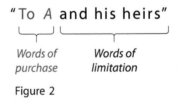

Figure 2

But, that was not always the case—as a brief historical digression will show. The legal significance of the words "and his heirs" changed throughout history. First, during early feudal times, a conveyance "To *A*" merely gave *A* an interest in the land during *A*'s lifetime (known as a "life estate" today), which returned

---

2. In some jurisdictions, escheat does not technically terminate the fee simple absolute, but simply passes it to the state as the "ultimate heir." William B. Stoebuck & Dale A. Whitman, The Law of Property (3d ed. 2000).

to the lord at *A*'s death. Next, by about 1100 the right of inheritance became recognized, and land descended to a tenant's heirs (usually, the eldest son) at the death of the tenant. However, the property thus passed by inheritance *only if* the lord included in the conveyance the magic words "and his heirs" (similar words would not suffice). As an incentive to encourage lords to convey inheritable estates, tenants often made a monetary payment to the grantor—which was a type of precursor to the modern estate tax. By about 1225, it became settled that the words "and his heirs" gave nothing to the heirs themselves, but were simply words of limitation indicating that *A* had received an estate of potentially infinite duration. As a result, *A* could then convey the property to a third party, and the heirs could not complain because "and his heirs" were not words of purchase granting them an independent property interest.[3] Finally, the Statute of Wills was enacted in 1540, which allowed landholders to devise their freehold lands by will. After that, courts began to relax rigid linguistic requirements, and they interpreted "To *A*" as conveying a fee simple absolute (even without the addition of the limitation "and his heirs"), as long as such interpretation appeared consistent with the intent of the testator.

Today, virtually all states have abolished the requirement of using words of limitation ("and his heirs") to create a fee simple absolute. Thus, "To *A*" is ordinarily sufficient to create a fee simple absolute in modern times. Nevertheless, many drafters continue to use "To *A* and his heirs" to avoid any potential ambiguity.

Fee tail: Like the fee simple absolute, the fee tail is inheritable. But unlike the fee simple, the line of descent is cut down to the "heirs of the body" (also called the "issue") of the grantee, which means all *lineal* offspring in the grantee's direct bloodline. Thus, the fee tail passes to the original grantee's children, then to the grantee's grandchildren, then to the grantee's great-grandchildren, and so on, potentially forever. (Notably, this excludes the grantee's *collateral* heirs, such as aunts, uncles, nephews, nieces, and others.) The grantor retains a *reversion.* That means that if the original grantee's lineal bloodline runs out, then the fee tail terminates and the land will revert back to the grantor (or to the grantor's heirs, if the grantor is no longer alive). Alternatively, by its own terms, the conveyance creating the fee tail might provide for a *remainder* to vest in a third party (usually another branch of the family) upon expiration of the original grantee's issue. We will learn more about reversions and remainders in the next section. The fee tail is said to be of a *lesser quantum* than the fee simple absolute because its potential duration is briefer.

Example 2.   *O* conveys, "To *A* and the heirs of his body."

After the passage of the Statute of Wills in 1540 and a more relaxed judicial approach to the language of wills (as opposed to inter vivos conveyances), "To *A*

---

3. Moynihan's Introduction to the Law of Real Property, *supra*, at 36; Stoebuck & Whitman, *supra*, at § 2.2.

and his issue" might also be sufficient to create a fee tail (in addition to the magic words used in Example 2).[4] It remains unclear whether "and the heirs of his body" constituted words of purchase or words of limitation.[5]

The fee tail can be the subject of a limited inter vivos conveyance, but this merely transfers an estate that lasts for the life of the original grantee, and upon that grantee's death, the property passes down the original grantee's lineal bloodline. Fees tail cannot be devised by will, because that would cut off the inheritance right of the original grantee's issue. Finally, the fee tail is inheritable, but only to the line of offspring specified in the original conveyance. For example, grantors could convey what was known as a *fee tail male* ("To *A* and the heirs male of his body"), a *fee tail female* ("To *A* and the heirs female of his body"), a *fee tail special* ("To *A* and the heirs of his body by spouse *X*"), or a *fee tail general* ("To *A* and the heirs of his body").

In essence, the fee tail functionally created a series of life estates, all within the lineal bloodline. It acted as a restraint on alienation because (as just discussed) no current holder of the estate could cut out the inheritance rights of the original grantee's issue. In England, the fee tail was an important mechanism for the preservation of family wealth because it kept what was often the family's most valuable asset—land—within the line of lineal descendants. But, the fee tail was not well received in the United States, at least after the time of the American Revolution, because it interfered with the free alienability of land, and also because it was associated with dynastic wealth—anathema to the value Americans placed on equality and widespread opportunity.

England abolished the fee tail in 1925. Likewise, most American jurisdictions have abolished the fee tail (or at least modified it). In many states, a conveyance that purports to create a fee tail is construed instead as conveying a fee simple absolute, but several variations are possible.

Life estate: The life estate endures for the life of a specified person, usually the grantee. For example, if *O* conveys Blackacre, "To *A* for life," then the property passes to *A* for the duration of *A*'s life.

> *Example 3.*   *O* conveys, "To *A* for life" or "To *A* for the life of *X*."

In other cases, a third party is used as the measuring life—say, *X*. In that case, *O* would convey Blackacre, "To *A* for the life of *X*." That language creates a life estate *pur autre vie* ("for the life of another"). "*To A*" are words of purchase, and "for life" (or, "for the life of *X*") are words of limitation.

---

4. Moynihan's Introduction, *supra*, at 53.
5. Danaya C. Wright, The Law of Estates and Future Interests 272 (Foundation Press 2015) (describing the ambiguity as "not particularly relevant today" but nevertheless an "interesting question of feudal land law that has yet to be settled").

Example 4. *O* conveys, "To *A* for life, then to *B*."

What happens when *A* (or *X*) dies? In many cases, the grant will create a *remainder* in a third party. In Example 4, *B* would become the owner at *A*'s death. If there is no such remainder, then *O* holds a *reversion* and the property will revert back to *O* at *A*'s death (or to *O*'s heirs or devisees if *O* is not alive at *A*'s death). In yet other cases, a court might decide that the conveyance did not create a life estate at all. We will explore the nature of this ambiguity in *White v. Brown*, below. The life estate is of a lesser quantum than the fee tail, which itself is of a lesser quantum than the fee simple absolute.

Nonfreehold estates: In the next chapter, we will see that there are four types of nonfreehold estates: the *term of years*, the *periodic tenancy*, the *tenancy at will*, and the *tenancy at sufferance*. For now, you should know that the non-freehold possessory estates form the foundation of the modern leasehold. In this chapter, we will introduce the *term of years* as a representative example of the leasehold.

Example 5. *O* conveys, "To *A* for 10 years" or "To *A* from January 1 to June 1."

The term of years is of definite duration, and begins on a specific calendar date or upon the happening of a specified event. It terminates on a specific calendar date or is computable by a formula. As with life estates and fees tail, *O* retains a reversion that will become possessory when the leasehold expires.

Example 6. *O* conveys, "To *A* for 10 years, then to *B*."

Alternatively, *O* could provide for a *remainder* in a third party, as in Example 6. Nonfreehold estates are said to be of a lesser quantum than fees simple absolute, fees tail, and life estates.

A Place to Start | Present Estates

	Fee Simple Absolute (FSA)	Fee Tail (FT)	Life Estate (LE)	Term of Years* (TOY)
Duration	• Potentially infinite	• Potentially infinite (until the grantee's lineal bloodline dies out)	• Endures for the life of the grantee (or another specified life)	• Definite duration • Begins on a specific date or at a specified event • Ends on a specific date or computable by formula

	Fee Simple Absolute (FSA)	Fee Tail (FT)	Life Estate (LE)	Term of Years* (TOY)
Corresponding future interest	• None	• Reversion in the grantor, *or* • Remainder in a grantee	• Reversion in the grantor, *or* • Remainder in a grantee	• Reversion in the grantor, *or* • Remainder in a grantee
Transferability in modern times	• Alienable inter vivos • Devisable • Inheritable	• Generally alienable inter vivos • Generally inheritable • (Subject to much state variability in modern times)	• Alienable inter vivos	• *See* Chapter 4
Miscellaneous	—	• The FT has been abolished or modified in most jurisdictions	—	One of four leasehold estates • Term of years • Periodic tenancy • Tenancy at will • Tenancy at sufferance
Magic words	• *To A and her heirs* • *To A* (creates FSA today; at common law, would have created only a LE)	• *To A and the heirs of his body*	• *To A for life* • *To A for the life of X*	• *To A for 10 years, beginning on January 1* • *To A for 6 months, beginning upon the completion of the premises*

*The term of years is used in the table above as an example of one of the more common types of leasehold estates. We will take a closer look at the leasehold estates in Chapter 4.

Test Your Understanding

For each example below, assume that *O*, who holds a fee simple absolute, made the following conveyances. Determine what type of present estate *O* conveyed at common law and, alternatively, in modern times. If the result is ambiguous, identify the source of the ambiguity and the potential estates that might have been created.

1. To *A*.
2. To *A* and her heirs.
3. To *A* and the heirs of his body.
4. To *A* to live in.
5. To *A* forever.
6. To *A* for the life of *X*.
7. To *A* for 10 days.

White v. Brown

559 S.W.2d 938 (Tenn. 1977)

Reading Guide

The distinction between the conveyance of a *fee simple absolute* and a *life estate* is not as straightforward as it might first appear to be. In the case below, Jessie Lide left a "holographic" will—a document wholly written in her own handwriting and not witnessed by others. The will failed to use the traditional legal terminology of present estates and future interests. Under such circumstances, how should a court interpret the will?

BROCK, J.

This is a suit for the construction of a will. The Chancellor held that the will passed a life estate, but not the remainder, in certain realty, leaving the remainder to pass by inheritance to the testatrix's heirs at law. The Court of Appeals affirmed.

Mrs. Jessie Lide died on February 15, 1973, leaving a holographic will which, in its entirety, reads as follows:

> April 19, 1972
>
> I, Jessie Lide, being in sound mind declare this to be my last will and testament. I appoint my niece Sandra White Perry to be the executrix of my estate.
>
> I wish Evelyn White to have my home to live in and <u>not</u> to be <u>sold</u>.
>
> I also leave my personal property to Sandra White Perry. My house is not to be sold.
>
> Jessie Lide

(Underscoring by testatrix).

Mrs. Lide was a widow and had no children. Although she had nine brothers and sisters, only two sisters residing in Ohio survived her. These two sisters quitclaimed any interest they might have in the residence to Mrs. White. The nieces and nephews of the testatrix, her heirs at law, are defendants in this action.

Mrs. White, her husband, who was the testatrix's brother, and her daughter, Sandra White Perry, lived with Mrs. Lide as a family for some twenty-five years. After Sandra married in 1969 and Mrs. White's husband died in 1971, Evelyn White continued to live with Mrs. Lide until Mrs. Lide's death in 1973 at age 88.

Mrs. White, joined by her daughter as executrix, filed this action to obtain construction of the will, alleging that she is vested with a fee simple title to the home. The defendants contend that the will conveyed only a life estate to Mrs. White, leaving the remainder[6] to go to them under our laws of intestate succession. . . .

I

Our cases have repeatedly acknowledged that the intention of the testator is to be ascertained from the language of the entire instrument when read in the light of surrounding circumstances. . . . But, the practical difficulty in this case, as in so many other cases involving wills drafted by lay persons, is that the words chosen by the testatrix are not specific enough to clearly state her intent. Thus, in our opinion, it is not clear whether Mrs. Lide intended to convey a life estate in the home to Mrs. White, leaving the remainder interest to descend by operation of law, or a fee interest with a restraint on alienation. Moreover, the will might even be read as conveying a fee interest subject to a condition subsequent (Mrs. White's failure to live in the home). . . .

In such ambiguous cases it is obvious that rules of construction, always yielding to the cardinal rule of the testator's intent, must be employed as auxiliary aids in the courts' endeavor to ascertain the testator's intent.

In 1851 our General Assembly enacted two such statutes of construction, thereby creating a statutory presumption against partial intestacy.

Chapter 33 of the Public Acts of 1851 (now codified as T.C.A. ss 64-101 and 64-501) reversed the common law presumption . . . that a life estate was intended unless the intent to pass a fee simple was clearly expressed in the instrument. T.C.A. s 64-501 provides:

> Every grant or devise of real estate, or any interest therein, shall pass all the estate or interest of the grantor or devisor, unless the intent to pass a less estate or interest shall appear by express terms, or be necessarily implied in the terms of the instrument.

---

6. [As we will see in section C, below, a future interest in the grantor (including one that passes to the grantor's heirs by intestate succession) should technically be called a *reversion*, and not a remainder.—Eds.]

Chapter 180, Section 2 of the Public Acts of 1851 (now codified as T.C.A. s 32-301) was specifically directed to the operation of a devise. In relevant part, T.C.A. s 32-301 provides:

> A will . . . shall convey all the real estate belonging to (the testator) or in which he had any interest at his decease, unless a contrary intention appear by its words and context.

Thus, under our law, unless the "words and context" of Mrs. Lide's will clearly evidence her intention to convey only a life estate to Mrs. White, the will should be construed as passing the home to Mrs. White in fee. . . .

II

Thus, if the sole question for our determination were whether the will's conveyance of the home to Mrs. White "to live in" gave her a life interest or a fee in the home, a conclusion favoring the absolute estate would be clearly required. The question, however, is complicated somewhat by the caveat contained in the will that the home is "not to be sold" a restriction conflicting with the free alienation of property, one of the most significant incidents of fee ownership. We must determine, therefore, whether Mrs. Lide's will, when taken as a whole, clearly evidences her intent to convey only a life estate in her home to Mrs. White.

Under ordinary circumstances a person makes a will to dispose of his or her entire estate. If, therefore, a will is susceptible of two constructions, by one of which the testator disposes of the whole of his estate and by the other of which he disposes of only a part of his estate, dying intestate as to the remainder, this Court has always preferred that construction which disposes of the whole of the testator's estate if that construction is reasonable and consistent with the general scope and provisions of the will. . . . A construction which results in partial intestacy will not be adopted unless such intention clearly appears. . . . It has been said that the courts will prefer any reasonable construction or any construction which does not do violence to a testator's language, to a construction which results in partial intestacy. . . .

The intent to create a fee simple or other absolute interest and, at the same time to impose a restraint upon its alienation can be clearly expressed. If the testator specifically declares that he devises land to A "in fee simple" or to A "and his heirs" but that A shall not have the power to alienate the land, there is but one tenable construction, viz., the testator's intent is to impose a restraint upon a fee simple. To construe such language to create a life estate would conflict with the express specification of a fee simple as well as with the presumption of intent to make a complete testamentary disposition of all of a testator's property. . . .

In our opinion, testatrix's apparent testamentary restraint on the alienation of the home devised to Mrs. White does not evidence such a clear intent to pass only a life estate as is sufficient to overcome the law's strong presumption that a fee simple interest was conveyed.

Accordingly, we conclude that Mrs. Lide's will passed a fee simple absolute in the home to Mrs. White. Her attempted restraint on alienation must be declared void as inconsistent with the incidents and nature of the estate devised and contrary to public policy. . . .

The decrees of the Court of Appeals and the trial court are reversed and the cause is remanded to the chancery court for such further proceedings as may be necessary, consistent with this opinion. Costs are taxed against appellees. . . .

HARBISON, J., dissenting.

With deference to the views of the majority, and recognizing the principles of law contained in the majority opinion, I am unable to agree that the language of the will of Mrs. Lide did or was intended to convey a fee simple interest in her residence to her sister-in-law, Mrs. Evelyn White. . . .

The testatrix appointed her niece, Mrs. Perry, executrix and made an outright bequest to her of all personal property. . . .

The will does not seem to me to be particularly ambiguous, and like the Chancellor and the Court of Appeals, I am of the opinion that the testatrix gave Mrs. White a life estate only, and that upon the death of Mrs. White the remainder will pass to the heirs at law of the testatrix. . . .

In the present case the testatrix knew how to make an outright gift, if desired. She left all of her personal property to her niece without restraint or limitation. As to her sister-in-law, however, she merely wished the latter have her house "to live in", and expressly withheld from her any power of sale. . . .

In my opinion, this interpretation conflicts more greatly with the apparent intention of the testatrix than did the conclusion of the courts below, limiting the gift to Mrs. White to a life estate. I have serious doubt that the testatrix intended to create any illegal restraint on alienation or to violate any other rules of law. It seems to me that she rather emphatically intended to provide that her sister-in-law was not to be able to sell the house during the lifetime of the latter a result which is both legal and consistent with the creation of a life estate. . . .

Notes

1. *The intent of the grantor:*   What was Jessie Lide's intent, according to the majority and the dissent, respectively? What evidence supports each view? What do you think Jessie Lide intended?

Jessie Lide and her co-workers at Deitch's (circa 1953)
Source: Knox County Public Library

2. *Practice pointer:*   According to Justice Brock, it was unclear whether Jessie Lide intended to convey to Evelyn White, (a) a life estate, (b) a fee simple absolute, or (c) a fee simple subject to a condition subsequent. Redraft the will to clearly convey each of those present estates, respectively. You might wish to postpone the third drafting exercise until after you have read the material in section B.2, below.

3. *The difficulties of sharing over time—waste:*   Suppose the court had determined that Evelyn White held a life estate, followed by a remainder in her nieces and nephews. If Evelyn ran into financial difficulties, would she be able to sell the house to take advantage of any equity that had accumulated in the property? Alternatively, would she be able to harvest any trees on the property, alter any farming practices on the land, extract minerals from beneath the property, and/or demolish (or significantly alter) the house?

Under the *law of waste*, such actions might subject Evelyn to damages or injunctive relief in favor of the holders of the future interest (generally, holders of vested remainders and reversions receive the most protection). Under the law of *voluntary waste*, holders of present estates are responsible for affirmative actions that cause unreasonable harm to the future interest holders. The law also holds possessors responsible for *permissive waste* if they fail to perform mandatory duties imposed for the benefit of the future interest holders. Such duties generally include the making of normal repairs to prevent substantial deterioration of the property.

We will return to the idea of waste in the next chapter, when we study land-lord-tenant law. Tenants can be liable for waste to their landlords, who hold a reversionary interest that follows the tenant's term of years or other leasehold estate. But why should the law care about waste? Professor Michael Pappas suggests that the doctrine applies in a variety of contexts, and that it serves five specific, and sometimes competing, societal values: economic efficiency, human flourishing, concern for future generations, stability and consistency, and ecology. *See* Michael Pappas, *Anti-Waste*, 56 Ariz. L. Rev. 741 (2014).

4. *The trust—avoiding limitations of the life estate:*   Today, estate plan-ners warn against the creation of legal life estates. In addition to the issue of waste described in the preceding note, the life tenant is constrained by numer-ous other considerations. For example, suppose that the court in *White v. Brown* had determined that Evelyn White received only a life estate, rather than a fee simple absolute. In that case, if Evelyn desired to sell, lease, mortgage, or otherwise manage the property, would she have been able to do so? In general, the answer is that she would not be permitted to take such actions without the consent of the remaindermen (some of whom might not yet be born or ascertainable).

As an alternative to the legal life estate, the life estate *held in trust* is a common tool used by modern estate planners. In that case, a life tenant (such as Evelyn White) would hold *equitable* title to the life estate, and a trustee would hold legal title to the property for the benefit of the owner of both the present estate (here, Evelyn) and the owners of the future interest. The trustee, pursuant to the terms of the trust, typically has broad powers to manage the property without judicial approval. And in many cases, the equitable life tenant herself has broader powers of alienation than would the owner of the tradi-tional life estate. *See* Danaya C. Wright, The Law of Estates and Future Interests: Cases, Exercises, and Explanations 175 (Foundation Press 2015).

2. Defeasible Present Estates

As you just learned, both the fee simple and the fee tail can potentially last forever; the life estate can last for a lifetime; and the term of years potentially endures for a specified length of time. Those are the absolute forms of each present estate. As a matter of terminology, an unqualified fee simple is said to be a *fee simple absolute* (or as a shorthand, a "fee simple"). For the other three types of present estates, you can assume that they are in their absolute form, unless indicated otherwise (it would be uncommon to encounter a reference to a "life estate absolute," a "fee tail absolute," or a "term of years absolute").

But, each of those present estates can be made *defeasible*, such that it will terminate earlier than it otherwise would, upon the occurrence of a specified condition or event that is uncertain to occur. Although defeasible estates date back to feudal times, they retain modern significance. Often, the condition or event relates to particular land uses that the grantor would like to encourage or restrict. For example, *O* might convey, "To *A*, provided that the land is never used for commercial purposes," or "To *A*, but if the property is ever used for coal mining, then to *B*." These types of restrictions have been overshadowed by another type of land use control that we will study later in the course—the restrictive covenant (Chapter 10). Less commonly, defeasibility provisions might be designed to encourage or restrict certain types of behavior by the owner of the land. For example, *O* might convey, "To my daughter *A*, provided that she does not drop out of college," or "To my son *A*, but if he ever takes up smoking, then to *B*." Defeasible estates are said to be *qualified*, but not of a lesser quantum than their absolute counterparts. Thus a defeasible fee simple absolute might last forever, but is qualified by a condition of defeasibility.

Notice that the penalty for violation of the condition is *forfeiture* of the present estate—a rather stiff penalty. As an alternative, many courts prefer to interpret ambiguous limitations as mere covenants protected by *contract law* remedies. In contrast, defeasible estates are protected by *property rules* that affect the state of the title. Why might that difference matter?

In Figure 1, notice the three types of defeasible estates: the estate *determinable*, the estate *subject to condition subsequent*, and the estate *subject to executory limitation*. We will examine each in more detail below. Because the fee simple is the estate that is most commonly made defeasible, we will use it as our example. As with all fees simple, the defeasible fees are freely alienable inter vivos, devisable, and inheritable, all subject to the conditions or limitations contained in the initial grant.

Fee simple determinable: The fee simple determinable (FSD) is a potentially infinite present estate qualified by a special limitation that will cause the estate to terminate *naturally* if the limitation is violated.

> *Example 7.*   *O* conveys, "To *A* so long as the property is used for residential purposes" or "To *A* while the premises are used for noncommercial purposes."

The limitation is expressed by words of *duration*, such as *during, until, while*, and *so long as.* As a technical drafting matter, the limitation is often contained right in the initial granting clause, not offset by punctuation.

When conveying a fee simple determinable, the grantor gives away less than the full fee simple absolute. The remnant retained by the grantor is known as a *possibility of reverter* (POR)—it is only a *possibility* of reverter, because at the time of the conveyance, it is uncertain whether the limitation will be violated. Under the examples above, if *A* opens a gas station on the premises, then the right to possession *automatically* reverts back to *O*, and *O's* possibility of reverter becomes a vested possessory right. The possibility of reverter arises by operation of law, even if *O's* retained interest is not expressly stated in the conveyance to *A*.

Fee simple subject to condition subsequent: The fee simple subject to a condition subsequent (FS/CS) is a potentially infinite estate limited by a condition that is uncertain to occur. The condition of defeasibility is expressed by *words of condition*, such as *but if, provided that*, and *on condition that*. As a matter of technical drafting, the condition subsequent is generally set off from the initial granting clause by a comma or other punctuation mark.

> *Example 8.*   *O* conveys, "To *A*, but if *A* divorces, *O* may re-enter and terminate the estate."

The corresponding future interest in *O* is known as the *right of entry* (ROE) (also called a *power of termination* or a *right of re-entry*). If the specified condition occurs, then *O* has an *elective* right to re-enter the premises and retake possession (in contrast to the fee simple determinable, which automatically returns to the grantor upon violation of the limitation). At the moment of such re-entry, *O's* future interest (a right of entry) becomes a present possessory interest—a fee simple absolute. Conceptually, the exercise of *O's* power to terminate is said to *divest* (cut short) the present estate (in contrast to the possibility of reverter which vests automatically after the natural termination of the fee simple determinable). This subtle distinction between divestment and natural termination is an historical remnant, but the distinction persists today.[7] The future interest in *O* is usually (but not always) stated explicitly. Otherwise, a reviewing court might interpret the grant as conveying a fee simple absolute, subject to a mere covenant protected by a contract remedy.

Fee simple subject to executory limitation: The fee simple subject to executory limitation (FS/EL) is a potentially infinite estate, qualified by a limitation (as with the fee simple determinable) or a condition subsequent (as with the fee simple on condition subsequent). As such, the qualification can be expressed either by *words of duration* or by *words of condition*. Importantly, the future interest is held by the grantee (in contrast to both the fee simple determinable

---

7. Danaya C. Wright, The Law of Estates and Future Interests 79-82 (Foundation Press 2015) ("Historically, [t]he power of termination . . . was essentially a contractual right to regain possession under certain limited circumstances rather than a reversionary property right").

and the fee simple on condition subsequent, in which the grantor *O* holds the future interest).

> *Example 9*   *O* conveys, "To *A* so long as *A* does not divorce, otherwise to *B*" or "To *A*, but if *A* divorces, then to *B*."

The future interest in a third party is called an *executory interest*, and must be stated explicitly in the conveyance. Like the fee simple subject to condition subsequent, the fee simple subject to executory limitation is generally *divested* (cut short) if the limitation is violated or the condition occurs.[8] But, like the possibility of reverter following a fee simple determinable, possession of the executory interest is said to vest *automatically* in the holder of the future interest (*B*). Thus, upon the moment of *A*'s divorce (if ever), *B*'s future interest (an executory interest in fee simple) automatically becomes a present possessory interest—a fee simple absolute.

Do labels matter?   As a general rule of construction, often courts prefer to construe ambiguous conveyances as fees simple absolute. Their next preference is to find fees simple limited by covenants (enforced by contractual remedies); next, fees simple subject to conditions subsequent; and finally, fees simple determinable. What policies might support these preferences?

Many of the subtle points mentioned in this section are deeply rooted in history, but even today they can be critically important. Consider at least three areas where the labels matter. First, the executory interest and the possibility of reverter *automatically* divest the preceding estate, and these future interests transform into present possessory estates at the moment the limitation is violated or the condition occurs. This can matter in terms of transferability, as we will see in *Mahrenholz v. County Board of School Trustees*, below. Second, suppose the specified limitation or condition is violated, and then fire destroys the property. Who bears the risk of loss? That would depend, in part, upon who owns the property. That, in turn, depends upon whether the future interest vested automatically, or whether it required elective action on the part of *O*. Finally, suppose that the specified limitation or condition is violated, but that the original grantee remains in possession of the property. The jurisdiction has a 10-year statute of limitations. At what point in time does it begin to run against the holder of a possibility of reverter, a right of entry, and an executory interest, respectively? (Hint: At what point in time does the original grantee's continued possession become *hostile* to the future interest holder's right of possession?) The answer varies according to whether the future interest vests

---

8. This is a slight over-generalization that ignores the following exception: If the preceding fee simple expires by the happening of an event, not a condition ("To *A* as long as *A* does not divorce, otherwise to *B*"), then one might say that the executory interest will take effect on the expiration of, not the divestment of, the preceding fee estate. *See* Moynihan's Introduction to the Law of Real Property 252-53 (Sheldon F. Kurtz, 5th ed. 2011).

automatically or requires action on the part of *O*. Which of the future interests would be more vulnerable to loss by adverse possession? Adverse possession aside, the grantor who delays too long in exercising the right of entry might be precluded from doing so under the defenses of waiver, estoppel, or laches.

A Place to Start	Defeasible Fee Simple Estates		
	FS Determinable (FSD)	FS Subject to Condition Subsequent (FS/CS)	FS Subject to Executory Limitation (FS/EL)
Who holds future interest?	• Grantor	• Grantor	• Grantee
Defeasibility	• Present estate terminates *naturally* if limitation violated • *Automatic* return to grantor	• Grantor may *divest* (cut short) present estate if condition violated • Grantor must *elect* to re-enter	• Normally *divests* (cuts short) the preceding estate • Possession *automatically* vests in grantee upon violation
Language of defeasibility	• Words of duration (*during, until, while, so long as . . .*)	• Words of condition (*but if, provided that, on condition that . . .*)	• Words of duration *or* • Words of condition
Transferability in modern times	• Alienable inter vivos • Devisable • Inheritable	• Alienable inter vivos • Devisable • Inheritable	• Alienable inter vivos • Devisable • Inheritable
Corresponding future interest	• Possibility of reverter (POR) • Can be stated explicitly or implied by law	• Right of entry (ROE) (also known as *power of termination* or *right of re-entry*) • Usually stated explicitly, otherwise courts might interpret as mere covenant enforceable in contract law	• Executory interest • Must be stated explicitly
Magic words	• *To A as long as A does not divorce, otherwise to O* • *To A while the property remains a smoke-free establishment*	• *To A, but if A divorces, O may re-enter and terminate the estate* • *To A, on condition that A does not divorce, otherwise O may reenter*	• *To A as long as A does not divorce, otherwise to B* • *To A, but if A divorces, then to B*

3. A System for Labeling Estates and Future Interests

As you work through the *Test Your Understanding* problems at the end of this subsection, here is a system that will help you work methodically through each problem. What present estates and future interests do the following conveyances create? In all examples in this chapter, assume that the grantor (or the testator) held a fee simple absolute before the conveyance or the will became effective.

Step 1—The parties: Identify potential estate holders in the order the conveyance (or will) lists them, as well as any language of limitation or condition. The conveyance must identify a series of grantees capable of owning the property in perpetuity. Therefore, if the conveyance does not specifically hold back a future interest in *O* (or in the testator, *T*), insert "*O?*" (or "*T?*") as a placeholder to remind yourself that someone must stand ready to possess the property in perpetuity.

Step 2—The present estate: Identify the holder and type of present estate. *Who* holds the right of possession immediately after the grantor (or testator) properly executes a deed (or will)? What general *type* of present estate did the grantor convey: fee simple, life estate, fee tail, or term of years? Do not worry about defeasibility at this point.

Step 3—The present estate—absolute or defeasible?   Determine whether the present estate is absolute or defeasible: There are two clues to guide you. First, look for words of duration (suggesting an estate determinable *or* an estate subject to executory limitation) or words of condition (suggesting an estate subject to condition subsequent *or* an estate subject to executory limitation). Second, notice whether the corresponding future interest is held by *O* (suggesting that the present estate is either an estate determinable *or* an estate subject to condition subsequent) or by a third party grantee (suggesting that the present estate is an estate subject to executory limitation). If the estate is not defeasible, then it is absolute. If you have more facts, then you should also be guided by the likely intent of the grantor.

Step 4—The future interests: Is the first future interest held by the grantor? If so, is it a possibility of reverter (following an estate determinable), a right of entry (following an estate subject to condition subsequent) or a reversion (following a fee tail, life estate, or term of years in its absolute form)? Alternatively, is it held by a third party grantee? If so, is it an executory interest (following an estate subject to executory limitation) or a remainder (following a fee tail, life estate, or term of years in its absolute form)? After you have identified the future interest, be sure to check whether it is held in fee simple, in fee tail, in a life estate, or in a term of years. For example, if *O* conveys, "To *A* for life, then to *B* for life," *B*'s future interest is a remainder *in a life estate*, which is then followed by a reversion in *O in fee simple absolute*. If there is more than one future interest, identify them one at a time in the order that they appear in the grant. We will take a closer look at future interests in section C, below.

Example 10:   *O* conveys, "To *A* and his heirs as long as Blackacre is used for school purposes."

Step 1—The parties: The conveyance specifically mentions only *A*, leaving *O* as a potential placeholder in case no prior vested estate in fee simple stands ready to take when all prior interests have ended. Notice also the limiting language "as long as" that qualifies *A*'s estate.

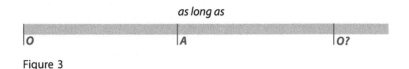

Figure 3

Step 2—The present estate: *A* takes the present estate immediately after *O* executes the conveyance. The words of purchase, "To *A* and his heirs" indicate that *A* holds some type of fee simple (either absolute or defeasible).

Figure 4

Step 3—The present estate—absolute or defeasible?   The conveyance contains words of duration ("as long as"), which suggest that *A* holds an estate determinable. Our hunch is confirmed by the fact that *O* holds the future interest, which is indeed the case with estates determinable. Notice that here *O* holds the future interest by default because the grant specifies no other possible taker.

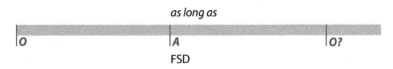

Figure 5

Step 4—The future interests: We have just identified *A*'s present estate as a fee simple determinable, which is always followed by a possibility of reverter. Therefore, *O* holds a possibility of reverter. Our hunch is confirmed by the observation that the law is willing to imply a possibility of reverter in *O*, even if not stated explicitly in the conveyance. Our initial uncertainty as to whether *O* holds a future interest has now been removed (and you can delete the question mark following *O*'s name on the diagram).

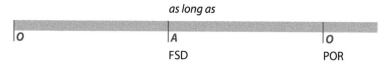

Figure 6

Example 11: Testator devises, "To *A* and her heirs, if and when *A* marries *B*." *T* dies, leaving *H* as his sole heir. At the time of *T*'s death, *A* is unmarried.

Step 1—The parties: Notice that this is a devise by will, rather than an inter vivos conveyance. We can insert the condition "if and when *A* marries *B*" at the beginning of *A*'s segment of the diagram because it appears to be a condition that must be satisfied before *A*'s interest vests in possession (we will learn more about such *conditions precedent* in the next section). We will also insert "*T*?" as a placeholder in case no prior vested estate in fee simple stands ready to continue throughout perpetuity when all prior interests end.

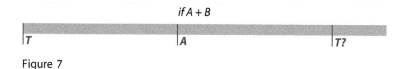

Figure 7

Step 2—The present estate: Notice carefully that *T* continues to hold the present estate in fee simple, *even after* an effective will has been drafted because the will does not take effect until the moment of *T*'s death (until that time, *T* can revoke the will or draft a replacement). When *T* dies, *H* steps in to take *T*'s place. In this example, *H* continues to hold the present estate as *T*'s successor because the right of possession does not pass to *A* until the condition precedent (her marriage to *B*) has been satisfied (if ever). We presume that *T* held a fee simple absolute in the absence of contrary evidence; therefore *H* likewise holds some type of fee simple estate.

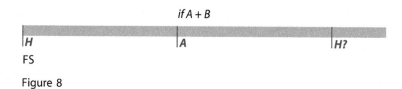

Figure 8

Step 3—The present estate—absolute or defeasible? Here, there are words of condition "if and when *A* marries *B*" that suggest *H*'s fee simple will be automatically divested upon such marriage by a right of entry (in the grantor) or an executory interest (in someone other than the grantor or testator). Because the future interest is held by *A* (a grantee), the present estate must be a FS/EL.

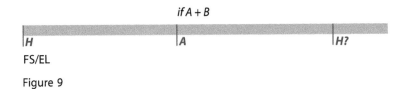

FS/EL

Figure 9

Step 4—The future interests: We have identified H's present estate as a fee simple subject to executory limitation, which is always followed by an executory interest. Therefore, A holds an executory interest. We will assume it is an executory interest *in fee simple absolute* because there is no language indicating otherwise. As such, there is no need for H to hold a future interest following A's executory interest in fee simple absolute. Either H's fee simple will continue forever (if A and B never marry), or it will be divested by A's executory interest. At the moment of A's marriage to B, A's future interest (an executory interest in fee simple absolute) will become a present possessory estate (a fee simple absolute).

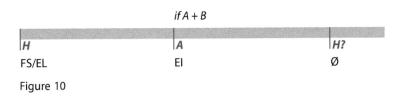

FS/EL   EI   Ø

Figure 10

Test Your Understanding

For each of the following conveyances, identify each estate and future interest. Unless otherwise stated, assume that O held a fee simple absolute prior to the conveyance.

1. O conveys, "To A and her heirs, but if alcohol is ever sold on the premises, then O has the right to re-enter and repossess the land."
2. O conveys, "To A and his heirs, but if A dies without issue living at his death, then to B and her heirs."
3. O conveys, "To A for life, but if B attains 21 during A's life, to B upon attaining 21."
4. O conveys, "To A and her heirs, A's interest to begin seven years from the date of this deed."
5. O conveys, "To the local school district for school purposes."
6. Recall that in *White v. Brown*, Jessie Lide made the following conveyance: "I wish Evelyn White to have my home to live in and not to be sold. . . . My house is not to be sold." Clearly redraft the conveyance to create a fee simple subject to condition subsequent.

Mahrenholz v. County Board of School Trustees

417 N.E.2d 138 (Ill. Ct. App. 1981)

Reading Guide

The outcome of this case turns on whether an ambiguous conveyance created a possibility of reverter or a right of entry. Pay attention to why the distinction matters. Notice also what evidence supports the court's conclusion.

JONES, J.

This case involves an action to quiet title to real property located in Lawrence County, Illinois. Its resolution depends on the judicial construction of language in a conveyance of that property. . . .

On March 18, 1941, W.E. and Jennie Hutton executed a warranty deed in which they conveyed certain land, to be known here as the Hutton School grounds, to the Trustees of School District No. 1, the predecessors of the defendants in this action. The deed provided that "this land to be used for school purpose only; otherwise to revert to Grantors herein." W.E. Hutton died intestate on July 18, 1951, and Jennie Hutton died intestate on February 18, 1969. The Huttons left as their only legal heir their son Harry E. Hutton.

The property conveyed by the Huttons became the site of the Hutton School. Community Unit School District No. 20 succeeded to the grantee of the deed and held classes in the building constructed upon the land until May 30, 1973. After that date, children were transported to classes held at other facilities operated by the District. The District has used the property since then for storage purposes only.

Earl and Madeline Jacqmain executed a warranty deed on October 9, 1959, conveying to the plaintiffs [Herbert and Betty Mahrenholz] over 390 acres of land in Lawrence County and which included the 40 acre tract from which the Hutton School grounds were taken. . . . The deed from the Jacqmains to the plaintiffs excepted the Hutton School grounds, but purported to convey the disputed future interest, with the following language:

> Also, except the following tract of land which was on the 18th day of March, [1941], by the said grantors (sic) conveyed to the Trustees of Schools of District No. One (1) of the Town of Allison, in the County of Lawrence and State of Illinois, and described as follows: (legal description) and containing one and one-half (1-1/2) acres, more or less; Reversionary interest to Grantees. . . .

On May 7, 1977, Harry E. Hutton, son and sole heir of W.E. and Jennie Hutton, conveyed to the plaintiffs all of his interest in the Hutton School land. . . . On September 6, 1977, Harry Hutton disclaimed his interest in the property in favor of the defendants. . . . The document further recited that it was made for the purpose of releasing and extinguishing any right Harry E. Hutton may have had in the "interest retained by W.E. Hutton and Jennie Hutton . . . in that deed to the Trustees of School District No. 1, Lawrence County, Illinois dated March 18, 1941, and filed on the same date. . . ." . . .

[The plaintiffs' first and second amended complaints were dismissed.]

The plaintiffs filed a third amended complaint on September 13, 1978. This complaint recited the interests acquired from the Jacqmains and from Harry Hutton. On March 21, 1979, the trial court entered an order dismissing this complaint. In the order the court found that the

> [W]arranty deed dated March 18, 1941, from W.E. Hutton and Jennie Hutton to the Trustees of School District No. 1, conveying land here concerned, created a fee simple subject to a condition subsequent followed by the right of entry for condition broken, rather than a determinable fee followed by a possibility of reverter.

Plaintiffs have perfected an appeal to this court.

The basic issue presented by this appeal is whether the trial court correctly concluded that the plaintiffs could not have acquired any interest in the school property from the Jacqmains or from Harry Hutton. Resolution of this issue must turn upon the legal interpretation of the language contained in the March 18, 1941, deed from W. E. and Jennie Hutton to the Trustees of School District No. 1: "this land to be used for school purpose only; otherwise to revert to Grantors herein." In addition to the legal effect of this language we must consider the alienability of the interest created and the effect of subsequent deeds.

The parties appear to be in agreement that the 1941 deed from the Huttons conveyed a defeasible fee simple estate to the grantee, and gave rise to a future interest in the grantors, . . . and that it did not convey a fee simple absolute, subject to a covenant. The fact that provision was made for forfeiture of the estate conveyed should the land cease to be used for school purposes suggests that this view is correct. . . .

The future interest remaining in this grantor or his estate can only be a possibility of reverter or a right of re-entry for condition broken. As neither interest may be transferred by will or by inter vivos conveyance (Ill. Rev. Stat., ch. 30, par. 37b), and as the land was being used for school purposes in 1959 when the Jacqmains transferred their interest in the school property to the plaintiffs, the trial court correctly ruled that the plaintiffs could not have acquired any interest in that property from the Jacqmains by the deed of October 9, 1959.

Consequently this court must determine whether the plaintiffs could have acquired an interest in the Hutton School grounds from Harry Hutton. The resolution of this issue depends on the construction of the language of the 1941 deed of the Huttons to the school district. As urged by the defendants and as the trial court found, that deed conveyed a fee simple subject to a condition subsequent followed by a right of re-entry for condition broken. As argued by the plaintiffs, on the other hand, the deed conveyed a fee simple determinable followed by a possibility of reverter. In either case, the grantor and his heirs retain an interest in the property which may become possessory if the condition is broken. We emphasize here that although sec. 1 of An Act relating to Rights of Entry or Re-entry for breach of condition subsequent and possibilities of reverter effective July 21, 1947 (Ill. Rev. Stat., ch. 30, par. 37b) provides that rights of re-entry for condition broken and possibilities of reverter are neither alienable or devisable, they are inheritable. . . . The type of interest held governs the mode of reinvestment with title if reinvestment is to occur. If the grantor had a possibility of reverter, he or his heirs become the owner of the property by operation of law as soon as the condition is broken. If he has a right of re-entry for condition broken, he or his heirs become the owner of the property only after they act to re-take the property.

It is alleged, and we must accept, that classes were last held in the Hutton School in 1973. Harry Hutton, sole heir of the grantors, did not act to legally retake the premises but instead conveyed his interest in that land to the plaintiffs in 1977. If Harry Hutton had only a naked right of re-entry for condition broken, then he could not be the owner of that property until he had legally re-entered the land. Since he took no steps for a legal re-entry, he had only a right of re-entry in 1977, and that right cannot be conveyed inter vivos. On the other hand, if Harry Hutton had a possibility of reverter in the property, then he owned the school property as soon as it ceased to be used for school purposes. Therefore, assuming (1) that cessation of classes constitutes "abandonment of school purposes" on the land, (2) that the conveyance from Harry Hutton to the plaintiffs was legally correct, and (3) that the conveyance was not pre-empted by Hutton's disclaimer in favor of the school district, the plaintiffs could have acquired an interest in the Hutton School grounds if Harry Hutton had inherited a possibility of reverter from his parents.

The difference between a fee simple determinable (or, determinable fee) and a fee simple subject to a condition subsequent, is solely a matter of judicial interpretation of the words of a grant. . . . A fee simple determinable may be thought of as a limited grant, while a fee simple subject to a condition subsequent is an absolute grant to which a condition is appended. . . .

. . . In the 1941 deed, though the Huttons gave the land "to be used for school purpose only, otherwise to revert to Grantors herein," no words of temporal limitation, or terms of express condition, were used in the grant.

The plaintiffs argue that the word "only" should be construed as a limitation rather than a condition. The defendants respond that where ambiguous language is used in a deed, the courts of Illinois have expressed a constructional preference for a fee simple subject to a condition subsequent. . . .

We believe that a close analysis of the wording of the original grant shows that the grantors intended to create a fee simple determinable followed by a possibility of reverter. Here, the use of the word "only" immediately following the grant "for school purpose" demonstrates that the Huttons wanted to give the land to the school district only as long as it was needed and no longer. The language "this land to be used for school purpose only" is an example of a grant which contains a limitation within the granting clause. It suggests a limited grant, rather than a full grant subject to a condition, and thus, both theoretically and linguistically, gives rise to a fee simple determinable.

The second relevant clause furnishes plaintiffs' position with additional support. It cannot be argued that the phrase "otherwise to revert to grantors herein" is inconsistent with a fee simple subject to a condition subsequent. Nor does the word "revert" automatically create a possibility of reverter. But, in combination with the preceding phrase, the provisions by which possession is returned to the grantors seem to trigger a mandatory return rather than a permissive return because it is not stated that the grantor "may" re-enter the land. . . .

. . . We are not persuaded by the cases cited by the defendants for the terms of conveyance in those cases distinguish them from the facts presented here. . . .

The defendants . . . direct our attention to the case of *McElvain v. Dorris* (1921), 298 Ill. 377, 131 N.E. 608. There, land was sold subject to the following condition: "This tract of land is to be used for mill purposes, and if not used for mill purposes the title reverts back to the former owner." When the mill was abandoned, the heirs of the grantor brought suit in ejectment and were successful. The Supreme Court of Illinois did not mention the possibility that the quoted words could have created a fee simple determinable but instead stated,

> Annexed to the grant there was a condition subsequent, by a breach of which there would be a right of re-entry by the grantor or her heirs at law. (Citations.) A breach of the condition in such a case does not, of itself, determine the estate, but an entry, or some act equivalent thereto, is necessary to revest the estate, and bringing a suit in ejectment is equivalent to such re-entry. . . .

It is urged by the defendants that *McElvain v. Dorris* stands for the proposition that the quoted language in the deed creates a fee simple subject to a condition subsequent. We must agree with the defendants that the grant in *McElvain* is strikingly similar to that in this case. However, the opinion in *McElvain* is ambiguous in several respects. First, that portion of the opinion which states that "Annexed to the grant there was a condition subsequent . . ." may refer to the provision quoted above, or it may refer to another provision not reproduced in that opinion. Second, even if the court's reference is to the quoted language, the holding may reflect only the court's acceptance of the parties' construction of the grant. . . . After all, as an action in ejectment was brought in *McElvain*, the difference between a fee simple determinable and a fee simple subject to a condition subsequent would have no practical effect and the court did not discuss it.

To the extent that *McElvain* holds that the quoted language establishes a fee simple subject to a condition subsequent, it is contrary to the weight of Illinois and American authority. A more appropriate case with which to resolve the problem presented here is *North v. Graham* (1908), 235 Ill. 178, 85 N.E. 267. Land was conveyed to trustees of a church under a deed which stated that "said tract of land above described to revert to the party of the first part whenever it ceases to be used or occupied for a meeting house or church." Following an extended discussion of determinable fees, the court concluded that such an estate is legal in Illinois and that the language of the deed did in fact create that estate.

Although the word "whenever" is used in the *North v. Graham* deed, it is not found in a granting clause, but in a reverter clause. The court found this slightly unorthodox construction sufficient to create a fee simple determinable, and we believe that the word "only" placed in the granting clause of the Hutton deed brings this case under the rule of *North v. Graham*.

We hold, therefore, that the 1941 deed from W.E. and Jennie Hutton to the Trustees of School District No. 1 created a fee simple determinable in the Trustees followed by a possibility of reverter in the Huttons and their heirs. Accordingly, the trial court erred in dismissing plaintiffs' third amended complaint which followed its holding that the plaintiffs could not have acquired any interest in the Hutton School property from Harry Hutton. We must therefore reverse and remand this cause to the trial court for further proceedings. . . .

Notes

1. *Interpreting ambiguous conveyances:* According to the court, what future interest did the Huttons convey to the school trustees by the 1941 warranty deed? What factors support the court's conclusion?

2. *Practice pointer—drafting with clarity:* Edit the 1941 conveyance so that it clearly creates a fee simple determinable. Then, redraft so that it clearly creates a fee simple subject to condition subsequent.

3. *Alienability of future interests:* Notice that Illinois law provided that possibilities of reverter and rights of entry were neither alienable nor devisable, but that they could be inheritable. This preference for inheritability is an historical remnant. We will see a similar preference for inheritance when we look at a variety of common law rules designed to enhance the marketability of land in section D, below.

4. *Much ado about nothing?* On remand and after trial, the court concluded that storage of school property constituted a "school purpose" within the meaning of the deed. *Mahrenholz v. County Bd. of School Trustees*, 544 N.E.2d 128 (Ill. Ct. App. 1989) (appeal after remand). This final resolution

occurred 15 years after the plaintiffs filed their first complaint. Can you redraft the condition in the original deed ("for school purpose only") in a way that would have avoided such protracted litigation in the first instance?

C. FUTURE INTERESTS

Section B introduced you to the main categories of future interests, which are shown in Figure 11. As you can see, three are held by the grantor (reversion, possibility of reverter, and right of entry) and two are held by grantees (executory interests and remainders). In turn, there are four subcategories of remainders (contingent remainders, vested remainders subject to divestment, vested remainders subject to open, and indefeasibly vested remainders). Altogether, then, there are eight types of future interests, as shown in the red boxes in Figure 11. From the moment an inter vivos conveyance or a devise by will takes effect, future interests are property rights entitled to legal protection. However, as the name "*future* interest" suggests, they will not *vest in possession* until some future date, if ever.

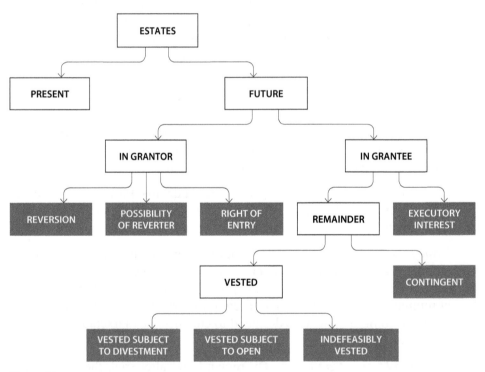

Figure 11

You can think of Figure 11 as a type of decision tree that will help you identify the various types of future interests. In this section, we will examine each of the following decision points. For now, here is a brief overview, which you can use as a reference:

Grantor or grantee? Who holds the future interest—the *grantor* or a *grantee*? If held by the grantor, then determine whether it is a reversion, possibility of reverter, or right of entry (using the analysis from the previous section).

Wait patiently or divest? If the future interest is held by a third party grantee, does it follow a fee tail, life estate, or term of years and wait patiently for that prior estate to end *naturally*? If so, then it is some type of remainder. Alternatively, does it *divest* the present estate? If so, then it is an executory interest.

Condition precedent or unascertained taker? If the future interest is some type of remainder, is there a *condition precedent* (pronounced *pre-SEE-dent*) or an *unascertained* grantee? If so, then it is a contingent remainder.

Condition subsequent? Is there a *condition subsequent*? If so, then it is a vested remainder subject to divestment.

Class gift? Is there a *class gift* with at least one ascertained member who has satisfied all conditions precendent? If so, then it is a vested remainder subject to open.

The remaining option: If you have exhausted all of the above categories, then the future interest is an *indefeasibly vested remainder*.

Work methodically through each of these decision points. You will likely find that the process of classifying estates and future interests is challenging, but also quite logical (and satisfying!).

1. The Basic Categories of Future Interests

In the absence of language to the contrary, assume that all future interests are held in fee simple absolute. But as we will see, when it is the future interest holder's turn to enjoy possession, the future interest transforms into a present possessory estate, which might take any of the absolute or defeasible forms we studied in the previous section. For example, suppose *O* conveys, "To *A* for life, then to *B* for life." In that example, *A* holds a life estate, and *B* holds a vested remainder *in a life estate* (and *O* holds a reversion in fee simple absolute by default). At *A*'s death, *B*'s future interest (vested remainder in a life estate) vests in possession and becomes a present possessory life estate.

Reversion: If a grantor conveys an estate of a lesser quantum than the grantor's original estate (or a series of lesser estates that do not add up to the size of the grantor's original estate), then the *grantor* retains some type of reversionary interest. As we have seen, if it follows an estate determinable, it is called a possibility of reverter; and if it follows an estate subject to condition subsequent, it is called a right of entry. Otherwise, the grantor's future interest is called a *reversion*. The reversion waits patiently for the *natural termination* of a preceding fee tail, life estate, or term of years, and then vests *automatically* in the grantor.

>   *Example 12.*   *O* conveys, "To *A* and the heirs of his body."

In Example 12, *O* retains a reversion. When *A*'s lineal bloodline dies out, if ever, then *O*'s reversion is ready to take over. That is, at the moment the last of *A*'s issue die off (if ever), then *O*'s future interest (a reversion in fee simple absolute) automatically becomes a present estate (a fee simple absolute) possessed by *O* (or by *O*'s successors if *O* is no longer alive). As a general rule, *O* retains a reversion unless there is, (1) a prior *vested* interest, (2) in *fee simple*, (3) that is ready to take possession *immediately* at the termination of all prior interests. Reversions are *uncertain* to become possessory and, in some cases, never vest in possession.

Possibility of reverter: As we saw in section B.2, the *grantor* always retains a possibility of reverter after conveying a fee simple determinable. Possession automatically vests in the grantor after the natural termination of the present estate (that is, upon violation of the special limitation).

Right of entry: As we saw in section B.2, the *grantor* always retains a right of entry after conveying a fee simple subject to condition subsequent. It *divests* the preceding estate, but requires the grantor to take action to do so.

Remainder: Remainders are future interests created in favor of *grantees*, and are capable of becoming possessory immediately upon the end of all prior estates. Remainders must be conveyed simultaneously with a present possessory estate less than the fee simple.

>   *Example 13.*   *O* conveys, "To *A* for life, and then to *B*."

In Example 13, *B* holds a remainder. But suppose instead that *O* conveys, "To *A* for life," and then later *O* transfers her reversion to *B*. We would continue to call the future interest a reversion (rather than a remainder) because it was not created simultaneously with *A*'s life estate.

>   *Example 14.*   *O* conveys, "To *A* for life, then to *B* if *B* has graduated from college."

Remainders wait patiently for the *natural* expiration of preceding estate (fees tail, life estates, or terms of years), at which time they must be *capable* of becoming possessory immediately. In Example 14, *B* holds a remainder. *B*'s interest is theoretically capable of becoming possessory immediately at *A*'s death, even if the circumstances make that unlikely (for example, if *B* is 80 years old and dropped out of college decades ago). Thus, suppose *B* graduates from college and then *A* dies. Upon graduation, *B*'s contingent remainder vests in *interest* and becomes a vested remainder. At the moment of *A*'s death, *B*'s future interest (a remainder in fee simple absolute) automatically vests in *possession* and becomes a present fee simple absolute. Remainders closely resemble reversions, except that they are held by grantees rather than by the original grantor. As we will see in section C.2, remainders come in four forms.

Executory interest: Executory interests were not recognized as legal interests prior to the enactment of the Statute of Uses in 1536, when the common law began to recognize that parties other than the grantor could hold divesting future interests. Today, executory interests are future interests in *grantees* (someone other than the grantor or testator) that *divest* (cut short) the preceding estate. As we saw in section B.2, an executory interest always follows a fee simple subject to executory limitation (or other present estate subject to executory limitation).

> *Example 15.*   *O* conveys, "To *A* as long as *A* does not divorce, otherwise to *B*" or "To *A*, but if *A* divorces, then to *B*."

> *Example 16.*   *O* conveys, "To *A* and his heirs, beginning one year from today."

As a matter of terminology, a *shifting* executory interest divests the interest of another grantee, whereas a *springing* executory interest divests an interest of the grantor. In Example 15, *B* holds a shifting executory interest that will divest *A*'s fee simple subject to executory limitation. In Example 16, *A* holds a springing executory interest that divests the grantor's interest. To understand why this is so, notice that *O* continues to retain possession of the present estate (a fee simple subject to executory limitation) for one year after the conveyance takes effect. One year after the conveyance, *A*'s future interest (an executory interest in fee simple) will spring up and divest the grantor's present estate. At that moment, *A*'s interest vests in possession and becomes a present fee simple absolute.

A Place to Start — Future Interests	Reversion (Rev)	Possibility of Reverter (POR)	Right of Entry (ROE)	Remainder (Rem)	Executory Interest (EI)
Who holds the interest?	• Grantor	• Grantor	• Grantor	• Grantee	• Grantee
Patient or impatient?	• Patiently waits for *natural* end of preceding FT, LE, or TOY	• Patiently waits for *natural* end of preceding estate determinable	• Impatient—divests preceding estate	• Patiently waits for *natural* end of preceding FT, LE, or TOY	• Impatient—divests prior estate

	Reversion (Rev)	Possibility of Reverter (POR)	Right of Entry (ROE)	Remainder (Rem)	Executory Interest (EI)
Right of possession	• Vests automatically when prior estate ends	• Vests automatically if prior estate terminates	• *O* must affirmatively retake possession	• Can become possessory upon expiration of all prior interests	• Automatically divests prior estate
Transferability	• Alienable inter vivos • Devisable • Inheritable	• Not alienable inter vivos in some states • Not devisable in some states • Inheritable	• Not alienable inter vivos in some states • Not devisable in some states • Inheritable	• Generally alienable inter vivos (but some limits may apply to contingent remainders) • Devisable • Inheritable	• Alienable inter vivos • Devisable • Inheritable
Miscellaneous	*O* retains a reversion in absence of prior vested interest in FS ready to take immediately at end of all prior interests	—	—	• Must be conveyed at same time as present estate	• *Shifting* EI divests another grantee • *Springing* EI divests the grantor
Examples	• *To A for life* (*O* retains a reversion)	• *To A while the property remains a smoke-free establishment* (*O* holds a POR)	• *To A, but if A divorces, O may re-enter and terminate the estate* (*O* holds a ROE)	• *To A for life, then to B* (*B* holds a remainder)	• *To A, but if A divorces, then to B* (shifting EI) • *To A, beginning one year from today* (springing EI)

2. Remainders—A Closer Look

You have now studied all of the basic categories of present estates and future interests. As a final refinement, this section introduces you to the four forms that remainders can take. To distinguish one from another, be sure to ask yourself the following questions in order, drawing from the decision tree suggested by Figure 11, above: (a) Is there a condition precedent or an unascertained taker? (b) Is there a condition subsequent? (c) Is there a class gift? More explanation follows.

Contingent remainder: A contingent remainder is subject to a condition precedent and/or is held by an unascertained person. A *condition precedent* is a requirement that must be satisfied before the remainder vests in possession.

> *Example 17.* O conveys, "To A for life, then to B if B graduates from law school."

In Example 17, A holds a life estate, and B holds a contingent remainder because it will not vest in possession unless the condition precedent has been satisfied (B must graduate from law school). Notice also that O retains a reversion in fee simple absolute because there is no prior *vested* interest in fee simple ready to take immediately at the end of A's life estate. If B graduates from law school while A is still alive, then the classification of B's future interest will change from "contingent" remainder to "vested" remainder, and O will no longer hold a reversion.

What happens if A dies and B has not yet graduated from law school (but might possibly do so in the future)? O's future interest (reversion in fee simple absolute) becomes a possessory fee simple estate subject to defeasance by B's future interest. How should we classify B's interest after A's death? B is a grantee, so B must hold a remainder or an executory interest. B does not hold a remainder, because B is not waiting patiently for O's present estate to end (O's fee simple is of potentially infinite duration). Therefore, B now holds a springing executory interest that will divest O's fee simple when (if ever) B graduates from law school and O holds a fee simple subject to executory limitation. Notice that this rather convoluted sequence of reclassifications at A's death could have been avoided if the initial conveyance had read, "To A for life, then to B if B has graduated from law school *by the time of A's death.*" In that case, if B had not graduated by the time of A's death, then B's contingent remainder would never become possessory and O would simply hold a fee simple absolute.

> *Example 18.* O conveys, "To A for life, then to A's oldest surviving child."

There is a second reason why remainders will be classified as contingent—if they are conveyed to *unascertained* takers. These include *heirs* (who cannot be ascertained until the moment of the ancestor's death), *widows and widowers* (who cannot be identified until the moment of the spouse's death because of the possibility of remarriage), those who have not yet been born, and the like. In Example 18, A holds a life estate, the oldest surviving child holds a contingent remainder in fee simple, and O retains a reversion in fee simple absolute. The remainder is contingent because the oldest surviving child cannot yet be ascertained (the current oldest child might predecease A, or A might not have any children at all at the time of A's death). Suppose A dies, leaving children B (age 10) and C (age 5). At the moment of A's death, we can ascertain that B is the next taker as the oldest surviving child. Therefore, B's future interest (a contingent remainder in fee simple) automatically vests in possession and becomes a present fee simple absolute (thereby divesting *O*'s reversion in fee simple absolute).

> *Example 19.*   *O* conveys, "To *A* for life, then to *B* and her heirs if *B* survives *A*; and if *B* does not survive *A*, then to *C* and his heirs."

It is possible for a conveyance to contain two contingent remainders, subject to conditions precedent that are the mirror opposites of one another—known as *alternative contingent remainders*. In Example 19, *B* holds a remainder because *B* is waiting patiently for *A*'s life estate to end. The remainder is *contingent* because it is subject to a condition precedent. But what happens if *A* dies and *B* is no longer alive? The property will then pass to *C* (or to *C*'s heirs) even if *C* is no longer living, because *C*'s condition only requires that *B* fails to survive *A*. Just like *B*, *C* has been waiting patiently for *A*'s life estate to terminate. Therefore *C* holds a remainder. It is contingent because it is subject to a condition precedent. It is an *alternative* contingent remainder, because its condition precedent is the mirror opposite of *B*'s condition precedent. Does *O* hold a reversion? As a practical matter, such a reversion will never become possessory because either *B* survives *A* (giving *B* a fee simple absolute at *A*'s death) or *B* does not survive *A* (giving *C* a fee simple absolute at *A*'s death). But as a formality, *O* retains a reversion because there is no prior *vested* interest in fee simple ready to take immediately at the end of *A*'s life estate.

Remember that all remainders wait patiently for the natural end of the preceding estate. Therefore, merely waiting for the present estate to expire (at *A*'s death) is not considered a condition precedent. For example, if *O* conveys, "To *A* for life, then to *B*," *B*'s remainder is vested, not contingent. *B* is waiting patiently for her turn at possession, and you should not consider *A*'s death as a condition precedent to the vesting of possession in *B*.

Vested remainder subject to divestment: A vested remainder subject to divestment is subject to a *condition subsequent.* The distinction between a condition precedent and a condition subsequent is rather formalistic, but can have significant consequences. As the names imply, a condition precedent generally appears before the language creating the remainder or within the granting clause, whereas a condition subsequent generally appears after the language creating the remainder (and is often set off by a comma or other punctuation mark).

> *Example 20.*   *O* conveys, "To *A* for life, then to *B*, but if *B* ever uses the property for commercial purposes, then to *C*."

In Example 20, *A* holds a life estate, *B* holds a vested remainder in fee simple subject to divestment, and *C* holds a shifting executory interest in fee simple. When *A* dies, *B*'s future interest (a vested remainder in fee simple subject to divestment) automatically vests in possession and becomes a present fee simple subject to executory limitation (and *C* continues to hold a shifting executory interest).

Vested remainder subject to open (also called vested remainder subject to partial divestment):   A remainder is vested subject to open when, (1) it is held by an open group or class of people (sometimes called a *class gift*); and (2) at least one living member who has satisfied all conditions precedent (if any) can be ascertained.

> *Example 21.*   *O* conveys, "To *A* for life, then to *B*'s children and their heirs."

In Example 21, suppose that at the time of the conveyance, *B* is alive and has one child, *C.* This is a class gift to the group made up of *B*'s children. Because at least one class member (*C*) is alive and ascertainable, the remainder is vested (and not contingent). If *B* has more children, then *C*'s interest will be reduced proportionately to share with such after-born children. Therefore, *C* holds a vested remainder in fee simple subject to open. Upon birth, the after-born children will divest (partially) *C*'s vested remainder in fee simple.

When does the class of "*B*'s children" close? There are two possibilities. First, under the *natural class closing rule*, the class will close physiologically when *B* dies. Before that time, even if *B* is elderly and infertile, the law will assume *B* is capable of having more children. Thus, suppose *A* dies while *B* is still alive. At that moment, *C*'s future interest (a vested remainder in fee simple subject to open) will vest in possession and become a present fee simple. Under the natural closing rule, *C*'s fee simple would be subject to executory limitation, and would remain defeasible throughout *B*'s life, in case *B* has more children entitled to share in the class gift. As a practical matter, this limits the marketability of *C*'s fee simple. To prevent this result, courts generally close the class under the *rule of convenience* once the interest vests in possession. The rule calls for the class to close as soon as at least one class member is entitled to possession—here, the class would close at *A*'s death because *C* would then be entitled to possession. *C* would then hold a fee simple absolute, and no after-born children of *B* would be permitted to share in the gift. The rule of convenience is a *rule of construction* (rather than a *rule of law*). That means that courts generally prefer to apply the rule of convenience, provided that there is no evidence that the grantor intended otherwise.

Indefeasibly vested remainder: If you have patiently worked through the decision tree set out at the beginning of section C and none of the previous classifications apply, then you can safely assume that the future interest is an indefeasibly vested remainder. Such a remainder is certain to become possessory at some point in the future.

> *Example 22.*   *O* conveys, "To *A* for 10 years, then to *B*."

In Example 22, *B* holds an indefeasibly vested remainder in fee simple. After 10 years pass, *B*'s interest will vest in possession and become a present fee simple absolute.

A Place to Start	A Closer Look at Remainders			
	Contingent (C-Rem)	Vested Subject to Divestment (V-Rem/ Divest)	Vested Subject to Open (V-Rem/ Open)	Vested Indefeasibly (V-Rem)
Condition?	• Precedent, *or* • Unascertained taker	• Subsequent	• None	• None
Miscellaneous	• Uncertain to become possessory	—	• Held by a group or class of people • At least one living member ascertained • No condition precedent	• Certain to become possessory
Examples	• To *A* for life, then to *B* if *B* graduates from college • To *A* for life, then to *A*'s oldest surviving child • To *A* for life, then to *B* and her heirs if *B* survives *A*; and if *B* does not survive *A*, then to *C* and his heirs	• To *A* for life, then to *B*, but if *B* ever uses the property for commercial purposes, then to *C*	• To *A* for life, then to *B*'s children and their heirs (*B* has 1 child)	• To *A* for 10 years, then to *B*

Test Your Understanding

For each conveyance below, identify the present estate and future interest(s) that it creates. Assume that the grantor (or testator) held a fee simple absolute at the time of the conveyance, unless stated otherwise. If the correct response is not clear, identify the source of the ambiguity and potential resolutions of that ambiguity.

1. To *A* for life, then to *B* for life.
2. To *A* for 10 years.

3. To *A* for 10 years, then to *B*.
4. To *A* for life, then to *B* and her heirs if *B* survives *A*.
5. To *A* for life as long as *A* does not ever smoke cigarettes.
6. To *A* and the heirs of his body, but if *A* ever smokes cigarettes, *O* may renter.
7. To *A* for life, then to *B* and her heirs if *B* reaches the age of 21. Identify the estates and future interests under each of the following scenarios: (a) *B* is 9 years old at the time of the conveyance; (b) *B* turns 12 and then *A* dies; (c) *B* turns 21 during *A*'s life.
8. To *A*, but if the premises are used for nonresidential purposes, then to *B* and his heirs.
9. To *A* so long as the premises are used for residential purposes, otherwise to *B* and his heirs.
10. By will, *T* devises, "To *A* for life, if and when *A* marries *B*." *T* dies, leaving *H* as his only heir. At the time of *T*'s death, *A* is unmarried.

D. ENHANCING MARKETABILITY: FIVE RULES

Suppose that *O* conveys, "To *A* for life, then to *B*'s heirs." This conveyance creates a life estate in *A* and a contingent remainder in *B*'s heirs. The common law disliked such contingent remainders because they created the risk of a gap in seisin (the precursor to the modern idea of ownership). As long as *B* is alive, *B*'s heirs cannot be ascertained. Thus, if *A* dies before *B*, it would be impossible to identify the heirs who were to be seised of the property. Moreover, such a conveyance limits the alienability of property. During *A*'s life, the most that *A* could convey to another would be a life estate *pur autre vie* (measured by *A*'s life). There would be no possibility that *A* and the unascertained heirs (including perhaps those who were not yet born) could join together to convey a fee simple absolute, as would be possible if the remainder had been vested and its takers ascertained.

The common law developed a number of rules to address this problem. The first four take aim squarely at contingent remainders. The fifth rule—the *rule against perpetuities*—casts a broader net, and potentially destroys contingent remainders as well as executory interests and vested remainders subject to open. As discussed below, many of these rules have limited applicability in modern times.

1. The Destructibility of Contingent Remainders Rule

The rule: A contingent remainder is destroyed if it does not vest in interest at or before the termination of the preceding freehold estate.

Example 23.   *O* conveys, "To *A* for life, then to *B*'s heirs."

Following the conveyance in Example 23, assume that *A* dies while *B* is still alive. The destructibility rule would destroy the contingent remainder in *B*'s heirs at the moment of *A*'s death because the class gift has not yet vested in interest—that is, it remains contingent. Seisin would shift back to *O* (or *O*'s successors if *O* is no longer alive) as a reversion in fee simple absolute. Because the rule destroyed the contingent remainder in *B*'s heirs, the remainder could not spring up out of *O*'s estate at *B*'s death (when the heirs could be ascertained). Notice the timing of the rule's operation—the contingent remainder will be destroyed (or not) at the moment the preceding freehold estate (*A*'s life estate) terminates. Not only did the destructiblity rule avoid the problem of a gap in seisin, but it also enhanced the marketability of land. When *A* died, *O*'s fee simple absolute would be easily transferable. Without the rule, *O* would hold a fee simple subject to a springing executory limitation in *B*'s unidentified heirs—an estate that would likely have little marketability.

Current status: The rule has been abolished by most states, thereby breathing new life into the potential restraints on alienation that the common law rule was designed to eliminate. Contingent remainders continue to play a prominent role in modern estate planning, primarily in long-term trusts.

2. The Doctrine of Merger

The rule: If a life estate and the next vested interest in fee simple *come into the hands* of the same person, the lesser estate merges into the larger. Merger will destroy intervening contingent remainders *unless* the life estate, contingent remainder, and next vested interest were all created by the same instrument. In that case, merger will not be applied to destroy the intervening contingent interest because that would run counter to the apparent intent of the grantor or testator, who took care to create three separate interests in the initial conveyance.

Example 24.   *O* conveys, "To *A* for life, then to *A* and her heirs."

In Example 24, *A* holds a life estate and a vested remainder in fee simple absolute. The life estate merges into that is, it is swallowed by) the vested remainder, and *A* holds a fee simple absolute. Although the grantor took care to create two separate interests in *A*, merger would likely not defeat the intent of the grantor because the practical result is the same—*A* (and *A*'s) successors hold an estate of potentially infinite duration.

Example 25.   *O* conveys, "To *A* for life, then to *B* and his heirs."

Suppose instead that *O* makes the conveyance in Example 25. Subsequently, *A* conveys the life estate to *B*, and both life estate and vested remainder have "come into the hands" of *B*. As a result, *B* now holds a life estate *pur autre vie* and a vested remainder in fee simple absolute. The lesser life estate merges into the larger remainder and *B* holds a fee simple absolute.

Example 26.   *O* conveys, "To *A* for life, then to *B* if *B* turns 21.

But what happens if an intervening contingent remainder separates the life estate and next vested interest? The conveyance in Example 26 creates a life estate in *A*, a contingent remainder in *B*, and a reversion in fee simple absolute in *O*. Subsequently, *O* conveys the reversion to *A*. The life estate and the next vested interest have now "come into the hands" of the same person—*A*. Under merger, the lesser life estate merges into the larger reversion (which, typically, will retain its original name even though it is now held by a grantee rather than by the grantor). As a consequence, merger destroys the intervening contingent remainder in *B*.

Current status: The simple, non-destructive version of the rule continues today (that is, a life estate will merge into a vested remainder in the same party, resulting in a fee simple absolute). But the application of the rule to destroy intervening contingent remainders has been abolished by most states. As asserted above, contingent remainders continue to play a prominent role in modern estate planning, primarily in long-term trusts, but the survivorship of contingent remainders (in most states today) means many properties are less alienable.

3. The Rule in Shelley's Case

The rule: If the same instrument gives a life estate to *A* and a remainder to "*A*'s heirs" or "the heirs of *A*'s body," then as a rule of law *A* takes the remainder (which merges with *A*'s life estate into a fee simple absolute) and the heirs take nothing. Notably, the rule only applies if both estates are legal or both estates are equitable. Notice also that this is a rule of law that can override a contrary intention of the grantor. Words such as "children" (rather than *heirs* or *heirs of the body*) do not invoke the rule's application.

Example 27.   *O* conveys, "To *A* for life, then to *A*'s heirs."

In Example 27, under the rule *A* holds both a life estate and a vested remainder in fee simple absolute. Notice what the rule accomplishes. First, it destroys contingent remainders by replacing the *contingent* remainder in *A*'s heirs (unascertained takers) with a *vested* remainder in *A* (a living, ascertained person). This destruction occurs *ab initio*—that is, "from the beginning"—at the moment the conveyance is properly executed, without waiting for subsequent events to unfold (as with the destructibility of contingent remainders rule).

Second, the rule requires *A*'s heirs to take by *inheritance* (which triggered the feudal equivalent of the modern inheritance tax), rather than by purchase. How does this happen? After operation of the rule, *A* holds both a life estate and a vested remainder in fee simple absolute. Under the *merger rule*, *A* would hold a fee simple absolute, which the heirs would then take by inheritance (unless *A* otherwise conveyed it during life or by will after the common law recognized such transfers).

Current status: The rule has been abolished in a majority of jurisdictions. In some states, however, the abolition was prospective only. Thus, you might encounter some old conveyances that remain subject to the rule because they were drafted at a time when the rule was still in effect in that jurisdiction.

4. The Doctrine of Worthier Title

The rule: If an inter vivos conveyance creates a remainder or executory interest in the heirs of the grantor, then the grantor has a reversion and the heirs take nothing. The so-called "testamentary branch" of the doctrine achieved a similar result with respect to devises by will.

> *Example 28.*   *O* conveys, "To *A* for life, then to the heirs of *O*."

In Example 28, *O* holds a reversion in fee simple absolute and the heirs take nothing. Historically, this was a rule of law that could override a contrary intention of the grantor. The rule served to destroy contingent remainders and executory interests from the moment the conveyance (or will) was properly executed. Like the rule in Shelley's Case, the doctrine prevented grantors (and testators) from avoiding feudal taxes on inheritance.

Current status: The inter vivos version of the rule has been abolished in a majority of jurisdictions. In jurisdictions where it remains in effect, often it is treated as a rule of construction that can be overridden by evidence of the grantor's intent.

5. The Rule Against Perpetuities

The rule: The most common statement of the rule dates back to its articulation by Professor John Chipman Gray of Harvard Law School: "No interest is good unless it must vest, if at all, not later than 21 years after some life in being at the creation of the interest."[9] In essence, the rule is a compromise that seeks to limit dead hand control for a reasonable period of time—roughly one generation into the future, when the next generation reaches the age of majority (21). The analysis under the rule can become quite complicated. Our goals here are simply to gain a basic understanding of the rule and to apply it to a few relatively straightforward situations. Let's examine each phrase of the rule in

---

9. John C. Gray, *The Rule Against Perpetuities* § 201 (4th ed. 1942).

isolation. Then, we will put them together and apply the rule to a variety of examples:

"No interest is good":   The rule against perpetuities takes aim at three future interests especially capable of generating uncertainty and limiting marketability: *contingent remainders, executory interests,* and *vested remainders subject to open.* As you just learned, the destructibility of contingent remainders rule could strike down certain late-vesting contingent remainders. But, the destructibility rule lost its force in England during the late 19th century, and in the United States has been abolished in most states today. Moreover, the rule against perpetuities is of broader scope than the destructibility rule. Not only does it render vulnerable two additional types of future interest (executory interests and vested remainders subject to open), but it also invalidates offending interests immediately, rather than waiting to see how events unfold (as under the destructibility rule, which waits until the present estate terminates to determine the validity of contingent remainders). For each example in this section, we assume that the destructibility rule is *not* in effect in the relevant jurisdiction, unless otherwise indicated.

"Unless it must vest, if at all":   In essence, the rule asks whether there is *any possibility,* however remote or absurd, that the vesting of a future interest will remain uncertain beyond the time period permitted by the rule. If so, then it is invalid from the moment of its creation, and the rule will strike out the offending future interest as if it had never been created. It only takes one such example of *what might happen* to invalidate a vulnerable future interest.

The word "vesting" has a particular meaning in the context of the rule against perpetuities. *Contingent remainders* vest when the taker is ascertained and when no conditions precedent remain unsatisfied. At that time, the remainder will change its name from "contingent" to "vested." *Executory interests* become vested under the rule when they become possessory. *Vested remainders subject to open* become vested when the class *closes* and when *every* member of the class has satisfied all conditions precedent.

"Not later than 21 years after some life in being at the creation of the interest":   This phrase sets forth the *perpetuities time period*—a type of measuring stick to determine whether the period of uncertainty will potentially last too long to be countenanced under the rule. The perpetuities period begins to run when a vulnerable future interest has been *created.* For inter vivos conveyances, interests are created at the moment an irrevocable transfer has been made (usually, at the time of delivery). In contrast, interests devised by will are created at the moment of the testator's death.

The rule relies on *lives in being* (LIBs). In theory, this refers to anyone in the world alive (or conceived, if later born alive) at the moment the vulnerable interest was created. In practice, however, we will limit our consideration of LIBs to all persons mentioned in the conveyance (and supporting factual background) who could potentially *affect the vesting* of the future interest. For example, in a conveyance to the class of "*A*'s children," if *A* is still alive, then she is a LIB who could potentially affect the vesting of the class gift by bearing more children. Overall, you can think of the length of the perpetuities measuring stick as *LIB + 21*.

Applying the rule: The analysis under the rule can be quite daunting. But perhaps you will find it to be more manageable if you follow this methodical approach:

- *Step 1—Identify the estates created by the conveyance:*   Identify each estate and future interest. Notice whether any of the future interests are of the type vulnerable to the rule—contingent remainders, executory interests, and vested remainders subject to open. There may be more than one. If so, evaluate the validity of each such future interest in turn.

- *Step 2—Identify when the perpetuities period begins to run:*   For inter vivos conveyances, the perpetuities period begins to run as soon as the grantor (*O*) makes an irrevocable transfer (in the absence of contrary evidence, you can assume that all designated conveyances are irrevocable). For devises by will, the perpetuities period begins to run as soon as the testator (*T*) dies.

- *Step 3—Identify the circumstances of vesting:*   For each vulnerable interest, identify under what circumstances it will "vest" (if at all) within the meaning of the rule.

- *Step 4—Embrace absurdity:*   The RAP is a rule that considers *what might happen*, rather than a rule that waits to see what actually does happen. As a consequence, the rule can invalidate future interests if they *might* vest too remotely under an identified scenario—no matter how absurd or how unlikely to occur. As the following examples will show, such invalidating scenarios tend to follow a pattern:

  a) *Births:* First, identify all lives in being listed in the conveyance. Then, imagine *after-born* persons—those who were born after the creation of the interest, and who therefore do not qualify as "some life in being at the creation of the interest." We will name such non-lives-in-being *X*.
  b) *Deaths:* Next, imagine that all lives in being die. As a result, all potential validating lives have come to an end.
  c) *Measure:* Finally, imagine that 21 years have passed after the death of all lives in being. Is it *possible* that the contingent interest might still vest at some later point in time? If so, the interest is void and should be stricken from the original grant as if it had never been created. Otherwise, the interest is valid.

- *Step 5—Be aware of risky situations:*   If any of the future interests are vulnerable under the rule, take a closer look to see if the conveyance creates a situation that is particularly prone to failure. Such situations include (among others):

a) *Age requirements:* Age requirements exceeding 21 year might create interests vulnerable to the rule (such as, "when *B* turns 22").
b) *Timeless conditions:* Timeless conditions that are uncertain to occur might create interests vulnerable to the rule (such as, "if the property ever ceases to be used for educational purposes").
c) *Unnamed persons:* Gifts to persons not specifically named or ascertained can be vulnerable (such as, "to *B*'s son" instead of "to *B*'s son, Bob").
d) *Class gifts* can create especially difficult situations (such as, "to the children of *A*"). Recall from section C.2, above, that classes close under the *rule of convenience* as soon as at least one class member is entitled to possession (unless the grantor intended otherwise). That happens when (1) the preceding estate ends, and (2) at least one class member satisfies all conditions precedent (if any). If the rule of convenience does not apply to a particular set of facts, then the class will close *naturally* at a later time. Notice that even after the class *closes* (which can occur under the rule of convenience when only one member has satisfied all conditions precedent), the rule against perpetuities also requires *every* class member to satisfy all conditions precedent before the interest "vests" under the rule.

Let's apply this five-step analysis to a series of examples. We will look at each of the risky situations identified under step five, above. But first, we'll begin with a situation that is generally safe from the rule.

> *Example 29 (self-validating gift).*   *O* conveys, "To *A* for life, then to *B* if *B* attains the age of 30." *B* is now 2 years old.

In Example 29, *A* takes a life estate, *B* takes a contingent remainder in fee simple (subject to the condition precedent of living to 30), and *O* holds a reversion in fee simple absolute. *B*'s contingent remainder is potentially vulnerable under the rule. We will assume this is an inter vivos conveyance because it was created by a grantor (*O*) rather than by a testator (who would be designated as *T*). Therefore, the perpetuities period begins to run now—because we assume *O* has made an irrevocable transfer in the absence of evidence to the contrary. *B*'s vulnerable contingent remainder will vest, it at all, when *B* turns 30 (thereby satisfying the condition precedent). At that time, *B*'s contingent remainder will become a vested remainder.

Is there any absurd sequence of events—no matter how unlikely—under which *B*'s contingent remainder might vest *beyond* the perpetuities period— that is, more than 21 years after all lives in being have ended (*A* and *B* die)? No, that is not possible because *B* qualifies as a life in being at the time the interest was created. If *B*'s interest ever vests, it *must do so* within *B*'s own lifetime—on *B*'s 30th birthday. Therefore, *B* is the validating life that saves *B*'s own contingent remainder from the rule.

> ***Example 30 (age requirements exceed 21 years)—possibly saved by the destructibility rule.***   *O* conveys, "To *A* for life, then to *A*'s first child who turns 30." *A* has one child, *B*, who is now 2 years old.

In Example 30, *A* has a life estate, the conveyance to *A*'s first child who turns 30 is a contingent remainder in fee simple, and *O* retains a reversion in fee simple absolute. The remainder is contingent for two reasons: (1) it is held by an unascertained person, and (2) it is subject to the condition precedent of turning 30 before any of *A*'s other children. Notice that *B*—whose name does not specifically appear in the grant—has a mere expectancy of taking the future interest. The contingent remainder is vulnerable to the rule, and the perpetuities period begins to run now. Contingent remainders vest under the rule when the taker has been ascertained, and when that person has satisfied all conditions precedent. Here, that means that the contingent remainder will vest when any child of *A* turns 30.

Is there any absurd scenario under which the contingent remainder might vest beyond the perpetuities period? Yes. First, imagine that *A* has an after-born child, *X* (who was not a life in being at the creation of the interest). Next, imagine that all lives in being die immediately thereafter—that is, both *A* and *B* die. Finally, imagine that 21 more years pass. Is it possible that the contingent interest will vest at some later period in time? Yes, because *X* is only 21 at this time, and might still live to be 30. Therefore, the conveyance was void from the start, as if it had been written like this: "To *A* for life, then to *A's* first child who turns 30." As a result, at *A*'s death, *O* takes the property in fee simple absolute. (Notice that the interest would have been valid if the condition precedent had stated, "then to *A*'s first child who turns 21").

However, the future interest will be valid if the jurisdiction still follows the destructibility of contingent remainders rule. Recall that such rule destroys contingent remainders that remain contingent when the prior estate ends. Under the destructibility rule, at *A*'s death, if none of *A*'s children has yet reached 30, the contingent remainder will be destroyed at that time. Therefore, there is no possibility that the remainder will vest outside the perpetuities period (that is, more than 21 years after the death of the lives in being—*A* and *B*). Therefore, the rule against perpetuities does not invalidate the contingent remainder ab initio, although the destructibility rule might later strike it down.

> ***Example 31 (timeless condition).***   O conveys, "To the City, but if it ceases to use the property for educational purposes, to *A* and his heirs."

In Example 31, the City takes a fee simple subject to executory limitation, and *A* takes a shifting executory interest in fee simple. *A*'s executory interest is vulnerable under the rule, and the perpetuities period begins to run now. Executory interests vest under the rule when they become possessory. Here, that means that *A*'s executory interest will vest, if at all, when the City ever stops using the property for educational purposes. It is not difficult to imagine circumstances under which *A*'s executory interest will vest too remotely to satisfy the rule, because the condition is timeless and not tied to any particular human lifespan. Thus, it is possible that all lives in being end (*A* dies), more than 21 years pass, and then the City stops using the property for educational purposes. Because of this possibility, *A*'s interest is void ab initio, as if the original conveyance had read, "To the City~~, but if it ceases to use the property for educational purposes, to *A* and his heirs~~." Because *A*'s executory interest is not enforceable under the rule against perpetuities, the City has a fee simple absolute.

> *Example 32 (gift to persons not specifically named or ascertained):* *O* conveys, "To *A* for life, then to *A*'s widow for life, and then to the heirs of *A*'s widow." *A* is 80 years old and is married to wife *B*.

Example 32 creates a life estate in *A*, a contingent remainder in a life estate in *A*'s widow (the widow cannot be ascertained until *A*'s death), a contingent remainder in fee simple in the widow's heirs (the heirs cannot be ascertained until the widow's death), and a reversion in fee simple absolute in *O*. Notice that *B* takes nothing under the conveyance, even though we anticipate that *B* will be *A*'s widow. Both contingent remainders are potentially vulnerable under the rule. The widow's interest is valid, because *A* can serve as the validating life. That is, the widow's interest will vest, if at all, immediately upon the death of *A* (who is a life in being at the creation of the interest).

Is the contingent remainder in the widow's heirs valid? Notice that it will vest (if at all) when we can ascertain the widow's heirs, which will be possible when both *A* and *A*'s widow die. This raises the classic property hypothetical known as the "unborn widow" problem. Consider the following absurd turn of events: First, *X* is born after the conveyance by *O*, making *X* ineligible to serve as a validating life (because *X* was not a life in being at the time of *O*'s conveyance). Next, suppose *A* and *B* divorce. Then, imagine that *X* grows up and marries *A* (despite their vast age disparity and *A*'s advanced age). Then, assume the death of all lives in being—*A* and *B*. This leaves *X* as *A*'s widow. Is it possible that *X* will live for more than 21 additional years, thereby delaying the vesting of the heirs' remainder beyond the perpetuities period? Certainly. As a result, the contingent remainder in the widow's heirs is void ab initio. Instead, *O* will take the property in fee simple absolute upon the death of *A*'s widow.

> *Example 33 (class gift):* *O* conveys, "To *A* for life, then to *A*'s children who reach 30." *A* has one child, *B*, who is 30 years old.

The conveyance in Example 33 creates a life estate in *A* and a vested remainder in fee simple subject to open in the class of *A*'s children. Recall that vested remainders subject to open are one of the three future interests that are vulnerable under the rule. Even though their name suggests that they are vested ("*vested* remainders subject to open"), the rule against perpetuities does not consider them to be vested until two criteria are satisfied. First, the class must close. Under the *natural closing* rule, the class will close at *A*'s death, because at that time *A* will no longer be capable physiologically of bearing more children. Under these facts, the *rule of convenience* will produce the same result, provided that *B* is still alive at *A*'s death. That is, the class will close under the rule of convenience when at least one member is entitled to possession. Here, *B* would be entitled to possession at the end of the preceding life estate—upon *A*'s death.

Second, for purposes of the rule against perpetuities, the class gift will not vest until *each* class member satisfies all conditions precedent—here, by turning 30. To determine whether the class gift is valid, you must understand the so-called *all or nothing* rule. Under that provision, the entire class gift is void if the interest of one class member might possibly violate the rule against perpetuities. Applying the all or nothing rule, the following absurd scenario would invalidate the class gift under the rule against perpetuities. First, suppose that *A* has an after-born child, *X*. Then assume that all lives in being die—first *A* dies, closing the class. Then *B* dies. Recall that vested remainders subject to open do not vest under the rule against perpetuities until the class closes and every member satisfies all conditions precedent. Therefore, we must also wait for *X* to turn 30. Because it is possible that will not happen for more than 21 years after the deaths of *A* and *B*, the entire class gift was void ab initio under the all or nothing rule. One commentator refers to the all or nothing rule as a "pernicious subrule." Moynihan's Introduction to the Law of Real Property 261 (Sheldon F. Kurtz, ed., 5th ed. 2011). Do you see why? Absent that subrule, *B*'s interest would have vested in possession at *A*'s death. At that moment, *B* (or *B*'s heirs, if *B* were no longer alive) would have been entitled to possession (recall that *B* had already turned 30, thereby satisfying the condition precedent).

Current status: Most states still follow some version of the rule against perpetuities, but often in a modified form. Three predominant modifications are discussed below:

- *Cy pres (pronounced SEE-pray):*   Under this equitable rule of construction, some courts will interpret a conveyance in a way that carries out the intent of the grantor as near as possible, while still saving interests that otherwise would be invalid under the rule against perpetuities.

- *Wait and see approach:*   Many jurisdictions allow events to unfold, rather than invalidate uncertain interests when created. In those jurisdictions, interests will be validated if they *actually* vest within a specified time period, such as the common law perpetuities period. In that case, if an interest actually vests during the identified lives in being (or within 21 years thereafter), then the interest will be declared valid, even if the rule against perpetuities would have produced a contrary result. In Example 32 above, the interest of "the heirs of *A*'s widow" would be valid under the wait and see approach if wife *B* in fact turned out to be *A*'s widow, as expected.

- *The Uniform Statutory Rule Against Perpetuities ("USRAP"):*   Under this uniform rule, a nonvested property right is invalid unless it is valid under the common law rule against perpetuities *or* if the interest actually vests or terminates within 90 years after its creation. The USRAP also permits courts to reform invalid interests in a way that carries out the intent of the grantor as near as possible. For example, a court could save an interest by vesting it within 90 years of its creation, thereby saving it from extinction. As of 2015, 28 states, the District of Columbia, and the U.S. Virgin Islands had enacted the USRAP. *See* http://www.uniformlaws.org/ (visited Oct. 3, 2015) (follow links to statutory rule against perpetuities).

A Place to Start | Five Rules

	Destructibility	Merger	Shelley's Case	Worthier Title	The RAP
Rule	C-Rem must vest at/before end of preceding freehold estate	If LE and next vested interest in FS *come into the hands* of the same person, the lesser estate merges into the larger	If same instrument gives a LE to *A* and a Rem to *A*'s heirs or the heirs of *A*'s body, then *A* takes the Rem and the heirs take nothing	If *inter vivos* conveyance gives a Rem or EI to *O*'s heirs, then *O* has a Rev and the heirs have nothing	No interest is good unless it must vest/fail within LIB + 21
Exceptions	—	Destroys intervening C-Rem unless all three interests created by same instrument	Applies only if both estates are legal, or both are equitable	Testamentary branch of doctrine also existed at common law	—
Vulnerable future interests	• C-Rem	• C-Rem	• C-Rem	• C-Rem • EI	• C-Rem • EI • V-Rem/ Open
Timing	Wait until end of preceding freehold estate	Effective if successive interests "come into the hands" of the same person	Interest void ab initio	Interest void ab initio	Interest void ab initio

	Destructibility	Merger	Shelley's Case	Worthier Title	The RAP
Rule of law?	Yes	Yes	Yes	Yes (historically)	Yes
Majority status	Rule abolished	Rule abolished (with respect to destruction of C-Rems)	Abolished (sometimes prospectively)	• *Inter vivos* branch abolished in most states (or treated as a rule of construction) • Testamentary branch abolished	• Various reforms in effect
Examples	*To A for life, then to B's heirs* (*B*'s C-Rem destroyed if not vested by *A*'s death)	*To A for life, then to B if B turns 21* (*B*'s C-Rem destroyed if Rev comes into *A*'s hands)	*To A for life, then to A's* ~~*heirs*~~	*To A for life, then to O's* ~~*heirs*~~	*To A for life,* ~~*then to A's first child who turns 30*~~ (*A* has one living child who is 2)

Test Your Understanding

The following problems are designed to test your understanding of the five common law rules discussed in this section. For each conveyance, identify the present estate and future interest(s) that it creates. If the problem contains a parenthetical explanation of subsequent events, identify how the identifications change (if at all) after those events occur. Then, determine whether any of the five common law rules would change the result (assuming that the rule applied in the relevant jurisdiction). If the correct response is not clear, identify the source of the ambiguity and potential resolutions of that ambiguity. Assume that the grantor (or testator) held a fee simple absolute at the time of the conveyance, unless stated otherwise.

1. *O* conveys, "To *A* for life, then to *B* if *B* gets married." (*B* is single at *A*'s death.)

2. *O* conveys, "To *A* for 10 years, then in fee simple to *B*'s children who survive *B*." (*B* dies in 5 years, leaving children *C* and *D*. Then, 10 years

expire.) (Assume instead that 10 years pass and *B* is still alive, with children *C* and *D*.)

3. *O* conveys, "To *A* for life, then to *B* for life if *B* is married, then to *C*." *B* is single at the time of the conveyance. (Later, *A* conveys her interest to *C*.)
4. *O* conveys, "To *A* for life, then to *B* for life, then to *A*'s heirs."
5. *O* conveys, "To *A* for life." (Later, during *A*'s life, *O* devises the reversion "to *A*'s heirs.")
6. *O* conveys, "To *A* for life, then to *O*'s daughter, *B*." (Then *O* dies, leaving *B* as his only heir.)
7. *O* conveys, "To *A* for life, then to the heirs of *O*." (*O* dies while *A* is still alive, devising all her property to Habitat for Humanity, a charitable organization.) (Then, *A* dies.)
8. *O* conveys, "To *A* for life, then to *B* if *B* attains the age of 30." *B* is 3 years old.
9. *O* conveys, "To the local fire department as long as it uses the property for the operation of a fire department, then to *A* and her heirs."
10. *O* conveys, "To *A* for life, then to her children for their lives, and then to her grandchildren." *A* is 80 years old and infertile. She has son and one grandchild.

Abrams v. Templeton

465 S.E.2d 117 (S.C. Ct. App. 1995)

Reading Guide

Even if a state has softened its common law rule against perpetuities by statute, interests created before such reform can still fall prey to the rule. This case demonstrates one method by which such interests can get a second chance at survival. As you read the case, think about how good legal advice could have prevented this litigation from erupting more than 80 years after Mary Ann Ramage executed her original will.

HEARN, J.

This case involves the construction of a 1914 will which violates the rule against perpetuities. Pursuant to S.C. Code Ann. § 27-6-60(B) (1991), the trial judge inserted a savings clause into a provision of the will to prevent a forfeiture. We affirm as modified.

The testator, Mary Ann Taylor Ramage, executed her will in 1914 and died in 1915. She was survived by her husband Frank, a son Albert, and various grandchildren. The testator's daughter, Alma Templeton, predeceased her, but left five surviving children. . . . In her will, the testator devised approximately one hundred and thirty acres of land to Alma's children (the Templeton side). The testator further devised a one hundred and sixty acre tract of land, the subject of this action:

> to my husband Frank Ramage during the term of his natural life and at his death . . . to my son Albert Ramage . . . to have, hold, and enjoy the same during his the said Albert Ramage's natural life, and at his death to his children to hold and enjoy during the term of their natural life and at their death their several interests to be divided among their children.

The trial judge found the provision of the testator's will which created a gift over to her great-grandchildren ("at their death their several interests to be divided among their children") was non-vested for the purposes of the rule against perpetuities. The gift over to the great-grandchildren was a class gift. *See* 61 Am. Jur. 2d *Perpetuities, etc.,* § 33 at 41 (While gifts to a class, where the class is open until some future time, are technically vested, if there are members of the class in being at the time of making the gift, from the standpoint of the perpetuity rule the gifts are on the same footing as purely contingent gifts, and are not regarded as vested until the final membership of the class is determined). Because the class could continue to expand during the lifetime of the testator's grandchildren, for purposes of the rule against perpetuities, it is considered nonvested because it remained "open" after the gift was made. . . .

S.C. Code Ann. § 27-6-60(B) (1991) provides:

> If a nonvested property interest . . . was created before July 1, 1987, and is determined in a judicial proceeding . . . to violate this State's rule against perpetuities as that rule existed before July 1, 1987, a court upon the petition of an interested person shall reform the disposition by inserting a savings clause that preserves most closely the transferor's plan of distribution and that brings that plan within the limits of the rule against perpetuities applicable when the nonvested property interest or power of appointment was created.

Both parties concede that the gift over to the testator's great-grandchildren violates the rule. . . .

The trial judge found that the testator's intended plan of distribution was to equally benefit each "side" of her family: Alma's descendants (the Templeton branch) and Albert's descendants (the Ramage branch). We agree.

Each branch of the family received approximately the same acreage. . . . A common sense reading of the provision dealing with the one hundred and sixty acre tract shows the testator intended to create successive life estates in her son and his children with the remainder over to their children. Clearly, the testator wanted this tract to stay with the Ramage branch of the family and not to include the Templeton branch which received other real and personal property.

In an attempt to bring the provision of the will within the limits of the perpetuities rule and to preserve the testator's intent, the trial judge inserted a savings clause as follows:

> I will, devise and bequeath to my son Albert Ramage all that certain tract of land situate in the county and state aforesaid, containing about one hundred sixty acres more or less . . . to have, hold, and enjoy the same during his the said Albert Ramage's natural life, and at his death to his children *who are alive at the time of my death* to hold and enjoy during the term of their natural life and at their death their several interests to be divided among their children.

As a result, the "measuring life" for the purposes of the perpetuities rule becomes the testator's grandchildren, all of whom were alive at the time of the testator's death and whose children, the testator's great-grandchildren, would have to be born during the lives of these grandchildren.

Albert had nine children (the testator's grandchildren). Five of these children survived Albert and had children, while the remaining four of his children died childless. The trial judge ordered, in accordance with the testator's presumed intent, the shares of the grandchildren who died without children to augment the share of those who had children. Therefore, he ordered that the entire interest in the one hundred sixty acre tract should pass one-fifth to each set of children of the five grandchildren who died with children.

Appellants, the testator's heirs-at-law in the Templeton branch, contend the gift over to the great-grandchildren was void as violative of the rule against perpetuities. Therefore, since the testator's grandchildren had only life estates in the property, at their deaths the remainder reverted back to the testator to pass to her heirs-at-law. We disagree.

To void the gift over to the great-grandchildren would be to invoke the drastic result S.C. Code Ann. § 27-6-60(B) sought to prevent. The South Carolina General Assembly adopted this statutory provision to avoid the remorseless application of the common law rule. The law abhors a forfeiture. The law abhors intestacy and will indulge every presumption in favor of the validity of the will. . . . Clearly, the statute mandates the courts attempt to reconstruct the will so as to save the gift rather than declare it void.

Appellants contend that if the entire gift is not void, they are entitled to at least their intestacy portion of the interest of the grandchildren who died childless. The law is clear that the ultimate fee in every tract of land must rest somewhere. . . . Title to real estate cannot be held in abeyance; it must be vested somewhere. . . . Therefore, appellants argue, because the testator's grandchildren had only life estates in the subject property, the testator must have retained the ultimate reversion subject to divestment if great-grandchildren were born to each of Albert's children. Since four of the testator's grandchildren died without children, and there was no residuary clause or alternative disposition of the interests of those who died childless, their four-ninths interests must revert back to the testator, and, therefore, pass by intestate succession to the testator's heirs-at-law.

We agree with appellants to the extent that the trial judge's savings clause, while it cures the perpetuities rule violation, leaves the four-ninths interest of the childless grandchildren "floating." However, we agree with the trial judge's finding that the testator intended to benefit both "sides" of her family equally and wanted all interest in the subject property to remain with Albert's descendants. Therefore, to effect the trial judge's order to augment the interests of the testator's great-grandchildren on Albert's side with the shares of those grandchildren who died childless, we modify the will to state:

> I will, devise and bequeath to my son Albert Ramage all that certain tract of land situate in the county and state aforesaid, containing about one hundred sixty acres more or less . . . to have, hold, and enjoy the same during his the said Albert Ramage's natural life, and at his death to his children *who are alive at the time of my death* to hold and enjoy during the term of their natural life and at their death their several interests to be divided among their children, *or if any of Albert Ramage's children die childless, his or her interest in default be divided among those who have children.*

This reconstruction of the testator's will no longer violates the rule against perpetuities and clearly effectuates the intent of the testator.

Accordingly, the order of the trial judge is affirmed as modified.

Notes

1. *The original conveyance:* Identify the interests created by the original conveyance. Why was the interest in the testator's grandchildren valid under the rule against perpetuities? Why was the interest in the testator's great-grandchildren invalid?

2. *The remorseless application of the common law rule:* Even in states that have modified (or abolished) the rule against perpetuities, the common law rule can still live on with respect to interests created by some older conveyances. Here, notice that South Carolina modified its common law rule against perpetuities *prospectively*, applying only to conveyances created after the effective date of the 1987 statutory modifications. Fortunately for the great-grandchildren on the Ramage side of the family, South Carolina law allowed for the reformation of older conveyances to save them from the common law rule.

3. *Practice pointer—cy pres and savings clauses:* Here, the court saved the testator's conveyance to her great-grandchildren by affirming the savings clause inserted by the trial court pursuant to its statutory authority. How did the clause inserted by the trial court solve the perpetuities problem? Beyond judicial use of savings clauses, careful drafters can avoid litigation altogether by

inserting savings clauses into the initial conveyance, will, or trust instrument to make sure that it will not violate the rule against perpetuities. We will take a closer look at savings clauses in the skills exercise of section F, below.

4. *The floating interest of the childless grandchildren:* Beyond the perpetuities savings clause drafted by the trial court, the appellate court also modified the will to address what it described as the problem of the floating interest of the childless grandchildren. What exactly was the problem? How did the court's modification resolve that problem? Do you agree with the court that its modification "clearly effectuates the intent of the testator"?

E. BEYOND THE BLACK LETTER: DEAD HAND CONTROL

Our study of estates and future interests has touched on fundamental questions of dead hand control, and the proper balance between the desires of testators and the desires of the living. On the one hand, many favor "testamentary freedom"—the right of people to distribute the wealth they amassed during their lives (whether through labor or gift) however they please at their deaths. *See* Lee-ford Tritt, *Sperms and Estates: An Unadulterated Functionally Based Approach to Parent-Child Property Succession*, 62 SMU L. Rev. 367 (2009). Among other things, they argue that such freedom serves as a powerful incentive for people to lead productive lives, knowing that they can pass the fruits of their labor on to their loved ones at their death. Others, however, worry that passing great amounts of wealth from generation to generation can be a strong disincentive for the receiving generation to lead productive lives. As Andrew Carnegie articulated in 1891, "[T]he parent who leaves his son enormous wealth generally deadens the talents and energies of the son, and tempts him to lead a less useful and less worthy life than he otherwise would." Joshua C. Tate, *Conditional Trusts and the Incentive Problem*, 41 Real Prop. Prob. & Tr. J. 445, 446 (2006). Further, they argue, too much dead hand control can be a shackle for the living and impose obstacles to the free use and alienation of property by the present generation. In general, though, courts have been reluctant to strike on public policy grounds testamentary restraints that condition inheritance on such things as the religious faith of one's chosen spouse. *See Feinberg v. Feinberg*, 919 N.E.2d 888 (Ill. 2009) (upholding clause of trust preventing the distribution of assets to descendants who marry outside the Jewish faith or whose spouses do not convert to Judaism, but expressing willingness to strike similar restraints that unreasonably restrict marriage in general or encourage divorce).

To stimulate your thinking on this subject, consider the case of the art collection of Albert C. Barnes, a collection with an estimated value of more than 20 billion dollars.

Portrait of Dr. Albert C. Barnes, Barnes Foundation, Merion
Photo by Carl Van Vechten (1940)
Source: Library of Congress

During his life, pharmaceutical tycoon Dr. Albert Coombs Barnes accumulated a remarkable and virtually priceless art collection at his Lower Merion Township, Pennsylvania property, including paintings by such masters as Picasso, Matisse, Cézanne, and Renoir. Barnes curated the collection in a highly quirky way beloved by many, but considered bizarre by others:

The realization of Barnes's intention relied on unconventional juxtapositions, thematic compositions and cultural associations. . . . Medieval painting merged with African sculpture, Post-Impressionists with Egyptian antiquities, Chinese scrolls with Baroque altarpieces, all juxtaposed with ordinary items and tools such as strike plates, fire irons, and soup spoons.

Heinrich Schweizer, *Settlor's Intent vs. Trustee's Will: The Barnes Foundation Case*, 29 Colum. J.L. & Arts 63, 76 (2005).

Barnes created a trust to be administered by the Barnes Foundation, and then donated his artwork to the Foundation. Among other things, the trust agreement required that after Barnes's death, (1) none of the pictures belonging to the collection should ever be loaned, sold or otherwise disposed of, except under very narrow circumstances, (2) "all the paintings shall remain in exactly the places they are at the time of the death of the Donor and his said wife," and (3) the Lower Merion property would continue to be used as an art school so that the art students could be inspired by the paintings. When the Foundation encountered financial difficulties, it sought judicial permission to modify some of the rigid dictates of the trust and to move the collection to a new building in nearby Philadelphia. Among other things, the move would make the collection more easily accessible to the general public. In one phase of the extensive litigation, the court noted the extraordinary public interest generated by the controversy:

At the outset, we must comment on the unprecedented public interest in this case. Since the filing of the original petition, rarely a day has gone by without a letter or phone call arriving at the undersigned's chambers from someone wanting to weigh in on this matter. Politicians, art scholars, financial experts, and former students have sent suggestions for saving The Foundation. Major newspapers have published endless dialogues of letters to the editors, as well as editorials endorsing one outcome or another, as if this were a political race. Even legal scholars, attorneys, and law professors, who know that cases are determined by applying the law to the evidence produced in court and *not* by public opinion, have sent unsolicited opinion letters for our edification. The court has studiously avoided being influenced by these outside forces; however, the experience has been unique.

In re Barnes Foundation, No. 58,788, 2004 WL 1960204, at *1 (Pa. Com. Pl. Jan. 29, 2004). Under the charitable trust doctrine of *deviation*, the court permitted the Foundation to modify some of the trust terms, thereby paving the way for the Foundation to remove the collection from the Lower Merion property. In 2012, the collection relocated to Philadelphia, and has since received more than one million visitors.

Discussion Questions

1. *The Barnes collection:* Apart from the nuances of trust law, do you think the Barnes Foundation should have been allowed to deviate from the

strict terms of the trust established by Dr. Barnes? If so, under what circumstances? What public interests, if any, can outweigh the express intent of Barnes as to the disposition of his property? For how long into the future should the artwork be considered the property of Barnes and subject to his control? For more information on the Barnes saga, *see* The Barnes Foundation, barnesfoundation.org; Jed Perl, *The Barnes Foundation's Disastrous New Home*, New Republic, Aug. 24, 2012.

2. *The vices and virtues of testamentary gifts:*   More broadly, do you tend to favor testamentary freedom, or do you favor restrictions on dead hand control? How would you balance those two competing concerns? Even more broadly, consider whether the transmission of vast amounts of wealth from one generation to the next is a good thing—even if unconstrained by restrictions purporting to modify the behavior or choices of the devisees. The right of descent, of course, is firmly established as a bedrock principle of our law. But, as a matter of public policy, does it ever have any negative consequences? A number of high-profile billionaires and millionaires have indicated that they will restrict the amount of wealth they will pass to their children. For example, Warren Buffet has stated that extremely wealthy people should leave their children "enough money so that they would feel they could do anything, but not so much that they could do nothing"[10] and Bill and Melinda Gates stated that children, "need to have a sense that their own work is meaningful and important."[11] Likewise, Facebook founder and CEO Mark Zuckerberg announced in 2015 that he would give away about 99% of his Facebook stock (worth some $45 billion) during his life to further the mission of "advancing human potential and promoting equality."

Beyond parental concerns for the well-being of their descendants, some claim that devise and inheritance contribute to the vast disparity in wealth between the upper and lower classes. Still others argue that up to 90% of social wealth derives from our collective heritage of scientific, technological, and other efforts, rather than from individual labor and ingenuity. *See* Gar Alperovitz & Lew Daly, Unjust Deserts: How the Rich Are Taking Our Common Inheritance (2008). The issues are highly divisive and emotionally charged. What do you think? How should property law respond to such difficult questions?

F. SKILLS PRACTICE: DRAFTING SAVINGS CLAUSES

Review *Abrams v. Templeton*, above. Notice how the court drafted a savings clause to protect a portion of a will that would have been invalidated by the rule

---

10. Richard I. Kirkland Jr., *Should You Leave It All to the Children?*, Fortune, Sept. 29, 1986.
11. Marcus Wohlsen, *Bill and Melinda Gates Aren't Leaving Their Kids Billions*, Wired, Mar. 19, 2012.

against perpetuities. The drafting of savings clauses involves a variety of considerations. In some instances, the attorney might develop a uniform, versatile clause that can prevent most problems. This approach has the advantage of cost-effectiveness in the drafting stage, but might not fit all situations. In addition, it does not always prevent the need for judicial involvement. For example, one such savings clause might assert,

> In any disposition in this instrument . . . I do not intend that there shall be any violation of the Rule Against Perpetuities or any related rule. If any such violation should inadvertently occur, it is my wish that the appropriate court shall reform the gift or appointment in such a way as to approximate most closely my intent, or intent of the appointor, within the limits permissible under such Rule or related rule.

David M. Becker, *If You Think You No Longer Need to Know Anything About the Rule Against Perpetuities, Then Read This!*, 74 Wash. U. L. Rev. 713, 735 n. 72 (1996), quoting W. Barton Leach, *Perpetuities: The Nutshell Revisited*, 78 Harv. L. Rev. 973, 986 (1965).

As an alternative, an attorney might develop a narrower clause that specifies a particular *actuating event* that triggers the clause, and then *redirects* the assets if that event occurs. For assets placed in trust, such a clause might read:

> All trusts created must terminate on the last day of the twenty-first year following the death of the survivor of all beneficiaries within this instrument who are in being at the estate owner's death. If any beneficiary or beneficiaries of principal are then living and have not yet received a share of the principal, the principal shall then be distributed to them in equal shares.

For complicated trusts, however, such a clause might miss the mark. That is, it might fail to create a broad enough safety net for some interests, or it might divest prematurely an interest that would have survived the rule against perpetuities. Becker, *supra*, at 737 n.78.

As a third approach, one might add a specific *savings phrase* to each provision of an instrument to make sure that the specified interest does not violate the rule against perpetuities. This is the approach that the *Abrams v. Templeton* court took in reforming the will before it, by adding the italicized language below:

> I will, devise and bequeath to my son Albert Ramage all that certain tract of land situate in the county and state aforesaid, containing about one hundred sixty acres more or less . . . to have, hold, and enjoy the same during his the said Albert Ramage's natural life, and at his death to his children *who are alive at the time of my death* to hold and enjoy during the term of their natural life and at their death their several interests to be divided among their children.

If the decedent had consulted an attorney before drafting her will, the insertion of such a phrase might have prevented the litigation that followed.

Task

For our purposes, the drafting of simple savings phrases will help you to think preventively and to avoid violations of the rule against perpetuities. Review the conveyances set forth in Examples 30 through 33 (in section D.5, above). In each case, the purported conveyance violated the rule against perpetuities. For each example, can you insert a simple clause that will protect the offending interest? As you do so, try to discern the apparent intent of the grantor and to effectuate that intent as closely as possible. In actual practice, client interviews would help you to gather such information about the grantor's intent.

G. CHAPTER REVIEW

1. Practice Questions[12]

Identify each estate and future interest created by the following conveyances. For these problems, do not apply the five common law rules that enhance marketability, as covered in section D, unless specifically instructed to do so.

1. *O* conveys, "To *A* for life, then to *B* and the heirs of his body, then to *C*'s children." At the time of the conveyance, *C* is alive and has one child, *D*.
2. *O* conveys, "To *A* and the heirs of her body."
3. *O* conveys, "To *A* and her heirs, but if she dies without having married, then to *B* and his heirs."
4. *O* conveys, "To *A* for life, then to *B* and her heirs, but if *B* ever drinks alcohol to *C* and his heirs."
5. *O* conveys, "To *A* for life, then to *B*'s children who are residing in Wyoming at the time of *A*'s death." At the time of the conveyance, *B* has one child, *C*, who is living in Wyoming.
6. *O* conveys, "To *A*, provided that *A* keeps the house in good repair, but if *A* does not keep the house in good repair, then *O* may retake the premises."
7. *O* conveys, "To *A* for life, then one day later to *B*." *A* dies. What estates and future interests did the original conveyance create? At the time of *A*'s death, what is the state of the title?
8. *O* conveys, "To *A* for life, then to *B*'s children." *B* has no children at the time of the conveyance.

---

12. Answers appear in the Appendix to this casebook.

9. *O* conveys, "To *A* for life, then to *B* for life if *B* gets married, then to *A* in fee simple absolute." What estates and future interests does the original conveyance create? How, if at all, does that change if you apply the five common law rules that enhance marketability?

10. Consider the same conveyance described in problem 9. Then suppose that *A* conveys to *C*, "all my interest." What is the state of the title if the five common law rules of marketability apply?

11. *O* conveys, "To *A* for life, then to such of *B*'s children who are 21 at *A*'s death." What estates and future interests does the conveyance create? Then *A* dies. *B* is alive and has one child, *C*, who is 15 years old. If the five common law rules apply, what is the state of the title after *A*'s death?

12. *O* conveys, "To *A* for life, then to the heirs of *O*." What estates and future interests does the conveyance create? What is the state of the title if the five common law rules of marketability apply?

13. *O* conveys, "To *A* for life, remainder to Harry, *A*'s heir." At *A*'s death, Harry is *A*'s only heir. What estates and future interests does the conveyance create? What is the state of the title at *A*'s death? If the five common law rules apply, what is the state of the title?

14. *O* conveys, "To *A* for life, then to such of *A*'s children who become comedians." What estates and future interests does the conveyance create? If the five common law rules of marketability apply, is the gift to "*A*'s children" valid? Why or why not?

2. Bringing It Home

Research your state's statutory law and find its relevant provisions, if any, on the issues listed below.

1. *The fee tail:* Has your state abolished or modified the fee tail by statute?

2. *Rules to promote marketability:* Has your state abolished or modified by statute, (a) the destructibility of contingent remainders rule, (b) the Rule in Shelley's Case, (c) the Doctrine of Worthier Title, and/or (d) the Rule Against Perpetuities? If so, are the amendments retroactive or prospective? If the latter, as of what effective date does the statute govern new conveyances?

3. *The Uniform Statutory Rule Against Perpetuities:* Has your state adopted the Uniform Statutory Rule Against Perpetuities? <u>Hint</u>: Go to the website of the Uniform Law Commission (http://www.uniformlaws.org), then follow links to *Acts,* then *Statutory Rule Against Perpetuities,* then *Legislative Fact Sheet.*

Landlord-Tenant Law

A. The Lease as Conveyance
B. The Lease as Contract
C. The Rights and Duties of the Parties
D. Beyond the Black Letter: Parking—There's an App for That!
E. Skills Practice: Client Counseling and Drafting a Residential Lease
F. Chapter Review

Chapter 4–Cases

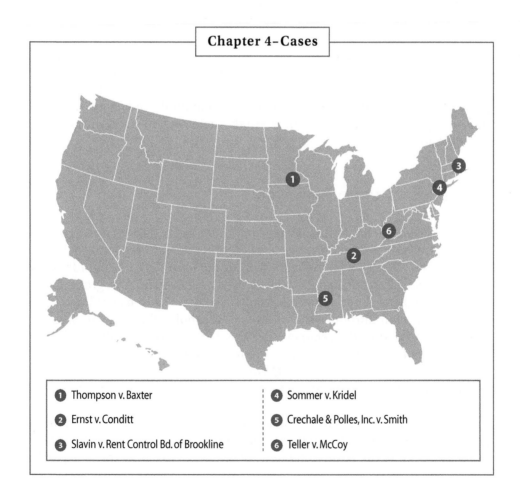

1. Thompson v. Baxter
2. Ernst v. Conditt
3. Slavin v. Rent Control Bd. of Brookline
4. Sommer v. Kridel
5. Crechale & Polles, Inc. v. Smith
6. Teller v. McCoy

Leaseholds, which date back to feudal times, are creatures of both property law and contract law. At first, leasehold agreements—like contracts—were recognized only as a type of *chattel* (an article of personal property). By about 1500, however, the leasehold took on a property dimension, and the law recognized it as a type of present possessory estate in real property—albeit of the *nonfreehold* variety lacking *seisin* (recall our discussion of these concepts from Chapter 3). The characterization of the lease as a *chattel real* reflects this historical contractual/property duality.

Over time, increasing urbanization rendered some aspects of the historical leasehold ill-suited to modern conditions. In response, landlords and tenants began to negotiate specific lease covenants tailored to their particular circumstances. With this reintroduction of a contractual element into the leasehold, its historical evolution came full circle. Further, courts and legislatures began to promote reform—primarily tenant-friendly measures—to expand the rights of residential tenants in response to a growing disparity of bargaining power between landlords and tenants. The federal Fair Housing Act of 1968 (FHA) is an important example of such legislative intervention, as we will see in section C.3, below.

Like the topic of estates and future interests, leaseholds involve multiple parties who *simultaneously* hold a legal interest in the same property, but who hold *consecutive* possessory rights. That is, the tenant has a present right to present possession, and the landlord holds a present right to future possession (a reversion) that takes effect upon the termination of the leasehold.

A. THE LEASE AS CONVEYANCE

In the previous chapter on estates and future interests, we considered the array of freehold present estates and future interests recognized by the common law. We also became familiar with the *term of years*, a nonfreehold present estate that could be followed by a reversion in the grantor or a remainder in a third party. In this chapter we will take a closer look at the term of years, and introduce the other two leaseholds that the common law recognized: the *periodic tenancy* and the *tenancy at will*. Each of these three leaseholds is classified as a *nonfreehold possessory* estate. We will also encounter the *tenancy at sufferance*, which is not a true tenancy at all, and is sometimes more accurately described as the "occupancy at sufferance."

First, the *term of years* (or, "tenancy for years") is an estate for a definite period of time. Despite the estate's name, the specified time period need not be measured in years. Rather, the term of years requires only that the parties can determine how long the leasehold will endure with reference to specific beginning and ending dates, or to a formula. The second estate, the *periodic tenancy*, is a leasehold of indefinite duration that continues until one of the parties provides adequate notice of termination to the other. The third leasehold, the *tenancy at will*, is also of indefinite duration. As its name implies, its defining characteristic is that either landlord or tenant can terminate the lease at will and at any time. Finally, the *tenancy at sufferance* arises when a tenant enters lawfully into the possession of land, but remains in possession wrongfully ("holds over") after the leasehold has terminated. Although little more than bare trespass, this "tenancy" does not count as hostile possession for purposes of adverse possession. Under the *holdover* doctrine, the landlord must make an *election of remedies*—either bring an action to evict the tenant as trespasser, or unilaterally bind the holdover tenant to a new lease.

Under some circumstances, it may be difficult to distinguish leases from other types of property interests. For example, a *license* is a revocable privilege to use another's property for a limited purpose, such as that held by an overnight guest at a hotel. Because licenses are revocable, they may bear some resemblance to the fragile tenancy at will. But unlike the tenancy at will and other leaseholds which are *possessory* estates (descended from the common law nonfreehold estates we saw in the last chapter), licenses are nonpossessory interests in property. On the other hand, it may also be difficult to distinguish leaseholds from freehold estates such as the life estate. The three tenancies, and other interests they resemble, are explored further in the first case of this chapter, *Thompson v. Baxter*.

But first, to familiarize yourself with the three leasehold estates, examine the *A Place to Start* box below. The entry labeled "Can a single party control the right of termination?" requires a bit of additional explanation at this point, with more to follow later in the chapter. The issue is whether the law permits the creation of leaseholds in which one specified party alone—either landlord or tenant—has the power to terminate the leasehold early, before its natural expiration. Such leaseholds are said to have a *unilateral power of termination* (or in some cases, a unilateral power of *early* termination before the lease expires of its own terms). Such arrangements might be fairly unremarkable in situations where the lease is of relatively brief duration. But what if the lease lasts much longer? In such cases, a unilateral power of termination vests considerably more power and control in one party than the other. Should the law allow such arrangements, provided the parties agree to them in the lease? What are the practical consequences from the perspective of the landlord and from the perspective of the tenant? *Thompson v. Baxter*, the chapter's first case, takes up this issue in more detail.

A Place to Start   Leaseholds

	Term of Years	Periodic Tenancy	Tenancy at Will
Duration	• Definite duration (even if not precisely determinable in advance)	• Indefinite duration	• Indefinite duration • May be terminated at the will of either party
Beginning	• Begins on specific calendar date or at happening of event	• Begins on specific calendar date or at happening of event	• When *T* enters with *L*'s assent
Termination and notice thereof	• Ends on specific calendar date or computable by formula • Generally, the parties are not required to give notice to terminate the leasehold	• Notice required to terminate • Without notice, lease automatically continues for another period • Common law required notice equal to length of period, up to maximum of 6 months; modern statutes may shorten required length of advance notice	• At common law, notice not required to terminate; today, many states impose a notice requirement by statute
Impact of death of *L* or *T*	• Lease continues and successors take over	• Lease continues and successors take over	• Lease terminates under presumption that mutual assent ends
Can a single party control the right of termination?	• Yes, lease may grant power of early termination to one party, but not the other	• No, not permissible	• If lease allows only *L* to terminate, courts usually imply reciprocal power in *T* • If lease allows only *T* to terminate, some courts imply reciprocal power in *L*; others treat as life estate in *T*
Other	• Statute of frauds generally applies to terms greater than	• Can be created expressly • Court may imply if *T* takes possession	• Can be created expressly, or court may imply if *T* takes

	Term of Years	Periodic Tenancy	Tenancy at Will
	one year such that the lease must be in writing to bind the parties • Tenancy can be defeasible, as by the creation of a term of years determinable, a term of years subject to condition subsequent, or a term of years subject to executory limitation	under lease for undefined period with periodic rent payments • If *T* "holds over" and *L* elects to treat as tenancy rather than trespass, majority treats as periodic tenancy • Tenancy can be defeasible	possession under lease for undefined period without periodic rent payments • In most cases, *T* not expected to pay rent
Example	*To T from 1/1/ 2017 to 2/5/2017*	*To T from week to week, beginning July 1*	*To T starting next Tuesday, for so long as the parties desire*

Test Your Understanding

1. *Categorize the leasehold:* What type of leasehold has been created in each example below? If the language is ambiguous, identify the source of the ambiguity, its impact on your classification, and what you think is the best resolution of the ambiguity. Unless otherwise stated, assume the lease specifies that it begins next Monday. (Hint: In appropriate cases, it will be helpful to recall the material on estates and future interests that we studied in the previous chapter.)

a) To *T* for one year, beginning upon the death of *B*.

b) To *T* for six months, beginning upon the completion of the rental premises.

c) To *T* for 10 years or until *T* sooner moves to Chicago.

d) To *T* starting next January 1 until *T* is discharged from military service.

e) To *T* starting next January 1 at an annual rent of $36,000, payable as $3,000 per month on the first day of each month.

f) To *T* for 10 years starting next January 1. The lessee shall have the right to cancel this lease at any time after five years have elapsed.

g) To *T* until *T* decides to move out.

h) To *T* from year to year beginning June 1, as long as *T* operates a coffee shop on the premises.

2. *Adequacy of notice:* In each example, assume the lease provided for a starting date of January 1. Did Tenant provide adequate notice to Landlord of the leasehold's termination? When does the lease terminate?

   a) To *T* for 1 year. (*T* moved out on December 31 without providing notice.)
   b) To *T* from year to year. (*T* provided notice on November 1.)
   c) To *T* for so long as the parties desire. (*T* moved out on May 1 without providing notice.)

Thompson v. Baxter

119 N.W. 797 (Minn. 1909)

Reading Guide

You just had a brief introduction to the three types of tenancies. Should courts recognize yet a fourth category—the lease for life? Consider this question from both the landlord's and the tenant's point of view.

BROWN, J.

Proceedings in forcible entry and unlawful detainer, instituted in justice court, where defendant [Charles Baxter] had judgment. Plaintiff [Helen A. Thompson] appealed to the district court, where a like result followed. From the judgment of that court she appealed to this court.

The action involves the right to the possession of certain residence property in the city of Albert Lea, and was submitted to the court below upon the pleadings and a stipulation of facts. It appears that plaintiff is the owner of the premises; that she acquired title thereto by purchase from a former owner, who had theretofore entered into a contract by which he leased and demised the premises to defendant at an agreed monthly rent of $22; and plaintiff's title is subject to all rights that became vested in defendant thereby. The lease, after reciting the rental of the premises and other usual conditions, contained upon the subject of the term of the tenancy, the following stipulation:

> To have and to hold the above-rented premises unto the said party of the second part [the tenant], his heirs, executors, administrators, and assigns, for the full term of while he shall wish to live in Albert Lea, from and after the 1st day of December, 1904.

The only question involved under the stipulation is the construction of this provision of the lease. Defendant has at all times paid the rent as it became due. . . . Appellant contends that the lease created either a tenancy at will, at sufferance, or from month to month, and that plaintiff could terminate the same at any time by proper notice. The trial court held, in harmony with defendant's contention, that the contract created a life estate in defendant, terminable only at his death or removal from Albert Lea. Appellant assigns this conclusion as error.

A determination of the question presented involves a construction of the lease and a brief examination of some of the principles of law applicable to tenancies at will, at sufferance, from month to month, and life estates. Deeds, leases, or other instruments affecting the title to real property are construed, guided by the law applicable to the particular subject, precisely as other contracts are construed, and effect given the intention of the parties. The contract before us, though somewhat peculiar and unusual as to the term of the tenancy intended to be created, is nevertheless clear and free from ambiguity. It granted the demised premises to defendant "while he shall wish to live in Albert Lea." The legal effect of this language is, therefore, the only question in the case.

Tenancies at will may be created by express words, or they may arise by implication of law. Where created by express contract, the writing necessarily so indicates, and reserves the right of termination to either party, as where the lease provides that the tenant shall occupy the premises so long as agreeable to both parties. Such tenancies arise by implication of law where no definite time is stated in the contract, or where the tenant enters into possession under an agreement to execute a contract for a specific term and he subsequently refuses to do so, or one who enters under a void lease, or where he holds over pending negotiations for a new lease. The chief characteristics of this form of tenancy are (1) uncertainty respecting the term, and (2) the right of either party to terminate it by proper notice; and these features must exist, whether the tenancy be created by the express language of the contract or by implication of law. An accurate definition is given in 1 *Wood on Landlord and Tenant* 43, in the following language:

> A tenant at will is one who enters into the possession of the lands or tenements of another, lawfully, but for no definite term or purpose, but whose possession is subject to termination by the landlord at any time he sees fit to put an end to it. He is called a tenant at will because he hath no certain or sure estate, for the lessor may put him out at what time it pleaseth him.

A tenancy at sufferance arises where the tenant wrongfully holds over after the expiration of his term, differing from the tenancy at will, where the possession is by the permission of the landlord. He has a naked possession without right, and, independent of statute, is not entitled to notice to quit. . . . In fact, this relation exists in all cases where a person who enters lawfully into the possession wrongfully holds possession after his estate or right has ended. A tenancy from month to month or year to year arises where no definite time is agreed upon and the rent is fixed at so much per year or month, as the case may be, and is terminable at the expiration of any period for which rent has been paid. This form of tenancy can never exist where the lease or contract prescribes a fixed time. The mere fact that rent is payable monthly does not alone determine the character of the tenancy. The monthly or yearly payments and an intention to limit the term to a month or year must in all cases concur to create this species of tenancy.

From these general principles of the law of tenancy it is quite clear that the lease under consideration does not come within either class mentioned. Its language does not expressly define it as a tenancy at will, and no such relation arises by implication, for the reason that the term is not indefinite, within the meaning of the law on this subject, nor is the right to terminate the lease reserved to the lessor. Indefiniteness or uncertainty as to the term of the lease is illustrated by instances where one occupies land by the naked permission of the owner, or a person who holds under a void deed, or where he enters under an agreement for a lease not yet executed, or under a lease until the premises are sold, and under various circumstances where no time is specifically agreed upon. In the lease under consideration the tenancy is limited by the time defendant shall continue to dwell in Albert Lea, and this limitation takes the case out of the class of tenancies at will. It is equally clear that a tenancy at sufferance was not created by the contract. There has been no wrongful or unlawful holding over after the expiration of the term. Nor does the rule of tenancy from month to month apply for the reasons already pointed out.

We therefore turn to the question, the turning point in the court below, whether the instrument created a life estate in defendant within the principles of law applicable to that branch of land titles. It is thoroughly settled that a life estate may be created by a deed, lease, or devise, either with or without a stipulation for the payment of rent. This class of tenancies differs in many essential respects from tenancies at will, or from year to year, or at sufferance; the principal distinction being that the former confers a freehold upon the tenant, and the latter a mere chattel interest. The lease under consideration embodies all the essentials of a life tenancy. It contains the usual words of inheritance, necessary at common law, running to defendant, "his heirs, executors, administrators, and assigns," and grants the right of occupancy for the term stated therein. Life estates or life tenancies are clearly defined in the books, and the lease here involved brings it within this class of estates. 1 *Taylor on Landlord and Tenant* 52, states the rule as follows:

> An estate for life may be created by express limitation or by a grant in general terms. If made to a man for a term of his own life, or for that of another person, he is called a "life tenant." But the estate may also be created by a general grant, without defining any specific interest, as where the grant is made to a man, or to a man and his assigns, without any limitation in point of time, it will be considered as an estate for life, and for the life of the grantee only. . . . Where made subject to be defeated by a particular event, and there is no limitation in point of time, it will be *ab initio* a grant for an estate for life, as much as if no such event had been contemplated. Thus, if a grant be made to a man so long as he shall inhabit a certain place, or to a woman during her widowhood, as there is no

certainty that the estate will be terminated by the change of habitation or by marriage of the lessees, the estate is as much an estate for life, until the prescribed event takes place, as if it had been so granted in express terms.

The author's statement of the law is sustained by the other writers on the subject, and by the adjudicated cases. . . . In *Mickie v. Wood's Ex'r*, 5 Rand. (Va.) 574, the grant was to continue so long as the tenant should pay the stipulated rent. It was held a life estate. A grant "so long as the waters of the Delaware shall run" was held in *Foster v. Joice*, 3 Wash. C.C. 498, to create a life estate. . . . The lease in the case at bar comes within the rule of these authorities, and the trial court properly held that it vested in defendant a life estate, terminable only at his death or his removal from Albert Lea.

Judgment affirmed.

Notes

1. *What is it?* Carefully review the court's explanation as to why the lease did not create a tenancy at will, a tenancy at sufferance, or a tenancy from month to month. Do you agree with the court's analysis? Of those three types of interests, which one do you think the lease language most closely describes? What is the relevance of the court's statement that the arrangement is "terminable only at [the tenant's] death or his removal from Albert Lea"?

2. *Practice pointer—clear drafting:* Suppose that you represent one of the parties in this case. Clearly redraft the lease language from the principal case so that it creates unambiguously: (a) a term of years, (b) a tenancy at will, (c) a tenancy at sufferance, (d) a tenancy from month to month, and (e) a life estate.

3. *The intent of the parties:* The court purported to honor the intention of the parties. Did it? It appears likely that the parties borrowed the language of their lease from a form book or another source, and modified only the language highlighted below in bold italics:

> To have and to hold the above-rented premises unto the said party of the second part [the tenant], his heirs, executors, administrators, and assigns, for the full term of ***while he shall wish to live in Albert Lea,*** from and after the 1st day of December, 1904.

What type of interest do you think the parties intended to create? Do you think the landlord really intended to give the tenant the right to remain on the premises for the rest of his life (provided he continued to make monthly payments to the landlord), without any right on the landlord's part to end the tenancy sooner? When a lease purports to give only the *landlord* the power of termination, most courts will imply a reciprocal power of termination in the tenant, and they will treat the arrangement as a tenancy at will. Powell on Real Property § 16.05(1) (Michael Allan Wolf, gen. ed. 2015). But when the lease gives the termination power to the *tenant* only, the law is not as clear. Some courts will imply a like power of termination in the landlord. *Id.*, citing *Dwyer v. Graham*, 457 N.E.2d 1239 (Ill. 1983); *Foley v. Gamester*, 170 N.E. 799 (Mass. 1930). Other courts, like the court in *Thompson v. Baxter*, treat the lease as creating a life estate.

4. *The lease for life:*   The court asserted, "[i]t is thoroughly settled that a life estate may be created by a deed, lease, or devise," and the court referred to both "life estates" and "life tenancies." But, is there such a thing as a *life tenancy*? Two commentators addressed this question by referring to the *numerus clausus* principle (which we introduced in Chapter 3):

> [O]ne issue implicating the [numerus clausus] doctrine that has arisen in several jurisdictions concerns the proper construction of an instrument that purports to grant a lease of property for the life of the tenant. Under the system of estates in land, there is no such thing as a "lease for life." One can create a life estate. And one can create a lease. But a lease must be either a term of years, a periodic tenancy, a tenancy at will, or a tenancy at sufferance. Thus, courts confronted with an instrument purporting to create a "lease for life" have typically asked which common-law box best matches the grantor's intentions: a life estate or a tenancy at will. . . .

Thomas W. Merrill & Henry E. Smith, *Optimal Standardization in the Law of Property: The Numerus Clausus Principle*, 110 Yale L.J. 1, 22 (2000). Do you think courts should recognize leases for life? Why or why not?

Albert Lea, Minnesota (c. 1908), named for Lieutenant Albert Lea, who mapped the area in 1835
Photograph by F. J. Bandholtz (1877-)
Source: Library of Congress

B. THE LEASE AS CONTRACT

If you are a tenant, have you ever read your lease carefully? You may be surprised to learn the legal significance of some of the provisions to which you agreed. Familiarize yourself with the following model lease developed by the state of Maine, and then answer the questions that follow. You might find it helpful to refer back to this document often as you read the cases in this chapter.

Model Landlord-Tenant Lease[1]

1. PARTIES TO THIS LEASE

The parties to the lease are: _____ (Landlord) and _____ (Tenant).

2. RESIDENCE LOCATION

This residence is a house _____, apartment _____, mobile home _____ (check one), located at _____.

3. LENGTH OF LEASE

A. *Initial Rental Period.* The landlord will rent this residence to the tenant for _____ months. This term shall begin on the _____ day of _____ 20_____, at noon.

B. *Extended Stay.* If the tenant has not moved out of the residence by 12 noon on the day the lease ends and has not signed with the landlord a new lease, then this lease becomes a continuing "tenancy at will" and the tenant will rent from month-to-month. All terms of this lease will remain in effect, except for terms that are in conflict with a State law regulating a tenancy at will. Either party can stop this month-to-month tenancy by giving to the other party at least 30-days written notice.

C. *No Extended Stay.* The landlord can refuse to allow the tenant to become a month-to-month tenant at the end of the lease. To do so he must so inform the tenant at least 30 days before the end of the initial Rental Period (paragraph A). The tenant must then leave the residence no later than the last day of the Initial Rental Period.

4. RENT PAYMENTS

A. *Rental Amount.* The total rental price for the term of this lease is $ _____, payable in installments of $ _____ per month. The tenant shall pay the rent for each month on the _____ day of that month.

B. *Paying the Rent.* The rent should be paid to: _____. The landlord can assess a penalty of _____% (up to 4%) of the monthly rent once payment is 15 or more days late.

5. SECURITY DEPOSIT

A. *Amount of Security Deposit.* The tenant has paid the landlord $ _____ as a Security Deposit. The Security Deposit is in addition to rental payments and should not be substituted by the tenant for unpaid rent. The landlord will hold the Security Deposit until the end of the residency. The Security Deposit remains the tenant's money. The landlord

---

1. This lease was adapted by the casebook editors from the Maine Attorney General's Model Landlord-Tenant Lease (revised January 22, 2015). *See* http://www.maine.gov/tools/whatsnew/attach.php?id=27935&an=1 (visited Apr. 28, 2015).

will keep the Security Deposit separate from the landlord's own money. The landlord will not require a Security Deposit of more than two months' rent.

B. *Return of the Security Deposit.* This Security Deposit may be used by the landlord after the tenancy has ended to repair damage to the residence and for the actual costs of unpaid rent, storing and disposing of unclaimed property, or utility charges the tenant owes to the landlord. The Security Deposit cannot be used to pay for routine cleaning or painting made necessary by normal wear and tear. The landlord will return the entire Security Deposit to the tenant at the end of the lease if the following conditions are met: (1) The apartment is in good condition except for (a) normal wear and tear or (b) damage not caused by the tenant, the tenant's family, invitees, or guests; (2) The tenant does not owe any rent or utility charges which the tenant was required to pay directly to the landlord; and (3) The tenant has not caused the landlord expenses for storage and disposing of unclaimed property.

If the landlord deducts money from the tenant's Security Deposit, the landlord will provide the tenant a list of the items for which the tenant is being charged and return to the tenant the balance of the Security Deposit. The landlord will return the Security Deposit, or the remaining balance, to the tenant no more than thirty (30) days after the tenancy ends.

6. MOVING IN

If the residence is not ready to move into on the day the rental period begins, the tenant may cancel the lease and receive a full refund. If the tenant chooses to wait until the residence is ready, then the rental period will begin with the first day the tenant moves in and the first month's rent payments will be proportionately reduced.

7. SERVICES PROVIDED BY THE LANDLORD

Utilities and services shall be paid by the parties as follows (check one):

UTILITIES / SERVICES	LANDLORD	TENANT
Electricity	_____	_____
Natural Gas	_____	_____
Trash Removal	_____	_____
Yard Maintenance	_____	_____
Snow Removal	_____	_____
Air Conditioning	_____	_____
Hot Water	_____	_____
Cold Water	_____	_____
Cable Television	_____	_____
Internet Services	_____	_____

8. TENANT RESIDENTIAL RESPONSIBILITIES

A. *Use Only as a Residence.* The tenant agrees that the residence will be used only as a residence, except for incidental use in trade or business (such as telephone solicitation of sales or arts and crafts created for profit). Such incidental uses will be allowed as long as they do not violate local zoning laws or affect the landlord's ability to obtain fire or liability insurance. The total number of persons residing in this residence cannot exceed

_____.

B. *Damage*. The tenant agrees not to damage the apartment, the building, the grounds or the common areas or to interfere with the rights of other tenants to live in their apartments in peace and quiet. Damage (other than normal wear and tear) caused by the tenant, the tenant's family, invitees, or guests shall be repaired by the tenant at the tenant's expense. Upon the tenant's failure to make such repairs the landlord, after reasonable written notice to the tenant, may make the repairs and the tenant shall be responsible to the landlord for their reasonable cost.

C. *Alterations*. No alteration, addition, or improvement to the residence shall be made by the tenant without the prior written consent by the landlord.

9. LANDLORD RESIDENTIAL RESPONSIBILITIES

A. *Legal Use of the Residence*. The landlord agrees not to interfere with the tenant's legal use of the residence.

B. *Residence Must Be Fit to Live In*. The landlord promises that the residence: (1) complies with applicable housing codes; (2) is fit to live in; and (3) is not dangerous to the life, health, or safety of the occupants. The landlord agrees to make all necessary repairs and take all necessary action to keep the residence fit to live in and to meet all applicable housing code requirements.

C. *Tenant's Rights if the Landlord Fails to Provide Services*

(1) *Unsafe conditions*. If there are conditions in the residence that threaten health or safety, state law allows the tenant to withhold rent and to use it to make minor repairs to the unsafe conditions or to purchase fuel oil during the heating season. Except in an emergency, before withholding rent the tenant must first provide 14 days prior written notice to the landlord and meet other state statutory requirements. The tenant cannot withhold more than $500 or one half of the monthly rent, whichever is the greater. This state law does not apply if the residence is in a building of 5 or fewer residences, one of which is occupied by the landlord.

(2) *Failure to provide utilities*. If the landlord fails to provide electric, gas, or water utilities as agreed to in Section 7 of this lease, State law allows the tenant to pay for these utilities and deduct the amount paid from the rent due.

(3) *Unlivable conditions*. If, through no fault of the tenant, the residence is so damaged that it cannot be lived in and because of the damage the tenant moves out, the tenant will not be liable for rent from the day of the damage and may cancel the lease on 3 days' notice.

10. LANDLORD ENTRY INTO THE RESIDENCE

Except for emergencies, the landlord may enter the apartment only during reasonable hours and after obtaining the tenant's consent at least 24 hours in advance. The tenant may not unreasonably withhold consent to the landlord to enter the residence.

11. DISTURBING THE PEACE

The tenant agrees not to cause or allow on the premises any excessive nuisance, noise, or other activity which disturbs the peace and quiet of neighbors or other tenants in the building or violates any state law or local ordinance. The landlord agrees to prevent other tenants and other persons in the building or common areas from similarly disturbing the tenant's peace and quiet.

12.   EVICTION FOR VIOLATIONS OF LEASE

A. *Notice of Violation.* Serious or repeated violations of the terms of this lease can result in termination of the lease and eviction of the tenant. Except for failure to pay rent (see paragraph B), if the tenant does not live up to the terms of this lease the following will occur:

(1) The landlord will deliver to the tenant a written notice describing the violation and demanding that the tenant cease the lease violation within 10 days of delivery of the notice.

(2) If the tenant does not comply within that 10-day period, the landlord will deliver to the tenant a second written notice that the lease will end within 30 days. On that day, the lease term automatically terminates and the tenant will leave the residence and return the keys to the landlord.

B. *Eviction for Failure to Pay Rent.* If the tenant is 14 days or more late in paying the rent the landlord may send a notice that states that the lease will end in 7 days, unless the tenant pays all overdue rent or late charges before that 7-day period ends. If the tenant fails to pay the rent, the lease term automatically terminates and the tenant will leave the residence and return the keys to the landlord.

C. *Notice of Termination.* The landlord must notify the tenant in writing when the lease is terminated. This notice must: (1) State the reasons for termination with enough specificity to allow the tenant to prepare a defense; (2) Advise the tenant that if a judicial proceeding for eviction is commenced, the tenant has the right to present a defense in that proceeding; and (3) Be served on the tenant by sending a prepaid first class properly addressed letter (return receipt requested) to the tenant at the residence or by delivering a copy of the notice to the residence.

D. *Forcible Eviction.* The landlord will not physically force the tenant out by removing the tenant's possessions or by changing the lock on the tenant's door or by any other method. The tenant can be forcibly removed from the residence only by a law enforcement officer after a Maine court has ordered eviction. The tenant will be given prior notice of the court eviction hearing and will have a chance to testify. Only after this hearing can the court order the tenant's forcible eviction.

13.   SUBLEASING

The tenant agrees not to sublease or assign this residence without the prior written consent of the landlord. Consent will not be withheld except for good reason.

14.   OCCUPANTS

The residents listed below shall be the sole occupants of the leased premises:

_____

_____

15. PETS

The tenant may _____ may not _____ (check one) maintain pets in the residence. If the tenant is allowed to have pets, only the following pets may live in the residence:

_____

_____

16. WHEN THE LEASE ENDS

When the lease ends, the tenant agrees to return the residence in the same condition as it was at the start of the lease, except for normal wear and tear. The tenant will have to pay for damage to the residence only if the damage was caused by the tenant or the tenant's family, invitees, or guests. The tenant must return the keys to the residence or else the tenant can be considered a "hold-over" tenant and still obligated to pay monthly rent.

17. OTHER AGREEMENTS

The landlord and the tenant also agree to the following:

_____

_____

_____

18. CONFLICT WITH STATE OR FEDERAL LAW

If any provision of this lease conflicts with state or federal law, then state law shall take precedence.

19. JOINT AND SEVERAL LIABILITY

The undersigned tenants are jointly and severally responsible and liable for all obligations under this agreement.

20. SIGNATURES

The tenant and landlord have each received identical copies of the lease, each copy signed and dated by both landlord and tenant.

_____   _____
(date)   (tenant)

_____   _____
(date)   (tenant)

_____   _____
(date)   (landlord)

Test Your Understanding

Assume that landlord and tenant have executed the above lease agreement. How does the lease address each of the following issues? Is the relevant provision fair and evenhanded, or does it favor either the landlord or the tenant above the other?

1. *The leasehold:* What type of leasehold does this document establish—a term of years, periodic tenancy, or tenancy at will? *See* Lease ¶(3).
2. *The security deposit:* To what purposes can the landlord apply the security deposit: to substitute for unpaid rent, to repair damage caused by the tenant, or for some other purpose? Under what circumstances can the landlord retain all or part of the security deposit? *See* Lease ¶(5).
3. *Additional roommates:* Assume the tenant is having difficulty paying the rent each month. Can the tenant ask a friend to move in to help pay the rent? Under what circumstances? *See* Lease ¶(14).
4. *Maintaining the premises:* Does the landlord have a duty to maintain the premises in good repair? If so, under what standard? If the landlord breaches this duty, what remedies are available to the tenant? *See* Lease ¶(9).
5. *The tenant's obligations:* What are the tenant's obligations under the lease? What are the landlord's remedies if the tenant is in breach of the agreement? *See* Lease ¶¶(8, 11, 12).
6. *Subleasing and assigning:* Can the tenant sublease the premises? Assign them? If so, under what circumstances? *See* Lease ¶(13).
7. *The termination of the lease:* What are the tenant's obligations when the lease expires? Must the tenant provide notice to the landlord in order to terminate the lease? *See* Lease ¶¶(3, 16).
8. *The irresponsible roommate:* Suppose that two friends sign the lease and agree to occupy the premises as roommates. Unknown to one of the tenants, the other has not been paying her share of the rent each month. Does this have any effect upon the responsible tenant who has been promptly paying his share of the rent? *See* Lease ¶(19).

C. THE RIGHTS AND DUTIES OF THE PARTIES

Numerous rights (and corresponding duties) attach to the landlord-tenant relationship, whether imposed by property law, contract law, statute, or constitution. This section examines the rights, duties, and remedies surrounding three key aspects of the leasehold—consecutive rights of possession, maintenance of the premises, and nondiscrimination in the selection and treatment of tenants.

1. Possession

A Place to Start | **Rights of Possession**

■ *Tenant's rights:*

■ *Delivery of possession:* Under the majority rule (the "English rule"), the tenant has a right to receive actual possession from the landlord at the beginning of the leasehold term, free from the presence of holdover tenants or others in wrongful possession. Under the minority rule (called the "American rule," despite its minority status), there is no implied warranty that the landlord will deliver actual possession, distinct from the legal right to possession.

■ *Sublease and assignment:* Tenants can *sublease* their possessory rights in the leasehold for a period less than its remaining duration, and retain a reversion at the end of the subtenant's possession. Tenants can also *assign* their interest to an assignee who will have the right of possession for the full remaining duration of the leasehold.

Periodic tenancies and terms of years are freely transferable by sublease or assignment unless the lease states otherwise. Tenancies at will and tenancies at sufferance generally cannot be subleased or assigned to others because they lack a definite possessory period. Lease provisions prohibiting subleases and/or assignments (or sometimes, prohibiting such transfers unless the landlord consents to them) are enforceable, but are strictly construed against the landlord because they impose restraints on alienation. For example, if a lease explicitly forbids only subleasing, courts would likely tolerate an assignment. Likewise, if the lease forbids subleases and assignments but does not specifically give the landlord authority to terminate the underlying lease upon transfer, some courts would uphold the transfer and award only damages to the landlord. Under the majority rule, the landlord under a *residential* lease has no duty to act reasonably when deciding whether or not to consent to a sublease or assignment. For commercial leases, however, under the modern trend the landlord may not unreasonably withhold consent.

■ *Landlord's rights:*

■ *The tenant who leaves too soon—abandonment:* If a tenant abandons before the leasehold terminates, the landlord has three options: (1) treat the lease as terminated by the tenant's abandonment (interpreted as an offer of surrender) and seek damages; (2) retake on the tenant's behalf and lease the premises to another, recovering any shortfall in rent from the abandoning tenant; or (3) stand by and do nothing, continuing to hold the original tenant responsible for rent payments. Although the traditional view permits all three options, the modern trend (now a majority, according to some sources) disfavors the third option, and instead requires the landlord to mitigate the tenant's damages in at least some circumstances by making reasonable efforts to re-let the premises. Powell on Real Property § 17.05[2] (Michael Allan Wolf, gen. ed. 2015). Under this view, the landlord's failure to mitigate provides the tenant with a defense to an action for rent.

■ *The tenant who stays too long—holdover:* The landlord holds a reversion that becomes possessory at the termination of the leasehold. If a tenant remains in possession after the leasehold ends (becoming a tenant at sufferance), within a reasonable time the landlord must make an *election of remedies,* and either (1) treat the tenant as a trespasser and bring an action to recover possession; or (2) impose a new tenancy on the holdover tenant, generally dating back to when the prior lease terminated and the holdover's possession became wrongful (this election may be implied by the landlord's acceptance of rent during the sufferance period). Most jurisdictions treat the new leasehold as a periodic tenancy. In some jurisdictions, the new period is equivalent to the original period or term (up to one year). In others, the new period corresponds to the way rent was calculated under the original lease (up to one year)—either the period for which rent was "reserved" (e.g., at an annual rent of $15,000) or the period between the payment of each installment (e.g., payable in installments of $1,250 on the first of each month).

See generally William B. Stoebuck & Dale A. Whitman, The Law of Property (3d ed. 2000), §§ 6.17, 6.20-.21, 6.59, 6.68-.71, 6.82.

DIGGING DEEPER: Do you think that the typical allocation of rights between landlords and tenants, as described above, is fair and even-handed? What changes, if any, would you recommend?

Ernst v. Conditt

390 S.W.2d 703 (Tenn. App. 1964), *cert. denied* (1965)

Reading Guide

Recall the historical evolution of the leasehold as incorporating elements of both contract and property. Even today, the modern tenant has both a contractual and a property relationship with the landlord. The following information will help you understand this case:

◆ *Privity of estate:* Landlord and tenant are said to be in *privity of estate* because they hold simultaneous interests in the same property: the tenant holds the present estate (a nonfreehold possessory leasehold) and the landlord holds the future interest (a reversion that become effective at the termination of the leasehold).

◆ *Privity of contract:* Landlord and tenant are also said to be in *privity of contract* because they signed the lease document, in which each made certain covenants to the other (such as the landlord's covenant to convey possession to the tenant for the lease term, and the tenant's covenant to pay rent).

CHATTIN, J.

Complainants, B. Walter Ernst and wife, Emily Ernst, leased a certain tract of land in Davidson County, Tennessee, to Frank D. Rogers on June 18, 1960, for a term of one year and seven days, commencing on June 23, 1960.

Rogers went into possession of the property and constructed an asphalt race track and enclosed the premises with a fence. He also constructed other improvements thereon such as floodlights for use in the operation of a Go-Cart track.

We quote those paragraphs of the lease pertinent to the question for consideration in this controversy:

> 3. Lessee covenants to pay as rent for said leased premises the sum of $4,200 per annum, payable at the rate of $350 per month or 15% of all gross receipts, whether from sales or services occurring on the leased premises, whichever is the larger amount. . . .

> 5. Lessee shall have no right to assign or sublet the leased premises without prior written approval of Lessors. In the event of any assignment or sublease, Lessee is still liable to perform the covenants of this lease, including the covenant to pay rent, and nothing herein shall be construed as releasing Lessee from his liabilities and obligations hereunder.

> 9. Lessee agrees that upon termination of this contract, or any extensions or renewals thereof, that all improvements above the ground will be moved at Lessee's expense and the property cleared. . . .

Rogers operated the business for a short time. In July, 1960, he entered into negotiations with the defendant, A. K. Conditt, for the sale of the business to him. During these negotiations, the question of the term of the lease arose. Defendant desired a two-year lease of the property. He and Rogers went to the home of complainants and negotiated an extension of the term of the lease which resulted in the following amendment to the lease, and the sublease or assignment of the lease as amended to Conditt by Rogers:

> By mutual consent of the parties, the lease executed the 18th day of June 1960, between B. Walter Ernst and wife, Emily H. Ernst, as Lessors, and Frank G. Rogers as Lessee, is amended as follows:

> 1. Paragraph 2 of said lease is amended so as to provide that the term will end July 31, 1962 and not June 30, 1961. . . .

> 5. Lessor hereby consents to the subletting of the premises to A. K. Conditt, but upon the express condition and understanding that the original Lessee, Frank K. Rogers, will remain personally liable for the faithful performance of all the terms and conditions of the original lease and of this amendment to the original lease.

> Except as modified by this amendment, all terms and conditions of the original lease dated the 18th day of June, 1960, by and between the parties shall remain in full force and effect.

> In witness whereof the parties have executed this amendment to lease on this the 4th day of August, 1960. [The signatures of B. Walter Ernst, Emily H. Ernst, and Frank D. Rogers appeared below this paragraph.]

For value received and in consideration of the promise to faithfully perform all conditions of the within lease as amended, I hereby sublet the premises to A.K. Conditt upon the understanding that I will individually remain liable for the performance of the lease. This 4th day of Aug, 1960. [The signature of Frank D. Rogers appeared below this paragraph.]

The foregoing subletting of the premises is accepted, this the 4th day of Aug. 1960. [The signature of A.K. Conditt appears below this paragraph.]

Conditt operated the Go-Cart track from August until November, 1960. He paid the rent for the months of August, September and October, 1960, directly to complainants. In December, 1960, complainants contacted defendant with reference to the November rent and at that time defendant stated he had been advised he was not liable to them for rent. However, defendant paid the basic monthly rental of $350.00 to complainants in June, 1961. This was the final payment received by complainants during the term of the lease as amended. The record is not clear whether defendant continued to operate the business after the last payment of rent or abandoned it. Defendant, however, remained in possession of the property until the expiration of the leasehold.

On July 10, 1962, complainants, through their Attorneys, notified Conditt by letter the lease would expire as of midnight July 31, 1962; and they were demanding a settlement of the past due rent and unless the improvements on the property were removed by him as provided in paragraph 9 of the original lease; then, in that event, they would have same removed at his expense. Defendant did not reply to this demand.

On August 1, 1962, complainants filed their bill in this cause seeking a recovery of $2,404.58 which they alleged was the balance due on the basic rent of $350.00 per month for the first year of the lease and the sum of $4,200.00, the basic rent for the second year, and the further sum necessary for the removal of the improvements constructed on the property. . . .

The Chancellor found the instrument to be an assignment. A decree was entered sustaining the bill and entering judgment for complainants in the sum of $6,904.58 against defendant. . . .

To support his theory the instrument is a sublease, the defendant insists the amendment to the lease entered into between Rogers and complainants was for the express purpose of extending the term of the lease and obtaining the consent of the lessors to a "subletting" of the premises to defendant. That by the use of the words "sublet" and "subletting" no other construction can be placed on the amendment and the agreement of Rogers and the acceptance of defendant attached thereto.

Further, since complainants agreed to the subletting of the premises to defendant "upon the express condition and understanding that the original lessee, Frank D. Rogers, will remain personally liable for the faithful performance of all the terms and conditions of the original lease and this amendment to the original lease," no construction can be placed upon this language other than it was the intention of complainants to hold Rogers primarily liable for the performance of the original lease and the amendment thereto. And, therefore, Rogers, for his own protection, would have the implied right to re-enter and perform the lease in the event of a default on the part of the defendant. This being true, Rogers retained a reversionary interest in the property sufficient to satisfy the legal distinction between a sublease and an assignment of a lease.

It is then urged the following rules of construction of written instruments support the above argument:

> Where words or terms having a definite legal meaning and effect are knowingly used in a written instrument the parties thereto will be presumed to have intended such words or terms to have their proper legal meaning and effect, in the absence of any contrary intention appearing in the instrument. 12 Am. Jur., Contracts, Section 238. . . .

As stated in complainants' brief, the liability of defendant to complainants depends upon whether the transfer of the leasehold interest in the premises from Rogers is an assignment of the lease or a sublease. If the transfer is a sublease, no privity of contract exists between complainants and defendant; and, therefore, defendant could not be liable to complainants on the covenant to pay rent and the expense of the removal of the improvements. But, if the transfer is an assignment of the lease, privity of contract does exist between complainants and defendant; and defendant would be liable directly and primarily for the amount of the judgment.

The general rule as to the distinction between an assignment of a lease and a sublease is an assignment conveys the whole term, leaving no interest nor reversionary interest in the grantor or assignor. Whereas, a sublease may be generally defined as a transaction whereby a tenant grants an interest in the leased premises less than his own, or reserves to himself a reversionary interest in the term.

The common law distinction between an assignment of a lease and a sublease is succinctly stated in the case of *Jaber v. Miller*, 239 S.W.2d 760 (Ark. 1951):

> If the instrument purports to transfer the lessee's estate for the entire remainder of his term it is an assignment, regardless of its form or of the parties' intention. Conversely, if the instrument purports to transfer the lessee's estate for less than the entire term—even for a day less—it is a sublease, regardless of its form or of the parties' intention.

The modern rule which has been adopted in this State for construing written instruments is stated in the case of *City of Nashville v. Lawrence*, 284 S.W. 882 (Tenn.):

> The cardinal rule to be followed in this state, in construing deeds and other written instruments, is to ascertain the intention of the parties.

. . . In the case of *Commerce Street Company v. Goodyear Tire & Rubber Company*, 215 S.W.2d 4 (Tenn. App. 1948), this Court said:

It is the duty of the court in the construction of contracts to ascertain the intention of the contracting parties, understand what they meant by the contract, and give effect to such understanding and meaning. All other rules of construction are only aids or helps in establishing the intention of the parties and their mutual understanding of the meaning of their contract. . . .

. . . It is our opinion under either the common law or modern rule of construction the agreement between Rogers and defendant is an assignment of the lease.

The fact that Rogers expressly agreed to remain liable to complainants for the performance of the lease did not create a reversion nor a right to re-enter in Rogers either express or implied. The obligations and liabilities of a lessee to a lessor, under the express covenants of a lease, are not in anywise affected by an assignment or a subletting to a third party, in the absence of an express or implied agreement or some action on his part which amounts to a waiver or estops him from insisting upon compliance with the covenants. This is true even though the assignment or sublease is made with the consent of the lessor. By an assignment of a lease the privity of estate between the lessor and lessee is terminated, but the privity of contract between them still remains and is unaffected. Neither the privity of estate or contract between the lessor and lessee are affected by a sublease.

Thus, the express agreement of Rogers to remain personally liable for the performance of the covenants of the lease created no greater obligation on his part or interest in the leasehold, other than as set forth in the original lease.

The argument that since the agreement between Rogers and defendant contains the words, "sublet" and "subletting" is conclusive the instrument is to be construed as a sublease is, we think, unsound:

> A consent to sublet has been held to include the consent to assign or mortgage the lease; and a consent to assign has been held to authorize a subletting. 51 C.J.S. Landlord and Tenant § 36, page 552.

Prior to the consummation of the sale of the Go-Cart business to defendant, he insisted upon the execution of the amendment to the lease extending the term of the original lease. For value received and on the promise of the defendant to perform all of the conditions of the lease as amended, Rogers parted with his entire interest in the property. Defendant went into possession of the property and paid the rent to complainants. He remained in possession of the property for the entire term. By virtue of the sale of the business, defendant became the owner of the improvements with the right to their removal at the expiration of the lease. . . .

It is our opinion the defendant, under the terms of the agreement with Rogers, had a right to the possession of the property for the entire term of the lease as amended, including the right to remove the improvements after the expiration of the lease. Rogers merely agreed to become personally liable for the rent and the expense of the removal of the improvements upon the default of defendant. He neither expressly, nor by implication, reserved the right to re-enter for a condition broken by defendant.

Thus, we are of the opinion the use of the words, "sublet" and "subletting" is not conclusive of the construction to be placed on the instrument in this case; it plainly appearing from the context of the instrument and the facts and circumstances surrounding the execution of it the parties thereto intended an assignment rather than a sublease.

It results the assignments are overruled and the decree of the Chancellor is affirmed with costs.

Notes

1. *Classifying the estate:* Review the categories of leasehold estates. What type of leasehold did the Ernsts originally convey to Rogers?

2. *Assignment v. sublease:* The court examines three clues as to whether the transfer by Rogers to Conditt was an assignment or a sublease. In which direction did each clue point, and what did the court conclude? In practical terms, why does it matter?

3. *A judicial blunder?* The court says, "If the transfer is a sublease, no privity of contract exists between complainants and defendant. . . . But, if the transfer is an assignment of the lease, privity of contract does exist between complainants and defendant. . . ." Is that an accurate statement of the law?

4. *A web of interests—privity of estate and privity of contract:* The court stated in *Ernst v. Conditt*, "By an assignment of a lease the privity of estate between the lessor and lessee is terminated, but the privity of contract between them still remains and is unaffected. Neither the privity of estate or contract between the lessor and lessee are affected by a sublease." What does that mean?

Recall the dual nature of a lease as both contract and conveyance of an estate in property. Those who hold consecutive possessory interests in the same property are said to be in *privity of estate* with one another—such as a tenant (holding the right to present possession) and a landlord (holding an adjoining reversionary interest in future possession). Landlord and tenant are also in *privity of contract* because both are parties to the lease agreement and are bound by the promises contained therein. If a tenant defaults on the obligation to pay rent, then the landlord can sue under either a privity of estate theory (that is, the landlord conveyed a possessory right in exchange for rent) or under a privity of contract theory (that is, through the lease the tenant made a contractual promise to pay rent). Using our web of interests metaphor first introduced in Chapter 1, you can imagine spiderlike threads linking landlord and tenant, representing either property duties (privity of estate) or contract duties (privity of contract).

In the original landlord-tenant relationship, landlord and tenant are connect by both property threads and contract threads, as suggested by the diagram below:

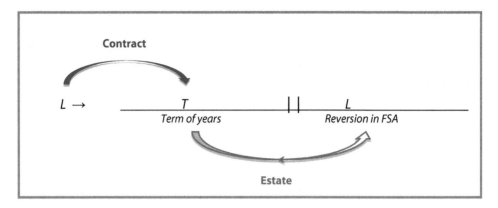

Figure 1

Now, suppose that the tenant *assigns* her estate to a second tenant, the assignee, for the entire balance of the leasehold. The assignee steps into the shoes of the tenant, and enters into privity of estate with the landlord. But the original tenant cannot throw off her contractual obligations to the landlord so easily, and she remains responsible for her contractual promises to him unless expressly released. Conversely, the assignee is not bound to the landlord under the contract unless the assignee expressly "assumes" the lease. The relations are as follows:

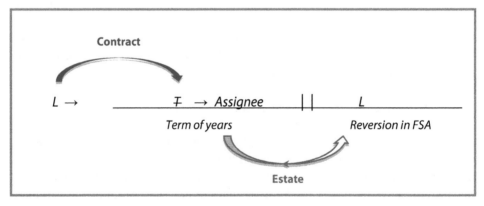

Figure 2

Finally, assume instead that the tenant *subleases* her possessory interest to a second tenant, the subtenant (*SubT*), retaining a reversionary interest in her own leasehold. As between the tenant and subtenant, there is both privity of estate and privity of contract, analogous to the relationship between the landlord and original tenant (depicted in the Figure 1 above). Unlike the assignment, here the tenant sublets to *SubT* for a period less than the entire balance of her leasehold. As a result, the original tenant and landlord remain in privity of estate because the original tenant's right to future possession of her leasehold adjoins the landlord's reversionary interest. At the same time, the original tenant also remains in privity of contract with the landlord, unless the landlord expressly released her from her contractual obligations. The sub-tenant is not bound to the landlord under the contract unless the subtenant expressly "assumed" the lease. The relations look like this:

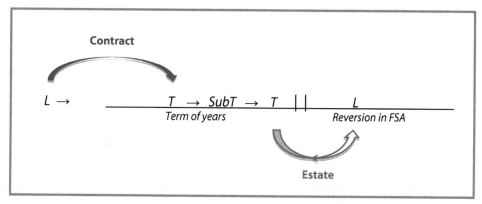

Figure 3

As a practical matter, the landlord must be linked to the second tenant in some way—either through privity of contract or through privity of estate—in order to have an action against the second tenant for nonpayment of rent. Ordinarily, that occurs only if the second tenant is an assignee (or if the second tenant expressly enters into privity of contract with the landlord). Suppose you temporarily move out of your apartment at the end of your first year of law school to take an externship in another city. If you can find a replacement tenant, will you *sublease* or *assign* your apartment for the summer? What legal consequences would follow from your choice?

Slavin v. Rent Control Bd. of Brookline

548 N.E.2d 1226 (Mass. 1990)

> #### Reading Guide
>
> In *Ernst v. Conditt*, the landlord agreed to the tenant's assignment of the lease to a second tenant. But what if the landlord does not agree to the transfer? Should courts *imply* a duty of reasonableness into each lease, prohibiting landlords from *unreasonably* withholding consent for a proposed sublease or assignment? Should it matter whether the lease concerns residential or commercial property?

O'CONNOR, J.

Article XXXVIII of the Brookline rent control by-law provides in relevant part as follows:

Section 9. Evictions. No person shall bring any action to recover possession of a controlled rental unit unless . . . the tenant has violated an obligation or covenant of his tenancy other than the obligation to surrender possession upon proper notice. . . . A landlord seeking to recover possession of a controlled rental unit shall apply to the board for a certificate of eviction. . . . If the board finds that the facts attested to in the landlord's petition are valid and in compliance with [this section], the certificate of eviction shall be issued. . . .

The plaintiff landlord applied to the defendant rent control board of Brookline (board) for a certificate of eviction seeking to evict the defendant tenant Barry Myers on the ground that Myers had violated an obligation of his tenancy. The lease states:

Occupancy of Premises—Tenant shall not assign nor underlet any part or the whole of the premises, nor shall [tenant] permit the premises to be occupied for a period longer than a temporary visit by anyone except the individuals specifically named in the first paragraph of this tenancy, their spouses, and any children born to them hereafter, without first obtaining on each occasion the assent in writing of Landlord.

After a hearing, the board found that the tenant had allowed an unauthorized person to occupy his apartment without first obtaining the landlord's written consent. Nonetheless, the board refused to issue the eviction certificate. The board based its refusal on its determination of law that, implicit in the lease provision requiring the landlord's consent prior to an assignment or a sublease or the permitting of other occupants, there is an "agreement on the part of the landlord to at least consider prospective tenants [and other permitted occupants] and not withhold consent unreasonably or unequivocally." The board found that the landlord had acted unreasonably because she had categorically refused to allow the tenant to bring in someone new after the original cotenant had moved out. Because of the landlord's unreasonable behavior, the board concluded that the tenant could not be said to have violated the lease.

The landlord obtained judicial review under G.L. c. 30A, § 14, and a judge in the Brookline Division of the District Court annulled the board's decision and ruled that the certificate of eviction should be issued. The judge concluded, contrary to the board's decision, that Massachusetts law permits a landlord to withhold consent in an arbitrary or unreasonable manner unless the landlord has expressly contracted not to do so. . . .

The board appealed, and the Appellate Division of the District Court affirmed the decision of the trial judge annulling the board's decision and ordering issuance of the certificate of eviction. . . .

The board filed a notice of appeal from the Appellate Division's decision and we granted the board's application for direct appellate review. We now affirm the Appellate Division's decision concerning the effect of the consent provision in the lease. . . .

The issue whether a tenant's obligation, as specified in a residential lease, to obtain the written consent of a landlord before assigning the lease or subletting or permitting other occupants implies as a matter of law an obligation on the landlord's part to act reasonably in withholding consent has not been decided by this court. . . .

In this case, . . . we must resolve the question whether the landlord may unreasonably withhold consent because here the board found that the landlord's unreasonable and categorical refusal to consent to any replacement tenant whatsoever excused any failure on the part of the tenant to request the landlord's consent.

A majority of jurisdictions subscribe to the rule that a lease provision requiring the landlord's consent to an assignment or sublease permits the landlord to refuse arbitrarily or unreasonably. . . . However, the board argues that the current trend is the other way, and cites numerous cases in support of that proposition. We note that every case cited by the board except two, which we discuss below, involved a commercial, not a residential, lease. Although the significance of the distinction between commercial and residential leases may be fairly debatable, we observe that in several of the cases cited by the board the court specifically states that its holding is limited to the commercial lease context.

Kruger v. Page Management Co., 432 N.Y.S.2d 295 (N.Y. 1980), is the only purely residential lease case cited by the board. We get little help from that case because the reasonableness requirement in New York has been statutorily imposed. The other noncommercial lease case cited by the board is *Sanders v. Tropicana*, 229 S.E.2d 304 (N.C. App. 1976). In that case, the court held that consent by the board of directors of a cooperative corporation to the transfer of the plaintiff's stock subscription and proprietary lease could not be unreasonably withheld. The relevance of *Sanders* to this case, however, was subsequently limited by *Isbey v. Crews*, 284 S.E.2d 534 (N.C. App. 1981), in which the same court that decided *Sanders* refused to imply a reasonableness requirement in a commercial lease. The court distinguished *Sanders* by saying that "[t]he Court's imposition of a 'reasonableness' limitation on the Board's discretion may be attributed to the fact that *Sanders* involved the alienability of corporate stock as well as of a leasehold. . . ." *Isbey*, 284 S.E.2d 534. The fact that no State court has acted to create a reasonableness requirement in a case involving only a residential lease, while not determinative, at least counsels us to be cautious about taking such a step.

The board argues that we should be guided by the commercial lease cases because the reasons for implying a reasonableness requirement in a residential lease are at least as compelling as in a commercial lease. Our review of the commercial lease cases, however, and particularly of the rationale that appears to have motivated the courts in those cases to adopt a reasonableness requirement, does not persuade us that we should adopt such a rule in this case, which involves a residential lease in a municipality governed by a rent control law.[2]

Two major concerns emerge from the commercial lease cases. First, courts have exhibited concern that commercial landlords may exercise their power to withhold consent for unfair financial gain. In several of the cases cited by the board, a commercial landlord refused to consent to a proposed subtenant and then attempted to enter into a new or revised lease for the same premises at a more favorable rental rate. However, in a rent control jurisdiction like Brookline there is little economic incentive to withhold consent in the residential lease context because the landlord has such limited control over the rent that can be charged.

The second concern that appears to have motivated the commercial lease decisions is a desire to limit restraints on alienation in light of the fact that "the necessity of reasonable alienation of commercial building space has become paramount in our ever-increasing urban society." *Homa–Goff Interiors, Inc. v. Cowden*, 350 So. 2d 1035, 1037 (Ala. 1977). However, this court has previously, albeit not recently, ruled that a commercial lease provision requiring a landlord's consent prior to an assignment, with no limitation on the landlord's ability to refuse, is not an unreasonable restraint on alienation. *68 Beacon St., Inc. v. Sohier*, 194 N.E. 303 (Mass. 1935). In light of our decision in *68 Beacon St., Inc.*, and in the absence of a demonstrable trend involving residential leases in other jurisdictions, we are not persuaded that there is such a "necessity of reasonable alienation of [residential] building space" that we ought to impose on residential landlords a reasonableness requirement to which they have not agreed. We are mindful that valid arguments in support of such a rule can be made, but there are also valid counter-arguments, not the least of which is that such a rule would be likely to engender a plethora of litigation about whether the landlord's withholding of consent was reasonable. The question is one of public policy which, of course, the Legislature is free to address. We note that the Legislature has spoken in at least four States: Alaska Stat. § 34.03.060 (1988); Del. Code Ann. tit. 25, § 5512(b) (1975); Haw. Rev. Stat. § 516-63 (1985 & Supp. 1988); N.Y. Real Property Law § 226-b (McKinney 1989). . . .

The decision of the Appellate Division annulling the board's decision and ordering issuance of the certificate of eviction is affirmed. . . .

Notes

1. *Practice pointer—drafting with clarity:*   Can you re-draft the lease from the principal case to avoid the ambiguity that gave rise to this litigation? What

---

2. [FN 3] We make no suggestion about the rule we might adopt in other contexts.

language would you suggest if you represented tenant Barry Myers? What language would you suggest if you represented landlord Slavin?

2. *A case of first impression:*   This was a case of first impression, leaving the court to rely on various policy considerations in choosing what rule should govern this case. The court discussed two rationales that may require landlords to act reasonably when withholding consent to sublease or assign commercial leases. What were they? Did the court find those rationales applicable to residential leases? Do you agree with the court's conclusion?

3. *Legislative v. judicial action:*   The court declined to rely on precedent from New York (*Kruger v. Page Management Co.*), stating, "We get little help from that case because the reasonableness requirement in New York has been statutorily imposed." Why do you think the court drew that distinction?

4. *The relevance of rent control—the example of Brookline, Massachusetts:*   Brookline, Massachusetts, a suburb just outside of Boston, had imposed rent control measures since the late 1960s. Just four years after the *Slavin* opinion was issued, Brookline terminated most aspects of its rent control program by voter referendum. In 1997, it ended the program altogether by terminating remaining protections for disabled, elderly, and low-income renters. *Rent Control: The Morning After*, The Economist, Apr. 30, 1998.

Suppose the same conflict had arisen in a jurisdiction without a rent control program. What result would the court reach? What do you think would be the best result? Rent control programs, which formed an important backdrop for the *Slavin* opinion, have had a long history. Today, although such programs are in decline, according to Professor Zachary Bray, they have been "among the most significant governmental programs designed to provide affordable housing in the United States." Zachary Bray, *The New Progressive Property and the Low-Income Housing Conflict*, 2012 B.Y.U. L. Rev. 1109, 1139-44 (2012).

Rent control programs have also been controversial:

> Over the course of their history in the United States, rent and eviction controls have taken two forms. The first type, sometimes called "first generation rent controls," involves straightforward caps on rents at a level below market rates. The second type, sometimes called "second generation rent controls," allows rent levels to be set more or less freely when tenants first occupy an apartment, but then limits subsequent increases as long as the tenant remains. Second generation rent controls may also contain eviction controls, which limit the permissible grounds for eviction and set procedures for local enforcement to prevent landlords from circumventing the substantive rent-increase restrictions by threatening to evict tenants who refuse to pay rent increases. . . . Today, both forms of rent control are dying out: only a few states contain municipalities with either type, and many states ban rent control outright.

> Critics of rent control argue that its popularity is dramatically dwindling both because it has failed in its main goal of making housing more affordable in high-cost markets, and because its many side effects have become more widely

acknowledged since the last wave of rent-control ordinances were enacted in the 1970s. The standard arguments against rent control are numerous and well developed: critics argue that rent control is highly inefficient and distorts housing markets; is a poorly focused and potentially unfair redistribution device; exacerbates the very housing shortages it is designed to reduce; reduces tenant mobility and increases commuting costs; leads to unnecessarily formalized relationships between landlords and tenants, crowding out the possibility for increased social capital; distorts landlords' incentives to maintain building quality, leading to dilapidation; and tends to reduce the possibility of cooperation and increase the possibility of nasty behavior between landlords and tenants. . . .

. . . The standard defense of rent control admits the potential efficiency losses picked out by many critics of rent control, but suggests that these potential losses may be offset by other gains of rent control, at least in certain situations. More specifically, the standard defense of rent control begins by suggesting, as a baseline, that most tenants generally ought to have a stronger interest in retaining their long-standing homes than most landlords ought to have with respect to their freedom of contract or the maintenance of their profit margins. However, according to the standard defense of rent control, this baseline rule does not apply to would-be tenants, because their potential property interest in a future tenancy has not yet become bound up, in meaningful, noncommercial ways, with their *personhood*. Thus, the standard defense suggests that rent and eviction controls may be justified, even in the face of some of the negative side effects identified by various critics, as long as those controls can be justified in terms of more significant benefits related to protecting property interests in *personhood* or existing communities.

Bray, at 1139-44 (italics supplied). Recall Justice Oliver Wendell Holmes' support for adverse possession in appropriate cases, because "[a] thing which you have enjoyed and used as your own for a long time, whether property or an opinion, takes root in your being" and compare it to the above references to *personhood*. Do you see any similarities between the two concepts? We will return to the personhood theory in Chapter 6.

Do you think rent control is a good idea? Can you think of additional approaches beyond the "first generation" and "second generation" controls described by Professor Bray? The problem of affordable housing continues, as we will see in Chapter 12 on zoning.

Sommer v. Kridel

378 A.2d 767 (N.J. 1977)

Reading Guide

In *Slavin v. Rent Control Board*, the Massachusetts Supreme Court declined to "rescue" the tenant from the terms of the contract he had signed, including a provision forbidding unapproved assignments and subleases. In the next case, The New Jersey Supreme Court considers rescuing the tenant from a different obligation—the duty to pay rent throughout the leasehold period specified in the contract, without exception for unforeseen circumstances or hardship. Does one situation present a more compelling case than the other for the tenant?

PASHMAN, J. for a unanimous Court.

We granted certification in these cases to consider whether a landlord seeking damages from a defaulting tenant is under a duty to mitigate damages by making reasonable efforts to re-let an apartment wrongfully vacated by the tenant. . . . We now reverse and hold that a landlord does have an obligation to make a reasonable effort to mitigate damages in such a situation. We therefore overrule *Joyce v. Bauman*, 174 A. 693 (E. & A. 1934) to the extent that it is inconsistent with our decision today.

This case was tried on stipulated facts. On March 10, 1972 the defendant, James Kridel, entered into a lease with the plaintiff, Abraham Sommer, owner of the "Pierre Apartments" in Hackensack, to rent apartment 6-L in that building.[3] The term of the lease was from May 1, 1972 until April 30, 1974. . . .

One week after signing the agreement, Kridel paid Sommer $690. Half of that sum was used to satisfy the first month's rent. The remainder was paid under the lease provision requiring a security deposit of $345. Although defendant had expected to begin occupancy around May 1, his plans were changed. He wrote to Sommer on May 19, 1972, explaining,

> I was to be married on June 3, 1972. Unhappily the engagement was broken and the wedding plans cancelled. Both parents were to assume responsibility for the rent after our marriage. I was discharged from the U.S. Army in October 1971 and am now a student. I have no funds of my own, and am supported by my stepfather.
>
> In view of the above, I cannot take possession of the apartment and am surrendering all rights to it. Never having received a key, I cannot return same to you.
>
> I beg your understanding and compassion in releasing me from the lease, and will of course, in consideration thereof, forfeit the 2 month's rent already paid.
>
> Please notify me at your earliest convenience.

Plaintiff did not answer the letter.

Subsequently, a third party went to the apartment house and inquired about renting apartment 6-L. Although the parties agreed that she was ready, willing and able to rent the apartment, the person in charge told her that the apartment was not being shown since it was already rented to Kridel. In fact, the landlord did not re-enter the apartment or exhibit it to anyone until August 1, 1973. At that time it was rented to a new tenant for a term beginning on September 1, 1973. The new rental was for $345 per month. . . .

---

3. [FN 1] Among other provisions, the lease prohibited the tenant from assigning or transferring the lease without the consent of the landlord. If the tenant defaulted, the lease gave the landlord the option of re-entering or re-letting, but stipulated that failure to re-let or to recover the full rental would not discharge the tenant's liability for rent.

Prior to re-letting the new premises, plaintiff sued Kridel in August 1972, demanding $7,590, the total amount due for the full two-year term of the lease. Following a mistrial, plaintiff filed an amended complaint asking for $5,865, the amount due between May 1, 1972 and September 1, 1973. . . . Defendant filed an amended answer to the complaint, alleging that plaintiff breached the contract, failed to mitigate damages and accepted defendant's surrender of the premises. He also counterclaimed to demand repayment of the $345 paid as a security deposit.

The trial judge ruled in favor of defendant. Despite his conclusion that the lease had been drawn to reflect "the settled law of this state," he found that "justice and fair dealing" imposed upon the landlord the duty to attempt to re-let the premises and thereby mitigate damages. He also held that plaintiff's failure to make any response to defendant's unequivocal offer of surrender was tantamount to an acceptance, thereby terminating the tenancy and any obligation to pay rent. As a result, he dismissed both the complaint and the counterclaim. The Appellate Division reversed in a per curiam opinion. . . .

[The Court recounted the facts of a companion case, *Riverview Realty Co. v. Perosio.*]

As the lower courts in both appeals found, the weight of authority in this State supports the rule that a landlord is under no duty to mitigate damages caused by a defaulting tenant. See *Joyce v. Bauman*, supra. . . .

Nevertheless, while there is still a split of authority over this question, the trend among recent cases appears to be in favor of a mitigation requirement. . . . The majority rule is based on principles of property law which equate a lease with a transfer of a property interest in the owner's estate. Under this rationale the lease conveys to a tenant an interest in the property which forecloses any control by the landlord; thus, it would be anomalous to require the landlord to concern himself with the tenant's abandonment of his own property.

For instance, in *Muller v. Beck*, 110 A. 831 (Sup. Ct. 1920), where essentially the same issue was posed, the court clearly treated the lease as governed by property, as opposed to contract, precepts.[4] The court there observed that the "tenant had an estate for years, but it was an estate qualified by this right of the landlord to prevent its transfer," and that "the tenant has an estate with which the landlord may not interfere." . . .

Yet the distinction between a lease for ordinary residential purposes and an ordinary contract can no longer be considered viable. As Professor Powell observed, evolving "social factors have exerted increasing influence on the law of estates for years." 2 Powell on Real Property (1977 ed.), s 221(1) at 180-81. The result has been that,

> [t]he complexities of city life, and the proliferated problems of modern society in general, have created new problems for lessors and lessees and these have been

---

4. [FN 3] It is well settled that a party claiming damages for a breach of contract has a duty to mitigate his loss.

commonly handled by specific clauses in leases. This growth in the number and detail of specific lease covenants has reintroduced into the law of estates for years a predominantly contractual ingredient. . . .

This Court has taken the lead in requiring that landlords provide housing services to tenants in accordance with implied duties which are hardly consistent with the property notions expressed in *Muller v. Beck*, supra. . . .

Application of the contract rule requiring mitigation of damages to a residential lease may be justified as a matter of basic fairness.[5] Professor McCormick first commented upon the inequity under the majority rule when he predicted in 1925 that eventually,

> the logic, inescapable according to the standards of a "jurisprudence of conceptions" which permits the landlord to stand idly by the vacant, abandoned premises and treat them as the property of the tenant and recover full rent, will yield to the more realistic notions of social advantage which in other fields of the law have forbidden a recovery for damages which the plaintiff by reasonable efforts could have avoided.

McCormick, *The Rights of the Landlord Upon Abandonment of the Premises by the Tenant*, 23 Mich. L. Rev. 211, 221-22 (1925). . . .

The pre-existing rule cannot be predicated upon the possibility that a landlord may lose the opportunity to rent another empty apartment because he must first rent the apartment vacated by the defaulting tenant. Even where the breach occurs in a multi-dwelling building, each apartment may have unique qualities which make it attractive to certain individuals. Significantly, in *Sommer v. Kridel*, there was a specific request to rent the apartment vacated by the defendant; there is no reason to believe that absent this vacancy the landlord could have succeeded in renting a different apartment to this individual.

We therefore hold that antiquated real property concepts which served as the basis for the pre-existing rule, shall no longer be controlling where there is a claim for damages under a residential lease. Such claims must be governed by more modern notions of fairness and equity. A landlord has a duty to mitigate damages where he seeks to recover rents due from a defaulting tenant.

If the landlord has other vacant apartments besides the one which the tenant has abandoned, the landlord's duty to mitigate consists of making reasonable efforts to re-let the apartment. In such cases he must treat the apartment in question as if it was one of his vacant stock.

As part of his cause of action, the landlord shall be required to carry the burden of proving that he used reasonable diligence in attempting to re-let the premises. . . . While generally in contract actions the breaching party has the burden of proving that damages are capable of mitigation, here the landlord

---

5. [FN 4] . . . However, we reserve for another day the question of whether a landlord must mitigate damages in a commercial setting.

will be in a better position to demonstrate whether he exercised reasonable diligence in attempting to re-let the premises. . . .

The *Sommer v. Kridel* case presents a classic example of the unfairness which occurs when a landlord has no responsibility to minimize damages. Sommer waited 15 months and allowed $4658.50 in damages to accrue before attempting to re-let the apartment. Despite the availability of a tenant who was ready, willing and able to rent the apartment, the landlord needlessly increased the damages by turning her away. While a tenant will not necessarily be excused from his obligations under a lease simply by finding another person who is willing to rent the vacated premises, . . . here there has been no showing that the new tenant would not have been suitable. We therefore find that plaintiff could have avoided the damages which eventually accrued, and that the defendant was relieved of his duty to continue paying rent. Ordinarily we would require the tenant to bear the cost of any reasonable expenses incurred by a landlord in attempting to re-let the premises, but no such expenses were incurred in this case. . . .

In assessing whether the landlord has satisfactorily carried his burden, the trial court shall consider, among other factors, whether the landlord, either personally or through an agency, offered or showed the apartment to any prospective tenants, or advertised it in local newspapers. Additionally, the tenant may attempt to rebut such evidence by showing that he proffered suitable tenants who were rejected. However, there is no standard formula for measuring whether the landlord has utilized satisfactory efforts in attempting to mitigate damages, and each case must be judged upon its own facts. . . .

The judgment in *Sommer v. Kridel* is reversed. . . .

Notes

1. *The landlord's duty:*   Articulate precisely the landlord's duty when seeking damages from a defaulting tenant. Note the lease's prohibition against assignments and transfers. What impact, if any, do you think that provision had on the court's holding? The court left open the question whether a landlord must mitigate damages in a commercial setting. *Should* such a duty attach to commercial landlords?

2. *Retroactivity:*   The trial judge concluded that the lease had been drawn to reflect the settled law of New Jersey at the time. At what point in time would the court's new standard bind the landlord? Would the result have been different (or, should it have been different) if the landlord had not turned down a ready, willing, and able tenant to replace defendant James Kridel?

3. *The landlord's remedies:*   The duty to mitigate serves as a defense to a landlord's claims against a defaulting tenant. But what are the underlying remedies that landlords can pursue? Recall the three remedies described in the "*A Place to Start*" box at the beginning of section C.1. Under the first option, the landlord can declare the lease terminated and seek "damages" from the tenant,

generally measured as the difference (if any) between the fair market value of the leasehold and the total rent reserved in the lease. This damage remedy is limited to a reasonable period of time, rather than the entire unexpired term. Under the second remedy, the landlord can retake on the tenant's behalf, find a substitute tenant, and recover from the defaulting tenant any deficiency between the original and substitute rental amounts. In such case, the landlord can *accelerate* the original rent owed, without waiting to sue the original tenant each month when the rent would have become due. Finally, under the third remedy, the landlord can hold the original tenant responsible for rent, unless modified by a duty to mitigate as imposed in *Sommer.* If allowed, the landlord can recover the full amount promised in the original lease. But, unless the lease contains an acceleration clause in accordance with the law of the jurisdiction, the landlord must bring multiple lawsuits to recover each rental installment after it comes due each month. Powell on Real Property § 17.05[2] (Michael Allan Wolf, gen. ed. 2015).

4. *A changing world—from trend to majority rule:* How would this case have come out under the common law? What had changed to justify a different result? The court stated (in 1977) that the trend favored imposing a mitigation requirement on landlords. Today, at least one treatise reckons that a majority of American jurisdictions now impose some duty on landlords to mitigate damages. Powell on Real Property § 17.05[2] (Michael Allan Wolf, gen. ed. 2015).

Crechale & Polles, Inc. v. Smith

295 So. 2d 275 (Miss. 1974)

Reading Guide

The previous case considered a tenant who abandoned too soon—defaulting on the lease before its expiration. This case considers the opposite situation—where the defendant overstays the lease term and becomes a "holdover tenant." In that situation, what are the rights of the parties?

RODGERS, J.

This action originated in the Chancery Court of the First Judicial District of Hinds County, Mississippi, pursuant to a bill for specific performance of a lease contract filed by Crechale and Polles, Inc., appellant herein. The court awarded the complainants one thousand seven hundred and fifty dollars ($1,750.00) in back rent payment, and seven hundred sixty dollars ($760.00) for damages to the leasehold premises, as well as costs incurred in the proceeding. From this judgment appellant files this appeal and appellees cross-appeal.

The testimony shows that on February 5, 1964, the appellant, Crechale and Polles, Inc., a Mississippi corporation, entered into a lease agreement with appellees, John D. Smith, Jr. and Mrs. Gloria Smith ("Smith"), with appellant as lessor and appellees as lessees. The lease was for a term of five (5) years commencing February 7, 1964, and expiring February 6, 1969, with rental in the amount of one thousand two hundred fifty dollars ($1,250.00) per month.

Smith was informed near the end of his lease that the new building which he planned to occupy would not be complete until a month or two after his present lease expired. With this in mind, he arranged a meeting with his landlord, Crechale, in late December, 1968, or early January, 1969, for the purpose of negotiating an extension of the lease on a month-to-month basis. The outcome of this meeting is one of the focal points of this appeal and the parties' stories sharply conflict. Crechale maintains that he told Smith that since he was trying to sell the property, he did not want to get involved in any month-to-month rental. Smith asserts that Crechale informed him that he was trying to sell the building, but that he could stay in it until it was sold or Smith's new building was ready. Smith's attorney drafted a thirty (30) day extension, but Crechale refused to sign it, saying, "Oh, go ahead. It's all right." Crechale denies that he was ever given the document to sign.

The following is a chronological explanation of the events which led to the subsequent litigation:

February 4, 1969—Smith sent a letter to Crechale confirming their oral agreement to extend the lease on a monthly basis.

February 6, 1969—Crechale wrote Smith denying the existence of any oral agreement concerning extension of the lease and requesting that Smith quit and vacate the premises upon expiration of the term at midnight, February 6, 1969. The letter also advised Smith that he was subject to payment of double rent for any holdover.

March 3, 1969—Smith paid rent for the period of February to March. The check was accepted and cashed by Crechale.

April 6, 1969—Smith paid rent for the period of March to April, but the check was not accepted by Chechale, because it was for "final payment."

April 7, 1969—Smith sent a telegram to Crechale stating that he was tendering the premises for purposes of lessor's inventory. The telegram confirmed a telephone conversation earlier that day in which Crechale refused to inventory the building.

April 19, 1969—Approximately three and one-half (3-1/2) months after the expiration of the lease, Crechale's attorney wrote Smith stating that since the lessee had held over beyond the normal term, the lessor was treating this as a renewal of the lease for a new term expiring February 6, 1974.

April 24, 1969—Smith again tendered the check for the final month's occupancy and it was rejected by Crechale.

April 29, 1969—Crechale's attorney wrote Smith again stating the lessor's intention to consider the lessees' holdover as a renewal of the terms of the lease.

There was no further communication between the parties until a letter dated May 15, 1970, from Crechale to Smith requesting that Smith pay the past-due rent or vacate the premises.

May 27, 1970-Smith's attorney tendered the keys to the premises to Crechale.

Subsequently, this lawsuit was filed by Crechale to recover back rent and damages beyond ordinary wear and tear to the leasehold premises. . . .

The appellant, Crechale and Polles, Inc., contends that the appellees became holdover tenants for a new term under the contract at the election of the landlord appellant, and that appellees owe appellant the rent due each month up to the filing of suit, less the rent paid; and, in addition thereto, it is entitled to specific performance of the holdover contract. This argument is based upon the general rule expressed in 3 Thompson on Real Property s 1024, at 65-66 (1959), wherein it is said:

> As a general rule, a tenancy from year to year is created by the tenant's holding over after the expiration of a term for years and the continued payment of the yearly rent reserved. . . . By remaining in possession of leased premises after the expiration of his lease, a tenant gives the landlord the option of treating him as a trespasser or as a tenant for another year. . . .

. . . An examination of the testimony in this case has convinced us that the appellant is not entitled to specific performance so as to require the appellees to pay rent for a new term of the rental contract as a holdover tenant for the following reasons.

After receiving a letter from one of the appellees in which appellee Smith confirmed an alleged agreement to extend the lease on a month-to-month basis, Crechale immediately wrote Smith and denied that there was such an agreement, and demanded that Smith quit and vacate the premises at the end of the lease.

In addition to the rule expressed in 3 Thompson on Real Property s 1024, above cited, another rule is tersely expressed in American Law of Property s 3.33, at 237 (1952) as follows: "When a tenant continues in possession after the termination of his lease, the landlord has an election either to evict him, treat him as a trespasser it is said, or to hold him as a tenant."

The letter from the appellant dated February 6, 1969, was an effective election on the part of appellant to terminate the lease and to treat the appellees as trespassers.

After having elected not to accept the appellees as tenants, the appellant could not at a later date, after failing to pursue his remedy to evict the tenants, change the election so as to hold the appellees as tenants for a new term.

It is pointed out by the text writer in 49 Am. Jur. 2d under the title of Landlord and Tenant that:

> After the landlord has once exercised his election not to hold the tenant for another term, his right to hold him is lost. On the other hand, if he has signified his election to hold the tenant for another term he cannot thereafter rescind such election and treat the tenant as a trespasser, since his election when once exercised is binding upon the landlord as well as the tenant. . . .

Although the landlord, appellant, expressly refused to extend the lease on a month-to-month basis, nevertheless, the appellant accepted and cashed the rent check for the month of February. The normal effect of such action by the landlord is tantamount to extension of the lease for the period of time for which the check was accepted, unless, of course, the landlord had elected to treat the tenant as a holdover tenant. . . .

On April 6, 1969, the tenants mailed a check for rent for the month of March accompanied by a letter stating that the enclosed check represented the final payment of rent. The next day the tenants tendered the lease premises to the landlord and requested an inventory of certain personal property described in the lease. The landlord refused to accept the tender and rejected the check as a final payment. On April 19, 1969 (three and one-half (3-1/2) months after the expiration of the lease) the landlord attempted to change its position. It then notified the tenants that it had elected to treat them as holdover tenants so as to extend the lease for another term.

We are of the opinion that once a landlord elects to treat a tenant as a trespasser and refuses to extend the lease on a month-to-month basis, but fails to pursue his remedy of ejecting the tenant, and accepts monthly checks for rent due, he in effect agrees to an extension of the lease on a month-to-month basis. . . .

The appellant contends that the decree of the trial court awarded inadequate damages to the appellant. The appellant fails, however, to point out any fact which would indicate to this Court wherein the decree of the trial court is manifestly wrong. We think that this issue of damages was a question of fact for the chancellor, and from an examination of the record we cannot say that the chancellor was manifestly wrong. . . .

We cannot agree with the cross-appellants' contention that the chancellor was manifestly wrong in awarding the amount of damages for the items set out in the decree of the chancery court. We have carefully examined each item in the light of the briefs, and we find no reversible error in the ruling of the trial court.

We hold, therefore, that the decree of the trial court should be and is hereby affirmed.

INZER, ROBERTSON, WALKER, AND BROOM, JJ., concur.

Notes

1. *Holdover tenants:*   What was the nature of the Smiths' interest when they first became "holdovers" by remaining in possession after the expiration of the original lease? What was the range of remedies available to Crechale and Polles upon the holding over by the Smiths? Which one did Crechale and Polles elect? What facts support that conclusion?

2. *The new tenancy:*   The court noted that the landlord "expressly refused to extend the lease on a month-to-month basis," and yet held that he "in effect agree[d] to an extension of the lease on a month-to-month basis." How can that be?

2. Maintaining the Premises

As we have seen, landlords and tenants have important rights (and duties) with respect to possession. Here, we take up a second set of rights and duties—those related to the physical condition of the premises. *See generally* William B. Stoebuck & Dale A. Whitman, The Law of Property (3d ed. 2000), §§ 6.23-.24, 6.30-.33, 6.38-.45.

| A Place to Start | The Condition of the Premises |

- *Tenant's rights:*

  - *The covenant of quiet enjoyment and constructive eviction:* Under the majority rule, in every lease, the landlord impliedly warrants that the tenant's possession will not be disturbed, either by the landlord or by a third party with a superior right to possession. As an extension of this warranty against actual physical eviction, acts or omissions of the landlord that render the premises substantially unsuitable for their intended purpose, or that substantially interfere with the tenant's quiet enjoyment of the premises, constitute a *constructive eviction* under the majority view. The tenant's obligations under the lease (such as the duty to pay rent) are *dependent* on the landlord's satisfaction of this implied *covenant of quiet enjoyment*; therefore, upon the landlord's breach, the tenant can choose to terminate the lease, provided that the tenant abandons the premises within a reasonable time (thereby completing the constructive "eviction").

  - *The implied warranty of habitability (IWH):* Under the common law doctrine of *caveat emptor* ("let the buyer [or lessee] beware"), the landlord had no duty to keep the premises in good repair. Under the majority view today, residential leases contain an *implied warranty of habitability* that the landlord will maintain the premises in "habitable" condition for the duration of the tenancy. In contrast to constructive evictions, tenants need not abandon the premises in order to pursue a remedy. Instead, if the landlord breaches the IWH, the tenant can remain in possession and pursue a variety of remedies. These remedies generally make the tenant's duty to pay rent *dependent*, at least in part, on the landlord's maintenance of habitable conditions.

- *Landlord's rights:*

  - *Avoidance of waste:* As we saw in the last chapter, the holders of present estates (such as tenants) have a duty to avoid waste for the benefit of the holders of future interests (here, landlords who hold reversionary interests). The doctrine of *affirmative waste* protects the landlord's reversionary interest from unauthorized voluntary acts by the tenant that cause permanent and substantial injury. Tenants also have a duty to avoid *permissive waste* by failing to take reasonable care of the premises, and instead must make minor repairs to avoid unwarranted deterioration. The scope of the tenant's duty varies by jurisdiction and can be affected by the corresponding duty in the landlord to maintain the habitability of the premises.

DIGGING DEEPER: Should courts imply lease terms beyond those that the parties negotiated, and if so, under what rationale? Substantively, how high should the implied standard be: what level of *habitability* should landlords maintain, and what level of *waste* should tenants avoid?

Teller v. McCoy

253 S.E.2d 114 (W. Va. 1978)

Reading Guide

Teller v. McCoy is a landmark decision recognizing the implied warranty of habitability in West Virginia.

◆ *Implied lease terms:* Should courts imply terms into the lease for which the parties did not bargain? If so, under what rationale?

◆ *The interplay of common law and statutory law:* Notice the relationship between statutory law and common law in *Teller*. What functions are better performed by the judiciary, and what functions are better left to the legislature?

McGRAW, J.

This proceeding is before us on certified question. Pursuant to W.Va. Code s 58-5-2, the Circuit Court of Logan County, West Virginia, certified to this Court the following questions of law upon the joint motion of the plaintiffs and defendant . . . :

1. Whether failure of a landlord to maintain rental premises in a habitable condition and otherwise remedy defects to the premises which render the residence uninhabitable is in violation of a landlord's implied warranty of habitability to a tenant? And if so, whether it is subject to waiver?

2. Whether a landlord's warranty of habitability and the tenant's covenant to pay rent are mutually dependent?

3. Whether failure of a landlord to maintain the premises in habitable condition constitutes a failure of consideration and a breach of the rental agreement?

4. Whether a landlord's breach allows to the tenant one or more of the following remedies: (a) a right of action or setoff for the difference between the agreed rent and the fair rental value of the premises in their defective condition; (b) after reasonable notice and opportunity to a landlord to correct the defective conditions, to repair the defects himself and deduct the repair cost from the rent; and (c) vacation of the premises terminating a tenant's obligation to pay rent, and (d) what damages, if any, are recoverable by the landlord or tenant in the event of breach of either party?

5. Whether a breach of the implied warranty of habitability is a defense to a landlord's action for rent, damages, or unlawful detainer [withholding of possession]?

I . . .

At common law, a lease for real estate was considered a conveyance or sale of an estate in land for a term. A burden of inspection was placed upon the tenant and fraud apart, there was no law against letting a tumble-down house. The only way that a tenant at common law could assure the fitness of a leasehold was by exacting an express covenant from the landlord that the property was to be fit for the purpose intended. Absent a statute to the contrary, it was uniformly held that there was no implied warranty of habitability or fitness for the purpose leased. . . .

These rules developed out of an agrarian economy beginning in the Middle Ages at a time when the land, not the simple buildings and fixtures, was the focal point of the transaction. . . . The rent was deemed to issue from the land itself without reference to the condition of the buildings or structures upon it. Thus, the rent was due even if the buildings were not habitable or fit for occupancy. This strict application of caveat emptor was consistent with the agrarian social setting under which the leasehold interests were created. It was accepted that the small, simple structures affixed to realty would be repaired by the farmer-tenant. . . .

But as society evolved, so did the setting under which the common law land-lord-tenant relationship existed. . . . The courts, recognizing that some tenants primarily seek living quarters and not land, implied a warranty of habitability into short-term leases of furnished dwellings. Where the lease was for an apartment or room that later was totally destroyed by fire, the courts discharged the tenant from future rent, again recognizing that the tenant's true object in such cases was not land, but a place to live. *Graves v. Berdan*, 26 N.Y. 498 (1863). . . .

[At common law, the] covenants in a lease were deemed to be independent, not dependent. Thus the duty of a tenant in possession to pay rent was accepted as essentially absolute. . . . But the courts implied into leases a "covenant of quiet enjoyment" to relieve a tenant from the obligation to pay rent when he was deprived of possession or disturbed by hostile claimants or defects in title. Under this doctrine, the landlord, through his acts or omissions, was deemed to "evict" the tenant by depriving him of the beneficial enjoyment of the demised premises. *Dyett v. Pendleton*, 8 Cow. 727 (N.Y. 1826). . . . Thus a tenant compelled to vacate any or all of an unfit and uninhabitable dwelling was deemed to be constructively "evicted" under law and was relieved from further rent liability.[6] . . . "This rule allowed the court to mitigate some of the

---

6. [FN 6] "Constructive eviction has proved an insufficient remedy for those most likely to have resort to it, low income tenants. The dilemma it raises for them is that they must continue to pay rent and endure the conditions of untenantability or abandon the premises and hope to find another dwelling which, in these times of severe housing shortage, is likely

injustices stemming from strict application of the independent covenants rule without repudiating the rule's basic premise that the lease was essentially a conveyance of a possessory interest in land for a term and not a contract for a dwelling suitable for human occupation." *Boston Housing Authority v. Hemingway*, 293 N.E.2d 831, 837 (Mass. 1973).

Certified Question No. 4(c) asks whether the landlord's failure to maintain the premises in a fit and habitable condition would allow the tenant to vacate the premises thereby terminating the obligation to pay rent. Constructive eviction . . . would afford the tenant that remedy.

Since W. Va. Const. art. 8, s 21 . . . hold[s] that drastic changes in the common law can be made only by the Legislature, we must next review those relevant changes that have been effectuated by statute. [The court reviewed numerous portions of state law addressing housing standards.] . . .

We therefore are compelled to agree completely with the following often-quoted passage from one of the pioneer American cases recognizing the implied warranty of habitability:

> . . . To follow the old rule of no implied warranty of habitability in leases would, in our opinion, be inconsistent with the current legislative policy concerning housing standards. The need and social desirability of adequate housing for people in this era of rapid population increases is too important to be rebuffed by that obnoxious legal cliché, caveat emptor. Permitting landlords to rent "tumbledown" houses is at least a contributing cause of such problems as urban blight, juvenile delinquency and high property taxes for conscientious landowners.

Pines v. Perssion, 111 N.W.2d 409, 412-13 (Wis. 1961).

We, therefore, hold that in a written or oral lease of residential premises, there is an implied warranty that the landlord shall at the commencement of a tenancy, deliver the dwelling unit and surrounding premises in a fit and habitable condition, and shall thereafter maintain the leased property in such condition.[7]

II

The Legislature's progressive abrogation of the common law no-repair rule was crystallized on March 11, 1978, when it added to our landlord-tenant

---

to be as uninhabitable as the last." *King v. Moorehead*, 495 S.W.2d 65 (Mo. Ct. App. 1973). . . . Even when alternative shelter is found, the tenant runs the risk of not being able to prove the abandoned premises were rendered uninhabitable and, consequently, might be held liable for substantial rent. Another pitfall in constructive eviction is that the tenant is deemed to "waive" the defects unless he abandons within a "reasonable time."

7. [FN 10] Twenty-nine states and the District of Columbia have adopted by statute or case law the implied warranty of habitability. . . . Most of these changes were antedated by the innumerable commentators who advocated adoption of the implied warranty. . . .

law . . . a new section which requires the landlord to deliver and maintain the rental dwelling unit in a fit and habitable condition.

This Court today, by implying a warranty of habitability into residential leases, intends in no way to impose upon the landlord a greater burden than that set forth by the Legislature in our new statute. The landlord's duty under the implied warranty and the statute are identical. That the case at bar arose before the effective date of the new statute is, then, of little consequence insofar as the landlord's duty is concerned. . . .

Mutual Dependency of Covenants

A lease under real property law was viewed as a conveyance for a term, and its covenants were not mutually dependent. Under such an interpretation, the duty to pay rent was not dependent upon the landlord's compliance with the terms of the lease. Thus, even if a landlord agreed in the lease to keep the premises in good repair, his failure to do so would not relieve the tenant of his independent duty to pay rent.

But this common law approach arose before the development in contract law of mutually dependent covenants. The authorities agree today that the modern lease is both a conveyance and a contract. . . .

In response to the second certified question, we hold that since a lease of a residential dwelling unit is to be treated and construed as any other contract, the covenant to pay rent and the warranty of habitability are mutually dependent.

Contractual Remedies

Upon recognizing that a lease for urban living quarters is essentially a contract, the courts have uniformly made available to the tenant faced with the material breach of warranty the same common law contract remedies of damages, reformation and rescission . . . We, too, so hold.[8]

Therefore in further answer to Certified Question No. 4(c) as to whether the tenant faced with the landlord's breach of the warranty can vacate the premises and thereby terminate his obligation to pay rent, we need look only to the

---

8. [FN 14] It appears, however, that the Legislature in the new W. Va. Code s 37-6-30(c) has specifically rendered unavailable the contract remedy of specific performance to a tenant "in arrears in payment of rent." This provision may tend to accelerate that which some say is the major underlying problem:

> The major limitations of the warranty of habitability lie in its inherent failure to mandate repair of the premises by the landlord, to provide enough money damages for tenants to make substantial repairs to deteriorated housing, and to be self-enforcing. A tenant may have to return to court month after month to obtain a rent abatement from a recalcitrant landlord. Because the economic sanction of the warranty of habitability is limited, moreover, tenants will often find that landlords would rather accept the abatement than make the repairs, thus leaving the tenant with a lower monthly rent but unimproved living conditions. Whether the rent reduction will be sufficient to allow the tenant to make the repairs personally will depend on the individual case.

A.B.A. Advisory Commission on Urban Growth, *Housing for All Under Law*, 596 (1978).

longstanding contract law of rescission. Breach of contract "so substantial as to tend to defeat the very object of the contract" . . . permits the injured party to rescind the contract. The warranty of habitability, a covenant upon which the very duty to pay rent depends, is certainly a vital and essential provision of the lease. Breach of this covenant, upon which the vitality of the lease depends, would entitle the lessee to rescind the lease, to vacate the premises and to be relieved of any further rental obligation. Because the typical residential tenant enters into a lease in order to obtain a habitable place to live, his failure to receive such a place to live would unquestionably justify rescission.

Certified Question 5 asks whether a breach of the implied warranty of habitability is a defense to a landlord's action for rent or damages. As is the case with many of the questions certified, the answer is to be found in the long-standing contract law of this jurisdiction. The answer to this particular question appears cogently in *Franklin v. Pence*, 36 S.E.2d 505, 50 (W. Va. 8 1945): "When the covenants are dependent and mutual, as here, a party who violates the contract cannot recover damages which result from its violation by the other party." Thus, breach by the landlord of the implied warranty of habitability, a material covenant upon which the duty to pay rent depends, may be raised as a defense in a landlord's action for rent. . . .

As to the "repair and deduct" inquiry in Certified Question 4(b), our research reveals that only one of the many cases adopting the implied warranty . . . allows the tenant this remedy. We feel at this time, as have apparently the majority of courts dealing with the issue, that the wide range of contract remedies available to the tenant are adequate to enforce fulfillment of the implied warranty. . . .

The Measure of Damages

But while it is widely accepted that a residential lease is to be treated as a contract and that the common law remedies for breach are applicable, the courts addressing the issue have had great difficulty formulating an appropriate measure of damages applicable to a breach of implied warranty. . . . Some courts adopt the "difference in value" approach. Under this method, the tenant's damages is measured by the difference between the fair market value of the premises if they had been as warranted and the fair rental value of the premises as they were during occupancy by the tenant in the unsafe and unsanitary conditions. . . . If the fair market value of an apartment in its defective condition is $100, yet would be worth $200 but for the breach of warranty, then the tenant sustains $100 per month in general damages. The actual monthly rent contracted for is irrelevant under this approach, except perhaps as evidence of the apartment's fair market value. The other approach to ascertaining damages is the "percentage reduction of use" method . . . under which the court reduced the tenant's rental obligation by a percentage corresponding to the relative reduction of use of the leased premises caused by the landlord's breach. Under this method, if the tenant, due to the landlord's breach, is denied the use of ten percent of an apartment renting for $200, then the tenant sustained damages of $20.00 per month.

We feel that neither approach should be the exclusive mode of assessing damages in such cases. Of the two, the "difference in value approach" is far more widely accepted and we adopt it, in part, as the measure of damages in cases involving the breach of the implied warranty of habitability. But, money damages so assessed, while appropriate in the commercial cases, are inadequate in most residential landlord-tenant tenant cases, since the residential tenant who endures a breach of the warranty of habitability normally does not actually lose only money. The typical residential tenant rents a dwelling for shelter, not profit. When the warranty is breached, he loses, instead, such intangibles as the ability to take a bath or use hot water as frequently as he would like, he may be forced to worry about the health of his children endangered by rats, roaches, or other undesirable pests, or he may be denied the use of certain rooms in the apartment because there is odor, severe water leakage, or no heat. . . .

Therefore, in response to the fourth certified question, we hold that when the warranty of habitability is breached, the tenant's damages are measured by the difference between the fair market value of the premises if they had been as warranted and the fair rental value of the premises as they were during the occupancy by the tenant in the unsafe and unsanitary condition. However, the tenant may additionally recover damages for annoyance and inconvenience proven to have resulted from the breach. . . .

The Implied Warranty at Trial

. . . [T]he determination of whether a landlord breached the warranty is a question of fact to be determined by the circumstances of each case. The breach must be of a substantial nature rendering the premises uninhabitable and unfit. Thus minor housing code violations or other deficiencies which individually or collectively do not adversely affect the dwelling's habitability or fitness would not entitle the tenant to a deduction in rent. In making the determination of whether the premises were uninhabitable and unfit, housing code violations and deficiencies should be scrutinized in light of such things as their nature, the length of time the persisted, their effect on safety and sanitation, the age of the structure, and the amount of rent charged.

Waiver

Allowing a tenant to "waive" the warranty could be tantamount to permitting the landlord to violate some statute, regulation or code enacted for the benefit of not only that tenant, but future tenants, adjoining tenants and landowners as well. . . .

Additionally, since "(i)t is fair to presume that no individual would voluntarily choose to live in a dwelling that had become unsafe for human habitation," *Bowles v. Mahoney*, 202 F.2d 320, 326 (D.C. Cir. 1952) (Bazelon, J. dissenting), we hold that waivers of the implied warranty of habitability are against public policy. Given the proliferation of "form leases" and the current scarcity of habitable dwellings, there exists a distinct danger that such waivers would become routine. If tenants seeking the scarce available shelter are compelled to waive their rights and accept uninhabitable dwellings, then the protection accorded by the implied warranty and the statutes could become meaningless.

III

This Court, along with many others, has concluded that the harsh common law rules of property, riddled historically with numerous exceptions, no longer exclusively govern the residential lease in light of legislative enactments and intent. . . .

Neely, J, concurring in part, dissenting in part. . . .

. . . I do agree with the majority's resolution of these questions insofar as they hold that before W. Va. Code, 37-6-30 (1978) became effective it would be proper to imply a covenant of habitability and that such covenant was not independent of the duty to pay rent. Everything else in the majority opinion is pure dicta and represents nothing more than the philosophy of the majority writer. . . .

The majority opinion would imply that everyone has a natural law right to accommodations which would reflect credit on the Ritz Hotel. Experience in the last thirty years, however, adequately demonstrates that the creation of new law does not usually create new wealth; in fact, wealth can be equitably redistributed only after, not before, it has been created. . . .

. . . The leading cases adopting an implied covenant of habitability arose predominantly in urban areas plagued by extensive ghettos in which slum dwellers were charged almost as much for slum housing as "middle class" people were charged for acceptable housing. Part of this phenomenon was the result of de facto racial discrimination, part of the urge of the poor to live in a hospitable community, and part of a lack of social skills which would permit the exploited to seek alternative accommodations. . . . Most of these areas make West Virginia's largest city of Charleston, which has a population well under eighty thousand, look like a virtual suburban haven. To the extent that deplorable conditions . . . exist in West Virginia they should be corrected; no person should be required to pay the same amount of money for a shack that he would pay for a modern apartment and no one should be permitted to be exploited in the market place because he is a different color or has any other background which engenders prejudice. However, a covenant of habitability cannot serve to correct every conceivable inconvenience that interferes with a tenant's enjoyment of leased premises. In my estimation, a covenant of habitability amounts only to a landlord's promise that if something is provided with a leased premise then it will work absent some specific disclaimer. For example, if an elevator is provided, the tenant can expect it to operate; if a toilet is provided, the tenant can expect it to flush; if a heater is provided, the tenant can expect it to heat; but, a tenant cannot expect a landlord to increase the size of rooms, provide elaborate lighting, or install the most expensive heating system ever devised by man.

I do not dispute for a moment that it would be wonderful if everyone could inhabit housing meeting both his taste and his budget but, unfortunately, the majority opinion cannot build houses, lower rents, or in any other way create more housing than already exists. Many people live in quarters which are less than luxurious because they cannot afford to pay more than what they already pay for rent. Ritz Hotel type housing cannot be provided where none otherwise exists unless someone pays for it. In our economy that means either (1) the landlord, (2) the tenant, or (3) the government. The government is trying to do its share, but its resources are limited. The landlord cannot make substantial renovations without passing his costs on to the tenant, and the tenant may then find that he has been given more luxury than he can afford. . . .

We do not do the people of this State a favor by taking dilapidated houses off the rental market if concomitantly we cannot provide alternative housing. Furthermore, we should not place ourselves in the position of the totalitarians who, allegedly, come to the Revolution intending to force feed strawberries and cream down the throats of everyone. . . .

MILLER, J., concurring in part and dissenting in part [omitted].

Notes

1. *Covenants of quiet enjoyment and constructive eviction, compared:* Carefully explain each doctrine; notice particularly how the two doctrines are similar and how they are different. From a tenant's perspective, what are the strengths of each? The limitations? Can the tenant waive the IWH? Why or why not?

2. *The remedy—retroactive or forward looking?* Is the implied warranty of habitability retroactive—that is, does it give the tenant a remedy for the rental of substandard housing during a period before the court announced the new standard of habitability? What is the court's rationale for taking this

approach? Recall *Sommer v. Kridel* (section C.1, above)—did it raise similar questions of retroactivity? How do the two situations compare?

3. *Majority and dissent:*   On what points did the majority and dissenting Justice Neely agree, and on what points did they disagree? Which position is more persuasive?

4. *A changing world—a revolution in the rights of the tenant and a housing market in flux:*   Beginning in the early 1970s, many common law principles of landlord-tenant law began to give way to accommodate the modern reality of urban tenants. As explained by one treatise, "This is particularly true of the law governing the rights of the tenant, a body of law in which profound, if not revolutionary, changes have occurred." Powell on Real Property § 16.01 (Michael Allan Wolf, gen. ed. 2015). The judiciary has been a "central moving force in the modernization of landlord-tenant law" through its application of modern contract principles to leases, including the doctrine of dependency of covenants (as applied in *Teller v. McCoy*), and the duty to mitigate damages (as applied in *Sommer v. Kridel). Powell* at §§ 16.01 & 16.02(1)(b).

The implied warranty of habitability, as well as the covenant of quiet enjoyment, affect a significant—and growing—segment of the population. As one commentator explains, the prospect of homeownership remains out of reach for many:

> Homeownership—long touted as the American Dream and promoted through government policies—is on the decline. Although more than 69% of Americans owned their homes in 2005, the financial crisis, plummeting property values, and rampant foreclosures have worked in combination to decrease that rate to 64.7% today [2014]. As the percentage of homeowners drops, the number of rental households increases significantly—five to ten million more Americans rent today than a decade ago. Previously, the primacy of homeownership as a policy and personal goal was both unchallenged and widespread, but economic realities of the past several years have tarnished the homeownership ideal. Furthermore, homeownership has increasingly become financially unattainable. Today's renters may either be unable to purchase a home or simply opt out of the property ownership model. The American Dream is in flux.

> Compared to owner occupants, renters represent a distinct demographic. Renters are typically younger and more likely to be unmarried and female. The median income of renters is lower than that of homeowners. Additionally, renters are more likely to be nonwhite. Moreover, many specific, vulnerable populations in our society are far more likely to rent than own their homes, including single mothers, new immigrants, and uneducated and unskilled persons. . . .

Andrea J. Boyack, *American Dream in Flux: The Endangered Right to Lease a Home*, 49 Real Prop. Tr. & Est. L.J. 203, 204-05 (2014) (arguing that private neighborhood covenants prohibiting the rental of homes harm the rights of would-be landlords, would-be tenants, and perpetuate broader social harms as well). Do you own your own home, or aspire to do so someday? Is it part of your "American dream"?

Problem

As we have seen, in deciding whether to adopt new common law rules, courts such as the *Teller* court frequently rely on policy analysis. Recall the Skills Practice exercise from Chapter 2 and its explanation of policy-based arguments. Then, reconstruct the following two policy arguments from *Teller*:

Majority: The majority declined to hold that tenants can waive the implied warranty of habitability. Complete the following policy argument:

> *If tenants can waive the IWH, then . . . , because. . . .*

What type of authority would bolster the policy prediction of the majority and of tenants?

Dissent: The dissent believed that experience over the 30 years preceding the decision demonstrated that the "the creation of new law does not create new wealth" and "a covenant of habitability cannot serve to correct every conceivable inconvenience that interferes with a tenant's enjoyment of leased premises." Complete the following policy argument:

> *If we take dilapidated houses off the market, then . . . , because. . . .*

What type of authority would bolster the policy prediction of the dissent and landlords?

3. Nondiscrimination

A variety of laws have sought to tackle discriminatory practices in the rental and sale of housing. The Civil Rights Act of 1866 admonished,

> All citizens of the United States shall have the same right, in every State and Territory, as is enjoyed by white citizens thereof to inherit, purchase, lease, sell, hold, and convey real and personal property.

42 U.S.C. § 1982. At first, § 1982 was used to stop governmental discrimination, but not to thwart discrimination by private parties. Two years after the enactment of § 1982, the Fourteenth Amendment to the U.S. Constitution was ratified in 1868. That amendment provides, "no state shall . . . deny to any person . . . the equal protection of the laws." Like the Civil Rights Act, the Fourteenth Amendment would not be applied to prohibit private discrimination until prodded by the U.S. Supreme Court about a century later. In the

landmark case of *Shelley v. Kraemer*, 334 U.S. 1 (1948), the Court held that state court *enforcement* of private racially restrictive covenants supplied the "state action" necessary to trigger the protection of the Fourteenth Amendment. (We will study *Shelley v. Kraemer* in Chapter 10.) Similarly, the Supreme Court decided *Jones v. Alfred H. Mayer Co.*, 392 U.S. 409 (1968), which held that Congress intended for § 1982 to prohibit both private and governmental discrimination.

Card showing African American slave reaching freedom.
Lithograph by H.L. Stephens (c. 1863)
Source: Library of Congress, LC-USZC4-2521

Even after these developments, important gaps remained in the legal framework outlawing public and private discrimination in the rental and sale markets for housing. Also in 1968, Congress passed the Fair Housing Act (FHA). Among other things, that legislation expands the range of protected classes and prohibited practices. The Fair Housing Act fills some, but not all, of the gaps remaining in the legal regime against housing discrimination.

The Fair Housing Act of 1968

42 U.S.C. §§ 3603, 3604

Reading Guide

- ◆ *Protected classes*: What seven classes of people does the Fair Housing Act protect?
- ◆ *Prohibited practices:* What practices does the Fair Housing Act prohibit?
- ◆ *Exemptions:* What types of properties does the Fair Housing Act exempt from its prohibitions? Why do you think Congress exempted such properties?
- ◆ *Sales and rentals:* Notice that the Fair Housing Act applies to both landlord-tenant transactions and to the sale of real estate (which we will consider in Chapter 7).

---

§ 3603. Effective dates of certain prohibitions. . . .

(b) **Exemptions:** Nothing in section 3604 of this title (other than subsection (c)) shall apply to—

(1) Any single-family house sold or rented by an owner: Provided, That such private individual owner does not own more than three such single-family houses at any one time: Provided further, That in the case of the sale of any such single-family house by a private individual owner not residing in such house at the time of such sale or who was not the most recent resident of such house prior to such sale, the exemption granted by his subsection shall apply only with respect to one such sale within any twenty-four month period: Provided further, That such bona fide private individual owner does not own any interest in, nor is there owned or reserved on his behalf, under any express or voluntary agreement, title to or any right to all or a portion of the proceeds from the sale or rental of, more than three such single-family houses at any one time: Provided further, That after December 31, 1969, the sale or rental of any such single-family house shall be excepted from the application of this subchapter only if such house is sold or rented (A) without the use in any manner of the sales or rental facilities or the sales or rental services of any real estate broker, agent, or salesman, or of such facilities or services of any person in the business

of selling or renting dwellings, or of any employee or agent of any such broker, agent, salesman, or person and (B) without the publication, posting or mailing, after notice, of any advertisement or written notice in violation of section 3604(c) of this title; but nothing in this proviso shall prohibit the use of attorneys, escrow agents, abstractors, title companies, and other such professional assistance as necessary to perfect or transfer the title, or

(2) Rooms or units in dwellings containing living quarters occupied or intended to be occupied by no more than four families living independently of each other, if the owner actually maintains and occupies one of such living quarters as his residence. . . .

§ 3604. Discrimination in the sale or rental of housing and other prohibited practices. . . . As made applicable by section 3603 of this title and except as exempted by sections 3603(b) and 3607 of this title, it shall be unlawful—

(a) To refuse to sell or rent after the making of a bona fide offer, or to refuse to negotiate for the sale or rental of, or otherwise make unavailable or deny, a dwelling to any person because of race, color, religion, sex, familial status,[9] or national origin.

(b) To discriminate against any person in the terms, conditions, or privileges of sale or rental of a dwelling, or in the provision of services or facilities in connection therewith, because of race, color, religion, sex, familial status, or national origin.

(c) To make, print, or publish, or cause to be made, printed, or published any notice, statement, or advertisement, with respect to the sale or rental of a dwelling that indicates any preference, limitation, or discrimination based on race, color, religion, sex, handicap, familial status, or national origin, or an intention to make any such preference, limitation, or discrimination.

(d) To represent to any person because of race, color, religion, sex, handicap, familial status, or national origin that any dwelling is not available for inspection, sale, or rental when such dwelling is in fact so available.

(e) For profit, to induce or attempt to induce any person to sell or rent any dwelling by representations regarding the entry or prospective entry into the neighborhood of a person or persons of a particular race, color, religion, sex, handicap, familial status, or national origin.

---

9. [Section 3602(k) defines "familial status" to mean "one or more individuals (who have not attained the age of 18 years) being domiciled with . . . a parent or another person having legal custody of such individual or individuals. . . ."—Eds.]

(f) (1) To discriminate in the sale or rental, or to otherwise make unavailable or deny, a dwelling to any buyer or renter because of a handicap[10] of . . . that person.

(2) To discriminate against any person in the terms, conditions, or privileges of sale or rental of a dwelling, or in the provision of services or facilities in connection with such dwelling, because of a handicap of . . . that person. . . .

(3) For purposes of this subsection, discrimination includes—

(A) a refusal to permit, at the expense of the handicapped person, reasonable modifications of existing premises occupied or to be occupied by such person if such modifications may be necessary to afford such person full enjoyment of the premises. . . .

(B) a refusal to make reasonable accommodations in rules, policies, practices, or services, when such accommodations may be necessary to afford such person equal opportunity to use and enjoy a dwelling; or

(C) in connection with the design and construction of covered multi-family dwellings for first occupancy after the date that is 30 months after September 13, 1988, a failure to design and construct those dwellings in such a manner that [is accessible]. . . .

Note

Going further—local ordinances: The federal Fair Housing Act provides a floor—a baseline of nondiscriminatory conduct for practices related to the rental or sale of real property. If they wish, states and local governments can provide additional layers of protection. In the following two examples, notice the interplay of federal, state, and local law.

§ 23.01.060 Discrimination in Selling, Renting, or Leasing Real Property Prohibited. (Portland, Oregon. Amended by Ordinance No. 175158, effective January 15, 2001.)

(A) It shall be unlawful to discriminate in selling, renting, or leasing real property on the basis of an individual's race, religion, color, sex, national origin, marital status, familial status, or disability, by committing any of the acts made

---

10. [Section 3602(h) defines "handicap" as "a physical or mental impairment which substantially limits one or more . . . major life activities, a record of having such an impairment, or being regarded as having such an impairment, but such term does not include current, illegal use of or addiction to a controlled substance. . . ."—Eds.]

unlawful under the provisions of Oregon Revised Statutes §§ 659.033 and 659.430.

(B) In addition, it shall be unlawful to discriminate in selling, renting, or leasing real property on the basis of an individual's sexual orientation, gender identity, source of income, or age if the individual is 18 years of age or older . . . by committing against any such individual any of the acts already made unlawful under Oregon Revised Statutes § 659.033 when committed against the categories of persons listed therein.

§ 5-1-51 Discrimination in sale or rental of housing. (Austin, Texas)

(A) A person may not refuse to sell or rent a dwelling to a person who has made a bona fide offer; refuse to negotiate for the sale or rental of a dwelling; or otherwise make unavailable or deny a dwelling to any person based on race, color, religion, sex, sexual orientation, gender identity, age, familial status, disability, marital status, student status, creed, or national origin.

(B) A person may not discriminate against a person in the terms, conditions, or privileges of sale or rental of a dwelling or in providing services or facilities in connection with the sale or rental, based on race, color, religion, sex, sexual orientation, gender identity, age, familial status, disability, marital status, student status, creed, or national origin.

(C) This section does not prohibit discrimination against a person because the person has been convicted under federal law or the law of any state of the illegal manufacture or distribution of a controlled substance, but does not permit discrimination based on a disability.

What, if anything, do the Portland and Austin municipal ordinances add to the federal Fair Housing Act? Can you think of any other classes of people that should be protected, or practices that should be prohibited?

Problem

Proving discriminatory intent: William Neithamer, a gay man who was HIV positive, viewed a townhouse advertised for rent by Brenneman Property Services. After Brenneman's agent showed the property to him, Neithamer submitted a rental application, credit references, and bank statements to the agent. He also told the agent that he had failed to make payments to some of his creditors a few years earlier, but that the reason was that several years ago he had devoted his financial resources to paying the medical bills of his partner, who died in 1994 of AIDS. Neithamer assured the agent that he had maintained good credit since 1994 and that the bank statements and credit references would confirm this. When the agent presented the application to Alida Stephens, the owner of the townhouse, she rejected it. Neithamer then offered to pay a second month's rent as an additional security, to obtain a co-signor for the lease, and/or to pre-pay one year's rent. Mrs. Stephens rejected all of these offers. Neithamer sued Brenneman and its agents, claiming that the defendants discriminated against him because of his sexual orientation and his medical disability in violation of the Fair Housing Act and in violation of the D.C. Human Rights Act (which forbids discrimination based on sexual orientation).

The court applied the following analytical framework, which had been used by several federal circuits to prove discrimination in cases where a plaintiff provided no *direct* evidence of discrimination:

> To establish a prima facie case of housing discrimination, the plaintiff must prove that: (1) he or she is a member of a statutorily protected class; (2) he or she applied for and was qualified to rent or purchase certain property or housing; (3) he or she was rejected; and (4) the housing or rental property remained available thereafter.
>
> The burden shifts to the defendants to offer a legitimate, non-discriminatory explanation for rejecting the plaintiff.
>
> If the defendants offer a reasonable and non-discriminatory explanation, then the burden shifts back to the plaintiff to establish that the defendants' explanation is pretextual and unworthy of credence.

The evidence shows that the property remained vacant as of the time the lawsuit was filed, and that the defendants sometimes rented property to applicants with poor credit. There is no evidence that the plaintiff specifically told the defendants of his sexual orientation, but the evidence shows that the defendants knew or suspected that he was gay. The evidence also demonstrates that the plaintiff was HIV positive, but the defendants deny that they ever knew or suspected that. The question is whether the plaintiff has provided enough evidence to give rise to an inference that the defendants perceived he was HIV positive.

Review the description of *fact-based analysis* from the Skills Practice exercise of Chapter 1 (section D). Then, carefully state the fact-based arguments that Neithamer must make to prevail in his action. Be sure to (1) read the *Neithamer* rule carefully, and (2) clearly list the facts that support each element of the rule. Has the plaintiff established a prima facie case? Can you think of a legitimate, nondiscriminatory explanation for rejecting the plaintiff that the defendants could offer? Would such explanation be believable, or would it likely be pretextual and unworthy of credence?

To help plaintiffs establish proof of a discriminatory motive, some courts adopt a burden-shifting framework, as described above. *See Neithamer v. Brenneman Property Services, Inc.*, 81 F. Supp. 2d 1, 4 (D.D.C. 1999) (applying burden-shifting framework of *McDonnell Douglas Corp. v. Green*, 411 U.S. 792, 802-05 (1973)). Going further, under the *disparate impact* theory of liability courts accept proof of discriminatory *effect*, rather than discriminatory *motive*, in appropriate cases. *See Texas Dep't of Housing and Community Affairs v. The Inclusive Communities Project*, 135 S. Ct. 2507 (2015) (holding disparate impact claims cognizable under the Fair Housing Act). We will take a closer look at disparate impact liability in Chapters 7 (real estate transactions) and 12 (zoning).

D. BEYOND THE BLACK LETTER: PARKING—THERE'S AN APP FOR THAT!

Can finding a parking space on crowded city streets become a peer-to-peer experience of the sharing economy (as we first discussed in Chapter 1)? Several startup companies have tried to make it so. MonkeyParking is a mobile application that allows a driver about to leave a parking spot on the street to auction it off to the highest bidder—typically for about $5, with MonkeyParking taking a 20% commission. The first car holds the spot until the second approaches, and then the two drivers switch places. Payment is made through an online transaction. Similar apps include Sweetch (a combination of "sweet" and "switch" parking spaces) and ParkModo.

MonkeyParking appeared in 2013 in San Francisco. In June 2014, the City Attorney issued a cease-and-desist order to the company, and also asked Apple to take down the mobile application from its App Store. The order asserted that the app violates a provision of the city code that specifically prohibits the buying, selling, or leasing of public on-street parking. It also claimed that the app "creates a predatory private market for public parking spaces," and it poses a safety hazard by encouraging cell phone use while driving, in violation of state law. MonkeyParking complied but, undaunted, soon announced plans to move to Santa Monica and Los Angeles. The company also announced a new version of its app that allows private driveway owners to rent out the public street space in front of their driveways for parallel parking (thereby blocking driveway access).

Critics claim that users of the apps hold public parking spaces hostage for private gain, and that they are selling something that they do not own. The app developers respond that users are simply sharing private information about the location of their vehicles; that the apps promote parking efficiency; and that cities should regulate, but not ban, the practice. *See* City & County of San Francisco, Office of the City Attorney, *News Release: Herrera Tells Monkey Parking to Drop Mobile App for Auctioning City Parking Spots*, June 23, 2014; Mike Billings, *San Francisco Tells Parking Startup to Stop Operations, Warns Two Others*, The Wall Street Journal, June 23, 2014.

Discussion Questions

1. *Property on the streets:*   Identify the precise right or service that mobile application users auction to others. Is it a property right? If so, is it a type of leasehold estate? If an app user has paid for metered parking and auctions off a space with time still left on the meter, could this be viewed as a sublease or assignment?

2. *Monkey business or the sharing economy?*   Are mobile applications like MonkeyParking a good idea? Are they an example of the sharing economy, or

an aberration from it? The founder of MonkeyParking argues that it should be regulated, not banned. Can you imagine any type of regulation that would be feasible and desirable?

E. SKILLS PRACTICE: CLIENT COUNSELING AND DRAFTING A RESIDENTIAL LEASE

Tyler just completed his first year of law school and is clerking for a law firm in Capital City, about two hours away from University City, where the state university (and law school) are located. The partners are so pleased with his work that they have already invited him to return to clerk again during the summer after his second year of law school. It is now August after Tyler's first year, and he took a weekend trip back to University City to look for a place to rent when school starts up again in the fall. He found a one-bedroom apartment that he really likes just a few blocks from the law school, located in the basement of a single-family home owned and occupied by Mrs. Lord. He would like the rent the apartment for his second and third years of law school. Ideally, he would like to move in about August 15 and move out a few months short of two years from now (right after graduation in early May). The rent is $700 per month, which is too much for him to pay next summer when he is working in Capital City again and also renting an apartment there. Luckily, though, Tyler has a lot of friends in University City and he is sure that he can find someone to live in the apartment next summer and take over the rent. His friend Thomas is a particularly good prospect. Thomas is a single father with occasional weekend custody of his son, so the pull-out sofa bed and fenced-in backyard would be perfect for Thomas and his son.

You are counsel for Mrs. Lord. You interviewed her last week and gathered the following information:

Mrs. Lord would like to rent to Tyler. She is impressed by his work history with the firm (with a job already lined up for next summer), and has received favorable reports back after checking his references and credit. Mrs. Lord is a widow and relies on the monthly income from the apartment. She has found that it is easiest to rent the apartment from August 15 to August 15, as students are returning to town for school. She would consider renting to Tyler for two years, during his second and third years of law school. She might be willing to accept a subletter or assignee for the summer months (after both his second and third years), but she is worried that Thomas (or another one of Tyler's friends) might not be as financially responsible and studious as Tyler, and might not make a good summer tenant.

You have scheduled another meeting with Mrs. Lord for the end of this week. Take note of the following steps as you prepare to counsel your client:

| A Place to Start | Skills: Client Counseling |

- *Clarify relevant issues and client interests:* Clarify the key legal issues posed by the client's problem. In addition, clarify the client's interests. Unlike a client's *position* (the outcome the client tells you she wants), *interests* reflect the reasons why the client has adopted a particular position, and typically incorporate client values, beliefs, and needs. For example, suppose a landlord's *position* is that she will not accept subleases or assignments. Her underlying *interests*, however, might be in maintaining a steady income stream, and in maintaining control over the selection of those who live in her apartment.

- *Articulate possible legal theories:* Identify all legal theories that might apply to your client's case. Challenge yourself to explain the law simply and clearly, yet accurately, as it applies to the facts of your client's case. Be sure to identify areas of uncertainty.

- *Identify client options:* Work with your client to "brainstorm" options to solve the problem. Think of as many potential courses of action as possible. Avoid becoming locked into your client's first articulated *position*, but instead keep her *interests* in mind as you develop a list of options together.

- *Explore consequences:* Explore the probable consequences of each option that you just identified. Working systematically through each option, be prepared to predict the likely legal outcome. Also be prepared to solicit your client's input as to the likely non-legal outcomes ("I liked that first young man who applied to rent my basement, but I worry that some of his nonstudent friends might just be too noisy to make good subtenants."). Then, work with your client to decide which course of action seems best able to maximize her *interests.*

Adapted from Leonard L. Riskin et al., Dispute Resolution and Lawyers 82-89 (abridged 5th ed. 2014).

As you finalize preparations for your meeting with Mrs. Lord, complete the following tasks.

Tasks

1. *Clarify relevant issues and interests:* Frame a tentative statement of your client's issues and interests to make sure you understand your client accurately. For example, the statement could take the form, "It seems to me that you are concerned about *issue* and hope to come to a resolution that is consistent with *interest x, interest y,* and *interest z,* is that right?" Riskin et al., *supra,* at 83.

2. *Articulate possible legal theories:*   In this situation, you can assume that the most relevant legal theory is the law of landlord and tenant. Prepare to explain to your client (a) the distinctions between terms of years, periodic tenancies, and tenancies at will; (b) the distinction between subleases and assignments; and (c) the meaning of joint and several liability. To prepare for this discussion, draft a brief outline of the points you will address with your client.

3. *Identify client options:*   Brainstorming with your client can generate a broad and creative range of options. But to prepare for your brainstorming session, generate a list of options on your own (you can expand and/or refine that list when you meet with Mrs. Lord later this week). Think of as many reasonable options as you can.

4. *Explore consequences:*   After each option appearing on the list you just generated, jot down your initial assessment of the likely legal consequences. Does this option seem likely to satisfy your client's *interest(s)*, and if so, which one(s)?

After you counsel Mrs. Lord, assume that she decides that she would like to continue discussions with Tyler about renting her apartment to him. Prepare a draft lease that can serve as the basis of her negotiations with Tyler. To do so, consider the following instructions:

A Place to Start | Skills: Drafting Documents

- ■ *Locate model documents:* Often, you do not need to write on a blank slate when drafting such routine documents as residential leases or contracts of sale. Search for a reputable source that has made model documents or forms available, such as state and local governments, the American Bar Association, or local bar associations. Such sources are usually evenhanded and fair to both sides; in addition, sources specific to your state will incorporate the law of your jurisdiction (you may also need to research local law). Here, you can begin with the model lease reproduced above in section B. You can assume that it was prepared by the Attorney General's Office in Mrs. Lord's state.

- ■ *Read the model document carefully:* Does the model document address all issues relevant to your client's situation? Are there any provisions that you would like to add or modify to reflect your client's interests?

- ■ *Modify the document as appropriate:* Produce a clean copy of the document that can serve as the basis of your client's negotiations.

Task

Relevant provisions from the model lease appear below. Amend, modify, and re-draft as necessary.

Lease Agreement

LENGTH OF LEASE

A. *Initial Rental Period.* The landlord will rent this residence to the tenant for _____ months. This term shall begin on the _____ day of _____ 20_____, at noon.

SECURITY DEPOSIT

A. *Amount of Security Deposit.* The tenant has paid the landlord $ _____ as a Security Deposit. The Security Deposit is in addition to rental payments and should not be substituted by the tenant for unpaid rent. The landlord will hold the Security Deposit until the end of the residency. The Security Deposit remains the tenant's money. The landlord will keep the Security Deposit separate from the landlord's own money. The landlord will not require a Security Deposit of more than two months' rent.

DISTURBING THE PEACE

The tenant agrees not to cause or allow on the premises any excessive nuisance, noise, or other activity which disturbs the peace and quiet of neighbors or other tenants in the building or violates any state law or local ordinance. The landlord agrees to prevent other tenants and other persons in the building or common areas from similarly disturbing the tenant's peace and quiet.

SUBLEASING

The tenant agrees not to sublease or assign this residence without the prior written consent of the landlord. Consent will not be withheld except for good reason.

OTHER AGREEMENTS

The landlord and the tenant also agree to the following:

_____

_____

_____

JOINT AND SEVERAL LIABILITY

The undersigned tenants are jointly and severally responsible and liable for all obligations under this agreement.

Signatures:

Mrs. Lord (landlord)

Tyler (tenant)

F. CHAPTER REVIEW

1. Practice Question[11]

Trading tenants: On January 1, 2010, Liam conveyed a leasehold in a commercial building that he owned, "To Alice and Bob for 10 years, for the sum of $5,000 per month." The agreement was duly signed and dated by the parties. Thereafter, Alice and Bob shared the premises for business purposes and promptly paid $5,000 to Liam on the first day of each month. On January 1, 2011, Bob duly executed a document stating "I hereby sublease to Braydon all my interest in the property for the period January 1, 2011 to December 31, 2019." Thereafter, Bob vacated the premises and Braydon moved his business into the building, sharing space with Alice. When Liam realized what had happened, he wrote Bob a letter that stated, "I withhold my consent to your sublease to Braydon and hereby terminate your tenancy." Alice and Braydon did not know of the letter, and continued to pay $5,000 to Liam on the first day of each month, and Liam cashed the checks. On January 1, 2012, Alice was in a serious car accident and died on the way to the hospital. Her valid will duly conveyed her entire estate to her daughter Ava, who promptly took over her mother's business operation in Liam's building. On February 1, 2012, Liam served Ava and Braydon with a notice to vacate the premises in 30 days and changed the locks on the building so that they could not enter. They refused to surrender the property and hired a locksmith to let them back into the building. Liam brought a legal action to evict Ava and Braydon. What should each of the parties argue? What are the precise property interests of each party? Who should win the lawsuit?

2. Bringing It Home

Research your state's statutory law and find its relevant provisions, if any, on the following topics:

1. *Model residential lease:* Does your state have a model residential lease available online, tailored to the applicable law of your state?

2. *Notice of termination:* Has the legislature modified the common law notice periods required to terminate leases in your jurisdiction?

3. *Security deposit:* For what purposes can the landlord hold a security deposit—for physical damages to the premises, for nonpayment of rent, and/or for something else?

---

11. Suggested responses appear in the Appendix to this book.

4. *Legal actions and attorney's fees:*   Has the legislature provided for an award of attorney's fees to the prevailing party in actions brought to enforce lease provisions? Is there a statutorily prescribed summary eviction procedure?

5. *Landlord's choice of remedies:*   If a tenant breaches the lease or wrongfully abandons the premises, what remedies can the landlord pursue? Is the landlord required to mitigate damages by trying to find a replacement tenant, or can the landlord stand by and do nothing, and continue to collect rent from the breaching tenant?

6. *Implied warranty of habitability:*   Has your state codified the common law implied warranty of habitability by statute? How should the standard of habitability be measured—by reference to local housing codes, or to some other specified standard?

7. *Nondiscrimination:*   Has your state (or local government) enacted legislation complementing the Fair Housing Act? If so, what additional classes are protected, or what additional actions are prohibited?

Concurrent Ownership and Marital Systems

A. Concurrent Ownership
B. Marital Property Systems
C. Beyond the Black Letter: New Forms of Concurrent Ownership
D. Skills Practice: Client Counseling and Negotiating a Tenants in Common Agreement
E. Chapter Review

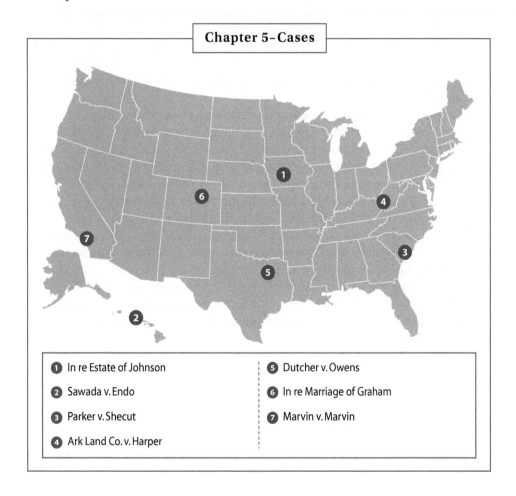

Chapter 5-Cases

1. In re Estate of Johnson
2. Sawada v. Endo
3. Parker v. Shecut
4. Ark Land Co. v. Harper
5. Dutcher v. Owens
6. In re Marriage of Graham
7. Marvin v. Marvin

In Chapters 3 and 4, we considered shared ownership across time, with two or more people holding successive rights of possession. In this chapter, we will study estates in which all owners share across space. As we will see, the law engages in a type of fiction known as the *unity of possession*—the idea that all owners have a right to possess the whole of the property at the same time. This might work well enough for a couple sharing ownership of the family home, or even several lawyers co-owning an office building, but it poses difficult challenges in cases where the owners wish to engage in incompatible activities on the same land, such as family retreat and coal mining operation (section A.2).

Concurrent ownership and marital systems are fascinating topics that shine a light on important pieces of our social history. We will consider such seemingly arcane questions as, "does one cotenant have the right to unilaterally sever the right of survivorship?" and "should the appreciation in value of property count as marital or separate property in an equitable distribution?" But, lurking behind such superficially dry questions is the broader story of property law's struggle to keep pace with social change. Among other things, we will examine the expansion of the rights of women and people of color to own and control property; the changing view of "family" from married couples with children, to unmarried cohabiting couples, to same-sex couples; and entirely new ownership arrangements including condominiums, cooperatives, and time-share housing.

What does concurrent ownership reveal about property law in general? By definition, concurrent ownership (and its characteristic unity of possession) runs counter to the Blackstonian ownership model that we considered in Chapter 1, with its view of property as "that sole and despotic dominion which one man claims and exercises over the external things of the world, in total exclusion of the right of any other individual in the universe." Likewise, concurrent ownership does not fit comfortably within the bundle of rights concept, the central premise of which is the right to exclude. Instead, another metaphor is needed to comprehend the intertwined property rights of potentially dozens of people in the same property at the same time. As you read this chapter, consider whether the web of interests metaphor is applicable, with its focus on both the subject of property rights (here, shared parcels of land in various configurations) and on the interconnected nature of owners' rights, responsibilities, and relationships.

A. CONCURRENT OWNERSHIP

1. Classifying the Estate

There are three types of concurrent estates. As a starting point for distinguishing one from another, we will rely on the concept of the *four unities*. If the *unity of time* exists, then the interest of all owners must vest at the same moment in time. If the *unity of title* exists, then all owners took title by the same instrument, such as a deed or a will (but taking simultaneously by inheritance does not satisfy the unity of title). If the *unity of interest* is present, then cotenants must hold equal shares, of equal duration. For example, *A*, *B*, and *C* must each hold an undivided ⅓ interest in Blackacre, and their interests must be of equal duration (for example, all hold in fee simple absolute, or all hold a term of years for 10 years). Finally, by definition, all cotenancies require the *unity of possession.* That is, even though each cotenant owns only a share of the property, each has an undivided right to occupy the entire property. This unity of possession is the core of concurrent ownership. As one court explained,

> It is admittedly a paradox, and perhaps an oxymoron, to state property could be divided in *undivided* one-half shares or interests. But it is consistently referred to in this manner, and the reason for doing so is that the individual tenants are entitled to possess the whole of the property while they remain co-tenants (therefore their possession is undivided), but should they choose to alienate the property, they only have a proportional interest . . . to alienate.

In re Estate of Johnson, 739 N.W.2d 493 (Iowa 2007) (excerpted below).

Tenants in common: The tenancy in common (TIC) is the default concurrent estate, and requires only the unity of possession. Because the unity of interest is not required, cotenants frequently own unequal shares of the property, generally corresponding to the percentage of the purchase price paid by each. An interest in a tenancy in common is freely transferable inter vivos, by will, and by inheritance. Because the unities of time and title are not required, the transferee takes over the transferor's place as a tenant in common, even though the transferee's interest vested at a later time than did the interests of the original cotenants, and even though the transferee's interest was conveyed by an instrument different than the original deed or other document that first created the tenancy in common. A modified form of the tenancy in common—the *tenancy in partnership*—evolved to fulfill the needs of business enterprises (we will leave the study of the tenancy in partnership to your upper level business law courses).

Joint tenants with a right of survivorship: Joint tenancies with a right of survivorship (JT/ROS or JT) require the satisfaction of all four unities, both at the initiation of the tenancy and throughout its duration. Joint tenants are said to hold *per my et per tout* ("by the half and by the whole")—that is, cotenants hold equal, undivided fractional shares of the estate as a whole. Despite the unity of title requirement, however, some jurisdictions will allow two or more persons to acquire a joint tenancy by adverse possession, provided they took under color of title—that is, pursuant to a defective instrument purporting to create a joint tenancy. Likewise, despite the unity of interest requirement, some jurisdictions will allow cotenants to own unequal fractional shares of the property. For example, if *A* pays ¾ of the purchase price, and *B* pays ¼ of the purchase price, some jurisdictions will nevertheless allow *A* and *B* to own the property as joint tenants, with *A* holding an undivided ¾ interest and *B* holding an undivided ¼ interest. In some modern jurisdictions, strict adherence to the four unities has been replaced with a test that relies on the intent of the parties, as considered in *In re Estate of Johnson* below.

Joint tenancies have an important feature—the right of survivorship (*ROS*). Upon the death of the first joint tenant, that tenant's share terminates. The remaining joint tenant(s) then become(s) the sole owner(s). Importantly, the decedent's share does not "pass" to the surviving joint tenant(s), but simply ends. Because of this, joint tenancies are often used as substitutes for wills, and avoid the need for probate. But note that only the surviving joint tenant(s) can take over the decedent's interest—joint tenants cannot pass their share by will or devise to others because there is no interest that survives their death. Conceptually, you can imagine that the cotenant's share simply disappears or evaporates at death, leaving nothing that can pass on to the decedent's successors. For this same reason, if only one joint tenant incurs a debt or conveys a mortgage interest to another, the debt or mortgage generally does not survive the death of that cotenant. Rather, the decedent's share terminates at death, leaving no property interest to secure the debt or mortgage. To avoid this situation, lenders (at least, sophisticated institutional lenders) routinely insist that all joint tenants sign mortgage documents so that the security interest in the property survives the early death of one of the mortgagors. If all cotenants die simultaneously, no owner remains to enjoy the right of survivorship. Instead, most jurisdictions allow the property to pass to the decedents' heirs or devisees, who will then hold the property as tenants in common.

Beware! Just when you think you have correctly categorized an estate as a joint tenancy, unilateral action by one of the cotenants can "sever" the right of survivorship. This can happen, for example, if one cotenant deeds her interest to another, thereby destroying the unities of time and title. As a consequence, the joint tenancy transforms automatically into the default estate—the tenancy in common. Severance, which can occur without the knowledge of the other joint tenant(s), destroys the ROS with dramatic consequences for the other joint tenant(s), a topic explored by *In re Estate of Johnson*, below.

Tenants by the entirety: Tenancies by the entirety (TBE) can exist only between married spouses, who hold the property as a unit, not by equal shares (*per tout et non per my*). The couple must be married before they can take title as tenants by the entirety; the property of an engaged couple, for example, does not automatically convert into entirety property upon their marriage. This type of tenancy cannot be created unless the tenants are married and the four unities are satisfied. William Blackstone recognized the tenancy by the entirety as a distinct estate in the late 18th century (although its origin dates back centuries earlier):

> If an estate in fee be given to a man and his wife, they are neither property joint-tenants, nor tenants in common; for husband and wife being considered as one in law, they cannot take the estate by moieties, but are seized of the entirety, *per tout et non per my*; the consequences of which is that neither the husband nor wife can dispose of any part without the assent of the other, but the whole must remain to the survivor.

William Blackstone, 2 Commentaries on the Laws of England 179 (9th ed. 1783). Historically, husbands held all rights to manage entirety property, to receive income from the property, or to transfer the property, leaving wives with little but the right of survivorship. However, states gradually began to expand the rights of women to own and control property in their individual names, thereby reducing the importance of the tenancy by the entirety. Moreover, the status of the tenancy by the entirety has "waned considerably," and has been abolished, restricted, or found to be unacceptable in many jurisdictions because of its "ground[ing] in the unity of spouses personified in the husband." Powell on Real Property § 52.01 (Michael Allan Wolf, gen. ed. 2015). The tenancy by the entirety was never recognized in community property states, which instead recognize *community property*, a unique form of co-ownership (*see* section B).

Like the joint tenancy, the tenancy by the entirety features a right of survivorship. However, the TBE right of survivorship is durable, and cannot be unilaterally destroyed by one spouse acting alone (for example, by purporting to transfer an interest in the property). Some jurisdictions presume that a grant to a married couple creates a tenancy by the entirety in the absence of a clear intent to the contrary. Tenancies by the entirety continue to be recognized in about half the states.

Miscellaneous issues: Two miscellaneous issues deserve mention: A single disgruntled tenant in common can petition the court for a *partition* that will divide the property into separate ownership, either by physically delineating separately owned parcels (*partition in kind*) or by ordering a sale, the proceeds from which will be divided among the former cotenants in accordance with their percentage share of ownership (*partition by sale*). Joint tenants can achieve the same result, but must first sever the joint tenancy into a tenancy in common, and then seek partition. In contrast, tenancies by the entirety cannot be partitioned, but the termination of shared ownership can be accomplished through divorce and its distribution of assets.

As a second miscellaneous point, notice that two or more people can have concurrent ownership of one of the estates or future interests that we studied in Chapter 3. For example, *A*, *B*, and *C* can own Blackacre as tenants in common for a term of years; or *A* and *B* can hold a vested remainder in fee simple absolute as joint tenants.

A Place to Start | Concurrent Estates

	Tenancy in Common	Joint Tenancy with ROS	Tenancy by the Entirety
Unities required?	Requires only unity of possession	Requires 4 unities	Requires 4 unities + marriage
Is there a right of survivorship?	No At death, each cotenant's share passes by will or intestate succession	Yes	Yes
Can the ROS be destroyed by one party acting alone?	N/A	• Yes • One JT can destroy the ROS by inter vivos conveyance (including the grant of a mortgage in a title theory state), thus severing the JT into a TIC	No
How can one cotenant's interest be transferred?	• Inter vivos conveyance • Devise • Inheritance	• Not allowed • Purported transfers may sever the ROS and transform estate into a TIC	Not allowed
Can one cotenant force a partition?	Yes	Yes (although this necessarily also involves a severance of the joint tenancy)	No
Other methods to terminate shared ownership?	• Mutual agreement	• Mutual agreement • Death	• Mutual agreement • Death • Divorce
Does debt of single cotenant survive debtor's death?	• Yes • The debt generally encumbers only the decedent's share (as passed to devisees or heirs)	Majority view: no	• Majority view: no

	Tenancy in Common	Joint Tenancy with ROS	Tenancy by the Entirety
Language creating cotenancy	• *To A, B, & C* • *To A & B as tenants in common*	• *To A & B as joint tenants, and not as tenants in common* • *To A, B, & C as joint tenants with a right of survivorship*	• *To Husband & Wife as tenants by the entirety* • *To A & B (if A & B are married, some states presume this creates a TBE)*

Test Your Understanding

What type of concurrent estate has been created in each example below? If the language is ambiguous, identify the source of the ambiguity, its impact on your classification, and what you think is the best resolution of the ambiguity. In addition, identify the interest of each cotenant after all hypothetical events have occurred.

1. Olivia sold her farm for $100,000, conveying it "To Aiden, Brittany, and Cody jointly." The three friends split the purchase price, with Aiden paying $25,000, Brittany paying $50,000, and Cody paying $25,000. Ten years later, Brittany died, devising all of her property to her daughter, Bianca.

2. In the example above, assume that Brittany conveyed a mortgage interest to First Bank before her death, to secure a loan that she needed to meet some other expenses. Aiden and Cody did not sign the mortgage instrument. Then, 10 years later, Brittany died, devising all of her property to her daughter, Bianca.

3. Omar conveyed his house "To Aiden, Brittany, and Cody as joint tenants, and not as tenants in common." The friends each paid ⅓ of the purchase price. Then, Aiden died. A few years later, Brittany died. What are the property interests? Assume instead that all three friends die at the same instant in an automobile accident. Aiden's will left his property to his son, Adam; Brittany's will left her property to her daughter, Bianca; and Cody died intestate leaving his son, Carter, as his only heir at law. What are the relevant property interests?

4. Omar conveyed his property to a married couple, "To Aiden and Brittany, as tenants by the entirety." Aiden mortgaged the property to First Bank, but Brittany did not sign the loan instrument. Then Aiden died, leaving a will that devised all of his property to Adam, his son from his first marriage.

5. Omar conveyed his property "To Aiden and Brittany for their joint lives, then to Aiden if Aiden survives Brittany, but if Aiden does not survive Brittany, then to Brittany." Subsequently, while Aiden and Brittany are both alive, Aiden conveyed a mortgage interest to Cody. Then, Aiden died.

In re Estate of Johnson

739 N.W.2d 493 (Iowa 2007)

Reading Guide

The common law doctrine of the four unities is the traditional measure of whether a joint tenancy has been created, and also whether it has been terminated. Can you think of any strengths or weaknesses of that doctrine? Would it be better if courts simply followed the intent of the parties? The next case takes up those questions.

CADY, J.

The right of survivorship makes joint tenancies a popular form of property ownership. Yet, the concomitant right of each joint tenant to destroy the joint tenancy, and thus the right of survivorship, is not always popular, particularly for the surviving joint tenant. As Hamlet observed in a different context, "ay, there's the rub"[1] and, in this case, the seeds of the issue presented. A district court decision found a joint tenant successfully exercised his right to destroy the right of survivorship prior to his death, and the surviving joint tenant appeals. We agree with the surviving joint tenant, now the executor of the surviving joint tenant's estate, and find the property remained in joint tenancy until the death of the joint tenant, at which time full title vested in the survivor. We reverse the district court's decision and remand.

Background Facts and Proceedings

Roy and Emogene Johnson purchased a home in Van Meter, Iowa, in 1963. They were married and took title to the home as joint tenants with the right of survivorship. They continued to live in their Van Meter home for over thirty-five years, where they raised a family and established the property as their homestead.

In the fall of 1998 Emogene suffered a severe stroke. The prognosis for her recovery was bleak, and she required intensive medical attention. Roy and the children felt Emogene would not live long, and they assumed Roy would survive her. Because of these circumstances, the family decided Emogene

---

1. [FN 1] William Shakespeare, *Hamlet*, act. 3, sc. 1, line 64.

should transfer title in her automobile to Roy, as well as her interest in the homestead.[2]

On November 24, 1998, Emogene purportedly executed a power of attorney in her hospital room. This document designated her daughters, Janice Johnson and Beverly Johnson Algoe, as attorneys-in-fact. The power of attorney authorized Janice and Beverly to sell Emogene's property. . . . On December 21, 1998, Janice and Beverly transferred the title for Emogene's car to Roy.

On that same day a quitclaim deed was drafted to convey Emogene and Roy's interest in their homestead solely to Roy. The deed stated "ROY N. JOHNSON and EMOGENE F. JOHNSON, husband and wife[,] do hereby Quit Claim to ROY N. JOHNSON all our right, title, interest, estate, claim and demand in the [homestead]." Roy signed the deed on December 21, and his signature was notarized. . . .

. . . Then on January 6, 1999, Janice signed the quitclaim deed on behalf of Emogene, as indicated by the notary's seal. The deed was recorded the same day.

The earlier assumptions made by the family that gave rise to the transfers of property were proven wrong when Roy suddenly passed away on December 17, 1999, survived by his ailing wife Emogene and the three children, Janice, Beverly, and William. Roy left a will that gave all of his property to his three children in equal shares, although he did not specifically disinherit Emogene. Janice was named executor of Roy's estate in his will, but Beverly took her place after Janice's death in June of 2004.

Beverly filed the final report in Roy's estate in June of 2005. . . . Emogene claimed the transfers of her car and her interest in the homestead were illegal because she was incompetent when the powers of attorney were executed.

The district court found Emogene was clearly incompetent at the time she signed the powers of attorney, which invalidated the transfer of her interest in the property to Roy under the deed. Nevertheless, the court held Roy unilaterally terminated the joint tenancy in the homestead by his act of conveying his interest to himself in fee simple because the deed constituted an expression of his intent to destroy the joint tenancy. . . .

As a result, the district court concluded title to the homestead was split between Emogene and Roy's estate as tenants in common in "undivided one-half" shares. . . . Emogene appealed the district court ruling concerning the title to the homestead.

Emogene died in March of 2007, during the pendency of this appeal. As a result, Emogene's son and executor of her estate, William Johnson, is the named appellant. . . .

---

2. [FN 2] The record suggests the family made these decisions to help Emogene qualify for Medicaid, although the decisions were likely based on erroneous assumptions.

Determining the Existence of Joint Tenancies in Iowa

Traditionally, questions concerning the existence of joint tenancies were answered by resorting to the "four unities" of interest, title, time, and possession. To create a joint tenancy the four unities had to be present—"[t]hat is, one and the same interest arising by the same conveyance, commencing at the same time and held by the one and the same undivided possession." *Switzer v. Pratt,* 23 N.W.2d 837, 839 (Iowa 1946). To sever or terminate[3] a joint tenancy, a joint tenant simply had to destroy one of the unities. *See Stuehm v. Mikulski,* 297 N.W. 595, 597 (Neb. 1941) ("The four unities heretofore listed must not only come into being with the creation of such an estate, but must also continue to exist while the estate exists, and the destruction of any one of them as to all holders will destroy the estate. . . .").

This common-law approach to the existence of joint tenancies began losing steam over fifty years ago. *See* R.H. Helmholz, *Realism & Formalism in the Severance of Joint Tenancies,* 77 Neb. L. Rev. 1, 1-2 (1998). Critics derided the approach as too formalistic, and declared it to be outdated. Moreover, critics recognized the four unities often worked, typically in conjunction with the common-law rule that a grantor could not also be a grantee, *see Riddle v. Harmon,* 162 Cal. Rptr. 530, 531-34 (Cal. App. 3d 1980) (recognizing how the four unities operate in conjunction with the "two-to-transfer" rule, and refusing to "adher[e] to [these] cumbersome feudal law requirements"), to "frustrate the legitimate expectations of too many joint tenants [or would-be joint tenants], and for no discernable purpose," Helmholz, at 2.

As a result, courts began adopting an alternative intent-based approach to determine the existence of joint tenancies. We recognized this approach many years ago and have gravitated towards it since that time. Today, the approach generally enjoys favorable acceptance among other courts and scholars as the more appropriate and realistic means for determining the existence of joint tenancies. . . .

---

3. [FN 5] Unfortunately, the words "sever" and "terminate" often appear side by side without any attempt to distinguish them. . . . The case law and commentary are less than clear on this point, but it is evident the terms are not perfectly synonymous. *Black's Law Dictionary* defines "severance" as "[t]he termination of a joint tenancy, usu[ally] by converting it into a tenancy in common." . . . Termination, on the other hand, is not usually defined, which can give rise to the belief that any destruction of a joint tenancy that is not a severance must be a termination, or that a severance is a special kind of termination.

This case highlights the need for clear terminology: the deed originally attempted to destroy the joint tenancy in favor of sole ownership in one party, and now one of the joint tenants alleges the attempted conveyance by deed operated to destroy the joint tenancy in favor of a tenancy in common among the former joint tenants. If either attempt prevailed, the joint tenancy would be destroyed, but the resulting ownership would be different in both how the property is held and by whom. While we acknowledge the two terms are not synonymous, we make no attempt to define the terms any further than describing the latter case as a severance, and the former as a termination. . . .

While we have not formally and expressly adopted the intent-based approach, we do so today. Our review of the case law and commentary confirms our position that strict reliance on the four unities is not the proper test for determining the existence of joint tenancies in Iowa. Instead, the intent of the parties should prevail when possible. In addition, we see no reason to distinguish our approach based on whether the joint tenancy is sought to be created, severed, or terminated. . . .

Although an intent-based test is the best and more realistic approach, we recognize it is not without its own difficulties, as this case illustrates. . . . Indeed, abandonment of the theoretical litmus test provided by the four unities may sacrifice some of the clarity it presumably provided. Clarity in the law is necessary, but we see no reason why it cannot be achieved under an intent-based approach when proper attention is paid to the individual facts and circumstances of each case. . . .

In drawing the contours of the intent-based test, it is important to recognize this approach does not simply permit a court to determine the intent of a party under the facts and then fulfill it.[4] . . . Instead, it seems fundamental that intent must be derived from an instrument effectuating the intent to sever the joint tenancy. Thus, we begin with the premise that intent unaccompanied by some action or instrument sufficient to corroborate and give effect to that intent will not create, sever, or terminate a joint tenancy. This approach, of course, leads us back to the district court holding that derived intent to sever from a deed characterized as a self-conveyance of one joint tenant.

Was the Joint Tenancy Severed in this Case?

The surrounding circumstances in this case inevitably point to a void deed. Under the common law, a void deed could not work a severance, but only because a failed conveyance could not disturb the original unities of time, title, interest and possession. Of course, we must decide if this same result occurs under an intent-based approach.

Emogene's incompetence rendered the conveyance of her interest invalid. . . .[5] Normally, Emogene's incompetence would not prohibit Roy from conveying his own property interest held in joint tenancy with her. However, the interest of a spouse in homestead property is protected by statute. . . . "A conveyance . . . of . . . the homestead, if the owner is married,

---

4. [FN 7] The "intent of the parties" typically refers to the intent of the joint tenants. . . . However, in cases of unilateral action, the "intent of the parties" really refers to just one joint tenant. Thus, in cases of unilateral severance, the question would be what the singular joint tenant's, or party's, intent was, rather than the parties' intent.

5. [FN 9] Of course, under the common law the conveyance of Roy's interest to himself would be invalid because it would violate the "two-to-transfer" rule. *See Riddle.* Iowa has, like most states, largely abandoned the common-law rule that prohibited conveyances between one person as grantor and grantee. . . .

is not valid, unless and until the spouse of the owner executes the same or a like instrument, or a power of attorney for the execution of the same or a like instrument." Iowa Code § 561.13 (2005). Roy was clearly attempting to convey the homestead, albeit his own interest to himself. Thus, the plain language of the statute prohibited Roy from doing so unless Emogene joined in the pursuit pursuant to the statute. The deed was totally void.

Notwithstanding, Roy's estate argues, as the district court held, a deed that is void or ineffective as a conveyance may nevertheless remain a viable source of intent to sever a joint tenancy with a spouse in homestead property because mere severance of the joint tenancy in homestead property only creates a tenancy in common and does not jeopardize or destroy the statutory homestead rights of the spouse. Instead, severance would only change the form of ownership without compromising the spouse's right of possession provided under the homestead statute. . . . We reject this application of the intent-based test for two core reasons.

First, it is obvious that Roy's intent under the deed in this case was to take sole title to the homestead, and the joint tenancy would have been destroyed, not severed, as a consequence of that intent. Under an intent-based test, it is fundamental that the underlying instrument must effectuate the intent to sever. At least one other court has found this distinction significant. *See Hayes v. Lewis*, 338 N.E.2d 102, 105 (Ill. Ct. App. 1975) ("The purpose of this attempt on behalf of defendant was not to sever the joint tenancy relationship so as to make the parties tenants in common. It was rather an attempt to eliminate entirely any interest on the part of plaintiff by vesting the entire ownership of the stock in defendant."). . . . We conclude it would be inappropriate to utilize an intent-based approach to achieve a result the parties never intended. As a result, Roy's lack of intent to sever the joint tenancy to create a tenancy in common with Emogene makes it unnecessary for us in this case to decide whether a spouse can unilaterally sever a joint tenancy in homestead property by means of a proper self-conveyance. . . .[6] The deed relied upon to supply intent did not express an intent to sever the joint tenancy.

Secondly, we are convinced an intent to sever a joint tenancy under the intent-based test must normally, if not in every instance, be derived from an

---

6. [FN 11] The district court found Emogene's incompetence only voided her transfer of her interest to Roy under the deed, yet the deed remained valid as a transfer by Roy of his interest to himself, which had the effect of severing the joint tenancy and creating a tenancy in common. The district court further found that the homestead statute did not stand as an impediment to the unilateral severance by Roy of the joint tenancy in homestead property because the severance of the joint tenancy by self-conveyance merely created a tenancy in common and did not jeopardize the purposes behind the homestead statute. The district court also found a contrary conclusion would have the effect of creating a tenancy in the entirety, a form of ownership we have refused to recognize in prior cases. These are questions we need not decide because the deed executed by Roy did not express an intent for the joint tenancy to be severed.

instrument that is legally effective to carry out the intent. While we have always recognized a conveyance will sever or terminate a joint tenancy, we have never recognized an invalid conveyance, i.e., a void deed, will do so. . . . We also find support for the proposition that an attempted conveyance by a void instrument, not necessarily a void deed, will not sever the joint tenancy despite an intent to do so.

The requirement for the intent under an intent-based analysis to be derived from a valid deed or similar instrument adds symmetry to the law and is consistent with our general principles governing property rights. In particular, we have never allowed a tenancy of any kind to be created without a valid deed or similar instrument. The same should hold true for the severance of a joint tenancy. . . .

Conclusion

In the final analysis, we think the circumstances of this case do not support a conclusion that the joint tenancy was severed. Not only was Roy's intent not aligned with the objective his estate seeks to accomplish in this proceeding, but it was accompanied by a void deed concerning homestead property. The district court erroneously determined the joint tenancy was severed. As a result, the property remained in joint tenancy, and Emogene's right of survivorship took effect upon Roy's death. The property should now be distributed in accordance with Emogene's will. We remand this case to the district court for proceedings consistent with this opinion.

Notes

1. *The ultimate gamble:* What does this case tell you about the potential fragility of the right of survivorship? One court has described the right of survivorship as,

> . . . a [mere expectancy that arises] only upon success in the ultimate gamble, survival, and then only if the unity of the estate has not heretofore been destroyed by voluntary conveyance . . . , by partition proceedings . . . , or by any other action which operates to sever the joint tenancy.

Tenhet v. Boswell, 554 P.2d at 330, 334 (Cal. 1976). Can you think of an alternative to joint tenancy that would guarantee that the surviving cotenant owns the property in fee simple absolute, even if the cotenants were not married?

2. *The common law four unities v. the intent-based approach:* The Iowa Supreme Court asserts that it was "obvious" that Roy intended to terminate, not merely sever, the joint tenancy. What difference does that make, and was Roy's intent really so clear? Compare the common law four unities doctrine to

the intent-based approach—what policies does each doctrine serve? Which test do you think is better? For a critique of the intent-based approach, *see* John V. Orth, *The Perils of Joint Tenancies*, 44 Real Property Tr. & Est. L.J. 427, 438-39 (2009) (asserting "[n]ot only is the substitution of an intent-based approach for the traditional four unities more complicated in application, but the consequences of a shift to intention as the sovereign test of the existence of a joint tenancy has not been thought through").

3. *Homestead property:*   Some state statutes or constitutions have homestead exemptions that protect "homestead property" (generally, the family residence) from the claims of specified creditors of either spouse, with some notable exceptions (for example, homestead property is generally not exempt from tax liens). In some states, a single spouse acting alone cannot alienate or encumber homestead property without the participation of the other. *See* 45 A.L.R. 395. What stance did the Iowa Code adopt? Did the court correctly interpret the statute at issue?

Problems

1. *Two to transfer?*   Frances Riddle and her husband, Jack, owned real property as joint tenants. Without her husband's knowledge, Mrs. Riddle executed a valid deed that granted to herself an undivided one-half interest in the subject property. The deed also provided, "The purpose of this deed is to terminate those joint tenancies formerly existing between the Grantor, Frances P. Riddle, and Jack C. Riddle, her husband." Mrs. Riddle then prepared a will disposing of her interest in the property. She died twenty days after executing the deed and will. Under the rule of *In re Estate of Johnson*, who would own the property? Is that a good result? *See Riddle v. Harmon*, 162 Cal. Rptr. 530 (Cal. Ct. App. 1980).

2. *Severance by mortgage?*   Brothers William and John Harms owned certain real estate as joint tenants. Without his brother's knowledge, John conveyed a mortgage interest to Carl and Mary Simmons, as security for a loan made by the Simmonses. John died about 10 years later, devising all of his real and personal property to Charles Sprague. Under the common law test discussed in *In re Estate of Johnson*, who owns the property at John's death? If the correct response is not clear, what issue must you resolve before you can answer the question?

As we will see in Chapter 7, when a person borrows money to purchase property, the borrower typically conveys a *mortgage* to the lender to secure repayment of the loan. In some states (*title theory* states), the mortgage conveys an actual real property interest to the lender, whereas in other states (*lien theory* states), it merely conveys a security interest to the lender. Does that help you answer the question? In a title theory state, who owns the property at John's death? In a lien theory state? *See Harms v. Sprague*, 473 N.E.2d 930 (Ill. 1984).

3. *Severance by lease?*   Raymond Johnson and Hazel Tenhet owned property as joint tenants. Without Hazel's knowledge or permission, Raymond
leased the property to Boswell for 10 years at $150 per year. Raymond died
three months after leasing the property to Boswell. Hazel, as the surviving
joint tenant, sought to enforce her right to sole ownership and possession of
the property and demanded that Boswell vacate the property. Will Hazel prevail
under the four unities doctrine? If the correct response is not clear, what issue
must you resolve before you can answer the question? *See Tenhet v. Boswell,*
554 P.2d 330 (Cal. 1976).

2. The Challenges of Shared Ownership

This section presents a brief overview of some of the default rules of cotenancies. However, the parties may enter into an agreement that alters these
rules—for example, they might agree not to mortgage the property, or not to
seek a partition of the property. Although such agreements might impose
restraints on alienation, courts usually uphold them if the restraints are reasonable in duration and purpose.

Unity of possession and ouster: The unity of possession applies to all types
of concurrent interests, giving each cotenant the right to possess the whole of
the premises. Because all cotenants have such a right, none can complain of the
others' presence, and a single cotenant in sole possession generally does not
owe rent to the other cotenants. Sometimes, however, one cotenant's possession is so complete that it constitutes an *ouster*—the exclusion of co-owners
from all or part of the premises. In that case, the excluded owners can bring an
action in ejectment, but may not resort to self-help in the interest of keeping
the peace. In some cases, the occupying owner will be liable to the others for
rent during the period of exclusion. If one cotenant ousts the others, then the
possession becomes hostile and the statute of limitations for *adverse possession*
begins to run. Without ouster, one cotenant in sole possession cannot extinguish the other cotenants' interests by adverse possession.

The condition of the premises—waste: In Chapters 3 and 4, we saw that
those who share property over time—including holders of present estates and
leaseholds—can be liable in waste to those entitled to future possession. Likewise, those who share property across space can be liable to one another for
waste. For example, a cotenant in sole possession (with or without ouster) who
damages the property will be liable to the other owners for waste, because that
owner has reduced the value of the other owners' interests in the property.

Finances: Who is entitled to the *rental income* that a property generates?
Although a single cotenant in exclusive possession does not owe rent to the
others (unless there has been an ouster), if one owner leases a portion of the
premises to an *outside* party, then the cotenant is liable to the others for their
share of the rents received, under the theory that the lessor is acting as agent for

the other cotenants. A single owner cannot grant the lessee exclusive possession of the premises because that would interfere with the other owners' possessory rights, and would likely constitute an ouster.

The question of *expenses* can also be a source of disagreement. If one cotenant makes *necessary* expenditures such as mortgage or tax payments, that owner generally has a right to recover a share of the expenses from the other cotenants. However, a cotenant that opts to make *elective* expenditures for repairs or improvements of the property usually cannot compel the others to contribute to the costs. In addition, the debts, mortgages, or other liabilities incurred by one cotenant alone generally cannot be satisfied from the interests of the other cotenants.

Partition—an exit strategy: Co-owners can voluntarily choose to terminate a concurrently held estate. In the absence of agreement, a single owner can petition a court for *partition*, even over the objection of the other owners. Tenancies by the entirety and community property cannot be partitioned, although if they can first be transformed into another type of concurrent interest, they can be partitioned subsequently. (Do not confuse partition, which terminates shared ownership altogether, with *severance*, which destroys a right of survivorship and transforms a joint tenancy into a tenancy in common.)

If the subject property can be divided physically into distinct segments, a court might order *partition in kind*. In theory, this is the preferred method of partition—state laws typically assert that partition must be accomplished in kind, unless the land is not reasonably susceptible to physical division and the parties will be unduly prejudiced by a judicial sale. Where the resultant segments of the property are unequal, a co-owner receiving a larger share may be required to make a cash payment (*owelty*) to the others to compensate for the lack of equality. If the property is not capable of physical division into parcels of equal value, a court can order a *partition by sale* and divide the proceeds among the co-owners in accordance with their respective ownership shares. Although courts often say that this is an extraordinary remedy to be exercised sparingly, partitions by sale are the dominant method employed today. Powell on Real Property § 50.07(5) (Michael Allan Wolf, gen. ed. 2015).

Legal actions: Cotenants can bring a variety of legal actions against one another. In an action for an *accounting*, one cotenant seeks to compel another to share benefits obtained from using, leasing, or otherwise exploiting the property (such as rents, profits, or proceeds from mining, logging, or similar activities). Through an action for *contribution*, a cotenant can seek reimbursement from another for a share of expenses incurred by the first cotenant, including taxes, mortgage payments, and homeowners association assessments. If the action is initiated by a cotenant in sole possession, some courts will give the non-occupying owner an "offset" for the fair market rental value, thereby reducing the contribution owed (even though, ordinarily, a cotenant in sole possession is not liable to the others for rent absent ouster).

Sawada v. Endo

561 P.2d 1291 (Haw. 1977)

Reading Guide

The tenancy by the entirety relies on a fictional unity of husband and wife. This case explores some of the complications that follow from that premise.

MENOR, J.

This is a civil action brought by the plaintiffs-appellants, Masako Sawada and Helen Sawada, in aid of execution of money judgments in their favor, seeking to set aside a conveyance of real property from judgment debtor Kokichi Endo to Samuel H. Endo and Toru Endo, defendants-appellees herein, on the ground that the conveyance as to the Sawadas was fraudulent.

On November 30, 1968, the Sawadas were injured when struck by a motor vehicle operated by Kokichi Endo. On June 17, 1969, Helen Sawada filed her complaint for damages against Kokichi Endo. Masako Sawada filed her suit against him on August 13, 1969. The complaint and summons in each case was served on Kokichi Endo on October 29, 1969.

On the date of the accident, Kokichi Endo was the owner, as a tenant by the entirety with his wife, Ume Endo, of a parcel of real property situate at Wahiawa, Oahu, Hawaii. By deed, dated July 26, 1969, Kokichi Endo and his wife conveyed the property to their sons, Samuel H. Endo and Toru Endo. This document was recorded in the Bureau of Conveyances on December 17, 1969. No consideration was paid by the grantees for the conveyance. Both were aware at the time of the conveyance that their father had been involved in an accident, and that he carried no liability insurance. Kokichi Endo and Ume Endo, while reserving no life interests therein, continued to reside on the premises.

On January 19, 1971, after a consolidated trial on the merits, judgment was entered in favor of Helen Sawada and against Kokichi Endo in the sum of $8,846.46. At the same time, Masako Sawada was awarded judgment on her complaint in the amount of $16,199.28. Ume Endo, wife of Kokichi Endo, died on January 29, 1971. She was survived by her husband, Kokichi. Subsequently, after being frustrated in their attempts to obtain satisfaction of judgment from the personal property of Kokichi Endo, the Sawadas brought suit to set aside the conveyance which is the subject matter of this controversy. The trial court refused to set aside the conveyance, and the Sawadas appeal.

The determinative question in this case is, whether the interest of one spouse in real property, held in tenancy by the entireties, is subject to levy and execution by his or her individual creditors. This issue is one of first impression in this jurisdiction.

A brief review of the present state of the tenancy by the entirety might be helpful. Dean Phipps, writing in 1951,[7] pointed out that only nineteen states and the District of Columbia continued to recognize it as a valid and subsisting institution in the field of property law. Phipps divided these jurisdictions into four groups. He made no mention of Alaska and Hawaii, both of which were then territories of the United States.

In the Group I states (Massachusetts, Michigan, and North Carolina) the estate is essentially the common law tenancy by the entireties, unaffected by the Married Women's Property Acts. As at common law, the possession and profits of the estate are subject to the husband's exclusive dominion and control. In all three states, as at common law, the husband may convey the entire estate subject only to the possibility that the wife may become entitled to the whole estate upon surviving him. As at common law, the obverse as to the wife does not hold true. Only in Massachusetts, however, is the estate in its entirety subject to levy by the husband's creditors. In both Michigan and North Carolina, the use and income from the estate is not subject to levy during the marriage for the separate debts of either spouse.

In the Group II states (Alaska, Arkansas, New Jersey, New York, and Oregon) the interest of the debtor spouse in the estate may be sold or levied upon for his or her separate debts, subject to the other spouse's contingent right of survivorship. Alaska, which has been added to this group, has provided by statute that the interest of a debtor spouse in any type of estate, except a homestead as defined and held in tenancy by the entirety, shall be subject to his or her separate debts.

In the Group III jurisdictions (Delaware, District of Columbia, Florida, Indiana, Maryland, Missouri, Pennsylvania, Rhode Island, Vermont, Virginia, and Wyoming) an attempted conveyance by either spouse is wholly void, and the estate may not be subjected to the separate debts of one spouse only.

In Group IV, the two states of Kentucky and Tennessee hold that the contingent right of survivorship appertaining to either spouse is separately alienable by him and attachable by his creditors during the marriage. The use and profits, however, may neither be alienated nor attached during coverture.[8]

It appears, therefore, that Hawaii is the only jurisdiction still to be heard from on the question. Today we join that group of states and the District of Columbia which hold that under the Married Women's Property Acts the interest of a husband or a wife in an estate by the entireties is not subject to the claims of his or her individual creditors during the joint lives of the spouses.

---

7. [FN 1] Phipps, *Tenancy by Entireties*, 25 Temple L.Q. 24 (1951).

8. [Under the common law, a woman's separate legal existence with respect to property rights ended upon marriage, and her legal rights and obligations were subsumed by those of her husband. As explained by Blackstone, "By marriage, the husband and wife are one person in law: that is, the very being or legal existence of the woman is suspended during the marriage, or at least incorporated and consolidated into that of the husband: under whose wing, protection, and *cover*, she performs every thing; and is therefore called . . . a *feme-covert*. . . ." William Blackstone, Commentaries on the Laws of England (1785).—Eds.]

In so doing, we are placing our stamp of approval upon what is apparently the prevailing view of the lower courts of this jurisdiction.

Hawaii has long recognized and continues to recognize the tenancy in common, the joint tenancy, and the tenancy by the entirety, as separate and distinct estates. That the Married Women's Property Act of 1888 was not intended to abolish the tenancy by the entirety was made clear by the language of Act 19 of the Session Laws of Hawaii, 1903 (now HRS § 509-1). The tenancy by the entirety is predicated upon the legal unity of husband and wife, and the estate is held by them in single ownership. They do not take by moieties, but both and each are seized of the whole estate.

A joint tenant has a specific, albeit undivided, interest in the property, and if he survives his cotenant he becomes the owner of a larger interest than he had prior to the death of the other joint tenant. But tenants by the entirety are each deemed to be seized of the entirety from the time of the creation of the estate. At common law, this taking of the "whole estate" did not have the real significance that it does today, insofar as the rights of the wife in the property were concerned. For all practical purposes, the wife had no right during coverture to the use and enjoyment and exercise of ownership in the marital estate. All she possessed was her contingent right of survivorship.

The effect of the Married Women's Property Acts was to abrogate the husband's common law dominance over the marital estate and to place the wife on a level of equality with him as regards the exercise of ownership over the whole estate. The tenancy was and still is predicated upon the legal unity of husband and wife, but the Acts converted it into a unity of equals and not of unequals as at common law. No longer could the husband convey, lease, mortgage or otherwise encumber the property without her consent. The Acts confirmed her right to the use and enjoyment of the whole estate, and all the privileges that ownership of property confers, including the right to convey the property in its entirety, jointly with her husband, during the marriage relation. They also had the effect of insulating the wife's interest in the estate from the separate debts of her husband.

Neither husband nor wife has a separate divisible interest in the property held by the entirety that can be conveyed or reached by execution. A joint tenancy may be destroyed by voluntary alienation, or by levy and execution, or by compulsory partition, but a tenancy by the entirety may not. The indivisibility of the estate, except by joint action of the spouses, is an indispensable feature of the tenancy by the entirety. . . .

We are not persuaded by the argument that it would be unfair to the creditors of either spouse to hold that the estate by the entirety may not, without the consent of both spouses, be levied upon for the separate debts of either spouse. No unfairness to the creditor is involved here. We agree with the court in *Hurd v. Hughes*, 109 A. 418, 420 (Ct. of Chancery of Delaware 1920):

> But creditors are not entitled to special consideration. If the debt arose prior to the creation of the estate, the property was not a basis of credit, and if the debt

arose subsequently the creditor presumably had notice of the characteristics of the estate which limited his right to reach the property.

We might also add that there is obviously nothing to prevent the creditor from insisting upon the subjection of property held in tenancy by the entirety as a condition precedent to the extension of credit. Further, the creation of a tenancy by the entirety may not be used as a device to defraud existing creditors.

Were we to view the matter strictly from the standpoint of public policy, we would still be constrained to hold as we have done here today. In *Fairclaw v. Forrest*, 130 F.2d 829, 833 (D.C. Cir. 1942) the court makes this observation:

> The interest in family solidarity retains some influence upon the institution (of tenancy by the entirety). It is available only to husband and wife. It is a convenient mode of protecting a surviving spouse from inconvenient administration of the decedent's estate and from the other's improvident debts. It is in that protection the estate finds its peculiar and justifiable function.

It is a matter of common knowledge that the demand for single-family residential lots has increased rapidly in recent years, and the magnitude of the problem is emphasized by the concentration of the bulk of fee simple land in the hands of a few. The shortage of single-family residential fee simple property is critical and government has seen fit to attempt to alleviate the problem through legislation. When a family can afford to own real property, it becomes their single most important asset. Encumbered as it usually is by a first mortgage, the fact remains that so long as it remains whole during the joint lives of the spouses, it is always available in its entirety for the benefit and use of the entire family. Loans for education and other emergency expenses, for example, may be obtained on the security of the marital estate. This would not be possible where a third party has become a tenant in common or a joint tenant with one of the spouses, or where the ownership of the contingent right of survivorship of one of the spouses in a third party has cast a cloud upon the title of the marital estate, making it virtually impossible to utilize the estate for these purposes.

If we were to select between a public policy favoring the creditors of one of the spouses and one favoring the interests of the family unit, we would not hesitate to choose the latter. But we need not make this choice for, as we pointed out earlier, by the very nature of the estate by the entirety as we view it, and as other courts of our sister jurisdictions have viewed it, "[a] unilaterally indestructible right of survivorship, an inability of one spouse to alienate his interest, and, importantly for this case, a broad immunity from claims of separate creditors remain among its vital incidents." *In re Estate of Wall*, 440 F.2d 215, 218 (D.C. Cir. 1971).

Having determined that an estate by the entirety is not subject to the claims of the creditors of one of the spouses during their joint lives, we now hold that the conveyance of the marital property by Kokichi Endo and Ume Endo, husband and wife, to their sons, Samuel H. Endo and Toru Endo, was not in fraud of Kokichi Endo's judgment creditors. Affirmed.

KIDWELL, J., dissenting. . . .

I find the logic of Appellant[s]' analysis convincing. While the authorities are divided, I consider that the reasoning of the cases cited by Appellant[s] best reconciles the Married Women's Act with the common law.

The majority reaches its conclusion by holding that the effect of the Married Women's Act was to equalize the positions of the spouses by taking from the husband his common law right to transfer his interest, rather than by elevating the wife's right of alienation of her interest to place it on a position of equality with the husband's. I disagree. I believe that a better interpretation of the Married Women's Acts is that offered by the Supreme Court of New Jersey in *King v. Greene*, 153 A.2d 49, 60 (N.J. 1959):

> It is clear that the Married Women's Act created an equality between the spouses in New Jersey, insofar as tenancies by the entirety are concerned. If, as we have previously concluded, the husband could alienate his right of survivorship at common law, the wife, by virtue of the act, can alienate her right of survivorship. And it follows, that if the wife takes equal rights with the husband in the estate, she must take equal disabilities. Such are the dictates of common equality. Thus, the judgment creditors of either spouse may levy and execute upon their separate rights of survivorship.

One may speculate whether the courts which first chose the path to equality now followed by the majority might have felt an unexpressed aversion to entrusting a wife with as much control over her interest as had previously been granted to the husband with respect to his interest. Whatever may be the historical explanation for these decisions, I feel that the resultant restriction upon the freedom of the spouses to deal independently with their respective interests is both illogical and unnecessarily at odds with present policy trends. Accordingly, I would hold that the separate interest of the husband in entireties property, at least to the extent of his right of survivorship, is alienable by him and subject to attachment by his separate creditors, so that a voluntary conveyance of the husband's interest should be set aside where it is fraudulent as to such creditors, under applicable principles of the law of fraudulent conveyances.

Notes

1. *Fraudulent conveyance:* The plaintiffs alleged that Mr. and Mrs. Endo's conveyance of real property to their sons should be set aside as fraudulent. Articulate precisely the argument that the plaintiffs would make in support of that claim. Conversely, what arguments would the Endo brothers make that the gift from their parents was valid? The court asserts, "No unfairness to the creditor is involved here." Do you agree? If not, would you favor a different result in this case?

2. *A unity of equals:* Both majority and dissent are concerned with ending the husband's common law dominance over the marital estate. What approach

does each favor? From the perspective of public policy, which view is preferable?

3. *A further complication—death:*   *Sawada* held that estates by the entirety are not subject to the claims of the creditors of a single spouse during the spouses' joint lives, but what happens at the death of the debtor-spouse? Does the survivor remain protected from the decedent's debts? By statute, Hawaii provides,

> After the death of the first of the spouses . . . , all real property . . . that was immune from the claims of their separate creditors . . . immediately prior to the individual's death shall continue to have the same immunity from the claims of the decedent's separate creditors as would have existed if the spouses . . . continued to hold the real property . . . as tenants by the entirety.

Hawaii Revised Statutes § 509-2(d).

4. *A changing world—women and property:*   Married women's property acts in every state abolish the husband's common law right of exclusive control over the spouses' real property. Some states also abolished the tenancy by the entirety, perceiving it as a relic of the husband's common law domination. As one commentator explains:

> The question has been raised whether the tenancy by the entirety serves a justifiable social purpose in modern times. Admittedly, this tenancy is an anomaly based on an anachronism. In situations where the marriage relationship is unstable, the tenancy can operate to the disadvantage of one or both of the spouses. The inability of either spouse to compel partition or to effectuate a severance, or in some states to convey a separate interest to a third person, can create a deadlock with respect to the property. The legitimate claims of creditors can be defeated in those jurisdictions which do not permit a levy of execution on the interest of the debtor spouse. Despite these objections, however, the tenancy by the entirety continues to be a popular form of co-ownership in several states and it is unlikely that appeals for its abolition will be heeded. In a sense, this peculiar form of marital co-ownership operates as a substitute for a community property system in the common-law states which still retain it.

Moynihan's Introduction to the Law of Real Property, ch. 9, § 7 (Sheldon F. Kurtz, ed. 5th ed. 2011). *See also* Powell on Real Property § 52.01(3) (Michael Allan Wolf, gen. ed. 2015) (describing the status of tenancy by the entirety in each of the fifty states and concluding that "[t]he approaches are so varied that no generalization is possible").

5. *The place—oligopoly in Hawaii:*   The court based its holding, in part, on the "concentration of the bulk of fee simple lands in the hands of a few" and on the shortage of single-family residential fee simple property in Hawaii. As the U.S. Supreme Court explained in a different case that arose in Hawaii,

> The Hawaiian Islands were originally settled by Polynesian immigrants from the western Pacific. These settlers developed an economy around a feudal land tenure system in which one island high chief, the ali'i nui, controlled the land and assigned it for development to certain subchiefs. . . . All land was held at the

will of the ali'i nui and eventually had to be returned to his trust. There was no private ownership of land.

. . . In the mid-1960's, after extensive hearings, the Hawaii Legislature discovered that, while the State and Federal Governments owned almost 49% of the State's land, another 47% was in the hands of only 72 private landowners. The legislature further found that 18 landholders, with tracts of 21,000 acres or more, owned more than 40% of this land and that on Oahu, the most urbanized of the islands, 22 landowners owned 72.5% of the fee simple titles. The legislature concluded that concentrated land ownership was responsible for skewing the State's residential fee simple market, inflating land prices, and injuring the public tranquility and welfare.

To redress these problems, the legislature decided to compel the large landowners to break up their estates. The legislature considered requiring large landowners to sell lands which they were leasing to homeowners. . . . [T]o accommodate the needs of both lessors and lessees, the Hawaii Legislature enacted the Land Reform Act of 1967 (Act), Haw. Rev. Stat., ch. 516, which created a mechanism for condemning residential tracts and for transferring ownership of the condemned fees simple to existing lessees. . . .

Hawaii Housing Authority v. Midkiff, 467 U.S. 229 (1984) (cited in *Kelo v. City of New London*, excerpted in Chapter 13). Did *Sawada v. Endo*'s interpretation of Hawaii's tenancy by the entirety address the problems described by *Hawaii Housing Authority v. Midkiff*? How?

Parker v. Shecut

562 S.E.2d 620 (S.C. 2002)

Reading Guide

The following tale of fighting sibling cotenants, unfortunately, is not unusual. As you read the case, consider what lessons it provides for parents who plan to leave their property to their children as tenants in common. Consider the case also from the perspective of siblings Bo and Anne. What, if anything, could they have done to avoid the problem that prompted this litigation?

PLEICONES, J.

We granted certiorari to consider the Court of Appeals' decision affirming the Master in Equity's determination that Respondent Marion A. Shecut, III, ("Bo") did not oust his co-tenant, Petitioner Anne S. Parker ("Anne"), from their jointly-owned beach house. We reverse and remand.

Facts

In October 1992 Mary Shecut died, leaving her estate of approximately $1.3 million dollars to her three children, Anne, Bo, and Defendant Winfield W.

Shecut ("Win"). Mary's will named Bo and Win executors of the estate. On April 6, 1993, Anne, Bo, and Win executed a written agreement ("private agreement") delineating how the substantial real property inherited from their mother would be divided. Under the private agreement, Win received the bulk of the family's farm property adjacent to his own residence, while Anne and Bo received, as tenants in common, some farmland, a beach house at Edisto Island (which is at the heart of the issue on appeal), and a number of commercial properties in Orangeburg County. Anne and Bo agreed to manage their properties together, and each deposited $3,000.00 in a banking account under the name Shecut Investments. The two apparently did not execute a partnership agreement or otherwise reduce their management agreement to writing.

Correspondence in the record suggests problems with the property arrangement between Anne and Bo began by early 1994. On February 15, 1994, Anne wrote Bo a letter offering to sever[9] the co-tenancy in some of their joint property, with each receiving sole ownership of a portion. She complained that some of the property was not "being utilized equally between us."

Despite Anne's complaints, she and Bo maintained the beach house as a rental property through 1995. Anne presented evidence that the beach house generated the following gross rents between 1993 and 1995:

YEAR	GROSS RECEIPTS
1993	$8,497.00
1994	$18,181.00
1995	$19,841.00

According to Bo, however, after taxes, insurances and other expenses, the beach house generated only $229.00 in income in 1995. Bo included this amount on his income taxes for 1995. He testified that he claimed no income for the years 1993 and 1994. A real estate appraiser, called by Anne, testified that the Edisto Island beach house was a break-even rental property. The appraiser added that the best use for the house, that is the most profitable use, was to sell it.

During the years the beach house was rented, Anne took one-half of its depreciation on her income tax returns. In 1995, Anne amended the agreement with Edisto Realty, the real estate company managing the beach house property, and had all rental checks mailed directly to her home in Atlanta.[10]

Upon receipt of the rental checks, Anne endorsed them over to the attorney for the mother's estate. According to Bo, during the year Anne received rental checks, taxes and other expenses on the property were not paid, and Edisto Realty had to pay some of the expenses on the beach house. Bo also testified

---

9. [Is "sever" the most appropriate word here? Can you suggest a more precise term of art?—Eds.]

10. [FN 2] Prior to this time rental checks had been mailed to Bo, payable to Shecut Investments.

that he retrieved a check for about $4,000.00 from Edisto Realty in June 1995 and kept the check.

In January 1996 Bo, without consulting Anne, made the beach house his primary residence, and ceased renting the house. Anne testified that Bo told her in March 1996 that she was not welcome to use the beach house. He also told her he changed the locks. Prior to this time, Anne had access to the beach house when it was not being rented.

Bo denied that he ever told Anne she was not welcome at the beach house. He testified she was always welcome as long as "she would behave." Anne testified that she visited the beach house as late as March 1997, and that she entered the house. She added that while there, she was confronted by police. She could not establish that Bo called the police or was in any way responsible for the police showing up at the house.

Anne visited the beach house on one occasion between May 1997 and November 1997 and discovered her keys no longer worked. As of the date of the second hearing, November 12, 1997, Anne no longer had a working key or access to the beach house.

Bo changed the locks after the house was vandalized on June 13, 1997. He admitted that after that date Anne no longer had a working key. Based on a conversation he had with Win, Bo suspected Anne committed the vandalism. Win testified that he had a telephone conversation with Anne wherein she admitted she vandalized the beach house. Anne denied vandalizing the house and maintained that she had not been at the house on or about June 13, 1997.

Following the November 12, 1997, hearing, the master ordered the property granted Anne and Bo in the private agreement divided in-kind, with the exception of the beach house, which he ordered sold at public auction. The proceeds were divided so as to equalize the in-kind distribution.[11] The master found Bo had not committed ouster and awarded Anne no rent for the time Bo was in exclusive possession of the house. The Court of Appeals affirmed, finding that "Anne offer[ed] no evidence of either ouster or exclusion. Accordingly, Bo does not owe Anne anything for his use of the beach house. . . ."

Issue

Did the Court of Appeals err in determining Anne had failed to show ouster by Bo?

Analysis

"'Ouster' is the actual turning out or keeping excluded a party entitled to possession of any real property." *Freeman v. Freeman*, 473 S.E.2d 467, 470 (S.C.

---

11. [FN 3] Specifically, the order practically awarded Bo $58,100 more of the proceeds of the beach house sale than Anne, not including attorney's fees.

Ct. App. 1996). "By actual ouster is not meant a physical eviction, but a possession attended with such circumstances as to evince a claim of exclusive right and title and a denial of the right of the other tenants to participate in the profits." *Woods v. Bivens*, 354 S.E.2d 909, 912 (S.C. 1987).

The acts relied upon to establish an ouster must be of an unequivocal nature, and so distinctly hostile to the rights of the other cotenants that the intention to disseize is clear and unmistakable. . . . Only in rare, extreme cases will the ouster by one cotenant of other cotenants be implied from exclusive possession and dealings with the property, such as collection of rents and improvement of the property. Where one co-tenant has ousted the other co-tenant, and kept them out by force, he is liable as a trespasser for the rental value of the property beyond his ownership share.

We do not agree with the Court of Appeals' conclusion that Anne produced no evidence of ouster or exclusion. In our view, the preponderance of the evidence demonstrates ouster. Bo's own testimony establishes that on or about June 13, 1997, he changed the locks to the beach house. Further, he testified that he had not given Anne a working key, nor did he have any intention of giving Anne a key unless the master ordered him to do so. Bo's actions in changing the locks and refusing to provide Anne with a key are so distinctly hostile to Anne's rights that Bo's intention to disseize is clear and unmistakable. Further, Bo's actions clearly evince his claim of exclusive right and a denial of Anne's right to use the property. Accordingly, we find that Bo ousted Anne on June 13, 1997.[12]

Because the evidence adduced at trial shows Anne was ousted from the beach house on June 13, 1997, we reverse the Court of Appeals' decision on this issue and remand to the master for a determination of damages, if any, due Anne from the date of ouster.

TOAL, C.J., MOORE, WALLER, and BURNETT, JJ., concurring.

Notes

1. *Ouster:* Define "ouster" and explain how its requisite acts go beyond those permitted under each co-owner's unity of possession. The court asserts, "The acts relied upon to establish an ouster must be of an unequivocal nature."

---

12. [FN 4] We disagree with the holding implicit in the master's order that because Bo believed Anne vandalized the beach house, he was justified in excluding her from the property. A co-tenant's suspicion that another co-tenant has vandalized jointly-owned property does not permit the suspicious co-tenant to take the law into his own hands and forcibly exclude his co-tenant. If Bo believed his co-tenant Anne wasted the property, he should have sought to enjoin her from doing so, rather than resorting to self-help.

What evidence did Anne present in this case, and did it unequivocally establish an ouster by her brother Bo?

2. *Fighting siblings:* What are the benefits and challenges of the tenancy in common? If Mary Shecut had known that her children Anne and Bo would fight over the family beach house after her death, do you think she would have altered the terms of her will? Similarly, if Anne and Bo had known their relationship would deteriorate, do you think they would have agreed to hold the beach house as tenants in common? Can you think of any better alternatives for the distribution of the mother's property?

3. *The place—Edisto Island:* Edisto Island, South Carolina, has a multicultural history of settlement by Native Americans (the Edistow tribe of the Cusabo Indians), English settlers (first arriving in 1683), and Spanish Jesuit Africans (enslaved and brought to the New World in about 1684 to labor on cotton plantations). Due to infestation by the boll weevil in the 1920s, cotton plantations failed. In the wake of cotton cultivation, seafood fishing, truck farming, and vacation resorts began to develop. *See generally* The Edisto Island Museum, *Explore Our History*.

Historic building on Edisto Island, Charleston County, S.C.
Photograph by C.O. Greene (Historic American Buildings Survey 1940)
Source: Library of Congress

Ark Land Co. v. Harper

599 S.E.2d 754 (W. Va. 2004)

Reading Guide

In the previous case, we saw a disagreement over the use of a beach house owned by brother and sister as tenants in common. There, the court ordered the property to be sold at a public auction, with the proceeds to be distributed between the two owners. But should the court have ordered the sale in the first place, particularly if one of the owners objected to it? This case takes a closer look at the issues surrounding judicial *partition.*

DAVIS, J.

This is an appeal by . . . [various members of the Caudill family] (hereinafter collectively identified as the "Caudill heirs"), appellants/defendants below, from an order of the Circuit Court of Lincoln County. The circuit court's order authorized a partition and sale of real property jointly owned by the Caudill heirs and Ark Land Company (hereinafter referred to as "Ark Land"), appellee/plaintiff below. Here, the Caudill heirs contend that the legal precedents of this Court warrant partitioning the property in kind, not a sale. After a careful review of the briefs and record in this case, we agree with the Caudill heirs and reverse the circuit court.

This is a dispute involving approximately 75 acres of land situate in Lincoln County, West Virginia. The record indicates that "[t]he Caudill family has owned the land for nearly 100 years." The property "consists of a farmhouse, constructed around 1920, several small barns, and a garden[.]" Prior to 2001, the property was owned exclusively by the Caudill family. However, in 2001 Ark Land acquired a 67.5% undivided interest in the land by purchasing the property interests of several Caudill family members. Ark Land attempted to purchase the remaining property interests held by the Caudill heirs, but they refused to sell. Ark Land sought to purchase all of the property for the express purpose of extracting coal by surface mining.

After the Caudill heirs refused to sell their interest in the land, Ark Land filed a complaint in the Circuit Court of Lincoln County in October of 2001. Ark Land filed the complaint seeking to have the land partitioned and sold. . . .

The dispositive issue is whether the evidence supported the circuit court's conclusion that the property could not be conveniently partitioned in kind, thus warranting a partition by sale. During the proceeding before the circuit court, the Caudill heirs presented expert testimony by Gary F. Acord, a mining engineer. Mr. Acord testified that the property could be partitioned in kind. Specifically, Mr. Acord testified that lands surrounding the family home did not have coal deposits and could therefore be partitioned from the remaining lands. On the other hand, Ark Land presented expert testimony which indicated that such a partition would entail several million dollars in additional costs in order to mine for coal.

We note at the outset that "[p]artition means the division of the land held in cotenancy into the cotenants' respective fractional shares. If the land cannot be fairly divided, then the entire estate may be sold and the proceeds appropriately divided." 7 Powell on Real Property, § 50.07[1] (2004). It has been observed that, "[i]n the United States, partition was established by statute in each of the individual states. Unlike the partition in kind which existed under early common law, the forced judicial sale was an American innovation." Phyliss Craig-Taylor, *Through a Colored Looking Glass: A View of Judicial Partition, Family Land Loss, and Rule Setting,* 78 Wash. U. L.Q. 737, 752 (2000). . . .

Partition by sale, when it is not voluntary by all parties, can be a harsh result for the cotenant(s) who opposes the sale. This is because "'[a] particular piece of real estate cannot be replaced by any sum of money, however large; and one who wants a particular estate for a specific use, if deprived of his rights, cannot be said to receive an exact equivalent or complete indemnity by the payment of a sum of money.'" *Wight v. Ingram-Day Lumber Co.,* 17 So. 2d 196, 198 (Miss. 1944) (quoting *Lynch v. Union Inst. for Savings,* 34 N.E. 364, 364-365 (Mass. 1893)). Consequently, "[p]artition in kind . . . is the preferred method of partition because it leaves cotenants holding the same estates as before and does not force a sale on unwilling cotenants." *Powell,* § 50.07[4][a]. . . . The laws in all jurisdictions "appear to reflect this longstanding principle by providing a presumption of severance of common ownership in real property by partition in kind[.]" Craig-Taylor, *supra. . . .*

In . . . *Consolidated Gas Supply Corp. v. Riley,* [247 S.E.2d 712 (W. Va. 1978)], this Court set out the following standard of proof that must be established to overcome the presumption of partition in kind:

> . . . [A] party desiring to compel partition through sale is required to demonstrate (1) that the property cannot be conveniently partitioned in kind, (2) that the interests of one or more of the parties will be promoted by the sale, and (3) that the interests of the other parties will not be prejudiced by the sale.

. . . [T]he circuit court addressed each of the three factors [of] *Consolidated Gas Supply Corp.* as follows:

> (14) . . . [I]t is clearly evident that the subject property's nature, character, and amount are such that it cannot be conveniently, (that is "practically or justly") partitioned, or divided by allotment among its owners. Moreover, it is just and necessary to conclude that such a proposal as has been made by the [Caudill heirs], that of allotting the manor house and the surrounding "bottom land" unto the [Caudill heirs], cannot be affected without undeniably prejudicing [Ark Land's] interests . . . ; and,

> (15) That while its uniform topography superficially suggests a division-in-kind, as proposed by Mr. Acord [the Caudill heirs' expert], the access road, the bottom

lands and the relatively flat home site is, in fact, integral to establishing the fair market value of the subject property in its entirety, as its highest and best use as mining property, as shown by the uncontroverted testimony of [Ark Land's] experts Mr. Morgan and Mr. Terry; and,

(16) . . . [I]t is undisputed that the remaining heirs, that are [the Caudill heirs] herein, do not wish to sell, or have the Court sell, their interests in the subject property, solely due to their sincere sentiment for it as the family's "home place". Other family members, however, did not feel the same way. Given the equally undisputed testimony of [Ark Land's] experts, it is just and reasonable for the Court to conclude that the interests of all the subject property's owners will not be financially prejudiced, but will be financially promoted, by sale of the subject property and distribution among them of the proceeds, according to their respective interests. The subject property's value as coal mining property, its uncontroverted highest and best use, would be substantially impaired by severing the family's "home place" and allotting it to them separately. . . . Accordingly, the Court does hereby conclude as a matter of law that the subject property should be sold as a whole in its entirety, and that it cannot be partitioned in kind by allotment of part and a sale of the residue.

We are troubled by the circuit court's conclusion that partition by sale was necessary because the economic value of the property would be less if partitioned in kind. We have long held that the economic value of property *may* be a factor to consider in determining whether to partition in kind or to force a sale. . . . However, our cases *do not* support the conclusion that economic value of property is the exclusive test for determining whether to partition in kind or to partition by sale. In fact, we explicitly stated in *Hale v. Thacker*, 12 S.E.2d 524, 526 (W. Va. 1940), "that many considerations, other than monetary, attach to the ownership of land, and courts should be, and always have been, slow to take away from owners of real estate their common-law right to have the same set aside to them in kind." . . .

Other courts have also found that monetary consideration is not the only factor to contemplate when determining whether to partition property in kind or by sale. In the case of *Eli v. Eli*, 557 N.W.2d 405, 409-410 (S.D. 1997), the South Dakota Supreme Court addressed the issue of the impact of monetary considerations in deciding whether to partition property in kind or by sale . . . :

[M]onetary considerations, while admittedly significant, do not rise to the level of excluding all other appropriate considerations. . . . The sale of property "without [the owner's] consent is an extreme exercise of power warranted only in clear cases." We believe this to be especially so when the land in question has descended from generation to generation. While it is true that the Eli brothers' expert testified that if partitioned, the separate parcels would sell for $50 to $100 less per acre, this fact alone is not dispositive. One's land possesses more than mere economic utility; it "means the full range of the benefit the parties may be expected to derive from their ownership of their respective shares." [internal citations omitted]. . . .

In view of the prior decisions of this Court, as well as the decisions from other jurisdictions, we now make clear and hold that, in a partition proceeding in which a party opposes the sale of property, the economic value of the property is not the exclusive test for deciding whether to partition in kind or by sale. Evidence of longstanding ownership, coupled with sentimental or emotional interests in the property, may also be considered in deciding whether the interests of the party opposing the sale will be prejudiced by the property's sale. This latter factor should ordinarily control when it is shown that the property can be partitioned in kind, though it may entail some economic inconvenience to the party seeking a sale.

In the instant case, the Caudill heirs were not concerned with the monetary value of the property. Their exclusive interest was grounded in the longstanding family ownership of the property and their emotional desire to keep their ancestral family home within the family.[13] It is quite clear that this emotional interest would be prejudiced through a sale of the property. . . .

The facts in this case reveal that, prior to 2001, Ark Land had no ownership interest in the property. Conversely, for nearly 100 years the Caudill heirs and their ancestors owned the property and used it for residential purposes.[14] In 2001 Ark Land purchased ownership rights in the property from some Caudill family members. When the Caudill heirs refused to sell their ownership rights, Ark Land immediately sought to force a judicial sale of the property. In doing this, Ark Land established that its proposed use of the property, surface coal mining, gave greater value to the property. This showing is self-serving. In most instances, when a commercial entity purchases property because it believes it can make money from a specific use of the property, that property will increase in value based upon the expectations of the commercial entity. This self-created enhancement in the value of property cannot be the determinative factor in forcing a pre-existing co-owner to give up his/her rights in property. To have such a rule would permit commercial entities to always "evict" pre-existing co-owners, because a commercial entity's interest in property will invariably increase its value. . . .

We are very sensitive to the fact that Ark Land will incur greater costs in conducting its business on the property as a result of partitioning in kind. However, Ark Land voluntarily took an economical gamble that it would be able to get all of the Caudill family members to sell their interests in the property. Ark Land's gamble failed. The Caudill heirs refused to sell their interests.

---

13. [FN 7] . . . While it may be true that the family members who sold their interest in the property did not have any emotional attachment to the family home, this fact cannot be dispositively attributed to the Caudill heirs. The interest of the Caudill heirs cannot be nullified or tossed aside, simply because other family members do not share the same sentiments for the family home.

14. [FN 8] No one lives permanently at the family home. However, the family home is used on weekends and for special family events by the Caudill heirs.

The fact that Ark Land miscalculated on its ability to acquire outright all interests in the property cannot form the basis for depriving the Caudill heirs of their emotional interests in maintaining their ancestral family home. The additional cost to Ark Land that will result from a partitioning in kind simply does not impose the type of injurious inconvenience that would justify stripping the Caudill heirs of the emotional interest they have in preserving their ancestral family home. *See* Syl. pt. 4, in part, *Croston v. Male,* 49 S.E. 136 (W. Va. 1904) ("Inconvenience of partition as one of the circumstances authorizing such sale, . . . is not satisfied by anything short of a real and substantial obstacle of some kind to division in kind, such as would make it injurious to the owners"). . . .

. . . We, therefore, reverse the circuit court's order requiring sale of the property. This case is remanded with directions to the circuit court to enter an order requiring the property to be partitioned in kind, consistent with the report and testimony of the Caudill heirs' mining engineer expert, Gary F. Acord.

MAYNARD, C.J., concurring, in part, and dissenting, in part.

I concur with the new law created by the majority in this case. That is to say, I agree that evidence of longstanding ownership along with sentimental or emotional attachment to property are factors that should be considered and, in some instances, control the decision of whether to partition in kind or sale jointly-owned property which is the subject of a partition proceeding.

I dissent in this case, however, because I do not believe that evidence to support the application of those factors was presented here. In that regard, the record shows that none of the appellants have resided at the subject property for years. At most, the property has been used for weekend retreats. While this may have been the family "homeplace," a majority of the family has already sold their interests in the property to the appellee. Only a minority of the family members, the appellants, have refused to do so. I believe that the sporadic use of the property by the appellants in this case does not outweigh the economic inconvenience that the appellee will suffer as a result of this property being partitioned in kind.

I am also troubled by the majority's decision that this property should be partitioned in kind instead of being sold because I don't believe that such would have been the case were this property going to be put to some use other than coal mining. For instance, I think the majority's decision would have been different if this property was going to be used in the construction of a four-lane highway. Under those circumstances, I believe the majority would have concluded that such economic activity takes precedence over any long-term use or sentimental attachment to the property on the part of the appellants. In my opinion, coal mining is an equally important economic activity. This decision destroys the value of this land as coal mining property because the appellee would incur several million dollars in additional costs to continue its mining operations. As a result of the majority's decision in this case, many innocent coal miners will be out of work. . . .

Notes

1. *Sentimental attachment to the home place:* The majority and dissent agree that emotional attachment to property is a relevant factor that courts can consider when determining what type of partition to order. The circuit court, in contrast, wanted to promote the "highest and best use" of the disputed property. Overall, how much weight should courts give to emotional, as opposed to economic, considerations? What does this case tell you about real property's dual nature as a fungible market commodity and a place of particular value to its owners?

2. *Majority rule—in theory, but not in practice:* Although concurrent ownership can be beneficial for as long as the co-owners get along, it poses perplexing challenges when one or more of the parties wants to exit from the shared ownership arrangement. If all owners can agree unanimously on an exit strategy, then the law will honor such voluntary termination of the cotenancy. But if the parties cannot agree, each individual owner has a right to petition a court to partition the property and put an end to shared ownership, even above the objections of the other owners. Courts repeatedly articulate a preference for partition in kind, as implemented in *Ark Land Co.*, and assert that a forced sale over the objection of some of the owners is an extraordinary remedy that should be awarded sparingly. Moreover, a forced sale can give short shrift to subjective values not easily captured by the market, nor reflected in the sales price.

In practice, however, it appears that courts more often partition property by sale. Powell on Real Property § 50.07(5) (Michael Allan Wolf, gen. ed. 2015) ("Most partitions today are indeed in the form of sale and division of proceeds."). What rationales support this judicial willingness to order partitions by sale? Some suggest that they avoid excessive "fragmentation." As Professor Michael Heller argues,

> . . . The American law of property encourages owners to subdivide resources freely. Hidden within the law, however, is a boundary principle that limits the right to subdivide private property into wasteful fragments. . . .
>
> The danger with fragmentation is that it may operate as a one-way ratchet: Because of high transaction costs, strategic behaviors, and cognitive biases, people may find it easier to divide property than to recombine it. . . . With too many owners of property fragments, resources become prone to waste either through overuse . . . or through underuse. . . .
>
> Consider two people who are tenants in common of a farm—each cotenancy is itself private property. To avoid overuse when owners' preferences conflict, property law interposes a nonwaivable "right to partition." However, when too

many co-owners share a farm, physical "partition in kind" can lead to uneconomically small lots and underuse. Judges prevent underuse by favoring "partition by sale" over "partition in kind," by dividing money rather than land among co-owners.

Michael A. Heller, *The Boundaries of Private Property*, 108 Yale L.J. 1163, 1165-67 (1999). Recall also our discussion of the problem of "fractionation" of Native American lands (in the notes after *Johnson v. M'Intosh* in Chapter 1). The federal government has attempted to remedy the fractionation problem by helping the tribes buy back land to be held in tribal trust ownership for uses benefitting tribal members. But that solution is not generally applicable beyond the tribal context.

Others support partitions by sale against the charge that the market cannot adequately translate subjective and emotional values into economic terms. According to Professors Bell and Parchomovsky,

> ... [E]ven where partition by sale is favored, co-tenants may bid for the sold property; thus, partition by sale allows a co-tenant who has developed enough of a subjective attachment to have become the highest value user to take control of the property by submitting the appropriate bid. Partition in kind, on the other hand, may destroy value in all of those cases where preservation of value is incompatible with changes in the underlying property's physical nature or the property's division among many users. ... An heirloom dish, for example, will lose its value if it is shattered in order to distribute the pieces among its co-owners. Similarly, when the co-owned asset is the family home, it cannot be partitioned in kind. ...

Abraham Bell & Gideon Parchomovsky, *A Theory of Property*, 90 Cornell L. Rev. 531, 551, 601-02 (2005).

What do you think? Should courts order partitions in kind or partitions by sale? How should they make that decision?

3. *Practice pointer—anticipating cotenant disputes:* How would you advise a client who had inherited property as a cotenant with numerous siblings? Can you think of any way to anticipate and minimize future cotenant disputes? *See* section D, below.

4. *The place—coal mining country:* The Caudill family faced a double challenge. First, the relatives had to navigate the difficulties of co-ownership. In their case, eight named heirs shared the family homestead with a mining company as tenants in common. Prior to the sale of a 67.5% interest to Ark Land Company, even more family members held shared title to the property. As a result, a dozen or so individuals had to agree on every aspect of the possession and use of the single farmhouse, several barns, garden, and surrounding acreage.

Perhaps even more challenging, the family property is located in Appalachian coal country, where opposing views about mining tear apart the fabric of the community, and pit neighbor against neighbor. Appalachia is one of the most impoverished regions of the country. West Virginia, home to the disputed property, ranked 49 out of 50 in per capita income, according to the 2000 U.S. census. Coal mining is an important industry in the state. In 2004, the year of the decision in *Ark Land Company*, West Virginia lagged behind only Wyoming in coal production. But over the preceding few decades, the introduction of highly mechanized surface mining techniques—so-called "mountaintop removal"—dramatically reduced the need for miners, and West Virginia's ranks of coal miners plummeted from 125,000 (in 1948) to 19,000 (2005). Under the practice, trees are clear-cut from the mountain peak, the rock is shattered with explosives to expose the coal seam underneath, and the fragmented mountain "overburden" is scooped up by huge draglines such as "Big John" (shown in the photograph) and packed into adjacent mountain valleys, in many cases by filling in existing stream beds. The Environmental Protection Agency estimates that at least 1,200 miles of mountain streams have been buried beneath mining waste. Ark Land Company wanted the Caudill property to expand one of its largest surface mines in the state—the 12,000-acre Hobet 21 mine.

The electric shovel "Big John" has a dragline as tall as a 20-story building and a scoop that can hold over 100 tons of rock and soil at a time. It was used at the Hobet 21 Mine, which Ark Land wanted to expand by purchasing the Caudill property.
Photograph by Lyntha Scott Eiler (1995)
Source: Coal River Folklife Project collection (AFC 1999/008), American Folklife Center, Library of Congress

It is easy to understand why county residents might value the mining industry for the jobs and economic benefits it provides, and why some of the Caudill family members would have been eager to sell out their ownership share to boost their family finances. On the other hand, the negative social, health, and environmental consequences of coal mining are well documented. *National Geographic* explained the risks posed in West Virginia and Kentucky by more than 250 coal mining wastewater impoundments, which the periodical described as "often perched precariously on the sides of the mountains":

> Variously referred to as slurry ponds, sludge lagoons, or waste basins, they impound hundreds of billions of gallons of toxic black water and sticky black goo, by-products of cleaning coal. . . . Mountain folk residing downhill from these ponds worry about what a flood of loose sludge might do—and has already done in a number of tragic cases.

> In Logan County [adjacent to Lincoln County, home of the Caudill property] in the winter of 1972, following two straight days of torrential rain, a coal-waste structure built by a subsidiary of the Pittson Coal Company collapsed and spilled 130 million gallons . . . into Buffalo Creek. The flood scooped up tons of debris and scores of homes as it swept downstream. Survivors recalled seeing houses bob by, atilt in the swift current, the doomed families huddled at their windows. The final count was 125 dead, 1,000 injured, 4,000 made homeless. The Pittston Company called the disaster an "act of God."

See John G. Mitchell, *When Mountains Move*, National Geographic (Mar. 2006); Environmental Protection Agency, *Mountaintop Mining/Valley Fills in Appalachia: Final Programmatic Environmental Impact Statement*, at 4 (Oct. 2005).

Uniform Partition of Heirs Property Act

National Conference of Commissioners on Uniform State Laws, © 2010

Reading Guide

> *Ark Land Co.* illustrated a widespread problem—what should courts do with property held by many (potentially dozens) of cotenants, when the owners cannot agree as to the use of the property? The problem is particularly widespread in lower- and middle-income communities where property owners often lack access to estate-planning attorneys and die intestate, thereby passing their property to numerous heirs as tenants in common under the states' laws of intestate succession. The Uniform Partition of Heirs Property Act is one attempt to address that problem. As of September 2015, the model legislation had been enacted by six states (Alabama, Arkansas, Connecticut, Georgia, Montana, and Nevada) and introduced in two others (Hawaii and South Carolina).

The Uniform Partition of Heirs Property Act (*UPHPA*) helps preserve family wealth passed to the next generation in the form of real property. Affluent families can engage in sophisticated estate planning to ensure generational wealth, but those with smaller estates are more likely to use a simple will or to die intestate. For many lower- and middle-income families, the majority of the estate consists of real property. If the landowner dies intestate, the real estate passes to the landowner's heirs as tenants-in-common under state law. Tenants-in-common are vulnerable because any individual tenant can force a partition. Too often, real estate speculators acquire a small share of heirs' property in order to file a partition action and force a sale. Using this tactic, an investor can acquire the entire parcel for a price well below its fair market value and deplete a family's inherited wealth in the process. UPHPA provides a series of simple due process protections: notice, appraisal, right of first refusal, and if the other co-tenants choose not to exercise their right and a sale is required, a commercially reasonable sale supervised by the court to ensure all parties receive their fair share of the proceeds.

§ 2. Definitions ...

(4) "Determination of value" means a court order determining the fair market value of heirs property under Section 6 or 10 or adopting the valuation of the property agreed to by all cotenants.

(5) "Heirs property" means real property held in tenancy in common which satisfies all of the following requirements as to the filing of a partition action:
   (A) There is no agreement in a record binding all the cotenants which governs the partition of the property;
   (B) One or more of the cotenants acquired title from a relative, whether living or deceased; and
   (C) Any of the following applies:
      (i) 20 percent or more of the interests are held by cotenants who are relatives;
      (ii) 20 percent or more of the interests are held by an individual who acquired title from a relative, whether living or deceased; or
      (iii) 20 percent or more of the cotenants are relatives. ...

§ 6. Determination of value

(a) Except as otherwise provided in subsections (b) and (c), if the court determines that the property that is the subject of a partition action is heirs property, the court shall determine the fair market value of the property by ordering an appraisal pursuant to subsection (d).

(b) If all cotenants have agreed to the value of the property or to another method of valuation, the court shall adopt that value or the value produced by the agreed method of valuation.

(c) If the court determines that the evidentiary value of an appraisal is outweighed by the cost of the appraisal, the court, after an evidentiary hearing, shall determine the fair market value of the property and send notice to the parties of the value.

(d) If the court orders an appraisal, the court shall appoint a disinterested real estate appraiser licensed in this state to determine the fair market value of the property assuming sole ownership of the fee simple estate. . . .

§ 7. Cotenant buyout

(a) If any cotenant requested partition by sale, after the determination of value under Section 6, the court shall send notice to the parties that any cotenant except a cotenant that requested partition by sale may buy all the interests of the cotenants that requested partition by sale.

(b) Not later than 45 days after the notice is sent under subsection (a), any cotenant except a cotenant that requested partition by sale may give notice to the court that it elects to buy all the interests of the cotenants that requested partition by sale.

(c) The purchase price for each of the interests of a cotenant that requested partition by sale is the value of the entire parcel determined under Section 6 multiplied by the cotenant's fractional ownership of the entire parcel. . . .

§ 8. Partition alternatives

(a) If all the interests of all cotenants that requested partition by sale are not purchased by other cotenants pursuant to Section 7, or if after conclusion of the buyout under Section 7, a cotenant remains that has requested partition in kind, the court shall order partition in kind unless the court, after consideration of the factors listed in Section 9, finds that partition in kind will result in [great] [manifest] prejudice to the cotenants as a group. In considering whether to order partition in kind, the court shall approve a request by two or more parties to have their individual interests aggregated.

(b) If the court does not order partition in kind under subsection (a), the court shall order partition by sale pursuant to Section 10 or, if no cotenant requested partition by sale, the court shall dismiss the action.

(c) If the court orders partition in kind pursuant to subsection (a), the court may require that one or more cotenants pay one or more other cotenants amounts so that the payments, taken together with the value of the in-kind distributions to the cotenants, will make the partition in kind just and proportionate in value to the fractional interests held. . . .

§ 9. Considerations for partition in kind

(a) In determining under Section 8(a) whether partition in kind would result in [great][manifest] prejudice to the cotenants as a group, the court shall consider the following:

(1) Whether the heirs property practicably can be divided among the cotenants;

(2) Whether partition in kind would apportion the property in such a way that the aggregate fair market value of the parcels resulting from the division would be materially less than the value of the property if it were sold as a whole, taking into account the condition under which a court-ordered sale likely would occur;

(3) Evidence of the collective duration of ownership or possession of the property by a cotenant and one or more predecessors in title or predecessors in possession to the cotenant who are or were relatives of the cotenant or each other;

(4) A cotenant's sentimental attachment to the property, including any attachment arising because the property has ancestral or other unique or special value to the cotenant;

(5) The lawful use being made of the property by a cotenant and the degree to which the cotenant would be harmed if the cotenant could not continue the same use of the property;

(6) The degree to which the cotenants have contributed their pro rata share of the property taxes, insurance, and other expenses associated with maintaining ownership of the property or have contributed to the physical improvement, maintenance, or upkeep of the property; and

(7) Any other relevant factor.

(b) The court may not consider any one factor in subsection (a) to be dispositive without weighing the totality of all relevant factors and circumstances.

§ 10. Open-market sale, sealed bids, or auction

(a) If the court orders a sale of heirs property, the sale must be an open-market sale unless the court finds that a sale by sealed bids or an auction would be more economically advantageous and in the best interest of the cotenants as a group.

(b) If the court orders an open-market sale and the parties, not later than 10 days after the entry of the order, agree on a real estate broker licensed in this state to offer the property for sale, the court shall appoint the broker and establish a reasonable commission. If the parties do not agree on a broker, the court shall appoint a disinterested real estate broker licensed in this state to offer the property for sale and shall establish a reasonable commission. The broker shall offer the property for sale in a commercially reasonable manner at a price no lower than the determination of value and on the terms and conditions established by the court.

(c) If the broker appointed under subsection (b) obtains within a reasonable time an offer to purchase the property for at least the determination of value . . . the sale may be completed in accordance with state law other than this [act].

(d) If the broker appointed under subsection (b) does not obtain within a reasonable time an offer to purchase the property for at least the determination
of value, the court, after hearing, may:
(1) Approve the highest outstanding offer, if any;
(2) Redetermine the value of the property and order that the property continue to be offered for an additional time; or
(3) Order that the property be sold by sealed bids or at an auction.
(e) If the court orders a sale by sealed bids or an auction, the court shall set terms
and conditions of the sale. If the court orders an auction, the auction must be
conducted under [insert reference to general partition statute or, if there is
none, insert reference to foreclosure sale].
(f) If a purchaser is entitled to a share of the proceeds of the sale, the purchaser is
entitled to a credit against the price in an amount equal to the purchaser's
share of the proceeds. . . .

Notes

1. *A web of interests—protecting "heirs property":*   Read the definition of
"heirs property" under § 2(5). Why do you think the drafters of the uniform act
selected this group of property owners as especially in need of legal protection?
What reforms does the act suggest, and what practical consequences would
follow from their implementation? Apply the uniform act to the facts of *Ark
Land Co. v. Harper*. Would the result have been the same?

2. *The problem of heirs property:*   What is the problem of heirs property
that the uniform act seeks to address? Among other things, heirs property
passes to successors without a will, in part as a relic of the Resconstruction
Era. Sarah Breitenbach, *Heirs' Property Challenges Families, States*, The PEW
Charitable Trust, Stateline (July 15, 2015) (explaining that during the Reconstruction era African-Americans gained property rights, but "often did not
create wills to establish formal ownership for future generations because
they were denied access to the legal system, did not trust it or could not afford
it"). As a consequence, owners lack a deed or formal record title to the property,
making it difficult to access the property's equity and to obtain the home
improvement loans often necessary to maintain the property. *Id.*

The threat of partition also renders heirs property fragile. As Professor
Thomas Mitchell, the reporter for the Uniform Act's drafting committee,
explains:

> A significant percentage of families who own heirs property poorly understand
> many of the legal rules governing tenancy-in-common ownership, which is not
> surprising given that many of the rules are counterintuitive and given that these
> families often lack access to basic legal services. . . . [O]ne study of such property

owners revealed that the overwhelming majority of these owners believed that their property was safe from a sale unless all of the cotenants would agree to sell. Therefore, many of these families wrongly assume that the large number of family members who own an undivided interest in the property serves as protection from the property being sold. Tragically, the first time many of these families learn about the actual rules governing tenancy-in-common ownership is after one of the cotenants threatens to file a partition action or, in many instances, after such a cotenant has filed a partition action. . . .

. . . African-Americans have been particularly at risk of losing their property as a result of partition sales because a substantial percentage of African-Americans who own land in the South own such properties under the default, tenancy-in-common rules, instead of under, for example, what is referred to as a tenancy-in-common agreement or TIC agreement. In fact, studies have documented that African-Americans have lost a significant amount of real property as a result of partition sales. . . . [The author also describes how the same pattern of land loss affects families who own land in Appalachia, middle-class white families, and Hispanic communities.]

Thomas W. Mitchell, *Reforming Property Law to Address Devastating Land Loss*, 66 Alabama L. Rev. 1, 28-33 (2014). *See also* Phyliss Craig-Taylor, *Through a Colored Looking Glass: A View of Judicial Partition, Family Land Loss, and Rule Setting*, 78 Washington U. L.Q. 737 (2000). Notice Professor Mitchell's reference to tenancy-in-common agreements as a desirable alternative to the tenancy in common default rules. We will consider such TIC agreements in section D, below.

3. Modern Applications: Condominiums, Cooperatives, and Time-Share Housing

Beyond the tenancy in common, joint tenancy, and tenancy by the entirety, several other types of shared ownership have been developed.

The condominium: The condominium is a form of concurrent ownership under which residents hold an undivided interest as *tenants in common* in the shared elements of the community (such as exterior walls, roof, swimming pool, and grounds) and also hold an interest in *fee simple absolute* in the interior of the unit. Each owner obtains separate financing for his or her individual unit. The condominium is a form of legal ownership and not a particular architectural configuration. Thus, condominiums can include freestanding houses, multi-unit buildings, or other types of structures. State statutes control many aspects of the creation and operation of condominium communities. In addition, most communities organize owners associations and adopt numerous rules and regulations known as "restrictive covenants" in an effort to promote a uniform environment. We will take a closer look at restrictive covenants in Chapter 10, below.

The cooperative: Although several variations exist, typically a nonprofit corporation owns the entire premises. Each resident is a *stockholder* in the corporation, and also holds a long-term *leasehold* interest in an individual unit or apartment. The corporation holds a single mortgage to finance the structure; if one stockholder defaults on payments, then all others must make up the shortfall owed to the lender. Like the condominium, cooperatives generally organize an owners association and adopt restrictive covenants. Cooperatives exist primarily as multi-unit buildings in urban areas.

The time-share housing: Under "deeded" time-share arrangements, each cotenant owns an interest in a specific unit to use at a *specific time each year* (such as the first week in June each year). This is a real property interest that can be sold, rented, or otherwise freely alienated. As with condominium ownership, all time-share owners together own the resort property. Marketed as a vacation alternative, time-share housing allows people to have an ownership stake in their vacation home (albeit, for a brief period of time each year) and to capture any associated appreciation in equity, rather than to pay for hotel rooms or other lodging. As a variation, one can own the *right to use* a particular unit for a specified time interval, which is an interest in *personal*, rather than real, property.

Dutcher v. Owens

647 S.W.2d 948 (Tex. 1983)

Reading Guide

This case provides a brief overview of the condominium form of ownership. It suggests yet another challenge of concurrent ownership—the allocation of liability for tort claims arising out of property elements owned in common.

RAY, J.

This is a case of first impression concerning the allocation of liability among condominium co-owners for tort claims arising out of the ownership, use and maintenance of "common elements." The defendant was found to be vicariously liable for the homeowners' association's negligence. The trial court ordered that the plaintiffs recover from the defendant an amount based upon the defendant's proportionate ownership in the condominium project. The court of appeals reversed in part the judgment of the trial court, holding "that each unit owner, as a tenant in common with all other unit owners in the common elements, is jointly and severally liable for damage claims arising in the common elements." 635 S.W.2d 208, 211. We reverse the judgment of the court of appeals and affirm the trial court's judgment.

J.A. Dutcher, a resident of San Diego, California, owned a condominium apartment in the Eastridge Terrace Condominiums, located in Dallas County, which he leased to Ted and Christine Owens. Ownership of the apartment includes a 1.572% *pro rata* undivided ownership in the common elements of the project. The Owenses suffered substantial property loss in a fire which began in an external light fixture in a common area.

The Owenses filed suit in Tarrant County against Dutcher, the Eastridge Terrace Condominium Association, Joe Hill Electric Company, IHS-8 Ltd. (the developer) and a class of co-owners of condominiums in Eastridge Terrace represented by the officers of the homeowners' association. All defendants with the exception of Dutcher obtained a change of venue to Dallas County. The case was tried before a jury, which found the following:

(1) The fire was proximately caused by the lack of an insulating box behind the light fixture in the exterior wall air space;
(2) The homeowners' association knew of this defect;
(3) The homeowners' association alone was negligent in failing to install an insulating box with knowledge of the defect; and
(4) The negligence of homeowners' association resulted in damage to the Owens' property in the amount of $69,150.00.

The trial court rendered judgment against Dutcher on the jury's verdict in the amount of $1,087.04. The award represents the amount of damages multiplied by Dutcher's 1.572% *pro rata* undivided ownership in the common elements of the Eastridge Terrace Condominium project.

By an agreed statement of facts filed with the court of appeals, the parties stipulated that the sole issue for determination on appeal was whether a condominium co-owner is jointly and severally liable or is liable only for a *pro rata* portion of the damages. Tex. R. Civ. P. 377(d).

In enacting the Texas Condominium Act (the Act), Tex. Rev. Civ. Stat. Ann. art. 1301a, the Texas Legislature intended to create "a new method of property ownership."[15] 1963 Tex. Gen. Laws, Ch. 191, § 26 at 512. A condominium is an estate in real property consisting of an undivided interest in a portion of a parcel of real property together with a separate fee simple interest in another portion of the same parcel. In essence, condominium ownership is the merger of two estates in land into one: the fee simple ownership of an apartment or unit in a condominium project and a tenancy in common with other co-owners in the common elements.

"General common elements" consist of, *inter alia,* the land upon which the building stands, the "foundations, bearing walls and columns, roofs, halls,

---

15. [FN 1] Condominium ownership is a tenure unknown at common law. Provisions for a form of condominium ownership can be found in the Roman civil law and the Napoleonic Code. 4B *Powell on Real Property* (Part III) ¶¶599, 633.1 *et seq.* (1976).

lobbies, stairways, and entrances and exits or communication ways; . . . [a]ll other elements of the building desirable or rationally of common use or necessary to the existence, upkeep and safety of the condominium regime, and any other elements described in the declaration. . . ." Tex. Rev. Civ. Stat. Ann. art. 1301a, § 2(*l*), subsections (1), (2) & (7). An individual apartment cannot be conveyed separately from the undivided interest in the common elements and *vice versa. Id.* § 9.

A condominium regime must be established according to the Act. The declaration must be filed with the county clerk, who must record the instrument in the Condominium Records. Once the declarant has complied with the provisions of the Act, each apartment in the project is treated as an interest in real property. Administration of the regime is established by the Act.

The condominium association or council is a legislatively created unincorporated association of co-owners having as their common purpose a convenient method of ownership of real property in a statutorily created method of ownership which combines both the concepts of separateness of tenure and commonality of ownership. The California Supreme Court has concluded that "the concept of separateness in the condominium project carries over to any management body or association formed to handle the common affairs of the project, and that both the condominium project and the condominium association must be considered separate legal entities from its unit owners and association members." *White v. Cox*, 95 Cal. Rptr. 259, 262 (Cal. App. 1971).

Given the uniqueness of the type of ownership involved in condominiums, the onus of liability for injuries arising from the management of condominium projects should reflect the degree of control exercised by the defendants. We agree with the California court's conclusion that to rule that a condominium co-owner had any effective control over the operation of the common areas would be to sacrifice "reality to theoretical formalism," for in fact a co-owner has no more control over operations than he would have as a stockholder in a corporation which owned and operated the project. *White v. Cox*, 95 Cal. Rptr. at 263. This does not limit the plaintiff[s'] right of action. The efficiency found in a suit directed at the homeowners' association and its board of directors representing the various individual homeowners, as well as any co-owner causally or directly responsible for the injuries sustained, benefits both sides of the docket as well as the judicial system as a whole.

Such a result is not inconsistent with the legislative intent. While the Act creates a new form of real property ownership, it does not address the issue of the allocation of tort liability among co-owners. Nevertheless, we are guided in our decision by the other provisions in the Act which appear *in pari materia,* and which proportionately allocate various financial responsibilities. For example, the Act provides for *pro rata* contributions by co-owners toward expenses of administration and maintenance, insurance, taxes and assessments. *Pro rata* provisions also exist for the application of insurance proceeds.

Respondents have cited us to two bills submitted in the legislature in 1981. The bills, which did not pass, included provisions for re-apportionment of liability on a *pro rata* basis. Inasmuch as each bill involved a complete revision of the Act, we cannot draw inferences of the legislature's intent from the failure of the bills to pass. Any such inference would involve little more than conjecture. The legislative history of the Act is so scant that the most that can be said is that the Act is silent as to the matter, and hence the legislative intent is unknown.

The theories of vicarious and joint and several liability are judicially created vehicles for enforcing remedies for wrongs committed. Justified on public policy grounds, they represent a deliberate allocation of risk.

Texas follows the rule that statutes in derogation of the common law are not to be strictly construed. Nevertheless, it is recognized that if a statute creates a liability unknown to the common law, or deprives a person of a common law right, the statute will be strictly construed in the sense that it will not be extended beyond its plain meaning or applied to cases not clearly within its purview. Since the Act is silent as to tort liability, we are dealing with rights and liabilities which are not creatures of statute but with the common law, which is our special domain. Hence, the rule we have reached is not a usurpation of the legislative prerogative. To the contrary, it is one reached in the public interest.

We hold, therefore, that because of the limited control afforded a unit owner by the statutory condominium regime, the creation of the regime effects a reallocation of tort liability. The liability of a condominium co-owner is limited to his *pro rata* interest in the regime as a whole, where such liability arises from those areas held in tenancy-in-common. The judgment of the court of appeals is reversed and the judgment of the trial court is affirmed.

Notes

1. *Who should pay?*   The trial court found that the homeowners association's negligence resulted in damage in the amount of $69,150 to the plaintiffs. Who should be responsible for paying those damages? Do you favor the trial court's approach (as affirmed by the Texas Supreme Court), the appellate court's approach, or some other approach to liability? *See* George L. Sutherland, *Cause of Action Against Condominium Association for Injury Suffered in Common Area of Condominium Development*, 30 Causes of Action 583 (1992 & 2015 Supp.); Jerry C.M. Orten & John H. Zacharia, *Allocation of Damages for Tort Liability in Common Interest Communities*, 31 Real Prop. Prob. & Tr. J. 647 (1997).

2. *Tort liability:*   As illustrated by the approach of the court of appeals, owners of individual condominium units face potentially broad tort liability for losses suffered on the common elements. This liability can be tempered by insurance or by statute. Mississippi law, for example, provides,

> The owners of a unit shall have no personal liability for any damages caused by the governing body on or in connection with the use of common areas. A unit owner shall be liable for injuries or damages resulting from an accident in his own unit to the same extent and degree that the owner of a house, an office, or a store would be liable for an accident occurring therein.

Miss. Code Ann. § 89-9-29(B). Similarly, under New Jersey law,

> A unit owner shall have no personal liability for any damages caused by the association or in connection with the use of the common elements. A unit owner shall be liable for injuries or damages resulting from an accident in his own unit in the same manner and to the same extent as the owner of any other real estate.

New Jersey Statutes § 46:8B-16(c). *See generally* Powell on Real Property § 54A.12(2)(a)(i) (Michael Allan Wolf, gen. ed. 2015). Do you think such statutes are desirable?

3. *The condominium form of ownership:*   Based on this brief introduction to condominiums—and perhaps on your own experience—what do you see as the advantages and disadvantages of condominium ownership? What does this case add to our consideration of the challenges of shared property? As one response to the challenges of shared ownership, most condominium developments impose legally binding covenants, conditions, and restrictions on all owners, as we will see in Chapter 10. *See generally* Donna S. Bennett, *Condominium Homeownership in the United States: A Selected Annotated Bibliography of Legal Sources*, 103 Law Library J. 249 (2011) (annotated bibliography tracing the legal development of condominium homeownership in the United States from its beginnings in the early 1960s).

B. MARITAL PROPERTY SYSTEMS

Two major systems govern the treatment of marital property in the United States. Although they take different approaches, both systems incorporate safeguards to promote fair treatment of each spouse and to protect the family, particularly upon divorce or death. In each system, it is important to distinguish *separate property*, which is owned and controlled by one spouse alone, from jointly held property (called *marital property* in the separate property system, and *community property* in the community property system). Here, we will simply provide a brief introduction to the marital property systems, leaving the details to upper-level courses on family law.

The separate property (or "common law") system: The majority approach is the *separate property* system (sometimes called the *common law* system), which developed from the common law of England. As its name implies, the separate property system gives each individual spouse considerable latitude to own and control *separate property* during and after the marriage.

A Place to Start | The Separate Property System

- *During marriage—separate v. marital property:*

  - *Separate property:* Separate property includes property acquired *before marriage*, such as real estate, automobiles, bank accounts, or stock (and its growth and dividends). In addition, it generally includes property acquired separately *during the marriage*, such as gifts, devises, inheritance, and wages.

  - *Marital property:* Separate property can be transformed ("transmuted") into marital property if the spouses so intend. For example, one spouse can convey separate property to the couple to be held as tenants in common, joint tenants, or tenants by the entirety. Separate property can also be transmuted if it is commingled with marital property and no longer separately traceable.

- *Death:* The surviving spouse is protected by:

  - *Laws of intestate succession:* State law governs the distribution of property in the absence of a will. Although they vary, state intestate succession statutes allocate a substantial share of the decedent's property at the time of death (the "estate") to the surviving spouse, and also provide for other survivors such as children (from present and former marriages) and surviving parents; or

  - *Elective share (or "forced share") provisions:* If the decedent's will is unfavorable, the surviving spouse can *elect* to take a statutorily prescribed share of the decedent's estate. As you might imagine, enterprising spouses at death's door have undertaken various actions in an attempt to undermine elective share statutes, such as transferring gifts *causa mortis* (Chapter 2). To counter such tactics, some states take a broad view of what constitutes the decedent's property at death (the so-called *augmented estate*). All separate property states (with the exception of Georgia) recognize elective shares, which range from one-third to one-half of the decedent's estate.

- *Dissolution of marriage—equitable distribution:* Upon divorce, most states require an *equitable distribution* of marital property, which is not necessarily an equal distribution. State laws specify relevant factors, including such things as the contribution to, and dissipation of, the marital assets by each spouse; the economic circumstances, sources of income, and employment prospects of each spouse after divorce; and child custody and support. Alternatively, if the parties negotiated a valid prenuptial agreement, it will control the distribution of property.

The community property system: Nine states located primarily in the west follow the *community property* system, which has been influenced by the civil law and its French and Spanish heritage: Arizona, California, Idaho, Louisiana, Nevada, New Mexico, Texas, Washington, and Wisconsin. In addition, couples in Alaska may elect to follow the community property system. One essential feature of the community property system is its recognition of a unique form of concurrent ownership—*community property*—that generally gives each spouse an extra measure of protection from the other's actions during the marriage, upon death, and upon divorce. Because this community property bears some resemblance to tenancies by the entirety, community property states do not recognize the tenancy by the entirety. Importantly, each spouse's earnings during marriage are community property, owned equally in undivided shares by both spouses.

A Place to Start | The Community Property System

■ **During marriage:**

  ■ **Separate property:** As in separate property jurisdictions, separate property generally includes property acquired *before* marriage and property acquired separately *during* the marriage by gift, devise, or inheritance (but not wages).

  ■ **Community property:** Community property includes all property, other than separate property, that either spouse acquires during the marriage. This includes each spouse's earnings, as well as property purchased with those earnings. In addition, separate property can be *transmuted* into community property if the spouses so intend, or if it is commingled with community property and no longer separately traceable. The couple owns community property equally and jointly, even if the property is titled in only one spouse. Community property is not subject to judicial partition.

■ **Death:** Although state variations exist, generally spouses are free to dispose of all of their separate property, and one-half of their community property by will. If a spouse dies without a will in a community property state, his or her share of the community property generally passes to the surviving spouse.

■ **Dissolution of marriage:** In some community property states, separate property must be awarded to its owner after divorce; in others, it is divided *equitably*. As to community property, most states require an *equitable distribution*, similar to the division of marital property required under the separate property system. Three states (California, Louisiana, and New Mexico), however, require an *equal* distribution of community property, awarding half to each former spouse. Alternatively, if the parties negotiated a valid prenuptial agreement, it will control the distribution of property in most states.

The following cases take a look at two issues related to the distribution of property upon divorce. First, does an education qualify as "property" to be divided among the divorcing spouses? Second, do the protections of the marital systems extend to the dissolution of relationships other than traditional marriages?

In re Marriage of Graham

574 P.2d 75 (Colo. 1978)

Reading Guide

In the words of the dissent, this case "presents the not-unfamiliar pattern of the wife who, willing to sacrifice for a more secure family financial future, works to educate her husband, only to be awarded a divorce decree shortly after he is awarded his degree." How should courts resolve the *degree-to-decree* dilemma? Should they treat a divorcing spouse's educational degree as "property," the value of which should be divided upon divorce?

LEE, J.

This case presents the novel question of whether in a marriage dissolution proceeding a master's degree in business administration (M.B.A.) constitutes marital property which is subject to division by the court. In its opinion . . . the Colorado Court of Appeals held that it was not. We affirm the judgment.

The Uniform Dissolution of Marriage Act requires that a court shall divide marital property, without regard to marital misconduct, in such proportions as the court deems just after considering all relevant factors. The Act defines marital property as follows:

> For purposes of this article only, "marital property" means all property acquired by either spouse subsequent to the marriage except:
>
> (a) Property acquired by gift, bequest, devise, or descent;
>
> (b) Property acquired in exchange for property acquired prior to the marriage or in exchange for property acquired by gift, bequest, devise, or descent;
>
> (c) Property acquired by a spouse after a decree of legal separation; and
>
> (d) Property excluded by valid agreement of the parties.

Section 14-10-113(2), C.R.S. 1973.

The parties to this proceeding were married on August 5, 1968, in Denver, Colorado. Throughout the six-year marriage, Anne P. Graham, wife and petitioner here, was employed full-time as an airline stewardess. She is still so employed. Her husband, Dennis J. Graham, respondent, worked part-time for most of the marriage, although his main pursuit was his education. He attended school for approximately three and one-half years of the marriage, acquiring both a bachelor of science degree in engineering physics and a master's degree in business administration at the University of Colorado. Following graduation, he obtained a job as an executive assistant with a large corporation at a starting salary of $14,000 per year.

The trial court determined that during the marriage petitioner contributed seventy percent of the financial support, which was used both for family expenses and for her husband's education. No marital assets were accumulated during the marriage. In addition, the Grahams together managed an apartment house and petitioner did the majority of housework and cooked most of the meals for the couple. No children were born during the marriage.

The parties jointly filed a petition for dissolution, on February 4, 1974, in the Boulder County District Court. Petitioner did not make a claim for maintenance or for attorney fees. After a hearing on October 24, 1974, the trial court found, as a matter of law, that an education obtained by one spouse during a marriage is jointly-owned property to which the other spouse has a property right. The future earnings value of the M.B.A. to respondent was evaluated at $82,836 and petitioner was awarded $33,134 of this amount, payable in monthly installments of $100.

The court of appeals reversed, holding that an education is not itself "property" subject to division under the Act, although it was one factor to be considered in determining maintenance or in arriving at an equitable property division.

The purpose of the division of marital property is to allocate to each spouse what equitably belongs to him or her. The division is committed to the sound discretion of the trial court and there is no rigid mathematical formula that the court must adhere to. . . .

The legislature intended the term "property" to be broadly inclusive, as indicated by its use of the qualifying adjective "all" in section 14-10-113(2). . . .

Nonetheless, there are necessary limits upon what may be considered "property," and we do not find any indication in the Act that the concept as used by the legislature is other than that usually understood to be embodied within the term. One helpful definition is "everything that has an exchangeable value or which goes to make up wealth or estate." *Black's Law Dictionary* 1382 (rev. 4th ed. 1968). In *Ellis v. Ellis*, 552 P.2d 506 (Colo. 1976), this court held that military retirement pay was not property for the reason that it did not have any of the elements of cash surrender value, loan value, redemption value, lump sum value, or value realizable after death. The court of appeals has considered other factors as well in deciding whether something falls within the concept, particularly whether it can be assigned, sold, transferred, conveyed, or pledged, or whether it terminates on the death of the owner.

An educational degree, such as an M.B.A., is simply not encompassed even by the broad views of the concept of "property." It does not have an exchange value or any objective transferable value on an open market. It is personal to the holder. It terminates on death of the holder and is not inheritable. It cannot be assigned, sold, transferred, conveyed, or pledged. An advanced degree is a cumulative product of many years of previous education, combined with diligence and hard work. It may not be acquired by the mere expenditure of money. It is simply an intellectual achievement that may potentially assist in the future acquisition of property. In our view, it has none of the attributes of property in the usual sense of that term.

Our interpretation is in accord with cases in other jurisdictions. We have been unable to find any decision, even in community property states, which appears to have held that an education of one spouse is marital property to be divided on dissolution. This contention was dismissed in *Todd v. Todd*, 78 Cal. Rptr. 131 (Cal. Ct. App. 1969), where it was held that a law degree is not a community property asset capable of division, partly because it "cannot have monetary value placed upon it." . . .

Other cases cited have dealt only with related issues. For example, in awarding alimony, as opposed to dividing property, one court has found that an education is one factor to be considered. *Daniels v. Daniels*, 185 N.E.2d 773 (Ohio Ct. App. 1961). In another case, the wife supported the husband while he went to medical school. *Nail v. Nail*, 486 S.W.2d 761 (Tex. 1972). The question was whether the accrued good will of his medical practice was marital property, and the court held it was not, inasmuch as good will was based on the husband's personal skill, reputation, and experience. Contra, *Mueller v. Mueller*, 301 P.2d 90 (Cal. Ct. App. 1956). . . .

The trial court relied on *Greer v. Greer*, 510 P.2d 905 (Colo. App. 1973), for its determination that an education is "property." In that case, a six-year marriage was dissolved in which the wife worked as a teacher while the husband obtained a medical degree. The parties had accumulated marital property. The trial court awarded the wife alimony of $150 per month for four years. The court of appeals found this to be proper, whether considered as an adjustment of property rights based upon the wife's financial contribution to the marriage, or as an award of alimony in gross. The court there stated that ". . . [i]t must be considered as a substitute for, or in lieu of, the wife's rights in the husband's property. . . ." We note that the court did not determine that the medical education itself was divisible property. The case is distinguishable from the instant case in that here there was no accumulation of marital property and the petitioner did not seek maintenance (alimony).

A spouse who provides financial support while the other spouse acquires an education is not without a remedy. Where there is marital property to be divided, such contribution to the education of the other spouse may be taken into consideration by the court. *Greer v. Greer*, *supra*. Here, we again note that no marital property had been accumulated by the parties. Further, if maintenance is sought and a need is demonstrated, the trial court may make an award based on all relevant factors. Certainly, among the relevant factors to be considered is the contribution of the spouse seeking maintenance to the education of the other spouse from whom the maintenance is sought. Again, we note that in this case petitioner sought no maintenance from respondent. The judgment is affirmed.

CARRIGAN, J., dissenting, joined by PRINGLE, C. J., and GROVES, J.

I respectfully dissent.

As a matter of economic reality the most valuable asset acquired by either party during this six-year marriage was the husband's increased earning capacity. There is no dispute that this asset resulted from his having obtained Bachelor of Science and Master of Business Administration degrees while married. These degrees, in turn, resulted in large part from the wife's employment which contributed about 70% of the couple's total income. Her earnings not only provided her husband's support but also were "invested" in his education in the sense that she assumed the role of breadwinner so that he would have the time and funds necessary to obtain his education.

The case presents the not-unfamiliar pattern of the wife who, willing to sacrifice for a more secure family financial future, works to educate her husband, only to be awarded a divorce decree shortly after he is awarded his degree. The issue here is whether traditional, narrow concepts of what constitutes "property" render the courts impotent to provide a remedy for an obvious injustice.

In cases such as this, equity demands that courts seek extraordinary remedies to prevent extraordinary injustice. If the parties had remained married long enough after the husband had completed his post-graduate education so that they could have accumulated substantial property, there would have been no problem. In that situation abundant precedent authorized the trial court, in determining how much of the marital property to allocate to the wife, to take into account her contributions to her husband's earning capacity.

A husband's future income earning potential, sometimes as indicated by the goodwill value of a professional practice, may be considered in deciding property division or alimony matters, and the wife's award may be increased on the ground that the husband probably will have substantial future earnings. *Todd v. Todd*, [*supra*] (goodwill of husband's law practice). . . .

Similarly, the wife's contributions to enhancing the husband's financial status or earning capacity have been considered in awarding alimony and maintenance. The majority opinion emphasizes that in this case no maintenance was requested. However, the Colorado statute would seem to preclude an award of maintenance here, for it restricts the court's power to award maintenance to cases where the spouse seeking it is unable to support himself or herself. Section 14-10-114, C.R.S. 1973.

While the majority opinion focuses on whether the husband's master's degree is marital "property" subject to division, it is not the degree itself which constitutes the asset in question. Rather it is the increase in the husband's earning power concomitant to that degree which is the asset conferred on him by his wife's efforts. That increased earning capacity was the asset appraised in the economist's expert opinion testimony as having a discounted present value of $82,000.

Unquestionably the law, in other contexts, recognizes future earning capacity as an asset whose wrongful deprivation is compensable. Thus one who tortiously destroys or impairs another's future earning capacity must pay as damages the amount the injured party has lost in anticipated future earnings. *Nemer v. Anderson*, 378 P.2d 841 (Colo. 1963). . . .

Where a husband is killed, his widow is entitled to recover for loss of his future support damages based in part on the present value of his anticipated future earnings, which may be computed by taking into account probable future increases in his earning capacity. *See United States v. Sommers*, 351 F.2d 354 (10th Cir. 1965). . . .

The day before the divorce the wife had a legally recognized interest in her husband's earning capacity. Perhaps the wife might have a remedy in a separate action based on implied debt, quasi-contract, unjust enrichment, or some similar theory. Nevertheless, the law favors settling all aspects of a dispute in a single action where that is possible. Therefore I would affirm the trial court's award. . . .

Notes

1. *From degree to decree:* Compare the opinions of the majority and the dissent—which promotes a more equitable result? In this case, the couple had not accumulated marital property during the relatively brief marriage. How did (or should) that affect the outcome of the case? How should courts resolve the degree-to-decree dilemma? If one spouse acquires "property" (a degree or enhanced earning ability) with the help of the other, should the owner-spouse owe anything to the supporting spouse upon divorce?

2. *Majority view:* In re Marriage of Graham represents the view of almost all states, under which professional degrees and licenses are not marital assets subject to distribution upon divorce. A few states hold otherwise. *See, e.g., O'Brien v. O'Brien*, 489 N.E.2d 712 (N.Y. 1985) (holding that husband's newly acquired license to practice medicine, acquired during the marriage, is marital property subject to equitable distribution under statutory scheme premised on the view of marriage as "an economic partnership to which both parties contribute as spouse, parent, wage earner or homemaker"); *Haugan v. Haugan*, 343 N.W.2d 796 (Wis. 1984). All is not lost for the supporting spouse, however. If the marriage endured long enough to generate marital assets, then some states regard the enhanced earning capacity that resulted from the degree or license, or the professional practice made possible by the professional degree as an asset subject to distribution when the marriage ends. *See, e.g., Mace v. Mace*, 818 So. 2d 1130 (Miss. 2002) (holding that although a professional degree is not marital property in Mississippi, the value of the professional practice made possible by the degree is marital property subject to equitable distribution). Other states will provide equitable relief to the supporting spouse through

restitution, rehabilitative alimony, reimbursement, and similar mechanisms. *See, e.g., Guy v. Guy*, 736 So. 2d 1042 (Miss. 1999); 3 A.L.R. 6th 447 (recognizing that supporting husband would be entitled to some reimbursement if he can demonstrate that he paid for former wife's education to obtain a nursing degree).

Marvin v. Marvin

557 P.2d 106 (Cal. 1976)

Reading Guide

Lee Marvin (1924-1987), a party to this case, was a prominent American actor and Academy Award winner who appeared in more than 60 movies. Likewise, *Marvin v. Marvin* is a prominent judicial opinion, with almost two thousand citations tallied by Westlaw. In the decade preceding the *Marvin* case, the U.S. census reported that the number of unmarried couples living together increased about eightfold. What does this case tell you about the relationship between property law and rapidly changing social conditions?

TOBRINER, J.

During the past 15 years, there has been a substantial increase in the number of couples living together without marrying. Such nonmarital relationships lead to legal controversy when one partner dies or the couple separates. [California] Courts of Appeal, faced with the task of determining property rights in such cases, have arrived at conflicting positions: two cases have held that the Family Law Act (Civ. Code, § 4000 et seq.) requires division of the property according to community property principles, and one decision rejected that holding. . . .

We conclude: (1) The provisions of the Family Law Act do not govern the distribution of property acquired during a nonmarital relationship; such a relationship remains subject solely to judicial decision. (2) The courts should enforce express contracts between nonmarital partners except to the extent that the contract is explicitly founded on the consideration of meretricious sexual services. (3) In the absence of an express contract, the courts should inquire into the conduct of the parties to determine whether that conduct demonstrates an implied contract, agreement of partnership or joint venture, or some other tacit understanding between the parties. The courts may also employ the doctrine of quantum meruit, or equitable remedies such as constructive or resulting trusts, when warranted by the facts of the case.

In the instant case plaintiff [Michelle Marvin] and defendant [Lee Marvin] lived together for seven years without marrying; all property acquired during this period was taken in defendant's name. When plaintiff sued to enforce a contract under which she was entitled to half the property and to support payments, the trial court granted judgment on the pleadings for defendant, thus leaving him with all property accumulated by the couple during their relationship. Since the trial court denied plaintiff a trial on the merits of her claim, its decision conflicts with the principles stated above, and must be reversed.

The factual setting of this appeal. . . .

Plaintiff avers that in October of 1964 she and defendant "entered into an oral agreement" that while "the parties lived together they would combine their efforts and earnings and would share equally any and all property accumulated as a result of their efforts whether individual or combined." Furthermore, they agreed to "hold themselves out to the general public as husband and wife" and that "plaintiff would further render her services as a companion, homemaker, housekeeper and cook to . . . defendant."

Shortly thereafter plaintiff agreed to "give up her lucrative career as an entertainer (and) singer" in order to "devote her full time to defendant . . . as a companion, homemaker, housekeeper and cook;" in return defendant agreed to "provide for all of plaintiff's financial support and needs for the rest of her life."

Plaintiff alleges that she lived with defendant from October of 1964 through May of 1970 and fulfilled her obligations under the agreement. During this period the parties as a result of their efforts and earnings acquired in defendant's name substantial real and personal property, including motion picture rights worth over $1 million. In May of 1970, however, defendant compelled plaintiff to leave his household. He continued to support plaintiff until November of 1971, but thereafter refused to provide further support. . . .

Plaintiff's complaint states a cause of action for breach of an express contract. . . .

Defendant first and principally relies on the contention that the alleged contract is so closely related to the supposed "immoral" character of the relationship between plaintiff and himself that the enforcement of the contract would violate public policy. . . .

Although the past decisions hover over the issue in the somewhat wispy form of the figures of a Chagall painting, we can abstract from those decisions a clear and simple rule. The fact that a man and woman live together without marriage, and engage in a sexual relationship, does not in itself invalidate agreements between them relating to their earnings, property, or expenses. . . .

In summary, we base our opinion on the principle that adults who voluntarily live together and engage in sexual relations are nonetheless as competent as any other persons to contract respecting their earnings and property rights. Of course, they cannot lawfully contract to pay for the performance of sexual services, for such a contract is, in essence, an agreement for prostitution and unlawful for that reason. But they may agree to pool their earnings and to hold all property acquired during the relationship in accord with the law governing community property; conversely they may agree that each partner's earnings and the property acquired from those earnings remains the separate property of the earning partner. . . .

Plaintiff's complaint can be amended to state a cause of action founded upon theories of implied contract or equitable relief. . . .

In *In re Marriage of Cary*, 109 Cal. Rptr. 862 (Cal. Ct. App. 1973), . . . the Court of Appeal held that, in view of the policy of the Family Law Act, property accumulated by nonmarital partners in an actual family relationship should be divided equally. . . .

Both plaintiff and defendant stand in broad agreement that the law should be fashioned to carry out the reasonable expectations of the parties. Plaintiff, however, presents the following contentions: that the decisions prior to *Cary* rest upon implicit and erroneous notions of punishing a party for his or her guilt in entering into a nonmarital relationship, that such decisions result in an inequitable distribution of property accumulated during the relationship, and that *Cary* correctly held that the enactment of the Family Law Act in 1970 over-turned those prior decisions. Defendant in response maintains that the prior decisions merely applied common law principles of contract and property to persons who have deliberately elected to remain outside the bounds of the community property system. *Cary*, defendant contends, erred in holding that the Family Law Act vitiated the force of the prior precedents. . . .

[The] . . . failure of the courts to recognize an action by a *nonmarital* partner based upon implied contract, or to grant an equitable remedy, contrasts with the judicial treatment of the *putative spouse*. Prior to the enactment of the Family Law Act, no statute granted rights to a putative spouse.[16] The courts accordingly fashioned a variety of remedies by judicial decision. Some cases permitted the putative spouse to recover half the property on a theory that the conduct of the parties implied an agreement of partnership or joint venture. Others permitted the spouse to recover the reasonable value of rendered ser-vices, less the value of support received. Finally, decisions affirmed the power of a court to employ equitable principles to achieve a fair division of property acquired during putative marriage. . . .

---

16. [FN 13] The Family Law Act, . . . classifies property acquired during a putative marriage as "quasi-marital property," and requires that such property be divided upon dissolution of the marriage in accord with Civil Code section 4800. [Section 4452 stated that if the "court finds that either party or both parties believed in good faith that the marriage was valid, the court should declare such party or parties to have the status of a *putative* spouse, and shall divide, in accordance with Section 4800, that property acquired during the union. . . ." (emphasis added).—Eds.]

Reviewing the prior decisions which had denied relief to the homemaking partner, the Court of Appeal [in *Cary*] reasoned that those decisions rested upon a policy of punishing persons guilty of cohabitation without marriage. The Family Law Act, the court observed, aimed to eliminate fault or guilt as a basis for dividing marital property. But once fault or guilt is excluded, the court reasoned, nothing distinguishes the property rights of a nonmarital "spouse" from those of a putative spouse. Since the latter is entitled to half the "quasi marital property" . . . , the Court of Appeal concluded that, giving effect to the policy of the Family Law Act, a nonmarital cohabitator should also be entitled to half the property accumulated during an "actual family relationship." . . .

In summary, we believe that the prevalence of nonmarital relationships in modern society and the social acceptance of them, marks this as a time when our courts should by no means apply the doctrine of the unlawfulness of the so-called meretricious relationship to the instant case. . . . To equate the nonmarital relationship of today to such a subject matter is to do violence to an accepted and wholly different practice.

We are aware that many young couples live together without the solemnization of marriage, in order to make sure that they can successfully later undertake marriage. This trial period, preliminary to marriage, serves as some assurance that the marriage will not subsequently end in dissolution to the harm of both parties. . . .

The mores of the society have indeed changed so radically in regard to cohabitation that we cannot impose a standard based on alleged moral considerations that have apparently been so widely abandoned by so many. Lest we be misunderstood, however, we take this occasion to point out that the structure of society itself largely depends upon the institution of marriage, and nothing we have said in this opinion should be taken to derogate from that institution. The joining of the man and woman in marriage is at once the most socially productive and individually fulfilling relationship that one can enjoy in the course of a lifetime.

We conclude that the judicial barriers that may stand in the way of a policy based upon the fulfillment of the reasonable expectations of the parties to a nonmarital relationship should be removed. . . . [I]n the absence of an express agreement, the courts may look to a variety of other remedies in order to protect the parties' lawful expectations.

The courts may inquire into the conduct of the parties to determine whether that conduct demonstrates an implied contract or implied agreement of partnership or joint venture, or some other tacit understanding between the parties. The courts may, when appropriate, employ principles of constructive trust or resulting trust. Finally, a nonmarital partner may recover in quantum meruit for the reasonable value of household services rendered less the reasonable value of support received if he can show that he rendered services with the expectation of monetary reward.

Since we have determined that plaintiff's complaint states a cause of action for breach of an express contract, and, as we have explained, can be amended to state a cause of action independent of allegations of express contract, we must conclude that the trial court erred in granting defendant a judgment on the pleadings. . . .

WRIGHT, C.J. and RIGHT, C.J., and McCOMB, MOSK, SULLIVAN, and RICHARDSON, JJ., concur.

CLARK, J. (concurring and dissenting).

Notes

1. *Meretricious relationships:* If Michelle Marvin could substantiate her claims on remand, to what would she be entitled? Alternatively, to what would she have been entitled if she and Lee had been married, or if she had been *putatively* married? Today, a "meretricious" relationship refers to a committed, intimate relationship. The Washington Supreme Court, for example, defined it as "a stable marital-like relationship where both parties cohabit with knowledge that a lawful marriage between them does not exist." *Connell v. Francisco*, 898 P.2d 831, 834 (Wash. 1995). The adjective, "meretricious," however, has a negative connotation, meaning, "(1) of or relating to a prostitute, or (2) tawdrily and falsely attractive." *Merriam-Webster Dictionary*. This negative aspect was reflected in an early California Supreme Court opinion, which distinguished a putative marriage from a meretricious or "sinful" relationship where "unmarried persons knowingly lived together." *Coats v. Coats*, 118 P. 441, 444-45 (Cal. 1911).

2. *More to the story:* This case established the then-groundbreaking principle that California would enforce express or implied contracts between unmarried partners for the division of property upon separation or the death of one of the partners. On remand, however, the trial court found that Lee Marvin had never agreed to share his property with Michelle, or to support her. Further, the court found that the couple had never agreed that Michelle would relinquish her professional career as a singer and entertainer to devote her attention to Lee as his companion and homemaker. *See Marvin v. Marvin*, 122 Cal. App. 3d 871, 873 (Cal. App. 1981). Despite the plaintiff's failure to prove her case on remand, *Marvin* had considerable influence on the rights of unmarried cohabitants' property rights, in both community property jurisdictions and separate property jurisdictions. *See* Powell on Real Property § 53.02 (Michael Allan Wolf, gen. ed. 2015). In addition, at least one jurisdiction applied *Marvin* to same-sex cohabiting couples. *See Gormley v. Robertson*, 83 P.3d 1042 (Wash. App. 2004).

3. *A changing world—same-sex marriage:* In the 1970s, *Marvin's* potential extension of the benefits of marriage to unmarried couples was considered quite remarkable. Later, the focus would shift to the issue of same-sex couples and same-sex marriage. In *Obergefell v. Hodges*, 135 S. Ct. 2584 (2015) (Kennedy, J., joined by Ginsburg, Breyer, Sotomayor, and Kagan, JJ.), the Court heard challenges brought by same-sex couples to laws in Michigan, Kentucky, Ohio, and Tennessee that defined marriage as a union between one man and one woman. The Court held:

> [T]he right to marry is a fundamental right inherent in the liberty of the person, and under the Due Process and Equal Protection Clauses of the Fourteenth Amendment couples of the same-sex may not be deprived of that right and that liberty. The Court now holds that same-sex couples may exercise the fundamental right to marry. No longer may this liberty be denied to them. . . . [T]he State laws challenged by Petitioners in these cases are now held invalid to the extent they exclude same-sex couples from civil marriage on the same terms and conditions as opposite-sex couples.

Id. at 2604-05.

There were three dissenting opinions. Chief Justice Roberts, joined by Justices Scalia and Thomas, argued:

> Although the policy arguments for extending marriage to same-sex couples may be compelling, the legal arguments for requiring such an extension are not. The fundamental right to marry does not include a right to make a State change its definition of marriage. And a State's decision to maintain the meaning of marriage that has persisted in every culture throughout human history can hardly be called irrational. In short, our Constitution does not enact any one theory of marriage. The people of a State are free to expand marriage to include same-sex couples, or to retain the historic definition.

Id. at 2611. In a separate dissent, Justice Scalia, joined by Justice Thomas, wrote:

> . . . I write separately to call attention to this Court's threat to American democracy. . . .

> The substance of today's decree is not of immense personal importance to me. The law can recognize as marriage whatever sexual attachments and living arrangements it wishes, and can accord them favorable civil consequences, from tax treatment to rights of inheritance. . . . It is of overwhelming importance, however, who it is that rules me. Today's decree says that my Ruler, and the Ruler of 320 million Americans coast-to-coast, is a majority of the nine lawyers on the Supreme Court. The opinion in these cases is the furthest extension in fact—and the furthest extension one can even imagine—of the Court's claimed power to create "liberties" that the Constitution and its Amendments neglect to mention. This practice of constitutional revision by an unelected committee of nine, always accompanied (as it is today) by extravagant praise of liberty, robs the People of the most important liberty they asserted in the Declaration of Independence and won in the Revolution of 1776: the freedom to govern themselves.

Id. at 2584. Justice Alito also filed a dissenting opinion, joined by Justices Scalia and Thomas:

> Until the federal courts intervened, the American people were engaged in a debate about whether their States should recognize same-sex marriage. The question in these cases, however, is not what States *should* do about same-sex marriage but whether the Constitution answers that question for them. It does not. The Constitution leaves that question to be decided by the people of each State.

Id. at 2640.

C. BEYOND THE BLACK LETTER: NEW FORMS OF CONCURRENT OWNERSHIP

As the Texas Supreme Court explained in *Dutcher v. Owens*, although Roman civil law and the Napoleonic Code recognized the condominium form of ownership, the common law did not recognize it. But in the United States, despite the *numerus clausus* principle, the states began to recognize new forms of concurrent ownership in the early 1960s, including the condominium, the cooperative, and time-share housing. Today, ever more variations of shared ownership have begun to emerge.

For example, building on the time-share model, *fractional ownership* allows multiple owners to use the same property for flexible periods of time. One commentator explains the popularity of this model in resort areas:

> [T]he use of fractional properties has grown extensively in popular vacation areas like Vail, Colorado. Globally, Vail is one of the most sought after resort properties, making even fractional ownership enormously expensive. This famous ski resort area offers fractional properties that range in price from $100,000 to the multi-millions, depending on the size of the fraction, the size of the residence, and location. The popularity of this resort area has helped to protect the investment of timeshare and fractional owners, unlike other locations. Notably, Vail has suffered very little with the mortgage crisis (likely because of the enormous number of buyers who pay in cash) and has been even less affected by the current U.S. housing slump. Vail is, essentially, the epitome of the timeshare [developer's] dream location.

Elizabeth A. Cameron & Salina Maxwell, *Protecting Consumers: The Contractual and Real Estate Issues Involving Timeshares, Quartershares, and Fractional Ownership*, 37 Real Estate L.J. 278, 280-81 (2009).

Personal property, too, can be divided into fractional ownership. For example, since about 1986, the fractional ownership of aircraft has attracted billions of dollars' worth of investment. In turn, these aircraft can be pooled together:

> In general terms, fractional ownership programs are multi-year programs covering a pool of aircraft, each of which is owned by more than one party and all of which are placed in a dry lease [without a crew] exchange pool to be made available to any program participant when the aircraft in which such participant owns an interest is not available. . . . By purchasing an interest in an aircraft that is part of the program, an owner gains round-the-clock access to a private jet at a fraction of the cost. In addition to access to the aircraft in which it owns an interest, it also has access to all other aircraft in the program, as well as the support of a management company that will handle all arrangements relating to maintenance, crew hiring, and all administrative details relating to the operation of a private aircraft.

Eileen M. Gleimer, *When Less Can Be More: Fractional Ownership of Aircraft—The Wings of the Future*, 64 J. Air Law & Commerce 979, 980 (1999). *See also* Eileen M. Gleimer, *The Regulation of Fractional Ownership: Have the Wings of the Future Been Clipped?*, 67 J. Air Law & Commerce 321 (2002). Today, more than seven million people in 95 countries own time-share and fractional property. Cameron & Maxwell, *supra*, at 278.

Assume that you graduated from law school, passed the bar, and began to work for a firm at a reasonable, but not extravagant, salary. You have always loved water sports and being out on the ocean. Recently, you have been presented with an opportunity to become a fractional owner of a yacht. Answer the following questions:

Discussion Questions

1. *Benefits and limitations of fractional ownership:* Based on what you have learned about concurrent interests in this chapter, make a list of the potential benefits and detriments of owning a fractional interest in the yacht, as well as potential alternatives to the fractional ownership arrangement. Be specific. How is fractional ownership different than the traditional forms of concurrent ownership? How is it different than time-share ownership? Can you think of any areas of legal concern that merit additional research before you make a decision whether or not to become a fractional owner of the yacht?

2. *Concurrent ownership evaluated:* Overall, after reading this chapter on concurrent ownership, do you think its benefits outweigh its detriments and risks? Why or why not?

D. SKILLS PRACTICE—CLIENT COUNSELING AND NEGOTIATING A TENANTS IN COMMON AGREEMENT

Roy Reynolds is a third-generation cattle rancher who owns a 5,000-acre spread in a broad valley just outside of a mountain ski resort. He has two children, Madelyn and Russ. Madelyn, her husband (Michael), and 15-year old son (Micah) help him work the ranch and live about 10 miles away in town. Russ, a lawyer who works in a metropolitan area several hours away, has no interest in living in the country or working as a rancher.

Roy is 65 years old and would like to retire from ranching and move into town (and maybe spend a few weeks each winter in Florida). One weekend, when Russ and his wife, Rena, were in town, Roy prepared a special family dinner (and also invited Madelyn and her family). As they were eating dessert, Roy surprised his children by handing them a formal looking piece of paper. It turned out to be a deed that conveyed the ranch, "To Madelyn and Russ together and jointly." The children hugged their father and thanked him profusely, and proceeded to discuss all his plans for a relaxing and productive retirement.

Later that evening, Madelyn and Michael discussed her father's surprising gift to them. Although Madelyn had expected to inherit the ranch (with Russ) someday, she had not anticipated her father's imminent retirement. Madelyn said, "Wouldn't it be wonderful if we could move into the ranch house after Dad gets settled in town? We could live there for free, instead of paying $2,000 each month to rent our house in town. We could save the extra money for Micah's college fund." Michael replied, "Yes, that would be great. But I still hope that Micah decides to come back home after college and help me work the ranch." Madelyn mused, "Well, he's still a teenager and doesn't really know what he wants to do with his life yet. I bet he'll go to college, maybe work for a few years after that, and then decide to come back home. Oh, and by the way, maybe we could use a little of the money we save on rent to remodel Dad's kitchen. He hardly ever cooks since mom died, and the kitchen could sure use an update!"

On the drive back to the city, Russ and Rena also discussed the weekend's surprising events. Russ said, "I've seen enough of these concurrent ownership situations to know that they can be trouble. We'd better sit down with Madelyn and work out an agreement." Rena responded, "Yes, that's true. I'm sure Madelyn can't wait to take over your dad's house—she's had her eye on it for years. She can't just live there for free if you own the house, too, can she? And if she did, she'd have to take over the mortgage and property taxes and all the expenses, wouldn't she?" "Well, that depends," said Russ. He added, "That property is a gold mine. It's close to a couple of ski resorts. I bet we could sell it to a resort condominium developer for millions!"

Madelyn and Russ have decided to work out a co-ownership agreement. Assume that you represent Madelyn (or alternatively, Russ, who has wisely decided to retain an attorney who specializes in property law). You interviewed your client last week and learned the above facts (to the extent they would be known to your client).

Tasks

You have scheduled another meeting with your client for next week. As you prepare to counsel your client, consider the following questions:

1. *Identify the estate:*   What type of concurrent estate did Roy convey to Madelyn and Russ?

2. *Default common law rules:*   What is the common law default rule for each of the following issues? Be prepared to explain the rule clearly to your client:

- *Possession:* Who is entitled to possession of the ranch home? If Madelyn and her family live there full time, must she pay rent to Russ?
- *Expenses:* Who is responsible for the payment of ranch expenses (mortgage, taxes, and other carrying expenses)? Does it matter if Madelyn and her family live there?
- *Profits:* Who is entitled to the ranch profits? Does it matter that Madelyn and her family work on the ranch?
- *Improvements:* Who decides whether or not improvements are made to the property (potentially including a remodeled kitchen)? Who pays for such improvements?
- *Termination of the cotenancy:* What happens if Madelyn and Russ cannot agree on the use and management of the property?
- *Transfer of individual interest:* Do Madelyn and Russ individually have the right to sell, lease, or mortgage his or her own share of the ranch? If so, what are the consequences for the other co-owner?

Suppose that you have met with your client and discussed each of the above issues. Now, your client would like to negotiate a tenant-in-common agreement with his or her sibling to clarify expectations and prevent future disputes. As you prepare to help your client negotiate such an agreement, take note of the following technique to assist with the negotiation:

| A Place to Start | Negotiation Technique—BATNA |

To test the strength of a proposed agreement, negotiators often think about the alternatives available if an agreement cannot be reached—the so-called "best alternative to a negotiated agreement" (BATNA)—a phrase introduced in Roger Fisher & William Ury, Getting to Yes (Penguin Books 1991).

For example, if a prospective purchaser of a new home cannot successfully negotiate a sales contract with the owner of Blackacre, what would happen? The purchaser has a variety of options, including buying a different property; forgoing purchase altogether and simply renting an apartment; or continuing to live in the purchaser's current home. Before negotiating with the owner of Blackacre, the prospective purchaser could perform the following BATNA analysis:

- List the alternatives
- Evaluate each alternative
- Select the best alternative available
- Measure the potential agreement against the best alternative

In the Blackacre example above, if the seller were willing to negotiate a contract that would put the buyer in a better position than the best alternative, then the buyer can confidently sign the contract, even if its terms are not ideal. Alternatively, if the best contract the buyer can negotiate is worse than the selected alternative, then the buyer can comfortably walk away from the deal.

Tasks

1. *List the alternatives:* In the counseling session you just completed, you identified the default common law rules for likely areas of conflict between Madelyn and Russ in the absence of an agreement. Considering those default rules as a whole, in the absence of an agreement, what are the likely alternatives if Madelyn and Russ reach a future impasse on any of those issues? List as many alternatives as possible.

2. *Evaluate each alternative:* Think about the consequences of each alternative. For example, if the disagreement were severe enough, would your client's co-owner petition a court for partition? Evaluate the consequences to your client if that occurs.

3. *Select the best alternative available:* If your client and the other owner disagree about the use and operation of the ranch, what is the best resolution of the conflict if no agreement is in place? Is it likely that the best alternative will be selected? Does your client have control over that choice?

4. *Measure the potential agreement against the best alternative:* There is not yet a potential agreement against which to measure the best alternative. Using the form below as a starting point, amend, modify, and draft potential terms of an agreement that would put your client in a better position than the best alternative resolution of an irreconcilable disagreement. It might be helpful to think of the six issues you discussed during your counseling session as a unified whole. Then, consider how your client could negotiate less than ideal terms for some of the issues, but still come out with an agreement that is preferable to your client's BATNA.

5. *Negotiation:* If time permits, your professor might pair you with opposing counsel. Negotiate the broad contours of an agreement, using the document below as a starting point. As an additional challenge, consider negotiating the precise agreement language for at least one of the six issues.

Tenants in Common Agreement

This agreement, made on this _____ day of _____, 2015, is made between *Madelyn* and *Russ*, hereinafter referred to as the "tenants in common."

Each of the tenants in common has an equal and undivided interest in the following property: *the Reynolds Family Ranch.*

The tenants in common have agreed to the following provisions:

(1) Possession: Each party holds an undivided right to possess the entire property and [neither party shall reside on the property full time] [either party can reside on the property full time] [Madelyn and her family shall be entitled to reside on the property full time, provided that. . . .] [other].

(2) Expenses: Expenses, including [mortgage payments, property tax, income tax from the ranch operations, other] shall be paid by [both tenants in common equally] [other].

(3) Profits: Any profits or losses derived from the operation of the property shall be shared [equally by the cotenants] [other].

(4) Improvements: Any improvement to the property [can be made only with the written approval of the other tenant in common] [can be made by either tenant in common, provided that such party pay the entire cost of the improvement] [other].

(5) Partition: Each of the tenants in common [waives] [does not waive] his or her right to bring any action for partition with respect to his or her undivided interest in the property. If the parties do not waive their rights, any such action for partition shall not request [a partition in kind] [a partition by sale.]

(6) Transfer of individual interest: Each of the cotenants [may] [may not] sell, lease, mortgage, or otherwise transfer or encumber his or her undivided interest in the property, if/unless: [the other party consents in writing] [the other party consents in writing, which consent shall not be unreasonably withheld] [the transfer is limited to members of the tenant in common's immediate family, defined as _____] [other provision].

Signed,

Madelyn

Russ

E. CHAPTER REVIEW

1. Practice Questions[17]

1. *Changes over time:*   Olivia conveyed property, "To Aiden, Brittany, and Cody as joint tenants with a right of survivorship." Subsequently, Cody conveyed all of his interest to Darren. What are the interests of Aiden, Brittany, Cody, and Darren? Subsequently, Aiden dies. What are the respective property interests after Aiden's death?

2. *The sisters and the townhouse:*   Two sisters, Ava and Bella, inherited a townhouse from their aunt. The deed to the property specified that Ava and Bella took title, "jointly, as tenants in common, with equal rights and interests in said land, and to the survivor thereof, in fee simple. To have and to hold the same unto the said parties hereto, equally, jointly, as tenants in common, with equal rights and interest for the period or term of their lives, and to the survivor thereof at the death of the other."

Ava moved into the townhouse and lived alone there for several years. At no time did she ever pay rent to her sister, Bella, who lived some distance away.

About a year ago, Ava entered into a written lease with Connor. The lease granted Connor a two-year lease term in the townhouse. Ava moved out and Connor took possession. Connor did not pay Ava the agreed monthly rent on a regular basis. Several months later, Ava died. At the time of her death she had not received rent for the townhouse for several months.

Ava left a valid will in which she left all her property to the Humane Society. Bella claims that she owns the property in fee simple absolute, and has filed a claim against the estate for one-half the rental value of the townhouse for the years Ava lived there alone. Bella also claims one-half of any rents paid by Connor. Finally, the Humane Society claims one-half of the townhouse, which Bella contends is hers alone.

a) Who owns the townhouse?
b) Is the estate liable to Bella for one-half the rental value of the townhouse for the period Ava was in possession?
c) Is the estate liable to Bella for one-half of any rent Ava collected from Connor?

2. Bringing It Home

Research your state's statutory law, and find its relevant provisions, if any, on the following topics:

---

17. Answers appear in the Appendix to this casebook.

   1. *Concurrent estates:*   Does your state have any legislation on tenancies in common or joint tenancies? Does it recognize tenancies by the entirety by statute?

   2. *Partition:*   Does your state have any legislation governing partition? Does it include a statutory test to determine the preferred method of partition? Has your state adopted the Uniform Partition of Heirs Property Act or something similar?

   3. *Homesteads:*   Does your state have a provision protecting homesteads from creditors' claims? What property is eligible? What exemptions are provided?

   4. *Marital systems:*   Are you in a separate property (also called common law) or community property jurisdiction? Is there an elective share (or "forced share") provision for a surviving spouse? If so, what is the share?

From Private Property to the Commons

Chapter 6–Cases

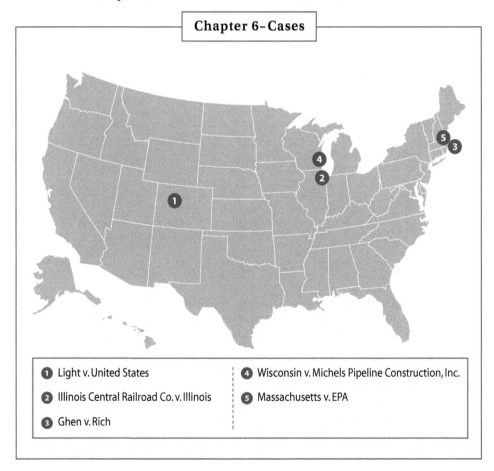

1. Light v. United States
2. Illinois Central Railroad Co. v. Illinois
3. Ghen v. Rich
4. Wisconsin v. Michels Pipeline Construction, Inc.
5. Massachusetts v. EPA

Our study of property has been expanding gradually to encompass an ever-increasing number of owners. In Chapters 1 and 2, we looked at individual property, beginning with one extreme end of the spectrum—Blackstone's idealized individual owner and his "sole and despotic dominion" over his property. In Chapters 3 through 5, we looked at property shared across time (estates and future interests, and landlord-tenant law) and space (concurrent and marital interests). In this chapter, we will pause and take stock of what you have already learned about private property held in individual ownership. Then, we will expand our understanding by introducing two additional ownership regimes. First, we will introduce *public property*—property that is owned by local, state, or federal governments. In addition, we will learn about *commons property*, the study of which will take us briefly beyond the landward borders of the United States to the seas, the atmosphere, and even outer space.

Professor Michael Heller provides the following illustration of what he calls the "standard trilogy" of property ownership. Michael A. Heller, *Three Faces of Private Property*, 79 Oregon L. Rev. 417, 421 (2000). In the illustration, *PP* refers to private property, *CP* refers to commons property, and *SP* refers to state property (also known to as public property):

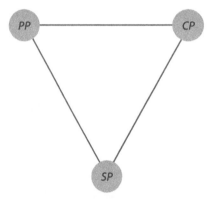

Figure 1
Source: Michael A. Heller

These three categories are fluid. That is, property can pass from one form of ownership to another. For example, under the *rule of capture*, commons property can become private property or public property (also known as "state property"). As we saw in Chapter 1, an unowned baseball can become the personal property of the first person to possess it, and an entire "unowned" continent can become the property of the European sovereign that first "discovered" it. Conversely, private property can become public property. In Chapter 1, we considered the Department of the Interior's efforts to return private property to the trust ownership of Native American tribes through a buy-back program (*see* note on *fractionation* following *Johnson v. M'Intosh*).

Further, Chapter 13's study of eminent domain will provide an additional example of the private-to-public property transformation.

As you read this chapter, keep three overarching considerations in mind. First, *what* is each ownership regime, and how does it differ from the others? The distinction may not be as simple as it first appears—the categories sometimes overlap and the ownership form of a particular piece of property can change over time. Second, *how* can each type of property be managed to maximize its benefits and minimize its challenges? For example, in the previous chapter on concurrent and marital interests, we noted some of the difficulties of shared ownership, but also some of its rewards when effectively managed—such as co-owners efficiently sharing property under a cotenants agreement, or families maintaining and enjoying together their historic home place (perhaps under the protection of state law modeled after the Uniform Partition of Heirs Property Act). How can law contribute to effective management of property? Finally, *why* does the law recognize each type of ownership—what benefits does it offer (and what challenges must it overcome)?

A. PRIVATE PROPERTY

What is private property? By now, you should have a pretty clear understanding of its contours, guided by the competing bundle of sticks and web of interests metaphors. In general, private property has a single owner who enjoys, among other things, strong rights of exclusion and transferability.

How can private property be managed to maximize its benefits to the owner, while similarly maximizing the benefits of owners of other private property, all without infringing unduly on the interests of society? Recall that in *State v. Shack* (Chapter 1), we encountered some constitutional limitations on the right to exclude in order to protect the competing rights (property and otherwise) of the migrant farmworkers employed and housed on the property. Can you think of any additional tools to maximize the benefits of private property and minimize its challenges? In Chapters 9-13 we will examine contractual, common law, statutory, and constitutional limits designed to protect one owner's full enjoyment of her property rights, without overly interfering with others' similar enjoyment of their property rights, or with the broader public interest.

So far, you have seen a wide variety of property rights—including rights in underground caves, deceased pets, human tissue, genetic material, stolen artwork, hidden drug money, and, of course, real estate. Now, let us pause to consider *why* society recognizes and protects private property in the first instance. Although many overlapping explanations are possible, the following five rationales are commonly considered to be among the main reasons why property rights exist. We will begin with three rationales that focus primarily on the benefits of private property to individuals, and then move outward to consider how property rights can serve the broader interests of society:

The labor rationale: John Locke's labor theory, which we first encountered in Chapter 1, posits a state of nature in which all property is unowned. Locke makes the case that *natural law*—predating any organized social order—allows individuals to sever private property rights from the commons by mixing in their labor with commons resources. His argument introduces an element of fairness, suggesting that laborers deserve to own the items that their toil and labor produced—such as acorns picked up under an oak, or apples gathered from trees in the commons.

The autonomy and liberty rationales: These justifications assert that the institution of private property gives each owner a sphere of personal autonomy—breathing space, if you will—to hold the problems of the world at abeyance and to enjoy a significant degree of freedom from interference by others. The right to exclude, as enforced by state trespass laws, is essential to the protection of autonomy. Using the familiar "home as castle" metaphor, Judge Jerome Frank explained:

> A man can still control a small part of his environment, his house: he can retreat thence from outsiders, secure in the knowledge that they cannot get at him without disobeying the Constitution. That is still a sizable hunk of liberty—worth protecting from encroachment. A sane, decent, civilized society must provide some such oasis, some shelter from public scrutiny, some insulated enclosure, some enclave, some inviolate place—which is a man's castle.

United States v. On Lee, 193 F.2d 306, 315-16 (2d Cir. 1951) (Frank, J., dissenting) (arguing that evidence of illegal drug sale obtained from hidden microphone smuggled onto defendant's property should be held inadmissible under the Fourth Amendment), *aff'd,* 343 U.S. 747 (1952), *rehearing denied,* 344 U.S. 848 (1952).

The personhood rationale: The personhood theory recognizes property rights because of their ability to facilitate self-development. As Professor Margaret Jane Radin explained:

> . . . The premise underlying the personhood perspective is that to achieve proper self-development—to be a person—an individual needs some control over resources in the external environment. The necessary assurances of control take the form of property rights. . . .

> Most people possess certain objects they feel are almost part of themselves. These objects are closely bound up with personhood because they are part of the way we constitute ourselves as continuing personal entities in the world. . . .

> One may gauge the strength or significance of someone's relationship with an object by the kind of pain that would be occasioned by its loss. On this view, an object is closely related to one's personhood if its loss causes pain that cannot be relieved by the object's replacement. If so, that particular object is bound up with

the holder. For instance, if a wedding ring is stolen from a jeweler, insurance proceeds can reimburse the jeweler, but if a wedding ring is stolen from a loving wearer, the price of a replacement will not restore the status quo—perhaps no amount of money can do so.

Margaret Jane Radin, *Property and Personhood*, 34 Stan. L. Rev. 957, 959 (1982). The personhood rationale involves "something more" than the autonomy and liberty rationales because it also conveys a "sense of connection with the external world" rather than isolation from it. *Id.* at 960. One of this book's recurrent themes—*the importance of place*—can be seen, in part, as logically related to the personhood theory. That is, both perspectives focus on the connection between people and property, and both emphasize the unique value of certain property that is not captured by market value alone.

The utilitarian and economic efficiency rationales: Based on the work of David Hume (1711-1776) and others, English philosopher Jeremy Bentham (1748-1832) advanced the principle of *utilitarianism*, under which actions should be based on their consequences. Actions are moral, he believed, if they bring about the greatest amount of happiness for the greatest number of people. In part, Bentham was reacting against the English tradition of the landed gentry, which passed its wealth from generation to generation to the exclusion of many.

The *economic efficiency* rationale for private property rights draws on utilitarianism. It argues that property rights should be *universal* in the sense that all rare and valuable resources should have an owner. It also calls for *exclusive* property rights that give their owners the right to exclude others. The rationale also emphasizes that property rights should be *transferable* and that restraints on alienation should be disfavored. If property has these three attributes, then society's overall wealth will be maximized (promoting something like Bentham's greatest happiness for the greatest number of people). This will occur, the theory continues, because the free market system will allocate scarce resources into the hands of those who value them the most, thereby ensuring that property will be put to its highest and best use, to the benefit of all.

The democracy rationale: Commentators from a variety of perspectives have linked property ownership with a robust democracy. Although viewpoints differ widely, there is considerable common ground. As Professor Joseph Singer suggested:

> Choosing to live in a free and democratic society that treats each person with equal concern and respect has enormous consequences for the basic structure of property law. But what those consequences are differs depending on one's normative framework. . . . [T]he ideals of equality, liberty, and democracy are not self-defining. . . . A libertarian framework . . . will interpret these basic values far differently than a liberal framework. . . . At the same time, it is crucial to understand that there is considerable and perhaps surprising overlap between

the libertarian and liberal perspectives—far more so than one would think if one focused on the polarized political rhetoric in the United States. At the very least, democracies require (1) that there be many owners, (2) that opportunities to acquire the property needed for a full human life are universally (and readily) available, and (3) that the scope of the powers granted to owners must be subject to rules that reflect both democratic processes and individual rights to liberty and to equal, dignified treatment.

Joseph William Singer, *Property as the Law of Democracy*, 63 Duke L.J. 1287, 1328 (2014)

Problem

From the previous chapters of this book, find at least one case that supports each of the five property rationales described above. For each case, describe the scope of protection that the court afforded to the subject property right; the court's rationale; and what limitations (if any) the court imposed to protect the rights of other property owners and the public interest.

B. PUBLIC PROPERTY

When governments own property, they generally hold it to promote the interests of the collective citizenry, rather than to specifically advance the needs or desires of selected individuals. As Professor Michael Heller explains,

> . . . [A] state property regime is similar to commons property in that no individual stands in a specially privileged position with regard to any resource, but is distinguished from commons property because the state has a special status or distinct interest—that of owner of all resources able to include or exclude all individuals, according to the rules of that particular state. In other words, the collective, represented usually by the state, holds all rights of exclusion and is the sole locus of decision-making regarding use of resources.

Michael A. Heller, *Three Faces of Private Property*, 79 Oregon L. Rev. 417, 418-21. The following two cases take a closer look at public property and the right to exclude.

Light v. United States

220 U.S. 523 (1911)

Reading Guide

This case concerns a dispute involving the Holy Cross Forest Reserve in Colorado. The reserves were the predecessors to the national forests. Today, the U.S.

Forest Service—which is located within the Department of Agriculture—manages 154 national forests and 20 grasslands in 44 states and Puerto Rico. According to the agency, its mission is "to sustain the health, diversity, and productivity of the nation's forests and grasslands to meet the needs of present and future generations." U.S. Forest Service, *About the Agency*, http://www.fs.fed.us/about-agency (visited June 8, 2015).

LAMAR, J.

[The Holy Cross Forest Reserve was established under the provisions of the Act of March 3, 1891. By that and subsequent statutes the Secretary of Agriculture was authorized to make provisions for the protection against destruction by fire and depredations of the public forest and forest reservations, and to "make such rules and regulations and establish such service as will insure the objects of such reservations; namely, to regulate their occupancy and use, and to preserve the forests thereon from destruction." 26 Stat. 1103 (1903). In pursuance of these statutes, regulations were adopted establishing grazing districts on which only a limited number of cattle were allowed. The regulations provided that a few head of cattle of prospectors, campers, and not more than ten belonging to a settler residing near the forest, might be admitted without permit; but, saving these exceptions, the general rule was that all persons must secure permits before grazing any stock in a national forest.]

On April 7, 1908, the United States, through the district attorney, filed a bill in the circuit court for the district of Colorado . . . alleging that the defendant, Fred Light, owned a herd of about 500 cattle and a ranch of 540 acres, located 2 1/2 miles to the east, and 5 miles to the north, of the reservation. This herd was turned out to range during the spring and summer, and the ranch then used as a place on which to raise hay for their sustenance. That between the ranch and the reservation was other public and unoccupied land of the United States; but, owing to the fact that only a limited number of cattle were allowed on the reservation, the grazing there was better than on this public land. For this reason, and because of the superior water facilities and the tendency of the cattle to follow the trails and stream leading from the ranch to the reservation, they naturally went direct to the reservation.

The defendant was enjoined from pasturing his cattle on the Holy Cross Forest Reserve, because he had refused to comply with the regulations adopted by the Secretary of Agriculture, under the authority conferred by the act of June 4, 1897 (30 Stat. 35, chap. 2), to make rules and regulations as to the use, occupancy, and preservation of forests. . . .

The bill alleged, and there was evidence to support the finding, that the defendant, with the expectation and intention that they would do so, turned his cattle out at a time and place which made it certain that they would leave the open public lands and go at once to the reserve, where there was good water and fine pasturage. When notified to remove the cattle, he declined to do so, and threatened to resist if they should be driven off by a forest officer. He justified this position on the ground that the statute of Colorado provided that a landowner could not recover damages for trespass by animals unless the property was inclosed with a fence of designated size and material. Regardless of any conflict in the testimony, the defendant claims that unless the government put a fence around the reserve, it had no remedy, either at law or in equity, nor could he be required to prevent his cattle straying upon the reserve from the open public land on which he had a right to turn them loose.

At common law the owner was required to confine his live stock, or else was held liable for any damage done by them upon the land of third persons. That law was not adapted to the situation of those states where there were great plains and vast tracts of uninclosed land, suitable for pasture. And so, without passing a statute, or taking any affirmative action on the subject, the United States suffered its public domain to be used for such purposes. There thus grew up a sort of implied license[1] that these lands, thus left open, might be used so long as the government did not cancel its tacit consent. *Buford v. Houtz*, 133 U. S. 320, 326 (1890). Its failure to object, however, did not confer any vested right on the complainant, nor did it deprive the United States of the power of recalling any implied license under which the land had been used for private purposes.

. . . "[T]he nation is an owner, and has made Congress the principal agent to dispose of its property. . . . Congress is the body to which is given the power to determine the conditions upon which the public lands shall be disposed of." *Butte City Water Co. v. Baker*, 196 U.S. 119, 126 (1904). "The government has, with respect to its own lands, the rights of an ordinary proprietor to maintain its possession and to prosecute trespassers. It may deal with such lands precisely as a private individual may deal with his farming property. It may sell or withhold them from sale." *Camfield v. United States*, 167 U.S. 518, 523 (1897). And if it may withhold from sale and settlement, it may also, as an owner, object to its property being used for grazing purposes, for "the government is charged with the duty and clothed with the power to protect the public domain from trespass and unlawful appropriation." *United States v. Beebe*, 127 U.S. 338 (1888).

The United States can prohibit absolutely or fix the terms on which its property may be used. . . . It is true that the United States do not and cannot hold property as a monarch may, for private or personal purposes. But that does not

---

1. [As we will see in Chapter 9, a license is revocable permission to use another's land in a manner that would otherwise constitute trespass.—Eds.]

lead to the conclusion that it is without the rights incident to ownership, for the Constitution declares, § 3, art. 4, that "Congress shall have power to dispose of and make all needful rules and regulations respecting the territory or the property belonging to the United States." The full scope of this paragraph has never been definitely settled. Primarily, at least, it is a grant of power to the United States of control over its property.

"All the public lands of the nation are held in trust for the people of the whole country." *United States v. Trinidad Coal & Coking Co.*, 137 U.S. 160 (1890). And it is not for the courts to say how that trust shall be administered. That is for Congress to determine. The courts cannot compel it to set aside the lands for settlement, or to suffer them to be used for agricultural or grazing purposes, nor interfere when, in the exercise of its discretion, Congress establishes a forest reserve for what it decides to be national and public purposes. In the same way and in the exercise of the same trust it may disestablish a reserve, and devote the property to some other national and public purpose. These are rights incident to proprietorship, to say nothing of the power of the United States as a sovereign over the property belonging to it. Even a private owner would be entitled to protection against wilful trespasses, and statutes providing that damage done by animals cannot be recovered, unless the land had been inclosed with a fence of the size and material required, do not give permission to the owner of cattle to use his neighbor's land as a pasture. They are intended to condone trespasses by straying cattle; they have no application to cases where they are driven upon unfenced land in order that they may feed there.

Fence laws do not authorize wanton and wilful trespass, nor do they afford immunity to those who, in disregard of property rights, turn loose their cattle under circumstances showing that they were intended to graze upon the lands of another.

This the defendant did, under circumstances equivalent to driving his cattle upon the forest reserve. He could have obtained a permit for reasonable pasturage. He not only declined to apply for such license, but there is evidence that he threatened to resist efforts to have his cattle removed from the reserve, and in his answer he declares that he will continue to turn out his cattle, and contends that if they go upon the reserve the government has no remedy at law or in equity. This claim answers itself.

It appears that the defendant turned out his cattle under circumstances which showed that he expected and intended that they would go upon the reserve to graze thereon. Under the facts, the court properly granted an injunction. The judgment was right on the merits, wholly regardless of the question as to whether the government had inclosed its property.

. . . The decree is therefore affirmed.

Notes

1. *A web of interests—private, public, commons:*   Identify the two forms of ownership mentioned in *Light*. <u>Hint:</u> Notice the mention of grazing permits. How can two distinct types of ownership coexist on the forest reserves?

2. *The trust metaphor:*   Can you piece together the respective roles of the public, Congress, and the U.S. Forest Service in the ownership and management of the forest reserves (today, the national forests)? Who owns the forest reserves? Who holds the ultimate authority to manage them? Who makes management decisions on a more pragmatic, day-to-day basis? And perhaps most importantly, *why* does the nation hold national forests in public ownership?

Recall our brief discussion of trusts from Chapter 3. Here, the Court cites precedent for the proposition that "[a]ll the public lands of the nation are held in trust for the people of the whole country." Trust language is quite common in natural resources law, and is often used as a metaphor to describe the nature of public ownership, rather than as a reference to a formal legal trust. With respect to the forest reserves, identify the trustee, the beneficiary, and the purposes of the trust.

3. *Private rights in public property:*   Should the Forest Service recognize private rights in the national forest reserves, such as the right to graze one's livestock pursuant to a permit? Do any of the rationales suggested in section A.1, above, provide such a justification?

4. *The federal public lands:*   The federal public lands are an extraordinary American institution. Of the 2.3 billion acres that make up the 50 states, the federal government holds title to more than 28% of the surface acreage (and additional subsurface acres containing valuable mineral deposits). Those lands came into federal ownership by cessions from the original 13 colonies, by purchase from foreign nations (such as the Louisiana Purchase from France in 1803), and by conquest (such as the conquest of Native American tribes discussed in *Johnson v. M'Intosh*, Chapter 1).

During the period of American settlement, the federal government surveyed the federal lands and conveyed some of them into private ownership, including grants to homesteaders, miners, the states, the railroads, and others. By about 1934, the federal policy of *disposition* gave way to a policy of *withdrawing* the remaining public lands from settlement, and often, *reserving* them for specified public purposes (such as the forest reserves in *Light*). Today, perhaps the better-known categories of federal lands include the national parks, the national forests, the national wildlife refuges, and so-called BLM lands (lands administered by the Bureau of Land Management for multiple uses, including grazing, mining, and recreation).

Public West, Private East

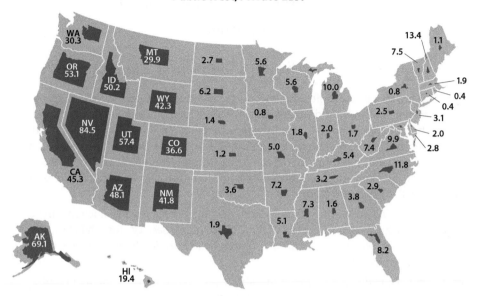

84.5 Percentage of public lands within each state

Figure 2
Source: University of Colorado Center of the American West
Atlas of the New West (William E. Riebsame, Gen. Ed. 1997)

5. *The Property Clause:*   Note the language of the Constitution's "Property Clause," art. 4, § 3: "Congress shall have power to dispose of and make all needful rules and regulations respecting the territory or the property belonging to the United States." Subsequent to *Light*, the U.S. Supreme Court turned its attention once again to the meaning of the Property Clause in the context of another grazing dispute. In *Kleppe v. New Mexico*, 426 U.S. 529 (1976), the state of New Mexico challenged Congress' authority under the Property Clause to enact legislation protecting wild, free-roaming horses and burros on federal lands because they competed for forage with privately owned livestock. In holding in favor of the United States' authority to manage not only the federal lands, but also the wildlife thereon, the Court opined,

> And while the furthest reaches of the power granted by the Property Clause have not yet been definitively resolved, we have repeatedly observed that "[t]he power over the public land thus entrusted to Congress is without limitations."

Kleppe, 426 U.S. at 538, *quoting United States v. San Francisco*, 310 U.S. 16 (1940). As the next case shows, states—like the federal government—can own property for the benefit of their citizens.

Illinois Central Railroad Co. v. Illinois

146 U.S. 387 (1892)

Reading Guide

Legal regimes in the United States and throughout the world have long recognized water, tidelands, and other types of submerged lands as a special type of property that should not fall into private ownership. As Roman law proclaimed, "And truly by natural right these be common to all: the air, the running water, and the sea, and hence the shores of the sea." Institutes of Justinian (codified circa 528 A.D.). This assertion of public ownership and control over certain resources is known as the *public trust doctrine*.

◆ The following case is a seminal decision that recognized the ancient public trust doctrine as part of the law of the United States. *See, e.g.*, Joseph L. Sax, *The Public Trust Doctrine in Natural Resource Law: Effective Judicial Intervention*, 68 Mich. L. Rev. 471 (1970).

◆ As you read *Illinois Central*, think about possible rationales for maintaining certain places in public, rather than private, ownership.

FIELD, J.

The object of the suit is to obtain a judicial determination of the title of certain lands on the east or lake front of the city of Chicago. . . .

The city of Chicago is situated upon the southwestern shore of Lake Michigan. . . . The growth of the city in subsequent years, in population, business, and commerce, required a larger and more convenient harbor, and the United States, in view of such expansion and growth, commenced the construction of a system of breakwaters and other harbor protections in the waters of the lake. . . . In the prosecution of this work there was constructed a line of breakwaters or cribs of wood and stone covering the front of the city between the Chicago river and Twelfth street, with openings in the piers or lines of cribs for the entrance and departure of vessels; thus inclosing a large part of the lake for the uses of shipping and commerce, and creating an outer harbor for Chicago. It comprises a space about one mile and one half in length from north to south, and is of a width from east to west varying from 1,000 to 4,000 feet. . . .

The state prays a decree establishing and confirming its title to the bed of Lake Michigan, and exclusive right to develop and improve the harbor of Chicago by the construction of docks, wharves, piers, and other improvements, against the claim of the railroad company that it has an absolute title to such submerged lands by the act of 1869, and the right, subject only to the paramount authority of the United States in the regulation of commerce, to fill all the bed of the lake within the limits above stated. . . .

Under the authority of this ordinance the railroad company located its tracks within the corporate limits of the city. Those running northward from Twelfth street were laid upon pilling in the waters of the lake. The shore line of the lake was at that time at Park Row, about 400 feet from the west line of Michigan avenue, and at Randolph street, about 112-$\frac{1}{2}$ feet. Since then the space between the shore line and the tracks of the railroad company has been filled with earth under the direction of the city, and is now solid ground. . . .

We proceed to consider the claim of the railroad company to the ownership of submerged lands in the harbor, and the right to construct such wharves, piers, docks, and other works therein as it may deem proper for its interest and business. The claim is founded upon the third section of the act of the [state] legislature of the state passed [on April 16, 1869]. . . .

The [legislation] in question has two objects in view [including the granting] to the railroad company submerged lands in the harbor. . . .

The act, if valid and operative to the extent claimed, placed under the control of the railroad company nearly the whole of the submerged lands of the harbor, subject only to the limitations that it should not authorize obstructions to the harbor, or impair the public right of navigation, or exclude the legislature from regulating the rates of wharfage or dockage to be charged. With these limitations, the act put it in the power of the company to delay indefinitely the improvement of the harbor, or to construct as many docks, piers, and wharves and other works as it might choose, and at such positions in the harbor as might suit its purposes, and permit any kind of business to be conducted thereon, and to lease them out on its own terms for indefinite periods. . . . A corporation created for one purpose, the construction and operation of a railroad between designated points, is by the act converted into a corporation to manage and practically control the harbor of Chicago, not simply for its own purpose as a railroad corporation, but for its own profit generally. . . .

The question, therefore, to be considered, is whether the legislature was competent to thus deprive the state of its ownership of the submerged lands in the harbor of Chicago, and of the consequent control of its waters; or, in other words, whether the railroad corporation can hold the lands and control the waters by the grant, against any future exercise of power over them by the state.

That the state holds the title to the lands under the navigable waters of Lake Michigan, within its limits, in the same manner that the state holds title to soils under tide water, by the common law, we have already shown; and that title necessarily carries with it control over the waters above them, whenever the lands are subjected to use. But it is a title different in character from that which the state holds in lands intended for sale. It is different from the title which the United States hold in the public lands which are open to pre-emption and sale. It is a title held in trust for the people of the state, that they may enjoy the navigation of the waters, carry on commerce over them, and have liberty of fishing therein, freed from the obstruction or interference of private parties. The interest of the people in the navigation of the waters and in commerce over them may be improved in many instances by the erection of wharves, docks, and piers therein, for which purpose the state may grant parcels of the submerged lands; and, so long as their disposition is made for such purpose, no valid objections can be made to the grants. It is grants of parcels of lands under navigable waters that may afford foundation for wharves, piers, docks, and other structures in aid of commerce, and grants of parcels which, being occupied, do not substantially impair the public interest in the lands and waters remaining, that are chiefly considered and sustained in the adjudged cases as a valid exercise of legislative power consistently with the trust to the public upon which such lands are held by the state.

But that is a very different doctrine from the one which would sanction the abdication of the general control of the state over lands under the navigable waters of an entire harbor or bay, or of a sea or lake. Such abdication is not consistent with the exercise of that trust which requires the government of the state to preserve such waters for the use of the public. The trust devolving upon the state for the public, and which can only be discharged by the management and control of property in which the public has an interest, cannot be relinquished by a transfer of the property. The control of the state for the purposes of the trust can never be lost, except as to such parcels as are used in promoting the interests of the public therein, or can be disposed of without any substantial impairment of the public interest in the lands and waters remaining. . . . A grant of all the lands under the navigable waters of a state has never been adjudged to be within the legislative power; and any attempted grant of the kind would be held, if not absolutely void on its face, as subject to revocation. The state can no more abdicate its trust over property in which the whole people are interested, like navigable waters and soils under them, so as to leave them entirely under the use and control of private parties, except in the instance of parcels mentioned for the improvement of the navigation and use of the waters, or when parcels can be disposed of without impairment of the public interest in what remains, than it can abdicate its police powers in the administration of government and the preservation of the peace. . . .

The harbor of Chicago is of immense value to the people of the state of Illinois, in the facilities it affords to its vast and constantly increasing commerce; and the idea that its legislature can deprive the state of control over its bed and waters, and place the same in the hands of a private corporation, created for a different purpose . . . is a proposition that cannot be defended.

The area of the submerged lands proposed to be ceded by the act in question to the railroad company embraces something more than 1,000 acres, being, as stated by counsel, more than three times the area of the outer harbor, and not only including all of that harbor, but embracing adjoining submerged lands, which will, in all probability, be hereafter included in the harbor. It is as large as that embraced by all the merchandise docks along the Thames at London; is much larger than that included in the famous docks and basins at Liverpool; is twice that of the port of Marseilles, and nearly, if not quite, equal to the pier area along the water front of the city of New York. And the arrivals and clearings of vessels at the port exceed in number those of New York, and are equal to those of New York and Boston combined. . . . It is hardly conceivable that the legislature can divest the state of the control and management of this harbor, and vest it absolutely in a private corporation. . . .

This follows necessarily from the public character of the property, being held by the whole people for purposes in which the whole people are interested. As said by Chief Justice Taney in *Martin v. Waddell*, 41 U.S. (16 Pet.) 367 (1842), "When the Revolution took place the people of each state became themselves sovereign, and in that character hold the absolute right to all their navigable waters, and the soils under them, for their own common use, subject only to the rights since surrendered by the constitution to the general government." . . .

It follows from the views expressed, and it is so declared and adjudged, that the state of Illinois is the owner in fee of the submerged lands constituting the bed of Lake Michigan, which the third section of the act of April 16, 1869, purported to grant to the Illinois Central Railroad Company, and that the act of April 15, 1873, repealing the same, is valid and effective for the purpose of restoring to the state the same control, dominion, and ownership of said lands that it had prior to the passage of the act of April 16, 1869. . . .

SHIRAS, J., dissenting [omitted].

Notes

1. *The trust metaphor again—the public trust doctrine:* What is the public trust doctrine? As in *Light v. United States*, the trust should be taken more as a metaphor than as a strict legal trust. Identify the trust property, the trustee, the beneficiaries, and the purposes of the trust. How does it compare to the trust considered in *Light*? The public trust is a complicated doctrine, and it has spawned much literature. Some even see the doctrine as a tool to protect the earth's atmosphere from activities leading to climate

change. *See, e.g.*, Symposium, *Public Trust Doctrine: Developments in the Public Trust*, 45 Environmental L. Rev. (vol. 2, 2015).

2. *A web of interests—private, public, commons:*   Identify the two forms of ownership mentioned in *Illinois Central*. <u>Hint</u>: Clearly articulate the exception carved out to the rule of the case. What are the purposes of the exception and what type of ownership does it allow? How can two types of ownership coexist in Lake Michigan? *See* Michael C. Blumm, *The Public Trust Doctrine and Private Property: The Accommodation Principle*, 27 Pace Envtl. L. Rev. 649 (2010) (arguing that the doctrine functions to mediate between public and private property rights).

3. *Private rights in state property:*   Should Illinois be allowed to recognize private rights in the bed of Lake Michigan? Do any of the rationales suggested in section A.1, above, provide such a justification?

4. *Navigablity:*   Determining the ownership of submerged lands can be a complex matter. *Illinois Central* concerned Lake Michigan, which a previous court had determined to be "navigable." Because of that previous determination, Illinois owned the lakebed outward from the state's borders (and other Great Lakes states similarly own a portion of the lakebed extending outward from their shores). Usually, the state's title to submerged lands begins at the *ordinary high water line* of navigable lakes and navigable rivers within or along the state's land borders, and extends outward beneath the waterbody.

Navigability is a term of art with a technical meaning, but in general, it applies to large waterbodies susceptible of use in their ordinary condition as highways for commerce in the customary modes of water travel. *See Utah v. United States*, 403 U.S. 9 (1971); *The Daniel Ball*, 77 U.S. (10 Wall.) 557 (1870). To further complicate the matter, navigability is usually judged by the conditions in place at the time the state entered the union, because it was at that moment that the full scope of the state's property was determined (as distinguished from federal or private property).

Apart from states fronting inland lakes such as Lake Michigan, the coastal states also own the submerged lands that extend seaward from their shores. The states own submerged lands starting at a baseline (often, the *ordinary high tide line*) and extending outward 3-9 nautical miles (depending on the state). Beyond that, under international law, the federal government exercises sovereignty over the "territorial seas" that extends 12 nautical miles from the baseline. International law also recognizes in each nation an "exclusive economic zone," generally extending 200 nautical miles from the baseline, in which the nation holds sovereign rights for purposes including exploring, exploiting, conserving, and managing natural resources. National Oceanic and Atmospheric Administration (NOAA), Office of Coastal Survey, *U.S.*

Maritime Limits & Boundaries, http://www.nauticalcharts.noaa.gov/csdl/mbound.htm (visited Sept. 27, 2015). We will save the complexities of navigability for upper level natural resources, environmental, and admiralty law courses. For our purposes, simply understand that the states own the submerged lands beneath navigable waters, generally beginning at a baseline of the ordinary high water line.

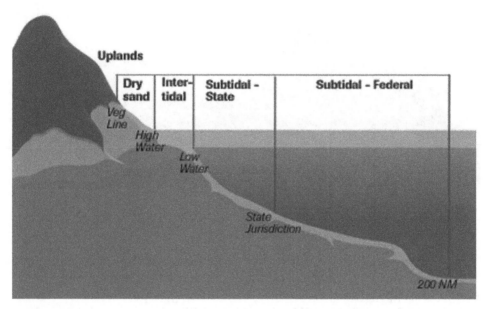

Figure 3
Source: The Nature Conservancy

5. *The place—Illinois Central Depot:*   Around 1832—in the early years of steam-powered locomotion—promoters suggested connecting the Illinois cities of Galena and Cairo by rail. Constructing a spur to Chicago was an afterthought, for at that time Chicago was a frontier settlement occupied by fewer than 200 settlers. The railroad line did not become financially feasible for almost two decades, when Illinois obtained a 2.5-million-acre federal land grant for the railroad under the authority of the newly passed Railroad Land Grant Act of 1850. See 9 Stat. 466 (Sept. 20, 1850). On February 10, 1851, the Illinois Central Railroad was chartered. By 1856, the Railroad had constructed a branch line leading to the growing city of Chicago. Because the initial *railroad* charter was limited to the state of Illinois, the Illinois Central continued south to New Orleans by means of a *steamboat* line on the Mississippi River. Samuel Clemens, who wrote under the name of Mark Twain, was perhaps the most celebrated steamboat pilot employed by the company.

Illinois Central Railway depot, Chicago, Ill. (demolished 1974)
Photograph by Detroit Publishing Co. (1900)
Source: Library of Congress

In Chicago, at first the Railroad was unable to obtain access through the core of the city. Instead, Illinois Central constructed a long trestle bridge to support its tracks above Lake Michigan parallel to the city's waterfront. On April 16, 1869, the state of Illinois conveyed more than 1,000 submerged acres to the Railroad, extending for one mile into the lake east of the trestle tracks and breakwater. Two years later, the city filled in the lakebed out to the trestle line, using debris from the great Chicago fire of 1871. In 1873, Illinois passed legislation purporting to repeal the 1,000-acre grant to the railroad, giving rise to the litigation considered above.

C. COMMONS PROPERTY

The third type of property ownership—commons property—has been described as "the residual category that theorists usually use when they describe a regime that is not private or state property." Michael A. Heller, *Three Faces of Private Property*, 79 Oregon L. Rev. 417, 418-21. In commons property, there are broad *use* rights, but no *exclusionary* rights. In Professor Heller's words, "every individual may use any object of property and no individual has the right to stop someone else from using the object." *Id.*

But can the forms of property ownership really be so neatly divided into three distinct categories—private, public, and commons? Recall our study of concurrent interests (joint tenancies, tenancies in common, and tenancies by the entirety). How should we classify those forms of ownership? On the one hand, they are not a comfortable fit with the idea of private property because there is no single property owner who can exclude all others. On the other hand, they do not seem to be commons property: although all co-owners have an undivided right to occupy the whole premises (and thus, their exclusionary rights are limited against one another), the co-owners retain the right to exclude the rest of the world. Are concurrent interests, perhaps, a private-commons hybrid?

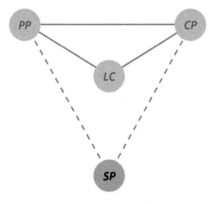

Figure 4
Source: Michael A. Heller

Professor Heller introduced the term *liberal commons* (LC)[2] to describe such hybrid ownership arrangements:

> Each is a legal invention that encourages people voluntarily to come together and create limited-access and limited-purpose communities dedicated to shared management of a scarce resource. Each offers internal self-governance mechanisms to facilitate cooperation and the peaceable joint creation of wealth, while simultaneously limiting minority oppression and allowing *exit*. For more and more resources, the old-fashioned image of sole private property has become impracticable and misleading; perhaps deterring people from creating even more successful variations on our theme.
>
> . . . [T]he idea of a liberal commons helps draw attention to a puzzle: why is there such a sharp contrast between existing liberal commons regimes and the unified hostility of legal theory and Anglo-American co-ownership law to *cooperation*? Our analytic tool can be deployed wherever people want to work

---

2. Professor Heller draws on the economics literature, in which "liberalism" refers to an ideological preference for placing economic decision-making in the hands of individuals rather than in the state or institutions.

together, but are prevented from doing so by background property rules premised on the old-fashioned Blackstonian image of private property and the unreflective hostility to cooperation built into the *tragedy of the commons* image.

79 Or. L. Rev. at 419-20, 427-29 (emphasis added). *See also* Hanoch Dagan & Michael A. Heller, *The Liberal Commons*, 110 Yale L.J. 549 (2001). Notice the reference to *exit*—how can co-owners exit from the shared ownership arrangement? <u>Hint:</u> Recall our study of the termination of joint tenancies and of marital estates. Notice also the reference to the *tragedy of the commons*—a concept that we will examine in the next excerpt.

The Tragedy of the Commons

Garrett Hardin, 162 Science 1243 (1968)

Reading Guide

Although written in 1968, *The Tragedy of the Commons* continues to be an enormously influential article across multiple disciplines, including ecology, health care, economics, population studies, geography, psychology, and sociology.

♦ *The tragedy:* As you read this excerpt, formulate a concise description of the tragedy that concerns the author, Garrett Hardin.

♦ *The solution:* Hardin suggests a number of potential solutions to the tragedy. Be sure to notice as many as possible. Which, if any, strike you as good options?

[A little-known pamphlet published in 1833 by William Forster Lloyd, a mathematical amateur, contains a scenario that] "[w]e may well call . . . 'the tragedy of the commons,' using the word 'tragedy' as the philosopher Whitehead used it: 'The essence of dramatic tragedy is not unhappiness. It resides in the solemnity of the remorseless working of things.'" . . .]

Tragedy of Freedom in a Commons

The tragedy of the commons develops in this way. Picture a pasture open to all. It is to be expected that each herdsman will try to keep as many cattle as possible on the commons. Such an arrangement may work reasonably satisfactorily for centuries because tribal wars, poaching, and disease keep the numbers of both man and beast well below the carrying capacity of the land. Finally, however, comes the day of reckoning, that is, the day when the long-desired goal of social stability becomes a reality. At this point, the inherent logic of the commons remorselessly generates tragedy.

As a rational being, each herdsman seeks to maximize his gain. Explicitly or implicitly, more or less consciously, he asks, "What is the utility *to me* of adding one more animal to my herd?" This utility has one negative and one positive component.

1) The positive component is a function of the increment of one animal. Since the herdsman receives all the proceeds from the sale of the additional animal, the positive utility is nearly +1.
2) The negative component is a function of the additional overgrazing created by one more animal. Since, however, the effects of overgrazing are shared by all the herdsmen, the negative utility for any particular decision-making herdsman is only a fraction of [the increment of one animal].

Adding together the component partial utilities, the rational herdsman concludes that the only sensible course for him to pursue is to add another animal to his herd. And another; and another. . . . But this is the conclusion reached by each and every rational herdsman sharing a commons. Therein is the tragedy. Each man is locked into a system that compels him to increase his herd without limit—in a world that is limited. Ruin is the destination toward which all men rush, each pursuing his own best interest in a society that believes in the freedom of the commons. Freedom in a commons brings ruin to all. . . .

In an approximate way, the logic of the commons has been understood for a long time, perhaps since the discovery of agriculture or the invention of private property in real estate. But it is understood mostly only in special cases which are not sufficiently generalized. Even at this late date, cattlemen leasing national land on the western ranges demonstrate no more than an ambivalent understanding, in constantly pressuring federal authorities to increase the head count to the point where overgrazing produces erosion and weed-dominance. Likewise, the oceans of the world continue to suffer from the survival of the philosophy of the commons. Maritime nations still respond automatically to the shibboleth of the "freedom of the seas." Professing to believe in the "inexhaustible resources of the oceans," they bring species after species of fish and whales closer to extinction.

The National Parks present another instance of the working out of the tragedy of the commons. At present, they are open to all, without limit. The parks themselves are limited in extent—there is only one Yosemite Valley—whereas population seems to grow without limit. The values that visitors seek in the parks are steadily eroded. Plainly, we must soon cease to treat the parks as commons or they will be of no value to anyone.

What shall we do? We have several options. We might sell them off as private property. We might keep them as public property, but allocate the right to enter them. The allocation might be on the basis of wealth, by the use of an auction system. It might be on the basis of merit, as defined by some agreed-upon standards. It might be by lottery. Or it might be on a first-come, first-served basis, administered to long queues. These, I think, are all the reasonable possibilities. They are all objectionable. But we must choose—or acquiesce in the destruction of the commons that we call our National Parks. . . .

Mutual Coercion Mutually Agreed Upon

The social arrangements that produce responsibility are arrangements that create coercion, of some sort. Consider bank-robbing. The man who takes money from a bank acts as if the bank were a commons. How do we prevent such action? Certainly not by trying to control his behavior solely by a verbal appeal to his sense of responsibility. Rather than rely on propaganda we . . . insist that a bank is not a commons; we seek the definite social arrangements that will keep it from becoming a commons. That we thereby infringe on the freedom of would-be robbers we neither deny nor regret.

The morality of bank-robbing is particularly easy to understand because we accept complete prohibition of this activity. We are willing to say "Thou shalt not rob banks," without providing for exceptions. But temperance also can be created by coercion. Taxing is a good coercive device. To keep downtown shoppers temperate in their use of parking space we introduce parking meters for short periods, and traffic fines for longer ones. We need not actually forbid a citizen to park as long as he wants to; we need merely make it increasingly expensive for him to do so. Not prohibition, but carefully biased options are what we offer him. A Madison Avenue man might call this persuasion; I prefer the greater candor of the word coercion.

. . . To many, the word coercion implies arbitrary decisions of distant and irresponsible bureaucrats; but this is not a necessary part of its meaning. The only kind of coercion I recommend is mutual coercion, mutually agreed upon by the majority of the people affected. . . .

An alternative to the commons need not be perfectly just to be preferable. With real estate and other material goods, the alternative we have chosen is the institution of private property coupled with legal inheritance. Is this system perfectly just? . . . An idiot can inherit millions, and a trust fund can keep his estate intact. We must admit that our legal system of private property plus inheritance is unjust—but we put up with it because we are not convinced, at the moment, that anyone has invented a better system. The alternative of the commons is too horrifying to contemplate. Injustice is preferable to total ruin. . . .

Notes

1. *The commons:* What does Hardin mean by "the commons"? He gives a variety of examples, including federal grazing lands, the seas, and national parks. In what ways are these commons alike? In what ways are they different? How does Hardin's definition compare to the forms of ownership suggested by Professor Heller?

2. *The tragedy and the solution:* What is the *tragedy* that concerns Hardin? What solutions does he suggest? As a matter of history, the suggestion of privatization has perhaps gained the most traction, followed by the idea of "mutual coercion mutually agreed upon." Which proposed solution do you prefer, and why?

3. *Tragedy or comedy?* Does commons property lead inevitably to tragedy? Professor Rose suggests that the answer is "no":

> . . . When things are left open to the public, they are thought to be wasted by overuse or underuse. No one wishes to invest in something that may be taken from him tomorrow. . . . All resort to snatching up what is available for "capture" today, leaving behind a wasteland. From this perspective, "public property" is an oxymoron: things left open to the public are not property at all, but rather its antithesis. . . .

> . . . [D]espite the power of the classical economic argument for private property, a curious cross-current has continually washed through American law. Our legal doctrine has strongly suggested that some kinds of property should not be held exclusively in private hands, but should be open to the public or at least subject to what Roman law called the *jus publicum*: the "public right." . . .

> [S]ervice to commerce was a central factor in defining as "public" such properties as roads and waterways. Used in commerce, some property had qualities akin to infinite "returns to scale." Thus here, the commons was not tragic, but comedic, in the classical sense of a story with a happy outcome. And customary doctrines suggest that commerce might be thought a "comedy of the commons" not only because it may infinitely expand our wealth, but also, at least in part, because it has been thought to enhance the sociability of the members of an otherwise atomized society. . . .

> . . . The British courts' acceptance of *customary claims*, especially those concerning recreation, suggested a rationale similar to scale economies. One example was the customary right claimed by some communities to hold periodic dances, a custom held good over a landowner's objections. At least within the community, the more persons who participate in a dance, the higher its value to each participant. Each added dancer brings new opportunities to vary partners and share the excitement. . . . Activities of this sort may have value precisely because they reinforce the solidarity and fellow-feeling of the whole community; thus the more members of the community who participate, even if only as observers, the better for all.

> In a sense, this is the reverse of the "tragedy of the commons": it is a *comedy of the commons*, as is so felicitously expressed in the phrase, "the more the merrier." . . . This quality is closely related to scale economies in industrial production: the larger the investment, the higher the rate of return per unit of investment.

> . . . One might think that many customary activities prior to the eighteenth-century enclosures—such as cutting peat or grazing animals on commons—involved consumptive uses in which each participant's use *diminishes* opportunities for the others. Recent economic history suggests, however, that even these traditional activities produced economies of scale: the commons were an integral part of a

mixed economic pattern in which (because of limited markets) labor-intensive individual cultivation and scale-economy commons livestock management were necessarily practiced together. . . .

The doctrines of custom, then, tell us why certain kinds of property—particularly those necessary to commerce—were presumed to be more valuable if access were open to all. . . .

. . . Our law consistently allocates that access to the public, because public access to those locations is as important as the general privatization of property in other spheres of our law. In the absence of the socializing activities that take place on "inherently public property," the public is a shapeless mob, whose members neither trade nor converse nor play, but only fight, in a setting where life is, in Hobbes' all too famous phrase, solitary, poor, nasty, brutish, and short.

Carol Rose, *The Comedy of the Commons: Custom, Commerce, and Inherently Public Property*, 53 U. Chi. L. Rev. 711 (1986) (emphasis added). *See also* Carol M. Rose, *Surprising Commons*, BYU L. Rev. (2015).

4. *More to the story:*   Hardin used the metaphor of the tragedy of the commons to express his concern over what he perceived as unchecked population growth. He wrote his article in the wake of World War II, when the United States experienced a period of unprecedented population growth—the so-called "baby boom." In 1946, there were 3.4 million births, an increase of almost 20% over the previous year. Annual births continued to increase, reaching a peak in 1957 of 4.3 million. When the baby boom ended by 1965, annual births dropped to below four million. Sandra L. Colby & Jennifer M. Ortman, *Current Population Reports* (U.S. Census Bureau, May 2014).

Beyond the context of population growth, Hardin's article has been cited extensively in the real property literature for its consideration of optimum patterns of land ownership and management. Three decades after publication of *The Tragedy of the Commons*, Hardin made an important clarification: that his analysis applied only to a subset of the commons—the *unmanaged* commons. Garrett Hardin, *Extensions of "The Tragedy of the Commons"*, 280 Science 682 (1998). What difference does that modifying adjective make?

Ghen v. Rich

8 F. 159 (D. Mass. 1881)

Reading Guide

When you first encountered tangible personal property in Chapter 1, you learned that *fugitive resources* are things that move under their own force (such as wild animals) or under the force of gravity (such as water, oil, and natural gas). Here, we will take a closer look at one type of fugitive resource—whales swimming in the ocean.

NELSON, D.J.

This is a libel to recover the value of a fin-back whale. The libellant lives in Provincetown and the respondent in Wellfleet. The facts, as they appeared at the hearing, are as follows:

In the early spring months the easterly part of Massachusetts bay is frequented by the species of whale known as the fin-back whale. Fishermen from Provincetown pursue them in open boats from the shore, and shoot them with bomb-lances fired from guns made expressly for the purpose. When killed they sink at once to the bottom, but in the course of from one to three days they rise and float on the surface. Some of them are picked up by vessels and towed into Provincetown. Some float ashore at high water and are left stranded on the beach as the tide recedes. Others float out to sea and are never recovered. The person who happens to find them on the beach usually sends word to Provincetown, and the owner comes to the spot and removes the blubber. The finder usually receives a small salvage for his services. Try-works are established in Provincetown for trying out the oil. The business is of considerable extent, but, since it requires skill and experience, as well as some outlay of capital, and is attended with great exposure and hardship, few persons engage in it. The average yield of oil is about 20 barrels to a whale. It swims with great swiftness, and for that reason cannot be taken by the harpoon and line. Each boat's crew engaged in the business has its peculiar mark or device on its lances, and in this way it is known by whom a whale is killed.

The usage on Cape Cod, for many years, has been that the person who kills a whale in the manner and under the circumstances described, owns it, and this right has never been disputed until this case. The libellant has been engaged in this business for ten years past. On the morning of April 9, 1880, in Massachusetts bay, near the end of Cape Cod, he shot and instantly killed with a bomb-lance the whale in question. It sunk immediately, and on the morning of the 12th was found stranded on the beach in Brewster, within the ebb and flow of the tide, by one Ellis, 17 miles from the spot where it was killed. Instead of sending word to Provincetown, as is customary, Ellis advertised the whale for sale at auction, and sold it to the respondent, who shipped off the blubber and tried out the oil. The libellant heard of the finding of the whale on the morning of the 15th, and immediately sent one of his boat's crew to the place and claimed it. Neither the respondent nor Ellis knew the whale had been killed by the libellant, but they knew or might have known, if they had wished, that it had been shot and killed with a bomb-lance, by some person engaged in this species of business.

The libellant claims title to the whale under this usage. The respondent insists that this usage is invalid. It was decided by Judge Sprague, in *Taber v. Jenny*, 1 Sprague, 315, that when a whale has been killed, and is anchored and left with marks of appropriation, it is the property of the captors; and if it is afterwards found, still anchored, by another ship, there is no usage or principle of law by which the property of the original captors is diverted, even though the whale may have dragged from its anchorage. . . .

In *Bartlett v. Budd*, 1 Low. 223, the facts were these: The first officer of the libellant's ship killed a whale in the Okhotsk sea, anchored it, attached a waif to the body, and then left it and went ashore at some distance for the night. The next morning the boats of the respondent's ship found the whale adrift, the anchor not holding, the cable coiled round the body, and no waif or irons attached to it. Judge Lowell held that, as the libellants had killed and taken actual possession of the whale, the ownership vested in them. In his opinion the learned judge says:

> A whale, being *ferae naturae*, does not become property until a firm possession has been established by the taker. But when such possession has become firm and complete, the right of property is clear, and has all the characteristics of property.

He doubted whether a usage set up but not proved by the respondents, that a whale found adrift in the ocean is the property of the finder, unless the first taker should appear and claim it before it is cut in, would be valid, and remarked that "there would be great difficulty in upholding a custom that should take the property of *A.* and give it to *B.*, under so very short and uncertain a substitute for the statute of limitations, and one so open to fraud and deceit." Both the cases cited were decided without reference to usage, upon the ground that the property had been acquired by the first taker by actual possession and appropriation.

In *Swift v. Gifford*, 2 Low, 110, Judge Lowell decided that a custom among whalemen in the Arctic seas, that the iron holds the whale was reasonable and valid. In that case a boat's crew from the respondent's ship pursued and struck a whale in the Arctic ocean, and the harpoon and the line attached to it remained in the whale, but did not remain fast to the boat. A boat's crew from the libellant's ship continued the pursuit and captured the whale, and the master of the respondent's ship claimed it on the spot. It was held by the learned judge that the whale belonged to the respondents. It was said . . . that the usage for the first iron, whether attached to the boat or not, to hold the whale was fully established; and he added that, although local usages of a particular port ought not to be allowed to set aside the general maritime law, this objection did not apply to a custom which embraced an entire business, and had been concurred in for a long time by every one engaged in the trade.

In *Swift v. Gifford*, Judge Lowell also said:

> The rule of law invoked in this case is one of very limited application. The whale fishery is the only branch of industry of any importance in which it is likely to be much used, and if a usage is found to prevail generally in that business, it will not be open to the objection that it is likely to disturb the general understanding of mankind by the interposition of an arbitrary exception.

I see no reason why the usage proved in this case is not as reasonable as that sustained in the cases cited. Its application must necessarily be extremely limited, and can affect but a few persons. It has been recognized and acquiesced in for many years. It requires in the first taker the only act of appropriation that is possible in the nature of the case. Unless it is sustained, this branch of industry must necessarily cease, for no person would engage in it if the fruits of his labor could be appropriated by any chance finder. It gives reasonable salvage for securing or reporting the property. That the rule works well in practice is shown by the extent of the industry which has grown up under it, and the general acquiescence of a whole community interested to dispute it. It is by [no] means clear that without regard to usage the common law would not reach the same result. . . . If the fisherman does all that is possible to do to make the animal his own, that would seem to be sufficient. Such a rule might well be applied in the interest of trade, there being no usage or custom to the contrary. . . . I hold the usage to be valid, and that the property in the whale was in the libellant.

The rule of damages is the market value of the oil obtained from the whale, less the cost of trying it out and preparing it for the market, with interest on the amount so ascertained from the date of conversion. As the question is new and important, and the suit is contested on both sides, more for the purpose of having it settled than for the amount involved, I shall give no costs.

Decree for libellant for $71.05, without costs.

Notes

1. *What type of ownership?* Why types of property ownership are relevant to the dispute in *Ghen v. Rich*—private, public, commons, or liberal commons? Explain.

2. *Why private property rights?* Why do we allow part of the commons to be privatized through the rule of capture? Consider the various rationales supporting private property, as set forth in section A, above. Do any of them explain why title should be awarded to the whaler? Conversely, can you think of any rationales why no individual should be able to claim the whale as private property? What are the likely consequences of the rule of capture with respect to whales?

3. *The role of custom:* What role did custom play in the court's decision? What are the advantages and disadvantages of applying customary principles to resolve disputes? In the context of water—another fugitive resource—the California Supreme Court in 1855 famously adopted the customary practices of the time as the state's principle of water allocation. In adopting the *prior appropriation doctrine*, essentially a rule of capture, the court stated:

> Courts are bound to take notice of the political and social condition of the country, which they judicially rule. . . . [A] system has been permitted to grow up by the voluntary action and assent of the population. . . . If there are, as must be admitted, many things connected with this system, which are crude and undigested, and subject to fluctuation and dispute, there are still some which a universal sense of necessity and propriety have so firmly fixed as that they have come to be looked upon as having the force and effect of *res judicata*.

Irwin v. Phillips, 5 Cal. 140 (Cal. 1855). Is that rationale convincing? Is it applicable to *Ghen v. Rich*?

4. *Governing the commons:*   Elinor Ostrom (1933-2012) was an American political economist who won the Nobel Prize in Economics in 2009 (shared with Oliver E. Williamson) for her work on the commons and related areas. Like Professor Rose, she studied the conditions under which common ownership might result in cooperation and mutual benefit, rather than tragedy. Professor Ostrom documented the following example of a fishing dispute in Alanya, Turkey, and the ingenious resolution devised by local fishers in the 1970s:

> Each September, a list of eligible fishers is prepared, consisting of all licensed fishers in Alanya, regardless of co-op membership. Within the area normally used by Alanya fishers, all usable fishing locations are named and listed. These sites are spaced so that the nets set in one site will not block the fish that should be available at the adjacent sites.

> These named fishing locations and their assignments are in effect from September to May. In September, the eligible fishers draw lots and are assigned to the named fishing locations.

> From September to January, each day each fisher moves east to the next location. After January, the fishers move west. This gives the fishers equal opportunities at the stocks that migrate from east to west between September and January and reverse their migration through the area from January to May.

> The system has the effect of spacing the fishers far enough apart on the fishing grounds that the production capabilities at each site are optimized. All fishing boats also have equal chances to fish at the best spots. Resources are not wasted searching for or fighting over a site. No signs of overcapitalization are apparent.

> The list of fishing locations is endorsed by each fisher and deposited with the mayor and local gendarme once a year at the time of the lottery. The process of monitoring and enforcing the system is, however, accomplished by the fishers themselves as a by-product of the incentive created by the rotation system. On a day when a given fisher is assigned one of the more productive spots, that fisher will exercise that option with certainty (leaving aside last-minute breakdowns in equipment). All other fishers can expect that the assigned fisher will be at the spot bright and early. Consequently, an effort to cheat on the system by traveling to a good spot on a day when one is assigned to a poor spot has little chance of remaining undetected. Cheating on the system will be observed by the very fishers who have rights to be in the best spots and will be willing to defend their rights using physical means if necessary. Their rights will be supported by

everyone else in the system. The others will want to ensure that their own rights will not be usurped on the days when they are assigned good sites. The few infractions that have occurred have been handled easily by the fishers at the local coffeehouse.

Although this is not a private-property system, rights to use fishing sites and duties to respect these rights are well defined. And though it is not a centralized system, national legislation that has given such cooperatives jurisdiction over "local arrangements" has been used by cooperative officials to legitimize their role in helping to devise a workable set of rules. That local officials accept the signed agreement each year also enhances legitimacy. The actual monitoring and enforcing of the rules, however, are left to the fishers. . . .

Elinor Ostrom, Governing the Commons: The Evolution of Institutions for Collective Action (Cambridge University Press 1990) (pp. 25, 32-33, 37-40). Professor Ostrom pointed to the Alanya fishery as but one example of many potential institutional arrangements devised to prevent a tragedy of the commons. She criticized "[b]oth the centralizers and the privatizers" because they "frequently advocate oversimplified, idealized institutions" while paying "little attention to how diverse institutional arrangements operate in practice." *Id.* Are you convinced that privatizing the commons or imposing central regulation are not necessarily the best approaches to the shared use of common pool resources?

Wisconsin v. Michels Pipeline Construction, Inc.

217 N.W.2d 339 (Wis. 1974)[3]

Reading Guide

Illinois Central Railroad Co. v. Illinois concerned the state's ownership of the bed of Lake Michigan and its duty to hold the lakebed and overlying waters in trust for the benefit of the people. Here, we will look at another aspect of water— the groundwater found in the rocks and pores beneath the surface of the earth. Is groundwater an example of a commons? Is it prone to tragedy, comedy, or cooperative management?

The trial court granted the demurrer of the defendants-respondents on the basis that the case of *Huber v. Merkel*, 94 N.W. 354 (Wis. 1903) established that there is no cause of action for interference with ground water. . . . In *Huber v. Merkel* an owner of real estate attempted to have another landowner in his vicinity enjoined from wasting and unreasonably using water from artesian

---

3. [Supplanted on rehearing by 219 N.W.2d 308 (Wis. 1974) (making ruling prospective only as applied to all but individually named defendants).—Eds.]

wells on the person's property. The defendant allowed his wells to flow continuously, the excess simply spilling on the ground and this adversely affected the artesian pressure of all the wells which tapped the same aquifer. This court held that it was the almost universal consensus of judicial opinion that:

> ... If the waters simply percolate through the ground, without definite channel, they belong to the realty in which they are found, and the owner of the soil may divert, consume, or cut them off with impunity. If, on the other [hand, the waters flow in a] defined channel, the rules which govern the use of surface streams apply; but the presumption is that the waters are percolating waters until it is shown that they are supplied by a definite, flowing stream.

... The *Huber* case did not discuss the basis or rationale for this common-law rule but merely asserted that this was the rule and adopted it. The case has been severely criticized. ... Much of the criticism was directed at the holding that even malice did not divest a landowner of his absolute right to the use of ground water. It is generally conceded that this aspect of the case was probably a misstatement or at least an extension of the cases which had applied the common-law or *English rule* up to that time. ...

What is the basis of the English or common-law rule? The basis for this rule of absolute ownership of percolating ground water was a feeling that the ways of underground water were too mysterious and unpredictable to allow the establishment of adequate and fair rules for regulation of competing rights to such water. So the English courts adopted the position that everyone was permitted to take and use all of which they could get possession. ...

Even in 1903 when the *Huber v. Merkel* case was written, the awe of mysterious, unknowable forces beneath the earth was fast becoming an outmoded basis for a rule of law. ... However, today scientific knowledge in the field of hydrology has certainly advanced to the point where a cause and effect relationship can be established between a tapping of underground water and the level of the water table in the area so that liability can be fairly adjudicated consonant with due process. Our scientific knowledge also establishes the interdependence of all water systems. ...

It makes very little sense to make an arbitrary distinction between the rules to be applied to water on the basis of where it happens to be found. There is little justification for property rights in ground water to be considered absolute while rights in surface streams are subject to a doctrine of reasonable use. The *Huber v. Merkel* case certainly gives no explanation of why a property right in ground water should be an exception to the general maxim—*sic utere tuo ut alienum non laedas*.[4]

Also, although at the time of the decision of *Huber v. Merkel* the English rule did probably prevail, it was not a common-law rule of venerable, entrenched

---

4. [FN 26] Use your own property in such a manner as not to injure that of another. [We will consider this maxim again when we study nuisance in Chapter 11.—Eds.]

and ancient origin. The first decisions which enunciated the doctrine were decided in the early 1840s only a short time before Wisconsin achieved statehood. . . . Soon thereafter other American jurisdictions began to reject the English common-law rule in favor of what has come to be known as the American rule or the reasonable use doctrine. . . . Now as pointed out in the appellant's brief there are twenty-five states which adhere to the reasonable use doctrine and three which have adopted the even broader correlative rights doctrine. Thus the weight of authority in this country no longer supports the English rule of absolute possession. . . .

For the reasons discussed above, we overrule our decision in *Huber v. Merkel* and for that reason we find it necessary to adopt a rule of law more in harmony with present scientific and legal principles.

What rule should this court now adopt as to the use of percolating ground water? There are three distinct doctrines applied in various American jurisdictions regarding rights in percolating water:

(a) *The English or common-law rule:* . . . [T]he person who owns the surface may dig therein, and apply all that is there found to his own purposes at his free will and pleasure; and if, in the exercise of such right, he intercepts or drains off the water collected from underground springs in his neighbor's well, this inconvenience to his neighbor falls within the description of *damnum absque injuria*, which cannot become the ground of an action. . . . There is one limitation that the actions may not be motivated by malice and waste of water can be actionable. Although framed in property language this doctrine is really a rule of capture. The landowner may sell and grant his right to withdraw the water to others.

(b) *Reasonable use*: As stated in *Corpus Juris Secundum:* "In some states, the rule of the common law followed in early decisions has given way to the doctrine of reasonable use limiting the right of a landowner to percolating water in his land to such an amount of water as may be necessary for some useful or beneficial purpose in connection with the land from which it is taken, not restricting his right to use the water for any useful purpose on his own land, and not restricting his right to use it elsewhere in the absence of proof of injury to adjoining landowners." . . .

(c) *Correlative rights*: Again *Corpus Juris Secundum* defines this doctrine as: "Under the rule of correlative rights, the rights of all landowners over a common basin, saturated strata, or underground reservoir are coequal or correlative, and one cannot extract more than his share of the water, even for use on his own land, where others' rights are injured thereby." . . . According to the appellant's brief only three states adhere to the correlative rights doctrine. This doctrine applies the basic rules of the reasonable use doctrine, but calls for apportionment of underground water where there is not a sufficient supply for all reasonable uses. We are not shown here that water conditions in Wisconsin are so critical as to necessitate the adoption of this doctrine. Also the administrative difficulties of a court trying to make such an apportionment would militate against its adoption.

The *reasonable use* doctrine has been widely adopted in the United States. However, a close reading of the language of the doctrine shows that it is not a very radical departure from the common-law rule. It still contains quite a broad privilege to use ground water. . . .

. . . [T]he term *reasonable* has a very special restricted meaning. A waste of water or a wasteful use of water is not unreasonable only if it causes harm, and a use of water that causes harm is nevertheless reasonable if it is made in connection with the overlying land. The withdrawal of water for use elsewhere for beneficial purposes such as municipal supply or domestic supply is not *reasonable* in this special sense, but such removal may be made without liability if no harm results. . . .

The *reasonable use* rule basically only affords protection from cities withdrawing large quantities of water for municipal utilities. The rule forces cities to pay those affected by such excessive use damages or the cost of new wells and pumping equipment and is very much in accord with policies of loss distribution and requiring the beneficiaries of harmful activities to pay the costs thereof. However, under the rule there is no apportionment of water as between adjoining landowners. If water is withdrawn for a beneficial use on the land from which it is taken there is no liability for any harm to adjoining property owners. In effect, the rule gives partial protection to small wells against cities or water companies, but not protection from a large factory or apartment building on the neighboring land.

We choose not to adopt any of the three rules here discussed, but rather to adopt the rule set forth in Tentative Draft No. 17 of the Restatement of the Law Second, Torts, as proposed on April 26, 1971, for adoption by the American Law Institute . . . :

> Analysis. The rule adopted in this Topic can be described as the American rule with its protection broadened. It gives more or less unrestricted freedom to the possessor of overlying land to develop and use ground water and it permits the grant and sale of ground water to persons who need water but do not possess land overlying it. It does not attempt to apportion the water among users except to the extent that the special conditions of underground streams and interconnected ground and stream water permit it to be done on a rational basis. It gives the protection of the American rule to owners of small wells harmed by large withdrawals for use elsewhere, but extends that protection in proper cases to harm done by large withdrawals for operations on overlying lands.

> The proposed . . . Restatement Second [§ 858A] reads as follows:

> A possessor of land or his grantee who withdraws ground water from the land and uses it for a beneficial purpose is not subject to liability for interference with the use of water by another, unless:

(a) The withdrawal of water causes unreasonable harm through lowering the water table or reducing artesian pressure,

(b) The ground water forms an underground stream, in which case the rules stated in secs. 850A to 857 are applicable, or

(c) The withdrawal of water has a direct and substantial effect upon the water of a watercourse or lake, in which case the rules stated in secs. 850A to 857 are applicable.

Thus the rule preserves the basic expression of a rule of nonliability—a privilege if you will—to use ground water beneath the land. The formulation of the exception to this basic rule recognizes that there is usually enough water for all users so that apportionment is not necessary but that the problem is who shall bear the costs of deepening prior wells, installing pumps, paying increased pumping costs, etc., necessitated by a lowering of the water table by a large user. The common law placed the burden of making improvements on each user. The *reasonable use* rule gives protection to existing wells if the water withdrawal is taken off the land for use elsewhere but not if the water is used for beneficial purposes on the overlying land. . . .

The comment on the meaning of *unreasonable harm* as used in the Restatement rule explains that as in other situations, reasonableness will vary with the circumstances. Later users with superior economic resources should not be allowed to impose costs upon smaller water users that are beyond their economic capacity. . . .

In adopting the rule proposed in the Restatement of Torts, we necessarily overrule the order of the trial court sustaining the demurrer here, and we remand for further proceedings in the trial court. . . .

Notes

1. *Groundwater law today:*   It is difficult to make an accurate assessment of the groundwater laws of each state. In many cases—particularly in the wetter eastern states where conflict is less frequent—there may be little or no directly applicable statutory or case law on the topic. Still, it is safe to generalize that a majority of the eastern states follow the reasonable use doctrine, and that a majority of the western states follow some variation of the prior appropriation doctrine, which follows the general maxim "first in time, first in right" (not discussed in *Michels Pipeline*). *See generally* Joseph W. Dellapenna, *Quantitative Groundwater Law*, in Waters and Water Rights (Amy K. Kelley, Editor-in-Chief).

Fewer than a handful of the states follow the English rule of absolute ownership rejected in *Michels Pipeline*. As a notable exception, Texas recently affirmed its adherence to the doctrine. In *Edwards Aquifer Authority v. Day*, 369 S.W.3d 814 (Tex. 2012), the Texas Supreme Court decided an issue of first impression: whether groundwater can be owned *in place*, even before an individual water user's well has *captured* a portion of the water contained in the aquifer. In deciding in the affirmative, the court extended the law of oil and gas to water:

> In our state the landowner is regarded as having absolute title . . . to the oil and gas in place beneath his land. The only qualification . . . is that it must be considered in connection with the law of capture and is subject to police regulations. The oil and gas beneath the soil are considered a part of the realty. Each owner of land owns separately, distinctly and exclusively all the oil and gas under his land and is accorded the usual remedies against trespassers who appropriate the minerals or destroy their market value.

369 S.W.3d at 831-32.

The court concluded that landowners have a constitutionally compensable interest in the groundwater beneath their property. *Id.* at 838. As a result, the state cannot regulate or restrict groundwater pumping or use, unless it pays "just compensation" under the Fifth Amendment to landowners whose groundwater pumping has been restricted. *See* Chapter 13 (considering the issue of regulatory takings and just compensation). Texas (or at least, parts of it) is among the driest states in the nation. Is the absolute ownership doctrine a good choice for allocating water among competing users in an arid state?

2. *Other fugitive resources—oil and gas:*   Like groundwater, oil and natural gas are fugitive resources that pose commons problems. As Professor Hannah Wiseman explains,

> Property rights in oil and gas are incredibly complex, involving ownership of fugitive resources in the form of oil and gas, which neighboring mineral owners compete to extract; access or use rights (easements) to the surface above the fugitive resource; and access or use rights to subsurface real property like rock or coal, which holds oil and gas within its pores. Sometimes, three or more different entities own these rights: A owns the surface—say, a tract called Oilacre; B owns the coal and certain other hard minerals beneath Oilacre, or the minerals below Oilacre to a particular depth; and C owns the oil and gas beneath Oilacre as well as the right to use the subsurface and surface as needed to extract oil and gas. To further complicate these property rights, although C technically owns the oil and gas, the pool of liquid resources sitting in rock pores underground is better conceptualized as a commons: under the common law rule of capture, whoever "traps" the oil and gas first by extracting it from rock and bringing it to the surface owns it. These numerous and varied property rights generate conflicts between neighboring mineral owners, between surface owners and mineral owners, and between owners of different layers of minerals beneath one property, among other conflicts. Exercising any one of these property rights can create externalities borne by other property owners and users, yet these other property owners and users often lack a protected property right or a seat at the table when mineral owners exercise their right to drill.

See Hannah J. Wiseman, *Coordinating the Oil and Gas Commons*, BYU L. Rev. 101, 104-05 (2015). Professor Wiseman explores a number of options to "better coordinate property rights to oil and gas, as well as government authority in this area" and concludes "by emphasizing the complexity of this area and the danger of definitively proposing one property-based or regulatory solution." *Id.* at 110.

Massachusetts v. Environmental Protection Agency

549 U.S. 497 (2007)

Reading Guide

Below, the Court considers a narrow question of statutory interpretation: Did Congress, through enactment of the Clean Air Act, intend for the Environmental Protection Agency to regulate the emission of carbon dioxide and other greenhouse gases as "air pollutants"? For our purposes, however, the question is broader: is the earth's atmosphere a global commons? If so, what is the best way to prevent a "tragedy of the commons" in the form of the harms associated with global climate change?

STEVENS, J., joined by KENNEDY, SOUTER, GINSBURG, and BREYER, JJ.

A well-documented rise in global temperatures has coincided with a significant increase in the concentration of carbon dioxide in the atmosphere. Respected scientists believe the two trends are related. For when carbon dioxide is released into the atmosphere, it acts like the ceiling of a greenhouse, trapping solar energy and retarding the escape of reflected heat. It is therefore a species—the most important species—of a "greenhouse gas."

Calling global warming "the most pressing environmental challenge of our time," . . . a group of States, . . . local governments, . . . and private organizations, . . . alleged in a petition for certiorari that the Environmental Protection Agency (EPA) has abdicated its responsibility under the Clean Air Act to regulate the emissions of four greenhouse gases, including carbon dioxide. Specifically, petitioners asked us to answer two questions concerning the meaning of § 202(a)(1) . . . of the Act: whether EPA has the statutory authority to regulate greenhouse gas emissions from new motor vehicles; and if so, whether its stated reasons for refusing to do so are consistent with the statute. . . .

Section 202(a)(1) of the Clean Air Act provides:

The [EPA] Administrator shall by regulation prescribe (and from time to time revise) in accordance with the provisions of this section, standards applicable to the emission of any air pollutant from any class or classes of new motor vehicles or new motor vehicle engines, which in his judgment cause, or contribute to, air pollution which may reasonably be anticipated to endanger public health or welfare. . . .

The Act defines "air pollutant" to include "any air pollution agent or combination of such agents, including any physical, chemical, biological, radioactive . . . substance or matter which is emitted into or otherwise enters the ambient air." 42 U.S.C. § 7602(g). "Welfare" is also defined broadly: among other things, it includes "effects on . . . weather . . . and climate."

When Congress enacted these provisions, the study of climate change was in its infancy. . . . In 1959, shortly after the U.S. Weather Bureau began monitoring atmospheric carbon dioxide levels, an observatory in Mauna Loa, Hawaii, recorded a mean level of 316 parts per million. This was well above the highest carbon dioxide concentration—no more than 300 parts per million—revealed in the 420,000-year-old ice-core record. . . . By the time Congress drafted § 202(a)(1) in 1970, carbon dioxide levels had reached 325 parts per million. . . .

In the late 1970s, the Federal Government began devoting serious attention to the possibility that carbon dioxide emissions associated with human activity could provoke climate change. . . .

In 1978, Congress enacted the National Climate Program Act . . . which required the President to establish a program to "assist the Nation and the world to understand and respond to natural and man-induced climate processes and their implications." . . .

Congress next addressed the issue in 1987, when it enacted the Global Climate Protection Act. . . . Finding that "manmade pollution—the release of carbon dioxide, chlorofluorocarbons, methane, and other trace gases into the atmosphere—may be producing a long-term and substantial increase in the average temperature on Earth," . . . Congress directed EPA to propose to Congress a "coordinated national policy on global climate change," . . . and ordered the Secretary of State to work "through the channels of multilateral diplomacy" and coordinate diplomatic efforts to combat global warming. . . .

Meanwhile, the scientific understanding of climate change progressed. In 1990, the Intergovernmental Panel on Climate Change (IPCC), a multinational scientific body organized under the auspices of the United Nations, published its first comprehensive report on the topic. Drawing on expert opinions from across the globe, the IPCC concluded that "emissions resulting from human activities are substantially increasing the atmospheric concentrations of . . . greenhouse gases [which] will enhance the greenhouse effect, resulting on average in an additional warming of the Earth's surface." . . .

Responding to the IPCC report, the United Nations convened the "Earth Summit" in 1992 in Rio de Janeiro. The first President Bush attended and signed the United Nations Framework Convention on Climate Change (UNFCCC), a nonbinding agreement among 154 nations to reduce atmospheric concentrations of carbon dioxide and other greenhouse gases for the purpose of "prevent[ing] dangerous anthropogenic [i.e., human-induced] interference with the [Earth's] climate system." . . . The Senate unanimously ratified the treaty. . . .

When a State enters the Union, it surrenders certain sovereign prerogatives. Massachusetts cannot invade Rhode Island to force reductions in greenhouse gas emissions, it cannot negotiate an emissions treaty with China or India, and in some circumstances the exercise of its police powers to reduce in-state motor-vehicle emissions might well be pre-empted. . . .

These sovereign prerogatives are now lodged in the Federal Government, and Congress has ordered EPA to protect Massachusetts (among others) by prescribing [the § 202] standards. . . .

The harms associated with climate change are serious and well recognized. Indeed, the [National Research Council] Report itself—which EPA regards as an "objective and independent assessment of the relevant science"—identifies a number of environmental changes that have already inflicted significant harms, including "the global retreat of mountain glaciers, reduction in snow-cover extent, the earlier spring melting of rivers and lakes, [and] the accelerated rate of rise of sea levels during the 20th century relative to the past few thousand years. . . ."

Petitioners allege that this only hints at the environmental damage yet to come. According to the climate scientist Michael MacCracken, "qualified scientific experts involved in climate change research" have reached a "strong consensus" that global warming threatens (among other things) a precipitate rise in sea levels by the end of the century, . . . "severe and irreversible changes to natural ecosystems," . . . a "significant reduction in water storage in winter snowpack in mountainous regions with direct and important economic consequences," *ibid.*, and an increase in the spread of disease. . . . He also observes that rising ocean temperatures may contribute to the ferocity of hurricanes. . . .

EPA nevertheless maintains that its decision not to regulate greenhouse gas emissions from new motor vehicles contributes so insignificantly to petitioners' injuries that the agency cannot be haled into federal court to answer for them. For the same reason, EPA does not believe that any realistic possibility exists that the relief petitioners seek would mitigate global climate change and remedy their injuries. That is especially so because predicted increases in greenhouse gas emissions from developing nations, particularly China and India, are likely to offset any marginal domestic decrease.

But EPA overstates its case. Its argument rests on the erroneous assumption that a small incremental step, because it is incremental, can never be attacked in a federal judicial forum. Yet accepting that premise would doom most challenges to regulatory action. Agencies, like legislatures, do not generally resolve massive problems in one fell regulatory swoop. . . .

While the Congresses that drafted § 202(a)(1) might not have appreciated the possibility that burning fossil fuels could lead to global warming, they did understand that without regulatory flexibility, changing circumstances and scientific developments would soon render the Clean Air Act obsolete. The broad language of § 202(a)(1) reflects an intentional effort to confer the flexibility necessary to forestall such obsolescence. . . . Because greenhouse gases fit well within the Clean Air Act's capacious definition of "air pollutant," we hold that EPA has the statutory authority to regulate the emission of such gases from new motor vehicles. . . .

ROBERTS, C.J., joined by SCALIA, THOMAS, and ALITO, JJ., dissenting

Global warming may be a "crisis," even "the most pressing environmental problem of our time."

. . . Indeed, it may ultimately affect nearly everyone on the planet in some potentially adverse way, and it may be that governments have done too little to address it. It is not a problem, however, that has escaped the attention of policymakers in the Executive and Legislative Branches of our Government, who continue to consider regulatory, legislative, and treaty-based means of addressing global climate change. . . .

[The dissent concludes that Massachusetts' lawsuit should be dismissed for lack of "standing" and that appropriate remedies should be fashioned by the executive and legislative branches of government.]

Note

The global commons: As we will see in the discussion problem in the next section, international law recognizes the atmosphere as one of four "global commons." Is the earth's atmosphere an example of a commons that is headed toward tragedy? In Garrett Hardin's hypothetical, the problem was that too many herdsmen (through their cattle) were "capturing" too much of the pasture's forage. How, if at all, does that apply to the problem of global climate change?

What solutions are possible to prevent a tragedy of the global commons? Should they occur at the state, federal, or international level? For an argument that too many potential regulators can lead to a "regulatory commons" and too little regulation, *see* William W. Buzbee, *Recognizing the Regulatory Commons: A Theory of Regulatory Gaps*, 89 Iowa L. Rev. 1 (2003).

D. BEYOND THE BLACK LETTER: MINING ASTEROIDS IN OUTER SPACE

Asteroids are minor planets—small, rocky masses that revolve around the sun. The National Aeronautics and Space Administration (NASA) developed plans for the first U.S. mission to return samples from an asteroid to Earth to launch in September 2016 and to reach the asteroid *Bennu* in October 2018. Scientific goals of the 14-year mission include learning about the earliest history of our solar system and developing mitigation plans for asteroid-Earth collisions—*Bennu* is potentially one of the most hazardous asteroids and has a relatively high probability of striking the earth in the late 22nd century. In addition, the mission will explore the economic development potential of asteroids, which contain resources including water, iron, nickel, cobalt, and precious metals (such as gold, platinum, and rhodium). According to NASA,

> Over the last hundred years, the human population has exploded from about 1.5 billion to more than seven billion, driving an ever-increasing demand for resources. . . .
>
> Asteroids could one day be a vast new source of scarce material if the financial and technological obstacles can be overcome. Asteroids are lumps of metals, rock and dust, sometimes laced with ices and tar, which are the cosmic "leftovers" from the solar system's formation about 4.5 billion years ago. There are hundreds of thousands of them, ranging in size from a few yards to hundreds of miles across. Small asteroids are much more numerous than large ones, but even a little, house-sized asteroid should contain metals possibly worth millions of dollars.

NASA, *New NASA Mission to Help Us Learn How to Mine Asteroids*, Aug. 8, 2013.

Billionaire entrepreneurs also hope to mine asteroids. *Planetary Resources—The Asteroid Mining Company*, founded by Google's chief executive and others, began working toward commercial asteroid mining in 2010, as explained by the company's website. *See* http://www.planetaryresources.com/asteroids/#asteroids-map (visited Sept. 27, 2015). But is it legal for private individuals or corporations to mine in outer space? A bill introduced in 2015, the *Space Resource Exploration and Utilization Act*, would have made it legal under domestic law. Among other things, the proposed legislation provided, "any asteroid resources obtained in outer space are the property of the entity that obtained such resources, which shall be entitled to all property rights thereto." The bill triggered heated debate, including questions as to its legality under international law.

Does international law permit the mining of asteroids? International law recognizes four global commons: the *High Seas*, the *Atmosphere*, *Antarctica*, and *Outer Space*. In the absence of a treaty to the contrary, international law regards the global commons as part of the common heritage of humankind, beyond appropriation by any single nation, and subject to the doctrine of open access to all. *See* United Nations Environment Programme, Division of Environmental Law and Conventions, *IEG of the Global Commons*, http://www.unep.org/delc/GlobalCommons/tabid/54404/ (visited Sept. 27, 2015). In 1967, the Outer Space Treaty[5] entered into force. It has been signed by

---

5. The Treaty's formal name is the *Treaty on Principles Governing the Activities of States in the Exploration and Use of Outer Space, including the Moon and Other Celestial Bodies. See* United Nations, Office for Outer Space Affairs, http://www.unoosa.org/oosa/en/ourwork/spacelaw/treaties/introouterspacetreaty.html (visited Sept. 27, 2015).

more than 100 nations, including the United States, Russia, and China. In part, the Treaty was a reaction to the Soviet Union's then newly emerging leadership in space exploration—in 1957, the Soviet Union launched Sputnik, the first artificial satellite put into orbit around the earth. The Outer Space Treaty sought to limit the use of outer space to peaceful purposes and to prohibit military uses such as the orbiting of weapons. United Nations, Office for Disarmament Affairs, *Outer Space, available at* http://www.un.org/disarmament/topics/outerspace/ (visited June 9, 2015).

When the Outer Space Treaty was negotiated in the mid-20th century, asteroid mining was simply not something the parties likely contemplated. Among other things, the Treaty contains the following provisions. How should its provisions be interpreted with respect to asteroid mining?

Article I: The exploration and use of outer space, including the Moon and other celestial bodies, shall be carried out for the benefit and in the interests of all countries, irrespective of their degree of economic or scientific development, and shall be the province of all mankind.

Outer space, including the moon and other celestial bodies, shall be free for exploration and use by all States[6] without discrimination of any kind, on a basis of equality and in accordance with international law, and there shall be free access to all areas of celestial bodies. . . .

Article II: Outer space, including the moon and other celestial bodies, is not subject to national appropriation by claim of sovereignty, by means of use or occupation, or by any other means.

Article V: States Parties to the Treaty shall regard astronauts as envoys of mankind in outer space and shall render to them all possible assistance in the event of accident, distress, or emergency landing on the territory of another State Party or on the high seas. . . .

Article VI: States Parties to the Treaty shall bear international responsibility for national activities in outer space, including the moon and other celestial bodies, whether such activities are carried on by governmental agencies or by non-governmental entities, and for assuring that national activities are carried out in conformity with the provisions set forth in the present Treaty. The activities of non-governmental entities in outer space, including the moon and other celestial bodies, shall require authorization and continuing supervision by the appropriate State Party to the Treaty. . . .

---

6. [Under international law, "States" refers to sovereign nations, such as the United States and the former Soviet Union. It does not refer to smaller units of government, such as the state of New York or the state of California.—Eds.]

Article IX: In the exploration and use of outer space, including the moon and other celestial bodies, States Parties to the Treaty shall be guided by the principle of co-operation and mutual assistance and shall conduct all their activities in outer space, including the moon and other celestial bodies, with due regard to the corresponding interests of all other States Parties to the Treaty. . . .

Article XI: In order to promote international co-operation in the peaceful exploration and use of outer space, States Parties to the Treaty conducting activities in outer space, including the Moon and other celestial bodies, agree to inform the Secretary-General of the United Nations as well as the public and the international scientific community, to the greatest extent feasible and practicable, of the nature, conduct, locations and results of such activities. . . .

Discussion Questions

1. *The global commons:* Under the Treaty, is outer space commons property (in the sense that we have been discussing), and if so, why? Point to specific treaty provisions in support of your response. Is outer space an example of a potential tragedy of the commons? What type of management approach does the Treaty adopt—the recognition of limited private property rights, mutual coercion, cooperation, or something else? Do you agree with the approach taken by the Treaty, or would you recommend modifications?

2. *Asteroids as fugitive resources:* Are asteroids a fugitive resource? If so, would any of the three groundwater rules discussed in *Wisconsin v. Michels Pipeline Construction Co.* provide a useful analogy for setting international policy on asteroid mining?

3. *Comedy of the commons:* Do asteroid mining and related activities present opportunities for a comedy of the commons? Thinking broadly about strategies for international diplomacy, can you think of any opportunities for cooperation presented by future Treaty negotiations?

4. *The legality of asteroid mining under international law:* Under the Treaty, can the United States or private American companies engage in asteroid mining? Can they claim ownership of resources and precious metals extracted from asteroids and brought back to Earth? What is the distinction between *use* and *appropriation* under the Treaty (*see* especially Article II)? For example, if a mining operation extracts virtually all of the content from a small asteroid, has the operation engaged in either *use* or *appropriation* of the asteroid? What approach would you prefer, being mindful of the fact that any rights or restrictions will apply not only to the United States, but also to other nations subject to the Treaty?

5. *Domestic law—the proposed Space Exploration and Utilization Act of 2015:* Was the proposed domestic legislation consistent with the international Treaty? Should Congress be concerned with international law? Should private investors be concerned? If a dispute arises internationally, what are the likely repercussions? Leaving international law aside, do you agree with the draft legislation's underlying policy?

E. SKILLS PRACTICE: STATUTORY LAW AND IMPLEMENTING REGULATIONS

Light v. United States (section B, above), involved the issue of whether a private rancher could graze his livestock on public lands owned by the United States without first obtaining a federal grazing permit. *Light* was decided in 1911, at which time there was a paucity of federal law on the topic. Today, the situation is the opposite—there are an overwhelming number of statutory and regulatory provisions that govern grazing on the federal lands. This is not uncommon in most areas of federal (and state) statutory law today, given the complexity of modern society.

Suppose that Frederica Light (a descendant of Fred Light) is your client, and she wants to know what requirements she must satisfy to graze her livestock on the federal lands. Recall that she lives in Colorado and wants to turn her livestock out onto the national forests—the successor to the forest reserves that her ancestor Fred wanted to use. Recall that the national forests are under the jurisdiction of the U.S. Forest Service, within the U.S. Department of Agriculture.

To prepare to counsel Frederica—and to gain a very basic introduction to statutory law and its implementation—we will examine two sources of law:

Federal statutory law—The Federal Land Policy & Management Act (FLPMA) of 1976: *Light* relied on statutes dating back to 1891 and 1903 through which Congress delegated rulemaking authority to the Forest Service to "make such rules and regulations . . . as will insure the objects of such reservations; namely, to regulate their occupancy and use, and to preserve the forests thereon from destruction." Today, the most relevant statutory authority is FLPMA,[7] 43 U.S.C. §§ 1701 *et seq.*, which governs federal lands managed by the U.S. Forest Service, and also those managed by the Bureau of Land Management. Through this law, Congress enacted a framework for federal land policy. But, as you might imagine, Congress is ill-equipped to deal with all of the on-the-ground details involved in running the nation's vast trove of federal lands. To provide assistance, Congress delegated considerable authority to the federal

---

7. [The acronym is generally pronounced, "FLIP-ma."—Eds.]

agencies to fill in the gaps of the statute and to come up with detailed plans to implement Congress' broad statutory scheme.

To find FLPMA, use an electronic database such as Westlaw™ or LexisNexis®. In WestlawNext™, for example, click on the content tabs "Federal Materials" and "United States Code Annotated (USCA)." Then, select "Title 43. Public Lands" and scroll down to "Chapter 35—Federal Land Policy and Management" and click on that tab. You should then see a table of contents for FLPMA. You would follow a similar (but not identical) process to find the statute on LexisNexis®. The questions below will prompt you to click on relevant sections of FLPMA to answer questions posed by your client. However, if you did not know which statutory section was relevant, you might find perusing the table of contents to be helpful.

Federal regulations—The Code of Federal Regulations (CFR): When Congress delegates rulemaking authority to federal agencies, they publish their draft and final rules in the *Federal Register*, which is the daily newspaper of the federal government containing federal agency regulations, proposed rules and public notices, executive orders, proclamations, and other presidential documents. The *Code of Federal Regulations* (CFR), in turn, codifies final rules by topic, rather than by date of publication. The regulations published in the CFR (assuming they have not been challenged in court and overturned) have the force of law.

Title 36, Part 222 of the CFR contains regulations related to "range management," and Subpart A covers "grazing and livestock use on the national forest system." To find that part of the CFR, select the "Regulations" content tab on WestlawNext™, then click on "Code of Federal Regulations (CFR)," and then click on "Title 36." Scroll down to "Chapter II—Forest Service, Department of Agriculture" and then click on "Part 222—Range Management." You should then see a table of contents for the grazing permit regulations issued by the Forest Service. You would follow a similar (but not identical) process to find the statute on LexisNexis®. The questions below will prompt you to click on relevant sections of the CFR to answer questions posed by your client, rancher Frederica Light.

Tasks

Refer to the statutory and regulatory provisions discussed above, and then answer the following questions.

1. *The secretaries:* Most grazing on federal lands takes place on federal lands administered by the Bureau of Land Management (under the Secretary of the Interior) and by the U.S. Forest Service (under the Secretary of Agriculture).

- Through FLPMA, did Congress delegate authority to one or both secretaries to issue rules and regulations governing grazing? Can the public participate in the promulgation of those regulations? *See* FLPMA §§ 1701(a)(5), 1702(g). *See also* 36 CFR § 222.3(c).

2. *Is a permit required?* Recall that the Court in *Light v. United States* asserted that ranchers could continue to graze their livestock on federal lands under "a sort of implied license . . . so long as the government did not cancel its tacit consent."

- Is that still an accurate statement of the law? *See* 36 CFR § 222.3(a).
- Do grazing permits confer private rights in public lands? *See* 36 CFR § 222.3(b).

3. *Grazing in Colorado:*

- What percentage of land in Colorado does the federal government own? *See* section B, above (Figure 2).
- What is the meaning of "grazing permit and lease" and can the Forest Service issue such a permit in Colorado? *See* FLPMA § 1702(o)&(p). *See also* 36 CFR § 222.51(a). Notice the various references to "eleven contiguous Western States" and "16 contiguous Western States"—why do you think the groupings vary in different parts of the statute and regulations?
- For how long will the permit last? *See* 36 CFR § 222.3(c)(1).
- Will your client be required to pay for the permit? *See* FLPMA § 1701(a)(9). *See also* 36 CFR § 222.50(a).

4. *Custom:* Can the customs of commercial livestock owners influence the government's administration of the grazing lands? *See* FLPMA §§ 1702(k), 1753(a)&(b). *See also* 36 CFR § 222.7(a). What impact might those provisions have on staving off a potential tragedy of the commons?

F. CHAPTER REVIEW

1. Practice Questions[8]

1. *Drilling for oil:* Jayden drilled an oil well on his land and began to produce thousands of barrels of oil per day. The well is located only 350 feet from the property of his neighbor Sarah. Sarah hired a consultant, who discovered that there was a vast deposit of oil beneath Sarah's land, which Jayden's well was pumping out. Sarah sued Jayden for damages, claiming that Jayden was taking her oil. Assume that Sarah can prove that the oil reservoir that Jayden was draining extends beneath her land. Assume also the jurisdiction has no

---

8. Answers appear in the Appendix to this casebook.

relevant legislation governing the extraction of oil. Which statement is most accurate?

A. Jayden should prevail under the rule of *Edwards v. Sims* (Chapter 1) and its maxim, *cujus est solum, ejus est usque ad coelum ad infernos.*

B. Jayden should prevail under the English (or common law) rule discussed in *Wisconsin v. Michels Pipeline Construction* if the court determines that oil is a fugitive resource.

C. Sarah should prevail under the rule in *Johnson v. M'Intosh* (Chapter 1) if she can prove that the consultant (as her agent) discovered the oil first.

D. Sarah should prevail under the rule of *Ghen v. Rich* because it is not possible for Jayden to first "kill" the oil, as was required of the whaler in *Ghen.*

2. *Owning a condominium:* Recall our study of condominium ownership from Chapter 5.A.3. Into which category of ownership do condominiums best fit, and why?

A. Private property

B. Public property

C. Commons property

D. Liberal commons property

3. *The Raging River and the power company:* Assume that the Raging River is "navigable" in the technical sense discussed in the note after *Illinois Central Railroad Co.* A large, private utility company wants to install hydroelectric power generating facilities in the riverbed. Can the state grant the utility the right to so use the riverbed?

A. Yes, but only if the state determines that the grant does not substantially impair the public interest in the lands and waters remaining.

B. Yes, because the riverbed is the state's property to convey as it wishes.

C. No, because the public trust doctrine forbids any private use of state property.

D. No, because the river is a commons over which the state has no authority to either grant or deny use rights.

2. Bringing It Home

1. *Federal lands:* Roughly what percentage of the land within your state is owned by the federal government? <u>Hint</u>: Refer to the map in Section B, Figure 2. Can you think of any purposes for which the federal government has reserved those lands? For example, are there any national forests, national parks, national wildlife refuges, or lands managed by the Federal Bureau of Land Management? Are you aware of any federal lands within your state that are used for grazing, as in *Light v. United States?*

2. *State submerged lands:*   Do you live or vacation in a coastal state? If so, what is the boundary between state-owned lands (held in trust for the public) and privately owned lands? States fall into three broad categories:

- *Mean high high water line states:* These states generally recognize the greatest expanse of public ownership, extending landward past the wet sand beach, and onto the dry sand up to the "mean high high water" line.
- *Mean high water line states:* These states recognize slightly less public ownership, extending up to the "mean high water line." In these states, the public can generally use the wet sand and areas seaward, but the dry sand beach can be privately owned.
- *Mean low low water line states:* These states recognize the least amount of public ownership, and allow both the dry sand and wet sand beach to be privately owned. Public ownership begins at the "mean low low water line" and extends seaward.

For more information, see the website of the National Geodetic Survey of the National Oceanic and Atmospheric Administration (NOAA) and the embedded illustration: http://www.ngs.noaa.gov/RSD/coastal/ (visited Sept. 28, 2015). For somewhat technical definitions of the various water lines, *see* NOAA Shoreline Website, *A Guide to National Shoreline Data and Terms: Glossary,* http://shoreline.noaa.gov/glossary.html (visited Sept. 28, 2015). Be aware that these determinations are approximate, and also subject to change by common law judicial opinions.

PART THREE

TRANSFERRING PROPERTY

Real Estate Transactions

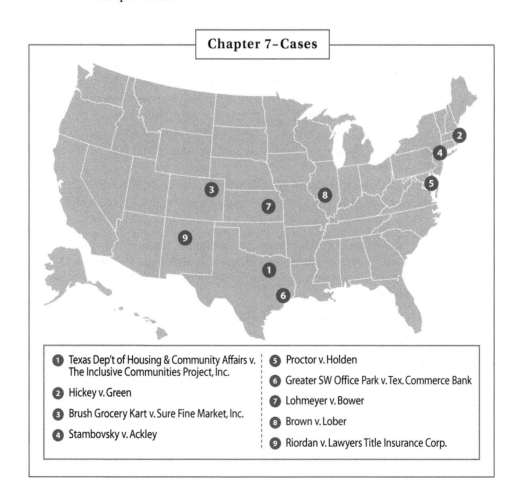

Chapter 7–Cases

1. Texas Dep't of Housing & Community Affairs v. The Inclusive Communities Project, Inc.
2. Hickey v. Green
3. Brush Grocery Kart v. Sure Fine Market, Inc.
4. Stambovsky v. Ackley
5. Proctor v. Holden
6. Greater SW Office Park v. Tex. Commerce Bank
7. Lohmeyer v. Bower
8. Brown v. Lober
9. Riordan v. Lawyers Title Insurance Corp.

In the previous chapters, we observed that the law favors the free transferability of property rights, and that it dislikes restraints on alienation. Our study of adverse possession demonstrated that the law even recognizes *involuntary* transfers of land and chattels under certain conditions. In this chapter, we will take a closer look at the process by which owners transfer their property to others, with a particular focus on *voluntary* transfers of *real* property.

The real estate transaction provides fertile ground for reconsidering *why* society recognizes and protects property rights. In the last chapter, we examined several justifications, including the labor rationale; the autonomy and liberty rationales; the personhood rationale; the utilitarian and economic efficiency rationales; and the democracy rationale. Drawing on such explanations, should we think of land primarily as a fungible market commodity—one that supplies an important source of wealth to its owners? If so, then perhaps the law should emphasize policies that maximize the market value of land and its efficient transfer, as suggested by the utilitarian and economic efficiency rationales. Alternatively, do particular parcels of land represent irreplaceable sanctuaries that become bound up with their owners' self-development and ability to thrive in the world? If so, then maybe the law should emphasize policies that maximize fairness and stability, as suggested by the personhood or autonomy/liberty theories of property. Or, can a single parcel of land simultaneously serve both of those purposes? We will see in section D, for example, that a mortgage lender and a borrower-owner each hold simultaneous legal interests in the same property. As you might imagine, the motivations and perceptions of each often diverge widely. How can the law accommodate both sets of interests, and should it do so?

The answers to these questions are likely to be complicated, in part because of what Professor Eduardo M. Peñalver refers to as land's "complexity" and "memory":

> ... In Karl Polanyi's words, "The economic function is but one of many vital functions of land." Instead, Polanyi argued, land "invests man's life with stability; it is the site of his habitation; it is a condition of his physical safety; it is the landscape and the seasons." ...

> On a deeper level, land derives its complexity directly from the intricacy of the social activities that take place upon it. Each parcel of land in a city will be unique, in a sense, because of the relationship it bears to the web of human interactions within which it is situated. ... In short, a crucial feature of land's complexity is its role as a template for—and a practically necessary ingredient in—the full spectrum of human aspiration and activity.

> In addition to its complexity, land has memory. Changes that human beings make to the land have a tendency to remain in place until they are affirmatively removed. And because the quantity of land is fixed, we are fated to live our lives

within a landscape that bears the indelible imprint of our forebears, even if we do not always recognize that imprint for what it is. . . .

Eduardo M. Peñalver, *Land Virtues*, 94 Cornell L. Rev. 821, 828-31 (2009).

It is no small task for the law to accommodate these multiple facets of real property—objective and subjective value, complexity, and memory. One common point of agreement, perhaps, is the importance of *information disclosure* in the real estate transaction. As you read this chapter and the next (on the recording system), pay attention to the law's various disclosure requirements, and their likely impact on the parties. Notice also the interplay of common law and statutory law, and how legislative enactments affect almost every aspect of the real estate transaction.

A. OVERVIEW OF THE REAL ESTATE TRANSACTION

1. The Timeline

We will break the real estate transaction into three stages, as illustrated below—the *contract formation* period, the *executory period*, and the *post-closing period*. This chapter will examine each stage of the real estate timeline in detail. For now, the following brief overview will give you a sense of the overall scope and progression of the typical real estate transaction.

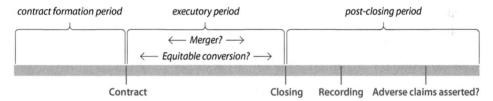

Figure 1

Contract formation:　First, during the *contract formation period*, the buyer searches for a suitable property, often with the aid of a real estate broker. If the buyer identifies such a property, then the buyer and the potential seller negotiate for the purchase and sale of real estate. If successful, this results in a signed, written document that satisfies the statute of frauds—or, less commonly, in an oral agreement that falls under an exception to the statute of frauds. In states that apply the doctrine of *equitable conversion*, upon the signing of the contract the buyer takes "equitable title" to the property, leaving the "legal title" in the seller. As we will see, this split of title can have important consequences. If the property is destroyed or damaged during the executory period, for example, the buyer might bear the risk of loss (even though the seller remains in possession), unless the contract provides otherwise.

Executory period: Next, during the *executory period*, the parties perform various tasks set forth in the contract, under a detailed time schedule set out in the contract. Among other things, as we will see, most contracts contain three "contingencies" that allow the buyer to perform certain investigations before finalizing the purchase: (1) investigate the physical condition of the premises, obtain a survey to make sure the property boundaries are located as expected, and determine whether the property is in a floodplain such that the buyer will have to arrange for a federal flood insurance policy (which is usually distinct from a typical homeowners insurance policy); (2) arrange for a mortgage or other financing, unless the buyer has enough resources to pay cash for the entire purchase price and does not need a loan; and (3) investigate the state of the title to make sure that the seller has good title, and obtain a commitment for title insurance that serves as a backup for title problems not disclosed by the search. The executory period ends with the *closing* of the contract. At the closing, the buyer (or the buyer's lender) gives the full purchase price to the seller, and the seller delivers a deed to the buyer. At this time, the buyer acquires the seller's entire property interest (and any split between legal and equitable title ceases).

In jurisdictions that follow the *merger doctrine*, all pre-closing promises "merge" into the final documents provided at closing. As a practical consequence, this means that the buyer must rely on warranties contained in the deed to replace any promises contained in the contract. Thus, it is essential that the buyer carefully inspect all closing documents to make sure that they comport with the contract warranties. For example, if the contract promises the buyer a "general warranty deed," then the buyer must take care to accept nothing less than the promised document. The merger rule appears to be in decline. In any case, the parties can contract around the merger rule and define what contract terms, if any, survive the closing of the contract and the delivery of the deed.

Post-closing period: The final stage is the *post-closing* period. The most critical events of this stage are the buyer's *recording* of the deed in the public records and the lender's recording of the buyer's mortgage. After closing and recording, problems can still occur. For example, parties holding competing claims to title may appear (such as one who holds an easement on the property, a lender that holds a prior mortgage on the property, or even someone who claims to hold superior title in fee simple absolute). Likewise, after closing and recording a buyer might default on loan payments, thereby triggering *foreclosure* proceedings upon the borrower's default (as considered in section D, below).

2. The Real Estate Broker

Real estate brokers perform a valuable service by matching prospective buyers and sellers with one another. Although some sellers market their property without a broker—known as *for sale by owner* (FSBO, pronounced *FIZZ-bo*) transactions—the majority of buyers and sellers use a broker. Among other things, brokers have access to vast amounts of market data, such as the "multiple listing service" (MLS), which is a restricted database of all properties listed for sale with a broker within a specified geographic area. Realtors share the MLS widely among themselves, but it is difficult for individual buyers and sellers to obtain this information. As a matter of terminology, real estate *agents* (or salespersons) usually work under real estate *brokers*. Both categories of real estate professionals are heavily regulated by the states, which establish educational standards and licensing examinations. The requirements for brokers are usually more extensive than those applicable to agents.

The representation:　Three issues involving brokers and agents deserve a brief mention as we begin our study of real estate transactions. First, whom does the broker represent—the seller, the buyer, both, or neither? Each of those options is possible, subject to varying restrictions imposed by state law. By far, most brokers represent *sellers*, a fact that might surprise many buyers who work closely with sellers' brokers in finding suitable properties. In such cases, the seller pays the broker's sales commission. (Can you think of any incentives that might create for brokers that are adverse to the buyer's interests?). Increasingly, however, it is common for buyers to have their own brokers, who work as *buyers agents*. Some states also allow brokers to serve as *dual agents*, and to represent both seller and buyer in the same transaction, provided that both parties consent to the arrangement. In all three of these situations, brokers act as fiduciary agents of their clients, and owe them duties of loyalty, disclosure, and confidentiality. As you might imagine, it is risky for brokers to engage in dual agent relationships, and to simultaneously satisfy their fiduciary obligations to both seller and buyer. As a fourth option, in some states brokers can serve as *transaction coordinators* who facilitate the sale (as by showing properties and preparing paperwork), but do not represent either party in a fiduciary capacity. To prevent confusion, most states require brokers to provide a written disclosure form expressly describing the broker's relationship to the buyer and to the seller.

The commission:　A second potential area of dispute concerns the broker's sales commission. Commissions generally range between 5% and 7% of the sales price, as negotiated by the seller and the seller's broker. For example, if a property sells for $100,000 and the parties have agreed to a 5% commission, then the seller's broker has earned $5,000 of the sales price (leaving the seller with the remaining $95,000). The seller's broker, however, generally shares the commission equally with the buyer's broker (amounting to a $2,500 commission for each). If the buyer has not retained a broker, then the seller's broker will usually retain the entire $5,000.

At what point in time does the broker earn the agreed commission? Under the majority rule, the broker earns the commission when the broker produces a buyer who is *ready, willing, and able* to purchase upon terms acceptable to the seller. As a practical matter, this usually occurs when the seller and prospective buyer sign a contract, even if the deal subsequently unravels. *See Fairbourn Commercial, Inc. v. American Housing Partners, Inc.*, 94 P.3d 292 (Utah 2004) (requiring seller to pay commission even though buyer did not proceed to closing, in part because the broker is not an insurer of the subsequent performance of the buyer). Notice the potential hardship suffered by the seller under the majority rule, particularly in cases where the sale falls apart absent any fault of the seller. To alleviate this burden, many majority rule jurisdictions recognize an exception based on the terms of the sales contract itself. That is, most real estate contracts give either buyer or seller the right to terminate the contract if certain specified conditions have not been satisfied (such as if the buyer has failed to qualify for a loan). In such cases, the contract itself might excuse the seller from the duty to pay a commission. Alternatively, sellers and brokers can negotiate around the majority rule by inserting a clause in the *listing agreement*—the contract under which a seller retains a broker to market a property—that the broker is not entitled to a commission unless the contract closes and the parties consummate the sale. In contrast to the majority rule and its exceptions, the minority rule (an increasing modern trend) requires sellers to pay the broker's commission only if the sale is finalized. *See Ellsworth Dobbs, Inc. v. Johnson*, 236 A.2d 843 (N.J. 1967). It is unclear whether brokers can negotiate for more favorable terms in jurisdictions that follow the minority rule.

The unauthorized practice of law: A third issue is whether any of the tasks performed by brokers impermissibly cross the line and represent the *unauthorized practice of law* by those who do not hold a legal license. Imagine a not-uncommon transaction in which neither seller nor buyer retains an attorney; further imagine that the buyer has not engaged the services of a buyer's broker. In such case, the seller's broker would likely put the buyer in touch with a mortgage company to determine if the buyer qualifies for a loan; present the seller and buyer with a standard form contract and assist each party in negotiating, completing, and executing the document; order a title commitment from an insurance company willing to issue an insurance policy to the buyer; order numerous inspections and reports (all of primary interest to the buyer); select an attorney to draft the deed that the seller will deliver to the buyer; and perform or facilitate numerous other actions that have potentially serious legal ramifications for the seller and the buyer. Should brokers be permitted to perform those quasi-legal actions?

On one hand, the absence of attorneys can save the parties hundreds, or even thousands, of dollars. Further, in many (if not most) cases, the transaction can proceed smoothly and efficiently under the practiced guidance of a reputable broker. On the other hand, brokers lack the training to recognize potential legal problems and to deal with non-routine circumstances that might arise. Further, the broker has a potential conflict of interest. As one court explained, the parties are relying on the broker "whose commission depends entirely on consummation of the transaction, and whose interest is primarily—in some cases it is fair to say exclusively—to get the contract signed and the deal closed." *In re Opinion No. 26 of the Committee of the Unauthorized Practice of Law*, 654 A.2d 1344 (N.J. 1995). The New Jersey Supreme Court neatly summarized the tension inherent in the unauthorized practice of law determination: "It would take a volume to describe each and every risk to which the seller and buyer [unrepresented by legal counsel] have exposed themselves without adequate knowledge. But it takes a very short sentence to describe what apparently occurs: the deal closes, satisfactory to buyer and seller in practically all cases, satisfactory both at the closing and thereafter." *Id.* Courts have reconciled the competing concerns of efficient, cost-effective transactions and risk minimization in a variety of ways. Most states allow brokers to prepare contracts of sale, provided that the brokers follow a standard form developed by attorneys in the state. Some states apply additional limitations, such as restricting the types of real estate forms that brokers can fill out, or requiring a notice to sellers and buyers of the risks they are assuming by forgoing the option of retaining legal counsel.

3. Discrimination in the Sale of Real Property

Various discriminatory practices in the sale of real property can contribute to segregated housing patterns and to the nation's racial inequality. As we first saw in our study of landlord-tenant law, critical tools to combat discrimination in both the rental and sale of real property include the Civil Rights Act of 1866, the Fourteenth Amendment to the U.S. Constitution, and the Fair Housing Act of 1968 (FHA). As the U.S. Supreme Court makes clear in the following case, housing practices are cognizable under the Fair Housing Act not only when the defendant has a discriminatory *intent*, but also when the defendant's practices have a disproportionately adverse *effect* on people that fall within the FHA's protected classes.

Texas Dep't of Housing & Community Affairs v. The Inclusive Communities Project, Inc.

135 S. Ct. 2507 (2015)

Reading Guide

♦ *Disparate impact liability:* In the following case, the Court considers the so-called *disparate impact* theory of liability, under which a plaintiff must prove discriminatory effect, rather than discriminatory motive. The case arises in the context of a state's program to provide affordable housing to its low-income residents—a topic we will take up later when we study zoning in Chapter 12.

♦ *Patterns of discrimination:* For now, we are concerned with the Court's description of our country's history of widespread discrimination in the

> housing market. As you read the Court's opinion, notice that historic (and potentially ongoing) patterns of discrimination include federal and state practices, "steering" by real estate agents, "redlining" by lending institutions, and actions by private individuals.

KENNEDY, J., joined by GINSBURG, BREYER, SOTOMAYER and KAGAN, J.J.

The underlying dispute in this case concerns where housing for low-income persons should be constructed in Dallas, Texas—that is, whether the housing should be built in the inner city or in the suburbs. This dispute comes to the Court on a disparate-impact theory of liability. In contrast to a disparate-treatment case, where a "plaintiff must establish that the defendant had a discriminatory intent or motive," a plaintiff bringing a disparate-impact claim challenges practices that have a "disproportionately adverse effect on minorities" and are otherwise unjustified by a legitimate rationale. *Ricci v. DeStefano*, 557 U.S. 557, 577 (2009). The question presented for the Court's determination is whether disparate-impact claims are cognizable under the Fair Housing Act (or FHA), 82 Stat. 81, as amended, 42 U.S.C. § 3601 *et seq.*

I

A

... The Federal Government provides low-income housing tax credits that are distributed to developers through designated state agencies. 26 U.S.C. § 42. Congress has directed States to develop plans identifying selection criteria for distributing the credits. ...

In the State of Texas these federal credits are distributed by the Texas Department of Housing and Community Affairs (Department). ...

The Inclusive Communities Project, Inc. (ICP), is a Texas-based nonprofit corporation that assists low-income families in obtaining affordable housing. In 2008, the ICP brought this suit against the Department and its officers in the United States District Court for the Northern District of Texas. As relevant here, it brought a disparate-impact claim under ... the FHA. The ICP alleged the Department has caused continued segregated housing patterns by its disproportionate allocation of the tax credits, granting too many credits for housing in predominantly black inner-city areas and too few in predominantly white suburban neighborhoods. ...

The District Court concluded that the ICP had established a prima facie case of disparate impact. It relied on two pieces of statistical evidence. First, it found "from 1999-2008, [the Department] approved tax credits for 49.7% of proposed non-elderly units in 0% to 9.9% Caucasian areas, but only approved 37.4% of proposed non-elderly units in 90% to 100% Caucasian areas." 749 F. Supp. 2d 486, 499 (N.D. Tex. 2010). ... Second, it found "92.29% of [low-income housing tax credit] units in the city of Dallas were located in census tracts with less than 50% Caucasian residents." *Ibid.*

The District Court then placed the burden on the Department to rebut the ICP's prima facie showing of disparate impact. . . . After assuming the Department's proffered interests were legitimate, . . . the District Court held that a defendant—here the Department—must prove "that there are no other less discriminatory alternatives to advancing their proffered interests," *ibid.* Because, in its view, the Department "failed to meet [its] burden of proving that there are no less discriminatory alternatives," the District Court ruled for the ICP. . . .

The Court of Appeals for the Fifth Circuit held, consistent with its precedent, that disparate-impact claims are cognizable under the FHA. . . . On the merits, however, the Court of Appeals reversed and remanded. . . . [T]he Court of Appeals held that it was improper for the District Court to have placed the burden on the Department to prove there were no less discriminatory alternatives for allocating low-income housing tax credits. . . .

. . . It is now appropriate to provide a brief history of the FHA's enactment and its later amendment.

B

De jure residential segregation by race was declared unconstitutional almost a century ago, *Buchanan v. Warley,* 245 U.S. 60 (1917), but its vestiges remain today, intertwined with the country's economic and social life. Some segregated housing patterns can be traced to conditions that arose in the mid–20th century. Rapid urbanization, concomitant with the rise of suburban developments accessible by car, led many white families to leave the inner cities. This often left minority families concentrated in the center of the Nation's cities. During this time, various practices were followed, sometimes with governmental support, to encourage and maintain the separation of the races: Racially restrictive covenants prevented the conveyance of property to minorities, *see Shelley v. Kraemer,* 334 U.S. 1 (1948); steering by real-estate agents led potential buyers to consider homes in racially homogenous areas; and discriminatory lending practices, often referred to as redlining, precluded minority families from purchasing homes in affluent areas. *See, e.g.,* M. Klarman, Unfinished Business: Racial Equality in American History 140-141 (2007). . . . By the 1960's, these policies, practices, and prejudices had created many predominantly black inner cities surrounded by mostly white suburbs. *See* K. Clark, Dark Ghetto: Dilemmas of Social Power 11, 21-26 (1965).

The mid-1960's was a period of considerable social unrest; and, in response, President Lyndon Johnson established the National Advisory Commission on Civil Disorders, commonly known as the Kerner Commission. Exec. Order No. 11365, 3 CFR 674 (1966-1970 Comp.). After extensive factfinding the Commission identified residential segregation and unequal housing and economic conditions in the inner cities as significant, underlying causes of the social unrest. *See* Report of the National Advisory Commission on Civil Disorders 91 (1968) (Kerner Commission Report). The Commission found that "[n]early two-thirds of all nonwhite families living in the central cities today live in neighborhoods marked by substandard housing and general urban blight." *Id.,* at 13. The Commission further found that both open and covert racial discrimination prevented black families from obtaining better housing and moving to integrated communities. . . . The Commission concluded that "[o]ur Nation is moving toward two societies, one black, one white—separate and unequal." *Id.,* at 1. To reverse "[t]his deepening racial division," *ibid.,* it recommended enactment of "a comprehensive and enforceable open-occupancy law making it an offense to discriminate in the sale or rental of any housing . . . on the basis of race, creed, color, or national origin." *Id.,* at 263.

In April 1968, Dr. Martin Luther King, Jr., was assassinated in Memphis, Tennessee, and the Nation faced a new urgency to resolve the social unrest in the inner cities. Congress responded by adopting the Kerner Commission's recommendation and passing the Fair Housing Act. The statute addressed the denial of housing opportunities on the basis of "race, color, religion, or national origin." Civil Rights Act of 1968, 804, 82 Stat. 83. Then, in 1988, Congress amended the FHA. Among other provisions, it created certain exemptions from liability and added "familial status" as a protected characteristic. *See* Fair Housing Amendments Act of 1988, 102 Stat. 1619.

II . . .

Recognition of disparate-impact claims is consistent with the FHA's central purpose. . . . The FHA . . . was enacted to eradicate discriminatory practices within a sector of our Nation's economy. . . .

These unlawful practices include zoning laws and other housing restrictions that function unfairly to exclude minorities from certain neighborhoods without any sufficient justification. Suits targeting such practices reside at the heartland of disparate-impact liability. See, *e.g.,* [*Town of Huntington*] *v. Huntington [Branch, National Association for the Advancement of Colored People]*, 488 U.S., [15,] at 16-18 [(1988)] (invalidating zoning law preventing construction of multifamily rental units); [*United States v.*] *Black Jack,* 508 F.2d [1179,] at 1182-1188 [(1974)] (invalidating ordinance prohibiting construction of new multifamily dwellings); *Greater New Orleans Fair Housing Action Center v. St. Bernard Parish,* 641 F. Supp. 2d 563, 569, 577-578 (E.D. La. 2009) (invalidating post-Hurricane Katrina ordinance restricting the rental of housing units to only "'blood relative[s]'" in an area of the city that was 88.3% white and 7.6% black). . . . Recognition of disparate-impact liability under the FHA also plays a role in uncovering discriminatory intent: It permits plaintiffs to counteract unconscious prejudices and disguised animus that escape easy classification as disparate treatment. In this way disparate-impact liability may prevent segregated housing patterns that might otherwise result from covert and illicit stereotyping.

But disparate-impact liability has always been properly limited in key respects that avoid the serious constitutional questions that might arise under the FHA, for instance, if such liability were imposed based solely on a showing of a statistical disparity. . . . The FHA is not an instrument to force housing authorities to reorder their priorities. Rather, the FHA aims to ensure that those priorities can be achieved without arbitrarily creating discriminatory effects or perpetuating segregation.

. . . [T]he underlying dispute in this case involves a novel theory of liability. . . . This case . . . may be seen simply as an attempt to second-guess which of two reasonable approaches a housing authority should follow in the sound exercise of its discretion in allocating tax credits for low-income housing. . . .

An important and appropriate means of ensuring that disparate-impact liability is properly limited is to give housing authorities and private developers leeway to state and explain the valid interest served by their policies. . . . [H]ousing authorities and private developers [must] be allowed to maintain a policy if they can prove it is necessary to achieve a valid interest. . . .

It would be paradoxical to construe the FHA to impose onerous costs on actors who encourage revitalizing dilapidated housing in our Nation's cities merely because some other priority might seem preferable. . . .

In a similar vein, a disparate-impact claim that relies on a statistical disparity must fail if the plaintiff cannot point to a defendant's policy or policies causing that disparity. A robust causality requirement ensures that "[r]acial imbalance . . . does not, without more, establish a prima facie case of disparate impact" and thus protects defendants from being held liable for racial disparities they did not create. *Wards Cove Packing Co. v. Atonio,* 490 U.S. 642, 653 (1989). . . .

. . . The Court holds that disparate-impact claims are cognizable under the Fair Housing Act. . . .

III

. . . Much progress remains to be made in our Nation's continuing struggle against racial isolation. In striving to achieve our "historic commitment to creating an integrated society," *Parents Involved, supra,* at 797 . . . , we must remain wary of policies that reduce homeowners to nothing more than their race. But since the passage of the Fair Housing Act in 1968 and against the backdrop of disparate-impact liability in nearly every jurisdiction, many cities have become more diverse. The FHA must play an important part in avoiding the Kerner Commission's grim prophecy that "[o]ur Nation is moving toward two societies, one black, one white—separate and unequal." Kerner Commission Report 1. The Court acknowledges the Fair Housing Act's continuing role in moving the Nation toward a more integrated society. . . .

The judgment of the Court of Appeals for the Fifth Circuit is affirmed, and the case is remanded for further proceedings consistent with this opinion.

THOMAS, J., dissenting [omitted].

ALITO, J., dissenting, joined by ROBERTS, C.J., and SCALIA and THOMAS, J.J. [omitted].

Notes

1. *Racial "steering" by real estate agents:*   *Steering* is the practice by which some real estate agents promoted housing segregation by declining to show properties in predominantly white neighborhoods to persons of color. The National Fair Housing Alliance (NFHA) uncovered evidence that steering is still practiced today. In 2015, the NFHA filed a housing discrimination complaint with the Department of Housing and Urban Development against a group of Mississippi real estate agents allegedly in violation of the FHA. As the NFHA explains,

> During [a] roughly year-long investigation, white and black testers posed as home buyers and contacted the company to view homes in Jackson, Mississippi. The testers were similarly-qualified and had similar housing preferences.

> According to the NFHA complaint, testing revealed that agents . . . discriminated on the basis of race. The agents steered the white home seekers away from inter-racial neighborhoods in Jackson, which is majority African American, and into majority white areas. . . . Conversely, the African American testers who inquired about properties in the Jackson area were often never called back and were generally provided very limited information.

National Fair Housing Alliance, *Press Release: National Fair Housing Alliance Investigation Reveals Race Discrimination in Jackson, Mississippi, Real Estate Market*, Sept. 9, 2015. Does steering violate the Fair Housing Act, and if so, which section? To answer that question, refer back to the FHA excerpt we studied in Chapter 4.C.3.

2. *Redlining and another FHA:*   Congress created the Federal Housing Administration (FHA) (now within the Department of Housing and Urban Development) in 1934 to stimulate the housing industry in the wake of the Great Depression. (Notice that "FHA" is used as an abbreviation for both the Federal Housing Administration and the federal Fair Housing Act.) In that capacity, the FHA was a "versatile tool," in the words of one analyst:

> The FHA was created in large part to inject liquidity into a moribund mortgage market. It succeeded wonderfully, with rapid growth during the late 1930s. The federal government repositioned it a number of times over the following decades to achieve a variety of additional social goals. These goals included supporting civilian mobilization during World War II; helping veterans returning from the

War; stabilizing urban housing markets during the 1960s; and expanding minority homeownership rates during the 1990s. It achieved success with some of its goals and had a terrible record with others.

David Reiss, *Underwriting Sustainable Homeownership: The Federal Housing Administration and the Low Down Payment Loan*, Georgia Law Review (2015-2016), *available at* http://ssrn.com/abstract=2652875 (visited Aug. 25, 2015). Although the FHA's policies produced public benefits—such as insuring residential loans to make them more widely available—the FHA also had an institutionalized policy of promoting segregated housing, thereby limiting those who could benefit from its programs:

> [F]rom its very beginning, the FHA had a major negative impact on . . . minority communities. . . . [T]he impact on minority households was quite intentional: the FHA reflected the widely-held prejudices and discriminatory practices already endemic in the all-white housing and mortgage-lending industries. One of the main such practices was the imposition of restrictive covenants that excluded blacks and other minorities. The FHA also drew red lines on its underwriting maps to cordon off blocks in which even a single non-white family lived. Such "redlined" blocks were not eligible for FHA-insured mortgages. The end result of such redlining was a massive disinvestment in cities with large black populations. . . . The link between bureaucratic redlining and the decline of cities was not fully made until the 1960s at which point many of the affected cities had become shadows of their former selves.

Id. Note the references to *restrictive covenants*, which historically included agreements prohibiting the sale of real property to nonwhite buyers. Judicial enforcement of the practice was declared unconstitutional in *Shelley v. Kraemer*, 334 U.S. 1 (1948). We will study restrictive covenants (and also *Shelley v. Kraemer*) in Chapter 10. *See also* National Public Radio, *Historian Says Don't "Sanitize" How Our Government Created Ghettos*, May 14, 2015 (discussing "explicit, racially purposeful policy . . . pursued at all levels of government" that created the "ghettos" in metropolitan areas around the country still existing today).

B. THE REAL ESTATE CONTRACT

Below is a typical real estate contract, as prepared by a state association of realtors. Review the contract, and then answer the questions that follow. Refer often to this sample purchase and sale agreement as you work your way through the topics in this chapter. This contract will also serve as the basis of the skills exercise in section G, below.

PURCHASE AND SALE AGREEMENT

(a) **BUYER NAME(s):** _____

(b) **SELLER NAME(s):** _____

(c) **PROPERTY ADDRESS and/or DESCRIPTION:** Buyer agrees to purchase and Seller agrees to sell the real property identified as:
_____
_____, _____ County, Tennessee.

(d) **PURCHASE PRICE: $**_____, _____ Dollars,
to be paid in cash or equivalent good funds at closing.

(e) **EARNEST MONEY: $** _____ valid check or money order payable to Escrow Agent: _____
_____, whose address is: _____,
will be promptly delivered to Escrow Agent **no later than 5:00 PM, three (3) calendar days after the Acceptance Date.**

(f) **CLOSING, EXPIRATION, & POSSESSION DATE:** _____. This is the date that the sale will
be closed, or this *Agreement* will expire on this date at 11:59 PM. If this is not a business day, this date will be extended to the
next business day. Any other change in this date must be agreed to **in writing** by all parties. Possession of the entire property will
be given to the Buyer at the time of closing, unless a different time of possession is agreed to in a separate *Occupancy Agreement*.

(g) **ITEMS INCLUDED OR EXCLUDED:** Included, if present, as part of the property sale: all real estate, buildings,
improvements, appurtenances (rights and privileges), and fixtures. **Fixtures** include all things which are attached to the
structure(s) by nails, screws, or other permanent fasteners, including, but not limited to all of the following, if present:
attached light fixtures and bulbs, ceiling fans, attached mirrors; heating and cooling equipment and thermostats; plumbing
fixtures and equipment; all doors and storm doors; all windows, screens, and storm windows; all window treatments
(draperies, curtains, blinds, shades, etc.) and hardware; all wall-to-wall carpet; all built-in kitchen appliances and stove; all
bathroom fixtures; gas logs, fireplace doors and attached screens; all security system components and controls; garage door
openers and all remote controls; swimming pool and its equipment; awnings; permanently installed outdoor cooking grills;
all fencing, landscaping and outdoor lighting; and mail boxes.
Other items included in the sale: _____
_____.
Items that are <u>not</u> included in the sale: _____.
Leased items:_____.

(h) **CLOSING COSTS:** Unless otherwise stated in Special Stipulations or Addenda, closing costs are to be paid as follows:
Seller must pay all Seller's existing loans, liens and related costs affecting the sale of the property, Seller's settlement fees,
real estate commissions, the balance on any leased items that remain with the property, and a **title insurance policy** with
Buyer to receive benefit of simultaneous issue. Any existing rental or lease deposits must be transferred to Buyer at closing.
Buyer must pay transfer taxes, deed and deed of trust recording fees, association transfer fees, hazard and any other
required insurance, Buyer's settlement fees, and **all Buyer's loan related or lender required expenses.**

(i) **PRORATIONS, TAXES & ASSESSMENTS:** The current year's property taxes, any existing tenant leases or rents,
association or maintenance fees, (and if applicable, any remaining fuel), will be prorated as of the date of closing. Taxes for
prior years and any special assessments approved before date of closing must be paid by Seller at or before closing. If
applicable, roll back taxes or any tax or assessment that cannot be determined by closing date should be addressed in
Special Stipulations or Addenda and will survive the closing.

(j) **HOME PROTECTION PLANS:** Home Protection plans available for purchase are **waived**, <u>unless</u> addressed in Special
Stipulations. Buyer and Seller understand that an administrative fee may be paid to the Real Estate Company if plan is purchased.

(k) **SPECIAL STIPULATIONS:** The following special stipulations, if in conflict with any language contained within the 3 pages of
this *Purchase and Sale Agreement*, will control: _____
_____
_____
_____
_____
_____
_____.

(l) **TIME IS OF THE ESSENCE:** The failure to meet specified time limits will be grounds for canceling this *Agreement*.

(m)**FAIR HOUSING AND EQUAL OPPORTUNITY:** This Property is being sold without regard to race, color, sex,
religion, disability, marital status, family status, sexual orientation, age, ancestry, or national origin.

Page 1 of 3

(n) **LOAN AND APPRAISAL CONTINGENCIES:** This *Agreement* is contingent on Buyer obtaining loan(s) of Buyer's choice. Buyer must deliver to Seller **no later than 5:00 PM, ten (10) calendar days after the Acceptance Date** a lender's conditional **commitment letter** proving that: loan application has been made; appraisal has been ordered; loan is <u>not</u> contingent on the sale of any other property (unless otherwise stated in *Agreement*); Buyer has necessary cash reserves; and providing reasonable assurance of Buyer's ability to obtain loan with rates, terms, payments and conditions acceptable to Buyer. Failure to timely provide commitment letter will be grounds for Seller to cancel this *Agreement* by delivering written *Notice* to Buyer, and all Earnest Money must be refunded to Buyer. *VA/FHA Loan Addendum* must be attached if Buyer seeks VA or FHA loan. If loan contingency is waived, Buyer must deliver proof of adequate funds within time period on Line 55. <u>**Appraisal Contingency**</u> - this *Agreement* is also contingent on the appraisal value equaling or exceeding the purchase price. **If any repairs are required by the lender,** Buyer must deliver to Seller a written list of lender required repairs. Seller must deliver to Buyer, no later than 5:00 PM, three (3) calendar days after receiving the repair list, a written *Notice* stating whether or not Seller will complete the repairs before closing at Seller's expense. If Seller does not agree to perform such repairs, or does not reply within the time limit, this *Agreement* will cancel and all Earnest Money must be refunded to Buyer **[see exception in (p)]. If, at anytime, the loan or appraisal contingency is not satisfied,** Buyer may cancel this *Agreement* by delivering to Seller a written *Notice of Cancellation*, along with supporting documentation, and all Earnest Money must be refunded to Buyer.

(o) **INSPECTION CONTINGENCY AND DUE DILIGENCE PERIOD:** This *Agreement* is contingent on Buyer's satisfaction with all property inspections and investigations. Buyer may use any inspectors of Buyer's choice, at Buyer's expense. Seller must permit Buyer, and Buyer's representatives and inspectors, reasonable access for inspections, with **all utilities in service at Seller's expense.** Buyer assumes all liability for any damage or loss caused by Buyer's or Buyer representatives' inspections or investigations of the property.
<u>**Due Diligence Period**</u>: **All inspections and investigations must be completed with response to Seller no later than 5:00 PM, ten (10) calendar days after the Acceptance Date.** *During* this due diligence period Buyer is strongly advised to:
(A) have a **professional home inspection** conducted by a licensed home inspector (at Buyer's expense), AND
(B) have a **wood destroying insect inspection** conducted by a licensed pest inspector (at Buyer's expense), AND
(C) investigate <u>all</u> matters itemized in the *Advisory to Buyers and Sellers* (which is an Addendum to this *Agreement*), AND
(D) perform any additional inspections and investigations desired, and verify any other matters of concern to the Buyer, AND
(E) if applicable, obtain a septic system inspection letter (available for a fee at TN Dept of Environment and Conservation).
<u>**Inspection Contingency Resolution**</u>: If Buyer is satisfied with all inspections and investigations, Buyer may deliver to Seller a *Notice of Release* of inspection contingency. If for **any** reason Buyer is **not** satisfied with the results of **any** inspection or investigation, the Buyer **must**, **within the Due Diligence Period** (Lines 74-75), deliver to Seller **either:**
(1) a written *Notice of Cancellation*, canceling this *Agreement*, and all Earnest Money must be refunded to Buyer, **OR**
(2) a written *Inspection Contingency Removal Proposal.* If Seller rejects Buyer's *Proposal* (or *Counterproposal*) by delivering a *Notice of Rejection* to Buyer, **or** if any *Counterproposal* is rejected by either party, **or** if a time limit for a written response to such is exceeded, this *Agreement* will cancel and all Earnest Money must be refunded to Buyer **[see exception in (p)].**
    - Any *Proposal, Counterproposal, Notice of Rejection,* or *Notice of Release* of inspection contingency must be in writing.
    - Any *Proposal* or *Counterproposal* must contain a time limit for responding (that is, an expiration date & time).
If it is discovered during the Due Diligence Period that any permanent structure on the property has an active wood destroying insect infestation, the Seller, upon Buyer's request, must **professionally treat infestation before closing at Seller's expense.** Repair of any damage from wood destroying insects must be negotiated in the *Inspection Contingency Removal Proposal.*

> **CAUTION TO BUYER:** Failure to deliver to the Seller either a written *Notice of Release* or *Notice of Cancellation*, or a written *Inspection Contingency Removal Proposal* <u>**within**</u> the Due Diligence Period described on Lines 74-75 will be considered to be an acceptance of the property **"as is,"** and the Inspection Contingency will be satisfied and no longer a part of this *Agreement*.

(p) **BUYER'S RIGHT TO REINSTATE:** If Seller refuses to complete the lender required repairs (Lines 63-66), or cancels this *Agreement* by rejecting an *Inspection Contingency Removal Proposal* (Lines 85-89), Buyer has the right to reinstate the *Agreement* by delivering to Seller a *Notice* stating that the Buyer will accept the property in its present "as is" condition. Buyer's *Notice* must be delivered to Seller **no later than 5:00 PM, three (3) calendar days after the delivery of Seller's *Notice*** of rejection, or if Seller has failed to respond, no later than 5:00 PM, three (3) calendar days after the Seller's deadline to reply.

(q) **FINAL INSPECTION & RISK OF LOSS:** Buyer has the right and responsibility to perform a final inspection before closing to determine that the property is in the same condition, other than ordinary wear, as when the *Agreement* was accepted (with Seller having responsibility to correct), and to see that any repairs agreed to be performed by Seller have been completed. Buyer may use inspectors. All utilities must be in service at Seller's expense. The closing of the sale confirms Buyer's acceptance of property condition. Seller is responsible for any loss or damage to the property before closing.

(r) **DISBURSEMENT OF EARNEST MONEY, AND ADEQUATE CONSIDERATION:** The Earnest Money will be applied towards the purchase price at closing. If any contingencies or conditions of this *Agreement* are not met and the *Agreement* is cancelled, all Earnest Money must be refunded to Buyer. If Seller fails to perform any obligation under this *Agreement*, all Earnest Money must be refunded to Buyer. If required, the Escrow Agent may file an interpleader action in a court of law, and recover expenses and reasonable attorney's fees, and will have no further liability as Escrow Agent. All parties acknowledge that the consideration given, including the promises exchanged, the time limitations imposed, and the notifications required, is sufficient and adequate in exchange for the Buyer's right to legally, properly, and in good faith cancel, reinstate or extend this *Agreement* in accordance with the other terms of this *Agreement*.

Page 2 of 3

(s) **TITLE, DEED, & SELLER REPRESENTATIONS:** Seller will convey to Buyer good and marketable title to the property by a valid general warranty deed. Seller, at Seller's expense, agrees to furnish Buyer at closing a title insurance policy. Title policy will be issued by company acceptable to Buyer and Buyer's lender. Buyer will receive benefit of simultaneous issue. <u>Seller represents</u> to the best of Seller's knowledge, unless otherwise disclosed, that: **property is not in a Special Flood Hazard Area or floodplain;** there are no violations of building, zoning or fire codes; there are no encroachments or violations of setback lines, easements or property boundary lines; and there are no boundary line disputes. If at anytime the title examination, mortgage loan inspection, survey, or other information discloses any such defects, or if the Buyer discovers that any representation in this *Agreement* is in fact untrue, Buyer may, by delivering written *Notice* to Seller, either (1) accept the Property with the defects, OR (2) cancel this *Agreement* and all Earnest Money must be refunded to Buyer, OR (3) Buyer may extend the closing date by up to 3 calendar days to perform additional due diligence, retaining the right to exercise option (1) or (2) above.

(t) **DEFAULT OR BREACH:** If either party fails to perform any obligation under this *Agreement*, the other party may do any or all of the following: (1) cancel the *Agreement* (2) sue for specific performance, (3) sue for actual and compensatory damages. Legal counsel is strongly recommended in such circumstances.

(u) **REAL ESTATE COMMISSIONS:** Seller authorizes closing company to debit Seller and pay commissions as follows at closing:
Real Estate Firm Name: _____ will receive _____% of the purchase price.
Licensee's Name and Contact Information: _____.
Other Real Estate Firm Name (if any): _____ will receive _____% of the purchase price.
Other Licensee's Name (if any) and Contact Information: _____.

(v) **ADDENDA, ATTACHMENTS, EXHIBITS, DISCLAIMERS, AND DISCLOSURES** (included if marked below):
☒ Confirmation of Agency Status (required with **all** Purchase and Sale Agreements)
☒ Advisory to Buyers and Sellers, or TAR Disclaimer Notice (required with **all** Purchase and Sale Agreements)
☐ Lead-Based Paint Disclosure (required for housing **constructed before 1978**)
☐ Personal Interest Disclosure & Consent (required if a **Licensee has a personal interest,** may be included in Confirmation of Agency)
☐ Occupancy Agreement (required if **possession is other than the time of closing**)
☐ VA/FHA Loan Addendum (required if sale involves **VA or FHA loan**)
☐ Impact Fees or Adequate Facilities Taxes Disclosure (required if sale is residential **new construction**)
☐ Subsurface Sewage Disposal System Permit Disclosure (required for newly constructed residential property with **septic system**)
☐ Addendum (extra page for additional Special Stipulations, if needed)
☐ Other: _____
*And **one** of the following three is required with **all** residential Purchase and Sale Agreements:*
☐ Tennessee Residential Property Condition Disclosure, OR
☐ Tennessee Residential Property Condition Exemption Notification, OR
☐ Tennessee Residential Property Condition Disclaimer Statement

(w) **METHOD OF EXECUTION AND DELIVERY:** Signatures and initials transmitted by fax, photocopy, or digital signature methods will be acceptable and treated as originals. This *Agreement* constitutes the sole and entire agreement between the parties. No verbal agreements, representations, promises, or modifications of this *Agreement* will be binding unless agreed to in writing by all parties. **Delivery** will be considered to have been completed as of the date and time a document is either (1) delivered in person, OR (2) transmitted by fax, OR (3) transmitted by email. Delivery of documents to the real estate Licensee assisting a party as that party's agent or facilitator (or to that Licensee's Broker) will be considered to be Delivery to that party.

(x) **ACCEPTANCE DATE AND BINDING CONTRACT:** The <u>Acceptance Date</u> will be the date of full execution (signing) of this *Agreement* by all parties, that is, the date one party accepts all the terms of the other party's written and signed *Offer* or *Counteroffer*, evidenced by the accepting party's signature and date on the *Offer* or *Counteroffer*. The Acceptance must be promptly communicated (by any reasonable and usual mode) to the other party, thereby making this *Agreement* a legally **Binding Contract**. Communications to the real estate Licensee assisting a party as that party's agent or facilitator (or to that Licensee's Broker) will be considered to be communication to that party. True executed copies of the Contract must be promptly delivered to all parties.

(y) **OFFER EXPIRATION DATE & TIME:** _____. If not Accepted by this date & time (or if blank, by the date and time on Lines 11-13), this *Offer* will expire. However, at any time before the other party's communication of Acceptance, the party making the *Offer* may **withdraw** the *Offer* by communicating the withdrawal to the other party, and confirm the withdrawal by the prompt delivery of a written *Notice of Withdrawal*.

Buyer makes this *Offer*.

X_____   X_____
  Buyer Signature   *Date & Time*   *Buyer Signature*   *Date & Time*

This *Offer* is: ☐Accepted   ☐Rejected   ☐Countered on this form   ☐Countered on a separate *Counteroffer* form

X_____   X_____
  Seller Signature   *Date & Time*   *Seller Signature*   *Date & Time*

*Tennessee Association of REALTORS®

Problems

Assume that buyer and seller have executed the above purchase and sale agreement. How does the contract address each of the following topics? Is the relevant provision fair and evenhanded, or does it favor the seller or the buyer?

1. *The buyers:* If the property will be sold to more than one new owner (such as to a couple, to siblings, or to business partners), can you think of any additional information the contract should contain? *See* Chapter 5, above (concurrent ownership). As you know, the federal Fair Housing Act prohibits certain types of discrimination in the sale or rental of real estate, and establishes certain "protected classes" of potential buyers and renters. This contract is stricter than federal law, and prohibits discrimination based on 11 classifications. List them. *See* contract ¶(m).

2. *The physical property:* What are "fixtures"? Who will own them when the sale is completed? *See* contract ¶(g). The property is in a federally designated floodplain and is vulnerable to flooding. Must the seller disclose this to the buyer? *See* contract ¶(s).

3. *Possession and risk of loss:* When is the buyer entitled to possession? *See* contract ¶(f). If the property is damaged before closing, who bears the risk of loss? *See* contract ¶(q).

4. *Deadlines:* The contract contains numerous deadlines for actions to be completed by the buyer and seller, respectively. What happens if one of the parties misses those deadlines? *See* contract ¶(l).

5. *The buyer's financing:* The buyer would like to obtain a conventional, 30-year, fixed-rate mortgage from an institutional lender, but can only qualify for an adjustable rate mortgage. *See* section D.1 of this chapter. Can the buyer rescind the contract? Must the seller return the earnest money? *See* contract ¶(n).

6. *The title:* What type of deed will the buyer receive at closing? Will the buyer receive a title insurance policy? Who will pay for it? *See* contract ¶¶(h) & (s). The buyer searches the public records and discovers that a neighbor has a recorded easement to park on a portion of the property. Can the buyer rescind the contract? *See* contract ¶(s). Assume instead that the buyer searches the public records, but she cannot find a recorded deed or other evidence of the seller's title. The seller informs her that he has acquired title by adverse possession, and provides credible evidence that he has satisfied all relevant requirements. Is that sufficient ground for the buyer to rescind the contract? *See* contract ¶¶(l) & (s).

7. *Default and remedies:* Two weeks after signing the contract, the seller receives a better offer and informs the buyer that the contract is canceled. Can the buyer force the seller to go through with the sale at the agreed contract price? *See* contract ¶(t).

1. The Statute of Frauds

The original English Statute of Frauds of 1677—entitled *An Act for the Prevention of Frauds and Perjuries*—required that contracts for the sale and purchase of real property must be in writing in order to be legally enforceable. As its name suggests, the statute was designed to guard against fraud and to minimize perjury. Every American state has adopted some version of the statute through legislation or judicial opinion. Although requirements vary, most jurisdictions require that the writing contain the *essential terms of the agreement,* as described in the *A Place to Start* box below. Despite the requirement of a written document, the form of the document can be quite informal. For example, even a notation jotted on a napkin and signed by the parties could be sufficient, provided that it contains the terms required by the jurisdiction. In most cases, however, the parties will fill in the blanks of standard-form real estate contracts that are widely available.

A Place to Start | **The Statute of Frauds**

- ***The requirements of the statute:*** In most jurisdictions, the written contract must include at least the following elements to be enforceable:
  - The identity of the parties
  - A description of the property
  - The sales price (in some cases, a formula such as "fair market value" might be sufficient)
  - The signature of *the party to be bound* (that is, the defendant in a lawsuit seeking enforcement)
- ***Exceptions to the statute of frauds:*** There are two potential exceptions to the statute of frauds, although courts often blur the distinction between the two:
  - ***The part performance exception:*** The party (either buyer or seller) seeking to enforce an oral agreement must prove that the *buyer* (1) paid all or part of the purchase price, (2) took possession of the property, and/or (3) made improvements to the property (requirements vary by jurisdiction). Sometimes, the parties will stipulate to the *existence* of an oral agreement (but one party may still assert the statute of frauds as a *defense* to enforceability). If the parties do not, some jurisdictions require proof that the buyer's actions were "unequivocally referable to the oral agreement"—a burden that has been criticized as almost impossible to satisfy. *See Martin v. Scholl,* 678 P.2d 274, 275 (Utah 1983) (requiring that the acts of performance are "not readily explainable on any other ground"); *Burns v. McCormick,* 135 N.E. 273 (N.Y. 1922) (strictly applying the requirement). The rationale for this exception is that the buyer's acts of performance provide evidence of an agreement sufficient to substitute for a written contract.

■ **The equitable estoppel exception:** The party seeking to enforce an oral agreement must prove that it (1) changed position in reasonable and detrimental reliance on the oral agreement, and (2) would suffer injustice if the agreement is not enforced. The rationale for this exception is rooted in equity and concern for fairness, such that one party can be *estopped* from asserting the statute of frauds as a defense to the enforcement of an otherwise valid oral agreement.

■ **Enforceability v. validity:** The statute of frauds does not automatically *invalidate* oral agreements, but instead makes them *unenforceable* in some cases (if not saved by an exception).

DIGGING DEEPER: As you read the materials in this section, consider why *part performance* is a misleading name for the first exception. Further, consider what it means to say an agreement is valid, but potentially unenforceable. Hint: Have you encountered "voidable" agreements in your Contracts class?

Hickey v. Green

442 N.E.2d 37 (Mass. Ct. App. 1982), *review denied*, 445 N.E.2d 156 (1983)

Reading Guide

The statute of frauds—exceptions: As you read this case, carefully distinguish between the *part performance* and *equitable estoppel* exceptions to the statute of frauds. Which exception is most relevant to the facts here? More broadly, what purpose does the statute of frauds serve? Why do courts nevertheless recognize exceptions to the statute?

CUTTER, J.

This case is before us on a stipulation of facts (with various attached documents). A Superior Court judge has adopted the agreed facts as "findings." We are in the same position as was the trial judge (who received no evidence and saw and heard no witnesses).

Mrs. Gladys Green owns a lot (Lot S) in the Manomet section of Plymouth. In July, 1980, she advertised it for sale. On July 11 and 12, Hickey and his wife discussed with Mrs. Green purchasing Lot S and "orally agreed to a sale" for $15,000. Mrs. Green on July 12 accepted a deposit check of $500, marked by Hickey on the back, "Deposit on Lot . . . Massasoit Ave. Manomet. . . . Subject to Variance from Town of Plymouth." Mrs. Green's brother and agent "was under the impression that a zoning variance was needed and [had] advised . . . Hickey to write" the quoted language on the deposit check. It turned out, however, by July 16 that no variance would be required. Hickey had left the payee line of the deposit check blank, because of uncertainty whether Mrs. Green or her brother was to receive the check and asked "Mrs. Green to fill in the appropriate name." Mrs. Green held the check, did not fill in the payee's name, and neither cashed nor endorsed it. Hickey "stated to Mrs. Green that his intention was to sell his home and build on Mrs. Green's lot."

"Relying upon the arrangements . . . with Mrs. Green," the Hickeys advertised their house on Sachem Road in newspapers on three days in July, 1980, and agreed with a purchaser for its sale and took from him a deposit check for $500 which they deposited in their own account.[1] On July 24, Mrs. Green told Hickey that she "no longer intended to sell her property to him" but had decided to sell to another for $16,000. Hickey told Mrs. Green that he had already sold his house and offered her $16,000 for Lot S. Mrs. Green refused this offer.

The Hickeys filed this complaint seeking specific performance. Mrs. Green asserts that relief is barred by the Statute of Frauds contained in G.L. c. 259, § 1. The trial judge granted specific performance. Mrs. Green has appealed.

The present rule applicable in most jurisdictions in the United States is succinctly set forth in Restatement (Second) of Contracts, § 129 (1981). The section reads,

> A contract for the transfer of an interest in land may be specifically enforced notwithstanding failure to comply with the Statute of Frauds if it is established that the party seeking enforcement, *in reasonable reliance on the contract* and on the continuing assent of the party against whom enforcement is sought, *has so changed his position that injustice can be avoided only by specific enforcement* (emphasis supplied).[2]

---

1. [FN 3] On the back of the check was noted above the Hickeys' signatures endorsing the check "Deposit on Purchase of property at Sachem Rd. and First St., Manomet, Ma. Sale price, $44,000."

2. [FN 6] Comments *a* and *b* to §129, read (in part): "*a.* . . . This section restates what is widely known as the 'part performance doctrine.' Part performance is not an accurate designation of such acts as taking possession and making improvements when the contract does not provide for such acts, but such acts regularly bring the doctrine into play. The doctrine is contrary to the words of the Statute of Frauds, but it was established by English courts of equity soon after the enactment of the Statute. Payment of purchase-money, without more, was once thought sufficient to justify specific enforcement, but a contrary view now prevails, since in such cases restitution is an adequate remedy. . . . Enforcement has . . . been justified on the ground that repudiation after 'part performance' amounts to a 'virtual fraud.' A more accurate statement is that courts with equitable powers are vested by tradition with what in substance is a dispensing power based on the promisee's reliance, *a discretion to be exercised with caution* in the light of all the circumstances . . . [emphasis supplied].

"*b.* . . . Two distinct elements enter into the application of the rule of this Section: first, the extent to which the evidentiary function of the statutory formalities is fulfilled by the conduct of the parties; second, the reliance of the promisee, providing a compelling substantive basis for relief in addition to the expectations created by the promise."

The earlier Massachusetts decisions laid down somewhat strict requirements for an estoppel precluding the assertion of the Statute of Frauds. . . . Frequently there has been an actual change of possession and improvement of the transferred property, as well as full payment of the full purchase price, or one or more of these elements.

It is stated in Park, Real Estate Law, § 883, at 334, that the "more recent decisions . . . indicate a trend on the part of the [Supreme Judicial C]ourt to find that the circumstances warrant specific performance." This appears to be a correct perception. *See . . . Orlando v. Ottaviani*, 148 N.E.2d 373 (Mass. 1958), where specific performance was granted to the former holder of an option to buy a strip of land fifteen feet wide, important to the option holder, and the option had been surrendered in reliance upon an oral promise to convey the strip made by the purchaser of a larger parcel of which the fifteen-foot strip was a part. . . .

The present facts reveal a simple case of a proposed purchase of a residential vacant lot, where the vendor, Mrs. Green, knew that the Hickeys were planning to sell their former home (possibly to obtain funds to pay her) and build on Lot S. The Hickeys, relying on Mrs. Green's oral promise, moved rapidly to make their sale without obtaining any adequate memorandum of the terms of what appears to have been intended to be a quick cash sale of Lot S. So rapid was action by the Hickeys that, by July 21, less than ten days after giving their deposit to Mrs. Green, they had accepted a deposit check for the sale of their house, endorsed the check, and placed it in their bank account. Above their signatures endorsing the check was a memorandum probably sufficient to satisfy the Statute of Frauds. . . . At the very least, the Hickeys had bound themselves in a manner in which, to avoid a transfer of their own house, they might have had to engage in expensive litigation. No attorney has been shown to have been used either in the transaction between Mrs. Green and the Hickeys or in that between the Hickeys and their purchaser.

There is no denial by Mrs. Green of the oral contract between her and the Hickeys. This, under § 129 of the Restatement, is of some significance.[3] There can be no doubt (a) that Mrs. Green made the promise on which the Hickeys so promptly relied, and also (b) she, nearly as promptly, but not promptly enough, repudiated it because she had a better opportunity. The stipulated facts require the conclusion that in equity Mrs. Green's conduct cannot be condoned. This is

---

3. [FN 9] Comment *d* of Restatement (Second) of Contracts, $129, reads "*d.* . . . Where specific enforcement is rested on a transfer of possession plus either part payment of the price or the making of improvements, it is commonly said that the action taken by the purchaser must be unequivocally referable to the oral agreement. But this requirement is not insisted on *if the making of the promise is admitted or is clearly proved.* The promisee *must act in reasonable reliance on the promise, before the promisor has repudiated* it, and the action must be such that the remedy of restitution is inadequate. If these requirements are met, *neither taking of possession nor payment of money nor the making of improvements is essential. . . .*" (emphasis supplied).

not a case where either party is shown to have contemplated the negotiation of a purchase and sale agreement. If a written agreement had been expected, even by only one party, or would have been natural (because of the participation by lawyers or otherwise), a different situation might have existed. It is a permissible inference from the agreed facts that the rapid sale of the Hickeys' house was both appropriate and expected. These are not circumstances where negotiations fairly can be seen as inchoate. . . .

We recognize that specific enforcement of Mrs. Green's promise to convey Lot S may well go somewhat beyond the circumstances considered in [our previous decisions] . . . where specific performance was granted. . . . We recognize also the cautionary language about granting specific performance in comment *a* to § 129 of the Restatement. . . . No public interest behind G.L. c. 259, § 1, however, in the simple circumstances before us, will be violated if Mrs. Green fairly is held to her precise bargain by principles of equitable estoppel, subject to the considerations mentioned below. . . .

The case . . . must be remanded to the trial judge for the purpose of amending the judgment to require conveyance of Lot S by Mrs. Green only upon payment to her in cash within a stated period of the balance of the agreed price of $15,000. The trial judge, however, in her discretion and upon proper offers of proof by counsel, may reopen the record to receive, in addition to the presently stipulated facts, a stipulation or evidence concerning the present status of the Hickeys' apparent obligation to sell their house. If the circumstances have changed, it will be open to the trial judge to require of Mrs. Green, instead of specific performance, only full restitution to the Hickeys of all costs reasonably caused to them in respect of these transactions (including advertising costs, deposits, and their reasonable costs for this litigation) with interest. . . .

Notes

1. *The requirements of the statute of frauds:*   Why did the Hickeys fail to satisfy the statute of frauds? Could they have asserted that the writing on their deposit check to Mrs. Green contained the essential terms? Consider instead the deposit check from the prospective purchaser of the Hickeys' home. Was that writing sufficient to enforce the agreement against the purchaser? Against the Hickeys?

2. *Exceptions to the statute of frauds:*   It is not uncommon for courts to collapse the *part performance* and *equitable estoppel* doctrines into a single exception or to otherwise blur the distinction between them. Patiently sift through the court's opinion, § 129 of the Restatement (Second) of Contracts, and the comments to § 129. In this case, which doctrine(s) did the court apply?

Make an argument on behalf of the Hickeys that the facts support a specific performance remedy under the part performance exception, and then make an argument under the equitable estoppel exception. Which argument is stronger, and why? Suppose instead that Mrs. Green had not stipulated that she entered into an oral agreement with the Hickeys. Can you still make a compelling argument under one or both exceptions on behalf of the Hickeys?

3. *Remedy and remand:* As you may know from your Contracts class, specific performance is an equitable remedy reserved for cases where damages would be inadequate—as where the subject of the contract involves a famous painting, a specific piece of property, or some other unique subject. In *Hickey v. Green*, why did the court remand the case to the trial judge? Among other things, the trial court was ordered to determine whether "circumstances have changed" and the "present status of the Hickeys' apparent obligation to sell their house." Suppose the trial judge finds that the Hickeys are no longer obligated to sell their current property. What will be the result, and why?

4. *Unrepresented parties:* It appears that Mrs. Green and the Hickeys entered into their agreement without professional representation. If the Hickeys had retained a real estate broker and/or an attorney, do you think they could have avoided this litigation?

5. *Electronic signatures:* The Electronic Signatures in Global and National Commerce Act of 2000 (*E-SIGN Act*) authorizes electronic signatures in cases involving transactions in or affecting interstate or foreign commerce. 15 U.S.C. §§ 7001-7031. Section 7001(a)(1) provides, "a signature, contract, or other record . . . may not be denied legal effect, validity, or enforceability solely because it is in electronic form" and preempts state laws to the contrary. In some cases, voice messages or e-mail messages can operate as legal signatures. Do such examples of electronic signatures satisfy the purposes of the statute of frauds? If not, what other policies do they promote?

2. Equitable Conversion

After the buyer and seller sign the contract of sale, a significant period of time can lapse before the contract is "closed." Who owns the property during this executory period? If the jurisdiction follows the *equitable conversion* doctrine, the buyer becomes the "equitable" owner from the moment the parties sign an enforceable agreement, leaving the seller with "legal" title and a claim for the purchase price secured by a lien on the property.

Startling consequences can flow from this conversion. Suppose the property is destroyed by fire, flood, or some other disaster. Many jurisdictions will treat the new *equitable* owner as the owner for virtually all purposes. As a result, the buyer might be forced to pay the full purchase price and complete the sale of the destroyed property, even if the seller continued to occupy the premises. Is that a good approach? Is it consistent with the parties' likely expectations at the time they signed the contract? The next case takes up those questions.

Brush Grocery Kart, Inc. v. Sure Fine Market, Inc.

47 P.3d 680 (Colo. 2002)

> ### Reading Guide
>
> ◆ *Equitable conversion and risk allocation:* When a buyer becomes the equitable owner of property, does it necessarily follow that the buyer assumes the risk of loss during the executory period?
>
> ◆ *Equitable conversion and specific performance:* Pay attention to the relationship between the doctrine of equitable conversion and the remedy of specific performance, under which a court orders completion of the sale, rather than making an award of damages.

COATS, J. . . .

In October 1992 Brush Grocery Kart, Inc. and Sure Fine Market, Inc. entered into a five-year "Lease with Renewal Provisions and Option to Purchase" for real property, including a building to be operated by Brush as a grocery store. Under the contract's purchase option provision, any time during the last six months of the lease, Brush could elect to purchase the property at a price equal to the average of the appraisals of an expert designated by each party.

Shortly before expiration of the lease, Brush notified Sure Fine of its desire to purchase the property and begin the process of determining a sale price. Although each party offered an appraisal, the parties were unable to agree on a final price by the time the lease expired. Brush then vacated the premises, returned all keys to Sure Fine, and advised Sure Fine that it would discontinue its casualty insurance covering the property during the lease. Brush also filed suit, alleging that Sure Fine failed to negotiate the price term in good faith. . . . Sure Fine . . . counterclaimed, alleging that Brush negotiated the price term in bad faith and was therefore the breaching party.

During litigation over the price term, the property was substantially damaged during a hail storm. With neither party carrying casualty insurance, each asserted that the other was liable for the damage. The issue was added to the litigation at a stipulated amount of $60,000. The court appointed a special master pursuant to C.R.C.P. 53 and accepted his appraised value of $375,000. The court then found that under the doctrine of equitable conversion, Brush was the equitable owner of the property and bore the risk of loss. It therefore declined to abate the purchase price or award damages to Brush for the loss.

Brush appealed the loss allocation, and the court of appeals affirmed on similar grounds. . . .

In the absence of statutory authority, the rights, powers, duties, and liabilities arising out of a contract for the sale of land have frequently been derived by reference to the theory of equitable conversion. . . . This theory or doctrine, which has been described as a legal fiction, is based on equitable principles that permit the vendee to be considered the equitable owner of the land and debtor for the purchase money and the vendor to be regarded as a secured creditor. The changes in rights and liabilities that occur upon the making of the contract result from the equitable right to specific performance. . . .

The assignment of the risk of casualty loss in the executory period of contracts for the sale of real property varies greatly throughout the jurisdictions of this country. What appears to yet be a slim majority of states, *see* Randy R. Koenders, Annotation, *Risk of Loss by Casualty Pending Contract for Conveyance of Real Property Modern Cases,* 85 A.L.R.4th 233 (2001), places the risk of loss on the vendee from the moment of contracting, on the rationale that once an equitable conversion takes place, the vendee must be treated as owner for all purposes. *See Skelly Oil v. Ashmore,* 365 S.W.2d 582, 588 (Mo. 1963) (criticizing this approach). Once the vendee becomes the equitable owner, he therefore becomes responsible for the condition of the property, despite not having a present right of occupancy or control. In sharp contrast, a handful of other states reject the allocation of casualty loss risk as a consequence of the theory of equitable conversion and follow the equally rigid "Massachusetts Rule," under which the seller continues to bear the risk until actual transfer of the title, absent an express agreement to the contrary. . . . A substantial and growing number of jurisdictions, however, base the legal consequences of no-fault casualty loss on the right to possession of the property at the time the loss occurs. *Koenders, supra,* §§ 6, 7. . . .

This court has applied the theory of equitable conversion in limited circumstances affecting title, *see Konecny v. von Gunten,* 379 P.2d 158 (Colo. 1963) (finding vendors incapable of unilaterally changing their tenancy in common to joint tenancy during the executory period of the contract because their interest had been equitably converted into a mere security interest and the vendee's interest into realty), and refused to apply it in some circumstances, *see Chain O'Mines [v. Williamson,]* 72 P.2d 265 [(Colo. 1937)] (holding that even if the doctrine applies to option contracts, no conversion would take place until the option were exercised by the party having the right of election). It has also characterized the theory as affording significant protections to purchasers of realty in Colorado. *See Dwyer v. Dist. Court,* 532 P.2d 725 (Colo. 1975) (finding personal jurisdiction over out-of-state vendee in part because of the protections afforded vendees of land in this jurisdiction during the executory period of the contract). It has never before, however, expressly relied on the theory of equitable conversion alone as allocating the risk of casualty loss to a vendee.

In *Wiley v. Lininger,* 204 P.2d 1083 [(Colo. 1949)], where fire destroyed improvements on land occupied by the vendee during the multi-year executory period of an installment land contract, we held, according to the generally accepted rule, that neither the buyer nor the seller, each of whom had an insurable interest in the property, had an obligation to insure the property for the benefit of the other. We also adopted a rule . . . that "the vendee under a contract for the sale of land, being regarded as the equitable owner, assumes the risk of destruction of or injury to the property *where he is in possession,* and the destruction or loss is not proximately caused by the negligence of the vendor." *Id.* (emphasis added). The vendee in possession was therefore not relieved of his obligation to continue making payments according to the terms of the contract, despite material loss by fire to some of the improvements on the property. . . .

Those jurisdictions that indiscriminately include the risk of casualty loss among the incidents or "attributes" of equitable ownership do so largely in reliance on ancient authority or by considering it necessary for consistent application of the theory of equitable conversion. *See Skelly Oil,* 365 S.W.2d at 592 (Stockman, J. dissenting) (quoting 4 Williston, *Contracts,* § 929, at 2607: "Only the hoary age and frequent repetition of the maxim prevents a general recognition of its absurdity."). . . . Under virtually any accepted understanding of the theory, however, equitable conversion is not viewed as entitling the purchaser to every significant right of ownership, and particularly not the right of possession. As a matter of both logic and equity, the obligation to maintain property in its physical condition follows the right to have actual possession and control rather than a legal right to force conveyance of the property through specific performance at some future date. . . .

The equitable conversion theory is literally stood on its head by imposing on a vendee, solely because of his right to specific performance, the risk that the vendor will be unable to specifically perform when the time comes because of an accidental casualty loss. It is counterintuitive, at the very least, that merely contracting for the sale of real property should not only relieve the vendor of his responsibility to maintain the property until execution but also impose a duty on the vendee to perform despite the intervention of a material, no-fault casualty loss preventing him from ever receiving the benefit of his bargain. Such an extension of the theory of equitable conversion to casualty loss has never been recognized by this jurisdiction, and it is neither necessary nor justified solely for the sake of consistency.

By contrast, there is substantial justification, both as a matter of law and policy, for not relieving a vendee who is entitled to possession before transfer of title, like the vendee in *Wiley,* of his duty to pay the full contract price, notwithstanding an accidental loss. In addition to having control over the property and being entitled to the benefits of its use, an equitable owner who also has the right of possession has already acquired virtually all of the rights of ownership and almost invariably will have already paid at least some portion of the contract price to exercise those rights. By expressly including in the contract for sale the right of possession, which otherwise generally accompanies transfer of title, . . . the vendor has for all practical purposes already transferred the property as promised, and the parties have in effect expressed their joint intention that the vendee pay the purchase price as promised. . . .

In *Wiley,* rather than adopting a rule to the effect that a vendee assumes the risk of casualty loss as an incident of equitable ownership, our holding stands for virtually the opposite proposition. Despite being the equitable owner, the vendee in that case was prohibited from rescinding only because he was already rightfully in possession at the time of the loss. While *Wiley* could be read to have merely resolved the situation under an installment contract for the sale of land that gave the vendee a right of immediate possession, the rule we adopted foreshadowed the resolution of this case as well. In the absence of a right of possession, a vendee of real property that suffers a material casualty loss during the executory period of the contract, through no fault of his own, must be permitted to rescind and recover any payments he had already made. . . .

Furthermore, where a vendee is entitled to rescind as a result of casualty loss, the vendee should generally also be entitled to partial specific performance of the contract with an abatement in the purchase price reflecting the loss. Where the damage is ascertainable, permitting partial specific performance with a price abatement allows courts as nearly as possible to fulfill the expectations of the parties expressed in the contract, while leaving each in a position that is equitable relative to the other. . . .

Here, Brush was clearly not in possession of the property as the equitable owner. Even if the doctrine of equitable conversion applies to the option contract between Brush and Sure Fine and could be said to have converted Brush's interest to an equitable ownership of the property at the time Brush exercised its option to purchase, neither party considered the contract for sale to entitle Brush to possession. Brush was, in fact, not in possession of the property, and the record indicates that Sure Fine considered itself to hold the right of use and occupancy and gave notice that it would consider Brush a holdover tenant if it continued to occupy the premises other than by continuing to lease the property. . . . Both the court of appeals and the district court therefore erred in finding that the doctrine of equitable conversion required Brush to bear the loss caused by hail damage.

At least under the circumstances of this case, where Brush chose to go forward with the contract under a stipulation as to loss from the hail damage, it was also entitled to specific performance with an abatement of the purchase price equal to the casualty loss. The judgment of the court of appeals is therefore reversed and the case is remanded for further proceedings consistent with this opinion.

Notes

1. *Three rules:* Clearly articulate the three rules identified by the court. What policy supports each rule—fairness, efficiency, or something else? Which rule do you think is best, and why?

2. *The influence of statutory law—the Uniform Vendor and Purchaser Risk Act:* The *Brush* court adopted the position of the Uniform Vendor and Purchaser Risk Act of 1935:

> Any contract hereafter made in this State for the purchase and sale of realty shall be interpreted as including an agreement that the parties shall have the following rights and duties, unless the contract expressly provides otherwise:
>
> (a) If, when neither the legal title nor the possession of the subject matter of the contract has been transferred, all or a material part thereof is destroyed without fault of the purchaser or is taken by eminent domain, the vendor cannot enforce

the contract, and the purchaser is entitled to recover any portion of the price that he has paid;

(b) If, when either the legal title or the possession of the subject matter of the contract has been transferred, all or any part thereof is destroyed without fault of the vendor or is taken by eminent domain, the purchaser is not thereby relieved from a duty to pay the price, nor is he entitled to recover any portion thereof that he has paid.

A number of states have adopted the act by judicial opinion, as in *Brush.* In addition, as of 2015, 12 states had adopted the act by statute. Uniform Law Commission, Vendor and Purchaser Risk Act (1935), www.uniformlaws.org (follow links to "Acts" and "Vendor and Purchaser Risk Act (1935)") (visited Aug. 1, 2015).

3. *Insurance:* Suppose that Sure Fine had maintained casualty insurance on the property, and that Brush decided to complete the sale, despite the hail damage. Would Brush be entitled to the proceeds from Sure Fine's policy? Under basic principles of insurance law, Sure Fine's policy is a *personal contract* between Sure Fine and the insurance company, and Brush has no rights under that agreement. Therefore, under a strict view, Sure Fine would be entitled to both the sales price from Brush *and* the insurance proceeds. Is that fair? How could Brush protect itself from such a possibility?

4. *Practice pointer:* Generally, the three rules described in *Brush* apply in the absence of an agreement to the contrary. Therefore, in the contract of sale, the parties should take care to allocate the risk of loss, to clarify which party is responsible for insuring the premises during the executory period, and to clarify whether the insuring party holds the proceeds in trust for the benefit of the other. Review the sample contract at the beginning of section B, above. Would the language of that contract be adequate to resolve the conflict in *Brush* without litigation? If you represented Brush and Sure Fine, respectively, what additional (or alternative) language would you have inserted into the contract to protect your client's interests?

Problems

Under the court's rule, is the buyer's bare possession enough to trigger equitable conversion and a shifting of the risk of loss? At what point in time is possession measured? Under that rule, would buyer or seller bear the risk of loss (or enjoy the gain) in each of the following situations?

1. *Zoning change:* Seller and buyer execute a sales contract for property that the buyer plans to develop into a gas station, and the buyer takes possession; before closing, the city changes its zoning ordinance in a way that would not allow the construction of a gas station.

2. *The surprisingly valuable farm:* Seller and buyer execute a sales contract on a rural farm, and the buyer takes possession; before closing, the buyer discovers oil and gas deposits beneath the land that potentially increase its value tenfold.

3. *A defective title:* Seller and buyer execute a sales contract, and the buyer takes possession; the title search has uncovered defects in the title, and the seller is working diligently to cure those defects; before closing, a hail storm destroys the property.

4. *The timing of the hail storm:* The hail damage occurred in 1992, soon after Brush opened its grocery store.

3. Remedies for Breach of Contract

Specific performance is considered an extraordinary remedy in most breach of contract cases. Nevertheless, courts have long awarded it as the favored remedy when the contract relates to the sale of *land.* As one court explained,

> The principle underlying the specific performance remedy is equity's jurisdiction to grant relief where the damage remedy at law is inadequate. The text writers generally agree that at the time this branch of equity jurisdiction was evolving in England, the presumed uniqueness of land as well as its importance to the social order of that era led to the conclusion that damages at law could never be adequate to compensate for the breach of a contract to transfer an interest in land. Hence specific performance became a fixed remedy in this class of transactions. . . . The judicial attitude has remained substantially unchanged. . . .

Centex Homes Corp. v. Boag, 320 A.2d 194 (N.J. Super. 1974). Refer back to the rationales justifying the existence and enforcement of property rights, as set forth in Chapter 6.A. Which rationale, if any, supports the view of the *Centex Homes* court? Beyond specific performance, courts award a variety of other remedies. To prevent litigation, prudent parties often stipulate in the sales contract the remedies to which each party will be entitled upon the other's default or breach.

A Place to Start | Remedies for Breach of Contract

Buyers and sellers, upon the other's default, can receive one or a combination of the following remedies:

- *Specific performance:* When awarding specific performance, a court orders the breaching party to carry out its obligations as set forth in the written contract. The court will award a non-breaching buyer title to the property upon payment of the contract sales price to the seller (the court can issue a decree effectively transferring title if the seller balks at executing a deed). A non-breaching seller is entitled to the contract sales price upon transfer of title to the buyer.

- *Damages:* Damage awards usually reflect the *benefit of the bargain*—the difference between the property's contract price and its market value at the time of breach (which is usually the date of closing). Other types of damage awards include *incidental damages* (expenses incurred in reliance on the breaching party's obligation to perform the contract, such as expenses for surveys, inspections, and attorney's fees); *consequential damages* (losses foreseeable at the time of contract execution); and *liquidated damages* (such as allowing the seller to retain a breaching buyer's earnest money deposit or down payment).

- *Rescission:* The remedy of rescission allows for the termination of the contract (and the parties' obligations thereunder) upon breach by either party.

- *Restitution:* If the contract is rescinded, both parties are entitled to be restored to their pre-contract position. The seller can recover possession (if the buyer took possession prior to closing), and the buyer can recover any payments made to the seller (such as an earnest money deposit or down payment).

DIGGING DEEPER: The fundamental rationale for the award of specific performance is the supposed uniqueness of land. Should that rationale apply to cases when the buyer defaults, as well as when the seller defaults? In instances of buyer default, should specific performance be available to force the buyer to complete the purchase of a single-family home, as well as to force the buyer to complete the purchase of one unit in a multi-unit condominium building?

Test Your Understanding

1. *Specific performance for the seller:* The usual rationale supporting specific performance is that monetary damages will not make the party whole. How does that rationale support equitable relief for the *seller*?

2. *Specific performance and damages compared—the seller's perspective:* From the buyer's perspective, it is easy to see the distinction between specific performance (the buyer acquires the desired property) and damages (the buyer receives a monetary award). But the distinction is less clear from the seller's point of view—both specific performance and the award of damages result in monetary relief to a non-breaching seller. Suppose the contract calls for the sale of property for $100,000. The buyer breaches, and the court awards *specific performance* to the seller. How much money will the seller receive? In contrast, suppose the court awards *damages* to the seller. Assume the market value of the property has remained stable in the relatively brief period between the execution of the contract and the date set for closing. How much will the seller receive? Suppose instead that the market value rises to $110,000 or declines to $90,000 in the interim. In each case, how much will the seller receive in damages? Based on financial considerations alone, which remedy would the

seller prefer? (And for that matter, which remedy might a court prefer to award?) If you represented the seller, what other factors would you consider in advising your client as to the best remedy to pursue?

C. THE PHYSICAL CONDITION OF THE PROPERTY

Review the sample contract that appears at the beginning of section B. What, if anything, does it say about the physical conditions of the premises and an *inspection contingency*? Under the common law doctrine of *caveat emptor*—"let the buyer beware"—a seller of real property was not liable for defects in the land or its structures, except in certain types of cases, such as where the seller had expressly warranted the condition of the premises; had engaged in active concealment or fraudulent misrepresentation; or had a confidential or fiduciary relationship with the buyer. Does the sample contract purport to apply or to alter the common law rule?

1. The Seller's Duty of Disclosure

Should the law require sellers to disclose physical property defects to potential buyers? If so, what sorts of defects should be revealed? For examples, should sellers be required to reveal the reported presence of *ghosts*?

Stambovsky v. Ackley

572 N.Y.S.2d (N.Y. App. Div. 1991)

> **Reading Guide**
>
> Under the common law rule of caveat emptor, sellers had no duty of disclosure. As you read this case, consider whether states should retain, modify, or abandon the common law rule. From a systemic perspective, what are the costs and benefits to the real estate market of required information disclosure?

RUBIN, J.

Plaintiff, to his horror, discovered that the house he had recently contracted to purchase was widely reputed to be possessed by poltergeists, reportedly seen by defendant seller and members of her family on numerous occasions over the last nine years. Plaintiff promptly commenced this action seeking rescission of the contract of sale. Supreme Court reluctantly dismissed the complaint, holding that plaintiff has no remedy at law in this jurisdiction.

The unusual facts of this case, as disclosed by the record, clearly warrant a grant of equitable relief to the buyer who, as a resident of New York City, cannot be expected to have any familiarity with the folklore of the Village of Nyack. Not being a "local," plaintiff could not readily learn that the home he had contracted to purchase is haunted. Whether the source of the spectral apparitions seen by defendant seller are parapsychic or psychogenic, having reported their presence in both a national publication ("Reader['s] Digest") and the local press (in 1977 and 1982, respectively), defendant is estopped to deny their existence and, as a matter of law, the house is haunted. More to the point, however, no divination is required to conclude that it is defendant's promotional efforts in publicizing her close encounters with these spirits which fostered the home's reputation in the community. In 1989, the house was included in a five-home walking tour of Nyack and described in a November 27th newspaper article as "a riverfront Victorian (with ghost)." The impact of the reputation thus created goes to the very essence of the bargain between the parties, greatly impairing both the value of the property and its potential for resale. The extent of this impairment may be presumed for the purpose of reviewing the disposition of this motion to dismiss the cause of action for rescission . . . and represents merely an issue of fact for resolution at trial.

While I agree with Supreme Court that the real estate broker, as agent for the seller, is under no duty to disclose to a potential buyer the phantasmal reputation of the premises and that, in his pursuit of a legal remedy for fraudulent misrepresentation against the seller, plaintiff hasn't a ghost of a chance, I am nevertheless moved by the spirit of equity to allow the buyer to seek rescission of the contract of sale and recovery of his downpayment. New York law fails to recognize any remedy for damages incurred as a result of the seller's mere silence, applying instead the strict rule of caveat emptor. Therefore, the theoretical basis for granting relief, even under the extraordinary facts of this case, is elusive if not ephemeral. . . .

From the perspective of a person in the position of plaintiff herein, a very practical problem arises with respect to the discovery of a paranormal phenomenon: "Who you gonna' call?" as the title song to the movie *Ghostbusters* asks. Applying the strict rule of caveat emptor to a contract involving a house possessed by poltergeists conjures up visions of a psychic or medium routinely accompanying the structural engineer and Terminix man on an inspection of every home subject to a contract of sale. It portends that the prudent attorney will establish an escrow account lest the subject of the transaction come back to haunt him and his client—or pray that his malpractice insurance coverage extends to supernatural disasters. In the interest of avoiding such untenable consequences, the notion that a haunting is a condition which can and should be ascertained upon reasonable inspection of the premises is a hobgoblin which should be exorcised from the body of legal precedent and laid quietly to rest.

It has been suggested by a leading authority that the ancient rule which holds that mere non-disclosure does not constitute actionable misrepresentation "finds proper application in cases where the fact undisclosed is patent, or the plaintiff has equal opportunities for obtaining information which he may be expected to utilize, or the defendant has no reason to think that he is acting under any misapprehension" (Prosser, Law of Torts § 106, at 696 [4th ed., 1971]). However, with respect to transactions in real estate, New York adheres to the doctrine of caveat emptor and imposes no duty upon the vendor to disclose any information concerning the premises . . . unless there is a confidential or fiduciary relationship between the parties . . . or some conduct on the part of the seller which constitutes "active concealment" (see, *17 East 80th Realty Corp. v. 68th Associates,* 173 A.D.2d 245, . . . [dummy ventilation system constructed by seller]; *Haberman v. Greenspan,* 368 N.Y.S.2d 717 [foundation cracks covered by seller]). Normally, some affirmative misrepresentation . . . or partial disclosure . . . is required to impose upon the seller a duty to communicate undisclosed conditions affecting the premises. . . .

Caveat emptor is not so all-encompassing a doctrine of common law as to render every act of non-disclosure immune from redress, whether legal or equitable. "In regard to the necessity of giving information which has not been asked, the rule differs somewhat at law and in equity, and while the law courts would permit no recovery of *damages* against a vendor, because of mere concealment of facts *under certain circumstances,* yet if the vendee refused to complete the contract because of the concealment of a material fact on the part of the other, equity would refuse to compel him so to do, because equity only compels the specific performance of a contract which is fair and open, and in regard to which all material matters known to each have been communicated to the other" (*Rothmiller v. Stein,* 38 N.E. 718 (N.Y.) [emphasis added]). Even as a principle of law, long before exceptions were embodied in statute law . . . the doctrine was held inapplicable to contagion among animals, adulteration of food, and insolvency of a maker of a promissory note and of a tenant substituted for another under a lease. . . . Where fairness and common sense dictate that an exception should be created, the evolution of the law should not be stifled by rigid application of a legal maxim.

The doctrine of caveat emptor requires that a buyer act prudently to assess the fitness and value of his purchase and operates to bar the purchaser who fails to exercise due care from seeking the equitable remedy of rescission. . . . It should be apparent . . . that the most meticulous inspection and the search would not reveal the presence of poltergeists at the premises or unearth the property's ghoulish reputation in the community. Therefore, there is no sound policy reason to deny plaintiff relief for failing to discover a state of affairs which the most prudent purchaser would not be expected to even contemplate. . . .

The case law in this jurisdiction dealing with the duty of a vendor of real property to disclose information to the buyer is distinguishable from the matter under review. The most salient distinction is that existing cases invariably deal with the physical condition of the premises . . . , defects in title . . . , liens against the property . . . , expenses or income . . . and other factors affecting its operation. No case has been brought to this court's attention in which the property value was impaired as the result of the reputation created by information disseminated to the public by the seller (or, for that matter, as a result of possession by poltergeists).

Where a condition which has been created by the seller materially impairs the value of the contract and is peculiarly within the knowledge of the seller or unlikely to be discovered by a prudent purchaser exercising due care with respect to the subject transaction, nondisclosure constitutes a basis for rescission as a matter of equity. Any other outcome places upon the buyer not merely the obligation to exercise care in his purchase but rather to be omniscient with respect to any fact which may affect the bargain. No practical purpose is served by imposing such a burden upon a purchaser. To the contrary, it encourages predatory business practice and offends the principle that equity will suffer no wrong to be without a remedy. . . .

. . . It has been remarked that the occasional modern cases which permit a seller to take unfair advantage of a buyer's ignorance so long as he is not actively misled are "singularly unappetizing" (Prosser, Law of Torts § 106, at 696 [4th ed. 1971]). Where, as here, the seller not only takes unfair advantage of the buyer's ignorance but has created and perpetuated a condition about which he is unlikely to even inquire, enforcement of the contract (in whole or in part) is offensive to the court's sense of equity. Application of the remedy of rescission, within the bounds of the narrow exception to the doctrine of caveat emptor set forth herein, is entirely appropriate to relieve the unwitting purchaser from the consequences of a most unnatural bargain.

Accordingly, the judgment of the Supreme Court . . . which dismissed the complaint . . . should be modified, . . . and the first cause of action seeking rescission of the contract reinstated, without costs.

SMITH, J. (dissenting).

[I]f the doctrine of caveat emptor is to be discarded, it should be for a reason more substantive than a poltergeist. The existence of a poltergeist is no more binding upon the defendants than it is upon this court. . . .

Notes

1. *New York's legislative reaction to* Stambovsky: After *Stambovsky*, New York enacted the Property Condition Disclosure Act of 2002 (colloquially known as the "haunted house" statute), which requires sellers to affirmatively disclose information about at least 48 conditions affecting residential properties. Among other things, the law requires disclosure of whether any or all of the property might be located in a designated floodplain. N.Y. Real Property Law § 462(10). Why might that be important to prospective buyers? Despite the long list of required disclosures, however, the remedy for failure to comply is weak.

See N.Y. Real Property Law § 465 ("In the event a seller fails to perform the duty . . . to deliver a disclosure statement prior to the signing by the buyer of a binding contract of sale, the buyer shall receive upon the transfer of title a credit of five hundred dollars against the agreed upon purchase price of the residential real property"). Do you agree with the approach taken by the New York legislature?

2. *A changing world—beyond caveat emptor:*   Under the modern trend, most states have created exceptions to caveat emptor, or rejected the doctrine altogether. A typical judicial formulation might require sellers to disclose defects that are (1) material, (2) latent, and (3) known or should be known to the seller. *See Johnson v. Davis*, 480 So. 2d 625 (Fla. 1985). State statutes can also modify the common law, such as the New York statute discussed above. To facilitate required disclosures, many states provide multi-page standardized disclosure forms to be completed by the seller prior to the acceptance of the contract. Although there is some variation, common required disclosures include structural defects; termite infestations; violations of local requirements (such as building codes and zoning laws); drainage problems; unstable soils; and environmental hazards (such as the presence of lead paint, hazardous materials, or underground storage tanks).

Some states also require sellers to disclose "stigmatizing" factors, such as the reputation as a haunted property; the fact that a death, murder, or other violent crime took place on the property; or that the seller had contracted HIV/AIDS. Conversely, there has also been a move against required disclosure of non-physical, stigmatizing, or psychological factors. For example, some state legislatures explicitly *exempt* from disclosure certain stigmatizing conditions. *See, e.g.,* N.Y. Real Property Law § 443-a (exempting from disclosure requirement the fact that the seller has been infected with certain non-communicable diseases; or the fact that a homicide, suicide, or felony took place on the premises); Fla. Stat. § 689.25 (exempting from disclosure requirement the fact that the property was the purported site of a homicide, suicide, or death, or the fact that an occupant of the property has received a diagnosis of HIV or AIDS infection).

3. *Caveat emptor light:*   Is there such a thing as *too much* disclosure? Dean Alex Johnson observes:

> [Some new disclosure] laws require inefficient disclosure of information by mandating the disclosure of all information, including that which is the product of deliberate investment and, relatedly, information that is equally available to both parties. As a result, and efficiently, *caveat emptor light* is emerging, which . . . is consistent with the economic theories requiring disclosure of information and correctly establishes the correct duty for disclosure of information from the knower, or vendor-seller, to the knowee, or vendee-buyer.

Alex M. Johnson, Jr., *An Economic Analysis of the Duty to Disclose Information: Lessons Learned from the Caveat Emptor Doctrine*, 45 San Diego L. Rev. 79,

83-84 (2008) (emphasis added). Dean Johnson coined the term "caveat emptor light" to describe two different reactions to expansive modern disclosure requirements mandated by the courts: (a) legislatively created mandatory disclosure forms, and (b) judicially or legislatively sanctioned options in some jurisdictions that allow the parties to contract to sell the property "as is" and without disclosure. *Id.* at 111-17. Do you agree that there can be too much disclosure? Should buyers be permitted to contractually agree to accept property "as is"?

4. *Timing issues—information disclosure and remedy:*   At what point in time should the disclosure requirement attach? One survey of *legislative* disclosure requirements revealed that statutes require disclosure to buyers before they make an offer (25% of disclosure statutes); before the seller accepts an offer (50% of disclosure statutes); or before closing the contract (25% of disclosure statutes). Stephanie Stern, *Temporal Dynamics of Disclosure: The Example of Residential Real Estate Conveyancing,* 57 Utah L. Rev. 57 (2005). What time is best? Professor Stern argues that cognitive psychology research supports a requirement of early disclosure:

> . . . First, research on behavioral compliance (also known as the lowball technique) shows that people who have made an overt or highly visible commitment to a course of action will tend to persist even when the costs subsequently increase. Second, psychologists have found "investment effects," where an initial expenditure of money, effort, or time created an increased tendency towards further investment in the same decision or venture. . . . Third, individuals "anchor" onto initial values so that the initial value, even when it is uninformative, influences the final judgment of price, probability, or other uncertain values. In negotiations, for example, individuals "anchor" onto initial offers and adjust suboptimally for subsequent information.

Id. at 57-58.

In terms of remedy, if the contract buyer discovers before closing that the seller has breached a disclosure duty, then the typical remedy would be rescission of the contract. For defects discovered after closing, the buyer will have a more difficult time obtaining a remedy, but in cases of serious defects might be able to recover money damages or (in rare cases) to rescind the entire transaction.

5. *The place—the haunted house on the Hudson:*   The May 1977 edition of Reader's Digest included a story by defendant Helen Herdman Ackley titled *Our Haunted House on the Hudson.* In it, she described her family's experience in an old 18-room Victorian home in Nyack, New York (about 20 miles north of New York City), overlooking the Hudson River. According to Ackley, soon after moving into the house, her family realized that it was haunted by a group of rambunctious, mischievous poltergeists. But long before the publication of Ackley's account, the area had a reputation for ghostly presences. Just across

the river, for example, Tarrytown, New York, was the storied site of the headless horseman featured in Washington Irving's 1820 short story, *The Legend of Sleepy Hollow*.

Drawing by Bill Batson
Source: Bill Batson, Nyack Sketch Log: A Legally Haunted House, Oct. 21, 2014

Years later, after Mrs. Ackley had been widowed, high property taxes and cold winters prompted her to put her house on the market with the plan of moving to Florida. Jeffrey and Patrice Stambovsky—a young couple from New York City who had not heard about the house's ghostly reputation—offered $650,000 for the property, and put down $32,500 as a deposit. However, after learning that the house was purportedly haunted, the couple did not appear at the real estate closing. Instead, as reported above, they sued Mrs. Ackley to rescind the contract and to obtain a refund of their earnest money. Mrs. Ackley soon found another buyer and packed up for Florida in 1991. *See* Robin M. Strom-Mackey, *Helen Ackley's Haunted House on the Hudson*, The Shore (Aug. 2, 2015); Mark Kavanagh, *The Ghost of Nyack*, Kavanagh Transit System (2010).

Problems

Under each of the following factual scenarios, would the *Stambovsky* rule require the seller to disclose the problem to the buyer? Apart from *Stambovsky*, do you think the seller *should* be required to reveal the information?

1. *The leaky roof:* The sellers know that their roof is prone to leaking. Past rains had stained the ceiling and caused the plaster around one of the window frames to buckle and peel.

2. *Prone to flooding:*   The property is in a floodplain that has a 1% chance of serious and potentially life-threatening flooding each year, according to publically available nationwide maps prepared by the Federal Emergency Management Agency (FEMA).

3. *A scratch on the floor:*   The seller's property has beautiful hardwood floors, except for one ugly scratch under the dining room table. A large area rug covers the scratch and makes for a comfortable dining area.

4. *Unreported hauntings:*   Contrary to the facts of *Stambovsky*, assume that Mrs. Ackley had observed ghostly happenings in her home, but had never reported them to *Reader's Digest* or to any other publication.

2. Flood Risk and Federal Insurance

As we have seen, the typical real estate contract contains three *contingencies* (inspection, financing, and title) that afford prospective buyers an opportunity to investigate various aspects of the sale property. Increasingly, buyers are evaluating the flood risk of property as part of the inspection contingency. As a useful resource, buyers can consult the flood hazard maps prepared by the Federal Emergency Management Agency (FEMA) for virtually all areas of the country. In particular, the FEMA flood maps identify high-risk floodplains and areas subject to coastal storm surge. The *high risk* or *special flood hazard areas* (sometimes misleadingly referred to as "hundred year floodplains") are those that have at least a one-in-four chance of flooding during a 30-year mortgage, which translates into a 1% chance of flooding in any given year. FEMA updates its flood hazard maps to reflect flood risk changes over time, including those triggered by new development and by environmental changes (such as global climate change and sea level rise). The costs of flooding can be significant. For example, FEMA estimates that the damage to a 2,000 square foot home caused by one inch of flooding could reach $20,000. *See* National Flood Insurance Program, *FloodSmart.gov: The Official Site of the NFIP*, https://www.floodsmart.gov/floodsmart/ (visited Oct. 4, 2015).

Flood risks also influence the financing contingency. If a buyer seeks to purchase property in a *special flood hazard area*, the buyer will not be able to obtain a mortgage from a federally regulated or federally insured lender unless the property is covered by federal flood insurance. Standard homeowners policies do not cover flooding, in large part because the risk is too great for private lenders to absorb. Instead, Congress established the National Flood Insurance Program (NFIP) in 1968, which today covers some five million policyholders. But the financial solvency of the NFIP is uncertain: in the wake of such massive storms as Hurricane Katrina (2005) and Hurricane Sandy (2012), the federal NFIP program owed more than $23 billion to the U.S. Treasury. Congress has struggled to deal with the highly politically charged issue of funding the program. For example, 2012 legislation that would have phased out federally subsidized premiums until policyholders paid the true cost of insuring their properties met with a massive political backlash amid evidence that some annual premiums could increase dramatically (up to $28,000 per year, in some extreme cases). In response, Congress retreated in 2014 by passing legislation that reinstated certain subsidies and slowed the rate of premium increases. Still, it seems likely that annual premiums will increase significantly until they reflect the true cost of insurance coverage. *See* U.S. Government Accountability Office (GAO), *National Flood Insurance Program*, http://www.gao.gov/highrisk/national_flood_insurance/why_did_study (visited Oct. 4, 2015); *See* Robert R.M. Verchick & Lynsey R. Johnson, *When Retreat is the Best Option: Flood Insurance After Biggert-Waters and Other Climate Change Puzzles*, 47 John Marshall L. Rev. 695, 711-12 (2013).

Problem

Suppose that you are a real estate attorney and are representing a buyer who is considering the purchase of a particular piece of property. What investigations would you undertake on behalf of your client with respect to the risk of flooding? List at least four areas of research that you would pursue, and possible sources of relevant data.

D. FINANCING—MORTGAGES AND FORECLOSURE

Review the sample contract that appears at the beginning of section B. What, if anything, does it say about the buyer's ability to obtain a mortgage loan and a *financing contingency*? Although some buyers can pay cash to purchase real property, most require a loan from a bank or other lender to finance their purchase.

1. The Mortgage

Assume that a buyer has signed a contract to purchase real property for $100,000. The buyer deposits $5,000 in *earnest money* into an *escrow account* to show good faith—a buyer who defaults on the contract risks losing the earnest money. Although highly variable, such deposits typically range from 3% to 10% of the purchase price. The buyer has available an additional $15,000 in savings. What happens next?

The buyer will apply for a loan in the amount of $80,000, taking care to satisfy all of the deadlines set out in the sales contract. To supplement the application, the lender will request information about the buyer's employment, earnings, job security, assets, credit rating, and the like. The lender will also order an *appraisal* of the subject property to make sure that it has not been overpriced (this would make it difficult for the lender to recover the remaining debt if the borrower defaulted on its payments and the property had to be sold at a foreclosure auction). If the lender's subsequent investigation suggests that the buyer is financially stable and will likely be able to repay the loan, then it will make a *loan commitment* to the buyer.

When it comes time to close the contract, the lender will pay the $80,000 directly to the seller (who will then be responsible for paying the broker's sales commission). To guarantee repayment of the loan, the borrower (the *mortgagor*) will provide two critical legal documents to the lender (the *mortgagee*): (1) a *promissory note*, which represents the buyer's *contractual* commitment to repay the loan, and (2) a *mortgage*, which gives the lender a *property* interest as security for the buyer's obligation to repay the debt. The lender's security interest is called a *lien*, which is an *encumbrance* upon the property that may render its title *unmarketable* to future purchasers until the entire loan is repaid (as considered below in section E.1). Promptly after closing, these two documents should be recorded in the public records.

In some cases as a mortgage alternative, the seller will provide financing—an arrangement known as an *installment land sale contract* (or *contract for deed*). This can be useful, for example, if the buyer does not qualify for a loan from an institutional lender. In this situation, upon execution of the agreement, the buyer acquires possession of the property and equitable title to the property. The buyer agrees to pay the purchase price and interest to the seller in periodic installments, usually monthly payments. The seller retains legal title until the buyer pays off the entire sum, and then the seller conveys a deed to the buyer. We will return to the installment land sale contract in section D.2's consideration of the foreclosure process. The following *A Place to Start* box provides additional information about mortgage documents. Use it as a reference as you read the cases that follow.

A Place to Start | **Mortgage Documents**

- **Loan commitment:** In the loan commitment, the lender agrees to make a loan according to specified terms:
  - **Amount:** The lender will specify the amount of the loan ($80,000 in our hypothetical).
  - **Interest rate:** In addition to paying back the loan amount (the *principal*), the borrower must also pay *interest*, which can be significant. For an $80,000 loan at 5% interest (to be repaid over 30 years), the borrower would pay more than $74,000 in interest (in addition to repaying the $80,000). Interest rates can be *fixed* over the life of the loan, or the buyer can have an *adjustable rate mortgage* (*ARM*) whose interest rate is periodically adjusted based a national credit market index.
  - **Repayment period:** Traditionally, the repayment period was 30 years—a rough approximation of one generation, and thought to be the length of time

a typical family might live in its home. Today, loans can be for much shorter periods of time (five years, for example), with a *balloon* (or large balance) due at the end of the period.

- **Repayment schedule:** This schedule determines how often and when payments are due (for example, the buyer must make monthly payments due on the first day of each month).

- **Promissory note:** This is the borrower's contractual commitment to repay the loan.

  - **Clarification of the loan commitment:** The note will provide additional detail, such as the amount of each payment and when it is due. For example, our hypothetical borrower of $80,000 at 5% for 30 years would owe 360 monthly payments of $429 each (which includes both interest and principal). The note might also contain a *prepayment clause* that allows early debt repayment in whole or in part without penalty. In times of falling interest rates, this would allow borrower's to refinance and pay off the existing high interest-rate mortgage without penalty.

  - **Scope of liability:** In some jurisdictions, a defaulting borrower is subject to personal liability if there is a deficiency after the mortgaged property has been sold at a foreclosure sale. In other jurisdictions, *anti-deficiency* legislation limits the lender's recovery to the proceeds from the foreclosure sale.

- **The mortgage:** The mortgage creates a *security interest* (known as a *lien*) in the subject property. If a borrower (the *mortgagor*) defaults on its loan payments, the lender (the *mortgagee*) can sell the property at a *foreclosure sale* to recover the outstanding debt.

  - **Title theory states—minority position:** In some states, the mortgage conveys legal title to the lender; legal title is held by the lender until the debt has been repaid in full. Under the harsh common law, even if the borrower faithfully repaid all but the last dollar of an $80,000 loan, the lender still held title and could take over the entire property upon the borrower's default (and retain all previous loan payments). Today, legislation moderates that result considerably.

  - **Lien theory states—majority position:** In other states, the lender holds only a *lien* against the property until the debt has been repaid, which gives the lender the right to foreclose if the borrower defaults.

  The distinction is of less significance today because states have passed protective legislation for borrowers. However, the distinction still retains some vitality in the context of concurrent ownership. *Recall* Chapter 5, in which we considered whether the conveyance of a mortgage interest by one joint tenant alone severed the other joint tenant's right of survivorship.

DIGGING DEEPER: What factors should the buyer consider when deciding whether to apply for a loan from a traditional lender or to approach the seller to negotiate an installment land sale contract? What are the potential benefits and risks to each party of such a contract?

Depending upon how they are structured, some loans place buyers at a greater risk of default than others, which in turn puts the buyers at risk of losing their properties through foreclosure. In Massachusetts, for example, the Attorney General brought a consumer protection enforcement action against a large commercial lender, claiming that it engaged in unfair and deceptive practices just before the Great Recession of 2007-2009 by originating certain *subprime* loans—those made to borrowers who generally would not qualify for traditional loans offered at prevailing interest rates. *Commonwealth v. Fremont Investment & Loan*, 897 N.E.2d 548 (Mass. 2008). The court identified a combination of four loan characteristics that made the loans practically "doomed to failure":

> (1) the loans were ARM [adjustable rate mortgage] loans with an introductory rate period of three years or less;[4] (2) they featured an introductory rate for the initial period that was at least three per cent below the fully indexed rate; (3) they were made to borrowers for whom the debt-to-income ratio would have exceeded fifty per cent had [the lender] measured the borrower's debt by the monthly payments that would be due at the fully indexed rate rather than under the introductory rate;[5] and (4) the loan-to-value ratio was one hundred per cent, or the loan featured a substantial prepayment penalty (defined . . . as greater than the [conventional prepayment penalty] . . . or a prepayment penalty that extended beyond the introductory rate period).[6]

The Massachusetts Supreme Court affirmed the trial court's preliminary injunction that restricted the lender's ability to foreclose on such "presumptively unfair" loans.

But should borrowers and lenders avoid loans with some or all of those characteristics in all cases? To the contrary, one commentator asserts that the conventional loan package eliminates *too* much risk from the borrower (at a cost that is passed on to the borrower), and that two characteristics of the traditional American mortgage "are highly expensive and suboptimal features for many consumers"—a long fixed-rate term and the ability to refinance (with no prepayment penalty). *See* Todd J. Zywicki, *The Behavioral Law and Economics of Fixed-Rate Mortgages (and Other Just-So Stories)*, 21 Supreme Court Economic Review 157 (2014). *See also* Andre K. Gray, *Caveat Emptor: Let the Borrower Beware of the Subprime Mortgage Market*, 11 U. Penn. J.

---

4. The loans "then adjusted every six months to a considerably higher variable rate for the remaining period of what was generally a thirty-year loan. Thus, borrowers' monthly mortgage payments would start out lower and then increase substantially after the introductory two-year or three-year period." *Id.* at 552.

5. The lender "generally required that borrowers have a debt-to-income ratio of less than or equal to fifty per cent—that is, that the borrowers' monthly debt obligations, including the applied-for mortgage, not exceed one-half their income." *Id.* at 552.

6. "As an additional feature to attract subprime borrowers, who typically had little or no savings, [the lender] offered loans with no down payment. Instead of a down payment, [the lender] would finance the full value of the property, resulting in a 'loan-to-value ratio' approaching one hundred per cent." *Id.* at 552.

L. & Soc. Change 195 (2007-2008) (arguing "[a]lthough the subprime mortgage market is risky and can potentially lead to abusive lending practices and harmful [effects] on consumers, subprime loans are not inherently abusive and can offer several benefits," and proposing solutions to help consumers make informed decisions when navigating the mortgage market).

In 2010, Congress established a new "Consumer Financial Protection Bureau," in part to prevent the kind of risky loans that helped to trigger to 2007 recession. Among other things, the Bureau enacted regulations that require mortgage servicers to counsel consumers before obtaining high-cost mortgages; to provide periodic notices of pending interest rate increases (as with ARMs); and to intervene early to assist delinquent borrowers. Is information disclosure a good solution to the problem of risky loans and their threat to the economy?

Proctor v. Holden

540 A.2d 133 (Md. App. 1988), *cert. denied*, 313 Md. 506 (1988)

Reading Guide

This case highlights the critical importance of the *financing contingency* in the contract of sale, and will also give you sense of how events unfold during the *executory phase* of the contract. As you read this case, consider what purpose the financing contingency serves from the perspective of both seller and buyer.

ALBERT, J.

This is an appeal by John P. and Deborah Proctor ... from a jury verdict entered in favor of Michael and Deborah Holden in the Circuit Court for Talbot County. Count I of appellees' Complaint alleged breach of contract by the Proctors for their failure to return the $20,000 deposit despite appellees' inability to obtain the financing provided for in the contract.[7] ...

April 1985, appellees Michael and Deborah Holden decided to relocate from Ocean City, Maryland to the Mid-Shore area. ... The Holdens contacted Charlotte Valliant, a real estate agent associated with appellant Freeman & Kagan,

---

7. [FN 2] A home purchaser may prefer an institutional loan over owner financing for several reasons. Among the more commonly stated reasons are: (1) A buyer may want to buy only if the judgment of a particular lender as to the property's value concurs with his own; (2) A buyer may want to borrow only from a lender whose practices in the event of default are known to be patient and reasonable; and (3) Lender's practices in permitting rapid pre-payment of loans vary widely, and a buyer might want to borrow only from a lender he knew would not seek to penalize pre-payment.

Inc., a real estate brokerage in Easton. For more than a month, Valliant showed the Holdens homes in the Talbot County area. . . .

On July 24, 1985, the Proctors signed a 24-hour listing agreement with Freeman & Kagan. Later that same day Michael and Deborah Holden visited the property where they met and spoke directly with Deborah Proctor for the first time. Asked about the possibility of owner-financing, Deborah Proctor responded that she would not hold any financing, and in addition she wanted settlement within 30 days. Michael Holden responded that even though he had already submitted a mortgage application to Magnet Mortgages 60 days was needed; after some discussion Proctor agreed.

Thereafter, Valliant prepared for the Holdens' signature a standard fill-in-the-blanks contract then in use by the Talbot County Board of Realtors. $210,000 was inserted in the blank for purchase price. In addition, a mortgage contingency clause was completed, which is set out in full *infra*. The contract also stated: "Time is of the essence of this agreement." The Holdens tendered a $20,000 deposit with their contract, to be held in an interest bearing account by the broker, Freeman & Kagan.

The Proctors accepted the contract on July 26, 1985. On approximately August 1, 1985, Delphine Amrhun of Magnet Mortgages telephoned Michael Holden to advise him that he would not qualify for a $150,000 30-year loan; moreover, she intimated that no lender employing standard . . . guidelines would qualify him for such a loan because of his high debt to earnings ratio. Amrhun later confirmed this in a letter to Holden dated August 8, 1985. Holden then submitted a mortgage application to Second National Building & Loan on August 9th, which similarly was rejected on August 12th. . . .

At the request of the realtors, Mr. Talbot Roe of United Mortgage contacted Holden. Mr. Roe stated that he could help the Holdens obtain a loan through a group of investors "who didn't care what the risk was." Holden testified that he was not interested in Roe's offer on the basis of his being told by two reputable banks that he could not afford the loan.

Holden notified Charlotte Valliant by letter of his inability to obtain financing and requested the return of his $20,000 deposit. In response, Tim Kagan of Freeman & Kagan, in a letter dated August 20, 1985, informed the Holdens that the Proctors had agreed to finance the purchase pursuant to the adjustable rate terms stated in the contract. . . . The Holdens rejected this offer of owner financing and again requested a refund of their deposit. The Proctors refused. Accordingly, Freeman & Kagan did not release the funds, and the Holdens filed suit against the Proctors to compel release of their deposit. . . .

The essence of appellants' argument is that the Holdens forfeited their right to the return of their deposit by not fulfilling their obligation under the financing clause. Specifically, appellants assert that appellees breached the contract (1) by not applying for a mortgage within five days of acceptance of the contract, and (2) by rejecting the Proctors' offer of owner financing. We disagree with both assertions.

The specific contract language underlying this dispute is paragraph 7, the "Financing Contingency," which reads:

> FINANCING CONTINGENCY—This contract is contingent upon the Buyer obtaining a Purchase Money Loan as follows:

> Amount borrowed at least *$150,000.00*. Interest rate not greater than *11%*. Period of amortization *30* years. Payments made on a *monthly* basis. Payoff of mortgage in *30* years. Required mortgage points paid by *buyer*. Adjustable rate mortgage starting at *10%* interest with a *4%* life cap. Buyer agrees to apply for said mortgage within five days of acceptance and to pay the normal closing costs in obtaining same. Buyer to receive mortgage commitment and approval on or before *Sept. 7, 1985*. Should Buyer be unable to obtain said mortgage and Buyer so notifies the Seller or his agent on said date this contract will be null and void of no force or effect, all deposits returned and all parties to this contract released of all liability hereunder.

Thus, the clause provides for both a fixed rate conventional mortgage and an adjustable rate mortgage. Appellants argue that the clause should be read in the disjunctive despite the omission of language to that effect. We see no error in the trial judge's determination that the financing contingency is ambiguous inasmuch as the terms are obviously inconsistent. Clearly the Holdens were not agreeing to obtain a mortgage with both a fixed rate and an adjustable rate. If read in the disjunctive, the terms of the mortgage are unclear: Does the language "Period of amortization *30* years. Payments made on a *monthly* basis. Payoff of mortgage in *30* years. Required mortgage points paid by *buyer*" sandwiched between the two types of mortgages apply to both, or only to the fixed rate mortgage? The court did not err in admitting extrinsic evidence to determine the parties' intent. . . . Thus, the next step, to determine whether the Holdens took bona fide, prompt and reasonable actions to procure financing, was a question properly presented to the jury.

Five Day Requirement

Next, appellant alleges that the "time is of the essence clause" superimposed upon the financing contingency compelled performance in the five day period following the contract's acceptance. According to appellants, the Holdens' mortgage application with Magnet Mortgages, originating before the Proctors accepted the contract, does not comply with the five-day requirement in the financing contingency. We disagree.

We have found no case precisely on point, but *Allview Acres v. Howard Investment Corp.*, 182 A.2d 793 (Md. 1962) is instructive. In *Allview Acres* the sale of a 104 acre parcel of land was contingent upon the seller's obtainment of a zoning reclassification. The issue before the Court of Appeals was whether the seller's application to the zoning board forty-two days *before* the contract was signed constituted compliance with the contract. Finding compliance, the court reasoned:

> We have found no case dealing with the question whether efforts, reasonable in themselves, were or were not a compliance with the contract when (absent any specific time stipulations in the contract) they were initiated before the contract was signed and were continued thereafter. In the circumstances of this case, we have no difficulty in concluding that the efforts were reasonable and did constitute a compliance with the contract. . . . Although the record does not show whether Manning, the original contract purchaser . . . knew that an application had previously been filed at the time he signed the contract, the time set for settlement and common business practice strongly suggest that the purchaser was aware that the application had been initiated and that the settlement date was set with that in mind. Moreover, the absence of a date specified before or after which an application was required to be made, persuasively suggests that the fact that the application was initiated prior to the date of the contract was to have no legal consequence in the transaction.
>
> Where, as here, the application was pending and had not been decided, it seems reasonably clear to us that such application was deemed to satisfy the requirement of the clause of the contract here in question. No possible advantage to either party and no greater prospect of success has been suggested—nor can we envision any—which might have been derived from filing the application after, instead of before, the execution of the contract.

Id. at 793.

The contingency at bar does contain a time limitation: "within five days of acceptance." The contract sets only an outside limit of five days for the buyer to make application. We do not construe this to mean that the application may not be initiated prior to acceptance of the contract. The purpose of the time limitation is to prevent a delay that jeopardizes the agreement. A buyer who delays in applying for a mortgage puts the settlement at risk. Setting an outside limit on the time for making a mortgage application protects the seller who is taking his house off the market. It also gives both parties peace of mind that the buyer is qualified and that settlement will take place on the stated date. . . . In the absence of specific language to the contrary, we cannot justify penalizing a buyer who acts responsibly by initiating the financing process in anticipation of making an offer to purchase property. . . . Indeed, Holden approached Magnet Mortgages three days after being told the Proctors had decided to sell. He testified, " . . . I initiated an application for a $150,000 loan. And my intention was to try to speed up the loan process in the event that we came to some kind of a deal on the house."

Moreover, the record indicates that Holden told Mrs. Proctor that he had applied for a loan at the time the two were negotiating a settlement date. . . . [W]e perceive no possible advantage to either party, and no greater chance of success had the Holdens filed their application after, instead of before, the execution of the contract. Indeed, after learning that their application had been rejected, the Holdens applied to Second National Building & Loan and were again rejected because of their debt/income ratio. Inasmuch as most banks follow the same guidelines, it was Holden's "understanding . . . that [he and his wife] would not qualify for any mortgage with any of those banks." The Holdens also followed up a lead from Ms. Valliant and contacted Miss Heath at Eastern Shore Mortgage. She too stated her bank would not approve the loan. . . .

[I]n the case at bar evidence was adduced in support of the Holdens' position that they did take "bona fide, reasonable and prompt action" to secure financing. Whether the Holdens complied with their contractual obligation to apply for a mortgage raised a jury question. The court did not err. *See Stevens v. Cliffs at Princeville Assoc.*, 684 P.2d 965, 971 (Hawaii 1984) (contract purchasers "are not obligated as a matter of law, to secure additional [lenders] in the event their bona fide loan applications are rejected for lack of sufficient income."). . . .

Sellers' Offer to Finance

On August 12th the Holdens sent Ms. Valliant a copy of their rejection letter from Magnet Mortgages. On the 13th, they did the same with their rejection from Second National and requested the return of their deposit. Thereafter, in a letter from Tim Kagan dated August 20th, the Holdens were informed that the Proctors were willing to finance the purchase. Kagan forwarded the Proctors' letter offering a $150,000 loan subject to the following terms:

> [W]e will provide a thirty (30) year (monthly payment of principal, interest, taxes and insurance) adjustable rate mortgage with an initial interest rate of 10%. The interest rate will be adjusted annually; any increase or decrease in the annual rate will not exceed two (2) percentage points. The rate will never be greater or less than four (4) percentage points above or below the initial (10%) rate. Three (3) points will be paid by purchasers at the time of settlement; and, the adjustable rate note will specify that it may not be assumed. . . .

The Holdens rejected this offer and the appellants now argue that this rejection breached the financing contingency. Appellants cite no law to support their contention that the appellees were required, as a matter of law, to accept owner financing. Instead, appellants argue again only that the contract was unambiguous and, therefore, the court erred in admitting appellees' evidence that the parties did not contemplate owner financing at the time of contract. Inasmuch as we have already held that the financing clause was ambiguous, this argument has no merit.

While there is no mention of owner financing in the contract, that fact alone is not decisive. There may be cases where owner financing, while not mentioned in the contract, may have been contemplated and indeed may be required. Under the facts of this case, we agree with the appellees that appellants were attempting "to force on him financing of the type that he did not desire or originally contemplate." *Tieri v. Orbell*, 162 A.2d 248, 250 (Penn. 1960). . . .

Notes

1. *The importance of the contingency clause:* Why would sellers and buyers, respectively, want the contract to include a financing contingency clause? Suppose the buyers had sufficient assets to purchase the Proctors' home without obtaining a loan. Would they still derive a benefit from a contingency clause? <u>Hint:</u> What types of information does the loan application process yield? Think of at least two types.

2. *Non-institutional lenders—sellers and investors:*   Why did the Holdens fail to qualify for a loan, and why would the Proctors be willing to finance the sale of the home, even after the Holdens failed to qualify for bank loans? Likewise, what would motivate the group of investors who "didn't care what the risk was"? Is it likely that the Proctors or the investors would give the Holdens the right to *prepay* the loan—that is, to exceed the required monthly installments to pay off the loan more quickly, or to refinance the loan with another lender (who would then pay off the first lender in full before the expiration of the original loan period)?

3. *Practice pointer:*   Suppose that you represent the Proctors. Redraft the mortgage contingency in a way that would protect their interests and avoid litigation. Then, suppose instead that you represent the Holdens, and redraft the mortgage contingency consistent with their interests. Be sure to anticipate the following possible events: (a) The buyers fail to qualify for a loan from a bank or conventional lender, but investor or seller financing is available; (b) The buyers qualify for an adjustable rate mortgage, but not for a conventional, self-amortizing loan.

2. Foreclosure

Recall our hypothetical buyer from section D.1 who obtained a loan for $80,000 to purchase a property priced at $100,000. Assume that the borrower promptly made the monthly mortgage payments until the loan balance had been paid down to $60,000. Then, the borrower became unemployed, ran into financial difficulty, and stopped making the monthly payments. What happens next?

The lender will provide written notice of the borrower's *default* and specify a time period during which the borrower can exercise its *equity of redemption* to avoid foreclosure. At this point, ideally, the lender would be willing to negotiate a loan *workout* to avoid foreclosure. If the parties fail to negotiate a workout, then the lender will initiate proceedings in accordance with state law to *foreclose* the borrower's equity of redemption—that is, to conduct a foreclosure auction to sell the property and to use the proceeds to pay off the remaining debt owed the lender. Two types of foreclosure sale are possible, depending upon state law and the terms of the mortgage documents: *judicial foreclosure* and *nonjudicial foreclosure* (also known as *power of sale foreclosure*). *See* Anna Kalinina, *A Grossly Inadequate Procedure: Non-Judicial Foreclosure in Texas*, 65 Baylor L. Rev. 1061 (2013) (listing judicial versus non-judicial permitted and required processes by state). Notably, both are a departure from the common law's *strict foreclosure*. The common law lender held legal title to the property until the loan was fully repaid (a concept that lingers today in *title theory* states). Therefore, upon the borrower's default, the lender simply took over the property without resort to an auction sale, and also retained all of the past loan payments.

From the auction purchaser's perspective, foreclosure property presents several risks. The successful bidder at the auction receives a bare deed that contains no warranties about the validity of the title to the property (this is similar to a *quitclaim* deed, which we will consider in section E). In addition, some states provide for a *statutory right of redemption* period during which the borrower can reacquire title to the property from the successful bidder at the auction. (Do not confuse this statutory right of redemption with the similarly-named "equity of redemption" discussed above.)

A Place to Start | **The Foreclosure Process**

Upon a borrower's *default*, the lender can initiate foreclosure proceedings in accordance with state law and the terms of the loan documents:

- **Equity of redemption:** During this period, the borrower can avoid foreclosure by paying off some or all of the remaining debt:
  - **Acceleration of debt:** In some cases, the borrower can redeem the property simply by bringing the overdue payments up to date. Routinely, however, the mortgage documents contain a clause that allows the lender to *accelerate the debt*, which means that the lender will demand payment of the entire loan balance, not just the overdue monthly payments. In our example, the borrower would be required to pay the entire $60,000 balance to avoid foreclosure.
  - **Loan workout:** Some lenders will be willing to waive the existing default and/ or to restructure the loan to reduce the amount the borrower owes each month (which would mean extending the life of the loan).

- **Foreclosure:**
  - **Common law strict foreclosure:** If the borrower did not pay off the full balance within a time permitted by courts of equity, then the borrower was forever barred from redeeming the property. Strict foreclosure is generally not permitted today.
  - **Judicial foreclosure:** Today, all states permit, and many states require, judicial foreclosures, which are lawsuits initiated by the lender that result in judicially supervised auctions. Judicial sales are time-consuming and expensive, but they are less likely to be challenged or invalidated after the fact.

■ *Nonjudicial (power of sale)* **foreclosure:** More than half the states permit nonjudicial foreclosures. If the mortgage documents include a *power of sale* provision, then the lender is authorized to conduct a sale without judicial supervision, provided it follows required statutory procedures and timelines (some states require that a trustee, rather than the lender, conduct the sale under a *deed of trust*).

■ *After the foreclosure sale:*

  ■ *Distributing the proceeds:* If the auction price exceeds the unpaid debt (and assuming there are no other lienholders), then the excess goes to the borrower. If the auction price is less than the loan balance, then the lender might seek an *antideficiency judgment*, if permitted by state law, to pay off the debt from the borrower's other assets. Some states limit such awards, however, particularly after nonjudicial foreclosures (because they were not subject to judicial oversight) or if the mortgaged property is the borrower's principal residence.

  ■ *Setting aside the foreclosure sale:* Courts will sometimes set aside the foreclosure sale, particularly if it did not comply with required statutory procedures. Other than that, in most jurisdictions, the borrower-mortgagor bears the difficult burden of showing that the sales price was so inadequate as to shock the court's conscience.

  ■ *Statutory right of redemption:* About half of the states prescribe a period of time following the foreclosure sale during which the borrower can reclaim title to the property from the successful auction bidder, typically by paying the purchase price, costs, and interests.

DIGGING DEEPER: Why would lenders be willing to negotiate *loan workouts?* If you represented a bank, would you recommend that it do so with defaulting borrowers? Further, what are the relative advantages and disadvantages of each type of foreclosure proceeding—*judicial* and *nonjudicial?* Why would a borrower (or lender) prefer one over the other, and how can those preferences be expressed in the mortgage documents?

Test Your Understanding

To understand the outcome of foreclosure sales, it is helpful to understand two basic premises: First, an owner's *equity* in real property equals the difference between the current market value of the property and the principal balance of all outstanding debt. As such, whether a borrower recovers equity (and if so, how much) after the foreclosure sale is highly dependent on the auction sales price. Second, foreclosing lenders have little interest in the mortgaged property beyond selling it at a price sufficient to recover the remainder of the debt owed. If the lender can acquire the property for an amount equal to (or less than) the loan balance, then the lender can walk away from the auction with title to the property and will not be required to come up with any additional money to complete the purchase. For this and other reasons, it is quite common for the lender to be the *only* bidder at a foreclosure sale and to bid no more than the amount of the remaining debt.

Recall the hypothetical situation described at the beginning of this subsection, under which the purchaser of a $100,000 property borrowed $80,000, and later defaulted on mortgage payments at a time when the loan balance had been paid down to $60,000. How much would the lender and the borrower, respectively, recover if the property sold at auction for (1) $30,000, (2) $60,000, or (3) $90,000? If you were the lender's attorney, how much would you counsel it to bid at the auction?

Greater Southwest Office Park, Ltd. v. Texas Commerce Bank Nat'l Assoc.

786 S.W.2d 386 (Tex. App. 1990), *superseded by statute*

Reading Guide

The following case will give you a sense of the mechanics of the foreclosure sale. As you read it, consider whether the foreclosure sale was fair in terms of both result and procedure. In addition, think about whether the court should be sympathetic to the defaulting borrower's plight. If so, on what basis?

WARREN, J.

Greater Southwest Office Park, Ltd. ("Greater Southwest") appeals from the trial court's order granting summary judgment to Texas Commerce Bank National Association ("the Bank"), and dismissing Greater Southwest's cause of action with prejudice.

Greater Southwest was the maker of a promissory note, in the original principal amount of $5,000,000, payable to the Bank. The note was secured by a deed of trust and security agreement, executed by Greater Southwest for the benefit of the Bank. In November of 1987, the Bank declared a default and posted the real property, which was the subject of the deed of trust, for foreclosure. On December 1, 1987, the Bank purchased the land at a public foreclosure sale for the sum of $4,847,903.96, which was the amount of the outstanding debt plus the costs of the sale. The Bank did not sue Greater Southwest for a deficiency balance; therefore, the holdings made in this opinion are not intended to express our opinion in cases involving a deficiency suit when the debtor is claiming that the lender grossly underbid on the foreclosed realty.

On May 16, 1988, Greater Southwest filed its original petition claiming that: (1) the fair market value of the real property foreclosed on by the Bank was $10,529,000; (2) the Bank bid an unconscionably low price for the property at the foreclosure sale; (3) Greater Southwest and the Bank were in a "trust arrangement," giving rise to a duty to make an honest effort to secure a fair price for the collateral at the foreclosure sale; and (4) this conduct constituted constructive fraud, actual fraud, and an intentional tort. Greater Southwest prayed for compensatory damages in the amount of $5,682,000, and exemplary damages in the amount of not less than $10,000,000.

. . . On October 5, 1988, Greater Southwest filed its first amended original petition, which reiterated the same complaints made in its original petition, added its complaint that the Bank engaged in a policy of not compensating debtors for the fair market value of foreclosed properties, and alleged that the Bank breached its duty of good faith and fair dealing.

The Bank filed a motion for summary judgment, claiming that it was entitled to summary judgment as a matter of law, on the ground that Greater Southwest had failed to state a cognizable cause of action. The court granted the Bank's motion for summary judgment, dismissing Greater Southwest's entire cause of action with prejudice, on December 2, 1988. . . .

Greater Southwest's entire cause of action rests on the premise that the Bank is liable to it in damages because it purchased the collateral at a foreclosure sale at a price that was less than fair or reasonable. Greater Southwest does not contend that the sale was irregular in any respect, nor does it seek to set aside the sale.

In the absence of irregularity that caused or contributed to the property being sold for a grossly inadequate price, mere inadequacy of consideration is not grounds for setting aside a trustee's sale. *American Sav. & Loan Ass'n v. Musick,* 531 S.W.2d 581, 587 (Tex.1975). . . .

Greater Southwest contends that the above rule does not apply to our case because it is suing, not to invalidate the sale, but for damages. To support this contention it relies on *Lee v. Sabine Bank,* 708 S.W.2d 582 (Tex. App.—Beaumont 1986, writ ref'd n.r.e.), and other cases involving the allowance of set-offs in suits for deficiencies, where it was alleged that the price bid by the lender was inadequate. In *Lee v. Sabine Bank,* Sabine Bank advanced Lee $500,000 to purchase a boat and for working capital; the bank retained a lien on the boat as security. With a balance of $404,000 still owing on the note, Lee defaulted. Sabine Bank purchased the boat at a judicial sale for $175,000, after crediting other pledged security and adding the expenses of sale and interest, leaving Lee with a balance of $226,064 owing under the terms of the note. Lee sued, seeking to prevent Sabine Bank from taking the other security pledged; Sabine Bank counterclaimed for the deficiency owed under the note. The trial court denied Lee's requested relief and awarded Sabine Bank judgment for its deficiency of $240,854. Lee claimed that the trial court erred by allowing him credit on the deficiency for the sales price bid by Sabine Bank, rather than the fair market value at the time of sale.

The court stated that "a lender who has secured collateral, whether personalty or realty is under a trust arrangement with the borrower, in the event of foreclosure, to make an honest effort to reduce the loan as much as possible by securing a fair price for the collateral." *Lee v. Sabine Bank,* 708 S.W.2d at 584. "[W]here there is a probable significant disparity between the sale price of the property and its fair market value, the borrower may contest the sale and present evidence contesting such." *Id.* at 585. It limited the rule to those cases where the lender or its surrogate was the purchaser at foreclosure. The court, however, affirmed the trial court because no evidence had been presented as to the market value of the ship at the time of the judicial sale.

First, we note that, because the *Sabine Bank* case did not concern realty, any comments by the court concerning the foreclosure of realty collateral is dicta. Second, we note that in our case, like *Sabine Bank,* no evidence was presented as to the fair market value of the collateral at the time of the foreclosure sale. . . .

Greater Southwest also relies on *Olney Sav. & Loan Ass'n v. Farmers Market of Odessa, Inc.,* 764 S.W.2d 869 (Tex. App.—El Paso 1989, writ pending), in its effort to extend the lender's liability. . . . The *Olney* opinion cited *Lee v. Sabine Bank* for the proposition that, since the bank was under a trust arrangement with the borrower, it must, in the event of a foreclosure, make an honest effort to reduce the loan as much as possible by securing a fair price for the collateral. . . . This rule was repudiated by Chief Justice Osborn in his concurring opinion and, possibly, by Judge Woodard in a concurrence without opinion. We are of the opinion that Chief Justice Osborn's concurrence correctly states the Texas rule regarding the lender's rights and duties under a foreclosure sale. We also agree with Judge Osborn's opinion that the rules are the same whether the lender or a third party is the successful bidder at a foreclosure sale. *Id.* at 873. . . .

We hold that: (1) in the absence of evidence of irregularity in the sale, causing the property to be sold for a grossly inadequate price, mere inadequacy of consideration is not grounds for setting aside a trustee's sale; (2) the rule applies whether the lender, its surrogate, or a third party is the buyer at the trustee's sale; and (3) the rule applies whether the borrower is seeking to set aside the trustee's sale or is suing for damages.

Because there was no irregularity alleged or shown in the trustee's sale, Greater Southwest's amended pleadings stated no cause of action against the Bank. Therefore, the trial court correctly dismissed the action. . . .

In Texas, a special relationship does not normally exist between a borrower and a lender, and when one has been found, it has rested on extraneous facts and conduct, such as excessive lender control over, or influence in, the borrower's business activities. [The borrower's] . . . mere subjective trust in the Bank, by itself, is not enough to transform the arms-length dealings of a debtor and creditor into a fiduciary relationship.

Each of appellant's points of error is overruled, and the judgment is affirmed.

Notes

1. *The adequacy of the sales price:* What was the auction sales price? How did it compare to the property's fair market value? How did it compare to the loan balance? Was the price adequate according to the court, and what rule did it follow? Do you agree with the court's conclusion?

2. *Adequacy of the proceedings:*   The court considered whether the sale involved any procedural irregularities—what might those include? Were any irregularities present here, and did they affect the outcome of the case?

3. *Remedies:*   What remedy did Greater Southwest seek? Two types are possible: First, the borrower can sue to invalidate the sale. If successful, the lender is free to conduct another sale. Second, the borrower can seek to recover damages for an inadequate sale. Why might a borrower seek one type of remedy rather than the other?

4. *Default under installment land sale contracts:*   Instead of conveying a mortgage to an institutional lender, suppose the buyer enters into an install-ment land sale contract for financing by the seller. What happens if the buyer is unable to make all required payments? In theory, perhaps, the seller should undertake the same steps as an institutional mortgagee to foreclose on the property, including all required safeguards to protect the interest of the buyer. In practice, however, the agreement may contain a *forfeiture* clause that, upon the buyer's default, calls for *liquidated damages* in the amount of the payments already received. A typical clause might provide: "Time is of the essence. Therefore, if the buyer fails to promptly and fully perform its obliga-tions, the seller, upon reasonable notice, may cancel the contract, repossess the property, and retain all payments and improvements made to date." As a buyer's attorney, would you advise your client to execute such an agreement? How, if at all, does the forfeiture provision resemble common law strict fore-closure, or a lease arrangement?

5. *A changing world—relief for defaulting borrowers:*   *Greater Southwest Office Park* represents a harsh (from the borrower's perspective)—and typical—approach to challenges to foreclosure sales. Still, other jurisdictions may provide more sympathetic treatment to borrowers. *Compare Murphy v. Financial Development Corp.*, 495 A.2d 1245 (N.H. 1985) (awarding damages to borrower where lender had reason to know that it could make a substantial profit on a quick turnaround sale, and holding that "[a] mortgagee . . . must exert every reasonable effort to obtain a fair and reasonable price under the circumstances").

Beyond sympathetic treatment by some courts, statutory reforms have sof-tened some of the harsher aspects of foreclosure, as present in *Greater South-west.* After the case, Texas amended its property code to include the following provision:

> (a) If the price at which real property is sold at a foreclosure sale under Section 51.002 [involving nonjudicial deed of trust foreclosures] is less than the unpaid balance of the indebtedness secured by the real property, resulting in a defi-ciency, any action brought to recover the deficiency must be brought within two years of the foreclosure sale and is governed by this section.

> (b) Any person against whom such a recovery is sought by motion may request that the court in which the action is pending determine the fair market value of

the real property as of the date of the foreclosure sale. . . . Competent evidence of value may include, but is not limited to, the following: (1) expert opinion testimony; (2) comparable sales; (3) anticipated marketing time and holding costs; (4) cost of sale; and (5) the necessity and amount of any discount to be applied to the future sales price or the cashflow generated by the property to arrive at a current fair market value.

(c) If the court determines that the fair market value is greater than the sale price of the real property at the foreclosure sale, the persons against whom recovery of the deficiency is sought are entitled to an offset against the deficiency in the amount by which the fair market value, less the amount of any claim, indebtedness, or obligation of any kind that is secured by a lien or encumbrance on the real property that was not extinguished by the foreclosure, exceeds the sale price. . . .

Tex. Property Code § 51.003 (enacted 1991).

Likewise, federal law provides relief in some cases. The Dodd-Frank Wall Street Reform and Consumer Protection Act of 2010 (*Dodd-Frank*) amended several federal consumer protection statutes affecting mortgages, and also created a new Consumer Financial Protection Bureau. Importantly, the federal law (with some exceptions) prohibits lenders from making residential mortgage loans unless the lender, "makes a reasonable and good faith determination, based on verified and documented information that, at the time the loan is consummated, the consumer has a reasonable ability to repay the loan, according to its terms. . . ." Truth in Lending Act, 15 U.S.C. §§ 1639c. If the lender subsequently conducts a nonjudicial foreclosure sale, the borrower can assert as a defense the lender's violation of the statutory provision. How, if at all, would the Texas and federal statutory provisions require a different outcome in *Greater Southwest Office Park* today?

E. TITLE SECURITY

It is critically important that buyers receive good title to their property—often described as *marketable title*. But how can the law assure buyers that there are no competing claims to the same property, and that the seller in fact has good title to convey? The scope of the challenge is immense, and the law has developed three principal mechanisms to address it. First, buyers (through their agents or attorneys) can conduct a *title examination* of the public records to assure themselves that the seller has good title to the property. Today, it is probably rare for buyers to go through this effort. Further, although the recording system followed in most jurisdictions is highly effective, it is not perfect. We will study the recording system in detail in the next chapter. Second, buyers contract for certain assurances from the seller. Ideally, the contract of sale will promise to convey marketable title through a *general warranty deed* that contains various seller *warranties* of title. Thus, even if the buyer's title search failed to uncover a problem (or if the buyer did not conduct a search), the seller can provide relief through an action to enforce the deed warranties. But, what if the seller can no longer be found or has insufficient assets to compensate the buyer? As a final method to assure good title, buyers routinely obtain *title insurance* issued by a commercial insurer, usually at the seller's expense. Today, this is the predominant method of providing title security. The insurance company will examine the public records for defects of title, and will compensate the buyer if title defects later surface (subject to specified exclusions from coverage). Although insurance provides a critical backup for the other two forms of title assurance, it also has various limitations.

We will study deed warranties and title insurance in the following materials (reserving the recording system for the next chapter). As you read on, notice that warranties and insurance are mechanisms to *allocate risk* in the face of *imperfect information*. Do they do a good job of instilling confidence in our real estate transaction system and assuring prospective buyers that they can be secure in the title to their new property? In addition, recall our study of adverse possession. What does that doctrine add to a buyer's security, if anything?

1. The Contract—The Promise of Marketable Title

Virtually all jurisdictions imply a seller's duty to provide *marketable* title (also called "good and marketable title" or "merchantable title"), unless the parties otherwise agree in the contract of sale. But what does that mean? In the modern world, it is unrealistic for buyers to expect perfect title free of any competing claims or restrictions whatsoever—including such ubiquitous things as zoning restrictions and utility rights-of-way. On the other hand, buyers should not be forced to take title that is less than they bargained for. The next case attempts to reconcile these competing concerns.

Lohmeyer v. Bower
———————————
227 P.2d 102 (Kan. 1951)

Reading Guide

- In *Stambovsky v. Ackley*, the court considered whether certain undisclosed *physical defects* in property gave buyers the right to rescind the contract before closing. Here, the court looks at a related issue: the types of *title defects* that give buyers the right to rescind.

- *Preview—restrictive covenants:* The court refers to "dedication restrictions," which are a type of *restrictive covenant*, a topic covered in Chapter 10. For now, you should know that such restrictions constitute a nonpossessory property right.

Parker, J.

This action originated in the district court of Lyon county when plaintiff filed a petition seeking to rescind a contract in which he had agreed to purchase certain real estate on the ground title tendered by the defendants was unmerchantable. The defendants Bower and Bower, husband and wife, answered contesting plaintiff's right to rescind and by cross-petition asked specific performance of the contract. . . . The case was tried upon the pleadings and stipulated facts by the trial court which rendered judgment for the defendants generally and decreed specific performance of the contract. The plaintiff appeals from that judgment. . . .

Plaintiff's petition alleges execution of the contract whereby he agreed to purchase Lot 37 in Berkley Hills Addition in the city of Emporia. . . . [A]fter execution of the agreement it came to his attention that the house on the real estate therein described had been placed there in violation of Section 5-224 of the Ordinances of the city of Emporia in that the house was located within approximately 18 inches of the north line of such lot in violation of the ordinance providing that no frame building should be erected within 3 feet of a side or rear lot line. It further avers that after execution of the agreement it came to plaintiff's knowledge the dedication of the Berkley Hills Addition requires that only a two story house should be erected on the lot described in the contract whereas the house located thereon is a one story house. It then states the violations of the city ordinance and the dedication restrictions were unknown to the plaintiff when he entered into the contract and that he would not have entered into such agreement if he had known thereof. It next alleges that after becoming aware of such violations plaintiff notified the defendants in writing thereof, demanded that he be released from his contract and that defendants refused such demand. Finally it charges that such violations made the title unmerchantable and asks that the agreement be cancelled and set aside and that all moneys paid by plaintiff under its terms be refunded.

[The answer of defendants Bower and Bower] . . . alleges performance of the contract, that plaintiff is in the possession of the property but has refused to pay the balance due on the purchase price, and that they are entitled to judgment for specific performance of the contract with directions to defendant Newcomer to pay them all sums paid him by plaintiff as escrow agent under its terms. . . .

Pertinent provisions of the contract, entered into between the parties, essential to disposition of the issues raised by the pleadings, read:

> . . . [T]he first party hereby agrees to sell unto the second party [the] following described real estate, . . . and to convey the . . . real estate to the second party by Warranty Deed with an abstract of title, certified to date showing good merchantable title or an Owners Policy of Title Insurance in the amount of the sale price, guaranteeing said title to party of the second part, free and clear of all encumbrances except special taxes subject, however, to all restrictions and easements of record applying to this property, it being understood that the first party shall have sufficient time to bring said abstract to date or obtain Report for Title Insurance and to correct any imperfections in the title if there be such imperfections. . . .

[The parties stipulated that] "defendants offered to purchase and convey to plaintiff two feet along the entire north side of the lot in controversy without charge and plaintiff refused such offer." . . .

. . . [I]t becomes apparent the all decisive issue presented by the pleadings and the stipulation is whether such property is subject to encumbrances or other burdens making the title unmerchantable and if so whether they are such as are excepted by the provision of the contract which reads "subject however, to all restrictions and easements of record applying to this property."

Decision of the foregoing issue can be simplified by directing attention early to the appellant's position. Conceding he purchased the property, subject to all restrictions of record he makes no complaint of the restrictions contained in the declaration forming a part of the dedication of Berkley Hills Addition nor of the ordinance restricting the building location on the lot but bases his right to rescission of the contract solely upon presently existing violations thereof. This, we may add, limited to restrictions imposed by terms of the ordinance, relating to the use of land or the location and character of buildings that may be located thereon, even in the absence of provisions in the contract excepting them, must necessarily be his position for we are convinced, although it must be conceded there are some decisions to the contrary, the rule supported by the better reasoned decisions, indeed if not by the great weight of authority, is that municipal restrictions of such character, existing at the time of the execution of a contract for the sale of real estate, are not such encumbrances or burdens on title as may be availed of by a vendee to avoid his agreement to purchase on the ground they render his title unmerchantable. . . .

On the other hand there can be no question the rule respecting restrictions upon the use of land or the location and type of buildings that may be erected thereon fixed by covenants or other private restrictive agreements, including those contained in the declaration forming a part of the dedication of Berkley Hills Addition, is directly contrary to the one to which we have just referred. Such restrictions, under all the authorities, constitute encumbrances rendering the title to land unmerchantable. . . .

In the instant case assuming the mere existence of the restrictions imposed by the provisions of section 5-224 of the ordinances of the city of Emporia do not constitute an encumbrance or burden and that the dedication restrictions fall within the exception clause of the contract providing Lot 37 was to be conveyed subject to all restrictions and easements of record applying thereto there still remains the question whether, under the stipulated facts, the restrictions imposed by such ordinance and/or the dedication declaration have been violated and if so whether those violations make the title to such property unmerchantable. . . .

There can be no doubt regarding what constitutes a marketable or merchantable title in this jurisdiction. This court has been called on to pass upon that question on numerous occasions. See our recent decision in *Peatling v. Baird*, 213 P.2d 1015, 1016 (Kan.), and cases there cited, wherein we held:

> A marketable title to real estate is one which is free from reasonable doubt, and a title is doubtful and unmarketable if it exposes the party holding it to the hazard of litigation.

To render the title to real estate unmarketable, the defect of which the purchaser complains must be of a substantial character and one from which he may suffer injury. Mere immaterial defects which do not diminish in quantity, quality or value the property contracted for, constitute no ground upon which the purchaser may reject the title. Facts must be known at the time which fairly raise a reasonable doubt as to the title; a mere possibility or conjecture that such a state of facts may be developed at some future time is not sufficient. . . .

Under the rule just stated, and in the face of facts such as are here involved, we have little difficulty in concluding that the violation of section 5-224 of the ordinances of the city of Emporia as well as the violation of the restrictions imposed by the dedication declaration so encumber the title to Lot 37 as to expose the party holding it to the hazard of litigation and make such title doubtful and unmarketable. It follows, since, as we have indicated, the appellees had contracted to convey such real estate to appellant by warranty deed with an abstract of title showing good merchantable title, free and clear of all encumbrances, that they cannot convey the title contracted for and that the trial court should have rendered judgment rescinding the contract. This, we may add is so, notwithstanding the contract provides the conveyance was to be made subject to all restrictions and easements of record, for, as we have seen, it is the violation of the restrictions imposed by both the ordinance and the dedication declaration, not the existence of those restrictions, that renders the title unmarketable. . . .[8]

. . . The authorities so hold, on the rationale, to which we subscribe, that to force a vendee to accept property which in its present state violates a building restriction without a showing that the restriction is unenforcible, would in effect compel the vendee to buy a lawsuit. . . .

Finally appellees point to the contract which, it must be conceded, provides they shall have time to correct imperfections in the title and contend that even if it be held the restrictions and the ordinance have been violated they are entitled to time in which to correct those imperfections. Assuming, without deciding, they might remedy the violation of the ordinance by buying additional ground the short and simple answer to their contention with respect to the violation of the restrictions imposed by the dedication declaration is that any changes in the house would compel the purchaser to take something that he did not contract to buy.

Conclusions heretofore announced require reversal of the judgment with directions to the trial court to cancel and set aside the contract and render such judgment as may be equitable and proper under the issues raised by the pleadings. . . .

---

8. [Is this an accurate statement of the law? Can you re-write this sentence so that it is consistent with the rest of the court's opinion?—Eds.]

Notes

1. *Encumbrances and marketability:*   What does *marketable title* mean under judicial precedent in Kansas? The Bowers' property was encumbered by two restrictions. How did the court's analysis differentiate, if at all, between each restriction's impact on marketability? What did the *violation* of each restriction add to the court's analysis of the property's marketability?

Jurisdictions do not agree on the definition of "marketability." There is widespread agreement that the mere existence of public restrictions (such as the zoning ordinance in *Lohmeyer*) does not destroy marketability. But beyond that, jurisdictions disagree as to such things as the impact of zoning *violations*, and whether various restrictions go to the quality of *title*, or whether they relate instead to the physical condition of the property. For example, *Lohmeyer* found that the property's location 18 inches too close to the lot line constituted a title defect, but other jurisdictions might find the defect to have no impact on title. *See generally* William B. Stoebuck & Dale A. Whitman, *The Law of Property* § 10.12 (3d ed. 2000).

2. *Marketability and adverse possession:*   Suppose the sellers held no deed to the property, but could make a good argument that they had acquired title by adverse possession. Could the buyer be forced to accept such title as "marketable"? Surprisingly, the answer may be "yes." Many jurisdictions recognize adverse possession as "marketable title," although it does not constitute "marketable *record* title" until the owners' title has been adjudicated by a court (as in a quiet title action) and relevant documentation (such as the court's decree) filed in the county records. *See Conklin v. Davi*, 388 A.2d 598 (N.J. 1978) (recognizing title by adverse possession as marketable). *Compare Tri-State Hotel Co. v. Sphinx Investment Co.*, 510 P.2d 1223 (Kan. 1973) (declining to recognize title by adverse possession as marketable).

3. *Practice pointer—waiving marketability:*   Plaintiff Lohmeyer waived his right to object to "all restrictions and easements of record." But how could he know at the time he signed the contract whether any of those recorded restrictions would be unacceptable to him? Consider the following alternative formulation of the relevant contractual language:

> Title to be conveyed shall be marketable and insurable, at regular rates, by any reputable title insurance company licensed to do business in the state, subject only to the encumbrances hereinabove set forth.

See Conklin v. Davi, 388 A.2d 598 (N.J. 1978). Would that version be preferable to Lohmeyer? Is it likely the Bowers would have agreed to such a provision? How does that provision shift the burden of information gathering between buyer and seller?

4. *Practice pointer—title security:*   Suppose you represented the buyer in *Lohmeyer v. Bower.* Would you have advised him to execute the contract as reprinted in the case? What changes would you recommend to better protect your client's interests? Try to make at least four recommendations.

2. The Deed—Title Warranties

The executory period ends at the closing, when the parties exchange important documents. Most notably, upon receipt of the purchase price from the buyer (or the buyer's lender), the seller conveys a deed to the buyer. There are three primary types of deeds.

- *General warranty deed:*   The general warranty deed offers the maximum amount of protection to the buyer. In it, the grantor warrants ("covenants") against all defects in title, whether or not they arose during the grantor's period of ownership. That is, the grantor's warranties extend throughout the entire period of the chain of title, up until the moment of deed delivery. The general warranty deed contains five or six warranties, as discussed below.
- *Special warranty deed:*   The special warranty deed is less favorable to buyers, and warrants only that from the moment the grantor acquired title, she did nothing to encumber the title or otherwise create a title defect.
- *Quitclaim deed:*   The quitclaim deed contains no warranties of title, but simply conveys to the buyer whatever title the seller holds.

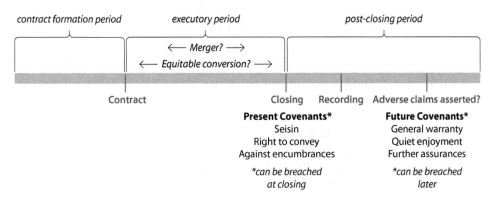

Figure 2

The deed contains important title warranties in the form of present and future *covenants of title.* As Figure 2 indicates, the *present covenants* are breached, if at all, at the moment the deed is delivered. The usual remedy for breach of a present covenant is the payment of damages, generally limited to the grantee's purchase price (and interest).

- *Covenant of seisin:*   This covenant warrants that the grantor is "seized" (holds both title and possession) of the estate the deed purports to convey in both quality (a fee simple absolute, for example) and quantity (100 acres, for example).

- *Covenant of the right to convey:*   This covenant is a promise that the grantor has the legal right to convey the estate described in the deed. For example, a grantor might hold equitable title as the beneficiary of a trust, but lack the right to transfer ownership (which authority is enjoyed by the trustee as the legal owner).

- *Covenant against encumbrances:*   Although not subject to a uniform definition in all jurisdictions, an *encumbrance* can be described as "any right to an interest in land which may subsist in third persons, to the diminution of the value of the land, not inconsistent with the passing of title." *Proffit v. Isley*, 683 S.W.2d 243 (Ark. Ct. App. 1979). Encumbrances include mortgages, leaseholds, easements, and other such interests. Most jurisdictions would find that an existing encumbrance breaches the covenant, *even if* the grantee actually knew of its existence at the time the deed was delivered. As an implied exception, however, some jurisdictions will preclude the grantee's recovery for the existence of encumbrances that are open and visible to the grantee.

The *future covenants*, as their name implies and as indicated on Figure 2, can be breached at some future point after the grantor has delivered the deed. The statute of limitations begins to run upon breach.

- *Covenant of quiet enjoyment:*   This is a promise that the grantee will not be disturbed in her quiet possession of the premises by one who is lawfully entitled to them. It is breached by an actual or constructive eviction from some or all of the property by one with superior title or by one claiming under the grantor. As with the present covenants, the grantee's remedy is generally an award of damages up to the amount of the purchase price (plus interest).

- *Covenant of general warranty:*   In most jurisdictions, this covenant is similar (if not identical) to the covenant of quiet enjoyment. It warrants that the grantor will defend against claims asserted by one with superior title or by one claiming under the grantor. The grantor is generally required to pay damages if the grantee suffers an actual or constructive eviction.

- *Covenant of further assurances:*   This covenant warrants that the grantor will provide whatever further assurances are necessary to perfect the grantee's title—such as executing additional documents. Unlike the above five covenants, which call for a damages remedy, specific performance is available if the grantor refuses to take additional action as warranted.

Review the following example of a general warranty deed. Note that it contains all six deed warranties.

General Warranty Deed

For valuable consideration, _____ ("Grantor")
(insert name and marital status of each Grantor)

hereby conveys and warrants to _____ ("Grantee"),
(insert name and marital status of each Grantee)

real property in _____ County, State, legally described as follows:

The Grantor, on behalf of himself, his heirs, and assigns ("the Grantor"), covenants to the Grantee, her heirs and assigns ("the Grantee") (1) that at the time of the making and delivery of the deed, the Grantor was lawfully seized of an indefeasible estate in fee simple in the premises, (2) that the Grantor has good right and full power to convey the same, (3) that the premises are free from all encumbrances, (4) that the Grantor forever warrants to the Grantee that the Grantor will defend the title thereto against all persons who may lawfully claim the same, (5) that the Grantor warrants to the Grantee the quiet and peaceful possession of such premises, and (6) that the Grantor warrants that he will execute any instrument necessary to provide further assurances of the title to the same on reasonable demand of the Grantee.

Grantor:

_____
(signature)

_____
(signature)

This instrument was acknowledged before me by _____
(insert name and marital status of each Grantor)

on _____, in testimony whereof I affix my seal.
  (month/day/year)

                    _____
                    (signature of notary)

                    My commission expires: _____

                    State of _____, County of _____

Brown v. Lober

389 N.E.2d 1188 (Ill. 1979)

┌───┐
│   **Reading Guide**   │
│   │
│   *Brown v. Lober* provides you with an opportunity to carefully distinguish the six │
│   deed covenants from one another. It also allows you to consider the practical │
│   ramifications of the distinction between present and future covenants. │
└───┘

UNDERWOOD, J.

. . . Plaintiffs [James and Dolly Brown] purchased 80 acres of Montgomery County real estate from William and Faith Bost and received a statutory warranty deed . . . , containing no exceptions, dated December 21, 1957. Subsequently, plaintiffs took possession of the land and recorded their deed.

On May 8, 1974, plaintiffs granted a coal option to Consolidated Coal Company (Consolidated) for the coal rights on the 80-acre tract for the sum of $6,000. Approximately two years later, however, plaintiffs "discovered" that they, in fact, owned only a one-third interest in the subsurface coal rights. It is a matter of public record that, in 1947, a prior grantor had reserved a two-thirds interest in the mineral rights on the property. Although plaintiffs had their abstract of title examined in 1958 and 1968 for loan purposes, they contend that until May 4, 1976, they believed that they were the sole owners of the surface and subsurface rights on the 80-acre tract. Upon discovering that a prior grantor had reserved a two-thirds interest in the coal rights, plaintiffs and Consolidated renegotiated their agreement to provide for payment of $2,000 in exchange for a one-third interest in the subsurface coal rights. On May 25, 1976, plaintiffs filed this action against the executor [Maureen Lober] of the estate of Faith Bost, seeking damages in the amount of $4,000.

The deed which plaintiffs received from the Bosts was a general statutory form warranty deed meeting the requirements of section 9 of "An Act concerning conveyances" (Ill. Rev. Stat. 1957, ch. 30, par. 8). That section provides:

> Every deed in substance in the above form, when otherwise duly executed, shall be deemed and held a conveyance in fee simple, to the grantee, his heirs or assigns, with covenants on the part of the grantor, (1) that at the time of the making and delivery of such deed he was lawfully seized of an indefeasible estate in fee simple, in and to the premises therein described, and had good right and full power to convey the same; (2) that the same were then free from all incumbrances; and (3) that he warrants to the grantee, his heirs and assigns, the quiet and peaceable possession of such premises, and will defend the title thereto against all persons who may lawfully claim the same. And such covenants shall be obligatory upon any grantor, his heirs and personal representatives, as fully and with like effect as if written at length in such deed. . . .

The effect of this provision is that certain covenants of title are implied in every statutory form warranty deed. . . .

. . . While the complaint could be more explicit, it appears that plaintiffs were alleging a cause of action for breach of the covenant of seisin. This court has stated repeatedly that the covenant of seisin is a covenant *in praesenti* and, therefore, if broken at all, is broken at the time of delivery of the deed. . . .

Since the deed was delivered to the plaintiffs on December 21, 1957, any cause of action for breach of the covenant of seisin would have accrued on that date. The trial court held that this cause of action was barred by the statute of limitations. No question is raised as to the applicability of the 10-year statute of limitations. . . . We conclude, therefore, that the cause of action for breach of the covenant of seisin was properly determined by the trial court to be barred by the statute of limitations since plaintiffs did not file their complaint until May 25, 1976, nearly 20 years after their alleged cause of action accrued.

In their post-trial motion, plaintiffs set forth as an additional theory of recovery an alleged breach of the covenant of quiet enjoyment. The trial court, without explanation, denied the motion. The appellate court reversed, holding that the cause of action on the covenant of quiet enjoyment was not barred by the statute of limitations. The appellate court theorized that plaintiffs' cause of action did not accrue until 1976, when plaintiffs discovered that they only had a one-third interest in the subsurface coal rights and renegotiated their contract with the coal company for one-third of the previous contract price. The primary issue before us, therefore, is when, if at all, the plaintiffs' cause of action for breach of the covenant of quiet enjoyment is deemed to have accrued.

This court has stated on numerous occasions that, in contrast to the covenant of seisin, the covenant of warranty or quiet enjoyment is prospective in nature and is breached only when there is an actual or constructive eviction of the covenantee by the paramount titleholder. . . .

The cases are also replete with statements to the effect that the mere existence of paramount title in one other than the covenantee is not sufficient to constitute a breach of the covenant of warranty or quiet enjoyment: . . . "[T]here is a general concurrence that something more than the mere existence of a paramount title is necessary to constitute a breach of the covenant of warranty." (*Scott v. Kirkendall* (1878), 88 Ill. 465, 467.) . . .

The question is whether plaintiffs have alleged facts sufficient to constitute a constructive eviction. They argue that if a covenantee fails in his effort to sell an interest in land because he discovers that he does not own what his warranty deed purported to convey, he has suffered a constructive eviction and is thereby entitled to bring an action against his grantor for breach of the covenant of quiet enjoyment. We think that the decision of this court in *Scott v. Kirkendall* . . . (1878), is controlling on this issue and compels us to reject plaintiffs' argument.

In *Scott*, an action was brought for breach of the covenant of warranty by a grantee who discovered that other parties had paramount title to the land in question. The land was vacant and unoccupied at all relevant times. This court, in rejecting the grantee's claim that there was a breach of the covenant of quiet enjoyment, quoted the earlier decision in *Moore v. Vail* (1855), 17 Ill. 185, 191:

> Until that time, (the taking possession by the owner of the paramount title,) he might peaceably have entered upon and enjoyed the premises, without resistance or molestation, which was all his grantors covenanted he should do. They did not guarantee to him a perfect title, but the possession and enjoyment of the premises.

Relying on this language in *Moore*, the *Scott* court concluded:

> We do not see but what this fully decides the present case against the appellant. It holds that the mere existence of a paramount title does not constitute a breach of the covenant. That is all there is here. There has been no assertion of the adverse title. The land has always been vacant. Appellant could at any time have taken peaceable possession of it. He has in no way been prevented or hindered from the enjoyment of the possession by any one having a better right. It was but the possession and enjoyment of the premises which was assured to him, and there has been no disturbance or interference in that respect. True, there is a superior title in another, but appellant has never felt "its pressure upon him."

Admittedly, *Scott* dealt with surface rights while the case before us concerns subsurface mineral rights. We are, nevertheless, convinced that the reasoning employed in *Scott* is applicable to the present case. While plaintiffs went into possession of the surface area, they cannot be said to have possessed the subsurface minerals.

> Possession of the surface does not carry possession of the minerals. . . . (Citation.) To possess the mineral estate, one must undertake the actual removal thereof from the ground or do such other act as will apprise the community that such interest is in the exclusive use and enjoyment of the claiming party.

Failoni v. Chicago & North Western Ry. Co., 195 N.E.2d 619, 622 (1964).

Since no one has, as yet, undertaken to remove the coal or otherwise manifested a clear intent to exclusively "possess" the mineral estate, it must be concluded that the subsurface estate is "vacant." As in *Scott*, plaintiffs "could at any time have taken peaceable possession of it. (They have) in no way been prevented or hindered from the enjoyment of the possession by any one having a better right." . . . Accordingly, until such time as one holding paramount title interferes with plaintiffs' right of possession (*e.g.*, by beginning to mine the coal), there can be no constructive eviction and, therefore, no breach of the covenant of quiet enjoyment.

What plaintiffs are apparently attempting to do on this appeal is to extend the protection afforded by the covenant of quiet enjoyment. However, we decline to expand the historical scope of this covenant to provide a remedy where another of the covenants of title is so clearly applicable. As this court stated in *Scott* . . . :

> To sustain the present action would be to confound all distinction between the covenant of warranty and that of seizin, or of right to convey. They are not equivalent covenants. An action will lie upon the latter, though there be no disturbance of possession. A defect of title will suffice. Not so with the covenant of warranty, or for quiet enjoyment, as has always been held by the prevailing authority.

The covenant of seisin, unquestionably, was breached when the Bosts delivered the deed to plaintiffs, and plaintiffs then had a cause of action. However, despite the fact that it was a matter of public record that there was a reservation of a two-thirds interest in the mineral rights in the earlier deed, plaintiffs failed to bring an action for breach of the covenant of seisin within the 10-year period following delivery of the deed. The likely explanation is that plaintiffs had not secured a title opinion at the time they purchased the property, and the subsequent examiners for the lenders were not concerned with the mineral rights. Plaintiffs' oversight, however, does not justify us in overruling earlier decisions in order to recognize an otherwise premature cause of action. The mere fact that plaintiffs' original contract with Consolidated had to be modified due to their discovery that paramount title to two-thirds of the subsurface minerals belonged to another is not sufficient to constitute the constructive eviction necessary to a breach of the covenant of quiet enjoyment.

Finally, although plaintiffs also have argued in this court that there was a breach of the covenant against incumbrances entitling them to recovery, we decline to address this issue which was argued for the first time on appeal. . . .

Accordingly, the judgment of the appellate court is reversed, and the judgment of the circuit court of Montgomery County is affirmed. . . .

Notes

1. *The statutory short-form deed:*   Many jurisdictions prescribe simplified deed language by statute. When used, courts will imply into the deed whatever covenants the statute specifies. Carefully read the language of the Illinois statute describing the jurisdiction's short-form warranty deed. Does it contain all six common law deed covenants? If not, does it matter in this case?

2. *Too late—the present covenants:*   Why was it too late for the Browns to bring an action against the Bosts (through the executor of Faith Bost's estate)? Statutes of limitation aside, carefully review each of the three present covenants. Which one(s), if any, clearly fit the facts of this case?

3. *Too soon—the future covenants:*   Why was it too soon for the Browns to bring an action against the Bost estate? What more is necessary? If you represented the Browns, what would you suggest they do now?

4. *Practice pointer—avoiding litigation:* What actions could the Bosts and the Browns, respectively, have taken to prevent this lawsuit? Would it have helped if the contract conveyed the property, "free and clear of all encumbrances, subject, however, to all restrictions and easements of record applying to this property"? Can you think of any additional deed language that could have prevented this conflict?

5. *Covenants running with the land:* In a majority of jurisdictions, the present covenants made by one seller do not "run with the land" for the benefit of future buyers. As a consequence, a buyer can sue only her immediate seller for a breach of the present covenants (rather than a former owner of the property). In contrast, future covenants do run with the land to future buyers. Suppose, for example, that *A* conveyed a general warranty deed to *B*, who conveyed a quitclaim deed to *C*. Later, *O*, the true owner, appears, exerts a lawful claim of superior title, and evicts *C* from the premises. Even though *B* made no warranties to *C* in the quitclaim deed, *A*'s general warranty deed to *B* contained all six covenants of title. Therefore, because *A*'s covenants run with the land to *B* and to her successors (including *C*), *C* can recover against *A* for breach of a future warranty, as long as the statute of limitations has not expired.

Problem

Obvious lake, not-so-obvious easement: The Housworths sold a 24-acre tract of land to the McMurrays by general warranty deed. There is a lake on a portion of the property. The dam that creates the lake (by backing up the flow of a natural stream) is located on an adjacent parcel of land in separate ownership. The owner of the dam holds a floodwater detention easement that allows him to use the Housworth (now McMurray) property to store excess streamflows on the property (which would have the practical effect of enlarging the lake and submerging more of the McMurray property). Although the easement is recorded in the public records, the McMurrays failed to conduct a title search prior to purchase, and therefore failed to discover the recorded easement. However, the dam is visible from their property. Later, after discovering the existence of the easement, the McMurrays sued the Housworths for breach of the covenant against encumbrances and the covenant of general warranty. What arguments will each party make? How should the court decide the case? What could each party have done to avoid the litigation? *See* McMurray v. Housworth, 638 S.E.2d 421 (Ga. App. 2006).

3. Title Insurance

We have just examined the seller's promises to convey good title, as embodied in the contractual commitment to deliver marketable title, and in the deed covenants. But those guarantees are imperfect—as illustrated by *Lohmeyer v.*

Bower and *Brown v. Lober*. Moreover, in some cases, the contractual promises merge into the deed warranties at closing. The next case considers an additional component of title security—the title insurance policy.

Riordan v. Lawyers Title Insurance Corp.

393 F. Supp. 2d 1100 (D.N.M. 2005)

Reading Guide

- ◆ *Deed warranties and title insurance compared:* Take note of the relative advantages and disadvantages of title insurance policies, as suggested by this case. How do they compare to the assurances provided by deed warranties?
- ◆ *The missing piece?* Do you think deed warranties and title insurance together provide adequate security of title? Can you think of anything else that would enhance the buyer's security?

BRACK, J.

Plaintiffs were owners of 160 acres of real property (hereinafter "Property") located in an "in-holding"[9] in the middle of the Sandia Mountain Wilderness of the Cibola National Forest near Albuquerque, New Mexico. Defendant issued an insurance policy (hereinafter "Policy") insuring Plaintiffs' title to the Property. Plaintiffs allege that they sustained a loss, covered by the Policy, as a result of lawsuit that they filed against the United States of America to declare a vehicular right of way to the Property. . . .

At all relevant times, the Property has been accessed by the Piedra Lisa Trail, which is a hiking and horse trail maintained by the United States Forest Service ("USFS"). The Property is located two and a half miles from the nearest paved road. The Piedra Lisa Trail was and is unsuitable for vehicular access. Mr. Riordan testified at his deposition that, at the time he purchased the Property in 1995, there were several former roads that had been used to access the Property, including roads that were accessible by jeep. Before Plaintiffs purchased the Property, the prior owner represented that he had accessed the Property by jeep over an access route other than the Piedra Lisa Trail. Mr. Riordan testified that a USFS employee informed Mr. Riordan that the Property had vehicular access and suggested the access route was near the original homestead on the Property.

On May 5, 1995, Riordan signed a Vacant-Land Purchase Agreement to purchase the property for $225,000. Prior to closing, Riordan visited the Property

---

9. [FN 1] In-holdings are lands surrounded by federally owned lands. *See* 16 U.S.C. § 3210(a).

by walking and riding his horse on the Piedra Lisa Trail. Plaintiffs closed on the Property on July 6, 1995.

Defendant issued the owner's policy of title insurance, effective September 11, 1995. The Policy provides in pertinent part:

> SUBJECT TO THE EXCLUSIONS FROM COVERAGE, THE EXCEPTIONS FROM COVERAGE CONTAINED IN SCHEDULE B AND THE CONDITIONS AND STIPULATIONS, LAWYERS TITLE INSURANCE CORPORATION . . . Insures . . . against loss or damage, not exceeding the Amount of Insurance stated in Schedule A, sustained or incurred by the insured by reason of:
>
> 1. Title to the estate or interest described in Schedule A being vested other than as stated therein;
>
> 2. Any defect and /or lien or encumbrance on the title;
>
> 3. Unmarketability of the title;
>
> 4. Lack of a right of access to and from the land.
>
> (Def. Ex. F.)

The Policy contains the following exclusion from coverage:

> The following matters are expressly excluded from the coverage of this policy and the Company will not pay loss or damage, costs, attorneys' fees or expenses which arise by reason of:
>
> 1(a) Any law, ordinance or government regulation . . . restricting, regulating, prohibiting or relating to (i) the occupancy, use, or enjoyment of the land. . . .
>
> (Def, Ex. F.)

The Plaintiffs brought the Primary Action to declare a vehicular right of way to the Property. The United States raised affirmative defenses in the primary action, but did not assert counterclaims against Plaintiffs. Defendant hired attorney Joseph Werntz to represent Plaintiffs in the Primary Action. In September 2002, the property appraised for $2.8 million. Thereafter, Plaintiffs sold the property to Sandia Pueblo for $1.3 million and a tax deduction for a $1.5 million charitable donation to the Pueblo. The Primary Action was dismissed as moot by stipulation on December 18, 2002. Plaintiffs made three demands for payment under the policy. The demands were rejected. . . .

Plaintiffs assert that the Policy insured against a lack of vehicular access to the Property. Defendant argues that the Policy covers a lack of a right of access, and does not insure the quality of that access. . . .

The Policy insures against loss caused by a "lack of right of access." Plaintiffs argue that this language should be construed to cover a lack of vehicular access based on their reasonable expectations. "An insurance contract should be construed as a complete and harmonious instrument designed to accomplish a reasonable end." *Knowles v. United Services Auto. Ass'n*, P.2d 394, 396 (N.M. 1992). The doctrine of reasonable expectations only applies where the policy terms are ambiguous. *Slack v. Robinson,* 71 P.3d 514, 517 (N.M. Ct. App. 2003). "Absent ambiguity, provisions of [an insurance] contract need only be applied, rather than construed or interpreted." *Richardson v. Farmers Ins. Co. of Ariz.,* . . . 811 P.2d 571, 572 ([N.M.] 1991). . . . The Policy insures against loss or damage sustained or incurred by the insured by reason of a lack of a right of access to and from the land. This language is clear and unambiguous. For this reason, the policy language controls and the doctrine of reasonable expectations is inapplicable.

Unambiguous insurance contracts must be construed in their usual and ordinary sense. . . . When the language in the policy is unambiguous, the New Mexico court "will not strain the words to encompass meanings they do not clearly express." *Gonzales v. Allstate Ins. Co.,* . . . 921 P.2d 944, 947-948 ([N.M.] 1996). The Policy insures against a lack of right of access; it does not insure that the Property has vehicular or any other type of access.

Although no New Mexico cases have addressed this point, courts in other jurisdictions have found that coverage for a "lack of right of access" to the insured property is not triggered where access is merely impractical or difficult as long as the right to access exists. *See Magna Enterprises, Inc. v. Fidelity National Title Ins. Co.,* . . . 127 Cal. Rptr. 2d 681, 684-685 (Ct. App. 2002); *Gates v. Chicago Title Ins. Co.,* 813 S.W.2d 10, 11-12 (Mo. Ct. App. 1991); *Krause v. Title & Trust Co. of Florida,* 390 So. 2d 805, 806 (Fla. Ct. App. 1980); *Title & Trust Co. of Florida v. Barrows,* 381 So. 2d 1088, 1090 (Fla. Ct. App. 1979); *Mafetone v. Forest Manor Homes, Inc.,* 34 A.D.2d 566, 567, 310 N.Y.S.2d 17 (N.Y. A.D. 1970). Plaintiffs admit that they had, and were never denied, a right to pedestrian access to and from the property over the Piedra Lisa Trail. Indeed, their right of access was mandated by federal law. *See* 16 U.S.C. § 3210(a).[10] Accordingly, there was no lack of right of access to the property that would trigger coverage under the policy.

Plaintiffs rely on *Marriott Financial Services, Inc. v. Capitol Funds, Inc.,* . . . 217 S.E.2d 551, 565 ([N.C.] 1975) in support of their claim of coverage. In *Marriott,* the court construed "right of access" to mean "without unreasonable restriction" and stated in dicta that pedestrian access was unreasonable in that case. *Id.* This dicta in *Marriott* has been roundly criticized. . . . Moreover, *Marriott* is inapposite to Plaintiffs' case. In *Marriott,* the subject property was adjacent to a heavily traveled city street in a commercial area. . . . The Property in this case is located in the middle of a wilderness area, two and a half miles from the nearest paved road. Thus, even if the *Marriott* dicta were applied to this case, pedestrian access to the Property was without unreasonable restriction.

---

10. [That section provides, ". . . [T]he Secretary shall provide such access to nonfederally owned land within the boundaries of the National Forest System as the Secretary deems adequate to secure to the owner the reasonable use and enjoyment thereof: *Provided,* That such owner comply with rules and regulations applicable to ingress and egress to or from the National Forest System."—Eds.]

Finally, the holding in *Marriott* does not support Plaintiffs' position. In *Marriott,* the court held that the claim was barred by the government action exclusion of the title insurance policy. The insured in that case was required to apply for a driveway permit with the city, but had never actually filed the application because of the city's stated intention not to approve the application if it were filed. . . . The *Marriott* court held that because the insured had not applied, access had not been denied, and even if the application had been submitted and rejected, coverage would still be excluded under the government action exclusion. *Id.*

The Policy in the instant case contains a similar government action exclusion. The Policy, excludes any claim that arises by reasons of "any law, ordinance or governmental regulation . . . restricting, regulating, prohibiting or relating to . . . the occupancy, use, or enjoyment of the land." (Def. Ex. F.) Plaintiffs complain that they were deprived of a right of access because the United States allegedly intended to reject any application for a special use authorization for vehicular access to the Property. However, Plaintiffs never applied for a special use permit, and they sold the property before obtaining a final determination in the Primary Action. Thus, *Marriott* does not support Plaintiffs' claim of coverage based on the government action exclusion.

Plaintiffs claim that the property was unmarketable is similarly unavailing. Defects in the physical condition of the property do not constitute unmarketability of title. . . . A difference exists between economic lack of marketability, which relates to physical conditions affecting the use of the property, and title marketability, which relates to defects affecting legally recognized rights and incidents of ownership. . . . Here, Plaintiffs had a right of access to the property at all relevant times. The fact that Plaintiffs were able to sell the property at a substantial profit militates against a determination that the title was unmarketable. Under these circumstances, the title was marketable.

Plaintiffs did not suffer a loss covered by the policy. Defendant's denial of coverage was justified. The remaining claims fail because there was no coverage under the policy. . .

WHEREFORE, IT IS ORDERED that Defendant's Motion for Summary Judgment . . . is GRANTED.

Notes

1. *The American Land Title Association:*   The American Land Title Association (ALTA), the national trade association for the title insurance industry, has developed a widely used standardized insurance form. The form also sets forth standardized exclusions from coverage, including losses due to the existence or violation of governmental regulations (such as zoning ordinances or building codes); unrecorded interests in the property (such as unrecorded easements); and matters that would be disclosed by a proper survey or inspection of

the premises (such as boundary irregularities or claims by adverse possessors). It is possible to negotiate for expanded coverage, in exchange for a higher premium. The insured (or often, the seller on behalf of the insured buyer) makes a one-time premium payment at the time the policy is issued.

2. *Marketable title:*   If the plaintiffs had challenged the property's title prior to completing their purchase of it in 1995, could they have rescinded the contract on the ground that the seller's title was unmarketable due to the lack of vehicular access to the property? Notice that the concept of marketability is relevant here, too, under paragraph (3) of the insurance policy. Is the *Riordan* court's view of marketability consistent with that of the court in *Lohmeyer v. Bower?*

3. *Cars in the wilderness?*   Why did the title insurance company retain an attorney to represent the plaintiffs in their earlier action against the United States to obtain a vehicular right of way to the property? It appears likely that the insurance company itself interpreted the "right of access" insured under paragraph (4) of the policy to mean *motorized* access by car or jeep. Should the company have undertaken such an obligation on property adjacent to a wilderness area?

This case concerns a private "in-holding" within a vast expanse of federal land—the more than 37,000 acre Sandia Mountain Wilderness in New Mexico, which is part of the 109-million-acre National Wilderness Preservation System. Through the Wilderness Act of 1964, 16 U.S.C. §§ 1131 *et seq.*, Congress established a system of wilderness on lands already in federal ownership "to secure for the American people of present and future generations the benefits of an enduring resource of wilderness" on federal land "retaining its primeval character and influence, without permanent improvements or human habitation." 16 U.S.C. § 1131(a) & (c). The use of motorized equipment and mechanical transport is generally prohibited on all wilderness lands, unless Congress provided an exception for a particular segment of wilderness, as by "grandfathering" in longstanding uses and practices.

After failing in the action against the United States, the insurance company took the opposite position—that the policy did *not* obligate it to insure motorized access. Why do you think the court held for the insurance company, despite the inconsistent positions the company advanced?

F. BEYOND THE BLACK LETTER: CLIMATE—THE NEXT REAL ESTATE BUBBLE?

The phrase "climate bubble" has been coined to mean climate-induced risks that threaten to diminish property values and to collapse real estate markets in vulnerable areas. As one scholar explains,

> The collapse of the housing bubble in 2008 led to the worst economic recession our country has experienced since the Great Depression. The housing and

financial crisis emerged from an unrealistic expansion of credit and artificially inflated home prices. . . . Low interest, low down payment loans were created and offered to buyers with dubious credit histories; demand exploded, prices accelerated, and a nation-wide bubble was created. By the time the stakeholders in this national lending and underwriting system figured out that housing prices outstripped demand, that prices were falling, and that mortgagors were unable to cover their monthly payments, it was too late, and in 2008 the bubble burst. . . .

Similarly, the Land Use Climate Bubbles that are emerging constitute a series of seemingly unrelated phenomena in different regions. . . . There are clear warning signs, not just in academic and governmental reports, but also on the ground in an increasingly large and disturbing number of places where real damage is being caused. The scale of this new bubble is perhaps much greater than that of the housing bubble; we risk ignoring the signals it is sending at our very great peril.

In numerous communities, property values are declining because of repeated flooding, continued threats of storm surges, sustained high temperatures, constant fear of wildfires, the lack of water in residential, commercial, and agricultural areas, and real concerns with mudslides in vulnerable areas. . . .

John R. Nolon, *Land Use and Climate Change Bubbles: Resilience, Retreat, and Due Diligence*, 39 William & Mary Envt'l L. & Policy Rev. 321 (2015).

The excerpt below from a Virginia newspaper provides a case study of the collapse of one such climate bubble in Norfolk, Virginia. As you read the excerpt, think about possible property law approaches and solutions to protect threatened areas and real estate markets.

Norfolk Sea Level Rise Takes Shine Off Waterfront Homes

Aaron Applegate, The Virginian-Pilot, Sept. 28, 2014

Soon after Mary-Carson and Josh Stiff got married last year, they began talking about buying a house. Josh, 30, wanted to live in Norfolk to be near his law office. Mary-Carson, 28, wasn't so sure. Sea level rise and the chronic flooding that plagues the city worried her. "My concern was, it might not be a wise place to invest in general," she said. Her worry was grounded in her work. . . . Mary-Carson has been immersed in sea level rise policy work for months. She's well-acquainted with the piles of studies, reports and charts that show Norfolk is one of the country's most vulnerable cities.

"I absolutely thought my dream home would be on the water," she said. "But knowing what I now know, my entire perception has changed. I think everyone in Hampton Roads has rose-colored glasses when it comes to a picturesque home on the waterfront, with a dock and a boat and a kayak. That life is sweet and has a place in my heart, but it's no longer what I dream about."

The newlyweds forged a compromise. They would search for a home in Norfolk to be near Josh's office. But it could not be in a flood plain, susceptible to rising seas, storm surge and escalating flood insurance prices.

Their decision is one glimpse into the changing dynamics of coastal real estate. A growing awareness of sea level rise and flooding, coupled with rising flood insurance premiums as the federal government phases out subsidies, has the potential to reshape segments of the Hampton Roads market.

No one, of course, knows exactly what the future holds, but there's consensus on the broad strokes. . . .

"Previously, people looked at the school district or maybe property taxes, but now they're also asking about flood insurance," said Michael McShane, an Old Dominion University professor specializing in risk management and flood insurance. "It's starting to worry people. It has become a new factor."

Committed to living in Norfolk, the Stiffs set out on a mission to find a home they loved away from the threat of water, a surprisingly challenging quest. Real estate agent Kathy Heaton found herself on the flip side of the growing concern, and perhaps at the forefront of a new trend. For months, the Nancy Chandler and Associates agent had been trying to sell a home in the desirable Norfolk neighborhood of Larchmont. The problem: Like many homes in that area, it's in a high-risk flood plain. Flood insurance could run up to $3,500 based on estimates she's seen. That would add almost $300 to a monthly mortgage, an amount many buyers Heaton has encountered would rather put into the cost of a home.

Regular homeowners insurance does not cover flooding. Homes in the flood plains with mortgages are required by lenders to have insurance from the subsidized National Flood Insurance Program. It is struggling financially, and reforms are steadily increasing rates—about 18 percent a year—until they represent coverage of the true cost of the risk.

The specter of flood insurance is making the Larchmont home, assessed at around $270,000, nearly impossible to sell. "We've probably had 35 showings, and everybody has walked out because of the flood insurance," Heaton said. The home is not unique in a city penetrated by tidal creeks with some of the highest rates of sea level rise in the country, a combination of sinking land and rising water.

About a quarter of properties in Norfolk—just over 17,000—are in high-risk flood plains, with values totaling 34 percent of the tax base, according to city figures. The number of homes that repeatedly flood, so-called "repetitive loss" properties, has increased from about 200 in 2002 to almost 900 today. . . .

Owners of these homes might be eligible for federal money to raise them above flood levels, but that money is competitive, and the option is not practical for all homes. Minor flooding, partly driven by sea level rise, has also been increasing around Norfolk, according to studies published this year by Old Dominion University scientists and the National Oceanic and Atmospheric Administration.

The Larchmont home has been so difficult for Heaton to sell that a creative solution is in the works that could be a model for flood zone homes in the future. The idea is to make changes to the home to reduce flood damage and drive down insurance rates. In this case, contractors would move the furnace, hot water heater and electric panel from the basement of the 1920s home into a newly created utility room in the upper part of the house. The basement would then be filled in, and vents would be added to allow floodwater to move in and then out from under the house. The work would cost about $15,000, said Mike Vernon, director of business development for Flood Mitigation Hampton Roads, a new company that would do the job. The seller and buyer would figure out how to split the cost, with the buyer's share getting wrapped into the mortgage as a type of renovation loan, he said. An insurance agent has estimated the improvements would lower flood insurance $392 a year. . . .

"The seller is now armed to negotiate with a buyer in a way that would allow them to move the house," Vernon said. His prediction for the long term: "The National Flood Insurance Program is going to mitigate America. The houses in the flood plains are either going to be washed away, mitigated, or they're going to be demolished."

Mary-Carson Stiff spent most of the year searching for homes that stayed clear of flood zone dilemmas. It took some work. "You're basically on your own," she said.

In Virginia, the burden of discovering potential problems is on the buyer, with a few exceptions. For example, sellers must disclose if a home is in an airplane noise zone or has defective drywall or has ever been used to manufacture meth. But they don't need to disclose if a home is in the flood zone or has been damaged in a flood; flood insurance claims for a home are not available to a potential buyer. The lack of information has led to deals falling through at the last minute, officials say, as buyers discover they need flood insurance that would dramatically increase mortgage payments.

"The regular homeowner, Joe Blow, might say, 'Hey, I can afford a $1,200 mortgage,' so he negotiates and gets the price down, and then he discovers he's also going to have a $300 a month flood insurance bill, and that pushes the cost over his limit, and he has to walk away," said Matthew Wall, the Virginia Department of Emergency Management's hazard mitigation officer. "It's not good for anyone." Wall and others have suggested Virginia change its rules so potential buyers are informed early of a home's flood plain status. . . .

Buyers may be on their own, but there are public resources to help. For example, the first thing Mary-Carson Stiff did with each home suggested by her real estate agent was plug the address into a city website that includes, among other things, whether a home is in a flood zone. It's called Norfolk Address Information Resource. "Every single house, I plug into Norfolk AIR," she said. "I don't even look at the pictures because I don't want to be disappointed." She looked at detailed maps developed by NOAA and Climate Central, a nonprofit that focuses on climate change news, which predict what areas will be covered by water as sea level rises.

Even if the state doesn't change disclosure rules, the private sector might come up with its own solutions. Real estate agents have no interest in seeing deals fall apart at the last minute, said Terry Gearhart, government affairs chairman of the Hampton Roads Realtors Association and a manager with Rose & Womble Realty Co. Some are informing buyers early with what's known as a "flooding addendum." "Every agent understands we're in an era of full disclosure," he said. "It's going to come out at some point. The lender is going to look at it. How anyone would benefit from hiding it, I don't know. The only time we get paid is when something closes." . . .

In late summer, the Stiffs' real estate agent told Mary-Carson about a home in the Colonial Place neighborhood they might want to check out. The flood plain crossed a small part of the parcel, but the home itself was not in it. Expensive flood insurance would not be required. Still, her first instinct was to pass because of the proximity to possible flooding. But after a long summer of fruitless searching, she agreed to take a look. The view from the porch made her a little nervous. She could see water, a tributary of the Lafayette River called Knitting Mill Creek. "It was like, 'I see you threatening,' " she recalled. On the other hand, the 1923 home was elevated on a ridge that put it well above flood level. Plus, they liked it. . . .

Even though they were not required to have flood insurance, they planned to buy a policy anyway. It will run about $400 year on the low-risk home, she said. Most real estate and insurance agents, city planners and emergency planners in Hampton Roads agree homeowners should buy flood insurance even if they're not in a flood plain. . . . The region has the highest percentage of homes outside a flood zone that are potentially uninsured and at risk for storm surge flooding—86 percent, or 340,000. . . .

The night before closing on the home, Mary-Carson and Josh Stiff drove to Colonial Place for what they imagined would be a romantic stroll around their new neighborhood. They parked at the house. It was a short walk. The street running parallel to Knitting Mill Creek, Mayflower Road, was impassable. A lunar high tide mixed with runoff from an earlier rainstorm had flooded it. They turned around, back toward the high ground of their new life.

Discussion Questions

1. *Bubbles at home:* Is your community faced with any climate-related threats? If so, what are they? Do you see signs of collapsing climate bubbles in your own community—that is, does the growing recognition of climate-related hazards threaten to reduce property values and make some properties difficult to sell?

2. *Impact of climate-related threats on the real estate market:* What are the potential impacts on the real estate market of climate-related threats, such as frequent floods, sea level rise, drought, wildfire, and mud slides? Consider, at a minimum, the following components of the real estate transaction:

- Property disclosures and the doctrine of caveat emptor
- Mortgage financing

- Property appraisals
- Insurance (casualty and flood)

3. *A changing world:* Commentators have suggested a variety of real estate–related approaches to reduce the risk of climate hazards. Which of the following measures, if any, do you think would be effective and desirable? Can you suggest other approaches that might also be possible?

- Information disclosure
- Adapting structures to accommodate periodic flooding
- Retreating to higher ground or out of the path of mudslides

G. SKILLS PRACTICE: REVIEWING PURCHASE OFFERS

Samir has listed his home for sale at $200,000. He has entered into a listing agreement with broker Beatrice, under which he has agreed to pay her a 7% sales commission upon the consummation of the sale of his property. Samir would like to close the contract as soon as possible, preferably within no more than five weeks, because he is being transferred out of town for work. His home is in excellent condition, with the exception of one area where the roof has been leaking for about the past three months. Beatrice held an open house last weekend, which was a great success. When she arrived in her office on Monday morning, the following two offers were awaiting.

Purchase and Sale Agreement

Buyer Name(s): Arthur and Alexandra Adams

Purchase Price: $ 200,000

Closing Date: This contract will close no later than five weeks after execution of this contract, provided that acceptable financing has been obtained by that time.

Loan and Appraisal Contingencies: This contract is contingent upon the Buyer obtaining a Purchase Money Loan as follows: Amount borrowed at least *$150,000.00*. Interest rate not greater than *5%*. Period of amortization *30* years. Payments made on a *monthly* basis. Buyer agrees to apply for said mortgage within five days of acceptance and to pay the normal closing costs in obtaining same. Should Buyer be unable to obtain said mortgage and Buyer so notifies the Seller or his agent on said date this contract will be null and void of no force or effect, all deposits returned and all parties to this contract released of all liability hereunder.

Inspection Contingency: This *Agreement* is contingent on Buyer's satisfaction with all property inspections and investigations (all at Buyer's expense), including a professional home inspection conducted by a licensed home inspector. All inspections and investigations must be completed with response to Seller no later than ten (10) calendar days after the Acceptance Date of this contract. Buyer assumes all liability for any damage or loss caused by Buyer's or Buyer representatives' inspections or investigations of the property.

Special Stipulations: None.

Buyer(s) makes this *Offer.*

Arthur Adams

Buyer signature

Alexandra Adams

Buyer signature

Purchase and Sale Agreement

Buyer Name(s): Bob and Belinda Brown

Purchase Price: $193,000 (cash)

Closing Date: This contract will close no later than five weeks after execution of this contract.

Loan and Appraisal Contingencies: None. The buyers will pay cash for the purchase price in full and will not seek to obtain a loan.

Inspection Contingency: None. The buyers will accept the property "as is."

Special Stipulations: The buyers are not represented by a real estate broker or agent.

Buyer(s) makes this *Offer:*

Bob Brown

Buyer signature

Betty Brown

Buyer signature

Tasks

1. *Evaluating the offers:*   You are legal counsel for Samir. Advise him as he evaluates which offer to accept. Identify as many factors as possible to distinguish the two offers from one another.

2. *Selecting quiet neighbors:*   The Browns are a retired couple, and they are planning a fairly extensive remodel of the property (Mr. Brown is a retired contractor). The Adams are a young couple with two children. Can Samir take those factors into consideration as he decides which offer to accept? In particular, he is leaning toward accepting the Browns' offer because he is worried that the Adams' young children will be noisy and upset his next door neighbors, who are elderly and in poor health. Advise Samir.

H. CHAPTER REVIEW

1. Practice Questions[11]

1. *The one-car Tudor:*   Blackacre was the site of a Tudor home with a one-car garage. Shan contracted to convey "marketable title" to Blackacre to Barbara "by warranty deed, free and clear of all encumbrances, subject to all restrictions and easements of record applying to this property." Through her title examination, Barbara learned that the property was subject to a private restrictive covenant requiring that any house erected on the lot must have at least a two-car garage. In Barbara's lawsuit to rescind the contract, what is the most likely result?
  A. Barbara will prevail because the mere existence of a private restrictive covenant makes title unmarketable.
  B. Barbara will prevail because the restrictive covenant has been violated.
  C. Shan will prevail because the contract waived Barbara's right to object to the restrictive covenant.
  D. Shan will prevail because the mere existence of a restrictive covenant or municipal ordinance does not make title unmarketable.

2. *Murder on the premises:*   Sofia contracted to sell her home to Benjamin. Many years earlier, a murder had been committed on the premises. Although Sofia was aware of that fact, she did not disclose it to Benjamin. If Benjamin learns of the murder and sues to rescind the contract, who will most likely prevail? The jurisdiction follows the modern trend with respect to the doctrine of caveat emptor.

---

11. Answers appear in the Appendix to this casebook.

    A. Benjamin will probably prevail because Sofia had a duty to disclose the circumstances of the murder to him.

    B. Benjamin will probably prevail if the court determines that the murder created a material defect in the premises.

    C. Sofia will probably prevail because the defect was not latent.

    D. Sofia will probably prevail under the majority rule of caveat rule.

3. *Backing out of his promise:* Sergio told Bridgette that he would sell his property at #1 Main Street to her for $100,000. Bridgette agreed, and wrote out a check to Sergio for $300. Bridgette duly signed and dated the check and wrote on the back, "down payment toward purchase of #1 Main Street for $100,000." Two weeks later, Sergio changed his mind and told Bridgette that he did not want to sell his property to her after all. If Bridgette sues Sergio for specific performance of the contract of sale and Sergio denies that he ever entered into a verbal agreement, what would be the most likely result?

    A. Bridgette will prevail because the check was a signed writing that contained both a description of the property and the total sales price.

    B. If Sergio admits that he made a verbal promise to Bridgette, then she will prevail because her action in bringing the lawsuit was unequivocally referable to the oral agreement.

    C. The court will enforce the contract unless restitution would be inadequate.

    D. The court will not enforce the contract because it failed to comply with the statute of frauds.

4. *Adverse possession:* Sapphire duly executed a contract for the sale of Blackacre to Brody. The contract provided that Sapphire would convey the property, "by warranty deed with an abstract of title, certified to date showing good marketable title, subject however to the encumbrances hereinabove set forth." At closing, Brody learned for the first time that Sapphire claimed that the validity of the title to a portion of the premises was based solely upon the doctrine of adverse possession. If Brody sues to rescind the contract, what is the most likely result?

    A. Sapphire will prevail because title acquired through adverse possession is a valid exception to the statute of frauds.

    B. Brody will prevail because a title acquired through adverse possession is not marketable title.

    C. Sapphire will prevail unless the contract provided that "time is of the essence."

    D. Brody will prevail unless Sapphire can convince the tribunal that the title to Blackacre is free from doubt and that all the elements of adverse possession have been satisfied.

2. Bringing It Home

Research your state's statutory law, and find its relevant provisions on the issues listed below:

1. *Equitable conversion:*   Has your state adopted the Uniform Vendor and Purchaser Risk Act, including its provisions on equitable conversion? <u>Hint</u>: *See* Uniform Law Commission, *Vendor and Purchaser Risk Act (1935)*, www.uni formlaws.org. Then, follow links to "Acts" and "Vendor and Purchaser Risk Act (1935)" to see if your state has adopted the model legislation.

2. *Property disclosures:*   Does your state mandate by statute the type of property defects that sellers must disclose (or, are not required to disclose) to prospective buyers? <u>Hint</u>: Find an online table of contents for your state's statutes. Then, search for a "real property" section (or similar), then search for a "conveyances of land" section (or similar), and then search for statutory provisions titled "disclosure."

3. *General warranty deeds:*   Does your state provide a simplified, standardized form for warranty deeds—sometimes called a *short-form warranty deed*? In these types of deeds, as in *Brown v. Lober*, use of the prescribed statutory language is sufficient to create a general warranty deed with all six covenants. <u>Hint</u>: Find an online table of contents for your state's statutes. Then, search for a "real property" section (or similar), then search for a "conveyances of land" section (or similar), and then search for statutory provisions titled "warranty deed," "short-form warranty deed," or similar.

The Recording System

A. The Chain of Title
B. The Recording Acts
C. Beyond the Black Letter: Evaluating the Recording System
D. Skills Practice: Drafting Tenant Estoppel Statements
E. Chapter Review

Chapter 8–Cases

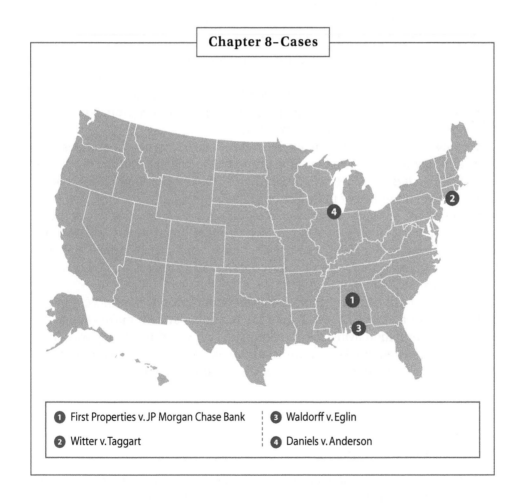

❶ First Properties v. JP Morgan Chase Bank   ❸ Waldorff v. Eglin

❷ Witter v. Taggart   ❹ Daniels v. Anderson

Why do we need a recording system? Every day in some large counties of the United States, hundreds (or even thousands) of deeds, mortgages, liens, easements, options to purchase, and similar documents are filed in the public records. Without an adequate recording system, it would be impossible for potential purchasers, banks evaluating loan applications, and others to determine whether the property in which they are interested is already owned or encumbered by someone else.

We will begin in section A by taking a close look at the recording system. First, we will consider how one goes about searching the public records to construct a chain of title. Then, we will look at documents that the law treats as "outside" the chain of title because even a diligent title search would fail to uncover them. As one treatise noted,

> This system is frugal in its expenditure of public funds and personnel. The government employees' only tasks are to receive, copy, index, and return the documents and to maintain the collection. The more demanding work of searching, analyzing, and reaching of legal conclusions from the instruments is left to the private users. The government makes no averment as to the state of the title.

William B. Stoebuck & Dale A. Whitman, The Law of Property 870 (3d ed. 2000). As a consequence, the system is far from perfect. As you may recall from the previous chapter, the prudent purchaser relies on two additional forms of title security to supplement the recording system—title insurance from a commercial entity and deed warranties from the seller.

Moving on, section B discusses the states' "recording acts"—statutes that resolve competing claims to the same property. We will see that the law favors *bona fide purchasers* (BFPs) who take title to property in good faith—that is, they take without notice of prior claims to the property. It is important to keep in mind that the law generally does not require parties to record their property interests. In fact, otherwise valid deeds or other instruments are binding between the original parties, even if they have not been recorded. But, the law creates an incentive for parties to record their instruments to protect themselves against subsequent claimants.

As you read this chapter, think about the importance of *information* in the real estate transaction. In general, does the recording system make *enough* (or *too much*) information available to the public? Can you think of any ways that the recording system could be improved? We will return to these questions in section C's *Beyond the Black Letter Law* discussion problem.

A. THE CHAIN OF TITLE

1. Searching the Chain of Title

As we have seen, in the contract of sale, the seller makes representations about the quality of the title that the buyer will receive at closing—such as, "good and marketable record title." During the executory phase of the contract, the buyer (through its attorney) will conduct a title search to verify that the seller indeed has marketable title that is not subject to any undisclosed or unacceptable defects. To do so, the attorney will search the *indexes* to the public records to find all documents relevant to the property's title, and then *read those documents* to make sure they do not adversely affect the title.

Alternatively, buyers often agree to accept title insurance policies instead of conducting their own title searches. Recall, for example, the sales contract in *Lohmeyer v. Bower* (Chapter 7) that promised that the seller would provide "an abstract of title showing good merchantable title *or* an Owners Policy of Title Insurance in the amount of the sale price." In such cases, the buyer relies on a professional title service that will search the indexes to locate relevant documents, and then compile an *abstract of title* (also called a *title plant*). The abstract summarizes the history of the property's ownership and also identifies claims against the property such as easements, mortgages, and liens. The buyer relies not only on the insurance company's title search, but also on its conclusion from that search that the title poses no unacceptable risks. But, as we saw in *Riordan v. Lawyers Title Insurance Corp.* in the previous chapter, the typical title insurance policy contains many exceptions from coverage, and the insurance company's tolerance of risk may be greater than that of any particular buyer.

The bulk of the public records affecting title are usually filed and indexed in the *county clerk and recorder's office* (or similarly named office). However, if the property's title has been impacted by bankruptcy, probate, divorce, or other proceedings, the title searcher will have to search those records, too (which might be stored in a separate physical location). There are two types of indexes: the *grantor/grantee* index, and the *tract* index. Increasingly, records are available through computer search. However, the process of digitizing decades and decades of old public records is slow, laborious, and expensive, and is far from completed in many jurisdictions.

A theoretically perfect title search would uncover the *root of title* as revealed by the earliest public records (or even go back to the United States or one of the original 13 states as grantor). Fortunately, many state *marketable title acts* limit the period of time that the search must cover to a period of usually 30-40 years. Some of those laws function as statutes of limitation that cut off the assertion of adverse claims after a specified period of time. Others purport to cure old title defects (rather than simply to bar the period of recovery). *See, e.g.,* Fla. Stat. § 712.04 ("[a]ny person ... who ... has been vested with any estate in land of record for 30 years or more ... shall have a marketable record title ... which shall be free and clear of all claims [with certain exceptions]"). To preserve property interests under such acts, long-term owners must periodically re-record evidence of their interests.

A Place to Start | Indexes to the Public Records

There are three recording systems for real property. By far, the grantor/grantee index is the most common, followed by the tract index system. A third system, Torrens registration, is used by a small and declining number of jurisdictions.

■ *Grantor/grantee index:* The oldest and most common system uses a *grantor/grantee* index. The system maintains two separate lists of conveyances, each organized alphabetically by the name of the relevant party. The *grantor* index lists alphabetically the names of all who grant property interests in a given year, whereas the *grantee* index lists alphabetically the recipients of those interests in a given year. Most jurisdictions consolidate their annual indexes periodically (perhaps every 5 or 10 years, depending on the size of the county).

■ *The tract index:* The title search process is much easier in jurisdictions that have a *tract index.* In such counties, the indexes are organized by *property*, rather than by *party* to the real estate transaction. A title searcher simply finds the file for the relevant property (usually organized by a unique identification number assigned to that parcel of land). The file should contain most or all documents affecting title to that tract. Very few states require all counties within their borders to maintain tract indexes. Among other things, the maintenance of a tract system requires expertise and judgment on the part of employees in the clerk and recorder's office. For each recorded instrument, they must carefully scrutinize the property description so that the transaction can be recorded on the index to the correct tract of land.

■ *The Torrens registration system:* The above two systems are *deed* systems that record property transactions, but leave it to the title searcher to determine the validity of the recorded instruments and, ultimately, the state of the title. The Torrens system, in contrast, is a *title registry* system (much like the automobile registration system) that gives conclusive proof of title, as well as a listing of all encumbrances on that title (easements, mortgages, and the like). The process is expensive and time consuming. Those seeking to register their title through this voluntary process must prove ownership through a judicial proceeding, after giving notice to all potentially affected parties claiming an interest in the same real property. The court will issue a decree declaring title and settling all outstanding claims, and the *registrar of titles* will file the original certificate of title in the appropriate registry and give a duplicate certificate to the owner. Subsequent transactions affecting the property must follow statutory procedures so that the registry can be updated appropriately.

DIGGING DEEPER: As you read the materials below, consider whether a tract index would have prevented or resolved the conflict. Also think about the role of electronic records, which more and more jurisdictions are compiling. Would an electronic system avoid all of the problems confronted in this chapter, or are there difficulties that even an electronic search could not avoid? Keep in mind that it can take decades for some large counties to digitize all of their existing paper records.

Suppose that your client wants to purchase real property currently owned by Emily Edwards. How will you search the title to uncover any possible encumbrances or adverse claims? Assume that the jurisdiction has a grantor-grantee index, but no tract index.

First, you will work backward in time to construct a *chain of title* of all record owners. To discover who sold the property to Edwards, search alphabetically under "Edwards" in the *grantee* index. Start with the current year and go back until you find the date of the deed that conveyed title to Edwards. You find a 2010 deed from Dion Dorsey to Emily Edwards. Next, search under "Dorsey" in the grantee index, starting with the year that he conveyed the deed to Edwards (2010) and continuing backward until you find the date that Dorsey received a deed to the property. Do *not* stop with the date on which Dorsey recorded his deed, which is typically later than receipt, but go backward until you find the year in which Dorsey received title (here, in 2003). You will learn that Dorsey purchased the property from Camilla Cruz in 2003. Search under "Cruz" in the grantee index, starting with the year she parted with title (2003), and work backward until you discover when (and from whom) Cruz received title (here, Cruz received a deed from *B* in 2000). Continue with this process until you have constructed a chain of title that goes back far enough in time to establish a *root of title* acceptable in your jurisdiction:

Figure 1

Second, you will reverse the process and search the *grantor* index forward in time. Start with the party representing the root of title—if the jurisdiction's marketable title act limits the search to 30 years, for example, then *A* would generally be the root of title. Search under "*A*" in the grantor index, beginning with the year in which *A* acquired a deed (1980), *not* the year in which *A* recorded the deed (which could be in a subsequent year). Continue forward in time until you find when the first (and hopefully, only) conveyance out from *A* (to *B* in 1995) was *recorded* (perhaps in 1996). Do not stop with the date on which *B* acquired a deed, because you might overlook adverse conveyances from *A* in the interval between *B*'s receipt and recording of the deed (1995-96). Next, look in the grantor index under "*B*" from the date *B* acquired a deed (1995) until the year the first conveyance out from *B* was recorded. You might discover, for example, that the first conveyance by *B* was *not* the deed to *C* (acquired and recorded in 2000). Instead, you might find that *B* conveyed a parking easement in the property to *X* in 1999:

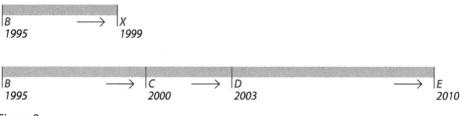

Figure 2

In that case, you should inform your client that the property is likely subject to *X*'s right to use the property for parking (depending on the relevant recording act). Continue with the process for searching under "*C*", "*D*", and "*E*", respectively, in the grantor index. For each, you will search the period of *record ownership*—from the date each owner acquired a property interest until the date that the first deed out from that owner was recorded by the next owner.

As the third stage of your search, you should obtain actual copies of each of the deeds and other instruments you identified in your search of the grantor and grantee indexes (which generally point you to the relevant book and page number on which such instruments can be found). Read those documents, noticing whether any irregularities appear on their face, or whether they contain cross-references to yet other documents that have not been recorded in the public records. It will also be necessary for you to identify types of interests that your county might record in a separate repository, such as tax liens, bankruptcy claims, and judgment liens.

Note carefully: The explanation above describes the minimum examination that a title searcher must undertake in a jurisdiction that uses a grantor-grantee index. Many jurisdictions take a more expansive view of what documents fall within the record chain of title, which means that title searchers must correspondingly expand their search, as discussed in the next subsection.

2. Matters Potentially "Outside" the Chain of Title

There are at least four ambiguous situations where a document can be physically present in the recorder's office, but might be difficult or impossible for title searchers to locate. In those cases, courts must determine whether the actual physical "recording" of the document should be given legal significance, such that the document is held to provide constructive notice to subsequent purchasers. This is important because the law protects *bona fide* purchasers—those who take title without notice of adverse claims (as we will consider in section B, below). Concerns for fairness and/or efficiency usually guide the inquiry, but the decisions are not consistent. Such ambiguous situations include: (1) *late recording*, (2) *early recording*, (3) the *wild deed* problem, and (4) the *common grantor* problem.

In each diagram below, (R) marks the point in time when a document is recorded, and (N) indicates that a grantee had actual notice or inquiry notice of a prior competing property interest. In the absence of such notations, assume that the grantee did not record her deed, and did not have notice of any prior conveyance of an interest in the property. In each situation, consider whether a tract index system could avoid the problem. As an important practical lesson, consider also what these examples tell you about the value of deed warranties and title insurance.

Late recording: Sometimes a grantee (here, *A*) delays recording her property interest until after her predecessor (here, *O*) conveys a deed to someone else (here, *B*). For example, suppose *O* conveyed a mortgage to *A*, who neglected to record. *O* then conveyed a deed to *B*, who knew about *A*'s mortgage interest (and who, therefore, suffered no injury from *A*'s late recording). *B* promptly recorded the deed. Next, *A* records the mortgage. Finally, *B* conveys to *C*, who has no knowledge of *A*'s interest, and who promptly records. Prior to purchasing the property, *C* conducted a standard title search under "*O*" in the grantor index, looking from the year in which *O* acquired title until the (apparently) first deed out from *O* was recorded (the conveyance to *B*). That search did not turn up the prior mortgage to *A*, which was recorded later. Should *C* be charged with notice of *A*'s prior interest?

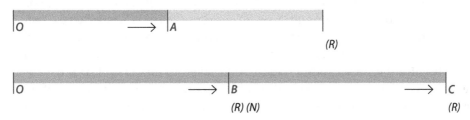

Figure 3

There is a split of authority as to whether the late recording provides constructive notice to title searchers. Some jurisdictions hold that *C* has notice of *A*'s mortgage from the public records, whereas others hold to the contrary. But to discover the mortgage, *C* would have to look under "*O*" in the grantor index from the date that *O* acquired title forward until the present date (not until the recording of the first deed out from *O*, the conveyance to *B*). Only such an expanded search would discover that *O* had made an earlier conveyance to *A*. If the jurisdiction recognizes late recording, then lawyers must routinely conduct such expanded searches.

Early recording: In other cases, a party (here, *X*) records a deed *before* that party's predecessor (here, *A*) actually acquired title to the property. For example, suppose *A* (who does not yet hold title, but who expects to receive a deed soon from *O*) conveys a deed to *X*, who promptly records. Soon thereafter, *O* conveys a deed to *A* (as expected), and *A* records promptly. Then, *A* conveys to *B*, who promptly records. Prior to purchasing the property, *B* conducted a standard title search under "*A*" in the grantor index, looking from the year in which *A* acquired title until the present time. That standard search failed to disclose that *before A* received title from *O*, *A* had conveyed an interest to *X*, who promptly recorded "early."

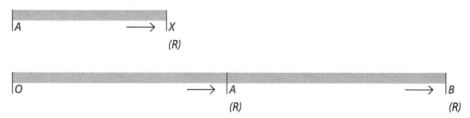

Figure 4

Most courts would hold that *B* is *not* charged with notice of the prior conveyance to *X*. To discover *X*'s interest, *B* would have to look under "*A*" in the grantor index starting well *before* (10 years? 50 years?) *A* acquired the deed from *O*. This would seem to place an unreasonable burden on *B*, so most jurisdictions would hold that *X*'s interest falls "outside" the chain of title.

Wild deeds: Suppose *O* conveys to *A*, who does not record. Then, *A* conveys to *B*, who records promptly. Next, *O* conveys the same property to *C*, who records promptly. Prior to accepting title, *C* conducted a standard title search, looking under "*O*" in the grantor index from the time *O* acquired title to the property until the present time. That search failed to link *O* to *A* or *B* because the *O* to *A* deed is not recorded in the public records. Because this chain of title has a missing link, all subsequent deeds (such as the one conveyed to *B*) are considered *wild*.

Figure 5

Virtually all jurisdictions hold that *B*'s deed is not properly "recorded" (even though it is physically somewhere in the public records building) so as to give *constructive notice*, unless all prior deeds in *B*'s chain of title have been recorded properly. It would be impossible for *C* to discover that *O* had made a prior conveyance to *A*, because that deed is not in the public records at all. *B*'s recorded deed is of no help because *B* is a stranger to *C* with no apparent connection to *O*. Therefore, *C* would have no reason to search under "*B*" in the public records. The lesson? *B* should not have purchased property from *A* without insisting that *A* first deposit her deed in the public records because a court will likely give priority to *C*'s interest over that of *B*. The wild deed problem is considered in *First Properties, L.L.C. v. JP Morgan Chase Bank*, below.

The common grantor problem: *O* is a developer who owns a large tract of land that he plans to develop into a high-end residential community. The tract is subdivided and *O* conveys Lot #1 to *A* who records promptly. *A* encumbers her property with a *restrictive covenant* (covered in Chapter 10, below), through which she promises that she and her successors will use her lot for residential purposes only. For his part, developer *O* promised in *A*'s deed, on behalf of himself and his successors, that his remaining property will be used for residential purposes only. Next, *O* conveys Lot #2 to *B*. *O* forgot to extract a residential-use-only promise from *B*, and *O* also neglected to promise on behalf of himself and his assigns that his remaining lots would be used for residential purposes only. *B* opens a restaurant.

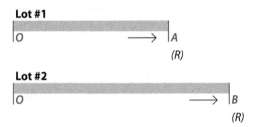

Figure 6

Can *A* enforce the residential-use-only promise against *B*? What type of title search would be required of *B* to discover that the use of her lot (Lot #2) had been restricted by *O*'s promise, as embodied in a deed within a *different* chain of title—that affecting Lot #1? Courts are split as to whether the limitation contained in *A*'s deed is binding upon *B*. This so-called common grantor problem is considered in *Witter v. Taggart*, below.

Other chain of title problems: Numerous other situations raise the issue of whether a document is recorded "within" (or "outside of") the chain of title, and therefore held to provide (or not to provide) constructive notice to those who come after. For example, like all humans, employees in the county recorder's office are fallible. On occasion, a document can be misindexed or lost. In other cases, the name of the grantor or the grantee might be misspelled, or one party might have numerous names not referenced in the index (such as a nickname, or a new name after marriage, divorce, or a legal name change). Jurisdictions split on many of these issues, making title insurance and seller's deed warranties essential supplements to assure security of title.

First Properties, L.L.C. v. JPMorgan Chase Bank

993 So. 2d 438 (Ala. 2008)

Reading Guide

◆ *The wild deed:* This case illustrates the problem of the wild deed. Notice whether the court treats the plaintiff's deed as *inside* or *outside* the chain of title.

◆ *Constructive notice:* Why does it matter if a deed or other title instrument is inside or outside the chain of title? As we will see in section B, below, documents outside the chain of title do not give constructive notice to subsequent claimants of the same property. As a result, courts will likely give priority to the claims of such subsequent bona fide purchasers over those holding wild deeds.

Sмith, J.

First Properties, L.L.C., appeals from a final judgment entered against it in an action filed by JPMorgan Chase Bank, National Association. We affirm.

On October 19, 1998, the Jefferson County fire district of Forestdale conducted a foreclosure sale on property located at 933 Heflin Avenue East in Birmingham. At the time of the sale, Ruthia Cullen Dumas held duly recorded title to the property. Apparently, the dues assessed by the fire district for fire-protection services were delinquent, and to satisfy the delinquency the fire district sold the property in accordance with the procedure outlined under "The Municipal Public Improvement Act".... [*S*]*ee also* § 12 of Act No. 79, Ala. Acts 1966 ..., which states that a service charge levied for fire districts in Jefferson County is "a personal obligation of the owner of the property served by the system," and creates a "lien against said property in favor of the district, which lien shall be enforceable by sale thereof in the same manner in which the foreclosure of a municipal assessment for public improvements is authorized."

With a bid of $603.45, the fire district was the highest bidder at the sale. The business manager of the fire district executed a deed purporting to convey the property from the fire district, as grantor, to the fire district, as grantee. The fire district then recorded the deed in the Jefferson County Probate Office on October 28, 1998. The deed was not listed in the grantor/grantee index, did not refer to Dumas as the owner of record, and contained what the trial court determined was an inadequate description of the property.

On November 9, 1999, Dumas secured a loan of $67,550 by executing a mortgage on the property in favor of First Franklin Financial Corporation. First Franklin recorded that mortgage in the Jefferson County Probate Office on January 13, 2000. On July 31, 2004, First Franklin assigned the mortgage to JPMorgan, and that mortgage was recorded on June 14, 2005.

On December 18, 2004, the fire district executed a quitclaim deed to the property to First Properties, in consideration of $2,851.25. The quitclaim deed listed Dumas as the owner of record before the foreclosure sale held on October 19, 1998. On December 23, 2004, First Properties recorded the quit-claim deed in the Jefferson County Probate Office.

On June 8, 2005, JPMorgan filed an action seeking a judgment declaring that it was a bona fide holder for value of the property without notice of the foreclosure sale by the fire district. JPMorgan claimed that it was entitled to status as a bona fide holder for value because, it alleged, the foreclosure deed to the fire district and the quitclaim deed from the fire district to First Properties were outside the chain of title and therefore did not serve as constructive notice to JPMorgan of the claimed interests of the fire district and First Properties. . . .

On November 29, 2006, the trial court entered a final order that included the following holdings:

> 1. JPMorgan is a bona fide encumbrancer of the property, for value, without notice of the foreclosure deed under which First Properties claims. As a result, the foreclosure sale and deed are ineffective as against JPMorgan. . . .
>
> 3. Alternatively, the legal description contained in the foreclosure sale notice and deed were defective, thus rendering the foreclosure sale and foreclosure deed invalid.
>
> 4. Alternatively, JPMorgan is entitled to redeem the property within three months from the date this order becomes final and, alternatively, for so long as its mort-gagor, Mrs. Dumas, holds possession of the property.

. . . First Properties filed a timely notice of appeal.

First Properties argues that the trial court erred in finding that JPMorgan is a "bona fide encumbrancer" for value.

"A bona fide purchaser is one who (1) purchases legal title, (2) in good faith, (3) for adequate consideration, (4) without notice of any claim of interest in the property by any other party. . . . Notice sufficient to preclude a bona fide purchase may be actual or constructive or may consist of knowledge of facts which would cause a reasonable person to make an inquiry which would reveal the interest of a third party. . . ." *Wallace v. Frontier Bank, N.A.,* 903 So. 2d 792, 797 (Ala.2004). . . . First Properties does not dispute that JPMorgan meets the first three requirements, *i.e.,* that JPMorgan purchased legal title in good faith for adequate consideration. First Properties contends, however, that JPMorgan did not purchase the property without notice of the fire district's and First Properties' claims to the property.

As noted, the fire district recorded the foreclosure-sale deed on October 28, 1998, before Dumas executed a mortgage on the property in favor of First Franklin. First Properties argues that First Franklin, which subsequently assigned the mortgage to JPMorgan, "was on constructive notice of all documents of record in the probate court," and, therefore, that JPMorgan had constructive notice of the foreclosure-sale deed.[1] . . . We disagree.

Although the fire district recorded the foreclosure-sale deed in the Jefferson County Probate Office on October 28, 1998, that deed does not list the record owner (Dumas). Thus, when the foreclosure-sale deed was indexed in the probate records the fire district was listed as both the grantor and the grantee, and the undisputed evidence before the trial court showed that a search of the grantor-grantee index in the Jefferson County Probate Office would not have uncovered the foreclosure-sale deed. Consequently, the foreclosure-sale deed is a "wild deed,"[2] outside the chain of title, and the fact that it was recorded did not impart constructive notice to First Franklin or to JPMorgan. As explained in *Wallace* . . . : "A purchaser is chargeable with notice of what appears on the face of the instruments *in his or her chain of title*. . . . However, *an instrument outside a purchaser's chain of title does not give constructive notice.*"

Accordingly, First Properties' argument that the foreclosure-sale deed provided constructive notice to JPMorgan is without merit. . . .

First Properties has not demonstrated that the trial court erred in holding that JPMorgan was a bona fide holder for value without notice of the foreclosure-sale deed. Accordingly, the trial court's judgment is due to be affirmed. . . .

---

1. [FN 1] More specifically, First Properties contends that JPMorgan was "put on constructive notice of anything of record in the probate court no matter how difficult to find those documents may be." . . . JP Morgan, in addition to citing legal authority that contradicts First Properties' argument in that regard, explains the impracticality of First Properties' position:

> First Properties argues that all documents recorded in a probate court impart constructive notice to any buyer. Under that logic, a buyer would be required to inspect all recorded documents in searching title to property. The average number of documents recorded daily in Jefferson County . . . is just under 1,000, amounting to approximately 260,000 per year. A 20-year search, therefore, would require review of 5,200,000 documents. The implications of First Properties' argument do not end there. It must be considered that such a search would include a duty to look [not only] for any instrument out of the record owner, but also for any document of any nature containing the legal description of the property. . . . First Properties would subject a title searcher to the duty of inspecting 5,200,000 documents and tracing millions of miles of calls in legal descriptions, handicapped by the even more severe burden of being subject to notice imparted by incomplete legal descriptions. . . .

2. [FN 2] *See* Robin Paul Malloy & Mark Klapow, *Attorney Malpractice for Failure to Require Fee Owner's Title Insurance in a Residential Real Estate Transaction*, 74 St. John's L. Rev. 407, 432 (2000): "A major pitfall in most recording systems involves the so-called wild deed. A wild deed is an instrument of conveyance that is literally recorded, but cannot be found by using the recordation index. Because it cannot be found, the wild deed poses a significant problem for searchers." . . .

Notes

1. *The wild deed:*   Describe at least three problems with the Fire District's purported recording of its deed. Did the court recognize the validity of such "recording" and should it have done so? Would this problem have arisen in a jurisdiction with a tract index?

2. *Practice pointer:*   What could First Properties have done to avoid this litigation and to protect its interest in the former Dumas property? What could JPMorgan have done?

3. *Two relatively innocent parties—the cheapest cost avoider:*   One way to think about the wild deed problem is the idea of the "cheapest cost avoider"—a concept derived from Guido Calabresi's seminal book, The Cost of Accidents: A Legal and Economic Analysis (1970). In the context of tort law, Calabresi reasoned that an optimal determination of liability would minimize the sum of the cost of accidents and the cost of avoiding them (including associated costs of administering the torts system). To promote this result, in appropriate cases Calabresi would assign tort liability to the party that could have avoided the subject harm most efficiently. In *First Properties v. JPMorgan Chase*, between the plaintiff and the defendant, who was the cheapest cost avoider? What action could that party have taken to avoid the problem in the first place? Did the court penalize the cheapest cost avoider here?

4. *Review—mortgages and foreclosure:*   Recall our study of mortgages and foreclosures from the previous chapter. Why do you think Ruthia Dumas remained in possession of the property, even though she no longer owned it after the foreclosure sale? Notice that the Dumas property sold for $603 at the foreclosure auction. Do you think such a sale would withstand judicial scrutiny if it had been challenged?

Witter v. Taggart

577 N.E.2d 338 (N.Y. 1991)

Reading Guide

◆ *The common grantor problem:* This case takes a closer look at the common grantor problem. Do you think the court came to the right conclusion?

◆ *The recording acts:* This case introduces the *recording acts*, which, according to the court, "protect the rights of innocent purchasers who acquire an interest in property without knowledge of prior encumbrances." The next subsection covers the recording acts in great detail. For now, try to get a sense of how the recording acts and the title search process work together.

BELLACOSA, J.

Plaintiff Witter and defendants Taggarts are East Islip neighboring property owners. Their homes are on opposite sides of a canal on the south shore of Long Island. Witter's home is north of the canal and the Taggarts' home and dock are across the canal on the south side. The Winganhauppauge or Champlin's Creek lies immediately west of both parcels. Their property dispute arose when the Taggarts erected a 70-foot long dock on their canal-side frontage. This was done after a title search revealed that their deed expressly permitted building the dock and reflected no recorded restrictions in their direct property chain against doing so. Witter complained of a violation of his scenic easement to an unobstructed view of the creek and an adjacent nature preserve, which he claims is protected by a restrictive covenant[3] contained in his chain of title. He sued to compel the Taggarts to dismantle and remove the dock and to permanently enjoin any such building in the future.

Supreme Court granted the Taggarts' motion for summary judgment dismissing Witter's complaint and denied Witter's cross motion for summary judgment. Relying principally on *Buffalo Academy of Sacred Heart v. Boehm Bros.*, 196 N.E. 42 (N.Y. 1935), the trial court held that the Taggarts are not bound by or charged with constructive notice[4] of a restrictive covenant which does not appear in their direct chain of title to the allegedly burdened land. . . .

The Appellate Division affirmed the instant case, reasoning that under *Buffalo Academy* . . . , the restrictive covenant contained in the chain of deeds to Witter's allegedly benefited parcel was outside the chain of title to the Taggarts' land and did not constitute binding notice to them. . . .

We granted Witter's motion for leave to appeal to decide whether the covenant recited in Witter's chain of title to his purported "dominant" land, which appears nowhere in the direct chain of title to the Taggarts' purported "servient" land, burdens the Taggarts' property. We agree with the lower courts that it does not, and therefore affirm the order of the Appellate Division.

The homes of these neighbors are located on lots which have been separately deeded through a series of conveyances, originally severed and conveyed out by a common grantor, Lawrance. Lawrance conveyed one parcel of his land to Witter's predecessor in title in 1951. The deed contained the restrictive covenant providing that "no docks, buildings, or other structures [or trees or plants]

---

3. [We will study easements and restrictive covenants in Chapters 9 and 10. Both give their holders (and their successors) a type of property right to use the land of another, or to prevent the owners (and their successors) from using their land in specified ways. The property interest burdened by a restriction is called the *servient* estate, and the property interest benefitted by a restriction is called the *dominant* estate.—Eds.]

4. [The presence or absence of notice is important under state *recording* acts, as considered in the next section. As we will see, "constructive notice" includes the type of notice that the public records provide to potential purchasers of property who conduct a proper title search.—Eds.]

shall be erected [or grown]" on the grantor's (Lawrance's) retained servient lands to the south "which shall obstruct or interfere with the outlook or view from the [dominant] premises" over the Winganhauppauge Creek. That deed provided that the covenant expressly ran with the *dominant* land. William and Susan Witter purchased the dominant parcel in 1963 by deed granting them all the rights of their grantor, which included the restrictive covenant. In 1984, Susan Witter transferred her interest to William Witter alone.

After common grantor Lawrance died, his heirs in 1962 conveyed his retained, allegedly servient, land to the Taggarts' predecessor in title. Lawrance's deed made no reference to the restrictive covenant benefiting the Witter property and neither did the heirs' deed to the Taggarts' predecessors. The restrictive covenant was also not included or referenced in any of the several subsequent mesne conveyances of that allegedly servient parcel or in the deed ultimately to the Taggarts in 1984. Quite to the contrary, the Taggarts' deed specifically permitted them to build a dock on their parcel.

Restrictive covenants are also commonly categorized as negative easements. They restrain servient landowners from making otherwise lawful uses of their property. . . . However, the law has long favored free and unencumbered use of real property, and covenants restricting use are strictly construed against those seeking to enforce them. . . .

The guiding principle for determining the ultimate binding effect of a restrictive covenant is that "[i]n the absence of actual notice before or at the time of . . . purchase or of other exceptional circumstances, an owner of land is only bound by restrictions if they appear in some deed of record in the conveyance to [that owner] or [that owner's] direct predecessors in title." *Buffalo Academy of Sacred Heart v. Boehm Bros.*, 196 N.E. 42 (N.Y. 1935). . . . Courts have consistently recognized and applied this principle, which provides reliability and certainty in land ownership and use. . . .

In *Buffalo Academy*, we held that a restrictive covenant did not run with the dominant land, but added that even if it did, the servient landowners were not bound because the deed to the servient land did not reflect the covenant. We noted that this rule is "implicit in the acts providing for the recording of conveyances." . . . The recording act . . . was enacted to accomplish a twofold purpose: to protect the rights of innocent purchasers who acquire an interest in property without knowledge of prior encumbrances, and to establish a public record which will furnish potential purchasers with actual or at least constructive notice of previous conveyances and encumbrances that might affect their interests and uses. . . .

The recording statutes in a grantor-grantee indexing system charge a purchaser with notice of matters only in the record of the purchased land's chain of title back to the original grantor. . . . *Buffalo Academy* recognized that a "purchaser is not normally required to search *outside* the chain of title" . . . , and is not chargeable with constructive notice of conveyances recorded outside of that purchaser's direct chain of title where, as in Suffolk County . . . , the grantor-grantee system of indexing is used. . . . This is true even if covenants are included in a deed to another lot conveyed by the same grantor. . . .

To impute legal notice for failing to search each chain of title or "deed out" from a common grantor "would seem to negative the beneficent purposes of the recording acts" and would place too great a burden on prospective purchasers (*Buffalo Academy of Sacred Heart v. Boehm Bros.*, . . . 196 N.E. 42). Therefore, purchasers like the Taggarts should not be penalized for failing to search every chain of title branching out from a common grantor's roots in order to unearth potential restrictive covenants. They are legally bound to search only within their own tree trunk line and are bound by constructive or inquiry notice only of restrictions which appear in deeds or other instruments of conveyance in that primary stem. Property law principles and practice have long established that a deed conveyed by a common grantor to a dominant landowner does *not* form part of the chain of title to the servient land retained by the common grantor. . . .

A grantor may effectively extinguish or terminate a covenant when, as here, the grantor conveys retained servient land to a bona fide purchaser who takes title without actual or constructive notice of the covenant because the grantor and dominant owner failed to record the covenant in the servient land's chain of title. . . . One way the dominant landowner or grantor can prevent this result is by recording in the servient chain the conveyance creating the covenant rights so as to impose notice on subsequent purchasers of the servient land. . . .

It goes almost without repeating that definiteness, certainty, alienability and unencumbered use of property are highly desirable objectives of property law. To restrict the Taggarts because of Lawrance's failure to include the covenant in the deed to his retained servient land, or for the failure by Witter's predecessors to insist that it be protected and recorded so as to be enforceable against the burdened property, would seriously undermine these paramount values, as well as the recording acts. . . .

[W]e hold that, consistent with long-standing precedents and property principles, the Taggarts did not have actual or constructive notice of this restrictive covenant because it was never included in their deed or direct chain of title. There being no other imputable constructive or inquiry notice, they are not bound by that covenant. . . .

Notes

1. *Practice pointer—expanding the title search:*   What type of title search would be required for the Taggarts to uncover the restrictive covenant affecting their lot? Would the common grantor problem arise in a tract index jurisdiction?

2. *The common grantor problem—searching one stem or all the branches?* *Witter v. Taggart* represents one view, but courts are divided. For whom did the court hold and why? Did the court penalize the cheapest cost avoider, or did it seek to advance other policies? Do you agree with the court's conclusion?

Problem

The sloppy subdivider: A developer owned a large tract of land, which was divided into numerous residential subdivision lots. Some of the purchasers (including the plaintiff Guillette) received deeds that contained single-family-residential-use-only restrictions "imposed solely for the benefit of the other lots shown" on a recorded subdivision plan. Those restricted deeds provided also that "the same restrictions are hereby imposed on each of said lots now owned by the seller." Other purchasers (including the defendant Daly Dry Wall) received deeds that failed to mention the restriction. Each deed was promptly recorded. In addition, *all* of the deeds referred to a recorded subdivision plan that identified the subdivision developer and showed the layout of all tracts in the subdivision, but that failed to mention the residential-use-only restriction. The defendant Daly Dry Wall bought a tract of land in the subdivision. Its deed contained no reference to any restrictions but did refer to the recorded subdivision plan. The defendant made no inquiry concerning restrictions and did not know of any development pattern. It had a title examination made. Later, it learned of the restrictions. Subsequently, it obtained a building permit to construct 36 apartment units on its lot. Guillette sued Daly Dry Wall to stop construction of the apartments.

Should the defendant be enjoined? Can this case be distinguished from *Witter v. Taggart? See Guillette v. Daly Dry Wall, Inc.,* 325 N.E.2d 572 (Mass. 1975) (enjoining construction of apartment building). Many courts follow the *Guillette* approach, whereas many others follow that of *Witter v. Taggart.* Which is preferable?

B. THE RECORDING ACTS

1. Overview of the Recording Acts

In some situations, a property owner (*O*) might convey an interest in the same property to more than one party. For example, as shown in Figure 7, *O* might convey a mortgage interest to American Bank (*A*), and then subsequently sell the property in fee simple absolute to *B*. Does *B* take subject to *A*'s mortgage interest? Or, *O* might lease the property to *A*, and then sell the property to *B*. In that case, must *B* honor *A*'s lease and accept *A* as a tenant? *O* might even sell the property to *A* (who, for a variety of reasons, does not take possession), and then later purport to sell the same property to *B*. Who has better title—*A* or *B*? It is possible that *O* is willfully engaging in fraud or double-dealing. But, it is just as likely that the property interests are not necessarily conflicting, or that *O* has simply made a mistake or forgotten about the prior conveyance.

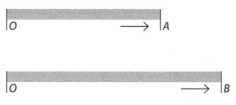

Figure 7

How should the law resolve the competing interests of *A* and *B*? Each state must struggle with this question as it drafts its recording statute. Notice, we are *not* asking whether *A* or *B* should have recourse against *O* for creating the problem in the first place (in most cases, they do have such recourse). Rather, as between two relatively innocent parties, which one should the law favor? In all of our examples, we will refer to the first line of conveyances as the first *chain of title* (or COT #1), and we will refer to the second line of conveyances as the second chain of title (or COT #2).

The common law default rule is *first in time, first in right*. That is, in each case above, *A*'s interest would be superior to that of *B* because *O* conveyed a property interest to *A* first. That sounds fair enough, but can you think of any circumstances under which the law should favor *B*? Some state statutes will favor *B*, but only if *A*'s interest is unrecorded *at the time* that *B* takes a property interest under the second conveyance. That is, because *A* failed to take simple measures to protect himself and to prevent future conflicts, some states will "rescue" *B* from the common law's rigid first in time rule. But, more is needed. As we consider below, in addition to *A*'s initial failure to record, *B* must, (1) *record* her property interest before *A* records (if ever), (2) pay value for the property and have no *notice* of *A*'s interest *at the time B* takes her property interest, or (3) satisfy both factors. The following *A Place to Start* box gives an overview of the recording acts. After you read that information, we will look at a number of examples to see how the recording acts operate in practice.

A Place to Start | **The Recording Acts and Notice**

- ***Recording acts:*** States follow one of the three following types of recording acts. The first—race statutes—are followed in less than a handful of jurisdictions.

  - ***Race recording acts:*** Under race statutes, a prior *unrecorded* conveyance is invalid against a subsequent purchaser (or sometimes all types of subsequent grantees, even donees) who *records* first.

  - ***Notice recording acts:*** Under notice statutes, a prior *unrecorded* conveyance is invalid against a subsequent *bona fide purchase* (that is, someone who (1) pays value for the property, and (2) takes a property interest without notice of the prior conveyance).

■ *Race-notice recording acts:* Under race-notice statutes, a prior *unrecorded* conveyance is invalid against a subsequent *bona fide purchaser* who *records first.*

■ *Types of notice:* Suppose *O* conveys an interest in Blackacre to *A*, and then subsequently conveys an interest in Blackacre to *B*. Under what circumstances will *B* be charged with notice of *A*'s prior interest?

■ *Actual notice:* As its name implies, *actual notice* means that a party is aware of the prior competing conveyance. For example, *B* would have actual notice if she had seen *A*'s deed, if *A* himself told *B* of his prior interest in the property, or under similar circumstances.

■ *Constructive notice—record:* A properly recorded property interest gives *constructive record notice* to all who take an interest in the property subsequent to the recording. For example, *B* would have constructive record notice of *A*'s prior claim if *A*'s deed is properly recorded in the public records, which *B* would find if she conducted a proper title search.

■ *Constructive notice—inquiry:* A party has *constructive inquiry notice* of a competing interest if there are facts sufficient to prompt a reasonable person to inquire further into the state of the title. For example, *B* might be charged with constructive inquiry notice of *A*'s prior claim if there were people on the property whose presence is not readily explained by the public records—are they tenants under an unrecorded lease, adverse possessors, or others with some potentially valid claim to possession or title?

DIGGING DEEPER: As you read the following material, keep two broad questions in mind. First, what policies should state recording acts promote—fairness, efficiency, or something else? Second, what (if anything) justifies the recording acts' rather extraordinary departure from the common law? After all, they can render the *first* owner's title subject to the claim of someone who came *later.*

Race jurisdictions: A few states will save *B* from the common law default rule *if* she records before *A* records—that is, if *B* can win the so-called *race to the courthouse* to file her deed in the public records. A typical race statute might assert:

A prior **unrecorded** conveyance is invalid against a subsequent **purchaser** who **records first.**

In Figure 8, as between *A* and *B*, whose claim receives priority?

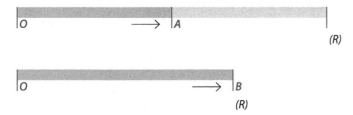

Figure 8

Under the race statute, we must ask three questions. First, was there a prior *unrecorded* conveyance in COT #1, measured as of the moment *B* took her property interest in COT #2? Yes. If not, then the statute simply does not apply and the common law rule governs. Although *A* eventually recorded his interest, he failed to do so *before B* took a competing property interest—in time for *B* to be aware of the potential problem and to make an informed decision. Second, did *B* qualify as a *purchaser*—a party who paid value for the property? Yes. In our examples, we will assume that *B* is a purchaser, unless the facts specifically indicate that *B* was a *donee*—one who acquired property at no cost, such as the recipient of a gift, an heir, or one who takes under a will. In some race jurisdictions (depending on how the statute is worded) even *donees* are entitled to protection. Finally, did *B* record before *A*? Yes. Therefore, in Figure 8, *B*'s interest has priority over *A*'s interest because the race statute rescued *B* from the common law default rule.

Conversely, suppose that *B* failed to record before *A* (even though *A*'s interest was unrecorded at the time of the conveyance to *B*). In that case, the race statute will not save *B* from the common law because she did not "record first" (in the words of the statute). As a result, *A* wins under the default common law rule. Be sure to notice that *A* cannot attribute his success to the race statute—it simply does not apply because *B* was unable to satisfy its requirements. Therefore, the default common law rule governs, to *A*'s advantage. What policies does the race statute promote?

Notice jurisdictions: Some state laws will save *B* from the common law default rule *if* she lacked notice of the prior conveyance to *A*, measured as of the moment *B* received her property interest. *B*'s victory will not be reversed if she later receives notice of *A*'s competing claim because the critical time is the moment *B* takes title—in time for *B* to be aware of the potential conflict and to make an informed decision.

A typical notice statute might assert:

> A prior **unrecorded** conveyance is invalid against a subsequent **purchaser** who **takes without notice**, or

> A prior **unrecorded** conveyance is invalid against a subsequent **bona fide purchaser (BFP).**

A *bona fide* purchaser is one who takes in good faith—that is, one who takes *without notice* of a prior competing conveyance. Therefore, *BFP* is a convenient shorthand to indicate one who both pays value ("purchaser"), and lacks notice ("bona fide") of a prior competing claim.

In Figure 8, does *A* or *B* have better claim to the property in a notice jurisdiction? Three questions are relevant under the notice statute. First, was there a prior *unrecorded* conveyance in COT #1, at the moment *B* took her property interest in COT #2? Yes (as discussed previously). Next, did *B* qualify as a *purchaser*? We will assume so (as discussed previously). Finally, is *B* a *bona fide* (good faith) purchaser? That is, did *B* "take" her property interest before (if ever) she had *notice* of *A*'s claim? Yes, because even a diligent title search prior to *B*'s acquisition of title would not have found *A*'s interest (which was not recorded until later), and there is no evidence that *B* had actual or inquiry notice. Therefore, under a notice statute, *B* is saved from the common law default rule and her interest is superior to that of *A*. What policies does the notice statute serve?

Race-notice jurisdictions: Some state laws will save *B* from the common law default rule if she recorded before *A*, *and* if she lacked notice of the prior conveyance to *A*. A typical race-notice statute might assert:

> A prior ***unrecorded*** conveyance is invalid against a subsequent ***purchaser*** who ***takes without notice*** and ***records first***, or

> A prior ***unrecorded*** conveyance is invalid against a subsequent ***bona fide purchaser (BFP)*** who ***records first.***

Again return to Figure 8. In a race-notice jurisdiction, does *A* or *B* have a better claim? As required under the race and notice statutes, first determine whether there was a prior *unrecorded* conveyance in COT #1, at the moment *B* took her property interest in COT #2. Yes (as discussed previously). Second, did *B* qualify as a *purchaser*? Yes (as discussed previously). Third, did *B* qualify as a *bona fide* (good faith) purchaser? Yes (as discussed previously). Finally, did *B* record first? Yes (as discussed previously). Therefore, under a race-notice statute, *B* is saved from the common law default rule and her interest receives priority over *A*'s interest.

Consider one further detail before you test your understanding of the recording acts with the problems below. How can you tell which type of recording act the jurisdiction applies? Often, the statutory language can be confusing. The key to deciphering the text is to work patiently through each clause of the statute and decide whether it applies to COT #1 or to COT #2. Not uncommonly, statutes locate the initial prerequisite for rescue from the common law (the presence of a *prior unrecorded conveyance*) in an awkward location within the text.

What type of recording act does the following statute represent?

> No conveyance, transfer, or mortgage of real property, or of any interest therein, nor any lease for a term of 1 year or longer, shall be good and effectual in law or equity against creditors or subsequent purchasers for a valuable consideration and without notice, unless the same be recorded according to law. . . . (Fla. Stat. § 695.01)

That language is an example of a *notice* statute. If you were confused, observe that the gray shading below marks the language applicable to COT #1. That language states the prerequisite for invocation of the statute: there must be a prior *unrecorded* conveyance in the first chain of title. The red text marks the language applicable to COT #2: the subsequent grantee seeking refuge from the default common law rule must qualify as a BFP.

> *No conveyance,* transfer, or mortgage of real property, or of any interest therein, nor any lease for a term of 1 year or longer, *shall be good* and effectual in law or equity against creditors or *subsequent purchasers for a valuable consideration and without notice, unless the same be recorded* according to law. . . . (Fla. Stat. § 695.01)

Test Your Understanding

In each example below, compare the final grantee in COT #1 against the final grantee in COT #2. Whose interest has priority under, (1) a race statute, (2) a notice statute, and (3) a race-notice statute? Why—because of the default common law rule or because of rescue under the statute? In the problems where a third party *C* has been introduced, the results may be ambiguous. In those cases, identify the potential outcomes, the result that you think is preferable, and why. Unless the illustration suggests otherwise, assume that each party failed to record, lacked actual or inquiry notice of a prior conveyance in the previous chain of title, and paid value for the property interest.

1. *Default or not?*   *O* conveys to *A*, who records promptly. Then *O* conveys to *B*, who records promptly.

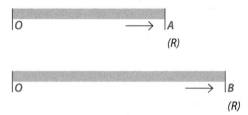

Figure 9

2. *The procrastinator:*   *O* conveys to *A*, then *O* conveys to *B*. Then, *A* records.

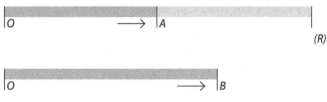

Figure 10

3. *The complacent purchaser:*   *O* conveys to *A*, then *O* conveys to *B*. Then, *A* records. Finally, *A* conveys to *C*. (Hint: Could *B* have done anything to protect her interest? If so, should *C*'s interest be entitled to priority over *B*'s interest?)

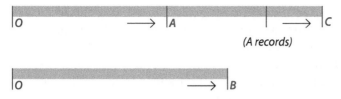

Figure 11

4. *The shelter rule:* O conveys to A, then O conveys to B, who records promptly. Then, A records. Finally, B conveys to C, who had actual notice of the conveyance from O to A. (<u>Hint:</u> Could B have done anything else to protect her interest? If not, should she be given priority over A?) The so-called *shelter rule* illustrated by this example is an integral part of the recording system and is applied in every jurisdiction. Can you imagine why? (<u>Hint:</u> First compare A to B. As between the two, B has superior title under any type of recording act. Why do the acts protect someone like B? Would those policies be undermined if B could not "shelter" C and pass on good title to C?

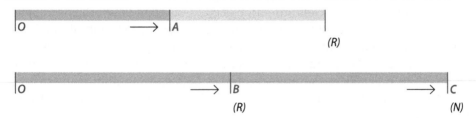

Figure 12

2. Protecting the Bona Fide Purchaser

In this subsection, we change our focus from the recording process to the beneficiaries of the recording system—*bona fide purchasers.* In the first case, we will examine the concepts of *good faith* and inquiry notice. In the second case, we will consider what it means to be a "purchaser" under an installment land sale contract.

Waldorff Insurance & Bonding, Inc. v. Eglin National Bank

453 So. 2d 1383 (Fla. Dist. Ct. App. 1984)

Reading Guide

What is encompassed within the notion of *inquiry notice*? Suppose a bank is about to acquire a mortgage interest in a multi-unit condominium building occupied by numerous parties. As the bank's attorney, what sort of title inquiry would you advise the bank to undertake?

Shivers, J.

Waldorff Insurance and Bonding, Inc. (Waldorff) appeals the supplemental final judgment of foreclosure entered against it in favor of Eglin National Bank (Bank) on a condominium unit. Appellant argues that the trial court erred in not finding its interest in the condominium unit superior to the liens of two mortgages held by the Bank. We agree and reverse.

Choctaw Partnership (Choctaw) developed certain properties in Okaloosa County by constructing condominiums. On June 8, 1972, Choctaw executed a promissory note and mortgage on these properties in the amount of $850,000. This indebtedness was later increased to $1,100,000. This note and mortgage was eventually assigned to appellee Bank on January 17, 1975. At that time, the principal balance remaining on this note and mortgage was $41,562.61.

Waldorff entered into a written purchase agreement with Choctaw for condominium unit 111 on April 4, 1973. Choctaw was paid $1,000 at that time as a deposit on Unit 111. The total purchase price of Unit 111 was to be $23,550. In April or May 1973, Waldorff began occupancy of the unit. Furniture worth $5,000 was purchased by Waldorff and placed in the unit. Waldorff continually occupied the unit for about 1-$\frac{1}{2}$ years thereafter, paying the monthly maintenance fee, the fee for maid service, the fee for garbage pick-up, and paying for repairs to the unit. At the time of the hearing in this case on February 21, 1983, the furniture was still in the unit, the utility bills and monthly maintenance fees were still paid by Waldorff, and Waldorff had the keys to the unit and controlled it.

On October 10, 1973, Choctaw executed a note and mortgage for the principal sum of $600,000 in favor of the Bank. Among the properties included in this mortgage was the condominium unit involved in the instant case, Unit 111.

On June 28, 1974, Choctaw executed yet another note and mortgage, this one in favor of the Bank for the principal sum of $95,000. This mortgage secured a number of units, one of which was Unit 111.

Choctaw was apparently a client of Waldorff, and in 1974, Choctaw owed Waldorff over $35,000 for insurance premiums. Choctaw agreed to consider the purchase price of Unit 111 paid in full in return for cancellation of the debt owed by Choctaw to Waldorff. Waldorff "wrote off" the debt, and Choctaw executed a quitclaim deed to Unit 111 in favor of Waldorff. The deed was recorded in March 1975.

In 1976, the Bank brought a foreclosure action against Choctaw, Waldorff and others. A final judgment of foreclosure was entered in September 1976, but that judgment did not foreclose Waldorff's interest in Unit 111. Instead, the 1976 final judgment explicitly retained jurisdiction to determine the ownership of Unit 111. A hearing was held on February 21, 1983. The issue at this hearing was whether Waldorff's occupancy, together with the purchase agreement, was sufficient notice so as to make Waldorff's interest in Unit 111 superior to that of the Bank. At this hearing, evidence was taken concerning the agreements between Choctaw and Waldorff and Waldorff's occupancy of Unit 111. There was evidence that condominium units other than 111 were also occupied and that many of these units were occupied by persons who had no legal interest in the units, *e.g.,* persons invited by Choctaw to occupy the units for a time as part of Choctaw's marketing campaign.

The trial court entered a supplemental final judgment of foreclosure which found that Waldorff's occupancy of Unit 111 was "equivocal" because Choctaw allowed at least 8 other condominium units to be furnished and used for occupancy by various persons. The trial court also found that Waldorff did not pay the consideration promised for Unit 111 because the debt owed by Choctaw to Waldorff was used as a bad debt write-off for federal income tax purposes rather than being credited to Choctaw. The trial court found that "even if defendant could establish some right to Unit 111 by occupancy, defendant failed to pay the agreed consideration for the quitclaim deed and, therefore, the conveyance is void." Based on these findings, the trial court held the Bank's mortgage liens superior to Waldorff's interest.

A contract to convey legal title to real property on payment of the purchase price creates an equitable interest in the purchaser. Beneficial ownership passes to the purchaser while the seller retains mere naked legal title. Subsequent successors to the legal title take such title burdened with the equitable interests of which they have either actual or constructive notice. . . . In the instant case, it appears clear that the April 4, 1973, Agreement to Purchase entered into between Choctaw and Waldorff vested equitable title in Waldorff. Therefore, the interests acquired by the Bank pursuant to the October 1973 and June 1974 mortgages would be subordinate to Waldorff's equitable interest if the Bank had either actual or constructive notice of that interest. . . .

In *Blackburn v. Venice Inlet Co.,* 38 So. 2d 43 (Fla.1948), the court stated:

> It is settled law in Florida that actual possession is constructive notice to all the world, or anyone having knowledge of said possession of whatever right the occupants have in the land. Such possession, when open, visible and exclusive, will put upon inquiry those acquiring any title to or a lien upon the land so occupied to ascertain the nature of the rights the occupants really have in the premises.

Id. at 46. . . . In the instant case, Waldorff was in open, visible and exclusive possession of Unit 111 at the time of the making of the October 1973 and June 1974 mortgages.

The trial court found, however, that Waldorff's possession of Unit 111 was "equivocal" because other units in the condominium project were occupied by persons who had no interest in the units. We do not agree with this analysis. Although many of the condominium units were held by a common grantor, Choctaw, the units were separate parcels intended to be alienated individually.

The mortgage executed on June 28, 1974, which secures both the $95,000 note and the $600,000 note of October 10, 1973, described the property mortgaged in terms of individual units, specifically including Unit 111. The status of other units within the condominium project, therefore, is irrelevant to the question of the possession of Unit 111. The issue in the instant case concerned only the rights of the parties involved in Unit 111, not the condominium project as a whole or any other individual units.

Appellee argues, however, that it would have been difficult to ascertain whether any person physically occupying any of the units in the project had a claim of ownership interest in the unit being occupied. Although we agree that it would be more inconvenient for a prospective lender to make several inquiries rather than a single one, we do not find this argument persuasive. We find the ancient, but oft-cited, case of *Phelan v. Brady,* 23 N.E. 1109 (N.Y. 1890), to be instructive in this matter. On May 1, 1886, Mrs. Brady took possession of a tenement building containing 48 apartments occupied by 20 different occupants as tenants from month to month. Her possession was pursuant to a contract for sale secured for her by her attorney. Three of the apartments were occupied by Mrs. Brady and her husband, who kept a liquor store in part of the building. Mrs. Brady began collecting rents immediately upon taking possession of the premises. Mrs. Brady's deed, however, was not recorded until August 26, 1886, subsequent to the recordation of Phelan's mortgage which had been executed by the record owner of the property on July 23, 1886. The court stated:

> At the time of the execution and delivery of the mortgage to the plaintiff, the defendant Mrs. Brady was in the actual possession of the premises under a perfectly valid, but unrecorded, deed. Her title must therefore prevail as against the plaintiff. It matters not, so far as Mrs. Brady is concerned, that the plaintiff in good faith advanced his money upon an apparently perfect record title of the defendant John E. Murphy. Nor is it of any consequence, so far as this question is concerned, whether the plaintiff was in fact ignorant of any right or claim of Mrs. Brady to the premises. It is enough that she was in possession under her deed and the contract of purchase, as that fact operated in law as notice to the plaintiff of all her rights. It may be true, as has been argued by plaintiff's counsel, that, when a party takes a conveyance of property situated as this was, occupied by numerous tenants, it would be inconvenient and difficult for him to ascertain the rights or interests that are claimed by all or any of them. But this circumstance cannot change the rule. Actual possession of real estate is sufficient to a person proposing to take a mortgage on the property, and to all the world, of the existence of any right which the person in possession is able to establish. . . .

We also agree with appellant that the trial court erred in finding that the conveyance of the property from Choctaw to Waldorff was void due to lack of consideration for the quitclaim deed. Although Waldorff may have erred in attempting to take a "bad debt" tax deduction after cancelling the debt Choctaw owed to Waldorff for insurance premiums, Choctaw was relieved from payment of that debt, and this constituted a valuable consideration flowing to Choctaw. . . .

The parties agree that the 1972 mortgage lien is superior to Waldorff's interest in Unit 111. . . . [T]he supplemental final judgment of foreclosure is reversed and the cause remanded for entry of a judgment consistent with this opinion. Reversed and remanded.

Notes

1. *The BFP—who is a "purchaser" for value?*   Notice that Waldorff "wrote off" Choctaw's debt rather than pay money in exchange for the quitclaim deed. What issue did this raise, and how did the court resolve it?

As one hornbook explains,

> A common problem is raised by the creditor who takes a mortgage . . . as further security for a pre-existing debt. . . . Unless the bank somehow changes its position detrimentally in return for the mortgage, as by granting an extension of time for repayment . . . or giving some other concession such as a reduction in interest rate, it will by the large majority of cases be deemed not to have given value under the recording acts. Hence, the bank's mortgage will be subordinate to any prior unrecorded conveyances the debtor has made. . . .

> . . . But consider the case of the creditor who has previously made an unsecured loan, and who later takes a deed of the land in full or partial satisfaction of the debt. The creditor's position here is superficially similar to one who takes a mortgage to secure an antecedent debt. . . . Yet there is a vast difference, for here the creditor has detrimentally changed legal position by treating the debt as satisfied, typically by cancelling the debtor's promissory note. . . . Surprisingly, a number of courts have misunderstood this distinction, and have found no value to have been paid. This is plainly incorrect; the creditor should be protected, and the more recent decisions adopt this view.

William B. Stoebuck & Dale A. Whitman, The Law of Property 881-82 (3d ed. 2000). Which situation did *Waldorff v. Eglin* involve? Did the court reach the correct result, according to Stoebuck and Whitman?

2. *The BFP—who takes "without notice"?*   In jurisdictions that follow *Waldorff v. Eglin*, what type of title investigation must a prospective purchaser (or mortgage lender) undertake? Is that a good result? There is a split of authority on the scope of inquiry required of would-be BFPs, but *Waldorff* is fairly representative. How could prospective purchasers protect themselves against potential ownership claims of persons in possession? We will look at one solution in the skills practice exercise in section D, below.

Daniels v. Anderson

642 N.E.2d 128 (Ill. 1994)

Reading Guide

Notice and race-notice recording acts protect bona fide purchasers. But at what point in time does one qualify as a BFP under an installment land sale contract?

FREEMAN, J.

. . . In March 1977, Daniels contracted with Anderson and Jacula to buy the Daniels Property. The written contract consisted of a preprinted form and a rider. . . . [that provided]:

> *Right to Purchase Additional Land.* Seller agrees that he shall grant Purchaser the first right to purchase (on the same terms and conditions, and for the same price, as any bona-fide offer in writing made to Seller) a tract of land approximately two acres in area [the Contiguous Parcel], being that piece adjacent to [the Daniels Property]. . . .

Daniels and his wife moved into the single-family home on the Daniels Property when they entered into the 1977 sales contract. In March 1979, the Daniels Property closed and the Danielses received a deed. This deed did not mention Daniels' . . . right of first refusal of the Contiguous Parcel. Daniels did not record the 1977 sales contract at this time.

In June 1979, Jacula and his wife acquired sole ownership of the Contiguous Parcel. . . .

In September 1985, Zografos contracted with the Jaculas to buy the Contiguous Parcel for $60,000. . . . Since Daniels had not recorded the 1977 contract by this time, a title search for this sale to Zografos reflected that Daniels did not have any interest in the Contiguous Parcel. Pursuant to the 1985 contract, Zografos paid the Jaculas $10,000 initially and delivered to them a judgment note on the balance. On February 18, 1986, Zografos paid $15,000 and, on March 22, he paid another $15,000. At the closing on August 22, Zografos paid the remaining $20,000. Shortly after that date, Zografos recorded a warranty deed to the Contiguous Parcel. . . .

Daniels brought this action in December 1989. Daniels sought the specific performance of his right of first refusal of the Contiguous Parcel. Daniels also sought damages from Jacula for breaching the 1977 contract and damages from Zografos for interfering with that contract. . . .

At the close of a hearing, the trial court found as follows. Daniels' right of first refusal of the Contiguous Parcel, as provided by the 1977 sales contract, was legally enforceable. Zografos had actual notice of Daniels' right prior to Zografos' purchase of that parcel. Therefore, Zografos was not a *bona fide* purchaser of the Contiguous Parcel and he took title thereto subject to Daniels' right. Also, Jacula breached the 1977 sales contract by selling the Contiguous Parcel to Zografos without first offering it to Daniels.

Based on these findings, the trial court entered a judgment that provided as follows. Zografos was ordered to convey the Contiguous Parcel to Daniels on the same terms and conditions as Zografos received the property. . . . Daniels was ordered to pay Zografos the full purchase price and reimburse him for approximately $11,000 in property taxes that Zografos had paid on the Contiguous Parcel during his ownership. . . .

The appellate court affirmed the trial court's judgment in all material respects. . . .

. . . [I]n this appeal [Zografos] contends . . . he was a *bona fide* purchaser of the Contiguous Parcel. . . .

Daniels sought, *inter alia,* the specific performance of his right of first refusal of the Contiguous Parcel. Specific performance refers to the very (hence specific) thing required by a contract. This equitable remedy stands in contrast to the remedy at law, which is the payment of money as a substitute for performance. Specific performance is based on the desire to do more perfect and complete justice, which the remedy at law would fail to give. Further, specific performance is generally not available as a matter of right. . . .

A contractual right of first refusal is a valuable prerogative. A landowner is under a duty not to sell to any third person without first offering the land to the promisee. The promisee has an enforceable right to such forbearance. . . . If the owner offers or accepts an offer to sell the land to a third person, thereby breaching the contract, the promisee may obtain specific performance. This would compel the owner to convey to the promisee on the same terms as with the third person, "*as long as there is no contract with an innocent purchaser.*" (Emphasis added.) 5A A. Corbin, Corbin on Contracts § 1197, at 377-78 (1964).

Zografos raises the defense that he was an innocent, or *bona fide,* purchaser. A *bona fide* purchaser is a person who takes title to real property in good faith for value without notice of outstanding rights or interests of others. A *bona fide* purchaser takes such title free of any interests of third persons, except such interests of which he has notice. . . .

Zografos testified that he did not know of Daniels' right of first refusal until Daniels' wife told him in June 1986. By that time, Zografos had already contracted to buy the Contiguous Parcel and had paid $40,000 of the $60,000 purchase price. The trial court found that Zografos was not a *bona fide* purchaser based solely on this June 1986 notice.

In the appellate court, Zografos contended that he was a *bona fide* purchaser of the Contiguous Parcel despite his June 1986 notice of Daniels' interest. Zografos invoked the doctrine of equitable conversion in support of his *bona fide* purchaser defense. He argued that although he did not take legal title to the Contiguous Parcel until August 1986, he became the equitable owner of the

Contiguous Parcel in September 1985, when he entered into the contract. . . . Thus, Zografos reasoned, he became a *bona fide* purchaser because he took equitable title prior to receiving the June 1986 notice of Daniels' interest. The appellate court concluded that Zografos waived this theory. . . .

. . . Zografos raised this theory for the first time on appeal. "It has frequently been held that the theory upon which a case is tried in the lower court cannot be changed on review, and that an issue not presented to or considered by the trial court cannot be raised for the first time on review." . . .

Zografos attempts to avoid this prohibition. He argues that although he may not have used the label "equitable conversion," his presentation in the trial court encompassed the doctrine. . . .

Zografos' attempt to avoid the waiver rule fails. Although the parties addressed the issue of when Zografos received notice of Daniels' right of first refusal, the doctrine of equitable conversion goes to when Zografos "owned" the Contiguous Parcel. The record shows that Zografos did *not* contend in the trial court that he *had already owned* the Contiguous Parcel prior to the June 1986 notice. Rather, he argued that the June 1986 notice, in the context of all of the circumstances, was insufficient to deny him the status of a *bona fide* purchaser.

. . . We agree with the appellate court that "Zografos' advancement of the [equitable conversion] doctrine constitutes a new theory of defense which he never raised below." . . .

We must next address, absent consideration of the equitable conversion doctrine, the issue of when during the executory stages of a real estate installment contract does the buyer become a *bona fide* purchaser. Zografos contends that, during this executory period, the buyer can rely solely on the public records and ignore even actual notice of an outstanding, unrecorded interest.

This contention is erroneous. The legal principles are quite established. As we earlier noted, a *bona fide* purchaser, by definition, takes title to real property *without notice* of the interests of others. . . . A buyer who, prior to the payment of *any* consideration receives notice of an outstanding interest, pays the consideration at his or her peril with respect to the holder of the outstanding interest. Such a buyer is not protected as a *bona fide* purchaser and takes the property bound by the outstanding interest. . . . The law reasons that consummation of the purchase, after notice of the outstanding interest, is a fraud upon the holder of that interest. . . .

Where a buyer receives notice of an outstanding interest subsequent to paying *some*, but prior to paying the full purchase price, authorities differ on whether the buyer is a *bona fide* purchaser. As the appellate court noted, some of the authorities state that partial payment of the consideration is insufficient to render the buyer a *bona fide* purchaser. . . .

However, a majority of jurisdictions have relaxed this harsh rule. Instead, they apply a *pro tanto* rule, which protects the buyer to the extent of the payments made prior to notice, but no further. . . .

Courts have identified at least three methods to apply this *pro tanto* protection. First, the most common method is to award the land to the holder of the outstanding interest and award the buyer the payments that he or she made. The second method is to award the buyer a fractional interest in the land proportional to the amount paid prior to notice. The third method is to allow the buyer to complete the purchase, but to pay the remaining installments to the holder of the outstanding interest.... Courts exercise considerable latitude in these cases, taking into account the relative equities of the parties. ...

In the present case, the trial court ordered Zografos to convey the Contiguous Parcel to Daniels and ordered Daniels to pay Zografos the full purchase price. The trial court also ordered Daniels to reimburse Zografos for the property taxes that Zografos had paid on the property. We agree with the appellate court that the trial court's disposition of this issue, between Daniels and Zografos, satisfied these well-settled principles of equity. ... We cannot say that the trial court abused its discretion. ...

Notes

1. *The recording acts:* What type of recording act does this jurisdiction follow? The court does not directly answer this question, so you will have to read between the lines. At what point in time does the court measure BFP status?

2. *Majority and minority rules:* The court follows the majority *pro tanto* rule. Do you think the majority rule is the best approach? Consider the three methods that courts use to apply the *pro tanto* rule. What are the relative strengths of each approach? Conversely, in a jurisdiction that follows the minority rule, what type of title search must purchasers conduct in order to maintain their status as *bona fide* purchasers?

3. *Review—installment land sale contract:* Recall our study of installment land sale contracts (Chapter 7). What are they? Why does it matter in this case that Zografos purchased under such an installment contract? Would the result have been the same if Zografos had obtained a conventional mortgage from a commercial lender?

4. *Review—equitable conversion:* Previously, we encountered the doctrine of equitable conversion in the context of allocating the risk of loss during the executory period under a contract of sale (Chapter 7.B.2) and determining the protections owed to a defaulting buyer under an installment land sale contract (Chapter 7.D.2). In each situation, did the doctrine favor the buyer or the seller, and how? If Zografos had been allowed to raise the defense in this case, would that have changed the outcome of the case?

C. BEYOND THE BLACK LETTER: EVALUATING THE RECORDING SYSTEM

Review the three real property indexing systems used in the United States. To help you think more deeply about those systems and their implications for title security in particular, and property law in general, formulate responses to the following questions.

Discussion Questions

1. *Benefits and costs:*   What are the benefits and costs of each system? Be specific. Be sure to consider the relative accuracy of each type of title system.

2. *What should be recorded?*   Keeping costs and benefits in mind, what types of titles should be recorded or registered? Beyond title to real property, should the recording system also provide for the registration of titles to personal property? If so, what should be included—valuable art (as considered in *O'Keeffe v. Snyder*, Chapter 2); automobiles; the lease to your apartment; your Property casebook? Does your university have a bicycle registration system? If so, do you use it (assuming you have a bicycle)? Why or why not? As an alternative to the *recording* of documents, should the determination of superior title instead be based on *possession*?

3. *What or whom should be protected?*   The grantor-grantee and tract index systems generally protect *bona fide* purchasers. In contract, the Torrens registry protects those who have gone through the judicial registration process, but with some potential statutory exceptions for unregistered (and possibly undiscoverable) interests deemed worthy of protection. As a matter of public policy, what should those protected interests be? Torrens systems might protect, for example, such "overriding interests" as public rights of way, utility easements, short-term leaseholds, certain mortgages (recognizing the importance of the lending industry to national economies), or the rights of persons in actual possession of the property. In your view, should recording systems protect specific *claimants* (such as BFPs), specific property *interests*, or something else? Consider difficulties of proof, fairness, efficiency, and other policies you deem important.

4. *Property, information, and secrecy:*   What is the relationship between property and information? Is there such a thing as *too little* disclosure, or *too much*? If you would like to read more on these topics, *see, e.g.,* Abraham Bell & Gideon Parchomovsky, *Of Property and Information*, Columbia L. Rev. (arguing that "[r]egistries and the information they contain are . . . the formative forces that shape the world of property"); Amnon Lehavi, *Property and Secrecy* (2015),

http://papers.ssrn.com/sol3/papers.cfm?abstract_id=2662852   (noting the "bourgeoning phenomenon of secret ownership in Manhattan's high-end condominiums" to mask a combination of American and foreign wealth and asking whether secrecy may become the new norm).

D. SKILLS PRACTICE: DRAFTING TENANT ESTOPPEL STATEMENTS

Review *Waldorff Insurance v. Eglin National Bank*. You represent Eglin National Bank. Your client has given developer Choctow Partnership two prior loans on the multi-unit condominium building described in that case in exchange for two promissory notes and mortgages. Choctow proposes to convey yet another promissory note and mortgage on the building to secure an additional loan. Your client has noticed that many of the units in the building appear to be occupied by various persons and businesses.

Tasks

1. *Preparing to interview persons in possession:*   Your client has asked you to interview persons in possession of units in the building to determine their legal status. Will you interview everyone in the building? What questions will you ask? You have searched the public records and uncovered recorded leases to several units in the building. Will you also interview the persons in possession of those units? If so, what information would you seek beyond that contained in the written and recorded leases?

2. *Drafting estoppel statements:*   Often, cautious buyers ask tenants to execute estoppel statements. In the statements, purchasers (or lenders, as in the case of *Waldorff v. Eglin*) seek to verify the precise rights of tenants, including any agreements with the current owner not reduced to writing. Further, purchasers have an interest in knowing that tenants are financially sound and will continue to pay rent until the expiration of their leases (which, in turn, assists purchasers in making their mortgage payments). What provisions would you include in such a statement? List them. *See, e.g.,* Mark A. Senn, *Estoppel Certificates*, American Law Institute Continuing Legal Education, June 11-12, 2012 (ST054 ALI-CLE 1507) (containing sample statements and describing the estoppel certificate as "a status report on the lease that confirms its effectiveness and terms, and the absence of defenses to it or claims under it"); Douglas S. Buck & Katherine R. Rist, *Using Wisconsin's Commercial Offer to Purchase Form*, 81 Wisconsin Lawyer 10 (2008).

E. CHAPTER REVIEW

1. Practice Questions[5]

1. *Aaron conveys Blackacre to Bianca, who does not record.* Aaron then executes a deed to Carlos purporting to convey Blackacre to Carlos. Carlos had no notice of the deed to Bianca and paid Aaron full value for the property. Bianca then records her deed, after which Carlos records his deed. At the time Carlos received his deed, Bianca was not in possession of Blackacre, but soon thereafter Carlos found her in possession of Blackacre. The jurisdiction's recording statute provides:

> Every conveyance of real property shall be void as to subsequent purchasers and incumbrancers who give value and take without notice, unless such conveyance is duly recorded before such subsequent purchase or incumbrance.

Carlos sues to eject Bianca. Who will prevail?
   A. Bianca will prevail because the jurisdiction has enacted a race statute.
   B. Bianca will prevail because the jurisdiction has enacted a race-notice statute.
   C. Carlos will prevail because the jurisdiction has enacted a notice statute.
   D. Bianca will prevail under the common law default rule.

2. *Oma conveyed Blackacre to Aaron.* The next day, Oma conveyed a deed to Blackacre to Bianca, who had no notice of the prior conveyance. Bianca promptly recorded her deed. Later, Aaron recorded his deed. Then, Bianca gave a deed to Blackacre to Carlos, who knew of the prior conveyance to Aaron. Carlos promptly recorded his deed. In a lawsuit between Aaron and Carlos, who will prevail?
   A. Carlos will prevail under the shelter rule.
   B. Aaron will prevail if the jurisdiction has enacted a race statute.
   C. Aaron will prevail if the jurisdiction has enacted a notice statute.
   D. Aaron will prevail under the common law default rule.

3. *Oma conveyed Whiteacre to Aaron.* The next day, Oma gave a deed to Whiteacre to Bianca, who took without notice of the prior conveyance. Then, Aaron recorded his deed, and subsequently gave a deed to the property to Carlos. Bianca then recorded her deed. Next, Carlos recorded his deed. In a lawsuit between Bianca and Carlos, who will prevail?
   A. Carlos will prevail if the jurisdiction has enacted a notice statute.
   B. Bianca will prevail if the jurisdiction has enacted a notice statute.

---

5. Answers appear in Casebook Appendix A.

C. Bianca will prevail if the jurisdiction has enacted a race-notice statute.
D. Bianca will prevail if the jurisdiction has enacted a race statute.

4. *Oma conveyed her property to Aaron who did not record.* Oma then conveyed her property to Bianca, who took without notice of the conveyance to Aaron, paid value, and recorded. Bianca then conveyed a deed to the property to Carlos, who knew of the prior conveyance to Aaron, did not pay value, and did not record. Does Aaron or Carlos have better title under each of the three types of recording acts?

5. *Oma conveyed her property to Aaron who did not record.* Oma then conveyed a deed to the same property to Bianca who paid value. One week after the conveyance, Oma told Bianca about the prior transfer to Aaron. Bianca immediately ran to the recorder's office and properly recorded her deed. Does Aaron or Bianca have better title under each of the three types of recording acts?

2. Bringing It Home

Research your state's statutory law, and find its relevant provisions on the issues listed below.

1. *Recording act:* What type of recording act does your jurisdiction follow?

2. *Marketable record title act:* Does your state have a marketable record title act? If so, what period of record is sufficient to establish marketable record title?

PART FOUR

THE SCOPE OF PROPERTY— RIGHTS AND RESTRICTIONS

Contractual Limits and Beyond: Easements

Chapter 9–Cases

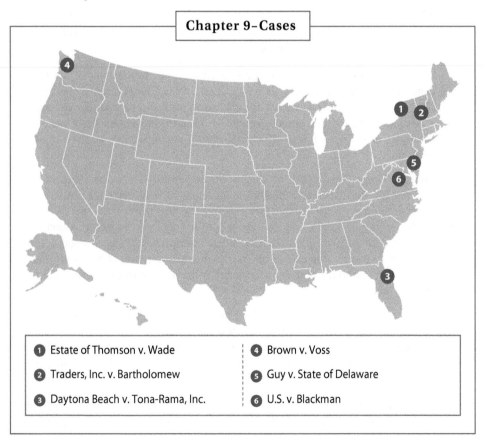

1 Estate of Thomson v. Wade

2 Traders, Inc. v. Bartholomew

3 Daytona Beach v. Tona-Rama, Inc.

4 Brown v. Voss

5 Guy v. State of Delaware

6 U.S. v. Blackman

In this chapter, we will study the topic of easements; in the next, we will learn about closely related arrangements known as *running covenants.* Together, easements and running covenants are often described as *servitudes.*

Easements are nonpossessory interests in the land of another. For example, *A* (fee simple owner of Blackacre) might grant neighbor *B* an easement to pass through Blackacre as a shortcut to the main road. Grounded in the intent of the parties, easements bear some resemblance to contracts. But they are more than contracts—they are also property rights that can be recorded in the jurisdiction's official registry of documents affecting land title, and their benefits and burdens generally pass to subsequent owners of the affected properties. Recall Chapters 3 through 6, which considered property shared over space or across time—estates and future interests, landlord-tenant law, concurrent ownership, marital interests, and the commons. Easements represent yet another type of shared property interest. In the example above, both *A* and *B* have certain legal rights to Blackacre: *A* holds a possessory fee simple estate in Blackacre, whereas *B* holds a nonpossessory use right in Blackacre.

Easements implicate the casebook theme "just passing through" and raise challenging questions of "dead hand" control, which we first encountered in Chapter 3's study of estates and future interests. In particular, why should easements and running covenants bind landowners subsequent to the original parties? As Professor Carol Rose suggests,

> Easements and covenants are second only to the "fee tail" or perhaps to "springing uses" as a symbol of the mindless formalism of traditional property law. . . . [W]hen we consider what easements and real covenants *do*—bind land owners to some previous owners' agreements in which the current owners have had no say—the puzzle is that a free and rational nation permits these legal arrangements at all. . . .
>
> [W]e tolerate these "dead hand" arrangements because they provide a long lasting security for land development and encourage property owners to invest in the long term improvements that are essential to the productive use of real estate. As Jeremy Bentham told us over a century ago, secure expectations of return are a *sina qua non* of enterprise; if the community wants to encourage my neighbor to invest time and effort in a solar heating panel, it had better let him agree with me that I and my successors will keep my trees from overshadowing his roof. . . .
>
> Many of the courts' complex distinctions help us to infer whether a new taker has voluntarily accepted the obligations of a servitude—an inference especially important in a society that aspires to conduct its affairs on the basis of free choice. Indeed, as rhetoric, *the inference of continuing or renewed assent* to some degree defuses the intergenerational conflict inherent in these long-lasting obligations.

Carol M. Rose, *Servitudes, Security, and Assent: Some Comments on Professors French and Reichman*, 55 S. Cal. L. Rev. 1403, 1403-04 (1982) (emphasis added).

As you read this chapter, think about the degree to which society tolerates (or restricts) such dead hand arrangements. Does the law governing the creation, scope, and termination of easements adequately address "dead hand" control? Do you agree with Professor Rose's suggestion that an inference of *continuing or renewed assent* can overcome some of the questions of dead hand control? Try to formulate tentative answers to these intractable questions as you read the following materials.

A. OVERVIEW

To begin our study of easements, it will be helpful for you to familiarize yourself with some basic vocabulary. After you review the *Test Your Understanding* box, try to work through the problems that follow, which challenge you to apply the new terminology to specific factual situations.

A Place to Start | **Terminology**

- *Appurtenant/in gross:* Easements *appurtenant* benefit land; easements *in gross* benefit people.

- *Dominant/servient:* The *dominant tenement* (also called *dominant estate*) is the tract of land benefitted by the easement, and the servient tenement is the burdened tract. Easements in gross have no associated dominant estates (because they benefit people, not land).

- *Affirmative/negative:* *Affirmative* easements permit their holders to make specified uses of the associated servient parcel; *negative* easements prohibit servient landowners from making specified uses of their own property. English and American common law disfavor negative easements, and grudgingly recognize only four types, which prohibit certain uses of the servient tenement:

  - *Blockage of light:* may not block light from windows on the dominant estate (many jurisdictions limit negative easements of light to those created *expressly*, rather than by *implication*);

  - *Blockage of air:* may not block air flow to dominant estate (many jurisdictions limit negative easements of air to those created *expressly*, rather than by *implication*);

  - *Removal of building support:* may not remove subjacent or lateral support from buildings on dominant estate; and

  - *Interference with streams:* may not interfere with the flow of water in *artificial* streams directed toward the dominant estate (principles of water law address conflicts involving *natural* streams).

- *Exclusive/nonexclusive:* Because easements are *nonpossessory* rights, their holders generally lack the ability to exclude others. Therefore, in the absence of evidence of the parties' contrary intent, an easement holder enjoys a *nonexclusive* right to use the servient tenement. That means that the holder cannot exclude the owner of the servient estate, nor prevent her from allowing others to use the servient estate in a manner not inconsistent with the easement holder's allowed uses.

- *Distinguish:* Be sure to distinguish easements from the following:
  - *Licenses:* Licenses are created when landowners give revocable permission (written or oral) to use their land in a manner that, absent permission, would constitute a trespass. Recalling the terminology of leases, you could think of licenses as "easements at will."
    - *Profits à prendre ("profits"):* Profits are nonpossessory interests that allow holders to remove things such as sand, minerals, wood, and water from the land of another.

DIGGING DEEPER: The terminology set forth above makes little sense until you apply it to specific factual scenarios, such as those contained in the problems below. As you do so, think about why landowners would voluntarily impose contractual limitations—often perpetual!—on the use of their own property. Should courts enforce such voluntary arrangements, even though they bind subsequent landowners who were not parties to the original agreement?

As we will see, the common law was quite reluctant to recognize *negative easements*, which give a functional land use "veto" power to their holder. Because such negative easements tend to make burdened property less desirable and marketable, the common law saw them as undesirable restraints on alienation. Moreover, unlike affirmative easements such as paths and rights-of-way, negative easements are virtually invisible to the naked eye. As such, they provide no inquiry notice to would-be purchasers of the burdened property. We will also see that the common law disfavored *easements in gross*, which it viewed as mere rights of personal enjoyment. As a result, such easements were not freely assignable or transferable to others. These two disfavored types of easements—negative easements and easements in gross—come together in the form of the modern *conservation easement*, which we will study in section D.

Test Your Understanding

Consult the *A Place to Start* text box above as you work through the following hypothetical: Amelia and Benjamin are neighbors. Their friend, Charlotte, rents an apartment several blocks away. Amelia is the fee simple owner of

Lot #1, which abuts the main highway. Benjamin is the fee simple owner of Lot #2, which borders a scenic and rugged mountain range on state-owned land. Lot #2 is "landlocked" and has no easy access to improved roads.

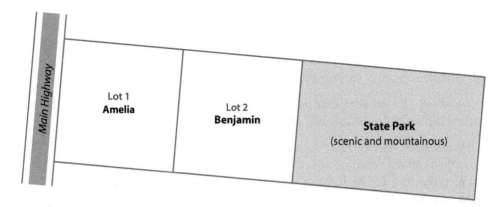

In each of the following situations, decide whether the parties have created an easement *appurtenant* or *in gross*. Is it *affirmative* or *negative*? Which lot is the *dominant tenement* (if any), and which is the *servient tenement*? If the result is ambiguous, identify the source of ambiguity.

1. Amelia grants Benjamin: "The right to cross Lot #1 for ingress and egress to Lot #2."
2. Amelia grants Charlotte, an avid hiker: "The right to cross Lot #1 to access the mountains." Benjamin grants an identical right for Charlotte to cross Lot #2.
3. In the early summer, the mountains are covered with wildflowers, some of which spill down onto Benjamin's lot. Amelia enjoys painting outdoor scenes, and Benjamin has told her that she is welcome to set up her painting supplies in a remote corner of his backyard. Benjamin also added, "While you're here, be sure to pick some flowers from my yard to put in a vase at your house." (Hint: Is the right to pick flowers an easement?)
4. Benjamin is going to build a guesthouse on his property. He knows that Amelia loves the mountain view from her home, and he promises Amelia, "The new structure will be only one story in height."
5. Benjamin invites Amelia and Charlotte to dinner at his home on Tuesday evening. (Hint: Does the invitation to attend the dinner create an easement?)
6. Charlotte's apartment building is undergoing extensive renovations over the next six months. Coincidentally, Amelia had planned to be on a business trip to another city during that same time period. Amelia grants Charlotte, "the right to reside in my home for the next six months." (Hint: Could this be something other than an easement?)

B. CREATION

Easements can be created in a variety of ways, generally grouped into the following four categories.

Express: Express easements are in writing and subject to the statute of frauds. However, verbal easements are sometimes enforced under the equitable *part performance* exception to the statute of frauds (recall chapter 7.B.1). We will consider express easements in section B.1, below.

Implied: Easements can be implied from *prior use* or from *necessity*, as further explored in section B.2, below.

Prescriptive easements: Easements can be created through *prescription*, a doctrine similar to that of adverse possession. The related doctrine of *custom* can give rise to a public right of use that is similar to an easement. Section B.3 examines these types of easements in detail.

Irrevocable licenses/easements by estoppel: License agreements accompanied by certain types of conduct can give rise to easements (or to their functional equivalent). *See* section B.4, below.

1. Express Easements

Many easements are created expressly by deed and are subject to the statute of frauds. Like other property instruments, such deeds (or other easement agreements) can be recorded in the jurisdiction's public records.

A Place to Start | **Express Easements**

- *Grant v. reservation:* Landowners can directly *grant* easements to other parties. Alternatively, landowners can convey real property interests to others, but *reserve* easements in favor of themselves. The common law disfavored the reservation of easements, and construed them strictly against grantors. Today, however, courts generally recognize reserved easements, provided there is evidence that the parties intended for the grantor to reserve such an easement.

- *Easement v. estate:* Sometimes, it can be difficult to determine whether a deed conveys an *easement* or an *estate* (such as a fee simple or a life estate), both of which permit the grantee to make certain uses of land. Courts often construe ambiguous grants narrowly as easements (which are nonpossessory *use* rights), rather than as estates (which are *possessory* rights).

Suppose a landowner *O* sells off a portion of his land to *A*. Can *O* reserve (or *except*) an easement in favor of himself? Instead, can he reserve an easement in favor of a third party *B*? The next case takes up those questions.

Estate of Thomson v. Wade

509 N.E.2d 309 (N.Y. 1987)

Reading Guide

The Thomson Estate's *Annex Parcel* is enviably situated on the St. Lawrence River, but has no access to the public road. The Estate unsuccessfully relied on two separate conveyances in an attempt to obtain a declaratory judgment that it held an easement across neighbor Judith A. Wade's inland property: the 1945 conveyance to Wade's predecessor, and the 1980 quitclaim to Thomson. As you read on, determine why each of those conveyances failed to create an express easement.

PER CURIAM.

Plaintiff, executrix of the estate of A. Graham Thomson, and defendant, Judith Wade, own adjoining parcels of land on the St. Lawrence River in the Village of Alexandria Bay. Plaintiff's property, on which a motel has been built, is known as the annex parcel and fronts on the river. Defendant owns the unimproved inland parcel, which is adjacent to plaintiff's and borders the public road.[1] Plaintiff claims an easement over defendant's parcel to the public road. Both parcels were previously owned by Edward John Noble, who, in 1945, separately conveyed them to different parties. Although Noble had always used defendant's parcel to gain access to the public road from the annex parcel, in transferring the annex parcel to plaintiff's predecessor-in-interest [the Thousand Islands Club], he did not convey an express easement appurtenant over defendant's parcel for the benefit of the annex parcel.

When Noble subsequently conveyed defendant's parcel to defendant's predecessor-in-interest, however, he "excepted and reserved" to himself personally, and to plaintiff's predecessor-in-interest, a right-of-way across defendant's parcel.

In the ensuing years, members of the public generally, and the various owners of the annex parcel, including plaintiff who purchased the parcel in 1954, used this right-of-way over defendant's land to reach the public road or the waterfront. When, in 1978, plaintiff erected a 50–room motel on the annex parcel, threatening an increase in traffic across defendant's property, defendant immediately sought to bar plaintiff's use of her property

---

1. [As the appellate court explained, the plaintiffs also owned the vacant Marsden House parcel, located on the other side of the Wade property from the Annex parcel. Edward John Noble originally owned all three parcels of land, which he conveyed into separate ownership in 1945. *See Estate of Thomson v. Wade*, 499 N.Y.S.2d 541 (App. Div. 1986).—Eds.]

to benefit the annex parcel. Plaintiff thereafter [in 1980] acquired from Noble's successor-in-interest, the Noble Foundation, a quitclaim deed to the right-of-way over defendant's property that Noble had reserved to himself.

In this declaratory judgment action, plaintiff claims title to an easement over defendant's property by express grant, relying not on its own deed to the annex parcel, but on the purported intent of Noble that the annex parcel benefit from an easement over defendant's property, as evidenced by his conveyance of defendant's parcel subject to a right-of-way in himself and in plaintiff's predecessor-in-interest. Plaintiff also relies on the express conveyance of Noble's personal right-of-way in the quitclaim deed from the Noble Foundation. The Appellate Division concluded that no express easement was created here. We agree.

It is axiomatic that Noble could not create an easement benefiting land which he did not own. Thus, having already conveyed the annex parcel, he could not "reserve" in the deed to defendant's predecessor-in-interest an easement appurtenant to the annex parcel for the benefit of plaintiff's predecessor-in-interest. The long-accepted rule in this State holds that a deed with a reservation or exception by the grantor in favor of a third party, a so-called "stranger to the deed", does not create a valid interest in favor of that third party. Plaintiff invites us to abandon this rule and adopt the minority view, which would recognize an interest reserved or excepted in favor of a stranger to the deed, if such was the clearly discernible intent of the grantor (*see, e.g., Willard v. First Church of Christ*, 498 P.2d 987 (Cal. 1972); *Restatement of Property* § 472, comment [b]).

Although application of the stranger-to-the-deed rule may, at times, frustrate a grantor's intent, any such frustration can readily be avoided by the direct conveyance of an easement of record from the grantor to the third party. The overriding considerations of the "public policy favoring certainty in title to real property, both to protect bona fide purchasers and to avoid conflicts of ownership, which may engender needless litigation" (*Matter of Violi*, 482 N.E.2d 29 (N.Y. 1985)), persuade us to decline to depart from our settled rule. We have previously noted that in this area of law, "where it can reasonably be assumed that settled rules are necessary and necessarily relied upon, stability and adherence to precedent are generally more important than a better or even a 'correct' rule of law" (*Matter of Eckart*, 348 N.E.2d 905 (N.Y. 1976)). Consequently, we hold here that any right-of-way reserved to plaintiff's predecessor-in-interest in the defendant's deed was ineffective to create an express easement in plaintiff's favor.

Additionally, inasmuch as the right-of-way reserved to Noble personally was not shown to be commercial in nature, the Appellate Division correctly determined that it could not be transferred to plaintiff in the quitclaim deed by the Noble Foundation. Thus, neither the reservation of an easement in gross in

Noble, nor the reservation of a right-of-way in plaintiff's predecessor-in-interest, entitles plaintiff to an express easement across defendant's property. . . . Accordingly, the order of the Appellate Division should be affirmed, with costs.

Notes

1. *Describe the easements:* Characterize the easements purportedly created by each of the two conveyances: Affirmative or negative? Appurtenant or in gross? Granted or reserved? How did each characterization influence the court?

2. *The "stranger to the deed" rule:* Clearly state the rule and its rationale. Is it a good rule? It remains the majority rule, although there is a growing trend toward its abandonment. *See* 4 Powell on Real Property § 34.04 (Michael Allan Wolf, gen. ed. 2015). How would a diligent title searcher find the purported reservation of an easement in favor of the Thousand Island Club? Would it appear under *Thousand Island Club* in the grantee index of the county's records?

3. *Alienability:* Why couldn't Noble transfer his personal right-of-way across the Wade property to the Thomsons? Think of at least two reasons.

4. *Practice pointer—drafting an express easement:* How could Noble's attorney have avoided the ambiguity that gave rise to this litigation? Make at least two suggestions for how an express easement could have been drafted to avoid the stranger-to-the-deed problem.

5. *The place—the Thousand Islands region of New York:* *Thomson v. Wade* was filed by the estates of father and son Captain Clarence S. Thomson (1876-1967) and A. Graham Thomson (1919-1969). The captain was co-owner of the Hotel Crossman, which he purchased in 1923 and operated until its demolition in 1962. As the court noted, a fifty-room motel was erected on the site in 1978, and today the property is home to "Capt. Thomson's Resort." During its storied history, the Hotel Crossman grew from its humble origins in 1848 as a fishermen's tavern to lodging for some 300 guests—hosting such dignitaries as President Martin Van Buren, President Grover Cleveland (before his presidency), Chief Justice Charles Evans Hughes, and businessman George Eastman (of Kodak fame). *See* Susan W. Smith, *A History of Recreation in the 1000 Islands,* http://oliver_kilian.tripod.com/1000islands/ (visited July 25, 2015); *Hotel Crossman: Landmark of the 1000 Islands Resort Area in Alexandria Bay, NY,* Watertown Daily Times, July 3, 1976.

Hotel Crossman, Thousand Islands (circa 1901)
Source: Library of Congress (LC-DIG-det-4a08221)

Alexandria Bay, located in New York's Thousand Islands region, is a well-loved destination for tourists and outdoor enthusiasts. Located on the south bank of the St. Lawrence River, the village enjoys panoramic views of almost 1,800 islands (some quite small) that outnumber its population (approximately 1,100 permanent residents, excluding some 15,000 warm-season visitors each year). After the Civil War, the area developed into a thriving vacation destination for many prominent visitors. Later, during the Prohibition era, local captains reportedly developed a vibrant business importing Canadian alcohol into the United States, eluding law enforcement by hiding in the St. Lawrence River's many inlets, and—in a pinch—throwing their illegal bounty overboard. Even today, divers reportedly find some of those hastily discarded bottles on the river's bottom. *See* http://www.visitalex bay.org/index.php/visitor-info/history/ (visited July 25, 2015).

Problem

Sunday drivers: Genevieve owned Lot #1 (which had a building on it) and adjacent Lot #2 (which was vacant). She was a member of the church across the street—the First Church of Christ Scientist—and allowed its members to use Lot #2 for parking during church services. She decided to sell Lot #2 to Willard, if the church could continue to use it for parking. The deed conveyed Lot #2 to Willard, "subject to an easement for automobile parking during church hours for the benefit of the church on the property at the southwest corner of the intersection of Hilton Way and Francisco Boulevard." Based on that ambiguous language, would you characterize the purported easement as appurtenant or in gross? Can you redraft the conveyance to clearly create an easement appurtenant? An easement in gross? If the jurisdiction follows the "stranger-to-the-deed rule" as articulated in *Thomson v. Wade*, is the easement valid? What could Genevieve have done to ensure that the church continued to enjoy parking privileges on Lot #2? *See Willard v. First Church of Christ Scientist*, 498 P.2d 987 (Cal. 1972).

2. Implied Easements

In addition to being created expressly, easements can also be created by implication in two circumstances. First, when *O* conveys a "landlocked" portion of his property to *A* and there is no reasonable way to access the property, courts will sometimes imply an easement by necessity across *O*'s retained property. Such easements are generally rooted in public policy favoring full and productive use of land, and perhaps also in the implication that the parties would have intended to create the easement had they thought about the issue.

Second, when *O* uses one portion of her land for the benefit of another portion of her land, if *O* subsequently divides the property and conveys only the benefitted (or only the burdened) portion of the land to *A*, courts will sometimes imply that the parties intended for the benefit and burden to continue, even though there is no longer unity of title for both portions of the property. Factual evidence of apparent, continuous, and necessary prior use gives rise to the reasonable implication that the parties *intended* that one parcel of land would continue to be used for the benefit of the other.

Notice that in both cases, the holder of the purported easement must demonstrate that one party originally owned both tracts of land *at the time* the necessity arose, or *at the time* of the prior use. That is, the claimant must demonstrate there had been *unity of title.* The requirements of implied easements are explained further in the *A Place to Start* box:

A Place to Start | **Implied Easements**

- ***Implied from necessity:*** The *grant* of an easement can be implied from necessity when a landowner conveys an interior portion of property, leaving the grantee with a "landlocked" tract with no reasonable means of access (except, perhaps, by boat or helicopter). Similarly, the *reservation* of an easement can be implied from necessity when a grantor's conveyance of the exterior portion of property leaves the grantor's remaining property landlocked. To prove an easement implied from necessity, a claimant generally must demonstrate:

■ *Unity of title:* The dominant and servient parcels must have been held in common ownership—demonstrating unity of title—*at the time* the parcels were severed, thereby creating the necessity for an easement. Courts will not imply an easement from necessity across the lands of a "stranger" (a third party).

■ *Necessity:* The required degree of necessity varies from jurisdiction to jurisdiction. Many require a showing of *strict necessity*, whereas others may be satisfied with a showing of something less (such as reasonable necessity). Easements implied from necessity endure for only so long as the necessity exists.

■ *Implied from prior use:* If a common owner uses one portion of the land (quasi-servient parcel) for the benefit of the remaining land (quasi-dominant parcel), a *quasi-easement* arises. If the common owner then subdivides the land and conveys one portion of it to another, the easement may continue by implication from the prior use. The claimant generally must demonstrate:

■ *Unity of title: At the time* of the prior use, the dominant and servient parcels were held in common ownership.

■ *Apparent:* The quasi-easement must have been *apparent* (at least upon careful inspection), thereby justifying the implication that the parties *intended* for the use to continue after the dominant and servient parcels were severed.

■ *Continuous:* The prior use must have been *continuous* (or sometimes, "permanent") to justify its continuation after severance of dominant and servient parcels.

■ *Necessity:* Not to be confused with the necessity requirement for easements implied from necessity alone, this element requires claimants to demonstrate that the prior use was important for the enjoyment of the dominant tract, or otherwise *reasonably necessary*. Courts have been reluctant to imply from prior use that the grantor *reserved* an easement in her own favor (as opposed to *granted* an easement in favor of another), but this hesitation has been less noticeable in modern times.

Traders, Inc. v. Bartholomew

459 A.2d 974 (Vt. 1983)

Reading Guide

This case provides an opportunity for you to distinguish the two types of implied easements from one another: (1) easements implied from prior use (which the court describes as "easements by implication"), and (2) easements implied from necessity (which the court calls "a way of necessity"). In addition, this case gives you a preview of *easements by prescription* and of the determination of the *scope* of easements, which we will study later in the chapter.

BILLINGS, J.

Plaintiff-appellant commenced a declaratory judgment action in Rutland Superior Court, seeking a determination whether a town highway located in the Town of Benson, and passing through to plaintiff's 121 acres of landlocked property, had been properly discontinued; and, in the alternative, whether a way of necessity existed across defendants-appellees Bartholomew's land affording plaintiff access to its 121 acre parcel. The trial court concluded that the town highway discontinuance proceedings in 1908 were in accordance with statutory requirements and thus valid. The court further found that plaintiff had a prescriptive easement along the former town highway, but that such easement was limited by past use to a strip of "sufficient width to accommodate a driveway for a single dwelling with appurtenant agricultural uses."

... [P]laintiff contends that the easement is properly one of necessity, not a prescriptive easement, and that it therefore exists without limitation as to prior use.

We turn first to the facts as found by the trial court. Prior to 1908, Town Highway 16 ran east and west, crossing the land now owned by the Bartholomews, and bordering the northern boundary of the 121 acre parcel now owned by plaintiff. On August 15, 1908, the selectmen of the Town of Benson discontinued the highway some distance west of the 121 acre parcel, and [transferred] the road to the owners on the north and south, one-half to each: the owners on the north took everything north of the centerline, and those on the south everything south of the centerline. . . .

... We . . . affirm the trial court's finding that . . . Highway 16 . . . was properly discontinued. . . .

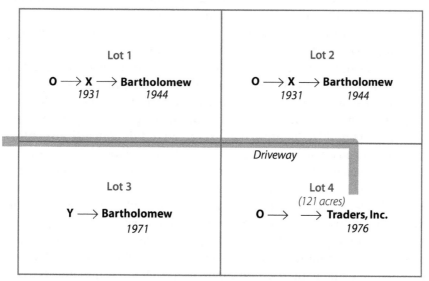

Source: Map supplied by casebook editors.

At the time of the discontinuance the disputed 121 acre southern parcel, now owned by plaintiff, as well as two other parcels north of the highway, now owned by the Bartholomews, were all commonly owned. At that time, given the single ownership, there was full access to the southern 121 acres through the parcel lying north of the old highway's centerline. In 1931, after having mortgaged the two northern parcels, the common owner lost them by a decree of foreclosure. By such action, the 121 southern acres were severed from the two northern parcels, thus landlocking the southern property. Ownership of the two northern properties devolved to defendants Bartholomew in 1944. In 1971, the Bartholomews purchased a lot south of the discontinued highway, adjacent to and just west of the 121 acre parcel. This lot came out of an entirely separate line of title, and was never part of the commonly owned lands. In 1976, after several transfers of title, plaintiff obtained ownership of the 121 acre land-locked parcel, with no right-of-way reserved in the deed.

The court below found that evidence was totally absent regarding the use made of the discontinued road up until 1943. However, in 1943 the Bartholomews purchased timber on the 121 acre parcel from its then owners, and used the road to remove the timber. In that same year, the then owners of the 121 acre parcel erected a small dwelling house on their land, and used the road until 1976 for ingress and egress, and for light agricultural purposes. In 1973, the Bartholomews built a gate at the westernmost point of the discontinued highway, thus blocking the way leading to plaintiff's 121 acre parcel. They did this with the apparent consent of the then owners, who continued to have access through the gate. Plaintiff, since acquiring ownership of the 121 acre parcel in 1976, has neither occupied the land for dwelling purposes, nor driven motor vehicles over the discontinued road.

The trial court found that by their use of the discontinued road during the period from 1943 to 1976, the prior owners of the 121 acre parcel had established a prescriptive easement to the portion of the roadway leading to their land. The court further found that the scope of the easement was limited by the use which created it: ingress and egress to and from a single dwelling house, with appurtenant agricultural uses. This easement passed to plaintiff through its predecessors in title. Plaintiff takes exception to this conclusion, contending that, for the purposes of determining the nature and scope of the easement, the relevant date was not 1943, when its predecessors commenced to use the roadway, but rather 1931, when the 121 acre parcel was severed by the foreclosure action and effectively landlocked. This severance, plaintiff argues, created a way of necessity twelve years prior to the actions giving rise to a prescriptive easement. Further, plaintiff urges the scope of a way of necessity is not limited by its prior use, but rather is coextensive with the full and reasonable present and future enjoyment of the dominant estate. The Bartholomews take the contrary position, contending first that plaintiff has not met the requirements of a way of necessity, and further that such a way is limited to the use at the time of the severance.

This Court has long since ruled that when, as a result of the division and sale of commonly owned land, one parcel is left entirely without access to a public road, the grantee of the landlocked parcel is entitled to a way of necessity over the remaining lands of the common grantor or his successors in title.

A way of necessity rests on public policy often thwarting the intent of the original grantor or grantee, and arises "to meet a special emergency . . . in order that no land be left inaccessible for the purposes of cultivation." *Howley v. Chaffee,* 93 A. 120, 122 (Vt. 1915). "Its philosophy is that the demands of our society prevent any man-made efforts to hold land in perpetual idleness as would result if it were cut off from all access by being completely surrounded by lands privately owned." 2 Thompson on Real Property § 362, at 382 (1980).

It is apparent from the cases cited and arguments propounded by defendants Bartholomew that they have confused the law regarding a way of necessity with the wholly distinct doctrine of easements by implication. . . . [T]he two are distinguishable by the circumstances which give rise to them, the policy bases which support them and the legal consequences which flow from them.

The Bartholomews correctly argue that there was a complete failure to prove the use made of the land by the common owner prior to and at the time of the severance. However, while such failure would be fatal to a finding of an easement by implication, it is totally irrelevant to a finding of a way of necessity. All that is required for the latter is the division of commonly owned land resulting in the creation of a landlocked parcel.

A review of the facts indicates that prior to the foreclosure action in 1931, there was unity of title in the two northern parcels and the 121 acre southern parcel. By the foreclosure decree a severance occurred by operation of law, thus leaving the 121 acre parcel landlocked. At that instant, a way of necessity arose over the lands severed for the benefit of the original grantor. This way did not (nor can it ever) lie over the Bartholomew's southern parcel to the west of the 121 acres, for those lands were never held in common with the other three parcels.

The Bartholomews raise two arguments against such a way: first, that if it did exist as of 1931, it was extinguished in 1971 by the operation of the state's so-called marketable title act, and in the alternative, they contend that any such way was extinguished in 1958, when the plaintiff's predecessors in title acquired a prescriptive easement over the way, thus eliminating the element of strict necessity. We dispose of these contentions in turn. . . .

[The court concluded that the easement falls within an exception to the state's marketable title act and was not barred by the failure to file statutory notice.]

Nor do we find merit in defendants' second argument, that the requisite necessity was lost in 1958, the date of the prescriptive easement found by the trial court. A prescriptive easement may only be acquired by hostile and adverse use for the fifteen year statutory period. In this case, plaintiff's predecessors acquired a way of necessity in 1943, through their grantor, the common owner. Thus, their use of the way was at no time adverse and could not ripen into a prescriptive easement. Consequently, the element of strict necessity remains.

Having found that plaintiff is entitled to a way of necessity over those lands of defendants Bartholomew which were originally held in common, we have also to decide its duration and scope.

As noted above, a way of necessity arises out of public policy concerns that land not be left inaccessible and unproductive. Therefore such a way exists only so long as the necessity which creates it: if, at some point in the future access to plaintiff's land over a public way becomes available, the way of necessity will thereupon cease. While this Court has not had occasion to pass on the scope of a way of necessity, we adopt what appears to be the sounder, majority rule on this issue. That is, since the easement is based on social considerations encouraging land use, its scope ought to be sufficient for the dominant owner to have the reasonable enjoyment of his land for all lawful purposes. Contrast *Read v. Webster,* 113 A. 814, 818 (Vt. 1921) (an easement by implication is limited to the use which gave rise to it, and can "neither be enlarged because of subsequent necessity nor cut down by a claim that some part of it was not indispensable.").

While the way of necessity is thus expansive, it may not grow to such proportions as to interfere materially with the reasonable uses of the servient estate. Thus, "it would seem to be coextensive with the reasonable needs, present and future, of the dominant estate for such right or easement, and to vary with the necessity, in so far as may be consistent with the full reasonable enjoyment of the servient tenement." *Tong v. Feldman,* 136 A. 822, 824 (Md. 1927). We recognize, however, that additional burdens will inevitably be imposed on the servient tenement as a consequence of the open-ended scope of a way of necessity. Therefore, we further hold that the grantee of the dominant estate who thus enlarges the scope of an existing way of necessity must bear those costs to the servient tenement reasonably attributable to such enlargement. These costs, which may include such items as necessary fencing, should be determined by the trial court along with such questions as the width and location of the easement.

It remains to determine the extent of the use of the way, its precise location, and its width. In addition, the court must assess those additional expenses to defendants Bartholomew which are reasonably attributable to the enlarged scope of the way, and charge them to plaintiff. For these purposes we must remand to the trial court. . . . Simply stated, the trial court must strive for a balancing of interests in fashioning the way, having before it evidence of the intended use of the land of both plaintiff and defendants Bartholomew.

The cause is remanded for determination of the use, location and width of the way, and those costs to be borne by plaintiff, pursuant to the opinions expressed herein. Affirmed in part, reversed in part, remanded.

Notes

1. *Easement implied from necessity:* The court held that the plaintiff acquired an easement implied from necessity. What rationale supports such a finding? What elements must be proved? What facts satisfy each element? Note carefully the issue of timing: what is the significance of the year 1931?

2. *Easement implied from prior use:* Why did the plaintiff fail to acquire an easement implied from prior use (imprecisely called "an easement by implication" by the court)? What time period is critical to this determination? What rationale could support the recognition of such an easement in other cases?

3. *Practice pointer—selecting a legal theory:* If you represented the plaintiff, which type of easement would you have claimed? Consider both your ability to prove the requisite elements, and the practical benefits each type of easement could provide to your client. Recall *Thomson v. Wade*, which introduced our study of express easements. Could Edward John Noble or the plaintiff have claimed an implied easement (either by necessity or from prior use) under the facts of that case?

4. *Preview—easement by prescription:* If a trespasser can prove elements analogous to those required by adverse possession, an easement by prescription may arise. What element of proof of adverse possession is analytically inconsistent with that required to prove an easement by prescription? (<u>Hint:</u> Recall that easements represent a type of property interest that requires the sharing of space.) We will look at easements by prescription in the next subsection.

5. *Grave matters—a bundle of sticks or a web of interests?* Suppose landowner *O* grants permission to bury the remains of *X* on *O*'s property (*X* was likely related to *O*). Many years later, *O* sells the property to *A*. Do the descendants of *X* have a right to visit *X*'s grave if *A* seeks to exclude them from the property? Make an argument as to why the descendants hold an easement in gross. What additional facts do you need as you formulate your argument?

For a discussion of such *graveyard rights, see* Alfred L. Brophy, *Grave Matters: The Ancient Rights of the Graveyard,* 2006 B.Y.U. L. Rev. 1469. Professor Brophy observes that two ancient and powerful ideas collide in the context of cemeteries on private property. The "conflict between the right to worship at our ancestors' graves and the right to exclude appears with increasing frequency these days, as landowners seek to develop land where cemeteries are located and descendants of people buried in the cemeteries seek to reclaim something of their heritage." This tension arises from a tangled web of private and communal interests. As the author outlines in his essay,

> We can see how the common law harmonized rights to exclude with other, overlapping community interests. It reminds us that while the rights of property (such as the right to exclude and to use property as one would like) are of critical

importance, there are limitations on those rights. [T]his Essay links this ancient right to the current discussion of memory of the era of slavery. It suggests that this right might be useful for descendants of enslaved people buried on private property.

The author reports that easements in gross to visit grave sites are "recognized by statute in about a fifth of states and by case law in many others." *Id.* at 1469-73. How should the law resolve this tension between interwoven community and private rights?

6. *The place—Vermont's ancient roads:*   Benson, Vermont was chartered in 1780. It is a rural town, with a population density of about twenty-three people per square mile. As described by one commentator, Vermont has an "ancient roads" problem—"the problem of legal highways that fell into disuse, were largely invisible to an observer on the ground, and increasingly clouded landowners' titles." *Traders, Inc. v. Bartholomew* confirmed that the road at issue—Town Highway 16—had been properly discontinued in 1908 (in Vermont, all public roads are technically defined as "highways"). The status of many other ancient roads, however, remained ambiguous. The Vermont legislature attempted to rectify this problem through 2006 legislation. *See* Alexander Hood, *Twists and Turns in Ancient Roads: As Unidentified Corridors Become a Reality in 2010, Act 178's Shortcomings Come into Focus,* 12 Vt. J. Envtl. L. 117 (2010).

3. Easements by Prescription

Acquiring an easement by prescription is similar to acquiring a possessory interest by adverse possession. Although the requisite elements vary from jurisdiction to jurisdiction, generally the claimant must prove all of the elements of adverse possession *except for* the element of exclusive use. Why is the notion of exclusivity incompatible with the very nature of easements?

A Place to Start   Easements by Prescription

To acquire an easement by prescription, the claimant must prove the following elements:

■ *Actual usage:* Recall that an adverse possessor obtains title only to the property actually possessed by the trespasser (unless the trespasser has *constructive* possession of additional property, as through *color of title*). Likewise, most courts limit prescriptive easements to the scope of actual usage during the prescriptive period. For the difficulties of making such a determination, *see Brown v. Raty*, 289 P.3d 156, 165 (Mont. 2012) (concluding that the district court erred in limiting the width of a cattle trail easement to 20 feet because "cattle do not simply walk in straight lines and remain within strict width limitations when being trailed through areas without fences").

- *Continuous and uninterrupted use for the statutory period:* The user must act continuously enough to provide reasonable notice to the servient landowner, who must fail to interrupt the use through physical obstructions or legal action. Users in privity with one another may tack their periods of use together to satisfy the relevant statute of limitations.

- *Hostile (adverse) use:* The use must be without the owner's permission, and wrongful (giving rise to a cause of action by the potential servient landowner against the adverse user). It is generally irrelevant whether the user acted in good faith or bad faith (that is, whether or not the user intended to violate the rights of the servient landowner).

- *Open and notorious use:* The use must be of such a character that a reasonably diligent landowner would have discovered the adverse use. If the servient landowner had actual notice of the use, then open and notorious usage is generally not required.

DIGGING DEEPER: Most American courts do not recognize *negative* prescriptive easements. Can you think why that might be the case?

Recall our study of public property from Chapter 6. Can one gain title to public property by adverse possession? In general, continuous use of property held in government ownership (federal, state, or local) does not ripen into ownership because statutes of limitation usually do not run against units of government. Likewise, the public generally cannot acquire prescriptive easements across government lands.

But what about private property? Can the public at large (or a group of people) gain easements by prescription? Again, this is usually not possible. The use of private property by the general public usually does not ripen into an easement, in part because it is difficult to determine the precise route that was adversely used by a collection of individuals. *But see, e.g., Concerned Citizens of Brunswick County Taxpayers Assn. v. North Carolina*, 404 S.E.2d 677, 683-84 (N.C. 1991) (requiring "substantial identity," not "definite and specific line of travel" to establish public prescriptive easement for access to ocean beach).

Daytona Beach v. Tona-Rama, Inc.

294 So. 2d 73 (Fla. 1974)

Reading Guide

Recall our discussion of the *public trust doctrine* from Chapter 6. There, we saw that certain public resources such as the oceans and other "navigable waters" are held by the states in trust for the benefit of all the people. As we learned, the line dividing public from private ownership is usually the *mean high tide line.* That is,

> the states generally own submerged coastal land and the wet sand beach in trust for the people, who may use the overlying waters for purposes including navigation, fishing, and commerce. Landward, the dry sand beach and uplands beyond the vegetation line can be privately owned.

ADKINS, C.J.

... Defendant has owned water front property in Daytona Beach, Florida, for more than 65 years and operated on the property an ocean pier extending 1,050 feet over the Atlantic Ocean as a recreation center and tourist attraction. Defendant provided such attractions as fishing space, helicopter flights, dances and skylift.

The tract of land upon which the pier begins extends 102 feet north and south along the ocean front and approximately 1,050 feet landward of the mean high water mark. This area of approximately 15,300 square feet is an area of dry sand and is covered by water only on rare occasions during extremely high tide and during hurricanes. Defendant secured a permit for and constructed the observation tower which precipitated this litigation. The circular foundation of the tower is 17 feet in diameter and the diameter of the tower is four feet. It occupies an area of approximately 225-230 square feet of the 15,300 square feet of land to which defendant holds record title. The observation tower is an integral part of the pier and can only be entered from the pier.

Oceanward and easterly of the dry sand area is the foreshore, that is, the area between the high and low water marks and is designated herein as the hard or wet sand area.

[A] building permit was issued by the City for construction of the tower after public hearings. After the permit was issued, the tower was constructed at a cost of over $125,000.

Plaintiff operated an observation tower near the site of the pier of defendant and protested the issuance of the permit. When work in connection with the erection of the tower had progressed to completion of test borings and other arrangements, plaintiff commenced this action against defendant for a declaratory judgment and injunctive relief to prevent the erection of defendant's public observation tower. Among other contentions, plaintiff alleged that by continuous use of the property for more than 20 years, the public had acquired an exclusive prescriptive right to the use of the land of defendant. ...

The land in question is a parcel of white, powdery sand running between the hard-packed driving surface of Daytona Beach and the existing seawalls. By stipulation of the parties, the land is above the normal high water mark and would be subject to being covered by the waters of the Atlantic Ocean only during hurricanes or extremely high tides.

We recognize the propriety of protecting the public interest in, and right to utilization of, the beaches and oceans of the State of Florida. No part of Florida is more exclusively hers, nor more properly utilized by her people than her beaches. And the right of the public of access to, and enjoyment of, Florida's oceans and beaches has long been recognized by this Court.

[We have said] in *White v. Hughes*, 190 So. 446, 448-50 (Fla. 1939) . . . :

> There is probably no custom more universal, more natural or more ancient, on the seacoasts, not only of the United States, but of the world, than that of bathing in the salt waters of the ocean and the enjoyment of the wholesome recreation incident thereto. The lure of the ocean is universal; to battle with its refreshing breakers a delight. Many are they who have felt the lifegiving touch of its healing waters and its clear dust-free air. Appearing constantly to change, it remains ever essentially the same. . . .

It is possible for the public to acquire an easement in the beaches of the State by the finding of a prescriptive right to the beach land. . . . However, in . . . the cases . . . relied upon by the District Court of Appeal . . . this Court declined to find such prescriptive right in the public because of the absence of an adverse nature in the public's use of private beach land. . . .

This Court in *Downing v. Bird*, 100 So. 2d 57 (Fla.1958), set forth the test for right of access by prescription:

> In either prescription or adverse possession, the right is acquired only by actual, continuous, uninterrupted use by the claimant of the lands of another, for a prescribed period. In addition, the use must be adverse under claim of right and must either be with the knowledge of the owner or so open, notorious, and visible that knowledge of the use by and adverse claim of the claimant is imputed to the owner. In both rights the use or possession must be inconsistent with the owner's use and enjoyment of his lands and must not be a permissive use, for the use must be such that the owner has a right to a legal action to stop it, such as an action for trespass or ejectment. . . .

In the case *sub judice*, the land in issue is occupied in part by the Main Street pier, a landmark of the Daytona Beach oceanfront for many years, and the land and pier are owned by the defendant. . . .

That portion of the land owned by defendant which is not occupied by the pier has been left free of obstruction and has been utilized by sunbathing tourists for untold decades. These visitors to Daytona Beach, including those who have relaxed on the white sands of the subject lands, are the lifeblood of the pier. As such, they have not been opposed, but have been welcomed to utilize the otherwise unused sands of petitioner's oceanfront parcel of land.

The sky tower, which was substantially completed when the trial judge's order halted it, consists of a metal tower rising 176 feet above the ocean and a 25-passenger, air-conditioned gondola which was to be boarded from the pier to rise, rotating slowly, to the top of the tower, remain rotating at the top for a few minutes, and then descend. The tower utilizes a circle of sand only 17 feet in diameter. . . .

The District Court [held that the prescriptive easement test has been met and that the tower should be removed]. . . . We cannot agree. The public has continuously, and over a period of several decades, made uninterrupted use of the lands in issue. However, neither the trial court, nor the District Court, reached the other requirement for prescription to be properly effective—adverse possession inconsistent with the owner's use and enjoyment of the land.

The use of the property by the public was not against, but was in furtherance of, the interest of the defendant owner. Such use was not injurious to the owner and there was no invasion of the owner's right to the property. Unless the owner loses something, the public could obtain no easement by prescription.

Even if it should be found that such an easement had been acquired by prescription, the defendant-owner could make any use of the land consistent with, or not calculated to interfere with, the exercise of the easement by the public. . . . The erection of the sky tower was consistent with the recreational use of the land by the public and could not interfere with the exercise of any easement the public may have acquired by prescription, if such were the case.

The beaches of Florida are of such a character as to use and potential development as to require separate consideration from other lands with respect to the elements and consequences of title. The sandy portion of the beaches are of no use for farming, grazing, timber production, or residency—the traditional uses of land—but has served as a thoroughfare and haven for fishermen and bathers, as well as a place of recreation for the public. The interest and rights of the public to the full use of the beaches should be protected. Two states, Oregon and Hawaii, have used the *customary rights doctrine* to afford the rights in beach property. *State ex rel. Thornton v. Hay*, 462 P.2d 671 (Ore. 1969); *In re Ashford*, 440 P.2d 76 (Haw. 1968). . . .

If the recreational use of the sandy area adjacent to mean high tide has been ancient, reasonable, without interruption and free from dispute, such use, as a matter of custom, should not be interfered with by the owner. However, the owner may make any use of his property which is consistent with such public use and not calculated to interfere with the exercise of the right of the public to enjoy the dry sand area as a recreational adjunct of the wet sand or foreshore area.

This right of customary use of the dry sand area of the beaches by the public does not create any interest in the land itself. Although this right of use cannot be revoked by the land owner, it is subject to appropriate governmental regulation and may be abandoned by the public. . . .

. . . The general public may continue to use the dry sand area for their usual recreational activities, not because the public has any interest in the land itself, but because of a right gained through custom to use this particular area of the beach as they have without dispute and without interruption for many years . . .

Boyd, J., dissenting.

... If this building be permitted to stand, then the owner might well next decide to erect a gargantuan hotel on the property, and the adjoining property owners, demanding equal protection of the law, might then begin to construct a series of hotels along the waterfront—similar to the series that now exists along the East side of Collins Avenue in Miami Beach. This would form a concrete wall, effectively cutting off any view of the Atlantic Ocean from the public. A repetition of the concrete wall created by such buildings would be extremely detrimental to the people of this State and to our vital tourism industry.

In my opinion, the trial court and the District Court of Appeal, First District, were correct in ordering the structure removed, for the reason that it encroaches upon the prescriptive rights of the public. ...

The majority opinion ably defines the law generally applicable to beach properties. The intermittent, occasional use of dry sand beach property by individuals or groups for recreational purposes does not establish prescriptive easements. If such were the law of this state, countless thousands of beach lots would have questionable titles. I dissent to the majority opinion only because the property here in question is totally unique in character by its treatment and use as a public beach for many decades. Only property having the same unique characteristics should be affected by any decision against this owner. ...

Ervin, J., dissenting. ...

What is overlooked by the majority is that as to prescriptive public coastal areas, navigable waters, tide lands and sovereignty lands, the judiciary has a positive and solemn duty as a last resort to protect the public's rights to the enjoyment and use of any of such lands. There is ample precedent of this Court to afford this protection, including those relating to the inalienable trust doctrine in ... navigable areas. ...

Mager, Associate Justice, dissenting, in part; concurring, in part [omitted].

Notes

1. *Easements by prescription v. customary rights access:*   Clearly describe the court's holding. Who "won" this case? What exactly did that party win? With respect to customary rights, why did the court recognize such a right for the public to use defendant's dry sand beach? How is a customary right different than an easement implied from prior use, or an easement implied from necessity? Courts have relied on a number of legal theories to allow the public to traverse—or even to use—the nation's dry sand beaches. Although they often describe such public rights as *easements,* other legal theories also recognize such a public right in appropriate cases. *See, e.g., Raleigh Avenue Beach Ass'n v. Atlantis Beach Club,* 879 A.2d 112 (N.J. 2005) (public trust doctrine); *Public Access Shoreline Hawaii v. Hawai'i County Planning Comm'n,* 903

P.2d 1246 (Haw. 1995) (custom), *cert. denied*, 517 U.S. 1163 (1996); *Gerwitz v. Long Beach*, 330 N.Y.S.2d 495 (Sup. Ct. 1972) (dedication); *Gion v. City of Santa Cruz*, 465 P.2d 50 (Cal. 1970) (implied dedication). *See also* Deborah Mongeau, *Public Beach Access: An Annotated Bibliography*, 95 Law Library J. 515 (2003).

2. *Access to public trust resources—overlapping public and private rights: Daytona Beach v. Tona-Rama* and other similar cases can be seen as an extension of the public trust doctrine. They pose the question of how the public can *access* public and common property. State ownership of submerged lands and control of the overlying waters would be of little benefit to the public if it could not access its public trust property (other than by boat). *Daytona Beach* considers two legal theories that potentially recognize public access rights across private dry sand beaches—prescription and custom.

But access works in both directions and private landowners have a reciprocal access challenge. What good is it to own oceanfront property if one cannot construct a pier or boat ramp to reach deep water, with foundations sunk into the public's submerged land? Most states recognize the right of riparian landowners (those who own property abutting natural watercourses) to "wharf out," provided their structures do not impede the public's right of navigation. *See* David H. Getches, Water Law in a Nutshell 46-48 (4th ed. 2009).

Main Street pier and sky tower (prior to 2012 demolition)
Photo by Christine A. Klein

3. *The place—Daytona Beach:*   Daytona Beach has been a prominent area for hundreds of years. In the early 16th century, Ponce de Leon's search for the fountain of youth led him to the natural springs just west of Daytona Beach. Three centuries later, Ohio tycoon Matthias Day built the area's first hotel and became Daytona's founding father. In 1946, Daytona hosted the first racially integrated spring training game, in which baseball great Jackie Robinson played. In 1959, one decade after the founding of NASCAR, Daytona saw the opening of the Daytona International Speedway, home to NASCAR's Daytona 500 race. Dubbed "the world's most famous beach," Daytona Beach includes more than twenty miles of white sand open to pedestrians and even to automobiles, in designated areas.

Problems

1. *Living on a golf course:*   The entryway to Hilda Weber's seven-acre lot in Los Angeles was steep, curving, and hazardous. To secure a safer entryway, Ms. Weber purchased from neighbor Bel-Air Country Club a long strip of land next to the sixth fairway of the club's golf course. Because errant balls landed frequently on the strip, the club inserted building restrictions in the deed conveyed to Ms. Weber, which required a 20-foot, no-build buffer zone, presumably to prevent injury from (and liability for) misdirected golf balls. Some years later, Ms. Weber sold her property to Conrad N. Hilton (renowned American hotelier and great-grandfather of Paris and Nicky Hilton). Hilton brought an action for declaratory relief that the building restrictions were invalid, and the country club counter-claimed that it had obtained a prescriptive easement to use a portion of the subject property as "rough" for its sixth fairway and for its members to enter the property to retrieve golf balls. The appellate court affirmed the district court's holding that the club had obtained a prescriptive easement. Based on your knowledge of the elements of prescriptive easements, what could Ms. Weber or Mr. Hilton have done to prevent the club's acquisition of such an easement, if anything? Should they have put up "no trespassing" signs? Erected a fence to exclude golf balls and golfers? Something else? *See MacDonald Properties, Inc. v. Bel-Air Country Club*, 72 Cal. App. 693 (Cal. App. 1977).

2. *Flying taxis in Alaska:*   Thomas Classen lived along the navigable Chena River in Alaska, and for many years operated an air taxi service from his home. To prepare for takeoff, he would taxi his floatplane down the river, continue under the bridge at University Avenue, and become airborne at some point after that (depending on the weight of his cargo). When the state of Alaska constructed a new downstream bridge that rose some thirty feet into the air, Classen could not dependably clear the new bridge during takeoff. As a result, he moved his business to the Fairbanks International Airport, at substantial expense. Classen sued the state for damages

arising from his business losses. The Alaska Supreme Court determined that Mr. Classen's complaint amounted to a claim for damages for interference with a purported prescriptive easement, and denied relief. Would such an easement be appurtenant or in gross? Affirmative or negative? What are the dominant and servient (if any) estates? Who owns those estates? Why do you think the court denied the plaintiff's claim? Think of at least two reasons rooted in traditional easement law. *See Classen v. Dept. of Highways*, 621 P.2d 15 (Alaska 1980).

4. Equitable Enforcement of License Agreements

Review the hypothetical factual scenario presented at the beginning of this chapter (section A). Suppose that Benjamin's property is vacant except for a small summer cabin. Benjamin accesses the cabin either by hiking in from the adjacent state park or by driving along a rough jeep trail that connects his property and the state park (the state park itself has public access to a main highway). Amelia tells Benjamin, "You don't have to use that old jeep road. You can drive through my property to get to your cabin." Can Benjamin rely on that permission (and perhaps winterize his cabin), or can Amelia later change her mind? Benjamin might be able to claim an *irrevocable license* (also called an *easement by estoppel*) if the elements described below are satisfied:

A Place to Start | Equitable Enforcement of License Agreements

- *License:* A license is revocable permission (verbal or written) to use the land of another in a manner that, absent permission, would constitute a trespass.

- *Irrevocable license/easement by estoppel:* To prove an irrevocable license, the claimant must prove (1) the landowner gave the claimant permission to use her land, (2) the claimant reasonably and detrimentally relied on the representation, as by expending money or labor to improve the property in a manner consistent with the existence of a license, and (3) it would be inequitable to revoke the license.

For how long will Benjamin's irrevocable license endure? Some sources suggest that irrevocable licenses continue for so long a time as the nature of the license calls for—an ambiguous standard that makes it risky for people like Benjamin to invest in improvements to the property. But other sources suggest that irrevocable licenses are better conceptualized as full-fledged easements that can only be terminated under traditional easement doctrine. *See* 4 Powell on Real Property §§ 34.24, 34.25 (Michael Allan Wolf, gen. ed. 2015); James W. Ely, Jr. & Jon W. Bruce, The Law of Easements and Licenses in Land §§ 11.7, 11.9. The Restatement (Third) of Property takes this approach and treats irrevocable licenses "the same as any other easement" unless the parties intended or reasonably expected otherwise. Further, the Restatement provides that the "duration of an easement by estoppel is the same as that of an expressly created easement. . . ." Restatement (Third) of Property, Servitudes, chapter 4 (Introductory Note) (2000).

Problem

The old haul road: In 1964, the Taylors bought a three-acre building site, on which they planned to construct a new residence. With the verbal permission of their adjacent neighbors, the Holbrooks, the Taylors used an old haul road that passed through the Holbrooks' property to assist in the construction. They used the roadway as ingress and egress for workmen from the main road, for hauling machinery and material to the building site, for the construction of the dwelling, and for making improvements generally to the premises. After construction of the residence, which cost $25,000, was completed, the Taylors continued to regularly use the roadway as they had been doing. With Mr. Holbrook's verbal permission, the Taylors widened the road, put in a culvert, and graveled part of it, at a cost of approximately $100. There was no other location over which a roadway could reasonably be built to provide an outlet for the Taylors. The neighbors' relationship deteriorated, and in 1970 the Holbrooks erected a steel cable across the roadway to prevent its use and also constructed "no trespassing" signs. The Taylors filed a lawsuit to require removal of the obstruction and to declare their right to the use of the roadway without interference. You represent the Taylors. Which type(s) of easement should they claim—express, implied (by necessity or by prior use), prescriptive, or by estoppel? For each theory that you select, identify the required elements, and then apply the law to the facts. *See Holbrook v. Taylor*, 532 S.W.2d 763 (Ky. 1976).

C. SCOPE, ASSIGNMENT, AND TERMINATION

1. The Scope of Easements

The *scope* of an easement circumscribes the uses that benefit and burden the respective properties and parties. The method by which an easement was created often affects its scope. In general, *the intention of the parties* governs the scope of express easements and easements implied from prior use. Alternatively, considerations of *public policy* usually govern the scope of prescriptive easements and irrevocable licenses. Courts cite to both measures when determining the scope of easements implied from necessity.

A Place to Start	The Scope of Easements

- *Express easements:*
  - *Normal development of the dominant estate:* Generally, courts presume that the parties contemplated that the scope of the easement would change with time and technological innovation to permit *normal development* of the dominant parcel. For example, an easement for telephone lines might also be allowed to service cable television or fiber-optic communication equipment.
  - *Benefit confined to dominant parcel:* The common law rigidly insisted that the benefit of an easement appurtenant must be confined to the dominant parcel and cannot be extended to other tracts of land, even if such extension would not increase the burden on the servient tenement.
- *Implied easements:* Like express easements, implied easements can generally expand to accommodate the *normal development* of the dominant parcel.
  - *Implied from necessity:* The scope must allow for *reasonably essential* uses of the dominant estate, determined in part by the intent of the parties, and in part by the public policy of promoting the beneficial use of land.
  - *Implied from prior use:* The intent of the parties can be determined by reference to the scope of the *quasi-easement* during the period when dominant and servient estates were held in common ownership. This is generally a matter of the intention of the parties.
- *Easements by prescription:*
  - *Scope:* Prescriptive easements are limited by the scope of the adverse use that was the basis of their creation. Throughout the prescriptive time period, it is likely that the adverse use demonstrated some variance. This inconsistency is common, and it challenges courts to discern enough of a pattern to justify the recognition of a prescriptive easement and to fix its contours. Courts are generally reluctant to permit the expansion of prescriptive easements to accommodate normal development.

Brown v. Voss

715 P.2d 514 (Wash. 1986)

Reading Guide

This is a long, sad tale of feuding neighbors. As you read about the dispute, think about what each party could have done to avoid the disagreement in the first place.

BRACHTENBACH, J.

The question posed is to what extent, if any, the holder of a private road easement can traverse the servient estate to reach not only the original dominant estate, but a subsequently acquired parcel when those two combined parcels are used in such a way that there is no increase in the burden on the servient estate. The trial court denied the injunction sought by the owners of the servient estate. The Court of Appeals reversed. We reverse the Court of Appeals and reinstate the judgment of the trial court.

In 1952 the predecessors in title of parcel A granted to the predecessor owners of parcel B a private road easement across parcel A for "ingress to and egress from" parcel B. Defendants acquired parcel A in 1973. Plaintiffs bought parcel B on April 1, 1977 and parcel C on July 31, 1977, but from two different owners. Apparently the previous owners of parcel C were not parties to the easement grant.

When plaintiffs acquired parcel B a single family dwelling was situated thereon. They intended to remove that residence and replace it with a single family dwelling which would straddle the boundary line common to parcels B and C.

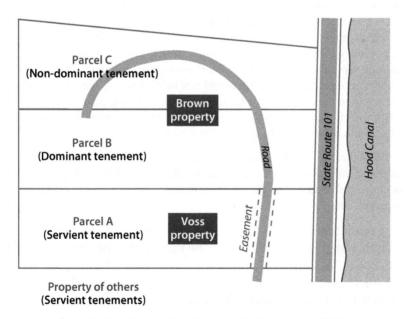

A portion of an exhibit depicts the involved parcels (map supplied by court, as modified by editors)

Plaintiffs began clearing both parcels B and C and moving fill materials in November 1977. Defendants first sought to bar plaintiff's use of the easement in April 1979 by which time plaintiffs had spent more than $11,000 in developing their property for building.

Defendants placed logs, a concrete sump and a chain link fence within the easement. Plaintiffs sued for removal of the obstructions, an injunction against defendant's interference with their use of the easement and damages. Defendants counterclaimed for damages and an injunction against plaintiffs using the easement other than for parcel B.

The trial court awarded each party $1 in damages. The award against the plaintiffs was for a slight inadvertent trespass outside the easement.

The trial court made the following findings of fact:

> The plaintiffs have made no unreasonable use of the easement in the development of their property. . . . Other than the trespass there is no evidence of any damage to the defendants as a result of the use of the easement by the plaintiffs. There has been no increase in volume of travel on the easement to reach a single family dwelling whether built on tract B or on [tracts] B and C. There is no evidence of any increase in the burden on the subservient estate from the use of the easement by the plaintiffs for access to parcel C.

> If an injunction were granted to bar plaintiffs access to tract C across the easement to a single family residence, Parcel C would become landlocked; plaintiffs would not be able to make use of their property; they would not be able to build their single family residence in a manner to properly enjoy the view of the Hood Canal and the surrounding area as originally anticipated at the time of their purchase and even if the single family residence were constructed on parcel B, if the injunction were granted, plaintiffs would not be able to use the balance of their property in parcel C as a yard or for any other use of their property in conjunction with their home. Conversely, there is and will be no appreciable hardship or damage to the defendants if the injunction is denied.

> If an injunction were to be granted to bar the plaintiffs access to tract C, the framing and enforcing of such an order would be impractical. Any violation of the order would result in the parties back in court at great cost but with little or no damages being involved. . . .

Relying upon these findings of fact, the court denied defendant's request for an injunction and granted the plaintiffs the right to use the easement for access to parcels B & C "as long as plaintiffs [sic] properties (B and C) are developed and used solely for the purpose of a single family residence."

The Court of Appeals reversed, holding:

> In sum, we hold that, in denying the Vosses' request for an injunction, the trial court's decision was based upon untenable grounds. We reverse and remand for entry of an order enjoining the use of the easement across parcel A to gain access to a residence any part of which is located on parcel C, or to further the construction of any residence on parcels B or C if the construction activities would require entry onto parcel C.

The easement in this case was created by express grant. Accordingly, the extent of the right acquired is to be determined from the terms of the grant properly construed to give effect to the intention of the parties. By the express terms of the 1952 grant, the predecessor owners of parcel B acquired a private road easement across parcel A and the right to use the easement for ingress to and egress from parcel B. Both plaintiffs and defendants agree that the 1952 grant created an easement appurtenant to parcel B as the dominant estate. Thus, plaintiffs, as owners of the dominant estate, acquired rights in the use of the easement for ingress to and egress from parcel B.

However, plaintiffs have no such easement rights in connection with their ownership of parcel C, which was not a part of the original dominant estate under the terms of the 1952 grant. As a general rule, an easement appurtenant to one parcel of land may not be extended by the owner of the dominant estate to other parcels owned by him, whether adjoining or distinct tracts, to which the easement is not appurtenant.

Plaintiffs, nonetheless, contend that extension of the use of the easement for the benefit of nondominant property does not constitute a misuse of the easement, where as here, there is no evidence of an increase in the burden on the servient estate. We do not agree. If an easement is appurtenant to a particular parcel of land, any extension thereof to other parcels is a misuse of the easement. . . . Under the express language of the 1952 grant, plaintiffs only have rights in the use of the easement for the benefit of parcel B. Although, as plaintiffs contend, their planned use of the easement to gain access to a single family residence located partially on parcel B and partially on parcel C is perhaps no more than technical misuse of the easement, we conclude that it is misuse nonetheless.

However, it does not follow from this conclusion alone that defendants are entitled to injunctive relief. Since the awards of $1 in damages were not appealed, only the denial of an injunction to defendants is in issue. Some fundamental principles applicable to a request for an injunction must be considered. (1) The proceeding is equitable and addressed to the sound discretion of the trial court. (2) The trial court is vested with a broad discretionary power to shape and fashion injunctive relief to fit the *particular facts, circumstances, and equities of the case before it.* Appellate courts give great weight to the trial court's exercise of that discretion. (3) One of the essential criteria for injunctive relief is actual and substantial injury sustained by the person seeking the injunction.

The trial court found as facts, upon substantial evidence, that plaintiffs have acted reasonably in the development of their property, that there is and was no damage to the defendants from plaintiffs' use of the easement, that there was no increase in the volume of travel on the easement, that there was no increase in the burden on the servient estate, that defendants sat by for more than a year while plaintiffs expended more than $11,000 on their project, and that defendants' counterclaim was an effort to gain "leverage" against plaintiffs' claim.

In addition, the court found from the evidence that plaintiffs would suffer considerable hardship if the injunction were granted whereas no appreciable hardship or damages would flow to defendants from its denial. Finally, the court limited plaintiffs' use of the combined parcels solely to the same purpose for which the original parcel was used—*i.e.,* for a single family residence.

... [T]he only valid issue is whether, under these established facts, as a matter of law, the trial court abused its discretion in denying defendants' request for injunctive relief. Based upon the equities of the case, as found by the trial court, we are persuaded that the trial court acted within its discretion. The Court of Appeals is reversed and the trial court is affirmed.

Dore, J., dissenting.

The majority correctly finds that an extension of this easement to nondominant property is a misuse of the easement. The majority, nonetheless, holds that the owners of the servient estate are not entitled to injunctive relief. I dissent.

The comments and illustrations found in the *Restatement of Property* § 478 (1944) address the precise issue before this court. Comment *e* provides in pertinent part that "if one who has an easement of way over Whiteacre appurtenant to Blackacre uses the way with the purpose of going to Greenacre, the use is improper even though he eventually goes to Blackacre rather than to Greenacre." Illustration 6 provides:

> By prescription, *A* has acquired, as the owner and possessor of Blackacre, an easement of way over an alley leading from Blackacre to the street. He buys Whiteacre, an adjacent lot, to which the way is not appurtenant, and builds a public garage one-fourth of which is located on Blackacre and three-fourths of which is located on Whiteacre. *A* wishes to use the alley as a means of ingress and egress to and from the garage. He has no privilege to use the alley to go to that part of the garage which is built on Whiteacre, and he may not use the alley until that part of the garage built on Blackacre is so separated from the part built on Whiteacre that uses for the benefit of Blackacre are distinguishable from those which benefit Whiteacre.

The majority grants the privilege to extend the agreement to nondominant property on the basis that the trial court found no appreciable hardship or damage to the servient owners. However, as conceded by the majority, any extension of the use of an easement to benefit a nondominant estate constitutes a misuse of the easement. Misuse of an easement is a trespass. The Browns' use of the easement to benefit parcel C, especially if they build their home as planned, would involve a continuing trespass for which damages would be difficult to measure. Injunctive relief is the appropriate remedy under these circumstances. ...

The Browns are responsible for the hardship of creating a landlocked parcel. They knew or should have known from the public records that the easement was not appurtenant to parcel C. In encroachment cases this factor is significant. As stated by the court in *Bach v. Sarich*, 445 P.2d 648 (1968): "The benefit of the doctrine of balancing the equities, or relative hardship, is reserved for the innocent defendant who proceeds without knowledge or warning that his structure encroaches upon another's property or property rights."

In addition, an injunction would not interfere with the Brown's right to use the easement as expressly granted, *i.e.*, for access to parcel B. An injunction would merely require the Browns to acquire access to parcel C if they want to build a home that straddles parcels B and C. . . .

I would affirm the Court of Appeals decision as a correct application of the law of easements. If the Browns desire access to their landlocked parcel they have the benefit of the statutory procedure for condemnation of a private way of necessity.[2]

Notes

1. *The holding—who won?*   Who "won" this case, and what precisely did that party win? Do you think the prevailing party was pleased with the outcome of the lawsuit? How will the court enforce its ruling and make sure that the Browns never use the easement to access the portion of their home located on parcel C? Precisely identify the point(s) of disagreement between the majority and the dissent. Overall, which opinion is more convincing?

2. *Preview—eminent domain:*   As we will see in Chapter 13, under certain circumstances, authorized *governmental* units can purchase property from unwilling sellers for "public use." As noted in the opinion, Washington law allows *private individuals* to "condemn" private ways of necessity, presumably requiring the payment of compensation. Is the Washington statute a good idea? What impact, if any, should it have on Washington's common law on easements by necessity?

3. **Traders, Inc. v. Bartholomew** *revisited:*   Review *Traders, Inc. v. Bartholomew*, in section B.2 above. How did the court distinguish between the scope of an easement implied from necessity and the scope of an easement implied from prior use? What policy considerations support the distinction?

4. *Practice pointer—a long, sad story:*   Often a client's success depends on how well the attorney is able to translate the client's story into a compelling narrative for the court. Which attorney did a better job in this case? Were the Vosses the "bad guys," preventing the Browns from building their dream home,

---

2. [The *Revised Code of Washington* § 8.24.010 provided: "An owner . . . of land which is so situate with respect to the land of another that it is necessary for its proper use and enjoyment to have and maintain a private way of necessity . . . through the land of such other, . . . may condemn and take lands of such other sufficient in area for the construction and maintenance of such private way of necessity. . . .—Eds.]

first by blocking the road with logs, concrete, and fencing, and later by defending their actions all the way up to the state supreme court (and asserting an overly formalistic counterclaim that the Browns unlawfully expanded the scope of the easement)? Even worse, according to the court, the Vosses apparently "sat by for more than a year while plaintiffs expended more than $11,000 on their project."

But, as is often the case, there were two sides to this story. Can you imagine any missing facts that might present the Vosses in a more sympathetic light? If you had been the Vosses' attorneys, what questions would you have posed to your clients in an attempt to uncover a more favorable narrative? According to a subsequent factual inquiry by a law professor, neither party was blameless. Like the Vosses, the Browns had poured their share of fuel on the fire that smoldered between the neighbors. In fact, Mr. Brown and Mr. Voss actually engaged in a physical altercation before the lawsuit was filed and Mr. Brown—younger by some fifteen years—allegedly knocked the older man to the ground and threatened him. The Browns purchased both properties (totaling about eight acres) without the benefit of a real estate agent or an attorney, and failed to educate themselves about the scope of their easement (which was appurtenant to parcel B only). Instead, they insisted that they should be able to build their "dream home" straddling both parcels, despite the nuances of easement law. They failed to clearly communicate their building plans to the Vosses, which may explain why the Vosses did not complain about the location of the structure for more than a year. The home they planned to build was significantly larger than parcel B alone could have accommodated. Moreover, it appears that parcel C was not "landlocked" after all, but had reasonable access to State Route 101.

As it turns out, litigation between the parties continued for about seven years. In the interim, the Browns suffered financial setbacks. They lost parcel B for failure to make payments under an installment land sale contract, and they lost parcel C for failure to pay taxes. By the time the Washington Supreme Court issued its opinion, they had moved to Alaska. The Vosses acquired title to parcel B, making them the owners of both parcels A and B. As a result, the long-disputed easement terminated under the doctrine of merger (*see* section C.3 below). *See* Elizabeth Samuels, *Stories Out of School: Teaching the Case of* Brown v. Voss, 16 Cardozo L. Rev. 1445 (1995). Zealous advocacy and litigation strategies aside, did either party really benefit from the litigation? How, if at all, could the attorneys have facilitated a more favorable resolution of this dispute?

2. The Assignment and Division of Easements

Suppose a landowner *O* grants her neighbor *A* the right to park on *O*'s property. Should *A* be able to assign that right to her friend *B* (or to a group of friends)? Should it matter whether the easement is for personal or for commercial purposes? Should it matter whether the easement was appurtenant to *A*'s lot or personal to *A*?

| A Place to Start | Assignment and Division of Easements |

- **Assignment:** Upon transfer of the servient property to a new owner, the *burden* generally runs with the land to the successor, unless the successor took the property without actual or constructive notice of the easement. Express easements can be recorded in the jurisdiction's public records (to notify successors, but it can be more difficult for purchasers to discover the existence of easements created by methods other than express, written grant or reservation.

  - **Easements appurtenant:** The *benefit* runs with the land to successors in interest to the dominant property.

  - **Easements in gross:** Today, most jurisdictions permit easement holders to assign or otherwise transfer the *benefit* to another if the easement is held for *commercial purposes*. Increasingly, personal easements can also be transferable if there is evidence that the grantor so intended. But according to one treatise, courts sometimes "unwisely" hold easements in gross to be nontransferable out of "a fear of resultant surcharge." *See* 4 Powell on Real Property § 34.16 (Michael Allan Wolf, gen. ed. 2015).

- **Division of the easement:** If an easement has been divided among the original holder and additional new holders, then courts must consider whether the burden has been impermissibly expanded. The issue is variously described as whether easements are *divisible*, *partially assignable*, *severable*, or *apportionable*.

  - **Easements appurtenant:** If the dominant tract is subdivided, then each new owner generally succeeds to the benefit of the easement, provided that any increase in burden can be justified as *normal development* within the scope of the original easement.

  - **Easements in gross:** Courts are more likely to permit multiple parties to use the easement if it is "exclusive," if there is evidence the grantor so intended, and/or if the court can fashion conditions to prevent an overburden (such as, the easement holders must act together as a single unit or as "one stock").

DIGGING DEEPER: Can you think of any policy reasons supporting the courts' relative reluctance to permit the transfer of easements in gross, as compared to easements appurtenant? Likewise, why should personal easements in gross be less transferable than commercial easements in gross?

Test Your Understanding

1. *From telephone lines to cable television:*   Detroit Edison, an electric utility, installed and maintained telephone poles and wires across Peter and Henrietta Heydon's property without their permission. At least fifteen years later, Detroit Edison entered into an agreement with MediaOne allowing it to place and maintain cable television lines on the same utility poles that continued to

support Detroit Edison's telephone lines. The Heydons sued Media One to enjoin it from installing cable lines across their property. What is the relevant issue? Be specific. If the court follows the modern trend, how should it resolve the dispute? *See Heydon v. MediaOne,* 739 N.W.2d 373 (Mich. App. 2007).

2. *Too many swimmers?* The Pocono Spring Water Ice Company owned lands on which a dam had been built, thereby creating artificial Lake Naomi. By express deed, the Company granted, "To Frank C. Miller, his heirs and assigns forever, the exclusive right to fish, boat, and swim on Lake Naomi." One year later, Frank granted to his brother, Rufus, by express deed, "To Rufus W. Miller, his heirs and assigns forever, [a]¼ interest in and to the fishing, boating, and bathing rights and privileges at, in, upon, and about Lake Naomi, which rights and privileges were granted and conveyed to me by the Pocono Spring Water Ice Company." Thereafter, the brothers formed a partnership, and together operated a summer church camp on the lake. Rufus died many years later, terminating the brothers' partnership. The executors of Rufus' estate planned to grant a license to a different church, allowing its 2,000 members to fish, boat, and swim in and around the lake. Fearing overcrowding and overuse of the lake, the Pocono Spring Water Ice Company brought suit against Rufus' executors, claiming that (a) the boating, bathing, and fishing privileges were not assignable by Frank C. Miller to Rufus W. Miller, and (b) even if the easement rights had been assignable, they were not divisible because this might subject the servient tenement to a greater burden than originally contemplated. Drawing upon what you have learned about easements in this chapter, how should the court decide each of these issues? *See Miller v. Lutheran Conference & Camp Association,* 200 A. 646 (Pa. 1938) (hypothetical facts modified slightly).

3. The Termination of Easements

Easements can be terminated, in whole or in part, through a wide variety of mechanisms. As you read through each of the following mechanisms, consider whether the method by which an easement was *created* affects the means by which it can be *terminated.*

A Place to Start | **Termination of Easements**

- **Expiration:** Easements can be time-limited in accordance with the terms of the instrument that created them (express easement) or the period of necessity (easements implied from necessity).
- **Release:** The holder can release the easement to the servient landowner, perhaps in exchange for a monetary payment or other type of benefit.

- *Abandonment:* The proponent of abandonment must demonstrate (1) a period of nonuse, and (2) actions or omissions indicating the easement holder's intent to abandon the easement (which can be inferred from a sufficient period of nonuse). Although intent is the touchstone, some courts tend to conflate nonuse and intent.

- *Estoppel:* Similar to abandonment, the holder can be estopped from asserting the existence of an easement upon a showing that the servient owner relied on conduct (action/inaction) of the holder that suggested an intent to relinquish use of the easement. Recall that estoppel theory can be employed to create (as well as to terminate) easements.

- *Prescription:* Just as easements can be created by prescription, so also can they be terminated by prescription if the servient landowner actually, continuously, hostilely, and open and notoriously prevents the easement holder from exercising the easement throughout the statutory period.

- *The recording system:* If the servient property is conveyed to a new owner who takes without notice of the easement, then the easement is potentially invalid against the new owner under the state's recording statute. Easement holders can protect themselves by recording their easements in the public records or otherwise providing notice of their easement.

- *Merger:* Easements appurtenant will terminate if the dominant and servient estates come into common ownership (unity of title) and use (unity of possession) because, by definition, easements involve the right to use the land of another.

DIGGING DEEPER: Can you group the above termination methods according to whether the triggering action (or inaction) must be taken by the holder of the easement, by the owner of the servient estate, by the parties together, or by some other means?

Guy v. State of Delaware

438 A.2d 1250 (Del. Super. 1981)

Reading Guide

This case gives you the opportunity to test a variety of easement termination mechanisms against a specific factual scenario. As you read the case, consider what policies are served by the termination of easements. In ambiguous cases, should courts err on the side of preservation or of termination?

TEASE, J.

Defendants Clifford and Mary Ennis move for summary judgment in this action for injuries received in an automobile accident.

On July 27, 1977, the Ennises conveyed to the State of Delaware, through the Department of Natural Resources and Environmental Control (DNREC), a parcel of farmland located on the northeast corner of the intersection of Routes 9 and 6 in Kent County. The farm was conveyed subject to easements of record; one of these, a so-called "daylighting" easement, had been deeded to the State of Delaware, through the Highway Department [DOT], in June of 1956. The easement required the Ennises not to obstruct the clear view over the land at the intersection of Routes 9 and 6.

The deed to the State set out several "reservations" in the Ennises, *i.e.*, the right to reside in the farmhouse and use all out-buildings for the remainder of their lives, exclusive trapping rights, the use of one goose blind site, and the right to grow corn or soybeans on all tillable acres. The option agreement from Ennis to the State, which preceded the sale, contained the same terms as the deed which followed it.

On August 28, 1977, one month after the sale to the State, plaintiffs' [the Guys'] vehicle collided with a vehicle driven by defendant Deborah Coverdale, who had failed to stop at a stop sign at the intersection of Routes 9 and 6. Plaintiffs contend that the accident could have been avoided, or the impact and resulting injuries greatly lessened, had their view at the northeast corner of the intersection not been obstructed by tall growths of corn and other vegetation. The farmland had been planted in corn by defendant George Wilson pursuant to an oral agreement between the Ennises and Wilson.

Plaintiffs' [first theory] of recovery [is] that the Ennises, by causing or allowing the clear view at the intersection to be obstructed . . . breached the covenants set out in the "daylighting" easement. . . .

. . . [T]he Ennises assert that they could have no liability under the easement agreement because the easement was a nullity after the farm's transfer to the State, or, if still in existence, it had been assigned to the State, thereby relieving the Ennises of all responsibility for keeping the land unobstructed.

The Ennises suggest three theories by which the easement may be considered a nullity. First, they argue that when the State, as owner of the dominant estate (the fee in the roadway), purchased the servient estate (the farm) the easement appurtenant was extinguished by merger. Clearly, this is the general rule.

Plaintiffs, however, contend that this case comes within an exception to the merger doctrine, which states that there is no merger absent unity of ownership and possession and enjoyment of the dominant and servient estates. Plaintiffs point out that the fee in the roadbed is owned by the Department of Transportation (DOT), successor to the Highway Department, and the fee in the farm by the DNREC. Further, these two state agencies hold title for different purposes—for highway purposes and for environmental purposes, respectively. Therefore, Plaintiffs argue, there was no unity of ownership and no merger of estates. . . . This attack on unity of ownership must fail; legal title to both estates is vested in the State, for the good of its citizens, and the fact of administration or supervision by different agencies of the State cannot destroy that unity.

Plaintiffs do, however, raise a contention fatal to extinguishment by merger. The deed to the state "reserved" certain life interests to the Ennises which left them in possession and control of the land as they had been prior to the sale. Their rights to reside on the farm, use all out-buildings, and till all tillable acreage, are exclusive of the State's rights, as fee owner, to possess and enjoy the land. The doctrine of merger does not operate where the fee in the servient estate is subject to an outstanding estate in possession.

. . . The important fact is that the State never had the unqualified right to possession and enjoyment—the right to enter upon the land and treat it in a manner consistent with full ownership of the fee.

The Ennises then argue that the easement is a nullity because it had been released by agreement with the State. This contention rests upon two circumstances. First, the easement was "excepted" from the rights to be transferred under the 90-day option agreement, but was not mentioned in the deed. However, the option agreement did no more than give the state notice that the easement existed as an encumbrance on title. Where the servient estate is purchased with notice of an easement, the purchaser takes title subject to the easement. Second, the Ennises argue that the deed reserves to them the right "to till all tillable acres of the farm." Extinguishment by release requires an express writing. The Ennises contend that the language of the deed permitting them to till all tillable acreage releases the easement and allows the planting of corn on the northeast corner of the intersection. This is, indeed, a strained construction; and in any case the use of the single word "all" does not amount to an express writing. As the Ennises themselves point out, the easement is not mentioned in the deed. It could not, therefore, have been expressly released by the State. . . .

The Ennises argue in the alternative that should the easement have vitality, as it does, then they were not responsible for maintaining it because it had been assigned to the State. While this is true, the Ennises are nonetheless bound by the covenant or promise made in 1956 not to obstruct the clear view while they were fee owners. The Ennises stand in the position of successors in interest to the promise contained in the easement by reason of their continued possession of the land. The easement creates a promise that the parties intended would run with the land by its express language ("for themselves, their heirs and assigns"). The Ennises may not now disclaim the burden of the promise they made.

For all of the above reasons, the Ennises' motion for summary judgment as to Count I of the complaint is denied. . . .

Notes

1. *Label the interests:*   Was the DOT's daylighting easement appurtenant or in gross? Affirmative or negative? Identify the servient and dominant (if any) tenements. If the DOT's goal was to maintain clear visibility at the intersection, was an easement the best tool to accomplish that purpose? Think of other alternatives the state could have pursued. Next, label the following interests created by the July 1977 conveyance: (a) the Ennises' right to reside in the farmhouse and use all out-buildings for the remainder of their lives, (b) exclusive trapping rights, (c) the use of one goose blind site, and (d) the right to grow corn or soybeans on all tillable acres.

2. *Potential termination of the easement:*   *Merger:* Why did the DNREC's ownership of the farm and the DOT's holding of the easement constitute unity of *title*? How did the court's ruling on that issue advance the policies behind the doctrine of merger, if at all? Conversely, why was there no unity of *possession* of the dominant and servient estates? What impact did that have on the potential extinguishment of the easement through merger? *Release:* Why did the court find that the state had not released its easement to the Ennises? What more would have been required to constitute an effective release?

Problems

1. *A gas line beneath the garage:*   Defendants purchased their lot in 1962. Pursuant to a valid express easement appurtenant granted to them by the Smiths, their neighbors to the east and the plaintiffs' predecessor in interest, the defendants ran the gas line servicing their residence east beneath the Smiths' lot and connected it with a meter located at the eastern border of the Smiths' lot. The defendants and the Smiths each retained a copy of the easement agreement for their personal records. The line is underground and no part of it is visible. Three gas meters are located on the boundary between the Smiths' lot and the property to the east: one of the meters services the Smiths, one services the defendants, and one services the Smiths' neighbor to the east. In 1980, the plaintiffs purchased the Smith property. Two years later, the plaintiffs inadvertently discovered the gas line as they were rebuilding their garage. You represent the plaintiffs, who brought suit to quiet title to their property and to require the defendants to remove the gas line from beneath their property. What arguments should you make on behalf of your client? What arguments do you anticipate that the defendants will make? As an alternative to litigation, can you counsel your clients as to other approaches that might achieve a satisfactory resolution of their concerns? *See generally Childress v. Richardson,* 670 S.W.2d 475 (Ark. App. 1984).

2. Grave matters, again: John and Sarah Frost owned a large acreage. They established a family graveyard on a portion of their property measuring about ⅓ of an acre. Over a period of about 100 years, a variety of Frost family members were buried there, including some of John and Sarah's grandparents, brothers, sisters, and an infant daughter. An uncle was the final person laid to rest in the graveyard. Throughout those 100 years, the property changed ownership several times, and finally came into the ownership of the Columbia Clay Company. Over time, all of the trees in and around the graveyard were cut down, and the spot has long since grown up in weeds, bramble, and blackberry bushes. No Frost family member has visited it in more than twenty years, and monuments or headstones can no longer be found. During the course of some excavation, defendant Columbia Clay accidentally unearthed some human bones, and immediately stopped its excavation. Descendants of John and Sarah Frost learned of the incident and sued Columbia Clay for $50,000 in damages and for a permanent injunction against the defendants' use of the ⅓ acre of its property where the Frost ancestors had been buried. What arguments would the plaintiffs make in support of their claims for relief? What defense will Columbia Clay assert? What policy issues are raised by this dispute? *See generally Frost v. Columbia Clay Co.,* 124 S.E. 767 (S.C. 1924).

D. CONSERVATION EASEMENTS

Easements can be used to protect values associated with environmental conservation and historic preservation. Suppose a ranching couple is about to retire, and all of their children have moved to the city and have no interest in returning to run the ranch. Development pressures are great, and the couple could sell the property for a significant amount of money to finance their retirement. And yet, they have worked the land for a lifetime, have a strong affinity for it, and would like to see it remain as a working ranch (or as open space and wildlife habitat). In mountainous areas of the west, for example, the close proximity of ski resorts creates a ready market for the development of ranches into condominium resorts and second homes. How can our retiring ranching couple derive money from their land without an outright sale for development?

So-called "conservation easements" represent a relatively modern and creative response to this question. The couple can sell or donate the right to develop the property—one of the sticks in the ranchers' bundle of rights—to a nonprofit organization (generally known as a "land trust") or a unit of government equipped to hold the conservation easement and monitor its enforcement. In turn, the couple will receive a financial benefit, such as the value of the forgone development rights, a federal income tax charitable deduction, a reduction of local property taxes (reflecting the reduced value of the ranch without its development rights), and/or a reduction of the inheritance tax that their heirs or devisees must pay. In most cases, the couple can continue to live on the ranch and even sell it, provided that they and their successors make a binding promise never to develop the property.

Who pays for the development rights? In the case of tax deductions, federal or local taxpayers foot the bill. If instead a nonprofit conservation organization purchases the conservation easement, then those who donate to that organization pay for that purchase. In exchange for these contributions, taxpayers and donors expect to receive a variety of benefits, as suggested by the definition of "conservation easement" in the Uniform Conservation Easement Act:

> "Conservation easement" means a nonpossessory interest of a holder in real property imposing limitations or affirmative obligations the purposes of which include retaining or protecting natural, scenic, or open-space values of real property, assuring its availability for agricultural, forest, recreational, or open-space use, protecting natural resources, maintaining or enhancing air or water quality, or preserving the historical, architectural, archaeological, or cultural aspects of real property.

Uniform Conservation Easement Act, § 1. The purchase of such easements represents an investment of many billions of dollars nationwide. In exchange, the public requires the easements to be perpetual in nature—similar to traditional easements and running covenants (which we will study in the next chapter). The Internal Revenue Service, for example, authorizes income tax deductions for charitable deductions only if the landowner "granted in perpetuity" the relevant use restriction on real property. *See* 26 U.S.C. § 170(a)(2)(C); Nancy A. McLaughlin, *Perpetual Conservation Easements in the 21st Century: What Have We Learned and Where Should We Go from Here?*, 2013 Utah L. Rev. 687, at 687.

The grant of conservation easements has gained rapid acceptance. Today, there are more than 1,700 active land trusts (local, state, and national) in the United States. Katie Chang, Land Trust Alliance, *2010 National Land Trust Census Report*. Together, they hold conservation easements encumbering an estimated 40 million acres of land in the country—an area roughly equivalent to that occupied by the state of Washington. National Conservation Easement Database, *What Is the NCED?, available at* http://conservationeasement.us (visited Oct. 19, 2015). For more information on the topic, *see, e.g.,* Federico Cheever & Nancy A. McLaughlin, *An Introduction to Conservation Easements in the United States: A Simple Concept and a Complicated Mosaic of Law*, 1 J. L. Property & Society 107 (2015); Jessica Owley, *Cultural Heritage Conservation Easements: Heritage Protection with Property Law Tools*, 49 Land Use Policy 177 (Dec. 2015).

Despite their broad acceptance today, conservation easements must overcome several common law hurdles on a state-by-state basis. Recall that the common law disfavored both negative easements and easements in gross—both of which describe conservation easements. Absent statutory intervention, then, conservation easements likely would not have been enforceable at common law. The next case considers such legislation.

United States v. Blackman

613 S.E.2d 442 (Va. 2005)

+---+
| **Reading Guide** |
| |
| ◆ *The interplay of common law and statutory law:* Every state has |
| adopted some type of legislation authorizing the creation of |
| conservation easements. In Virginia and other states, many common |
| law conservation easements were created *before* state statutes |
| explicitly recognized such novel arrangements. Should those older |
| easements be valid? |
| |
| ◆ *What is an easement?* This case raises the broader question, *what |
| is an easement?* We will return to this question in section E's |
| discussion problem. |
+---+

KOONTZ, J.

The Green Springs Historic District (the "District") is an area of roughly 14,000 acres in Louisa County that was settled in the 1700s. Much of the land in this area has historically been used for agricultural purposes, and this agricultural setting remains today. Because the land has been continuously farmed for almost three centuries, many of the homes and farms have been preserved in their original context with little alteration.

In the early 1970s, the Commonwealth of Virginia bought two hundred acres of land in the Green Springs area with the intention of building a prison. There was much local opposition, and some landowners expressed the belief that the prison would damage the character of their historic community. Reacting to this opposition, the then-governor of Virginia announced in 1972 that the state would not build the prison facility in the area if that area could be preserved. In response to the governor's challenge, local citizens organized a non-profit group dubbed Historic Green Springs, Inc. ("HGSI"), which obtained donations of easements for land conservation and historic preservation from landowners and initiated an effort to have the area designated as a National Historic Landmark District. The Green Springs Historic District was listed on the National Register of Historic Places in March of 1973, and was ultimately designated as a National Historic Landmark in 1974.

By a "Deed of Easement" dated March 19, 1973 (the "Easement"), D.L. Atkins and Frances Atkins granted to HGSI an assignable easement over several parcels of their property, including Eastern View Farm. The Easement states in part that,

> in consideration of the grant to the Grantee of similar easements in gross by other owners of land in the said Green Springs Historic District for similar purposes, the Grantors [D.L. Atkins and Frances Atkins] do hereby grant and convey to the Grantee [HGSI] an easement in gross restricting in perpetuity, in the

manner hereinafter set forth, the use of the following described tracts of land, together with the improvements erected thereon.

In 1978, HGSI decided to convey its entire portfolio of easements to the United States. . . . The National Park Service ("NPS") now administers these easements. . . . The Easement at issue provides that the manor house on Eastern View Farm:

> will be maintained and preserved in its present state as nearly as practicable, though structural changes, alterations, additions, or improvements as would not in the opinion of the Grantee fundamentally alter its historic character or its setting may be made thereto by the owner, provided that the prior written approval of the Grantee to such change, alteration, addition, or improvements shall have been obtained. . . .

Peter F. Blackman ("Blackman") purchased Eastern View Farm on July 1, 2002. . . . Blackman, *inter alia,* seeks to remove the existing front porch on the manor house, replace the siding, and create an addition. In support of these intended alterations, Blackman submitted several sets of renovation plans to the NPS for review, but the NPS repeatedly denied certain aspects of his plans. Rather than working with the NPS for final approval of his plan, Blackman's attorney stated in a letter dated January 13, 2004 that Blackman would "commence the Rehabilitation at a time of his choosing, without further notice to [NPS], in accordance with the attached elevations." Subsequently, Blackman removed the porch from his house. The United States filed the complaint in this case June 14, 2004, and on June 16, 2004 Judge James C. Turk issued a temporary restraining order restraining Blackman . . . unless he has first obtained written approval from the National Park Service.

In defense of his actions, Blackman argues that, *inter alia,* the original deed of easement granted to HGSI was invalid because at the time it was purportedly created, Virginia law did not recognize any kind of negative easement in gross, including such easements for the purpose of land conservation and historic preservation.

In its order, the district court correctly states that we have not directly addressed the issue of the validity of negative easements in gross in our prior decisions. While also correctly noting that only certain types of easements were recognized at common law, the district court references the statement in *Tardy v. Creasy,* 81 Va. (6 Hans.) 553, 557 (1886), that "there are many other easements which have been recognized, and some of them have been of a novel kind," for the proposition that prior to 1973 "*Tardy* leaves open the possibility that other easements, including negative easements related to land conservation and historic preservation, would be valid if sufficiently related to the land." . . .

. . . By the brief of *amici curiae* filed in this case, we are advised that at least seven other charitable entities hold conservation or historic preservation easements, many of them easements in gross, conveyed prior to 1973. Underlying the issue is a degree of apparent conflict between the common law preference for unrestricted rights of ownership of real property and the public policy of this Commonwealth as expressed in Article XI of the Constitution of Virginia, ratified by the people of this Commonwealth in 1970, that "it shall be the policy of this Commonwealth to conserve . . . its historical sites and buildings." . . .

Negative easements, also known as servitudes, do not bestow upon the owner of the dominant tract the right to travel physically upon the servient tract, which is the feature common to all affirmative easements, but only the legal right to object to a use of the servient tract by its owner inconsistent with the terms of the easement. In this sense, negative easements have been described as consisting solely of "a veto power."

At common law, an owner of land was not permitted at his pleasure to create easements of every novel character and annex them to the land so that the land would be burdened with the easement when the land was conveyed to subsequent grantees. Rather, the landowner was limited to the creation of easements permitted by the common law or by statute. The traditional negative easements recognized at common law were those created to protect the flow of air, light, and artificial streams of water, and to ensure the subjacent and lateral support of buildings or land.

Easements, whether affirmative or negative, are classified as either "appurtenant" or "in gross." An easement appurtenant, also known as a pure easement, has both a dominant and a servient tract and is capable of being transferred or inherited. It frequently is said that an easement appurtenant "runs with the land," which is to say that the benefit conveyed by or the duty owed under the easement passes with the ownership of the land to which it is appurtenant. The four negative easements traditionally recognized at common law are, by their nature, easements appurtenant, as their intent is to benefit an adjoining or nearby parcel of land.

In contrast, an easement in gross, sometimes called a personal easement, is an easement "which is not appurtenant to any estate in land, but in which the servitude is imposed upon land with the benefit thereof running to an individual." At common law, easements in gross were strongly disfavored because they were viewed as interfering with the free use of land. . . . For an easement to be treated as being in gross, the deed or other instrument granting the easement must plainly manifest that the parties so intended.

Because easements in gross were disfavored by the common law, they could neither be transferred by the original grantee nor pass by inheritance. By statute, however, Virginia long ago abrogated common law restrictions on the transfer of interests in land "by declaring that any interest in or claim to real estate may be disposed of by deed or will." *Carrington v. Goddin*, 54 Va. (13 Gratt.) 587, 599-600 (1857). Pursuant to this statutory change in the common law rule, currently embodied in Code § 55-6, we have recognized that an affirmative easement in gross is an interest in land that may be disposed of by deed or will. . . . Since 1962, Code § 55-6, in pertinent part, has expressly provided that "[a]ny interest in or claim to real estate, *including easements in gross,* may be disposed of by deed or will." (Emphasis added). . . .

Code § 55-6 unambiguously speaks to "easements in gross" as interests in real estate capable of disposition by deed or will. There is no suggestion in this language that the statute was intended to apply only to affirmative easements in gross and not to negative easements in gross. The significance of this statutory change in the common law is manifest. Easements in gross, whether affirmative or negative, are now recognized interests in real property, rather than merely personal covenants not capable of being disposed of by deed or will as was the case under common law. Moreover, as pertinent to the present inquiry, such was the case well before 1973 in this Commonwealth.

The 1962 amendment and clarification of Code § 55-6 with regard to the transferability of easements in gross has facilitated, in part, Virginia's long recognition of the value of conserving and preserving the natural beauty and historic sites and buildings in which it richly abounds. In 1966, the General Assembly enacted the Open-Space Land Act, 1966 Va. Acts ch. 461. This Act, currently found in Code §§ 10.1-1700 through -1705, is intended to encourage the acquisition by certain public bodies of fee simple title or "easements in gross or such other interests in real estate" that are designed to maintain the preservation or provision of open-space land. By definition, open-space land includes land that is preserved for "historic or scenic purposes." Code § 10.1-1700. . . . These statutes evince a strong public policy in favor of land conservation and preservation of historic sites and buildings.

As noted above, this public policy was expressly embodied in Article XI of the Constitution of Virginia which, since 1970, has provided:

> § 1. To the end that the people have clean air, pure water, and the use and enjoyment for recreation of adequate public lands, waters, and other natural resources, it shall be the policy of the Commonwealth to conserve, develop, and utilize its natural resources, its public lands, and its historical sites and buildings. Further, it shall be the Commonwealth's policy to protect its atmosphere, lands, and waters from pollution, impairment, or destruction, for the benefit, enjoyment, and general welfare of the people of the Commonwealth. . . .

In further support of this public policy, the General Assembly in 1988 enacted the Virginia Conservation Easement Act ("VCEA"), Code §§ 10.1-1009 through -1016. In pertinent part, as defined in the VCEA a conservation easement is "a nonpossessory interest of a holder in real property, whether easement appurtenant or in gross . . . the purposes of which include retaining or protecting natural or open-space values of real property . . . or preserving the historical, architectural or archaeological aspects of real property."

Mindful of this background, we now consider the validity of the negative easement in gross granted to HGSI by the Atkinses in the 1973 deed and subsequently conveyed, with the Atkinses' concurrence, to the United States in

1978. The validity of that easement is dependent upon whether it was a type of negative easement that would have been recognized by the law of Virginia in 1973. For the reasons that follow, we conclude that the 1973 deed created a valid easement.

Blackman contends that a negative easement in gross for the purpose of land conservation and historic preservation was not valid in this Commonwealth until 1988 with the enactment of the VCEA. The thrust of this contention is that the VCEA would have been unnecessary if such easements were already valid. We are not persuaded by this contention.

. . . Code § 55-6 since at least 1962 has recognized easements in gross, whether affirmative or negative, as interests in real property capable of being transferred by deed or will. Because easements in gross were not transferable at common law and, indeed, were strongly disfavored, it is self-evident that this statute materially changed the common law and recognized "interest[s] in or claim[s] to real estate" beyond those traditionally recognized at common law. Moreover, in the subsequent 1966 enactment of the Open-Space Land Act, the General Assembly specifically recognized easements in gross when it authorized acquisition by certain public bodies of easements in gross in real property which is preserved for historic purposes. Such easements under that Act, under certain circumstances, would be negative easements in gross. Accordingly, while we continue to be of opinion that "the law will not permit a land-owner to create easements of every novel character and attach them to the soil," *Tardy*, 81 Va. (6 Hans.) at 557, the easement at issue in the present case is not of a novel character and is consistent with the statutory recognition of negative easements in gross for conservation and historic purposes.

. . . Moreover, as referenced by the *amici curiae* in their brief, it is a matter of public record that conservation easements or similar interests in land, far from being unique to the Historic Green Springs conservation effort, have been in common use in Virginia for many years before the adoption of the VCEA.

In enacting the VCEA, the General Assembly undertook to comprehensively address various land interests that can be used for conserving and preserving the natural and historical nature of property. In so doing, the General Assembly addressed the use of such easements in a manner consistent with Code § 55-6, the Open-Space Land Act, and the public policy favoring land conservation and preservation of historic sites and buildings in the Commonwealth as expressed in the Constitution of Virginia. The readily apparent purpose of the VCEA was to codify and consolidate the law of conservation easements to promote the granting of such easements to charitable organizations. When so viewed, it is clear that the VCEA did not create a new right to burden land by a negative easement in gross for the purpose of land conservation and historic preservation. Rather, it facilitated the continued creation of such easements by providing a clear statutory framework under which tax exemptions are made available to charitable organizations devoted to those purposes and tax benefits and incentives are provided to the grantors of such easements. . . .

For these reasons, we hold that the law of Virginia in 1973 did recognize as valid a negative easement in gross created for the purpose of land conservation and historic preservation. . . .

Notes

1. *The Uniform Conservation Easement Act:* The court considered the validity of a 1973 conservation easement, created some 15 years before the adoption of the Virginia Conservation Easement Act of 1973. What did the court hold, and why? Are you convinced by its logic? The retroactivity problem is widespread. Most states had an extensive body of common law conservation easements in place before they ever passed an authorizing conservation statute. Today, every state has adopted legislation recognizing conservation easements. Of those, 21 states (and the District of Columbia and the U.S. Virgin Islands) have adopted the Uniform Conservation Easement Act developed by the Uniform Law Commission. *See* http://www.uniformlaws.org/ (follow links to "legislative fact sheet") (visited Oct. 19, 2015). Section 5 provides that the model legislation "does not invalidate any interest, whether designated as a conservation or preservation easement or as a covenant, equitable servitude, restriction, easement, or otherwise, that is enforceable under other law." The drafters included Section 5 to ensure that statutory recognition of conservation easements would not be used as a mechanism to invalidate previous conservation tools—such as pre-statutory, common law conservation easements.

2. *Ecosystem services:* Why are citizens (through their taxes) and land trusts willing to pay others to maintain the environmental, historic, and cultural values of their land by forgoing the right to develop the property? A growing literature on *ecosystem services* addresses this question. As one article explains,

> Nature is important [to humans] not only for environmental protection, but also for economic productivity, fiscal soundness, community life, and governance. We tend to take nature's ecological systems—or ecosystems—for granted, but they provide critically valuable services to society and to urban areas. Ecosystems help to control natural hazards and climatic threats, such as storm surges and floods, temperature variation, and wind. Ecosystems provide clean water by filtering out pollutants from storm water runoff, streams and rivers, aquifers, and drinking water supplies. They provide refuge and reproduction habitat for plants and animals, thereby facilitating biodiversity. Ecosystems create recreational opportunities and a sense of place, which contribute to our quality of life by enhancing human physical and psychological health. Additionally they facilitate food production and local food economies. Well-functioning ecosystems are not only better able to adapt to disturbances, but also strengthen the resilience and adaptive capacity of human communities and cities to withstand environmental alterations or catastrophes.

James Salzman et. al., *The Most Important Current Research Questions in Urban Ecosystem Services,* 25 Duke Envtl. L. & Policy Forum 1, 2-3 (2014). *See also* J.B.

Ruhl, *In Defense of Ecosystem Services,* 32 Pace Envtl. L. Rev. 306, 335 (2015); Gretchen C. Daily, Nature's Services: Societal Dependence on Natural Ecosystems (1997).

3. Is it really an easement?   Numerous characteristics of the Park Service's easement would have violated the common law, and yet the court (and Virginia's legislation) recognizes such arrangements as "easements." The discussion problem in the next section challenges you to think more deeply about exactly what qualifies as an *easement.*

E. BEYOND THE BLACK LETTER: CONSERVATION EASEMENTS— WHAT'S IN A NAME?

In *United States v. Blackman,* the Virginia Supreme Court struggled to determine whether a novel agreement to promote land conservation and historic preservation qualified as an *easement.* In so doing, it chronicled several historic restrictions the common law placed on easements. In addition, the court noted the tension between the common law's reluctance to permit landowners "to create easements of every novel character and attach them to the soil" and the state's modern public policy (as incorporated in the state's constitution) favoring clean air, pure water, and the use and enjoyment of natural resources.

Some authorities argue that "easement" is a misnomer in this context. The U.S. Internal Revenue Service—which provides income tax deductions under section 170(h) of the Internal Revenue Code as an incentive for the donation of such property interests—calls them "perpetual conservation restrictions." *See* 26 C.F.R. § 1.170A-14. The general editor of Powell on Real Property argues that the IRS terminology should be adopted widely:

> The confusion between easements of the "traditional" and "conservation" varieties . . . is just one in a long line of situations in which the decision to allow often significantly dissimilar concepts to share the same name has led to unfortunate consequences. . . .
>
> . . . Statutory and uniform law drafters who piggy-backed on the early efforts of practitioners and government officials anxious to preserve view corridors and to provide other benefits for which traditional [law] proved inadequate— chiefly and most importantly the drafters of the Uniform Conservation Easement Act (UCEA)—were straightforward in their efforts to cherrypick the best attributes of traditional servitudes, while discarding troublesome disabilities, in order to achieve their admirable legislative goals. Fortunately, this is not an area in which the wheel needs to be reinvented, as the federal tax law already provides a clear, functional, descriptive term . . . —*perpetual conservation restrictions.* The fact that a significant percentage of conservation "easements" are created to meet federal tax eligibility criteria provides even further support for a smooth shift to a less problematic label.

Michael Allan Wolf, *Conservation Easements and the "Term Creep" Problem*, 2013 Utah L. Rev. 787, 788-89 (2013). But Professor Wolf's campaign likely faces an uphill battle. As we saw, the Uniform Conservation Easement Act, whose terminology he criticizes, has been widely adopted. What do you think is the best way to describe this type of property interest? In the next chapter, we will study one candidate for an alternative name—the *restrictive covenant*.

Discussion Questions

1. *Common law restrictions on easements:*   Review the challenged easement at issue in *United States v. Blackman*. Identify at least four characteristics that called into question its characterization as an "easement" and its overall validity. Why do you think the common law imposed each of those restrictions? What does each one reveal about the common law's view of easements in particular, and property in general?

2. *The common law of easements—mindless formalism or vigilant protector?*   Review the insights of Professor Carol Rose, reproduced at the beginning of this chapter. Do they help you critique the common law's hesitation over conservation easements as either "mindless formalism" or vigilant protector of property rights—or perhaps, a bit of each?

3. *The numerus clausus principle, revisited:*   In Chapter 3's study of estates and future interests, we encountered the *numerus clausus* principle and its refusal to recognize new form of property rights. How does that principle apply to the potential expansion of easements? Does it apply to statutory modifications, as well as to common law evolution? Do the *numerus clausus* restrictions make sense in the context of conservation easements—why or why not?

4. *What's in a name?*   The label "conservation easement" is probably here to stay but is that really an accurate description of the type of property interest challenged in *Blackman*? In the first discussion question, you were asked to identify at least four ways in which conservation "easements" depart from the model of traditional easements. Should the label "easement" be stretched to accommodate such conservation interests, or should different terminology be used? Why, if at all, does the name matter?

F. SKILLS PRACTICE: DRAFTING AN EASEMENT

Steve and Emily live at #1 Main Street, together with their dog, Tagger. Steve and Emily's lot is quite small and there is no convenient yard area for Tagger's use. Their next-door neighbor to the east, Brian, lives at #3 Main Street. Brian's lot includes a fairly extensive west side yard that he does not use. Instead, Brian uses his backyard and east side yard for a garden and an outdoor seating area. Steve and Emily have asked Brian if they could acquire an easement for Tagger to use Brian's west side yard. Brian is willing to help out Steve and Emily, but he wants to be sure that his own legal rights are adequately protected. Among other things, he wants to be sure that he can continue to access the west yard to put up his storm windows each season.

Tasks

You are counsel for Steve and Emily (or, alternatively, for Brian). As you prepare to counsel your client, consider the questions below. Can you think of any additional considerations that might be relevant? Then, review the pre-printed "Easement Agreement" that follows. With your client's particular interests in mind, modify the agreement as necessary. If time permits, your professor might then have you negotiate the final easement language with counsel for the opposing party.

1. *The character of the easement:* Will this be an easement appurtenant or in gross? What portion of Brian's property will be burdened by the easement? Who (or what property) will be benefitted by the easement?

2. *The duration and termination:* Will the easement be perpetual such that it benefits and burdens the parties' successors? Alternatively, will it be defeasible? If so, will it expire at the end of a specific time period or upon the occurrence of a specified condition?

3. *The purpose, scope, and divisibility of the easement:* What is the purpose of the easement? Can it change over time in accordance with reasonably foreseeable developments? What happens if Steve and Emily get an additional pet? What if they rent their basement room to a tenant with a pet? What if they decide to open a doggie day care center on their property?

4. *Exclusiveness:* May Brian continue to use his west yard, and if so, for what purposes? May Brian grant to other neighbors or friends the right to use his west yard for their pets or for other purposes?

5. *Grantor's rights and duties:* Who will mow, clean, and maintain the west side yard?

6. *Grantees' rights and duties:* May Steve and Emily put up a fence or exercise other rights on Brian's west yard? If so, who will bear the costs? Do they assume any maintenance, repair, or other duties?

7. *Liability and insurance:* Who will maintain insurance on the west side yard? Who will be responsible if exercise of the easement results in injury or property damage?

Easement Agreement

This agreement is made between _____ ("Grantor") and _____ ("Grantee").

The Grantor is the owner of certain real property commonly known as, and more fully described as follows (the servient estate): _____ .

The Grantee is the owner of certain real property, commonly known as _____ (the dominant estate).

Creation of easement: In consideration of $___ Grantor hereby grants to Grantee an easement on and across the following-described portion of the servient estate: _____ .

Character of easement: It is the intention of the parties that the easement granted is [appurtenant to the dominant estate] [in gross for the benefit of _____].

Duration and termination: This Agreement is made expressly for the benefit of, and shall be binding on, the heirs, successors in interest, and assigns of the respective parties. [This easement shall endure for ____ years.] [This easement shall terminate if the purposes of the easement cease to exist, are abandoned by Grantee, become impossible to perform, or if _____.]

Purpose, scope, and divisibility: The easement is granted for the purpose of _____ . It is expressly agreed that the easement, rights, and privileges conveyed to Grantee are limited by _____ .

Exclusiveness: The easement, rights, and privileges granted by this easement are [exclusive, and Grantor will not convey any other easement or conflicting rights within the area covered by this easement] [nonexclusive, and Grantor retains the right to convey similar easements to other persons deemed proper by the Grantor].

Grantor's rights and duties: Grantor may continue to use the surface of the land subject to this easement for all purposes that do not interfere with the Grantee's use of the easement, including, but not limited to _____ .
Grantor shall have the duty to maintain and repair the property subject to the easement, including the duty to _____ .

Grantee's rights and duties: Grantee shall have the right to maintain access to the easement by removing encroaching vegetation or _____ .
Grantee shall have the duty to repair and maintain the property subject to the easement, including the duty to _____ .

Attorney's Fees: If legal action is initiated by either party for the purpose of enforcing or interpreting this agreement, or to compel the recording of a release, the prevailing party shall be entitled to recover from the losing party reasonable expenses, attorney's fees, and costs.

Executed this ___ day of _____, 20___.

Grantor: *Brian*

Grantees: *Steve* and *Emily*

G. CHAPTER REVIEW

1. Practice Questions[3]

1. *The buried utility cable:*   Laura owns a large parcel of land. She has constructed her home on the eastern portion of the property, and has run a private utility cable underground that connects with the City's utility poles at the western edge of the property. Later, Laura divides her property in two and sells the western half to Van. Van discovers the utility cable buried beneath his property, disconnects it, and digs up the portion that is buried beneath his land. Laura, who is now without electricity, sues Van to enjoin him from interfering with her utility cable. What is the most likely result of the lawsuit?

   A. Laura will prevail if she can show that the existence of the underground cable should have been apparent to Van, and that the continued use of the underground cable beneath Van's land is reasonably necessary to Laura's use and enjoyment of her property.

   B. Van will prevail because he destroyed Laura's unity of title when he purchased the western tract from her.

   C. Van will prevail because Laura is claiming an easement by reservation, rather than by grant.

   D. Laura will prevail because her property is "landlocked."

2. *Driving through the neighbor's property:*   Amy and Brian are neighbors. For many years, Amy has allowed Brian to use a road on the south end of her property in order to reach the main road. Amy sells her property to Anita through a valid deed stating that the conveyance was "subject to an easement for the benefit of my neighbor Brian to reach the main road from his property." What interest, if any, does Brian have in Anita's property?

   A. Brian has an easement by prescription, provided that he has used the road for the required statutory time period.

   B. Brian's easement across Amy's property terminated when she sold it to Anita.

   C. Brian has an express easement across Anita's property.

   D. Brian has no easement across Anita's property if the jurisdiction follows the common law "stranger to the deed" rule.

3. *A lakefront resort:*   Sam owns Wild Lake, and by written instrument has granted Breta "the exclusive right to develop the lake as a commercial resort." Through a proper written instrument, Breta thereafter grants to Susan, "her heirs and assigns forever, a one-fourth interest in the exclusive right to develop the lake as a commercial resort." What interest, if any, does Susan hold in Wild Lake?

---

3. Answers appear in the Appendix to the casebook.

A. Susan has no valid interest in Wild Lake because the covenant does not "touch and concern" Wild Lake.

B. Susan has a valid one-fourth interest in Breta's resort, provided that the assignment to Susan does not increase the burden on the servient estate beyond that originally intended by Sam.

C. Susan has no valid interest in Breta's resort because commercial easements in gross cannot be assigned or transferred to others.

D. Susan has no valid interest in Breta's resort because commercial easements appurtenant cannot be assigned or transferred to others.

4. *A change of plans:*   Charlotte owns Lot #1, which is bordered on the south by a major roadway. Her neighbor Steve owns Lot #2, which is directly north of Lot #1. Steve also owns Lot #3, which is directly north of Lot #2. Steve planned to build a home on Lot #2, and through a valid written conveyance Charlotte had granted Steve an easement across Lot #1 "for ingress to and egress from Lot #2." Steve, however, changed his mind and constructed his home on Lot #3. He regularly used the easement through Lot #1 in order to reach his new home on Lot #3. The neighbors' relationship deteriorated over time, and Charlotte erected a fence across the easement path that blocked Steve's ability to reach her land and the road beyond. Steve sued for removal of the fence and an injunction against Charlotte's interference with the use of the easement. What is the most likely result?

A. Steve will prevail because it was reasonably foreseeable that he might build a home on Lot #3.

B. Steve will prevail because he has an express easement created by a valid written conveyance.

C. Charlotte will prevail because Steve is seeking to unreasonably expand the burden on Lot #1.

D. Charlotte will prevail because Lot #3 is not the dominant estate.

2. Bringing It Home

Research your state's statutory law, and find its relevant provisions on the issues listed below. Can you recommend any additions or changes to your state's statutory treatment of easements? If so, what and why?

1. *Negative easements:*   Recall the four types of negative easements generally recognized at common law. Does your state recognize any additional types of negative easements by statute? *See, e.g.,* Indiana Code § 32-23-4 (establishing requirements for the creation of "solar easements," defined as "an easement obtained for the purpose of exposure of a solar energy device or a passive solar energy system to the direct rays of the sun").

2. *Easement by prescription:*   Often, state statutes prescribe a length of time that adverse use must continue in order to ripen into an "easement by

prescription" without specifically using that phrase. Review the table of contents to your state's statutes. Under what category would you expect to find the prescriptive period? <u>Hint</u>: recall Chapter 2's consideration of adverse possession. What function did the statutory period serve?

3. *Easements in gross:*   Can you find any statutory provisions governing the alienability or divisibility of easements in gross? Does your state provide statutory recognition of easements to visit grave sites? *Recall Traders, Inc. v. Bartholomew* (note 5 following case).

4. *Private condemnation of easements:*   Some states provide remedies where landowners are unwilling to grant certain types of easements deemed important to society. This can be viewed as a type of private eminent domain (Chapter 13). Washington, for example, authorized the condemnation of private ways of necessity. *See* Revised Code of Washington, § 8.24.010 (quoted in a footnote to the *Brown v. Voss* excerpt). Does your state have any such provision?

5. *Conservation easements:*   Every state has some type of statutory authorization for conservation easements. How does your state handle the retroactivity issue—does it validate such easements created *before* the statute explicitly expanded the common law quartet of negative easements to include those with a conservation purpose? <u>Hint</u>: First, see if your state has adopted the Uniform Conservation Easement Act (in whole or in part). Go to the website listing the uniform statutes promulgated by the Uniform Law Commission, then follow links to the "Conservation Easement Act" and "Legislative Fact Sheet." *See* http://www.uniformlaws.org/Acts.aspx. If your state has not adopted the uniform Act, then find an online table of contents to your state's statutory law. Search for some type of conservation easement legislation, looking under key words including *conservation, easements, conservation restriction* and *conservation servitude.*

Contractual Limits and Beyond: Running Covenants

A. Real Covenants
B. Equitable Servitudes
C. Termination and Nonenforcement of Covenants
D. Modern Applications: Common Interest Communities and Conservation Easements
E. Beyond the Black Letter: Forever Is a Long Time
F. Skills Practice: Policy-Based Arguments
G. Chapter Review

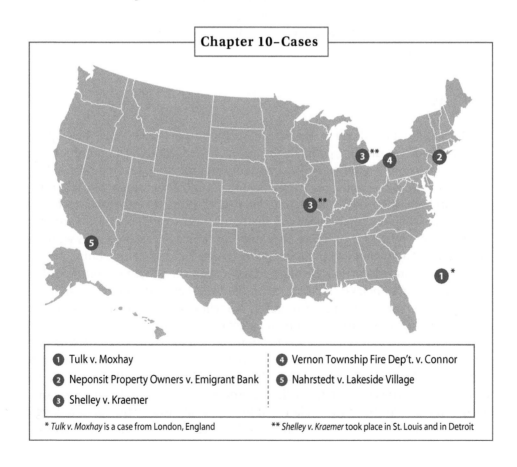

Chapter 10-Cases

❶ Tulk v. Moxhay
❷ Neponsit Property Owners v. Emigrant Bank
❸ Shelley v. Kraemer

❹ Vernon Township Fire Dep't. v. Connor
❺ Nahrstedt v. Lakeside Village

* *Tulk v. Moxhay* is a case from London, England   ** *Shelley v. Kraemer* took place in St. Louis and in Detroit

In the previous chapter, you learned about one type of servitude—the easement. Here, we will learn about a second type of servitude—the covenant. In general, "covenant" simply refers to a contract or an agreement. But when agreements affect land and when the original promising parties intend to bind their successors, then such agreements are called *running covenants*. Like easements, covenants are rooted in contract, but rise to the level of property rights. Like other property rights, for example, they can be recorded in the county records, and their condemnation by eminent domain requires compensation. Also like easements, covenants are nonpossessory in nature. But unlike easements, the benefits and burdens of covenants do not automatically attach to the land and bind successors unless the covenants satisfy certain technical requirements that we will study in this chapter.

Covenants take two forms—*real covenants* and *equitable servitudes*. The distinctions among easements and the two types of covenants are largely a product of history. In general, easements developed first, followed by real covenants, and then by equitable servitudes. As the courts restricted the use of one device in the name of promoting marketability, the next evolved. Today, some argue that the complex distinctions are unnecessary. Indeed, the drafters of Restatement (Third) of Property, Servitudes, argue that the technical distinctions among the three categories should give way to a uniform law of servitudes. After you learn more about covenants, think about whether you agree with that suggestion.

A. REAL COVENANTS

During the period when the law of running covenants was developing, England had two distinct judicial systems: law and equity. The common law courts, entrusted to a judiciary independent from the king, favored rigid adherence to precedent—principles of law developed in earlier cases. But when the common law courts were unable to deliver relief, often for extremely-technical reasons, or when monetary relief was inadequate, frustrated plaintiffs turned to the king's chancellor to provide an equitable remedy in accordance with his conscience. Today in the United States, the federal courts handle both law and equity cases, and almost all the states have a uniform system of courts for law and equity. Nevertheless, the distinction between law and equity continues to permeate the law of running covenants. We will begin by looking at so-called *real covenants*, which are also known as covenants *running at law.*

Suppose that landlord *A* leases property to tenant *B* for two years. *B* promises in the duly-executed lease, "On behalf of myself, my heirs, and assigns, I will keep the property in good repair and I will never use the premises for commercial purposes." Later, *A* sells the property to *C* (who takes over as landlord) and *B* assigns the entire balance of the leasehold to *D*, who opens a doggie daycare center on the premises and lets the yard become overgrown. Does *C* have a remedy against *D*? Notice that neither one was a party to the original covenant. As a matter of terminology, the original party making the promise and bearing its burden (*B*) is known as the *promisor* (or *covenantor*), and the original party receiving the benefit of the promise (*A*) is the *promisee* (or *covenantee*).

Let's begin by analyzing the nature of *B*'s promises to *A*.

Affirmative or negative?   An *affirmative* promise involves the promisor's agreement to *perform a specified act* (or undertake a specified duty). A *negative* promise requires the promisor to *refrain from acting* in an otherwise legally permissible manner. Here, *B*'s promise to keep the property in good repair is affirmative, whereas the promise to refrain from commercial uses of the property is negative.

Easement or covenant?   Running covenants are intimately related to easements appurtenant—one hornbook calls them "first cousins." William B. Stoebuck & Dale A. Whitman, The Law of Property § 8.13 (3d ed. 2000). Like such easements, one parcel of land is burdened for the benefit of another. Less commonly, a covenant might benefit a person rather than a tract of land—an arrangement that resembles an easement in gross. The distinction between easements and running covenants is rooted in history and based on logic that may no longer apply well in some situations today. As a result, sometimes it can be very difficult to tell the difference between running covenants and easements.

Focus first on the affirmative promise. As we saw in the last chapter, affirmative *easements* give their holders the right to *use the land of another*. In contrast, affirmative *covenants* involve promises to *perform specified acts*. Here, *B*'s promise to keep the property in good repair is an affirmative covenant. Next, focus on the negative promise. Both negative covenants and negative easements require the covenantor to *refrain from acting* in an otherwise legally permissible way. The two are virtually indistinguishable, except that the common law recognized only four types of negative easements, those that prevented interference with another's light, air, building support, or with artificial streamflow. If a negative promise fits into one of these four categories, it is likely a negative easement; otherwise, it is likely a negative covenant. Here, the promise to refrain from commercial use of the property is a negative covenant (also called a "restrictive covenant").

Now, let's turn to the question of whether the burden of *B*'s promise runs to *D*, and whether the benefit of the promise (and the right to enforce the promise) runs from *A* to *C*. As a tradition, law school professors have long used a diagram similar to Figure 1 to illustrate the various relationships between the original covenanting parties and their successors. The arrow from *B* to *A* (to the right of the red shaded bar) indicates that *B* made a promise to *A*. In many instances, the parties make *mutual promises* to one another. In that case, the unidirectional arrow should be replaced with dual-directional arrows. If the covenant satisfies a variety of requirements, as indicated on Figure 1, then it will "run" to successors. Let's examine the requirements one at a time.

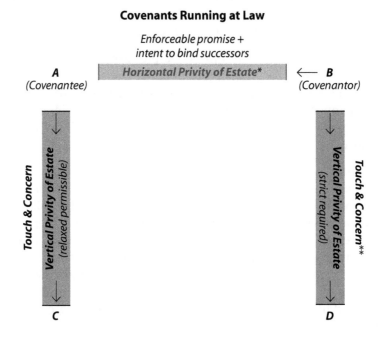

Covenants Running at Law

Enforceable promise +
intent to bind successors

A (Covenantee) — Horizontal Privity of Estate* ⟵ *B* (Covenantor)

Touch & Concern — Vertical Privity of Estate (relaxed permissible) — C

Vertical Privity of Estate (strict required) — Touch & Concern** — D

* The four types of horizontal privity of estate are: 1) landlord/tenant relationship (England);
2) simultaneous/mutual privity; 3) successive privity; and 4) privity not required (R3d)

** In some jurisdictions, the burden does not run if the benefit is in gross.

Figure 1

The original covenant: Like any contract, an enforceable covenant must be in writing and comply with the statute of frauds (or one of its exceptions). In practice, these requirements are usually satisfied easily. One potential obstacle occurs when the covenant appears within a deed transferring land—typically only the seller signs the deed. But what if the *buyer*'s promises appear within the deed (which has not been signed by the buyer)? Many courts circumvent this problem by assuming that the buyer/promisor's signature is implied from acceptance of the deed. The original covenanting parties must also *intend* to bind their successors. Typically, parties make this explicit through boilerplate language. For example, the parties can explicitly covenant "on behalf of themselves, their successors, and assigns."

Horizontal privity of estate: In addition to their contractual relationship, the original covenanting parties (*A* and *B*) must have engaged in a property transaction. The concept of *horizontal privity of estate* (shown by the red shaded bar in Figure 1) captures this property relationship. As a shorthand notation, some sources on running covenants simply refer to "privity," but they likely mean privity of estate rather than privity of contract. Recall that we have previously examined the concept of *privity* in connection with adverse possession and landlord-tenant law. Most jurisdictions require one of four types of horizontal privity. Because terminology is often inconsistent, focus on the underlying nature of the arrangement.

- *Landlord-tenant relationship:* Early English cases required the covenanting parties to be in a landlord-tenant relationship at the time the promise was made.
- *Simultaneous (or mutual) privity:* Early cases in Massachusetts (and perhaps in Nevada) required that the covenanting parties held simultaneous interests in the affected property at the time the covenant was made, or that the instrument containing the covenant itself created such simultaneous interests. Simultaneous privity includes a landlord-tenant relationship (as in the early English cases), but more broadly includes also parties to an easement (the owners of the dominant and servient estates); the holders of a present estate and future interest in the same land; and cotenants.
- *Successive privity:* Under this view, there is horizontal between the grantor and grantee of an interest in property, provided that the covenant is contained within the deed. Successive privity is the most commonly required form of privity today and is recognized in nearly all of the states.
- *Restatement (Third) of Property, Servitudes:* The Restatement would abolish the requirement of horizontal privity.

Vertical privity of estate: Similarly, the concept of *vertical privity of estate* (shown by the gray shaded bars in Figure 1) refers to any subsequent conveyances by *A* or *B* to successors. The adjectives *horizontal* and *vertical* simply refer to the diagramming convention of aligning the original parties along the horizontal axis, and their successors along a vertical axis. But beyond that, the critical question is whether any particular covenant is a mere contract binding only on the original parties, or whether it "runs with the land" to successors. More precisely, the issue is whether the burden and benefit of the covenant run with an *estate* in the land. As captured by one colorful phrase, "real covenants run along with estates as a bird rides on a wagon":

> [Real covenants] run with *estates* in land. That is, the burden passes with a transfer of the estate the covenantor held in the burdened land; and the benefit passes with a transfer of the estate, or at least some lesser estate carved out of the estate, that the covenantee held in the benefited land. It is, therefore, more precise to say that the respective *estates*, and not "lands," are benefited and burdened. As the quaint phrase puts it, real covenants run along with estates as a bird rides on a wagon.

William B. Stoebuck & Dale A. Whitman, The Law of Property § 8.17 (3d ed. 2000), quoting Powell on Real Property ¶670 (P. Rohan rev. ed. 1990).

- *Strict standard:* In its strictest sense, vertical privity exists only when a successor takes the *entire estate* (fee simple, life estate, etc.) of the original covenanting party (even if a lesser acreage). As shown in Figure 1, strict vertical privity is generally required for the burden to bind successors.

- *Relaxed standard:* Some courts will also find that vertical privity exists where a successor takes a lesser possessory estate carved out of the estate of the original covenanting party (that is, either a freehold estate or a lease). Notice that adverse possessors would not satisfy this standard because they start a new chain of title and do not succeed to the interest of the prior possessor. As a result, perhaps counter-intuitively, the possession of a trespasser can ripen into a title free of the benefits and burdens of the covenant. As shown on Figure 1, relaxed vertical privity is generally sufficient to allow the benefit to run to successors.

The promise "touches and concerns" land: In general, the covenant must affect the parties as owners of *estates in land*, rather than in their personal capacity (at least on the burden side). A direct physical connection between the covenant and the land is usually not required—such as a promise to trim the trees on the property. Instead, courts consider whether the covenant affects the estate's use, utility, or economic value. Under the strictest view, the burden will not run if the benefit is *in gross* (that is, if the benefit is personal and does not touch and concern land). Courts have struggled especially with promises to pay money (which do not seem to directly touch and concern land). But, if the payment is a substitute for an act that touches and concerns land—such as homeowner dues applied toward maintenance work—then the requirement might be satisfied.

Notice of the burden: There is no independent limitation that covenants burden only those who take property with notice of their existence. However, as you might recall from Chapter 8, state recording acts (in *notice* and *race-notice* jurisdictions) invalidate prior unrecorded conveyances against subsequent purchasers who take without notice of the covenant.

Remedy—money damages: At common law, courts awarded money damages for past breaches of real covenants. Today, the equitable remedy of injunction might also be awarded to prevent future breaches where the legal remedy of damages would be ineffective (as where unique property interests cannot be adequately protected by the backward-looking damages remedy). As a broad generalization, if the plaintiff seeks money damages, then you should analyze the agreement as a real covenant running at law.

Today, real covenants retain considerable vitality in the context of landlord-tenant law. Otherwise, they have been substantially displaced by the law of equitable servitudes (considered later in the chapter). *See generally* Stoebuck & Whitman, *supra*, at §§ 8.14-8.21.

A Place to Start | **Covenants Running at Law—Requirements**

- *The original covenant:*
  - Enforceable agreement that complies with the statute of frauds
  - Intent to bind successors
- *Horizontal privity of estate:*
  - Landlord-tenant relationship
  - Simultaneous (or mutual) privity, or
  - Successive privity
- *Vertical privity of estate:*
  - *Strict standard:* Generally required for burden to run
  - *Relaxed standard:* Generally sufficient for benefit to run
- *Touch and concern land:* Both benefit and burden must touch and concern the land
- *Remedy:* Usually money damages

Test Your Understanding

Unless instructed otherwise, assume that Amelia and Benjamin are neighbors who own in fee simple absolute Lot #1 and Lot #2, respectively. Lot #1 abuts the main highway, whereas Lot #2 is "landlocked" with no easy access to improved roads. The "State Park" is mountainous and scenic.

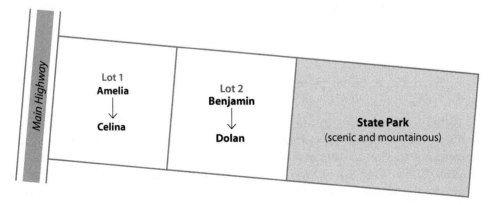

Figure 2

In each of the following situations, decide whether the parties have created an easement or a covenant, and whether it is affirmative or negative. Then determine whether the burden runs to Dolan, or whether the benefit runs to Celina, as relevant. Assume that each promise is contained in a valid written, recorded instrument that complies with the statute of frauds.

1. Benjamin grants Amelia, "The right to cross Lot #2 to access the State Park." Subsequently, Benjamin sells Lot #2 to Dolan, and Amelia sells Lot #1 to Celina.

2. Assume that Benjamin owns both Lot #1 and Lot #2 (contrary to Figure 2). He leases Lot #1 to Amelia, "For five years, beginning on the first day of next month." Benjamin plans to build a fence on the boundary line between Lot #1 and Lot #2, but he knows that it would be difficult for Amelia to keep the fence in good repair. He promises, "I, Benjamin, as owner of Lot #2, will keep the fence in continuous good repair." Subsequently, Benjamin sells Lot #2 to Dolan.

3. As in the original fact pattern, Amelia and Benjamin are neighbors, who own their lots in fee simple absolute. Benjamin plans to build an addition to his home, but he knows that Amelia likes looking out and opening her windows to enjoy the sunshine, fresh air, and mountain views. He promises Amelia, "Any structure hereinafter constructed on Lot #2 will be limited to one story in height." Subsequently, Benjamin sells Lot #2 to Dolan.

4. Amelia and Benjamin execute a valid agreement in which each promises, "My lot shall be used for residential purposes only." Subsequently, Amelia sells her lot to Celina, and Benjamin leases his lot to Dolan, who opens a restaurant on the property.

5. Assume that Amelia owns both Lot #1 and Lot #2. She conveys Lot #2, "To Benjamin as long as the land is used for residential purposes only." Subsequently, Benjamin sells his lot to Dolan, who opens a restaurant on the property. What consequence follows, if any, from Dolan's violation of the residential-use-only restriction?

B. EQUITABLE SERVITUDES

When the law of running covenants reached the English courts of equity, they considerably relaxed the common law's requirements for covenants to run to successors. Figure 3 illustrates the requirements for *covenants running in equity*, which are known as *equitable servitudes*. How do the requirements differ from those required for covenants to run at law?

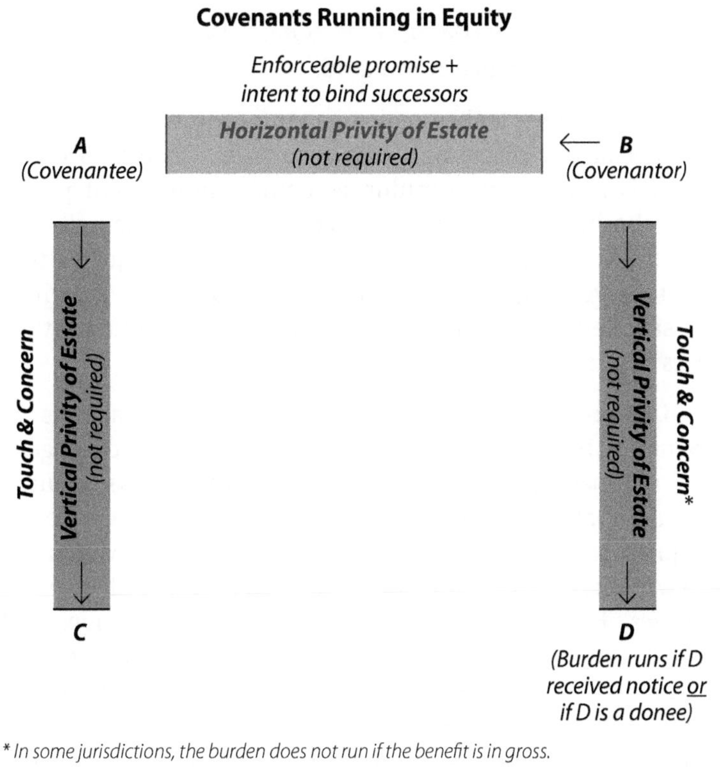

Covenants Running in Equity

Enforceable promise +
intent to bind successors

Figure 3

The original covenant: Like covenants running at law, equitable servitudes must arise from an enforceable promise that evidences the intent to bind successors.

Horizontal privity of estate: Horizontal privity is not required in equity. Thus, mere neighbors can enter into agreements that will bind successors, independent of any sort of land transaction or relationship among them.

Vertical privity of estate: Equitable servitudes run to subsequent users, even if they are not in vertical privity of estate with the original covenanting parties. Like easements, equitable servitudes "sink their roots into the soil" and *run with the land,* rather than with *estates in land* (as do real covenants). William B. Stoebuck & Dale A. Whitman, The Law of Property §§ 8.22 and 8.27 (3d ed. 2000). Because equitable servitudes run with the land itself, all who are on the land are bound by the servitude. This would include those who are in strict or relaxed vertical privity with the original covenanting parties (as with real covenants); contract purchasers who do not yet hold legal title; the parties to nonpossessory interests such as easements; and perhaps even adverse possessors.

The promise "touches and concerns" land: As with real covenants, the promise must touch and concern the land.

Notice of the burden: Unlike real covenants, equity does impose a notice requirement. Recall our discussion of notice from Chapter 8's study of the recording acts. For covenants running in equity, subsequent possessors are not bound by the burden unless they take with notice (actual, constructive, or inquiry) of the covenant *or* if they are "donees" that acquired the property for free (by inter vivos gift, will, or inheritance). In other words, when all other elements are satisfied, only *bona fide purchasers* without notice of the covenant can escape its burden.

Remedy—injunction: Injunction against future breach is the most common remedy. In rare cases, courts have awarded damages for past breaches. As a broad generalization, if the plaintiff seeks equitable relief, then you should analyze the agreement as an equitable servitude.

Today, equitable servitudes have overshadowed real covenants in importance. As we will see, they take on a prominent role in so-called *common interest communities.* However, if plaintiffs seek money damages rather than injunctive relief, they must generally proceed under the stricter real covenant theory. The *A Place to Start* box shows the requirements of covenants running in equity. As with real covenants, be sure to apply the elements separately to test the running of the benefit and the running of the burden, respectively.

A Place to Start | **Equitable Servitudes—Requirements**

- *The original covenant:*
  - Enforceable agreement that complies with the statute of frauds
  - Intent to bind successors
- *Horizontal privity of estate:* Not required
- *Vertical privity of estate:* Not required
- *Notice of covenant:* Burden does not run to *bona fide purchasers* without notice of the covenant
- *Touch and concern land:* Both benefit and burden must touch and concern the land
- *Remedy:* Usually injunction against future breach

Test Your Understanding

Review the test your understanding problems accompanying Figure 2, above. Applying the standards of equitable servitudes, determine for each problem whether the benefit and the burden run to the successors of the original covenanting parties.

Tulk v. Moxhay

(1848) 41 Eng. Rep. 1143 (P.C.)

Reading Guide

In this landmark case, the king's chancellor departed from the common law courts in the treatment of covenants running with the land. How would the common law courts have decided this case? Did the chancellor reach a more equitable result? Be sure to notice which legal requirements the chancellor abolished, modified, or added.

In the year 1808 the Plaintiff, being then the owner in fee of the vacant piece of ground in Leicester Square, as well as of several of the houses forming the Square, sold the piece of ground by the description of "Leicester Square garden or pleasure ground, with the equestrian statue then standing in the centre thereof, and the iron railing and stone work round the same," to one Elms in fee: and the deed of conveyance contained a covenant by Elms, for himself, his heirs, and assigns, with the Plaintiff, his heirs, executors, and administrators,

> that Elms, his heirs, and assigns should, and would from time to time, and at all times thereafter at his and their own costs and charges, keep and maintain the said piece of ground and square garden, and the iron railing round the same in its then form, and in sufficient and proper repair as a square garden and pleasure ground, in an open state, uncovered with any buildings, in neat and ornamental order; and that it should be lawful for the inhabitants of Leicester Square, tenants of the Plaintiff, on payment of a reasonable rent for the same, to have keys at their own expense and the privilege of admission therewith at any time or times into the said square garden and pleasure ground.

The piece of land so conveyed passed by divers mesne conveyances into the hands of the Defendant, whose purchase deed contained no similar covenant with his vendor: but he admitted that he had purchased with notice of the covenant in the deed of 1808.

The Defendant having manifested an intention to alter the character of the square garden, and asserted a right, if he thought fit, to build upon it, the Plaintiff, who still remained owner of several houses in the square, filed this bill for an injunction; and an injunction was granted by the Master of the Rolls to restrain the Defendant from converting or using the piece of ground and square garden, and the iron railing round the same, to or for any other purpose than as a square garden and pleasure ground in an open state, and uncovered with buildings.

Leicester Square (1874), looking from the west side toward the Alhambra Theatre.
Notice the equestrian statue and surrounding iron railing that Elms promised to keep in good repair.
Source: Leicester Square Garden, *Illustrated London News, July 4, 1874 (artist unaccredited)*

COTTENHAM, THE LORD CHANCELLOR.

That this Court has jurisdiction to enforce a contract between the owner of land and his neighbour purchasing a part of it, that the latter shall either use or abstain from using the land purchased in a particular way, is what I never knew disputed. Here there is no question about the contract: the owner of certain houses in the square sells the land adjoining, with a covenant from the purchaser not to use it for any other purpose than as a square garden. And it is now contended, not that the vendee could violate that contract, but that he might sell the piece of land, and that the purchaser from him may violate it without this Court having any power to interfere. If that were so, it would be impossible for an owner of land to sell part of it without incurring the risk of rendering what he retains worthless. It is said that, the covenant being one which does not run with the land, this Court cannot enforce it; but the question is, not whether the covenant runs with the land, but whether a party shall be permitted to use the land in a manner inconsistent with the contract entered into by his vendor, and with notice of which he purchased. Of course, the price would be affected by the covenant, and nothing could be more inequitable than that the original purchaser should be able to sell the property the next day for a greater price, in consideration of the assignee being allowed to escape from the liability which he had himself undertaken. . . .

That the question does not depend upon whether the covenant runs with the land is evident from this, that if there was a mere agreement and no covenant, this Court would enforce it against a party purchasing with notice of it; for if an equity is attached to the property by the owner, no one purchasing with notice of that equity can stand in a different situation from the party from whom he purchased. . . .

With respect to the observations of Lord Brougham in *Keppell v. Bailey* [(2M. & K. 547)], he never could have meant to lay down that this Court would not enforce an equity attached to land by the owner, unless under such circumstances as would maintain an action at law. If that be the result of his observations, I can only say that I cannot coincide with it.

I think the cases cited before the Vice-Chancellor and this decision of the Master of the Rolls perfectly right, and, therefore, that this motion [to discharge the Master's order] must be refused, with costs.

Notes

1. *The promises:* Elk made three promises to Tulk. Carefully articulate each, and explain whether it gave rise to an easement or a covenant, and whether the obligation was affirmative or negative.

2. *The requirements:* If this case had been decided in a court of law (rather than equity), would Moxhay have been bound by the burden of Elms' promises? In the court of equity, what requirements did the chancellor set forth, and how does each requirement promote an equitable result?

3. *More to the story—Leicester Square, London:* From its earliest years, the area that would become Leicester Square has been the subject of controversy, where competing pressures for development and preservation played out. In 1630, the Second Earl of Leicester bought a portion of St. Martin's Field, then a commons used by parish inhabitants for cattle grazing, laundry drying, and other domestic activities. Over the protest of the parishioners, the earl constructed a grand residence (that remained standing until 1791) at the north end of what would eventually become Leicester Square. Over the years, other building controversies erupted. The king transferred some of the land to private developers who turned the commons into a wealthy residential neighborhood. The core remained open as a private central garden for use by the surrounding residents. A gilded likeness of George I astride a horse graced the center of the garden. By the mid-19th century when the Tulk dispute began to

simmer, the square had become commercialized and the garden was overgrown and untended.

WYLD'S GREAT GLOBE
LEICESTER SQUARE
1851

An Early View of the Great Globe Without the Galleries
Print by Thomas H. Shepherd (Dec. 31, 1850)

Both Tulk and Moxhay passed away not long after the case was decided. The Moxhay family sold the garden to James Wyld, a well-known geographer, under an agreement that allowed him to build "Wyld's Great Globe"—an enormous building that housed a 60-foot high replica of the earth. Pursuant to their agreement, Wyld maintained the Globe for 10 years, and then removed it. Thus, although the garden had escaped development by Moxhay, it succumbed for a decade to Wyld's garish plans. In yet another twist to the story, Leicester Square's history came full circle—from commons, to private garden, and back to public space. In 1874, Baron Albert Grant bought the park, restored the garden, and donated it to the City of Westminster (a borough of London). Since that time, the city has owned and operated Leicester Square as a public park. Today, the square is surrounded by cinemas, and is the site of the London Film Festival each year. *See* Walter Thornbury, "Leicester Square," in Old and New London, volume 3 (1878); James Charles Smith, *Tulk v. Moxhay: The Fight to Develop Leicester Square*, in Property Stories 170 (Gerald Korngold & Andrew P. Morris eds. 2d ed. 2009).

Neponsit Property Owners' Ass'n, Inc. v. Emigrant Industrial Sav. Bank

15 N.E.2d 793 (N.Y. 1938)

Reading Guide

The equitable servitude paved the way for widespread use of subdivision covenants, a device that makes possible the modern *common interest community* (section D, below). Over time, such communities have come to provide a wide variety of private services and amenities beyond those supported by local tax dollars. To finance those improvements, homeowners covenant on behalf of themselves and their successors to make periodic payments to a *homeowners association* (HOA) authorized to levy private assessments for the maintenance of the community.

In the case below, the Neponsit Realty Company was ahead of its time in developing an exclusive beachfront community on New York's popular Rockaway peninsula in the early 20th century. But the legal enforceability of its homeowner covenants was far from certain at the time for two primary reasons. First, it was unclear whether a *promise to pay money* satisfied the requirement that running covenants must touch and concern the land. In addition, some early cases, particularly in New York and New Jersey, disfavored the running of *affirmative* covenants that affirmatively required the promisor to take a specified action (as opposed to negative covenants through which the parties merely agreed to refrain from certain actions). *Neponsit*'s resolution of these two issues represents the modern view.

LEHMAN, J.

The plaintiff, as assignee of Neponsit Realty Company, has brought this action to foreclose a lien upon land which the defendant owns. The lien, it is alleged, arises from a covenant, condition or charge contained in a deed of conveyance of the land from Neponsit Realty Company to a predecessor in title of the defendant. The defendant purchased the land at a judicial sale. The referee's deed to the defendant and every deed in the defendant's chain of title since the conveyance of the land by Neponsit Realty Company purports to convey the property subject to the covenant, condition or charge contained in the original deed. . . .

It appears that in January, 1911, Neponsit Realty Company, as owner of a tract of land in Queens county, caused to be filed in the office of the clerk of the county a map of the land. The tract was developed for a strictly residential community, and Neponsit Realty Company conveyed lots in the tract to purchasers, describing such lots by reference to the filed map and to roads and streets shown thereon. In 1917, Neponsit Realty Company conveyed the land now owned by the defendant to Robert Oldner Deyer and his wife by deed which contained the covenant upon which the plaintiff's cause of action is based.

That covenant provides:

> And the party of the second part [the buyer] for the party of the second part and the heirs, successors and assigns of the party of the second part further covenants that the property conveyed by this deed shall be subject to an annual charge in such an amount as will be fixed by the party of the first part [Neponsit Realty Company], its successors and assigns, not, however exceeding in any year the sum of four ($4.00) Dollars per lot 20x100 feet. The assigns of the party of the first part may include a Property Owners' Association which may hereafter be organized for the purposes referred to in this paragraph, and in case such association is organized the sums in this paragraph provided for shall be payable to such association. . . . Such charge shall be . . . be devoted to the maintenance of the roads, paths, parks, beach, sewers and such other public purposes as shall from time to time be determined by the party of the first part, its successors or assigns. . . . These covenants shall run with the land and shall be construed as real covenants running with the land until January 31st, 1940, when they shall cease and determine. . . .

There can be no doubt that Neponsit Realty Company intended that the covenant should run with the land and should be enforceable by a property owners association against every owner of property in the residential tract which the realty company was then developing. The language of the covenant admits of no other construction. Regardless of the intention of the parties, a covenant will run with the land and will be enforceable against a subsequent purchaser of the land at the suit of one who claims the benefit of the covenant, only if the covenant complies with certain legal requirements. These requirements rest upon ancient rules and precedents. The age-old essentials of a real covenant, aside from the form of the covenant, may be summarily formulated as follows: (1) It must appear that grantor and grantee intended that the covenant should run with the land; (2) it must appear that the covenant is one "touching" or "concerning" the land with which it runs; (3) it must appear that there is "privity of estate" between the promisee or party claiming the benefit of the covenant and the right to enforce it, and the promisor or party who rests under the burden of the covenant. . . .

. . . [The covenant in this case] is an affirmative covenant to pay money for use in connection with, but not upon, the land which it is said is subject to the burden of the covenant. Does such a covenant "touch" or "concern" the land? These terms are not part of a statutory definition, a limitation placed by the State upon the power of the courts to enforce covenants *intended* to run with the land by the parties who entered into the covenants. Rather they are words used by courts in England in old cases to describe a limitation which the courts themselves created or to formulate a test which the courts have devised and which the courts voluntarily apply. In truth such a description or test so formulated is too vague to be of much assistance and judges and academic scholars alike have struggled, not with entire success, to formulate a test at once more satisfactory and more accurate. "It has been found impossible to state any absolute tests to determine what covenants touch and concern land and what do not. The question is one for the court to determine in the exercise of its best judgment upon the facts of each case." *Clark on Covenants and Interests Running with Land*, p. 76.

Even though that be true, a determination by a court in one case upon particular facts will often serve to point the way to correct decision in other cases upon analogous facts. Such guideposts may not be disregarded. It has been often said that a covenant to pay a sum of money is a personal affirmative covenant which usually does not concern or touch the land. Such statements are based upon English decisions which hold in effect that only covenants, which compel the covenanter to submit to some *restriction on the use* of his property, touch or concern the land, and that the burden of a covenant which requires the covenanter to do an affirmative act, even on his own land, for the benefit of the owner of a "dominant" estate, does not run with his land. . . . [I]n many jurisdictions of this country the narrow English rule has been criticized and a more liberal and flexible rule has been substituted. In this State the courts have not gone so far. We have not abandoned the historic distinction drawn by the English courts. So this court has recently said: "Subject to a few exceptions not important at this time, there is now in this state a settled rule of law that a covenant to do an affirmative act, as distinguished from a covenant merely negative in effect, does not run with the land so as to charge the burden of performance on a subsequent grantee [citing cases]. This is so though the burden of such a covenant is laid upon the very parcel which is the subject-matter of the conveyance." *Guaranty Trust Co. of New York v. New York & Queens County Ry. Co.*, 170 N.E. 887, 892 (N.Y. 1930), opinion by Cardozo, C. J.

. . . [The courts have] pointed out that there were some exceptions or limitations in the application of the general rule. Some promises to pay money have been enforced, as covenants running with the land, against subsequent holders of the land who took with notice of the covenant. It may be difficult to classify these exceptions or to formulate a test of whether a particular covenant to pay money or to perform some other act falls within the general rule that ordinarily an affirmative covenant is a personal and not a real covenant, or falls outside the limitations placed upon the general rule. At least it must "touch" or "concern" the land in a substantial degree, and though it may be inexpedient and perhaps impossible to formulate a rigid test or definition which will be entirely satisfactory or which can be applied mechanically in all cases, we should at least be able to state the problem and find a reasonable method of approach to it. It has been suggested that a covenant which runs with the land must affect the legal relations—the advantages and the burdens—of the parties to the covenant, as owners of particular parcels of land and not merely as members of the community in general, such as taxpayers or owners of other land. That method of approach has the merit of realism. The test is based on the effect of the covenant rather than on technical distinctions. Does the covenant impose, on the one hand, a burden upon an interest in land, which on the other hand increases the value of a different interest in the same or related land?

Even though we accept that approach and test, it still remains true that whether a particular covenant is sufficiently connected with the use of land to run with the land, must be in many cases a question of degree. A promise to pay for something to be done in connection with the promisor's land does not differ essentially from a promise by the promisor to do the thing himself, and both promises constitute, in a substantial sense, a restriction upon the owner's right to use the land, and a burden upon the legal interest of the owner. On the other hand, a covenant to perform or pay for the performance of an affirmative act disconnected with the use of the land cannot ordinarily touch or concern the land in any substantial degree. Thus, unless we exalt technical form over substance, the distinction between covenants which run with land and covenants which are personal, must depend upon the effect of the covenant on the legal rights which otherwise would flow from ownership of land and which are connected with the land. The problem then is: Does the covenant in purpose and effect substantially alter these rights? . . .

Looking at the problem presented in this case . . . and stressing the intent and substantial effect of the covenant rather than its form, it seems clear that the covenant may properly be said to touch and concern the land of the defendant and its burden should run with the land. True, it calls for payment of a sum of money to be expended for "public purposes" upon land other than the land conveyed by Neponsit Realty Company to plaintiff's predecessor in title. By that conveyance the grantee, however, obtained not only title to particular lots, but an easement or right of common enjoyment with other property owners in roads, beaches, public parks or spaces and improvements in the same tract. For full enjoyment in common by the defendant and other property owners of these easements or rights, the roads and public places must be maintained. In order that the burden of maintaining public improvements should rest upon the land benefited by the improvements, the grantor exacted from the grantee of the land with its appurtenant easement or right of enjoyment a covenant that the burden of paying the cost should be inseparably attached to the land which enjoys the benefit. It is plain that any distinction or definition which would exclude such a covenant from the classification of covenants which "touch" or "concern" the land would be based on form and not on substance.

Another difficulty remains. Though between the grantor and the grantee there was privity of estate, the covenant provides that its benefit shall run to the assigns of the grantor who "may include a Property Owners' Association which may hereafter be organized for the purposes referred to in this paragraph." The plaintiff has been organized to receive the sums payable by the property owners and to expend them for the benefit of such owners. Various definitions have been formulated of "privity of estate" in connection with covenants that run with the land, but none of such definitions seems to cover the relationship between the plaintiff and the defendant in this case. The plaintiff has not succeeded to the ownership of any property of the grantor. It does not appear that it ever had title to the streets or public places upon which charges which are payable to it must be expended. It does not appear that it owns any other property in the residential tract to which any easement or right of enjoyment in such property is appurtenant. It is created solely to act as the assignee of the benefit of the covenant, and it has no interest of its own in the enforcement of the covenant.

The arguments that under such circumstances the plaintiff has no right of action to enforce a covenant running with the land are all based upon a distinction between the corporate property owners association and the property owners for whose benefit the association has been formed. If that distinction may be ignored, then the basis of the arguments is destroyed. How far privity of estate in technical form is necessary to enforce in equity a restrictive covenant upon the use of land, presents an interesting question. Enforcement of such covenants rests upon equitable principles, and at times, at least, the violation "of the restrictive covenant may be restrained at the suit of one who owns property or for whose benefit the restriction was established, irrespective of whether there were privity either of estate or of contract between the parties, or whether an action at law were maintainable." *Chesbro v. Moers*, 134 N.E. 842, 843 (N.Y. 1922). . . . We do not attempt . . . now . . . to formulate a definite rule as to when, or even whether, covenants in a deed will be enforced, upon equitable principles, against subsequent purchasers with notice, at the suit of a party without privity of contract or estate. . . . There is no need to resort to such a rule if the courts may look behind the corporate form of the plaintiff.

The corporate plaintiff has been formed as a convenient instrument by which the property owners may advance their common interests. We do not ignore the corporate form when we recognize that the Neponsit Property Owners' Association, Inc., is acting as the agent or representative of the Neponsit property owners. . . . Only blind adherence to an ancient formula devised to meet entirely different conditions could constrain the court to hold that a corporation formed as a medium for the enjoyment of common rights of property owners owns no property which would benefit by enforcement of common rights and has no cause of action in equity to enforce the covenant upon which such common rights depend. . . . In substance if not in form the covenant is a restrictive covenant which touches and concerns the defendant's land, and in substance, if not in form, there is privity of estate between the plaintiff and the defendant. . . .

Notes

1. *The basics:* Is this case about a real covenant or an equitable servitude, and how do you know? Be careful—the response is not as straightforward as it

first appears. According to the court, what requirements must be satisfied for the burden to run to defendant Emigrant Industrial Savings Bank? List the facts that support each requirement.

2. *The touch and concern requirement:* Even under the relaxed standards of equity, covenants must "touch and concern" land in order to run to successors. Yet despite the requirement's pivotal importance in both legal and equitable cases, courts rarely articulate a clear test or rationale for the requirement. What test did the court articulate here, and what is its underlying rationale? Identify at least one inconsistency in the court's position.

3. *Covenants to pay money:* Today, there is broader agreement that covenants to pay homeowners dues satisfy the touch and concern requirement. There is also agreement that leasehold covenants to pay rent satisfy the requirement. Beyond that, the decisions are still in some disarray as to whether other types of promises to pay money touch and concern land, including covenants to purchase insurance, covenants to pay real estate taxes and assessments, and landlord covenants to refund security deposits. *See* William B. Stoebuck & Dale A. Whitman, The Law of Property §§ 8.15, 8.24 (3d ed. 2000).

4. *Affirmative covenants:* It is now clearly established that both affirmative and negative covenants can run with land, both at law and in equity. *See* Stoebuck & Whitman, *supra*, at §§ 8.15, 8.24; Powell on Real Property § 60.04(3)(a) (Michael Allan Wolf, gen. ed. 2015).

5. *Seeking symmetry—the "burden won't run if the benefit is in gross" rule:* There is a split of authority as to whether a burden runs to successors if the benefit does not touch and concern the land—that is, if the benefit is "in gross." Some courts interpret such a covenant as being a mere "personal" contract incapable of binding successors. What could be the rationale for such a rule? Does it potentially apply to the facts of *Neponsit*?

C. TERMINATION AND NONENFORCEMENT OF COVENANTS

Running covenants present a puzzle. Although they are real property rights (of the nonpossessory variety), they can be deemed unenforceable, or even terminated, over the objection of some or all of their holders. Can you recall other examples of property rights that can be restricted or terminated involuntarily? This vulnerability of covenants reflects, in part, their hybrid contract-property status. Courts will refuse to enforce covenants—like contracts—that they perceive to be in violation of public policy (and on other grounds, as explained in this section). Their vulnerability also provides a good illustration of the web of interests metaphor. Because the benefits and burdens of covenants extend well beyond the original parties, courts sometimes look beyond those original parties' intentions when determining the continuing validity of covenants. Courts will refuse to enforce restrictions, or even declare covenants to be terminated, through a variety of overlapping mechanisms, including (but not limited to) those listed below. Be sure to compare the list below to the methods available to terminate easements, which we considered in the previous chapter.

A Place to Start | **Termination and Nonenforcement**

- *Expiration:* Covenants can be time-limited in accordance with the terms of the instruments that created them or by state law.

- *Release:* The beneficiaries of the covenant can execute a formal release, generally in the form of a written, recorded instrument.

- *Abandonment:* If there are substantial failures to comply with and enforce a covenant, a court might hold that the parties intend to abandon the restriction.

- *Merger:* If the burdened and benefitted parcels come into common ownership, then the covenant terminates.

- *The recording system:* A bona fide purchaser who takes the burdened property without actual or constructive notice of the covenant is generally not bound by the burden.

- *Equitable doctrines:* Relief can be awarded under such doctrines as acquiescence, unclean hands, laches, and estoppel.

- *Changed conditions (also known by names such as "change of neighborhood" and "change in circumstances"):* Courts will refuse to enforce covenants that have become outmoded due to a change of neighborhood conditions. They look to such factors as whether there have been substantial and widespread violations of the covenant, whether the restriction can no longer serve its intended purpose, and whether it has become impossible for the restriction to provide the intended benefits. Many, but not all, courts require that changed circumstances result in actual physical changes *within* the neighborhood protected by the covenant, and not merely produce some effect on the transition properties at the edge. Although some courts view the doctrine as equitable and available only to preclude injunctive relief, other courts will declare the covenant itself to be terminated.

- *Violation of law or public policy:* Courts will refuse to enforce covenants that violate law or public policy.

DIGGING DEEPER: Some have suggested that the continuing vitality of a particular covenant should depend on whether there is evidence that new owners voluntarily agreed to assume the burden (or benefit) at the time they acquired an interest in the subject property. Is that a good approach? How many new owners need to show their ongoing acceptance of the covenant? Do any of the above termination mechanisms reflect that approach?

Shelley v. Kraemer

334 U.S. 1 (1948)

Reading Guide

◆ Racially restrictive covenants played a shameful and widespread role in real estate practices throughout the first half of the 20th century (as we saw in Chapter 7). In this landmark decision, the U.S. Supreme Court declared the enforcement of such covenants unconstitutional.

◆ The Court confronted the issue of whether racially restrictive covenants fall within the "state action" doctrine, which you may have studied in Constitutional Law. As you read the case, consider where the Court drew the line between private discrimination (wrong, but not necessarily unconstitutional) and discrimination by the state (unconstitutional). Is there any characteristic of running covenants that makes their enforcement resemble state, rather than private, action?

VINSON, C.J.

These cases present for our consideration questions relating to the validity of court enforcement of private agreements, generally described as restrictive covenants, which have as their purpose the exclusion of persons of designated race or color from the ownership or occupancy of real property. Basic constitutional issues of obvious importance have been raised.

The first of these cases comes to this Court on certiorari to the Supreme Court of Missouri. On February 16, 1911, thirty out of a total of thirty-nine owners of property fronting both sides of Labadie Avenue between Taylor Avenue and Cora Avenue in the city of St. Louis, signed an agreement, which was subsequently recorded, providing in part:

> . . . the said property is hereby restricted to the use and occupancy for the term of Fifty (50) years from this date, so that it shall be a condition all the time and whether recited and referred to as [sic] not in subsequent conveyances and shall attach to the land, as a condition precedent to the sale of the same, that hereafter no part of said property or any portion thereof shall be, for said term of Fifty-years, occupied by any person not of the Caucasian race, it being intended hereby to restrict the use of said property for said period of time against the occupancy as owners or tenants of any portion of said property for resident or other purpose by people of the Negro or Mongolian Race.

The entire district described in the agreement included fifty-seven parcels of land. The thirty owners who signed the agreement held title to forty-seven parcels, including the particular parcel involved in this case. At the time the agreement was signed, five of the parcels in the district were owned by Negroes. . . .

On August 11, 1945, pursuant to a contract of sale, petitioners Shelley, who are Negroes, for valuable consideration received from one Fitzgerald a warranty deed to the parcel in question. The trial court found that petitioners had no actual knowledge of the restrictive agreement at the time of the purchase.

On October 9, 1945, respondents, as owners of other property subject to the terms of the restrictive covenant, brought suit in Circuit Court of the city of St. Louis praying that petitioners Shelley be restrained from taking possession of the property and that judgment be entered divesting title out of petitioners Shelley and revesting title in the immediate grantor or in such other person as the court should direct. The trial court denied the requested relief. . . .

The Supreme Court of Missouri sitting en banc reversed. . . .

The second of the cases under consideration comes to this Court from the Supreme Court of Michigan. The circumstances presented do not differ materially from the Missouri case. . . .

Petitioners have placed primary reliance on their contentions, first raised in the state courts, that judicial enforcement of the restrictive agreements in these cases has violated rights guaranteed to petitioners by the Fourteenth Amendment of the Federal Constitution and Acts of Congress passed pursuant to that Amendment.[1] . . .

I

Whether the equal protection clause of the Fourteenth Amendment inhibits judicial enforcement by state courts of restrictive covenants based on race or color is a question which this Court has not heretofore been called upon to consider. . . .

It is well, at the outset, to scrutinize the terms of the restrictive agreements involved in these cases. . . . Not only does the restriction seek to proscribe use and occupancy of the affected properties by members of the excluded class, but as construed by the Missouri courts, the agreement requires that title of any person who uses his property in violation of the restriction shall be divested. . . .

. . . Use of the properties for residential occupancy, as such, is not forbidden. The restrictions of these agreements, rather, are directed toward a designated class of persons and seek to determine who may and who may not own or make use of the properties for residential purposes. The excluded class is defined wholly in terms of race or color . . . .

---

1. [FN 4] The first section of the Fourteenth Amendment provides: "All persons born or naturalized in the United States, and subject to the jurisdiction thereof, are citizens of the United States and of the State wherein they reside. No State shall make or enforce any law which shall abridge the privileges or immunities of citizens of the United States; nor shall any State deprive any person of life, liberty, or property, without due process of law; nor deny to any person within its jurisdiction the equal protection of the laws."

It cannot be doubted that among the civil rights intended to be protected from discriminatory state action by the Fourteenth Amendment are the rights to acquire, enjoy, own and dispose of property. Equality in the enjoyment of property rights was regarded by the framers of that Amendment as an essential pre-condition to the realization of other basic civil rights and liberties which the Amendment was intended to guarantee. . . .

But the present cases . . . do not involve action by state legislatures or city councils. Here the particular patterns of discrimination and the areas in which the restrictions are to operate, are determined, in the first instance, by the terms of agreements among private individuals. Participation of the State consists in the enforcement of the restrictions so defined. The crucial issue with which we are here confronted is whether this distinction removes these cases from the operation of the prohibitory provisions of the Fourteenth Amendment.

Since the decision of this Court in the *Civil Rights Cases*, 109 U.S. 3 (1883), the principle has become firmly embedded in our constitutional law that the action inhibited by the first section of the Fourteenth Amendment is only such action as may fairly be said to be that of the States. That Amendment erects no shield against merely private conduct, however discriminatory or wrongful. . . .

We conclude, therefore, that the restrictive agreements standing alone cannot be regarded as a violation of any rights guaranteed to petitioners by the Fourteenth Amendment. So long as the purposes of those agreements are effectuated by voluntary adherence to their terms, it would appear clear that there has been no action by the State and the provisions of the Amendment have not been violated.

But here there was more. These are cases in which the purposes of the agreements were secured only by judicial enforcement by state courts of the restrictive terms of the agreements. . . .

II

That the action of state courts and of judicial officers in their official capacities is to be regarded as action of the State within the meaning of the Fourteenth Amendment, is a proposition which has long been established by decisions of this Court. That principle was given expression in the earliest cases involving the construction of the terms of the Fourteenth Amendment. Thus, in *Commonwealth of Virginia v. Rives*, 100 U.S. 313, 318 (1879), this Court stated:

> It is doubtless true that a State may act through different agencies,—either by its legislative, its executive, or its judicial authorities; and the prohibitions of the amendment extend to all action of the State denying equal protection of the laws, whether it be action by one of these agencies or by another.

In Ex parte Commonwealth of Virginia, 100 U.S. 339, 347 (1880), the Court observed: "A State acts by its legislative, its executive, or its judicial authorities. It can act in no other way." . . .

The short of the matter is that from the time of the adoption of the Fourteenth Amendment until the present, it has been the consistent ruling of this Court that the action of the States to which the Amendment has reference, includes action of state courts and state judicial officials. Although, in construing the terms of the Fourteenth Amendment, differences have from time to time been expressed as to whether particular types of state action may be said to offend the Amendment's prohibitory provisions, it has never been suggested that state court action is immunized from the operation of those provisions simply because the act is that of the judicial branch of the state government.

III . . .

We have no doubt that there has been state action in these cases in the full and complete sense of the phrase. The undisputed facts disclose that petitioners were willing purchasers of properties upon which they desired to establish homes. The owners of the properties were willing sellers; and contracts of sale were accordingly consummated. It is clear that but for the active intervention of the state courts, supported by the full panoply of state power, petitioners would have been free to occupy the properties in question without restraint.

These are not cases, as has been suggested, in which the States have merely abstained from action, leaving private individuals free to impose such discriminations as they see fit. Rather, these are cases in which the States have made available to such individuals the full coercive power of government to deny to petitioners, on the grounds of race or color, the enjoyment of property rights in premises which petitioners are willing and financially able to acquire and which the grantors are willing to sell. . . .

The enforcement of the restrictive agreements by the state courts in these cases was directed pursuant to the common-law policy of the States as formulated by those courts in earlier decisions. . . . The judicial action in each case bears the clear and unmistakable imprimatur of the State. We have noted that previous decisions of this Court have established the proposition that judicial action is not immunized from the operation of the Fourteenth Amendment simply because it is taken pursuant to the state's common-law policy. Nor is the Amendment ineffective simply because the particular pattern of discrimination, which the State has enforced, was defined initially by the terms of a private agreement. State action, as that phrase is understood for the purposes of the Fourteenth Amendment, refers to exertions of state power in all forms. And when the effect of that action is to deny rights subject to the protection of the Fourteenth Amendment, it is the obligation of this Court to enforce the constitutional commands.

We hold that in granting judicial enforcement of the restrictive agreements in these cases, the States have denied petitioners the equal protection of the laws and that, therefore, the action of the state courts cannot stand. . . .

Nor do we find merit in the suggestion that property owners who are parties to these agreements are denied equal protection of the laws if denied access to the courts to enforce the terms of restrictive covenants and to assert property rights which the state courts have held to be created by such agreements. The Constitution confers upon no individual the right to demand action by the State which results in the denial of equal protection of the laws to other individuals. And it would appear beyond question that the power of the State to create and enforce property interests must be exercised within the boundaries defined by the Fourteenth Amendment. . . .

The historical context in which the Fourteenth Amendment became a part of the Constitution should not be forgotten. Whatever else the framers sought to achieve, it is clear that the matter of primary concern was the establishment of equality in the enjoyment of basic civil and political rights and the preservation of those rights from discriminatory action on the part of the States based on considerations of race or color. Seventy-five years ago this Court announced that the provisions of the Amendment are to be construed with this fundamental purpose in mind. . . . Reversed.

REED, JACKSON, and RUTLEDGE, J.J. took no part in the consideration or decision of these cases.

Notes

1. *The common law:* Review the covenant at issue in *Shelley*. Did the respondents seek to enforce it as a real covenant or as an equitable servitude? The lower courts in Missouri held that it was the intention of the parties to the restrictive agreement that all property within the district was to be covered by the restrictions; but because the owners of some of the parcels did not sign the agreement, it never became final and complete and was of no force. *See Kraemer v. Shelley*, 198 S.W. 2d 679, 681 (Mo. 1946). The Missouri Supreme Court reversed, finding that the agreement intended to cover only the property of those owners who signed it, and that the failure of some neighbors to sign was not fatal. *Id.* If you represented the petitioners who sought to prevent enforcement of the covenants, what additional arguments would you have made that the covenant did not satisfy the common law requirements necessary for it to bind the Shelleys, as successors to the original covenantor?

2. *Constitutional law—the state action doctrine:* Long before *Shelley*, the Court had interpreted the prohibitions of the Fourteenth Amendment as applicable only to actions by the states or their representatives. *See The Civil Rights Cases*, 109 U.S. 3 (1883) (asserting, "[i]t is State action of a particular character that is prohibited" and "[i]ndividual invasion of individual rights is not the subject-matter of the amendment"). The rationale for the doctrine has not been consistently developed, although the Supreme Court has justified it as one that "preserves an area of individual freedom by limiting the reach of

federal law and federal judicial power." *Lugar v. Edmondson Oil Co.*, 457 U.S. 922, 936 (1982). The doctrine has been subject to considerable criticism. Professor Charles Black, for example, described it as "a conceptual disaster area" that has set scholars on "a torchless search for a way out of a damp echoing cave." Charles L. Black, Jr., *Foreword: "State Action," Equal Protection, and California's Proposition 14*, 81 Harv. L. Rev. 69, 95 (1967). After *Shelley*, the Court retreated somewhat from its position on state action. *See Lugar*, 457 U.S. at 928, 937, 939 n.21 (1982) (recognizing that "the party charged with the deprivation [of a federal right] must be a person who may fairly be said to be a state actor" and rejecting the notion "that a private party's mere invocation of state legal procedures" satisfies the state-actor requirement).

3. *Two FHAs—The Federal Housing Administration and the Fair Housing Act:* Recall from Chapter 7 that Congress created the Federal Housing Administration (FHA), an agency now within the Department of Housing and Urban Development, in 1934 to stimulate the housing industry in the wake of the Great Depression. Although the agency did much good in some areas, as by providing insurance for residential loans, it also played a role in institutionalizing discriminatory housing practices. In particular, it encouraged (and sometimes required) racially restrictive covenants in deeds conveying property subject to FHA-insured mortgages to avoid what it called the "adverse influence" on housing value caused by the mixing of "inharmonious racial groups." *See* Carol Rose, *Shelley v. Kraemer*, in Property Stories 206 (Gerald Korngold & Andrew P. Morriss, eds., 2d ed. 2009).

We have also studied another *FHA*—the federal Fair Housing Act of 1968. Review that statute, as considered in Chapters 4 and 7. If the facts of *Shelley* had taken place after the statute was in force, what arguments could the petitioners have made under the FHA? Be specific, citing to relevant statutory language and supporting facts.

4. *More to the story:* The Shelley House in St. Louis, Missouri, was built in 1906 and remains a private residence today. In 1930, the Shelley family had moved from Mississippi to St. Louis in the hope of finding better opportunities for themselves and for their six children. The Shelleys wanted to buy a house for their large family and went to their pastor, Robert Bishop, for advice. Pastor Bishop himself purchased a suitable house on Labadie Avenue, but did so through a fictional straw party—the purportedly white Mrs. Geraldine Fitzgerald. Then, the fictitious Mrs. Fitzgerald purported to convey a warranty deed to the Shelleys. Bishop took this convoluted approach for two reasons. First, it was easier for a white person (Mrs. Fitzgerald) to secure financing in the 1940s. Second, the seller had been one of the original signatories to the racial covenant. By first securing title in the fictional Mrs. Fitzgerald, Bishop hoped to break the 1911 covenant with a transaction between a willing white seller (albeit fictional) and a willing buyer. *See* Clement E. Vose, Caucasians Only: The Supreme Court, the NAACP, and Restrictive Covenant Cases 110, 112 (University of California Press, 1959).

The Shelley House, 4600 Labadie Avenue
Source: Wikimedia Commons

Shelley v. Kraemer was a unanimous decision, which was important to Chief Justice Vinson. As his clerk reported, "[h]e was apprehensive about the consequences, both to the Court and the country, of a decision invalidating the enforcement of racial covenants announced by a tribunal fragmented as to result or constitutional theory." Justices Reed, Jackson, and Rutledge did not participate. According to Justice Vinson's clerk, "[n]one stated publicly his reasons for the withdrawal, but it was generally assumed that each of the three Justices owned property burdened by a racial covenant." Francis A. Allen, *Remembering* Shelley v. Kraemer: *Of Public and Private Worlds*, 67 Wash. U. L. Rev. 709, 721 (1989). While briefs written by NAACP counsel stressed the destructive psychological effects of racially restrictive covenants, the Court decided the case on constitutional grounds. *See* John R. Howard, The Shifting Wind: The Supreme Court and Civil Rights from Reconstruction to *Brown* 291 (State University of New York Press, 1999). *See also* Kevin Boyle, Arc of Justice: A Saga of Race, Civil Rights, and Murder in the Jazz Age (2005) (narrative history of the struggle for integrated housing in Detroit, recounted through the lens of a sensational murder trial in which the defendant was represented by legendary attorney Clarence Darrow).

In *Shelley*, the challenged covenants' constitutional infirmities prevented judicial enforcement of their provisions. Beyond the question of constitutional infirmity, the next case considers common law doctrines that can result in the nonenforcement or termination of running covenants under some circumstances.

Vernon Township Volunteer Fire Dept., Inc. v. Connor

855 A.2d 873 (Pa. 2004)

Reading Guide

Today, the running of covenants has particular relevance in subdivisions. Developers, or the homeowners themselves, frequently impose uniform restrictions to promote their vision of an ideal community. But change is inevitable: circumstances evolve inside and outside of the neighborhood, and land ownership eventually passes from the original covenanting parties to their successors. Should the covenants remain in force, or should they give way to contemporary conditions? Is there a principled way to respond to these questions?

Vernon Township explores the *changed conditions* doctrine. As you read the case, consider the purpose of the doctrine and exactly whose interests it is designed to protect. Think about whether the majority or the dissent does a better job of applying the doctrine.

NEWMAN, J.

In these consolidated cases, . . . landowners within the Culbertson Subdivision [Appellants] . . . appeal from an Order of the Superior Court reversing an

Order of the Court of Common Pleas of Crawford County (trial court). The trial court had granted Judgment in favor of Appellants and against the Vernon Township Volunteer Fire Department, Inc. (Fire Department), a non-profit Pennsylvania Corporation, in an action to quiet title and for declaratory relief. For the reasons discussed herein, we reverse the Order of the Superior Court and remand the case so that the Superior Court can consider the Fire Department's remaining unaddressed issue concerning the applicability of the principles of estoppel, laches, and waiver to the instant matter.

In a document dated May 15, 1946 entitled "Restrictions" (Agreement), all of the property owners of the Culbertson Subdivision signed a restrictive covenant prohibiting the sale of alcoholic beverages on their land. The Agreement provides in relevant part that:

> ... [W]e, the undersigned owners of the legal and/or equitable title of certain lots, pieces or parcels of land situate, lying and being in Vernon Township, Crawford County, Pennsylvania ... do hereby mutually covenant and agree with each other that from and after the date hereof, *no vinous, spirituous, malt or brewed liquors, or any admixture thereof, shall be sold, or kept for sale,* on any of said lots, pieces or parcels of land, or on any part thereof, or in any building, or any part thereof, now or hereafter erected thereon. ...

> This agreement shall be binding upon our respective heirs, executors, administrators, successors, assigns, lessees, tenants and the occupiers of any of said lots, pieces or parcels of land, and is hereby specifically declared to be a covenant running with the lots, pieces or parcels of land held by the respective signers thereof, or in which we, or any of us, have an interest.

(Reproduced Record (R.R.) at 365a) (emphasis added). The intent of the original signatories, as set forth in the Agreement, is "to protect each for himself and for the common advantage of all, our health, peace, safety and welfare and that of our successors in title. ..." The Agreement was duly recorded. ...

On July 3, 1997, the Fire Department purchased a 3.25-acre parcel of land within the Culbertson Subdivision for the purpose of building a new truck room and social hall that would sell alcohol to its patrons. This newly acquired parcel is located approximately 2,000 feet from the Fire Department's existing truck room and social hall in Vernon Township. At the time of purchase, the Fire Department did not have actual notice of the restrictive covenant banning the sale of alcoholic beverages on the land. However, the Fire Department did have constructive notice of the restrictive covenant from a title search that its attorney conducted. Nevertheless, the alcohol restriction was not brought to the attention of the Fire Department until November of 1999, well after it had already commenced building the new social hall.

At the time that the Agreement was executed, the Culbertson Subdivision was bounded on the north by the Viscose Corporation, which operated a large manufacturing plant. ... Currently, the former site of the Viscose Corporation is now the Crawford County Industrial Park, which houses a variety of small commercial businesses and offices. The remainder of the restricted tract is bounded by wooded land to the northwest, the Cussewago Creek to the south and west, and the City of Meadville to the east.

Presently, there are no establishments within the Culbertson Subdivision that possess liquor licenses. The closest alcohol-serving establishment is the Fire Department's current social hall, which is located in Vernon Township, approximately one-half mile from the restricted lots. In addition, there are two bars located within two miles of the restricted tract. One bar is situated approximately one and one-half miles away in Vernon Township, and the other is approximately two miles away in the City of Meadville.

Upon learning of the restrictive covenant, the Fire Department stopped construction of the new social hall and sought to have all of the property owners within the restricted tract sign a Limited Release of Restrictions.[2] The owners of sixty-eight of the seventy-seven parcels within the Culbertson Subdivision signed the Limited Release of Restrictions and agreed to waive enforcement of the restrictive covenant as to the 3.25-acre parcel purchased by the Fire Department. The owners of three parcels neither signed the release nor sought to enforce the restrictive covenant. The remaining six parcel owners, now Appellants in this matter, refused to sign the Limited Release of Restrictions. As a result, the Fire Department brought the instant action at law seeking to quiet title to its parcel. In particular, the Fire Department sought to have the restrictive covenant prohibiting the sale of alcoholic beverages invalidated because changed conditions in the immediate neighborhood effectively rendered the restriction obsolete. . . .

. . . As a general matter, restrictive covenants on the use of land interfere with an owner's free use and enjoyment of real property and, therefore, are not favored by the law. Because land use restrictions are not favored in the law, they are to be strictly construed, and "nothing will be deemed a violation of such a restriction that is not in plain disregard of its express words. . . ." *Jones v. Park Lane for Convalescents, Inc.*, 120 A.2d 535, 537 (Pa. 1956). Although the law may disfavor restrictions on an owner's free use and enjoyment of real property, restrictive covenants are legally enforceable.

A landowner may limit his or her private use and enjoyment of real property by contract or agreement. It is a fundamental rule of contract interpretation that the intention of the parties at the time of contract governs and that such intent must be ascertained from the entire instrument. This same principle of contract law is equally applicable to the interpretation of restrictive covenants.

---

2. [FN 8] The Limited Release of Restrictions . . . provides in relevant part: "[T]he following owners of certain lots or parcels of land hereinafter mentioned in Vernon Township, Crawford County, Pennsylvania and for the mutual considerations contained hereafter and for the sum of $1.00 . . . do hereby release, abandon and extinguish any and all restrictions contained in [the Agreement] insofar as said restrictions relate to property . . . owned by the Vernon Township Fire Department. . . .

In order to ascertain the intentions of the parties, restrictive covenants must be construed in light of: (1) their language; (2) the nature of their subject matter; (3) the apparent object or purpose of the parties; and (4) the circumstances or conditions surrounding their execution. Typically, we will enforce a restriction if a party's actions are in clear defiance of the provisions imposed by the covenant. Moreover, we will enforce a restrictive covenant where it is established that the restriction is still of substantial value to the owners of the restricted tract.

As an initial matter, we note that a property owner has the duty to become aware of recorded restrictions in the chain of title and will be bound to such restrictions even absent actual notice. . . . The covenant was duly recorded in Crawford County Agreement Book 26, page 9, on June 10, 1946, and easily accessible via title search. The Fire Department clearly had constructive notice of the restrictive covenant; therefore, it cannot now avoid the consequences of such restriction because of its own lack of due diligence. This being the case, the restriction is enforceable unless the Fire Department can establish that the restrictive covenant has been discharged.

In order to discharge the covenant, the burden of proof is on the Fire Department to show that the original purpose of the restriction has been materially altered or destroyed by changed conditions, and that a substantial benefit no longer extends to Appellants by enforcement of the restriction. As a general rule, a restrictive covenant may be discharged if there has been acquiescence in its breach by others, or an abandonment of the restriction. In addition, changes in the character of a neighborhood may result in the discharge of a restrictive covenant. Where changed or altered conditions in a neighborhood render the strict adherence to the terms of a restrictive covenant useless to the dominant lots, we will refrain from enforcing such restrictions. This is based on the general rule that "land shall not be burdened with permanent or long-continued restrictions which have ceased to be of any advantage. . . ." *Daniels v. Notor*, 133 A.2d 520 (Pa. 1957). In considering changed conditions in a neighborhood, the word "neighborhood" is a relative term, and only the immediate, and not the remote, neighborhood should be measured. . . .

. . . [I]n reaching its decision, the trial court specifically evaluated the significance of other liquor-serving establishments located outside of the restricted tract. . . . Specifically, the trial court noted:

> Plaintiff presented evidence that two bars were now located within the neighborhood. One is to the East on Lincoln Avenue, at least a mile away, in the city of Meadville, and the other is the current Fire Department social hall, about a half a mile away, across the Creek and up a wooded hill. Neither is in the immediate neighborhood of the restricted lots. Accordingly, there is no change in the neighborhood making the restriction obsolete.

. . . [T]he relevant inquiry concerning changes to the immediate neighborhood is whether such changes alter or eliminate the benefit that the restriction was intended to achieve. In determining whether changed circumstances rendered enforcement of the present alcohol restriction useless, we find guidance in *Benner v. Tacony Athletic Association,* 196 A. 390 (Pa. 1938). The Court noted that "the fact that commercial establishments have crept in here and there does not impair the utility of the restriction against the sale of beer or liquor; that restriction, to the residents of the neighborhood, has a desirability and an object unaffected by the encroachments of business." In upholding the enforceability of the restrictive covenant, the Court stated that "[i]t is only when violations are permitted to such an extent as to indicate that the entire restrictive plan has been abandoned that objection to further violations is barred." *Id.* at 393.

Contrary to the argument of the Fire Department and the holding of the Superior Court, the existence of three other liquor-serving establishments located outside of the Culbertson Subdivision does not warrant a finding of changed circumstances to invalidate the restrictive covenant. Similar to *Benner,* the changes in the immediate neighborhood did not affect the benefit conferred upon Appellants by the alcohol restriction. These changes, which involved the introduction of establishments serving alcohol in the immediate neighborhood, but outside of the restricted tract, did not impair the utility of the covenant to the residents of the Culbertson Subdivision. . . . As *Benner* recognized, changed conditions outside of the restricted tract do not necessarily impair the value of an alcohol restriction to the residents of the restricted tract. The stated purpose of the restrictive covenant was to protect the "health, peace, safety and welfare" of the occupants of the land by preventing the sale of alcoholic beverages within the tract. The original signatories clearly intended to protect themselves and their heirs from the vices of alcohol consumption by restricting the sale of alcohol within the Culbertson Subdivision. As the trial court noted, "[i]f people are not drinking at establishments in the neighborhood, they are not exhibiting objectionable behavior which accompanies over-drinking, like public drunkenness and driving under the influence." Thus, Appellants will continue to benefit from the restriction as long as alcohol is not sold within the restricted tract.

In determining that the restrictive covenant no longer had substantial value to Appellants, the Superior Court found it significant that a majority of the property owners within the restricted tract agreed to release the alcohol restriction. Moreover, the Superior Court noted that Appellants testified that they did not rely upon the restrictive covenant when purchasing their property. However, the restriction clearly benefits Appellants by hindering the nuisances that inherently result from the sale and consumption of alcoholic beverages. Furthermore, the factual record reflects that alcoholic beverages have never been sold within the restricted tract since the covenant was signed in 1946. . . .

Because the alleged changed conditions in the immediate neighborhood did not affect the benefits conferred by the restrictive covenant, the Superior Court erred by refusing to enforce the alcohol restriction. . . .

CASTILLE, J., dissenting.

... When determining whether conditions have changed to such an extent as to invalidate the restriction, courts must look to the immediate neighborhood, which includes adjoining tracts of land.

The Majority, like the trial court, focuses on the fact that there are presently no establishments with liquor licenses within the specific confines of the Culbertson Subdivision and dismisses the presence in the immediately adjoining neighborhood of two bars and the Fire Department's existing social hall, which is located a mere 2,000 feet from the parcel on which the Fire Department seeks to build its new truck room and social hall. ... In one breath, the Majority states that it must consider not only the restricted tract but also the surrounding neighborhood and notes that three other alcohol-serving establishments exist in the immediate neighborhood. Then, in the next breath, the Majority essentially determines that the presence of those other establishments is irrelevant to its inquiry because the only relevant area is the Culbertson Subdivision itself. ...

... That 71 of the 77 purportedly affected owners find no value to the covenant and the other six did not rely upon the covenant in purchasing their properties is a clear signal that the covenant lacks significant value to the subdivision owners at this time. Anachronisms need not persist for their own sake. Accordingly, I would affirm the Superior Court's decision discharging the restrictive covenant in this case.

SAYLOR, J., dissenting [omitted].

Notes

1. *Neighborhood as a relative term—inside vs. outside the neighborhood:* What is the relevant neighborhood to be evaluated under the changed circumstances doctrine according to the majority and the dissent, respectively? Does the majority's view rigidly freeze a neighborhood in time, and preserve an "anachronism" for its own sake, as the dissent alleges? On the other hand, does the dissent's approach encourage the "domino effect" by allowing outside forces to slowly chip away at the Culbertson subdivision until they have penetrated its core?

Although courts vary considerably in their application of the changed conditions doctrine, the majority's approach in *Vernon Township* is representative of that taken by many courts. As one treatise explains,

> It might well be assumed that one purpose of the [covenant restrictions] was to guard against the encroachment of external changes; certainly [covenant restrictions] were not intended to operate in the *unrestricted area* and consequently should not be affected by any changes occurring therein. It has been held that where there are changes *outside of* but adjacent to a particular tract subject to

uniform restrictions, the covenant will be enforced in equity unless the change is so substantial that the usefulness of the covenant has been destroyed.

3 Tiffany Real Prop. § 875 (3d ed.) (updated Sept. 2015) (emphasis added).

2. *The "holdout" issue and remedy:*   Notice that the owners of 68 of the 77 lots within the subdivision agreed to waive enforcement of the alcohol restriction for one dollar, and 3 other owners appeared ambivalent as to its enforcement. If you represented the Fire Department, how would you have advised it to deal with the 6 so-called *holdout* owners who refused to budge? Should it have offered to pay them more than one dollar for their release of the covenant, and if so, how much more? Why would any holdout owner be willing to be the first one to agree to take the offer? If one holdout agreed to this arrangement, what effect do you think it would have on the remaining 5 holdouts? After the court issued its opinion, would the holdouts have even more leverage to command a higher price?

3. *Practice pointer—searching title:*   Recall our study of the recording system from Chapter 8. How could the Fire Department's attorney have failed to discover the restrictive covenant during the title search? What would a prudent title search involve when the relevant parcel is located within a subdivision? Conversely, what could the original covenanting parties have done to ensure that future title searchers would easily find the covenant?

4. *More to the story:*   The Vernon Fire Department's website indicates that it continues to have a vibrant social hall in adjoining Meadville that sponsors such events as Sunday breakfast buffets, evening entertainment, and raffles. A photograph of the hall shows a half-dozen or so beer taps protruding above its bar counter. Does the availability of a nearby alcohol-serving venue support or detract from the application of the changed circumstances doctrine? *See* http://vernontownshipvfd.com/station27/ (visited July 9, 2015).

D. MODERN APPLICATIONS: COMMON INTEREST COMMUNITIES AND CONSERVATION EASEMENTS

1. Common Interest Communities

One important modern application of covenants is the common interest community. So-called CICs are a type of housing development in which all owners share common land and facilities—such as swimming pools, clubhouses, landscaped areas, roads, and parking structures—but privately own their individual home or unit. Variations include both suburban-style subdivisions and highly dense, often high-rise urban condominiums. A homeowners association (HOA), through its elected representatives, usually governs the community, as you saw in *Neponsit v. Emigrant Sav. Bank.*

Through a recorded "declaration" or "master deed," the developer creates the homeowners association and the initial set of rules—generally known as covenants, conditions, and restrictions (CC&Rs). Later, the homeowners (directly, or through their elected representatives on the HOA board of directors) can amend the declaration and its CC&Rs by a super-majority vote, or can enact additional rules by majority vote. Homeowners associations have considerable authority: they can levy assessments (such as monthly dues to maintain the common elements of the community) and can regulate such things as pet ownership, parking, exterior building colors, and roofing materials. Some have likened them to mini-governments. The original and amended declarations generally take the form of equitable servitudes that run with the land to bind future homeowners in the community. Today in the United States, about 66.7 million people (about 21% of the population) live in more than 333,000 common interest communities. *See* Community Associations Institute, *National and State Statistical Review for 2014*, http://www.cairf.org/research/factbook/ (follow link to 2014 statistical review) (visited July 12, 2015). In many states, common interest communities are heavily regulated by statutory enactments.

Common interest communities are a type of *commons*, which we first encountered in Chapter 6. There, we observed that certain forms of shared ownership—including marital property, concurrent estates, and condominiums—are vulnerable to overexploitation (termed the *tragedy of the commons* by ecologist Garrett Hardin). But CICs incorporate elements of both solutions to the tragedy suggested by Hardin: private ownership and regulation. At least in theory, then, CICs are an example of what Professor Michael Heller calls the *liberal commons*—in which owners are free to exit the shared arrangement, and are also free to cooperate. As such, common interest communities should provide valuable opportunities for community interaction (termed the *comedy of the commons* by Professor Carol Rose). *See* Chapter 6.C (containing excerpts by Hardin, Heller, and Rose).

Many proponents of common interest communities would agree with this assessment. They observe that shared ownership makes available a wide range of privately financed amenities, and often results in lower housing costs. Other benefits include the efficiency of collective management and maintenance, and a sense of community. Critics disagree. They argue that many HOAs abuse their authority by enacting overly intrusive regulations, and that over-regulation can lead to bland homogeneity. Further, overzealous rule enforcement can subject noncompliant homeowners to serious fines and litigation. As Professor Paula Franzese explained,

> [A] significant lure of common interest communities is found in the desire to live in a "nice environment." Residents equate "niceness" with cleanliness, orderliness, image, the preservation of property values, a sense of community, and "hassle-free living." These latter desires—to feel that one belongs and to live in peace—have yielded, in numerous instances, to the litigious realities that

excessive regulation and aggressive enforcement mechanisms can inspire. . . . [Such measures] can stymie the formation of authentic community, transforming the relevant inquiry of resident relations from "how is my neighbor doing" to the far less desirable "*what* is my neighbor doing?"

Paula Franzese, *Privatization and Its Discontents: Common Interest Communities and the Rise of Government for "The Nice,"* 37 Urban Lawyer 335, 337 (2005).

The case below offers a glimpse into the difficulties of private governance—including the question of whether courts should uphold challenged rules and restrictions. Beyond that brief consideration, we will leave further study of common interest communities to upper level courses on real estate law, community association law, and the like.

Nahrstedt v. Lakeside Village Condominium Association

878 P.2d 1275 (Cal. 1994)

Reading Guide

◆ *The reasonableness of CIC rules:* When challenges to CC&Rs and association rules reach the courts, judges generally defer to those restrictions under some type of "reasonableness" test. That is, most courts will uphold such restrictions *if* they are reasonable, or *unless* they are unreasonable. But, the reasonableness test is not as straightforward as one might imagine. This case explores the nuances of that test.

◆ *Skills practice—policy-based argument:* This case forms the basis of the skills exercise in section F, which focuses on policy-based arguments. As you read this case, take note of the policies that each party claims its position will advance, and the sources of authority that supposedly uphold those claims.

KENNARD, J. . . .

Lakeside Village is a large condominium development in Culver City, Los Angeles County. It consists of 530 units spread throughout 12 separate 3-story buildings. The residents share common lobbies and hallways, in addition to laundry and trash facilities.

The Lakeside Village project is subject to certain covenants, conditions and restrictions (hereafter CC & R's) that were included in the developer's declaration[3] recorded with the Los Angeles County Recorder . . . at the inception of the

---

3. [As the court explained in an omitted footnote, "The declaration is the operative document for a common interest development, setting forth, among other things, the restrictions on the use or enjoyment of any portion of the development. In some states, the declaration is also referred to as the 'master deed.' "—Eds.]

development project. Ownership of a unit includes membership in the project's homeowners association, the Lakeside Village Condominium Association (hereafter Association), the body that enforces the project's CC & R's, including the pet restriction, which provides in relevant part: "No animals (which shall mean dogs and cats), livestock, reptiles or poultry shall be kept in any unit."[4]

In January 1988, plaintiff Natore Nahrstedt purchased a Lakeside Village condominium and moved in with her three cats. When the Association learned of the cats' presence, it demanded their removal and assessed fines against Nahrstedt for each successive month that she remained in violation of the condominium project's pet restriction.

Nahrstedt then brought this lawsuit against the Association, its officers, and two of its employees, asking the trial court to invalidate the assessments, to enjoin future assessments, . . . and to declare the pet restriction "unreasonable" as applied to indoor cats (such as hers) that are not allowed free run of the project's common areas. . . .

. . . In its supporting points and authorities, the Association argued that the pet restriction furthers the collective "health, happiness and peace of mind" of persons living in close proximity within the Lakeside Village condominium development, and therefore is reasonable as a matter of law. The trial court . . . dismissed Nahrstedt's complaint. . . .

A divided Court of Appeal reversed the trial court's judgment of dismissal. In the majority's view, the complaint stated a claim for declaratory relief based on its allegations that Nahrstedt's three cats are kept inside her condominium unit and do not bother her neighbors. According to the majority, whether a condominium use restriction is "unreasonable," as that term is used in [California Civil Code] section 1354, hinges on the facts of a particular homeowner's case. Thus, the majority reasoned, Nahrstedt would be entitled to declaratory relief if application of the pet restriction in her case would not be reasonable. . . .

II . . .

Use restrictions are an inherent part of any common interest development and are crucial to the stable, planned environment of any shared ownership arrangement. (Note, *Community Association Use Restrictions: Applying the Business Judgment Doctrine* (1988) 64 Chi. Kent L. Rev. 653, 673 [hereafter Note, *Business Judgment*]. . . . The viability of shared ownership of improved real property rests on the existence of extensive reciprocal servitudes, together with the ability of each co-owner to prevent the property's partition. (. . . Note, *Business Judgment, supra,* [suggesting that medieval building societies, an early

---

4. [FN 3] The CC & R's permit residents to keep "domestic fish and birds."

form of shared real property ownership, had failed for lack of enforceable regulations].) . . .

Thus, subordination of individual property rights to the collective judgment of the owners association together with restrictions on the use of real property comprise the chief attributes of owning property in a common interest development. As the Florida District Court of Appeal observed in *Hidden Harbour Estates, Inc. v. Norman* (Fla. Dist. Ct. App.1975) 309 So. 2d 180, a decision frequently cited in condominium cases:

> [I]nherent in the condominium concept is the principle that to promote the health, happiness, and peace of mind of the majority of the unit owners since they are living in such close proximity and using facilities in common, each unit owner must give up a certain degree of freedom of choice which he [or she] might otherwise enjoy in separate, privately owned property. Condominium unit owners comprise a little democratic sub-society of necessity more restrictive as it pertains to use of condominium property than may be existent outside the condominium organization.

(*Id.* at pp. 181-182). . . .

In states lacking . . . legislative guidance, some courts have adopted a standard under which a common interest development's recorded use restrictions will be enforced so long as they are "reasonable." . . . Others would limit the "reasonableness" standard only to those restrictions adopted by majority vote of the homeowners or enacted under the rulemaking power of an association's governing board, and would not apply this test to restrictions included in a planned development project's recorded declaration or master deed. Because such restrictions are presumptively valid, these authorities would enforce them regardless of reasonableness. . . .

III . . .

. . . [W]hen enforcing equitable servitudes, courts are generally disinclined to question the wisdom of agreed-to restrictions. This rule does not apply, however, when the restriction does not comport with public policy. . . . (*See Shelley v. Kraemer* (1948) 334 U.S. 1 [racial restriction unenforceable]). . . .

. . . Application of the test requires the accommodation of two policies that sometimes conflict: "One of these is that [persons] should be required to live up to their promises; the other that land should be developed to its normal capacity." (*Ibid.*) . . .

[W]e now turn to [California Civil Code] section 1354. . . . [U]nder subdivision (a) of section 1354 the use restrictions for a common interest development that are set forth in the recorded declaration are "enforceable equitable servitudes, unless unreasonable." In other words, such restrictions should be enforced unless they are wholly arbitrary, violate a fundamental public policy, or impose a burden on the use of affected land that far outweighs any benefit.

This interpretation of section 1354 is consistent with the views of legal commentators as well as judicial decisions in other jurisdictions that have applied a presumption of validity to the recorded land use restrictions of a common interest development. . . . In general, . . . enforcement of a common interest development's recorded CC & R's will both encourage the development of land and ensure that promises are kept, thereby fulfilling both of the policies identified by the Restatement. . . .

When courts accord a presumption of validity to all such recorded use restrictions and measure them against deferential standards of equitable servitude law, it discourages lawsuits by owners of individual units seeking personal exemptions from the restrictions. This also promotes stability and predictability in two ways. It provides substantial assurance to prospective condominium purchasers that they may rely with confidence on the promises embodied in the project's recorded CC & R's. And it protects all owners in the planned development from unanticipated increases in association fees to fund the defense of legal challenges to recorded restrictions. . . .

There is an additional beneficiary of legal rules that are protective of recorded use restrictions: the judicial system. Fewer lawsuits challenging such restrictions will be brought, and those that are filed may be disposed of more expeditiously, if the rules courts use in evaluating such restrictions are clear, simple, and not subject to exceptions based on the peculiar circumstances or hardships of individual residents in condominiums and other shared-ownership developments.

. . . Our social fabric is founded on the stability of expectation and obligation that arises from the consistent enforcement of the terms of deeds, contracts, wills, statutes, and other writings. To allow one person to escape obligations under a written instrument upsets the expectations of all the other parties governed by that instrument (here, the owners of the other 529 units) that the instrument will be uniformly and predictably enforced.

The salutary effect of enforcing written instruments and the statutes that apply to them is particularly true in the case of the declaration of a common interest development. As we have discussed, common interest developments are a more intensive and efficient form of land use that greatly benefits society and expands opportunities for home ownership. In turn, however, a common interest development creates a community of property owners living in close proximity to each other, typically much closer than if each owned his or her separate plot of land. This proximity is feasible, and units in a common interest development are marketable, largely because the recorded declaration of CC & R's assures owners of a stable and predictable environment.

Refusing to enforce the CC & R's contained in a recorded declaration, or enforcing them only after protracted litigation that would require justification of their application on a case-by-case basis, would impose great strain on the social fabric of the common interest development. It would frustrate owners who had purchased their units in reliance on the CC & R's. It would put the owners and the homeowners association in the difficult and divisive position of deciding whether particular CC & R's should be applied to a particular owner. Here, for example, deciding whether a particular animal is "confined to an owner's unit and create[s] no noise, odor, or nuisance" is a fact-intensive determination that can only be made by examining in detail the behavior of the particular animal and the behavior of the particular owner. Homeowners associations are ill-equipped to make such investigations, and any decision they might make in a particular case could be divisive or subject to claims of partiality. . . .

V

Under the holding we adopt today, the reasonableness or unreasonableness of a condominium use restriction that the Legislature has made subject to section 1354 is to be determined *not* by reference to facts that are specific to the objecting homeowner, but by reference to the common interest development as a whole. As we have explained, when, as here, a restriction is contained in the declaration of the common interest development and is recorded with the county recorder, the restriction is presumed to be reasonable and will be enforced uniformly against all residents of the common interest development *unless* the restriction is arbitrary, imposes burdens on the use of lands it affects that substantially outweigh the restriction's benefits to the development's residents, or violates a fundamental public policy. . . .

Nahrstedt's complaint alleges no facts that could possibly support a finding that the burden of the restriction on the affected property is so disproportionate to its benefit that the restriction is unreasonable and should not be enforced. . . .

. . . [W]e discern no fundamental public policy that would favor the keeping of pets in a condominium project. There is no federal or state constitutional provision or any California statute that confers a general right to keep household pets in condominiums or other common interest developments. . . . Nor does case law offer any support for the position that the recognized scope of autonomy privacy encompasses the right to keep pets: courts that have considered condominium pet restrictions have uniformly upheld them. . . .

We reverse the judgment of the Court of Appeal, and remand for further proceedings consistent with the views expressed in this opinion.

ARABIAN, J., dissenting. . . .

. . . Beyond dispute, human beings have long enjoyed an abiding and cherished association with their household animals. Given the substantial benefits derived from pet ownership, the undue burden on the use of property imposed on condominium owners who can maintain pets within the confines of their units without creating a nuisance or disturbing the quiet enjoyment of others substantially outweighs whatever meager utility the restriction may serve in the abstract. It certainly does not promote "health, happiness [or] peace of mind" commensurate with its tariff on the quality of life for those who value the companionship of animals. Worse, it contributes to the fraying of our social fabric. . . .

Both recorded and unrecorded history bear witness to the domestication of animals as household pets.[5] Throughout the ages, dogs and cats have provided human beings with a variety of services in addition to their companionship—shepherding flocks, guarding life and property, hunting game, ridding the house and barn of vermin. . . . Emotionally, they allow a connection full of sensation and delicacy of feeling.

Throughout the ages, art and literature, as well as mythology, depict humans in all walks of life and social strata with cats and dogs, illustrating their widespread acceptance in everyday life.[6] . . . Closer to home, our own culture is populated with examples of the well-established place pets have found in our hearts and homes.[7] . . .

What is gained from an uncompromising prohibition against pets that are confined to an owner's unit and create no noise, odor, or nuisance?

To the extent such animals are not seen, heard, or smelled any more than if they were not kept in the first place, there is no corresponding or concomitant benefit. . . .

The proffered justification is all the more spurious when measured against the terms of the pet restriction itself, which contains an exception for domestic fish and birds. A squawking bird can readily create the very kind of disturbance supposedly prevented by banning other types of pets. At the same time, many animals prohibited by the restriction, such as hamsters and the like, turtles, and small reptiles, make no sound whatsoever. Disposal of bird droppings in common trash areas poses as much of a health concern as cat litter or rabbit pellets, which likewise can be handled in a manner that avoids potential problems. . . .

In determining the "burden on the use of land," due recognition must be given to the fact that this particular "use" transcends the impersonal and mundane matters typically regulated by condominium CC & R's, such as whether someone can place a doormat in the hallway . . . , and reaches the very quality of life of hundreds of owners and residents. Nonetheless, the

---

5. [FN 5] Archeologists in Israel found some of the earliest evidence of a domesticated animal when they unearthed the 12,000-year-old skeleton of a woman who was buried with her hand resting on the body of her dog. (Clutton-Brock, Dog (1991) p. 35.) . . . Cats were known to be household pets in Egypt 5,000 years ago and often mummified and entombed with their owners. (Clutton-Brock, Cat (1991) p. 46.) . . .

6. [FN 7] For example, poetry runs the gamut from the doggerel of Ogden Nash to T.S. Eliot's "Old Possum's Book of Practical Cats."

7. [FN 10] The President and his family often set a national example in this regard. Chelsea Clinton's cat "Socks" is only the latest in a long line of White House pets, including Franklin Roosevelt's "Fala" and the Bushes' "Millie."

majority . . . essentially consider only one criterion to determine enforceability: was the restriction recorded in the original declaration? If so, it is "presumptively valid," unless in violation of public policy. Given the application of the law to the facts alleged and by an inversion of relative interests, it is difficult to hypothesize any CC & R's that would not pass muster. Such sanctity has not been afforded any writing save the commandments delivered to Moses on Mount Sinai, and they were set in stone, not upon worthless paper. . . .

Owning a home of one's own has always epitomized the American dream. More than simply embodying the notion of having "one's castle," it represents the sense of freedom and self-determination emblematic of our national character. Granted, those who live in multi-unit developments cannot exercise this freedom to the same extent possible on a large estate. But owning pets that do not disturb the quiet enjoyment of others does not reasonably come within this compromise. Nevertheless, with no demonstrated or discernible benefit, the majority arbitrarily sacrifice the dream to the tyranny of the "commonality." . . .

Notes

1. *The reasonableness test—judicial interpretation of statutory law:* How did the court interpret California Civil Code § 1354? What test did it use to determine whether a restriction is "unreasonable"? How did the court allocate the burden of proof? What opposing interpretation does the dissent favor? Which interpretation better implements the plain meaning of the statutory text and/or the likely intent of the legislators? Would the court afford the same degree of deference to declarations recorded by the developer, rules adopted by a majority of the homeowners, and rules adopted by the board of directors of the homeowners association? Should it?

2. *Facial challenges vs. as-applied challenges:* Under principles of administrative law, citizens can challenge rules promulgated by governmental agencies. Here, we saw residents challenging the enforcement of a pet restriction by the condominium association, which performs many quasi-governmental functions. Although the categories are not always mutually exclusive, a *facial challenge* is typically one that alleges that the challenged rule or statute is invalid under all possible circumstances, and seeks the remedy of invalidating the rule itself, once and for all. In contrast, an *as-applied* challenge alleges that the offending rule is invalid as applied to the facts of the plaintiff's case. If successful, this type of challenge will result in an injunction prohibiting enforcement of the rule against the plaintiff, but leaves the rule intact to be applied in other circumstances. Overall, plaintiffs find it more difficult to successfully bring a facial challenge, but the remedy is broader. In *Nahrstedt*, did the plaintiff bring a facial or an as-applied challenge? As a matter of strategy, why do you think the

plaintiff chose one type of challenge over the other? Conversely, how did the defendant association urge the court to frame the nature of the challenge? Which approach did the court take, and why? Did it affect the outcome of the case?

3. *More to the story—statutory amendment:*   In 2000, six years after the court decided *Nahrstedt*, the California legislature added a new § 1360.5 to the Civil Code that provides:

> (a) No governing documents shall prohibit the owner of a separate interest within a common interest development from keeping at least one pet within the common interest development, subject to reasonable rules and regulations of the association. . . .

> (b) For purposes of this section, "pet" means any domesticated bird, cat, dog, aquatic animal kept within an aquarium, or other animal as agreed to between the association and the homeowner.

> (c) If the association implements a rule or regulation restricting the number of pets an owner may keep, the new rule or regulation shall not apply to prohibit an owner from continuing to keep any pet that the owner currently keeps in his or her separate interest if the pet otherwise conforms with the previous rules or regulations relating to pets.

> (d) For the purposes of this section, "governing documents" shall include, but are not limited to, the conditions, covenants, and restrictions of the common interest development, and the bylaws, rules, and regulations of the association.

> (e) This section shall become operative on January 1, 2001, and shall only apply to governing documents entered into, amended, or otherwise modified on or after that date.

If § 1360.5 had been in effect at the time the facts of *Nahrstedt* occurred, how would that have affected the outcome of the case, if at all? If you represented the defendant association, what arguments would you make that the pet restriction was valid, despite the applicability of § 1360.5? *See Villa de las Palmas Homeowners Ass'n v. Terifaj*, 90 P.3d 1223, 1234-34 (Cal. 2004).

2. Conservation Easements Revisited

The last chapter introduced you to "conservation easements," which are recognized in every state by statute. In our discussion, we raised the question of whether conservation easements are true *easements*, or whether they represent some other type of legal arrangement. Now that you have gained some familiarity with running covenants, let us return to that question as an opportunity to synthesize the materials on easements and covenants—together, known as *servitudes*. Briefly review Chapter 9 (sections D and E) to refresh your understanding of conservation easements, and then answer the following questions.

Discussion Questions

1. *Easement, servitude, or something else?* As you saw in the previous chapter, many state statutes and the Uniform Conservation Easement Act refer to such conservation arrangements as "easements." Alternatively, the U.S. Internal Revenue Code § 170(h) (which provides income tax deductions to donors of conservation easements), refers to them as "perpetual conservation restrictions." In yet a third variation, Restatement (Third) of Property, Servitudes refers to them as "servitudes." *See id.* at §§ 1.6, 4.3(4), and 7.11. Which label is a better fit?

2. *Practical consequences:* From a practical perspective, does it matter whether conservation agreements are classified as easements, covenants, or something else? Among other things, consider potential differences of creation and termination.

E. BEYOND THE BLACK LETTER: FOREVER IS A LONG TIME

Throughout this book, we have periodically considered how property law involves a tension between current and future owners. Many believe that the current owner should have relatively unfettered freedom to control the use of property, its ownership, and even the behavior of its owners far into the future. Through the use of the defeasible fee (Chapter 3), for example, the current owner could convey a parcel of land, "to *X*, but if *X* divorces, then to *Y*." Likewise, many favor "testamentary freedom" under which a testator can devise property to a series of specified owners upon the testator's death. Others disagree, and chafe against lingering restrictions attached by former owners. The common law's disfavor of restraints on alienation and the Rule Against Perpetuities, for example, are designed to strike down (or at least restrict) such limitations.

As we have seen, the law of easements and covenants embodies a similar tension. Should a promise between two landowners today control the behavior subsequent owners of the property, and if so, for how long? For example, should an agreement among neighbors require future neighborhood residents to refrain from pet ownership or to pay homeowners dues? If future homeowners buy into the neighborhood with knowledge of such obligations, does that mean that they voluntarily embrace those obligations? And why would rational landowners agree, in the first place, to restrict their property rights indefinitely, or perhaps even in perpetuity? The following discussion questions challenge you to formulate a consistent, principled stance on these issues.

Discussion Questions

1. *The present vs. the future:* In general, do you favor expansive rights for the current owners of property, or do you think that current owners should

have only a limited ability to bind future owners? Is your answer the same in the context of estates and future interests, easements, running covenants, conservation easements, and common interest community restrictions? If not, can you articulate a principled distinction to justify your response?

2. *The role of the courts:*   Should the courts be willing to terminate (or enjoin enforcement of) easements and covenants, or should they be reluctant to do so? Who should bear the burden of proof—the party favoring termination, or the party opposing it? When circumstances make it impossible, impracticable, or illegal to implement the original terms of an easement or covenant, should courts exercise a power analogous to *cy pres* to remake the agreement to carry out the intention of the drafters as near as possible, rather than terminate the servitude altogether (recall our discussion of *cy pres* from Chapter 3)?

F. SKILLS PRACTICE: POLICY-BASED ARGUMENTS

In *Nahrstedt v. Lakeside Village Condominium Association,* both the majority and the dissent were heavily influenced by policy-based arguments, which we first introduced in the skills exercise in Chapter 2. Review the case, as well as the following template for policy-based arguments, and then perform the tasks set forth below.

A Place to Start: **Policy-Based Arguments**

A strong policy argument generally takes the form, "If the court adopts position *X,* the result will promote policy *Y because.* . . ."

■ *Articulate your position:* Clearly set forth the rule or outcome that you would like the court to adopt on behalf of your client.

■ *Predict positive outcomes:* What are the broader ramifications of your position, beyond the facts of your case? What types of benefits will it promote? Benefits fall into a number of categories, including the following:

  ▪ *Support for the judicial system:* Does your position support or improve the efficiency and fairness of the courts? For example, by rejecting your opponent's claim, a court might avoid the "slippery slope" of an overwhelming number of similar claims for relief.

  ▪ *Respect for separation of powers:* Does your position show deference to the most capable and appropriate branch of government as decision-maker under the facts of the case? For example, one party might argue that the courts are better suited to resolving the issue at hand, whereas the other party might argue that the issue should be decided by the legislature.

- ■ *Promotion of economic efficiency:* Does your position promote economic efficiency?

- ■ *Promotion of the public interest:* Does your position advance desirable social goals, values, or policies?

■ *Provide authority supporting your prediction:* Be sure to provide authority for your prediction that if the court adopts position *X*, then desirable consequence *Y* will follow. Sources of authority include publications, theories, and data from fields such as the following:

- ■ Law

- ■ Psychology and sociology

- ■ History

- ■ Medicine

- ■ Economics

Tasks

1. *Articulate your client's position:* Decide whether you will represent plaintiff Natore Nahrstedt or defendant Lakeside Village Condominium Association. Carefully articulate your client's position as to whether the no-pet restriction is "unreasonable" under the California Civil Code.

2. *Identify policies:* What policies support your client's position? For each policy, identify whether it is rooted in concern for the justice system, respect for institutional competence, economic policy, public policy positions, or something else.

3. *Cite to authority:* Based on a careful reading of the case, upon what authority did your client rely to demonstrate that its preferred outcome would promote important policies? Did it rely on psychology, sociology, history, medicine, economics, or something else?

4. *Can you do better?* For each policy argument suggested by the case excerpt, can you formulate a stronger version? Challenge yourself to redraft each argument several times until you have a concise, clear statement. Did the party (or the court) supply convincing supporting authority? If not, what types of sources should the attorneys have investigated in the search for appropriate authority?

G. CHAPTER REVIEW

1. Practice Questions[8]

1. *Good fences make good neighbors:*   Abu promised his neighbor Martha, on behalf of himself, "his heirs, and assigns," that he would keep his fence in good repair. What type of legal interest have the parties created, if any?
   A. Abu's promise creates an easement appurtenant.
   B. Abu's promise creates a negative easement.
   C. Abu's promise creates an affirmative covenant.
   D. Abu's promise creates an easement by estoppel.

2. *The deteriorating fence:*   Abu made a promise to his neighbor Martha, on behalf of himself, "his heirs, and assigns," that he would keep his fence in good repair. Subsequently, Martha sold her property to Mia, and Abu allowed his fence to deteriorate. Can Mia sue Abu for money damages caused by his failure to maintain the fence?
   A. Yes, if Abu's original promise was enforceable.
   B. Yes, because Martha's easement was transferred to Mia.
   C. No, because there was no horizontal privity between Abu and Martha.
   D. No, because there was no vertical privity between Martha and Mia.

3. *Fix that fence!*   Abu made a promise to his neighbor Martha, on behalf of himself, "his heirs, and assigns," that he would keep his fence in good repair. Subsequently, Martha sold her property to Mia, and Abu allowed his fence to deteriorate. Can Mia sue Abu for injunctive relief to require him to maintain the fence?
   A. Yes, if Abu's original promise was enforceable.
   B. Yes, because Martha's easement was transferred to Mia.
   C. No, because there was no horizontal privity between Abu and Martha.
   D. No, because there was no vertical privity between Martha and Mia.

4. *No fences make good neighbors?*   Zelda promised her neighbor Lucas that she would never erect a fence between their two properties. Which statement is most accurate?
   A. Zelda's promise has created a negative covenant.
   B. Zelda's promise has created an easement appurtenant.
   C. Zelda's promise has created a negative easement.
   D. Zelda's promise has created an affirmative covenant.

5. *The buried wetland:*   Sophia owns two adjacent tracts of land. Tract #1 is mainly covered with wetlands. Sophia sold Tract #2 to Mason, in a deed that promised on behalf of Sophia, "her heirs, and assigns," that she would never

---

8. Answers appear in the casebook Appendix.

develop Tract #1 in a way that would destroy the natural wetlands. Subsequently, Sophia leased her property for 99 years to Sara, who promptly began to fill in the wetland in preparation for constructing a new home on the site. Then, Mason leased his property to Micah. Which statement is most accurate? Assume that the original promise between Sophia and Mason was valid and enforceable.

A. Micah cannot enjoin Sara from destroying the wetland because there was no horizontal privity between Mason and Sophia.

B. Micah cannot recover damages from Sara for the destruction of the wetland because there was no horizontal privity between Mason and Sophia.

C. Micah cannot enjoin Sara from destroying the wetland because there is no vertical privity between Sophia and Sara.

D. Micah cannot recover damages from Sara for the destruction of the wetland because there is no vertical privity between Sophia and Sara.

2. Bringing It Home

Research your state's statutory law, and find its relevant provisions on the issues listed below. Can you recommend any additions or changes to your state's statutory treatment of running covenants? If so, what and why?

1. *The elements of running covenants:* Does your state statutorily codify the required elements for covenants to run to successors? Does it set forth the circumstances under which covenants will be terminated or declared unenforceable? Does it authorize use of the *cy pres* doctrine and allow courts to remake covenants, and if so, under what circumstances?

2. *Common interest communities:* Because of the potential for abuse, common interest communities are highly regulated in most states. Does your state have a statutory section devoted to CICs? If so, how does it define a common interest community? Does the statute contain some type of "reasonableness" test to determine whether challenged restrictions are valid? Does a uniform test apply to restrictions contained in the developer's original declaration and to subsequently enacted restrictions?

Common Law Limits:
Trespass and Nuisance

Chapter 11–Cases

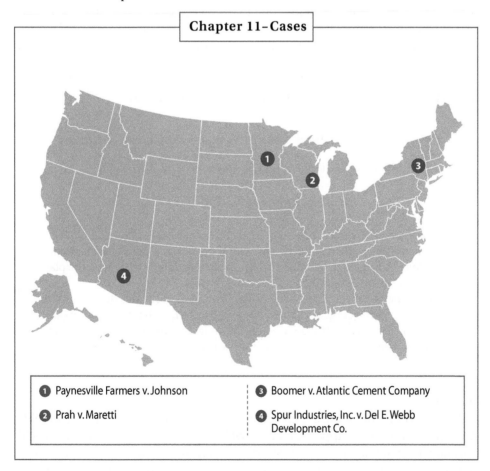

1 Paynesville Farmers v. Johnson

2 Prah v. Maretti

3 Boomer v. Atlantic Cement Company

4 Spur Industries, Inc. v. Del E. Webb
   Development Co.

In this final part of the book, we have been examining legal doctrines and mechanisms that limit the use of property. In Chapters 9 and 10, we studied servitudes, which include easements and running covenants. There, we saw that landowners sometimes enter into voluntary agreements that limit not only how they can use their own property, but also restrict their successors' use of the land. We observed that servitudes straddle the line between contract and property law. In this chapter we will turn to two common law restrictions on land use—trespass and nuisance. Like servitudes, these doctrines implicate two areas of the law—property and tort law.

A. TRESPASS

Trespass is the wrongful interference with possessory rights in land. Notably, trespass involves a *physical invasion* that interferes with the right of exclusive possession. The Great Onyx Cave case in Chapter 1—*Edwards v. Sims*—gave you a brief introduction to trespass. As you may recall, in that case the plaintiff landowner sought damages and an injunction against his neighbor who had developed and exhibited an underground cave that extended beneath the plaintiff's property.

Often, it can be difficult to distinguish trespass from nuisance. The following case explores some distinctions between the two doctrines.

Paynesville Farmers Union Coop. Oil Co. v. Johnson

817 N.W.2d 693 (Minn. 2012), *cert. denied*, 133 S. Ct. 1249 (2013).

Reading Guide

Trespass traditionally occurs when a tangible object enters the plaintiff's land without permission, thereby interfering with the plaintiff's right of exclusive *possession*. Nuisance, in contrast, traditionally involves an interference with the plaintiff's right to *use and enjoy* land.

Suppose that a conventional farmer's application of pesticides drifted onto the fields of a neighboring organic farmer, thereby threatening that farmer's "organic" certification. This case considers whether those facts give rise to a claim of trespass and/or nuisance. Why might it matter which theory is applicable?

GILDEA, C.J.

This action involves alleged pesticide contamination of organic farm fields in central Minnesota. Appellant Paynesville Farmers Union Cooperative Oil Company ("Cooperative") is a member owned farm products and services provider that, among other things, applies pesticides to farm fields. Respondents

Oluf and Debra Johnson ("Johnsons") are organic farmers. The Johnsons claim that while the Cooperative was spraying pesticide onto conventionally farmed fields adjacent to the Johnsons' fields, some pesticide drifted onto and contaminated the Johnsons' organic fields. The Johnsons sued the Cooperative on theories including trespass, nuisance, and negligence per se and sought damages and injunctive relief. . . .

We turn first to the question of whether, as the district court held, the Johnsons' trespass claim fails as a matter of law. . . .

. . . In Minnesota, a trespass is committed where a plaintiff has the "right of possession" to the land at issue and there is a "wrongful and unlawful entry upon such possession by defendant." . . . Actual damages are not an element of the tort of trespass. . . . In the absence of actual damages, the trespasser is liable for nominal damages. . . . [B]ecause trespass is an intentional tort, reasonableness on the part of the defendant is not a defense to trespass liability. . . .

We have not specifically considered the question of whether particulate matter can result in a trespass. The "gist of the tort" of trespass, however, is the "intentional interference with rights of exclusive possession." Dan B. Dobbs, *The Law of Torts* § 50 at 95 (2000). . . . [T]he defendant's entry must be done "by means of some physical, tangible agency" in order to constitute a trespass. James A. Henderson, Jr. et al., *The Torts Process* 386 (7th ed. 2007). . . .

When people or tangible objects enter the plaintiff's land without permission, these entries disturb the landowner's right to exclusively possess her land. . . . But the disruption to the landowner's exclusive possessory interest is not the same when the invasion is committed by an intangible agency, such as the particulate matter at issue here. . . . Such invasions may interfere with the landowner's use and enjoyment of her land, but those invasions do not require that the landowner share possession of her land in the way that invasions by physical objects do. . . .

The court of appeals forged new ground in this case and extended Minnesota trespass jurisprudence when it held that a trespass could occur through the entry of intangible objects, such as the particulate matter at issue here. . . . The court looked outside Minnesota to support the holding it reached. . . . (citing *Borland v. Sanders Lead Co.*, 369 So. 2d 523 (Ala. 1979); *Bradley v. Am. Smelting & Ref. Co.* . . . 709 P.2d 782 (1985)).

In *Bradley*, the Washington Supreme Court held that particulate matter deposited on the plaintiff's land from the defendant's copper smelter could constitute a trespass. . . . And in *Borland*, the Alabama Supreme Court upheld a trespass claim based on the defendant's "emission of lead particulates and sulfoxide gases" that the plaintiffs alleged accumulated on their property. . . .

. . . [G]iven that "the ambient environment always contains particulate matter from many sources," the expansion of the tort of trespass in cases such as *Bradley* and *Borland* to include invasions by intangible matter potentially "subject[s] countless persons and entities to automatic liability for trespass absent any demonstrated injury."... *Borland,* 369 So. 2d at 529.... To guard against that result, the courts in both *Bradley* and *Borland* required that it be reasonably foreseeable that the intangible matter "result in an invasion of plaintiff's possessory interest," and that the invasion caused "substantial damages" to the plaintiff's property.... This formulation of trespass, however, conflicts with our precedent defining the elements of trespass. Under Minnesota trespass law, entry upon the land that interferes with the landowner's right to exclusive possession results in trespass whether that interference was reasonably foreseeable or whether it caused damages....

... [T]he rule in those cases also blurs the line between trespass and nuisance. Traditionally, trespasses are distinct from nuisances: "[t]he law of nuisance deals with indirect or intangible interference with an owner's use and enjoyment of land, while trespass deals with direct and tangible interferences with the right to exclusive possession of land." Dobbs, *supra,* § 50 at 96. But in cases like *Bradley* and *Borland,* the courts "call[ ] the intrusion of harmful microscopic particles" a trespass and not a nuisance, and then "us[e] some of the techniques of nuisance law to weigh the amount and reasonableness of the intrusion." Dobbs, *supra,* § 50 at 96....

But the Johnsons argue that *Bradley* and *Borland* reflect the modern view of trespass and urge us to likewise abandon the traditional distinctions between trespass and nuisance when considering invasions by particulate matter. We decline the Johnsons' invitation.... Our trespass jurisprudence recognizes the unconditional right of property owners to exclude others through the ability to maintain an action in trespass even when no damages are provable.... The rule the Johnsons advocate, and that the court of appeals adopted, erodes this right because it imposes on the property owner the obligation to demonstrate that the invasion causes some consequence.... Imposing this restriction on a trespass claim is inconsistent with our precedent that provides a remedy to a property owner "for any trivial trespass."... And requiring that a property owner prove that she suffered some consequence from the trespasser's invasion before she is able to seek redress for that invasion "offends traditional principles of ownership" by "endanger[ing] the right of exclusion itself." *Adams,* 602 N.W.2d at 217, 221 (declining to recognize a trespass claim for dust, noise, and vibrations emanating from defendant's mining operation).

Moreover, it is not necessary for us to depart from our traditional understanding of trespass because other causes of action—nuisance and negligence—provide remedies for the type of behavior at issue in this case.... Indeed, if a defendant's emission of particulate matter causes enough damage to meet the court of appeals' "[discernible] and consequential amounts" element, ... the emission will also likely be an unreasonable interference with plaintiff's use and enjoyment of his land, and therefore constitute a nuisance....

Our review of cases from other jurisdictions reveals that courts have abandoned the distinction between trespass and nuisance, at least in part, because courts generally favor allowing parties to vindicate wrongs and, in many jurisdictions, actions for trespass have a longer statute of limitations than actions for nuisance. . . . But there is no statute of limitations difference in Minnesota. Generally, both trespass and nuisance have a 6–year statute of limitations. . . . Simply put, the policy concerns that have compelled other jurisdictions to abandon the traditional view of trespass are not present in Minnesota.

In summary, trespass claims address tangible invasions of the right to exclusive possession of land, and nuisance claims address invasions of the right to use and enjoyment of land. The Johnsons do not allege that a tangible object invaded their land. The Johnsons' claim is that the Cooperative's actions have prevented them from *using* their land as an organic farm, not that any action of the Cooperative has prevented the Johnsons from possessing any part of their land. The Johnsons' claim is one for nuisance, not trespass. We therefore hold that the district court did not err in concluding that the Johnsons' trespass claim failed as a matter of law. . . .

PAGE, J., dissenting. . . .

The court holds that Minnesota does not recognize claims for trespass by particulate matter. I disagree with the breadth of the court's holding. The term "particulate matter" encompasses a variety of substances, but the court's one-size-fits-all holding that particulate matter can never cause a trespass fails to take into account the differences between these various substances. The Environmental Protection Agency defines "particulate matter" as "a complex mixture of extremely small particles and liquid droplets" "made up of a number of components, including acids (such as nitrates and sulfates), organic chemicals, metals, and soil or dust particles." United States Envtl. Prot. Agency, http://www.epa.gov/pm/ (last updated June 28, 2012). Some particles are sufficiently large or dark to be observable, "such as dust, dirt, soot, or smoke." . . . In terms of size, the largest "inhalable coarse particles" are 10 micrometers in diameter; that is one-seventh the diameter of a strand of human hair. . . . It seems to me that differences in size, quantity, and harmfulness of varying types of particulate matter will have an effect on whether the invasion by the substance causes a trespass. For example, if someone causes harmful dust to enter a person's land and that dust settles on the person's land and interferes with the owner's possession of the land, it would seem that a trespass has occurred. However, if that person were to cause car exhaust, which presumably dissipates quickly in the air, to enter a person's land, it would seem that a trespass would not occur.

The distinction between trespass and nuisance should not be based on whether the object invading the land is tangible or intangible. Whereas that distinction may have been logical at times when science was not as precise as it is now, that distinction is not sound today. *See, e.g., Martin v. Reynolds Metals Co.,* 342 P.2d 790, 793 (Or. 1959) (suggesting that one explanation for the historical adherence to a distinction between tangible and intangible invasions of land was that "science had not yet peered into the molecular and atomic world of small particles"). . . .

The proper distinction between trespass and nuisance should be the nature of the property interest affected. . . . As other courts have suggested, the same conduct may constitute both trespass and nuisance. . . . Thus, while the court concludes that invasion by an intangible object never interferes with a property owner's possessory rights, I conclude that in some circumstances it may, particularly when that intangible object is actually a substance that settles on the land and damages it. . . .

Rather than adopt a categorical conclusion that particulate matter can never cause a trespass, I conclude, as discussed above, that it may constitute a trespass under some circumstances. Here, on the record presented at this stage in the litigation, it is not clear to me whether the pesticides in this case constituted a trespass. Therefore, I would allow the suit to go forward and permit the record to be developed to resolve that question. . . .

Notes

1. *Trespass v. nuisance:*   What are the elements of trespass? Did the plaintiff allege sufficient facts to support a claim of trespass? The court also gave a brief overview of nuisance (which we will consider in more depth in the following section). Based on that brief introduction, what appear to be the important elements of nuisance?

2. *Majority and dissent:*   According to the majority and dissent, respectively, what is the distinction between trespass and nuisance? Which view did you find more convincing? Is the distinction simply an historical remnant from a time when "science had not yet peered into the molecular and atomic world of small particles" or does the distinction retain vitality today?

Problem

Blasted rocks: Suppose a quarry operator sets off frequent, loud dynamite explosions to blast apart rock formations, and fragments routinely fly onto the neighboring property. Do the facts support a claim for trespass and/or nuisance, and why?

B. NUISANCE

A private nuisance is "a nontrespassory invasion of another's interest in the private use and enjoyment of land." Restatement (Second) of Torts, Nuisance § 821D. Although a fairly simple formulation, the nuisance definition can be difficult to apply. As a starting point, recall William Blackstone's absolutist view of property, which we first considered in Chapter 1. As applied to nuisance, the Blackstonian inquiry would be quite simple: If the actions of one landowner interfere with another landowner's use and enjoyment of property, then the first landowner's actions must be stopped. In Blackstone's words,

> [I]f one does any other act, in itself lawful, which yet being done in that place necessarily tends to the damage of another's property, it is a [nuisance]: for it is incumbent on him to find some other place to do that act, where it will be less offensive.

3 William Blackstone, Commentaries *217-18, *cited in* Louise A. Halper, *Untangling the Nuisance Knot*, 26 Boston College Environmental Affairs L. Rev. 89, 100, 102 (1998). Blackstone's approach operates as a rule of strict liability (a topic which you will likely study in your Torts class) because the action would be halted, even if the actor was not negligent and had no intent to harm the other. This approach works well to guard against potentially abusive power imbalances. That is, even the humblest homeowner can demand a protected sphere of use and enjoyment, even against the mightiest of enterprises.

On the other hand, failure to tolerate any interference with another's land use and enjoyment can prevent socially beneficial actions—such as the development of important new industries that generate negative externalities that spill over onto surrounding properties. In essence, the Blackstonian view freezes existing land uses in place and makes new uses difficult. As the Industrial Revolution got underway, and as the agricultural economy yielded to an industrial market economy, many began to perceive strict liability nuisance as an impediment to progress. One could say that strict liability required industry to "internalize" its "externalities" by bearing the costs of its impact on neighboring properties.

How did American courts respond to the challenge posed by changing social conditions? To determine whether the defendant's conduct generates a nuisance, American judges follow one of two approaches. Some courts use the *utilitarian balancing test* adopted by the Restatement (Second) of Torts § 826(a), which weighs the gravity of the harm inflicted on the plaintiff against the utility of the defendant's conduct. This approach facilitates development: The social utility of a multi-million dollar industry that provides jobs and useful products throughout the region almost inevitably outweighs the gravity of the harm suffered by nearby landowners, at least in the eyes of judges ushering in America's industrial era. Other courts follow the *substantial interference test* (also called the *threshold test*): If the degree of harm suffered by the plaintiff is substantial—that is, it rises above a level that an average plaintiff should be expected to tolerate—then the defendant is liable in nuisance. Section § 826(b) of the Restatement (Second) sets forth a version of this test. You can think of this test as a plaintiff's second chance, and a way to dull the harsh effects of the pure balancing test of § 826(a). Note carefully that in both cases it is the *interference* with the plaintiff's property interests that is the nuisance, and not the defendant's action itself. The elements of nuisance are considered more fully in the following *A Place to Start* box.

A Place to Start | **The Elements of Private Nuisance**

To establish a nuisance, the plaintiff must prove that the defendant caused a nontrespassory, substantial and unreasonable interference with the plaintiff's use and enjoyment of land.

■ ***The plaintiff's interest:*** The plaintiff must have some type of interest in the land purportedly affected by the nuisance. A possessory interest alone is generally sufficient, even if it is of brief duration (such as a short-term lease). In some cases, even adverse possession will be sufficient.

■ ***The nature of the interference:*** The defendant's conduct must cause a *nontrespassory* interference with the plaintiff's *use and enjoyment* of land— triggered by such things as noise, odors, vibrations, dust, and light. Be sure to distinguish trespass, which involves a physical invasion that interferes with the right of exclusive possession. The distinction has to do with the *interest* invaded (the right to use and enjoy vs. the right exclude), and the *type* of invasion (by intangible forces vs. physical forces). The distinction is not always clear because modern scientific knowledge informs us that dust, fumes, and noise all have a physical aspect (for example, sound waves involve the movement of energy).

■ ***The level of interference:*** Not every petty annoyance or inconvenience rises to the level of nuisance. The plaintiff must demonstrate that the defendant's activity causes a *substantial* interference that produces significant harm to a plaintiff of average sensitivity. In addition, the interference must be *unreasonable*. Note carefully: Some cases and sources evaluate whether the defendant's conduct is unreasonable; the better view is to consider whether the *interference* caused by the defendant's conduct is unreasonable. Unreasonableness is usually judged under one of the following tests:

■ ***The Restatement (Second) utilitarian balancing test:*** The interference is unreasonable if the gravity of the harm outweighs the social utility of the defendant's conduct; *or*

■ ***The threshold (or substantial harm) test:*** If the interference is more than the plaintiff should be expected to bear, then it is unreasonable.

■ ***The defendant's intent:*** In addition to the above factors, most courts also consider the nature of the conduct itself, and require that it is one of the following:

■ ***Intentional conduct:*** In most cases, the defendant must act intentionally. This simply means that the defendant intended to take action (such as, the defendant intended to build a house), *not* that the defendant intended to harm the plaintiff (that is, the plaintiff does not need to prove that by building a house the defendant intended to cast a shadow on the plaintiff's rooftop solar collectors); *or*

■ *Negligent, reckless, or unusually hazardous conduct:* Even in the absence of intentional conduct, the defendant will sometimes be held responsible for interferences caused by negligent, reckless, or unusually hazardous conduct. The interferences caused by this type of conduct are best analyzed as typical torts, and many property cases and commentators omit them from separate analysis as nuisances.

DIGGING DEEPER: As you read this chapter, pay careful attention to the individual and broader social consequences of the courts' determinations. Do they promote fairness, efficiency, or some other policy?

In this chapter, we will focus on *private* nuisance. Despite its similar name, *public* nuisance is a distinct legal principle that addresses an unreasonable interference with a right common to the general public—including threats to public health, safety, morals, comfort, and convenience. Most actions to enjoin public nuisances are brought by public officials on behalf of the general public. In some cases, however, individuals can sue for damages if they suffer harm distinct in kind (not merely degree) from that suffered by the general public. We will see an example of this in *Spur Industries*, excerpted in section B.2 below.

1. Entitlements and Liability

To understand how courts determine whether or not a nuisance exists, it is helpful to consider the concept of *entitlements*. A seminal article by Guido Calabresi and A. Douglas Melamed explains,

> The first issue which must be faced by any legal system is one we call the problem of "entitlement." Whenever a state is presented with the conflicting interests of two or more people, or two or more groups of people, it must decide which side to favor. Absent such a decision, access to goods, services, and life itself will be decided on the basis of "might makes right"—whoever is stronger or shrewder will win. Hence the fundamental thing that law does is to decide which of the conflicting parties will be entitled to prevail. The entitlement to make noise versus the entitlement to have silence, the entitlement to pollute versus the entitlement to breathe clean air, the entitlement to have children versus the entitlement to forbid them—these are the first order of legal decisions.

Guido Calabresi & A. Douglas Melamed, *Property Rules, Liability Rules, and Inalienability: One View of the Cathedral*, 85 Harv. L. Rev. 1089, 1090 (1972).

Suppose a plaintiff landowner complains of pollution from defendant's factory. Using the language of entitlements, if a court determines that the impact of the pollution is a nuisance, that court has decided (explicitly or implicitly) that the *plaintiff* holds an entitlement to be free from pollution. Conversely, a determination that the action does not create a nuisance means that the *defendant* is entitled to continue polluting, even if it causes harm to the plaintiff. In such case, it is likely the court has concluded that the plaintiff ought to put up with the inconvenience because the factory confers a significant benefit on society.

How should courts decide to whom entitlements should be awarded? There are a variety of answers to this question, including fairness and efficiency. Under the *fairness* view, plaintiffs should be protected from unreasonable harm or, at least, should be compensated if the defendant profits at their expense. Under the *efficiency* view, courts should strive to minimize costs to society as a whole by maximizing social benefits and minimizing social costs. In the words of Calabresi and Melamed (in the context determining liability for accidents),

> Economic efficiency asks that we choose the set of entitlements which would lead to that allocation of resources which could not be improved in the sense that a further change would not so improve the condition of those who gained by it that they could compensate those who lost from it and still be better off than before. This is often called Pareto optimality. . . . [E]conomic efficiency asks for that combination of entitlements to engage in risky activities and to be free from harm from risky activities which will most likely lead to the lowest sum of accident costs and of costs of avoiding accidents.

Id. at 1093-94. We will return to Calabresi & Melamed's analysis in section B.2 below, when we consider the question of remedy.

The Restatement (Second) of Torts, Nuisance

The American Law Institute (1979), Chapter 40

<hr>

Reading Guide

The Restatement (Second) of Torts, Nuisance, provides a useful starting point for our study of nuisance. Our purpose here is not to memorize the Restatement provisions, but simply to use it as a basis for thinking carefully about the nuances of nuisance law.

<hr>

§ 821D Private Nuisance

A private nuisance is a nontrespassory invasion of another's interest in the private use and enjoyment of land. . . .

§ 821F Significant Harm

There is liability for a nuisance only to those to whom it causes significant harm, of a kind that would be suffered by a normal person in the community or by property in normal condition and used for a normal purpose.

§ 822 General Rule

One is subject to liability for a private nuisance if, but only if, his conduct is a legal cause of an invasion of another's interest in the private use and enjoyment of land, and the invasion is either

(a) intentional and unreasonable, or
(b) unintentional and otherwise actionable under the rules controlling liability for negligent or reckless conduct, or for abnormally dangerous conditions or activities.

Comment: ... (b) Failure to recognize that private nuisance has reference to the interest invaded and not to the type of conduct that subjects the actor to liability has led to confusion. ...

§ 825 Intentional Invasion—What Constitutes

An invasion of another's interest in the use and enjoyment of land or an interference with the public right, is intentional if the actor

(a) acts for the purpose of causing it, or
(b) knows that it is resulting or is substantially certain to result from his conduct.

§ 826 Unreasonableness of Intentional Invasion

An intentional invasion of another's interest in the use and enjoyment of land is unreasonable if

(a) the gravity of the harm outweighs the utility of the actor's conduct, or
(b) the harm caused by the conduct is serious and the financial burden of compensating for this and similar harm to others would not make the continuation of the conduct not feasible.

§ 827 Gravity of Harm—Factors Involved

In determining the gravity of the harm from an intentional invasion of another's interest in the use and enjoyment of land, the following factors are important:

(a) the extent of the harm involved;
(b) the character of the harm involved;
(c) the social value that the law attaches to the type of use or enjoyment invaded;
(d) the suitability of the particular use or enjoyment invaded to the character of the locality; and
(e) the burden on the person harmed of avoiding the harm.

§ 828 Utility of Conduct—Factors Involved

In determining the utility of conduct that causes an intentional invasion of another's interest in the use and enjoyment of land, the following factors are important:

(a) the social value that the law attaches to the primary purpose of the conduct;
(b) the suitability of the conduct to the character of the locality; and
(c) the impracticability of preventing or avoiding the invasion. . . .

Prah v. Maretti

321 N.W.2d 182 (Wis. 1982)

Reading Guide

Although nuisance is an old doctrine, plaintiffs have attempted to press it into service to respond to new challenges. In this case, the court considered whether the shading of rooftop solar panels constitutes a nuisance.

◆ *Reasonableness test:* Notice which test the court adopted to determine whether the interference suffered by the plaintiff was unreasonable—the balancing test, the threshold test, or some other test. Consider whether (and how) that choice affected the outcome of the case.

◆ *Entitlement:* As you read the case, clearly articulate the right claimed by the plaintiff, and the opposing right claimed by the defendant. Notice to which party the court assigned the entitlement, and why.

ABRAHAMSON, J.

. . . According to the complaint, the plaintiff is the owner of a residence which was constructed during the years 1978-1979. The complaint alleges that the residence has a solar system which includes collectors on the roof to supply energy for heat and hot water and that after the plaintiff built his solar-heated house, the defendant purchased the lot adjacent to and immediately to the south of the plaintiff's lot and commenced planning construction of a home. The complaint further states that when the plaintiff learned of defendant's plans to build the house he advised the defendant that if the house were built at the proposed location, defendant's house would substantially and adversely affect the integrity of plaintiff's solar system and could cause plaintiff other damage. Nevertheless, the defendant began construction. The complaint further alleges that the plaintiff is entitled to "unrestricted use of the sun and its solar power" and demands judgment for injunctive relief and damages. . . .

... Plaintiff's home was the first residence built in the subdivision, and although plaintiff did not build his house in the center of the lot it was built in accordance with applicable restrictions. Plaintiff advised defendant that if the defendant's home were built at the proposed site it would cause a shadowing effect on the solar collectors which would reduce the efficiency of the system and possibly damage the system. To avoid these adverse effects, plaintiff requested defendant to locate his home an additional several feet away from the plaintiff's lot line, the exact number being disputed. Plaintiff and defendant failed to reach an agreement on the location of defendant's home before defendant started construction. The Architectural Control Committee and the Planning Commission of the City of Muskego approved the defendant's plans for his home, including its location on the lot. ...

... [T]he circuit court concluded that the law of private nuisance requires the court to make "a comparative evaluation of the conflicting interests and to weigh the gravity of the harm to the plaintiff against the utility of the defendant's conduct. The circuit court concluded: "A comparative evaluation of the conflicting interests, keeping in mind the omissions and commissions of both Prah and Maretti, indicates that defendant's conduct does not cause the gravity of the harm which the plaintiff himself may well have avoided by proper planning." ...

... We consider first whether the complaint states a claim for relief based on common law private nuisance. This state has long recognized that an owner of land does not have an absolute or unlimited right to use the land in a way which injures the rights of others. The rights of neighboring landowners are relative; the uses by one must not unreasonably impair the uses or enjoyment of the other.[1] When one landowner's use of his or her property unreasonably interferes with another's enjoyment of his or her property, that use is said to be a private nuisance.

---

1. [FN 5] [T]his court [has] quoted with approval Dean Prosser's description of the judicial balancing of the reciprocal rights and privileges of neighbors in the use of their land:

> ... The defendant's privilege of making a reasonable use of his own property for his own benefit and conducting his affairs in his own way is no less important than the plaintiff's right to use and enjoy his premises. The two are correlative and interdependent, and neither is entitled to prevail entirely, at the expense of the other. Some balance must be struck between the two. The plaintiff must be expected to endure some inconvenience rather than curtail the defendant's freedom of action, and the defendant must so use his own property that he causes no unreasonable harm to the plaintiff. The law of private nuisance is very largely a series of adjustments to limit the reciprocal rights and privileges of both. In every case the court must make a comparative evaluation of the conflicting interests according to objective legal standards, and the gravity of the harm to the plaintiff must be weighed against the utility of the defendant's conduct.

Prosser, *Law of Torts*, sec. 89, p. 596 (2d ed. 1971) (Citations omitted).

The private nuisance doctrine has traditionally been employed in this state to balance the rights of landowners, and this court has recently adopted the analysis of private nuisance set forth in the Restatement (Second) of Torts. The Restatement defines private nuisance as "a nontrespassory invasion of another's interest in the private use and enjoyment of land." Restatement (Second) of Torts sec. 821D (1977). The phrase "interest in the private use and enjoyment of land" as used in sec. 821D is broadly defined to include any disturbance of the enjoyment of property . . . :

> The phrase "interest in the use and enjoyment of land" is used in this Restatement in a broad sense. It comprehends not only the interests that a person may have in the actual present use of land for residential, agricultural, commercial, industrial and other purposes, but also his interests in having the present use value of the land unimpaired by changes in its physical condition. Thus the destruction of trees on vacant land is as much an invasion of the owner's interest in its use and enjoyment as is the destruction of crops or flowers that he is growing on the land for his present use. "Interest in use and enjoyment" also comprehends the pleasure, comfort and enjoyment that a person normally derives from the occupancy of land. Freedom from discomfort and annoyance while using land is often as important to a person as freedom from physical interruption with his use or freedom from detrimental change in the physical condition of the land itself.

Restatement (Second) of Torts, Sec. 821D, Comment *b*, p. 101 (1977). . . .

. . . In essence, the defendant is asking this court to hold that the private nuisance doctrine is not applicable in the instant case and that his right to develop his land is a right which is *per se* superior to his neighbor's interest in access to sunlight. This position is expressed in the maxim *cujus est solum, ejus est usque ad coelum et ad infernos,* that is, the owner of land owns up to the sky and down to the center of the earth. The rights of the surface owner are, however, not unlimited. *U.S. v. Causby,* 328 U.S. 256, 260-61 (1946).

. . . At English common law a landowner could acquire a right to receive sunlight across adjoining land by both express agreement and under the judge-made doctrine of "ancient lights." Under the doctrine of ancient lights if the landowner had received sunlight across adjoining property for a specified period of time, the landowner was entitled to continue to receive unobstructed access to sunlight across the adjoining property. Under the doctrine the landowner acquired a negative prescriptive easement and could prevent the adjoining landowner from obstructing access to light.

Although American courts have not been as receptive to protecting a landowner's access to sunlight as the English courts, American courts have afforded some protection to a landowner's interest in access to sunlight. American courts honor express easements to sunlight. American courts initially enforced the English common law doctrine of ancient lights, but later every state which considered the doctrine repudiated it as inconsistent with the needs of a developing country. . . .

... Many jurisdictions in this country have protected a landowner from malicious obstruction of access to light (the spite fence cases) under the common law private nuisance doctrine. If an activity is motivated by malice it lacks utility and the harm it causes others outweighs any social values. This court was reluctant to protect a landowner's interest in sunlight even against a spite fence, only to be overruled by the legislature. Shortly after this court upheld a landowner's right to erect a useless and unsightly sixteen-foot spite fence four feet from his neighbor's windows, *Metzger v. Hochrein*, 83 N.W. 308 (Wis. 1900), the legislature enacted a law specifically defining a spite fence as an actionable private nuisance. Thus a landowner's interest in sunlight has been protected in this country by common law private nuisance law at least in the narrow context of the modern American rule invalidating spite fences. *See, e.g.,* ... Restatement (Second) of Torts, sec. 829 (1977).

This court's reluctance in the nineteenth and early part of the twentieth century to provide broader protection for a landowner's access to sunlight was premised on three policy consideration. First, the right of landowners to use their property as they wished, as long as they did not cause physical damage to a neighbor, was jealously guarded.

Second, sunlight was valued only for aesthetic enjoyment or as illumination. Since artificial light could be used for illumination, loss of sunlight was at most a personal annoyance which was given little, if any, weight by society.

Third, society had a significant interest in not restricting or impeding land development. This court repeatedly emphasized that in the growth period of the nineteenth and early twentieth centuries change is to be expected and is essential to property and that recognition of a right to sunlight would hinder property development. ...

... These three policies are no longer fully accepted or applicable. They reflect factual circumstances and social priorities that are now obsolete.

First, society has increasingly regulated the use of land by the landowner for the general welfare. *Euclid v. Ambler Realty Co.*, 272 U.S. 365 (1926).[2] ...

Second, access to sunlight has taken on a new significance in recent years. ... Access to sunlight as an energy source is of significance both to the landowner who invests in solar collectors and to a society which has an interest in developing alternative sources of energy.[3]

---

2. [We will consider *Euclid* in Chapter 12. As we will see, modern comprehensive zoning can serve as a mechanism to minimize private nuisances.—Eds.]

3. [FN 11] State and federal governments are encouraging the use of the sun as a significant source of energy. In this state the legislature has granted tax benefits to encourage the utilization of solar energy. ... *See also* Ch. 354, Laws of 1981 (eff. May 7, 1982) enabling legislation providing for local ordinances guaranteeing access to sunlight. The federal government has also recognized the importance of solar energy and currently encourages its utilization by means of tax benefits, direct subsidies and government loans for solar projects. ...

Third, the policy of favoring unhindered private development in an expanding economy is no longer in harmony with the realities of our society. The need for easy and rapid development is not as great today as it once was, while our perception of the value of sunlight as a source of energy has increased significantly.

Courts should not implement obsolete policies that have lost their vigor over the course of the years. The law of private nuisance is better suited to resolve landowners' disputes about property development in the 1980s than is a rigid rule which does not recognize a landowner's interest in sunlight. . . . We read [our precedents] as an endorsement of the application of common law nuisance to situations involving the conflicting interests of landowners and as rejecting *per se* exclusions to the nuisance law reasonable use doctrine.

. . . We therefore hold that private nuisance law, that is, the reasonable use doctrine as set forth in the Restatement, is applicable to the instant case. Recognition of a nuisance claim for unreasonable obstruction of access to sunlight will not prevent land development or unduly hinder the use of adjoining land. It will promote the reasonable use and enjoyment of land in a manner suitable to the 1980s. That obstruction of access to light might be found to constitute a nuisance in certain circumstances does not mean that it will be or must be found to constitute a nuisance under all circumstances. The result in each case depends on whether the conduct complained of is unreasonable.

Accordingly we hold that the plaintiff in this case has stated a claim under which relief can be granted. . . . In order to be entitled to relief the plaintiff must prove the elements required to establish actionable nuisance, and the conduct of the defendant herein must be judged by the reasonable use doctrine. . . .

The circuit court concluded that because the defendant's proposed house was in conformity with zoning regulations, building codes and deed restrictions, the defendant's use of the land was reasonable. This court has concluded that a landowner's compliance with zoning laws does not automatically bar a nuisance claim. . . .

The judgment of the circuit court is reversed and the cause remanded for proceedings not inconsistent with this opinion.

Callow, J., (dissenting).

. . . I would submit that any policy decisions in this area are best left for the legislature. "What is 'desirable' or 'advisable' or 'ought to be' is a question of policy, not a question of fact. What is 'necessary' or what is 'in the best interest' is not a fact and its determination by the judiciary is an exercise of legislative power when each involves political considerations." *In re City of Beloit*, 155 N.W.2d 633 (1968). . . .

... I examine with interest the definition of nuisance as set out in the Restatement (Second) of *Torts* and adopted in the majority opinion: "A private nuisance is a nontrespassory *invasion* of another's interest in the private use and enjoyment of land." Restatement (Second) of *Torts* sec. 821D (1977) (emphasis added). ... I do not believe the defendant's "obstruction" of the plaintiff's access to sunlight falls within the definition of "invasion," as it applies to the private use and enjoyment of land. Invasion is typically synonymous with "entry," "attack," "penetration," "hostile entrance," "the incoming or spread of something unusually hurtful." Webster's Third International Dictionary, 1188 (1966). Most of the nuisance cases arising under this definition involve noxious odors, smoke, blasting, flooding, or *excessive light* invading the plaintiff's right to the use of enjoyment of his property. *See* Prosser, Law of Torts, sec. 89, 591-92 (4th ed. 1971).

In order for a nuisance to be actionable in the instant case, the defendant's conduct must be "intentional and unreasonable."[4] It is impossible for me to accept the majority's conclusion that Mr. Maretti, in lawfully seeking to construct his home, may be intentionally and unreasonably interfering with the plaintiff's access to sunlight. In addressing the "unreasonableness" component of the actor's conduct, it is important to note that "[t]here is liability for a nuisance only to those to whom it causes significant harm, of a kind that would be suffered by a normal person in the community or by property in normal condition and used for a normal purpose." Restatement (Second) of *Torts* sec. 821F (1979). The comments to the Restatement further reveal that "[if] normal persons in that locality would not be substantially annoyed or disturbed by the situation, then the invasion is not a significant one, even though the idiosyncrasies of the particular plaintiff may make it unendurable to him." *Id.* Comment d. ...

I conclude that plaintiff's solar heating system is an unusually sensitive use. In other words, the defendant's proposed construction of his home, under ordinary circumstances, would not interfere with the use and enjoyment of the usual person's property. ...

... I believe the facts of the instant controversy present the classic case of the owner of a solar collector who fails to take any action to protect his investment. There is nothing in the record to indicate that Mr. Prah disclosed his situation to Mr. Maretti prior to Maretti's purchase of the lot or attempted to secure protection for his solar collector prior to Maretti's submission of his building plans to the architectural committee. Such inaction should be considered a significant factor in determining whether a cause of action exists. ...

---

4. [FN 5] Unintentional conduct may also be actionable if the plaintiff asserts negligence or recklessness or if an abnormally dangerous condition or activity exists. Restatement (Second) of *Torts* sec. 822(b) (1979). The plaintiff's complaint does not specify whether the defendant's conduct was intentional, negligent, or reckless.

Notes

1. *The elements of nuisance:*

- *Nontrespassory interference with the use and enjoyment of land:* Notice the Restatement (Second)'s use of the word *invasion* (in contrast to the common law's general use of the word *interference*). What does this mean, according to Justices Abrahamson and Callow, respectively? Is there a potential conflict between the adjective *nontrespassory* and the noun *invasion*? In each of the examples cited by the dissent (noxious odors, smoke, blasting, flooding, excessive light), is the alleged interference both nontrespassory and invasive?

- *Substantial interference:* Compare the perspectives of Justices Abrahamson and Callow on the requirement of a substantial interference. What sorts of evidence would be relevant on remand, according to each?

- *Unreasonable interference:* Compare the perspectives of Justices Abrahamson and Callow on the unreasonable interference requirement. For each, decide whether the justice favors a balancing test or a threshold test, and does that matter to the justice's preferred outcome? Explain how the following factors affect the analysis of each justice: (a) whether the defendant's construction was lawful; (b) the *ad coelum* doctrine as modified by *United States v. Causby* (which we considered in Chapter 1); (c) whether the use was unusually sensitive; and (d) at what point in time the defendant learned about the existence of the plaintiff's solar panel system.

2. *A changing world—from illumination to energy production:* According to Justice Abrahamson, the early American judicial reluctance to provide broader protection for a landowner's access to sunlight reflects factual circumstances and social priorities that are now obsolete. Do you agree? Is nuisance law capable of adapting to changing circumstances? What elements of nuisance law are particularly important in this context? Does the majority's holding (and adoption of the Restatement (Second) reasonable use doctrine) promote the law of nuisance's ability to adapt to modern circumstances?

3. *The ancient lights doctrine:* The court describes the ancient lights doctrine as one that recognizes *negative prescriptive easements*. Recalling our study of easements from Chapter 9, explain why the rights recognized under the ancient lights doctrine constitute *negative* easements, and also why they constitute *prescriptive* easements. Why do you think the doctrine of ancient lights was repudiated in American jurisdictions? The court suggests this was because it was inconsistent with the needs of a developing country. Can you think of other reasons, recalling the common law's treatment of negative easements?

4. *Trespass and nuisance compared:*   Trespass law deals in absolutes in its vigilant protection of a landowner's exclusive right of possession against even slight invasions. Similarly absolutist, early nuisance law was based on strict liability: That is, actors were responsible for the harm they caused, whether they acted intentionally, negligently, or even accidentally. Today a plaintiff must prove more and demonstrate that the defendant engaged in some type of tortious conduct. In most cases, the defendant's conduct must be intentional—in the sense that the defendant intended for the action to occur, but not necessarily that the defendant intended to invade or interfere with the plaintiff's use of its property. Less commonly, negligent, reckless, or ultrahazardous conduct can also give rise to liability. Overall, trespass is a regime that tolerates no interference with the plaintiff's rights, whereas nuisance struggles to make some reasonable accommodation between the defendant's right to act and the plaintiff's right to be free from interference. *See generally,* Restatement (First) of Torts, ch. 40, *Scope and Introductory Note* (historical information).

5. *More to the story:*   While awaiting a jury trial on remand, the parties settled their dispute. In response to the case, the Wisconsin legislature enacted into law a bill recognizing solar rights. *See Landmark Solar Lawsuit Dismissed by Agreement*, The Milwaukee Journal, Jan. 20, 1984. Today, Wisconsin law provides:

> (1) **Purpose:** The purpose of this section is to promote the use of solar and wind energy by allowing an owner of an active or passive solar energy system or a wind energy system to receive compensation for an obstruction of solar energy by a structure outside a neighbor's building envelope as defined by zoning restrictions in effect at the time the solar collector or wind energy system was installed.

> (2) **Definitions:** In this section: (a) "Building envelope" means the 3-dimensional area on a lot on which building is permitted, as defined by the existing ground level and by any applicable height restriction, setback requirement, side yard requirement or rear yard requirement, notwithstanding any provisions for variances, special exceptions or special or conditional uses in effect in the city, town or village in which the lot is located. . . .

> **Comments:** . . . The effect of the statute is to freeze the "building envelope" of adjacent properties. The building envelope is defined as the 3-dimensional area on a lot, based on zoning existing at the time that the solar collector is installed. . . . The owner of the solar collector is entitled under the statute to rely on that fixed building envelope as dictating the maximum structure that may be installed on the property. After installation of the solar collector, the building envelope is fixed and no structure may be constructed beyond the building envelope that interferes with the solar collector, even if subsequent zoning amendments would permit a larger structure. . . .

Wis. Stat. Ann. § 700.41 (solar and wind access); *see also* Wis. Stat. Ann. § 66.0403(2)&(7) (instituting system of solar and wind access permits, and providing damages for "impermissible interference" with such permits). The solar energy provisions apply to obstructions that came into existence after May 7, 1982, and the wind energy system provisions apply to obstructions that came into existence after May 7, 1994.

Problem

Skills review—policy-based arguments: Should the law of nuisance protect a landowner's interest in sunlight? Construct at least four policy arguments why or why not. Remember to clearly articulate your preferred rule; identify policies that the rule will advance; and provide authority (or, identify the types of authority that you would need) to demonstrate that adherence to your rule would indeed result in the desired policy outcomes.

2. The Remedy for Nuisance

After the inquiry into liability, courts must determine what remedy to award. Before you read farther, pause here and quickly list the possible remedies that you think might be available to a court.

How many remedies did you think of? At least three approaches come easily to mind: First, if the defendant has not created a nuisance, then courts will provide no remedy and dismiss the complaint. Second, courts can issue injunctions against nuisance. Third, judges can award damages, rather than injunctive relief, to plaintiffs. But, might there be yet a fourth potential remedy?

Recall our discussion of *entitlements* from the previous subsection: Courts can award an entitlement to either the plaintiff or to the defendant. Guido Calabresi & A. Douglas Melamed, *Property Rules, Liability Rules, and Inalienability: One View of the Cathedral*, 85 Harv. L. Rev. 1089, 1090 (1972). Moreover, as you have probably observed in most of your first-year classes, two broad types of civil remedies are possible: injunction (which can be described as a "property rule") and damages (which can be described as a "liability rule"). As Calabresi and Melamed explained,

> Whenever society chooses an initial entitlement it must also determine whether to protect the entitlement by property rules [or] by liability rules. . . . In our framework, much of what is generally called private property can be viewed as an entitlement which is protected by a property rule. No one can take the entitlement to private property from the holder unless the holder sells it willingly and at the price at which he subjectively values the property. Yet a nuisance with sufficient public utility to avoid injunction has, in effect, the right to take property with compensation. In such a circumstance the entitlement to the property is protected only by what we call a liability rule: an external, objective standard of

value is used to facilitate the transfer of the entitlement from the holder to the nuisance.[5]

Id. at 1105-1106.

Reviewing these two sets of binary options—two potential entitlement holders, and two broad categories of remedy—Calabresi and Melamed reasoned that there must be four, not three, possible remedies for nuisance. They identified the logically missing fourth remedy: If the defendant creates a nuisance, courts should be able to enjoin the defendant's activity, but only if the *plaintiff pays damages* to indemnify the defendant for its costs of moving, shutting down, or otherwise stopping the nuisance. *Id.* at 1106. This latter remedy is an unusual combination of injunctive and damages relief, and will be explored further in the cases that follow. If we wanted to develop a visual illustration of Calabresi and Melamed's analysis, it would look like the grid in Figure 1. Review *Prah v. Maretti*. Into which box does its remedy fit? <u>Hint</u>: Notice the procedural posture of the case, and explain why it makes the *Prah* remedy potentially fit into two of the boxes in Figure 1.

Remedy	Entitlement in Plaintiff (Landowner)	Entitlement in Defendant (Actor)
Property Rule (Injunction)	Defendant's conduct enjoined	Defendant's harmful conduct can continue (complaint dismissed)
Liability Rule (Damages)	Plaintiff entitled to damages for defendant's past conduct; defendant's harmful conduct can continue if defendant willing to pay damages	Defendant's harmful conduct can continue; but if *plaintiff* willing to indemnify defendant, then court will enjoin conduct (reverse damages)

Figure 1

Our brief discussion of Calabresi & Melamed's article cannot do justice to its complexity and nuance. Those who are interested would do well to read the entire article, as well as critiques of the article. *See, e.g.,* Phyliss Craig-Taylor, *Through a Colored Looking Glass: A View of Judicial Partition, Family Land Loss, and Rule Setting,* 78 Wash. U. L.Q. 737, 762-64 (2000) (considering the remedy of judicial partition by sale to terminate concurrent property interests

---

5. Calabresi & Melamed also recognized a third type of rule that protects entitlements—a rule of inalienability—that forbids or severely restricts the ability to sell certain entitlements, such as the right to be free from slavery or the right to retain one's kidneys (thereby precluding the ability to sell one's kidneys to the highest bidder). *Id.* at 1111-115.

as an example of a quasi-liability rule and criticizing such approach as allowing the "nonconsensual taking of property by the highest bidder"); Richard A. Epstein, *A Clear View of the Cathedral: The Dominance of Property Rules*, 106 Yale L.J. 2091, 2092 (1997); Louis Kaplow & Steven Shavell, *Property Rules Versus Liability Rules: An Economic Analysis*, 109 Harv. L. Rev. 713 (1996).

Boomer v. Atlantic Cement Co.

257 N.E.2d 870 (N.Y. 1970)

Reading Guide

Can nuisance law effectively address the problem of air pollution? Pay attention to the remedy fashioned by the court in the case that follows. Even though this case is more than 40 years old, it is still cited as a landmark decision because of the remedy the court devised. Think about the consequences—both good and bad—that the court's remedy likely produced.

BERGAN, J.

Defendant operates a large cement plant near Albany. These are actions for injunction and damages by neighboring land owners alleging injury to property from dirt, smoke and vibration emanating from the plant. A nuisance has been found after trial, temporary damages have been allowed; but an injunction has been denied.

The public concern with air pollution arising from many sources in industry and in transportation is currently accorded ever wider recognition accompanied by a growing sense of responsibility in State and Federal Governments to control it. Cement plants are obvious sources of air pollution in the neighborhoods where they operate.

But there is now before the court private litigation in which individual property owners have sought specific relief from a single plant operation. The threshold question raised by the division of view on this appeal is whether the court should resolve the litigation between the parties now before it as equitably as seems possible; or whether, seeking promotion of the general public welfare, it should channel private litigation into broad public objectives. . . .

Effective control of air pollution is a problem presently far from solution even with the full public and financial powers of government. In large measure adequate technical procedures are yet to be developed and some that appear possible may be economically impracticable.

It seems apparent that the amelioration of air pollution will depend on technical research in great depth; on a carefully balanced consideration of the economic impact of close regulation; and of the actual effect on public health. It is likely to require massive public expenditure and to demand more than any local community can accomplish and to depend on regional and interstate controls.

A court should not try to do this on its own as a by-product of private litigation and it seems manifest that the judicial establishment is neither equipped in the limited nature of any judgment it can pronounce nor prepared to lay down and implement an effective policy for the elimination of air pollution. This is an area beyond the circumference of one private lawsuit. It is a direct responsibility for government and should not thus be undertaken as an incident to solving a dispute between property owners and a single cement plant—one of many—in the Hudson River valley.

The cement making operations of defendant have been found by the court of Special Term to have damaged the nearby properties of plaintiffs in these two actions. That court . . . accordingly found defendant maintained a nuisance and this has been affirmed at the Appellate Division. The total damage to plaintiffs' properties is, however, relatively small in comparison with the value of defendant's operation and with the consequences of the injunction which plaintiffs seek.

The ground for the denial of injunction [below], notwithstanding the finding both that there is a nuisance and that plaintiffs have been damaged substantially, is the large disparity in economic consequences of the nuisance and of the injunction. This theory cannot, however, be sustained without overruling a doctrine which has been consistently reaffirmed in several leading cases in this court and which has never been disavowed here, namely that where a nuisance has been found and where there has been any substantial damage shown by the party complaining an injunction will be granted.

The rule in New York has been that such a nuisance will be enjoined although marked disparity be shown in economic consequence between the effect of the injunction and the effect of the nuisance.

The problem of disparity in economic consequence was sharply in focus in *Whalen v. Union Bag & Paper Co.*, 101 N.E. 805 (N.Y.). A pulp mill entailing an investment of more than a million dollars polluted a stream in which plaintiff, who owned a farm, was "a lower riparian owner." The economic loss to plaintiff from this pollution was small. This court, reversing the Appellate Division, reinstated the injunction granted by the Special Term against the argument of the mill owner that in view of "the slight advantage to plaintiff and the great loss that will be inflicted on defendant" an injunction should not be granted. . . .

. . . The rule laid down in that case, then, is that whenever the damage resulting from a nuisance is found not "unsubstantial," *viz.*, $100 a year, injunction would follow. . . .

The court at Special Term . . . found the amount of permanent damage attributable to each plaintiff, for the guidance of the parties in the event both sides stipulated to the payment and acceptance of such permanent damage as a settlement of all the controversies among the parties. The total of permanent damages to all plaintiffs thus found was $185,000. . . .

This result at Special Term and at the Appellate Division is a departure from a rule that has become settled; but to follow the rule literally in these cases would be to close down the plant at once. This court is fully agreed to avoid that immediately drastic remedy; the difference in view is how best to avoid it.[*]

One alternative is to grant the injunction but postpone its effect to a specified future date to give opportunity for technical advances to permit defendant to eliminate the nuisance; another is to grant the injunction conditioned on the payment of permanent damages to plaintiffs which would compensate them for the total economic loss to their property present and future caused by defendant's operations. For reasons which will be developed the court chooses the latter alternative.

If the injunction were to be granted unless within a short period—*e.g.,* 18 months—the nuisance be abated by improved methods, there would be no assurance that any significant technical improvement would occur.

The parties could settle this private litigation at any time if defendant paid enough money and the imminent threat of closing the plant would build up the pressure on defendant. . . .

Moreover, techniques to eliminate dust and other annoying by-products of cement making are unlikely to be developed by any research the defendant can undertake within any short period, but will depend on the total resources of the cement industry nationwide and throughout the world. The problem is universal wherever cement is made.

For obvious reasons the rate of the research is beyond control of defendant. If at the end of 18 months the whole industry has not found a technical solution a court would be hard put to close down this one cement plant if due regard be given to equitable principles.

On the other hand, to grant the injunction unless defendant pays plaintiffs such permanent damages as may be fixed by the court seems to do justice between the contending parties. All of the attributions of economic loss to the properties on which plaintiffs' complaints are based will have been redressed.

The nuisance complained of by these plaintiffs may have other public or private consequences, but these particular parties are the only ones who have sought remedies and the judgment proposed will fully redress them. The limitation of relief granted is a limitation only within the four corners of these actions and does not foreclose public health or other public agencies from seeking proper relief in a proper court. It seems reasonable to think that the risk of being required to pay permanent damages to injured property

---

[*] Respondent's investment in the plant is in excess of $45,000,000. There are over 300 people employed there.

owners by cement plant owners would itself be a reasonable effective spur to research for improved techniques to minimize nuisance. . . .

Thus it seems fair to both sides to grant permanent damages to plaintiffs which will terminate this private litigation. The theory of damage is the "servitude on land" of plaintiffs imposed by defendant's nuisance. (*See United States v. Causby*, 328 U.S. 256, 261, 262, 267 (1946), where the term "servitude" addressed to the land was used by Justice Douglas relating to the effect of airplane noise on property near an airport.) . . .

This should be placed beyond debate by a provision of the judgment that the payment by defendant and the acceptance by plaintiffs of permanent damages found by the court shall be in compensation for a servitude on the land. . . .

The orders should be reversed, . . . and the cases remitted to Supreme Court . . . to grant an injunction which shall be vacated upon payment by defendant of such amounts of permanent damage to the respective plaintiffs as shall for this purpose be determined by the court.

JASEN, J., dissenting.

I agree with the majority that a reversal is required here, but I do not subscribe to the newly enunciated doctrine of assessment of permanent damages, in lieu of an injunction, where substantial property rights have been impaired by the creation of a nuisance.

It has long been the rule in this State, as the majority acknowledges, that a nuisance which results in substantial continuing damage to neighbors must be enjoined. . . . To now change the rule to permit the cement company to continue polluting the air indefinitely upon the payment of permanent damages is, in my opinion, compounding the magnitude of a very serious problem in our State and Nation today. . . .

The harmful nature and widespread occurrence of air pollution have been extensively documented. Congressional hearings have revealed that air pollution causes substantial property damage, as well as being a contributing factor to a rising incidence of lung cancer, emphysema, bronchitis and asthma.

The specific problem faced here is known as particulate contamination because of the fine dust particles emanating from defendant's cement plant. The particular type of nuisance is not new, having appeared in many cases for at least the past 60 years. . . . This type of pollution, wherein very small particles escape and stay in the atmosphere, has been denominated as the type of air pollution which produces the greatest hazard to human health. We have thus a nuisance which not only is damaging to the plaintiffs, but also is decidedly harmful to the general public.

I see grave dangers in overruling our long-established rule of granting an injunction where a nuisance results in substantial continuing damage. In permitting the injunction to become inoperative upon the payment of permanent damages, the majority is, in effect, licensing a continuing wrong. It is the same as saying to the cement company, you may continue to do harm to your neighbors so long as you pay a fee for it. Furthermore, once such permanent damages are assessed and paid, the incentive to alleviate the wrong would be eliminated, thereby continuing air pollution of an area without abatement. . . .

In a day when there is a growing concern for clean air, highly developed industry should not expect acquiescence by the courts, but should, instead, plan its operations to eliminate contamination of our air and damage to its neighbors.

Accordingly, the orders of the Appellate Division, insofar as they denied the injunction, should be reversed, and the actions remitted to Supreme Court, Albany County to grant an injunction to take effect 18 months hence, unless the nuisance is abated by improved techniques prior to said date.

Notes

1. *The entitlement:* Clearly describe the right claimed by the plaintiff and the opposing right claimed by the defendant. To which party did the court assign the entitlement?

2. *The remedy:* What remedy did the court award. Can you fit it into one of the boxes in Figure 1, above? The court thought that its remedy "seems fair to both sides"—do you agree? The court observed that there were many similar cement plants in the Hudson River valley. What types of incentives did the court's choice of remedy create for them? The court claimed that its selected remedy would redress "all of the attributions of economic loss" to the plaintiffs' property. Are there any non-economic losses that should be considered? In jurisdictions that follow *Boomer*, can you imagine any set of facts that would merit injunctive relief? How, if at all, does the court's approach differ from that taken by Restatement (Second) § 826(b)?

3. *Was there a nuisance?* Did the court apply the balancing test or the threshold test to determine whether the defendant's conduct created an unreasonable interference? How, if at all, did the choice of test affect the outcome of the case?

4. *A web of interests—air pollution:* The court viewed this private nuisance dispute as affecting the "general public welfare" and extending into "an area beyond the circumference of one private lawsuit." What aspects of the public welfare does this case implicate? List as many aspects as possible. In the absence of comprehensive statutory regulation, should nuisance law address the external impacts of one party's pollution upon the nearby community?

The *Boomer* nuisance complaint was filed about five years before Congress established the modern regulatory framework to control air pollution through the Clean Air Act of 1970 ("CAA"). Although air pollution still poses significant challenges—particularly the release of greenhouse gases that contribute to global climate change—the CAA has enjoyed remarkable success. The Environmental Protection Agency estimates that in its first 20 years alone, the CAA prevented more than 200,000 premature deaths and 18 million cases of respiratory illness in children. Overall, the EPA claims that for every dollar spent, the law has yielded more than $40 of benefits in return. *See* Lisa Jackson, EPA Administrator, *Remarks on the 40th Anniversary of the Clean Air Act*, Sept. 14, 2010.

5. *Preview—eminent domain:* The court suggested that its remedy created a "servitude" on the land of the plaintiffs, which allowed the defendant to continue to interfere with the plaintiffs' use and enjoyment of their property. Is this a voluntary or involuntary "sale" of the plaintiffs' property rights? In the usual case, servient property owners will voluntarily agree to impose burdens on their land only if they receive in return compensation that they deem to be fair. In Chapter 13, we will see that eminent domain can work a forced sale of a property interest, but generally only governmental authorities possess the power of eminent domain. Does this case authorize eminent domain by a private entity, with judicial approval?

Spur Industries, Inc. v. Del E. Webb Development Co.

494 P.2d 700 (Ariz. 1972)

Reading Guide

Like *Boomer*, this 1970s case is still considered a landmark decision because of the unusual remedy the court imposed. Try to determine into which box of the Figure 1 grid this remedy best fits.

CAMERON, VICE C.J. . . .

. . . The area in question is located in Maricopa County, Arizona, some 14 to 15 miles west of the urban area of Phoenix. . . .

Farming started in this area about 1911. . . . By 1950, the only urban areas in the vicinity were the agriculturally related communities of Peoria, El Mirage, and Surprise located along Grand Avenue. . . .

In 1956, Spur's predecessors in interest . . . developed feed-lots, about 1/2 mile south of Olive Avenue. . . . The area is well suited for cattle feeding and in 1959, there were 25 cattle feeding pens or dairy operations within a 7 mile radius of the location developed by Spur's predecessors. . . .

In May of 1959, Del Webb began to plan the development of an urban area [for senior citizens] to be known as Sun City. For this purpose, the Marinette and the Santa Fe Ranches, some 20,000 acres of farmland, were purchased for $15,000,000 or $750.00 per acre. This price was considerably less than the price of land located near the urban area of Phoenix, and . . . was a factor influencing the decision to purchase the property in question.

By September 1959, Del Webb had started construction of a golf course south of Grand Avenue and Spur's predecessors had started to level ground for more feedlot area. In 1960, Spur purchased the property in question and began a rebuilding and expansion program extending both to the north and south of the original facilities. By 1962, Spur's expansion program was completed and had expanded from approximately 35 acres to 114 acres. . . .

Accompanied by an extensive advertising campaign, homes were first offered by Del Webb in January 1960 and the first unit to be completed was south of Grand Avenue and approximately 2-1/2 miles north of Spur. By 2 May 1960, there were 450 to 500 houses completed or under construction. At this time, Del Webb did not consider odors from the Spur feed pens a problem and Del Webb continued to develop in a southerly direction, until sales resistance became so great that the parcels were difficult if not impossible to sell. . . .

By December 1967, Del Webb's property had extended south to Olive Avenue and Spur was within 500 feet of Olive Avenue to the north. . . . Del Webb filed its original complaint alleging that in excess of 1,300 lots in the southwest portion were unfit for development for sale as residential lots because of the operation of the Spur feedlot.

Del Webb's suit complained that the Spur feeding operation was a public nuisance because of the flies and the odor which were drifting or being blown by the prevailing south to north wind over the southern portion of Sun City. At the time of the suit, Spur was feeding between 20,000 and 30,000 head of cattle, and the facts amply support the finding of the trial court that the feed pens had become a nuisance to the people who resided in the southern part of Del Webb's development. The testimony indicated that cattle in a commercial feedlot will produce 35 to 40 pounds of wet manure per day, per head, or over a million pounds of wet manure per day for 30,000 head of cattle, and that despite the admittedly good feedlot management and good housekeeping practices by Spur, the resulting odor and flies produced an annoying if not unhealthy situation as far as the senior citizens of southern Sun City were concerned. . . .

. . . [T]he citizens of Sun City . . . are [not] represented in this lawsuit and the suit is solely between Del E. Webb Development Company and Spur Industries, Inc.

May Spur Be Enjoined?

The difference between a private nuisance and a public nuisance is generally one of degree. A private nuisance is one affecting a single individual or a definite small number of persons in the enjoyment of private rights not common to the public, while a public nuisance is one affecting the rights enjoyed by citizens as a part of the public. To constitute a public nuisance, the nuisance must affect a considerable number of people or an entire community or neighborhood. . . .

Where the injury is slight, the remedy for minor inconveniences lies in an action for damages rather than in one for an injunction. Moreover, some courts have held, in the "balancing of conveniences" cases, that damages may be the sole remedy. See *Boomer v. Atlantic Cement Co.*, 257 N.E.2d 870 (N.Y. 1970). . . .

We have no difficulty, however, in agreeing with the conclusion of the trial court that Spur's operation was an enjoinable public nuisance as far as the people in the southern portion of Del Webb's Sun City were concerned.

[Section] 36-601, subsec. A reads as follows:

Section 36-601. Public nuisances dangerous to public health: (A) The following conditions are specifically declared public nuisances dangerous to the public health: (1) Any condition or place in populous areas which constitutes a breeding place for flies, rodents, mosquitoes and other insects which are capable of carrying and transmitting disease-causing organisms to any person or persons.

By this statute, before an otherwise lawful (and necessary) business may be declared a public nuisance, there must be a "populous" area in which people are injured:

. . . [I]t hardly admits a doubt that, in determining the question as to whether a lawful occupation is so conducted as to constitute a nuisance as a matter of fact, the locality and surroundings are of the first importance. . . . A business which is not *per se* a public nuisance may become such by being carried on at a place where the health, comfort, or convenience of a populous neighborhood is affected. . . . What might amount to a serious nuisance in one locality by reason of the density of the population, or character of the neighborhood affected, may in another place and under different surroundings be deemed proper and unobjectionable. . . .

MacDonald v. Perry, 255 P. 494, 497 (Ariz. 1927).

It is clear that as to the citizens of Sun City, the operation of Spur's feedlot was both a public and a private nuisance. They could have successfully maintained an action to abate the nuisance. Del Webb, having shown a special injury in the loss of sales, had a standing to bring suit to enjoin the nuisance. . . . The judgment of the trial court permanently enjoining the operation of the feedlot is affirmed.

Must Del Webb Indemnify Spur? . . .

In addition to protecting the public interest, . . . courts of equity are concerned with protecting the operator of a lawful, albeit noxious, business from the result of a knowing and willful encroachment by others near his business.

In the so-called "coming to the nuisance" cases, the courts have held that the residential landowner may not have relief if he knowingly came into a neighborhood reserved for industrial or agricultural endeavors and has been damaged thereby:

> Plaintiffs chose to live in an area uncontrolled by zoning laws or restrictive covenants and remote from urban development. In such an area plaintiffs cannot complain that legitimate agricultural pursuits are being carried on in the vicinity, nor can plaintiffs, having chosen to build in an agricultural area, complain that the agricultural pursuits carried on in the area depreciate the value of their homes. . . .
>
> People employed in a city who build their homes in suburban areas of the county beyond the limits of a city and zoning regulations do so for a reason. Some do so to avoid the high taxation rate imposed by cities, or to avoid special assessments for street, sewer and water projects. They usually build on improved or hard surface highways, which have been built either at state or county expense and thereby avoid special assessments for these improvements. It may be that they desire to get away from the congestion of traffic, smoke, noise, foul air and the many other annoyances of city life. But with all these advantages in going beyond the area which is zoned and restricted to protect them in their homes, they must be prepared to take the disadvantages.

Dill v. Excel Packing Company, 331 P.2d 539, 548, 549 (Kan. 1958). . . .

Were [Del] Webb the only party injured, we would feel justified in holding that the doctrine of "coming to the nuisance" would have been a bar to the relief asked by Webb, and, on the other hand, had Spur located the feedlot near the outskirts of a city and had the city grown toward the feedlot, Spur would have to suffer the cost of abating the nuisance as to those people locating within the growth pattern of the expanding city. . . .

We agree, however, with the Massachusetts court that:

> The law of nuisance affords no rigid rule to be applied in all instances. It is elastic. It undertakes to require only that which is fair and reasonable under all the circumstances. In a commonwealth like this, which depends for its material prosperity so largely on the continued growth and enlargement of manufacturing of diverse varieties, "extreme rights" cannot be enforced. . . .

Stevens v. Rockport Granite Co., 104 N.E. 371, 373 (Mass. 1914).

There was no indication in the instant case at the time Spur and its predecessors located in western Maricopa County that a new city would spring up, full-blown, alongside the feeding operation and that the developer of that city would ask the court to order Spur to move because of the new city. Spur is required to move not because of any wrongdoing on the part of Spur, but because of a proper and legitimate regard of the courts for the rights and interests of the public.

Del Webb, on the other hand, is entitled to the relief prayed for (a permanent injunction), not because [Del] Webb is blameless, but because of the damage to the people who have been encouraged to purchase homes in Sun City. It does not equitable or legally follow, however, that [Del] Webb, being entitled to the injunction, is then free of any liability to Spur if [Del] Webb has in fact been the cause of the damage Spur has sustained. It does not seem harsh to require a developer, who has taken advantage of the lesser land values in a rural area as well as the availability of large tracts of land on which to build and develop a new town or city in the area, to indemnify those who are forced to leave as a result.

Having brought people to the nuisance to the foreseeable detriment of Spur, Webb must indemnify Spur for a reasonable amount of the cost of moving or shutting down. It should be noted that this relief to Spur is limited to a case wherein a developer has, with foreseeability, brought into a previously agricultural or industrial area the population which makes necessary the granting of an injunction against a lawful business and for which the business has no adequate relief.

It is therefore the decision of this court that the matter be remanded to the trial court for a hearing upon the damages sustained by the defendant Spur as a reasonable and direct result of the granting of the permanent injunction. . . .

Notes

1. *Public v. private nuisance:*   Review the distinction between private and public nuisance, as discussed in the narrative at the beginning of section B, above. Recall that a private, non-governmental plaintiff in a public nuisance action must demonstrate a "special injury" in order to bring the lawsuit. What was Del Webb's "special injury"? Alternatively, can the homeowners themselves bring a public nuisance claim?

2. *The remedy:*   What are the strengths and weaknesses of the remedy imposed by the court? How did the court assess the relative blameworthiness of the parties, and do you agree? Should courts apply this remedy broadly in the future? If so, under what circumstances?

3. *Coming to the nuisance:*   States vary in their treatment of plaintiffs who come to the nuisance. In some cases, it might serve as a defense to the plaintiff's lawsuit. In other cases, as *Spur*, it might influence the court's choice of remedy. In most cases, however, the fact that the plaintiff came to the nuisance is one factor that a court will consider in determining whether the interference caused by the defendant's conduct was unreasonable under the circumstances. What approach does the Restatement (Second) of Torts, Nuisance, take?

4. *Right-to-farm laws:*   In reaction to nuisance lawsuits, every state has enacted *right-to-farm* laws that provide farmers and ranchers with some measure of protection from nuisance lawsuits. National Agricultural Law Center, *States' Right-To-Farm Statutes*, http://nationalaglawcenter.org/

state-compilations/right-to-farm/ (visited July 29, 2015). For example, with certain qualifications, Missouri law provides,

> No agricultural operation . . . shall be deemed to be a nuisance, private or public, by any changed conditions in the locality thereof after the facility has been in operation for more than one year, when the facility was not a nuisance at the time the operation began. An agricultural operation protected pursuant to the provisions of this section may reasonably expand its operation in terms of acres or animal units without losing its protected status so long as all county, state, and federal environmental codes, laws, or regulations are met by the agricultural operation. . . .

Mo. Rev. Stat. § 537.295(1).

However, at least one such statute has been declared unconstitutional because it effectively grants farmers an easement to interfere with the use and enjoyment of neighboring properties, and provides no compensation to the affected properties. *See Bormann v. Kossuth County*, 584 N.W.2d 309 (Iowa 1998) (holding statutory nuisance immunity provision appearing at Iowa Code, § 352.11(1) unconstitutional under the Takings Clause of the federal constitution), *cert. denied*, 525 U.S. 1172 (1999). Are right-to-farm laws a good idea? If so, should nuisance immunity be expanded to protect additional types of land uses beyond farming?

Problem

Airplanes and power lines: A wholesale distributor bought 16 acres of land. With all required approvals, it developed a private airstrip on its property for use in delivering its products nationwide. About 10 years later, a local energy utility, with all required approvals, constructed a 115-foot high, 230,000 volt transmission line about 150 feet from the distributor's airstrip. The utility claimed that operation of the airstrip was a nuisance because it created an unreasonable risk that one of the aircraft would trespass into its airspace and strike the transmission line. The court granted an injunction against operation of the airstrip, which according to the distributor, would destroy its business. Should the distributor receive damages or other compensation from the utility? In answering, consider whether the facts are analogous to, or distinguishable from, the facts of *Spur Industries. See generally Brenteson Wholesale, Inc. v. Arizona Public Service Co.*, 803 P.2d 930 (Ariz. App. 1990).

C. BEYOND THE BLACK LETTER—DO DRONES CREATE A NUISANCE?

Drones—also known as "unmanned aerial vehicles" (UAVs)—include a variety of unpiloted aircraft. Dating back to at least World War II, military drones have been used in warfare to supplement human-piloted aircraft. Drones can be used for nonmilitary purposes, too. Commercial applications include use in agriculture, construction, mining, television and film production, and other industries. Drones also have potential applications for commercial package delivery. For example, Amazon obtained a patent in 2015 for an "unmanned aerial vehicle delivery system," and is developing plans for a future "Prime Air" service that would deliver packages to customers within 30 minutes after placement of an order. Hobby and recreational users also fly drones—generally in airspace below 400 feet. Beginner models can be purchased for under $100, and models equipped with high-definition cameras are available for a few hundred dollars more.

Although drones hold great promise for a variety of uses, they are not without peril. Commercial aircraft have reported near misses with drones, and some aviation safety experts claim it is not a matter of *if*, but *when* there will be a collision. Landowners complain that drones overhead (particularly those equipped with cameras) interfere with their privacy, and "Peeping Tom" activities have been reported. In a few cases, irate homeowners have shot drones out of the sky above their property.

Lawmakers have struggled to keep up with the growing interest in drones. The *Federal Aviation Administration* (FAA) *Modernization and Reform Act of 2012* instructed the Secretary of Transportation to develop "a comprehensive plan to safely accelerate the integration of civil unmanned aircraft systems into the national airspace system" within three years. In the interim, recreational uses were largely unregulated, subject only to FAA safety guidelines. Most commercial uses, in contrast, were banned by the FAA unless commercial users obtained individual authorization from the FAA. In addition to federal legislation, at least half the states have enacted laws on the topic. Many states seek to facilitate the beneficial uses of drones while simultaneously promoting safety and protecting privacy, but other efforts have not been quite so measured. In at least two states, frustrated lawmakers debated proposals that would allow homeowners to shoot down drones over their property, or that would provide for the issuance of hunting licenses to take aim at drones (those proposals did not become law). *See generally*, Federal Aviation Administration, *Unmanned Aircraft Systems*, https://www.faa.gov/uas/ (visited Aug. 5, 2015); National Conference of State Legislatures, *Current Unmanned Aircraft State Law Landscape*, July 28, 2015, http://www.ncsl.org/research/transportation/current-unmanned-aircraft-state-law-landscape.aspx; Mark Bowden, *How the Predator Drone Changed the Character of War*, Smithsonian Magazine, Nov. 2013.

For the following question, assume that there are no applicable federal or state laws in your jurisdiction that govern drones.

WMCH Drone
Photo by Clément Bucco-Lechat (December 1, 2013)
Source: Wikimedia Commons

Discussion Questions

1. *Do drones create a nuisance?*   Suppose your clients are annoyed by repeated recreational drone flights over their property. If they can identify the owner/operator of the drone, would you advise them to bring an action in nuisance (public or private) or in trespass? What additional facts would you need in order to advise your clients? What legal elements would your clients have to satisfy in order to successfully prosecute their claim?

2. *A changing world—new technologies:*   Recall the challenges and opportunities posed by new technologies in *Prah* (rooftop solar panels) and *Boomer* (potential for improved technology to reduce dust emissions by cement plants). Is common law, statutory law, or a combination of both, better equipped to manage conflicts posed by such new technologies? What would be the best approach in the case of drones? Do you see them as a social benefit, a potential nuisance, or something in between?

D. SKILLS PRACTICE: CLIENT COUNSELING—THE SMOKING NEIGHBOR

You interviewed your client Margery last week and learned that she has owned and occupied a condominium at Finch's Landing for the past five years. Finch's Landing is organized as a condominium community, and features a common swimming pool, tennis courts, and a small park. Each condominium unit shares one wall and a common entry hall with one adjacent unit. The opposite wall (farthest from the attached unit) opens onto a screened porch in each unit. Margery very much enjoys living at Finch's Landing and hopes to stay for a long time. In fact, she even considered adding four-season windows to her screened porch to add extra square footage to her home. But, when she learned that the window installation would cost about $1,000, she decided to put off the renovation until she could save up some money. Margery works as a public-health nurse, and her home is conveniently located close to her work.

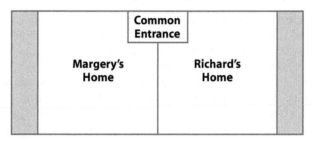

Figure 2

About six months ago, Margery's next-door neighbor sold her condominium to Richard. At first, Margery and Richard had struck up a neighborly relationship, and it seemed as if they might become good friends. But Richard was under pressure to complete a big project at work and was experiencing a great deal of stress. Margery began to smell cigarette smoke emanating from Richard's condominium, possibly coming through the common wall or through the common entry hall. Margery says that the smoke has aggravated her asthma and that she no longer enjoys being at home because of the fumes. In addition, Margery told you that she missed several days at work as a consequence. "I've always been sensitive to smoke," Margery explained. "And I just hate to see Richard smoke himself to death—I've seen too many smoking-related illnesses and deaths at work! And second-hand smoke—that's just as bad as smoking yourself!"

Margery approached Richard about the problem and he said, "Yeah, I know, I've taken up smoking again because of this tough project at work. I'd like to quit, but don't know if I have the willpower to quit again." Richard agreed to smoke outside on his screened porch only. But, as the cold weather set in, Richard has been smoking inside more and more. Margery discussed the issue with Richard several times, but he has been less receptive to her requests. Their friendship has chilled considerably, and a feeling of animosity has developed between them.

The condominium association does not have a rule regulating smoking. However, the city has an ordinance that bans smoking in public places, and asserts that "[s]moking in any form is a nuisance and a public health hazard."

Margery told you, "I don't really like lawyers (no offense to you) and I hate to think of suing Richard. But honestly, I can't stand the smell anymore and don't know what to do. I want to sue him to make him stop blowing his smoke right into my home—I don't know why he thinks he has the right to endanger my health like that!"

You have another meeting with Margery scheduled for next week in which you plan to counsel her as to her possible range of options. To prepare for that meeting, first review the following information on client counseling.

Skills | **Client Counseling—Interests, Not Positions**

■ *Clarify relevant legal issues and client interests*: Clarify the key legal issues posed by the client's problem. In addition, clarify the client's interests. Unlike a client's *position* (the outcome the client tells you she wants), *interests* reflect the reasons why the client has adopted a particular position, and typically incorporate client values, beliefs, and needs. For example, the interests of a client who wants to enjoin operations of the neighboring business as a nuisance might be to avoid the adverse impacts of the business (noise, fumes); to punish the business ("It can't treat the neighbors like this—I'll shut it down!"); to encourage the entire industry to adopt better pollution-control mechanisms; to protect the market value of her home ("I want to take a new out-of-state job, but I'll never be able to sell my house with that nuisance next door"); or to gain an advantage over a competitor's business.

■ *Articulate possible legal theories:* Identify all legal theories that might apply to your client's case. Challenge yourself to explain the law simply and clearly, yet accurately, as it applies to the facts of your client's case. Be sure to identify areas of uncertainty.

■ *Identify client options:* Work with your client to "brainstorm" options to solve the problem (including both litigation and non-litigation alternatives). Think of as many potential courses of action as possible. Avoid becoming locked into your client's first articulated *position*, but instead keep her *interests* in mind as you develop a list of options together.

■ *Explore consequences:* Explore the probable consequences of each option that you identified. Working systematically through the options, be prepared to predict the likely legal outcome of each. Also be prepared to solicit your client's input as to the likely non-legal outcomes ("If the business is shut down, I've heard that five of my close neighbors will be out of work" or "If the business is shut down, I've heard that a new, clean high-tech operation is ready to make a bid to buy the building and to start hiring" or "If I get at least $400,000 dollars, I think I could afford to move my family to a better location"). Then, work with your client to decide which course of action seems best able to maximize the *interests* of your client.

Adapted from Leonard L. Riskin et al., Dispute Resolution and Lawyers 82-89 (abridged 5th ed. 2014).

Tasks

1. *Clarify relevant issues and interests:*   Frame a tentative statement of your client's issues and interests to make sure you understand your client accurately. For example, the statement could take the form, "It seems to me that you are concerned about *issue A* and hope to come to a resolution that is consistent with *interest x, interest y,* and *interest z,* is that right?" Riskin et al., *supra.,* at 83.

2. *Articulate possible legal theories:*   What legal theory or theories might be relevant to Margery's case—trespass, private nuisance, public nuisance, or something else? From a cursory review, it is unclear whether or not your state has adopted the Restatement (Second) of Torts, Nuisance. Prepare to explain to Margery what legal claims her facts support, and what remedies might be available to her. To prepare for this discussion, draft a brief outline of the points you will address with your client.

3. *Identify client options:*   Brainstorming with your client can generate a broad and creative range of options. But to prepare for your brainstorming session, generate a list of options on your own (you can expand and/or refine that list when you meet with Margery next week). Think of as many reasonable choices as you can, including non-litigation options such as a negotiated agreement or other such action.

4. *Explore consequences:*   After each option appearing on the list you just generated, jot down your initial assessment of the likely legal consequences. Does this option seem likely to satisfy your client's *interests,* and if so, which one(s)?

E. CHAPTER REVIEW

1. Practice Questions[6]

1. *The siren and the birds:*   Abigail owns a cabin in a secluded area near the top of a mountain ridge. Although there is a cell phone transmission tower fairly close to her cabin, she can only see it from one side of her property where the trees are thin. From all other angles, she has beautiful, unobstructed views. Five years ago, Abigail began to spend most of her time at the cabin, because her employer implemented a new policy that allows her to work from home four days each week. When not working, Abigail spends most of her time outdoors bird watching and enjoying the quiet mountain setting. Last year, the cell phone provider that owns the transmission tower leased space to the county to

---

6. Answers appear in the Appendix to this casebook.

install an emergency alert siren system, which the county tests for 15 minutes each week. The county chose the site because its high elevation allows the warning siren to be heard from every location in the county. The periodic tests of the siren are so loud that Abigail must go indoors and close her windows. She also worries that the area's bird population will decline if the siren tests continue. Abigail would like to bring a legal action against the cell phone provider and the county. Does she have any valid claims (you can ignore any issues of the county's potential immunity from lawsuits)? Explain.

2. *The elements of private nuisance:*   Identify one or more of the following that are *not* elements of a private nuisance claim:
  A. An unlawful use of land by the defendant.
  B. An indirect interference with the plaintiff's use and enjoyment of property resulting from the defendant's actions.
  C. An unreasonable and substantial interference with plaintiff's enjoyment of land.
  D. An intent by the defendant to interfere with the plaintiff's enjoyment of land.

3. *The plaintiff:*   Identify the party least likely to be able to bring a nuisance action:
  A. An adverse possessor on the land affected by the defendant's private nuisance.
  B. The son of an owner of land affected by the defendant's private nuisance.
  C. The owner of a life estate in land affected by the defendant's private nuisance.
  D. The owner of land affected differently than surrounding properties by the defendant's public nuisance.

2. Bringing It Home

Research your state's statutory law, and find its relevant provisions, if any, on the following topics:

1. *Determination of nuisance:*   Has your state enacted legislation governing the determination of whether or not an activity creates a nuisance? Has it adopted any of the Restatement (Second) of Torts, Nuisance, provisions, such as the utilitarian balancing test of § 826(a)?

2. *Solar easements:*   Does your state have any legislation concerning conflicts over rooftop solar panels? If so, does the legislation assign an entitlement to the solar panel owner (the right to sunlight) or to neighbors (the right to build in accordance with local zoning ordinances, even if solar installations are shaded)?

3. *Right-to-farm legislation:*   Does your state provide statutory protection from nuisance liability for farming and ranching operations? If so, what approach does it take, and do you think it appropriately reconciles competing interests?

4. *Drones:*   Does your state have any legislation governing the recreational or commercial use of drones? Is it addressed as an aspect of nuisance, trespass, privacy, or some other topic?

Statutory Limits: Zoning

A. Introduction to Zoning
B. What Can Be Regulated?
C. Beyond the Black Letter: Urban Agriculture
D. Skills Practice: Drafting Zoning Regulations
E. Chapter Review

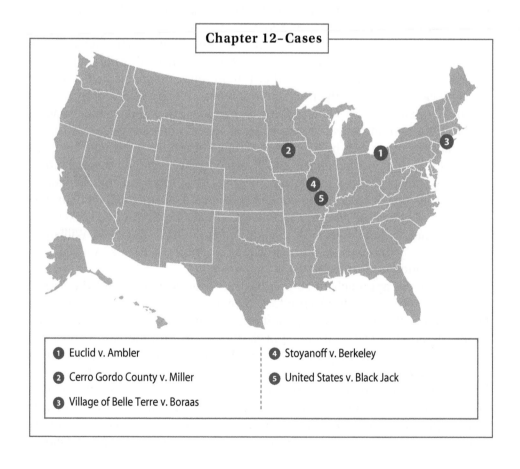

Chapter 12-Cases

1. Euclid v. Ambler
2. Cerro Gordo County v. Miller
3. Village of Belle Terre v. Boraas
4. Stoyanoff v. Berkeley
5. United States v. Black Jack

As we have seen, land use can be controlled by private agreements (easements and running covenants) and by the courts through the law of trespass and nuisance. But most communities today have chosen to engage in broad, comprehensive planning that goes beyond such piecemeal efforts. Through the local *zoning ordinance*, communities determine in great detail how land may be used within their borders.

In part, zoning was a reaction to late 19th century industrialization and rapid population growth, which led to miserable urban conditions, at least for those without means. Many city dwellers packed into tenement housing, where they were surrounded by noise, air pollution, poor sanitation, and disease. In some places, skyscrapers began to dominate the landscape, cutting off sunlight and airflow. A broad coalition of reformers called for change. These included social reformers, who sought to ease the suffering of the urban poor; proponents of the so-called *City Beautiful* movement, who favored aesthetic controls and urban planning to promote attractive, functional, and humane cities; commercial interests, who wanted to physically distance themselves from factories and working-class immigrants; and the wealthy, who wanted to live apart from multi-family and low-income housing.

Zoning's basic impulse is to *segregate* land uses thought to be incompatible, such as residential life and industrial operations. Many laud zoning for its protection of the family home and all that it represents, neighborhood character, property values, and orderly urban development. Others criticize zoning for its potential unfairness to some, ability to exclude low-income and minority people from certain areas, economic inefficiency, and interference with the free market. Zoning can be all of these things—both for good and for ill. As you read this chapter, challenge yourself to recognize both the potential pitfalls of zoning, but also the benefits that it offers. For more on the debate, *see* Stephen Clowney, *A Walk Along Willard: A Revised Look at Land Use Coordination in Pre-Zoning New Haven*, 115 Yale L.J. 116 (2005); Bradley C. Karkkainen, *Zoning: A Reply to the Critics*, 10 J. Land Use & Envtl. L. 45 (1994); William A. Fischel, The Economics of Zoning Laws: A Property Rights Approach to American Land Use Controls (1985).

The national approach to zoning has not been stagnant, and the system itself has come full circle in an effort to remedy some of its own problems. For example, although the segregation of uses might promote residential tranquility, it can also lead to urban sprawl, overreliance on the automobile, and the inability to walk from one place to another. In response, the *new urbanism* and *smart growth* movements have sought to re-introduce some mixed uses into communities, to make them walkable, and to use design to facilitate human interactions (such as by including the once ubiquitous front porch to housing plans). Likewise, zoning can lead to the separation of people by race or economic status. In response, *inclusionary zoning* and *affordable housing* efforts have sought to expand opportunity for more people. These are fascinating topics that mirror broader social currents, and you can study them in more detail in upper level courses on land use planning and local government law.

Zoning is all about place—it regulates on-the-ground uses of individual parcels of land in specific neighborhoods. You will notice that two of this chapter's cases took place in St. Louis. Our brief look at the history of that place will help you to understand why events transpired as they did, and why those same challenges might plague other places in the country. Zoning also provides insights into the web of interests metaphor—courts have upheld zoning's authority to restrict private landowners' use of their property, but only when justified by sufficient public interest considerations. Thus, a web of interests influences the use of any particular tract of land.

A. INTRODUCTION TO ZONING

New York City adopted the nation's first comprehensive zoning ordinance in 1916. As is still common today, the city developed, (1) a zoning *map*, that (2) divided the city into *zones* or districts, and (3) listed the *uses* permissible in each zone. By the 1920s, zoning had caught on throughout the United States, and almost half of the states had adopted *enabling acts* that delegated authority to local governments to adopt and enforce zoning ordinances. Such delegation is necessary because zoning is an exercise of the state's police power to protect the public health, safety, and welfare.

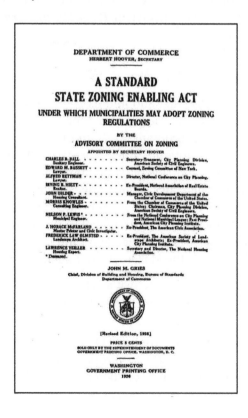

To facilitate local zoning, the U.S. Department of Commerce developed the *Standard Zoning Enabling Act* (SZEA) in 1924 as model legislation that the states could easily adopt (and adapt, as desired, to their particular circumstances). Among other things, the act contemplated that the *city council* (or other local government body with legislative authority) would hold public hearings and then enact its zoning ordinance into law. The legislative body would be assisted by at least two administrative bodies. First, the *zoning commission* (or similarly named body) would divide the community into zones and develop a proposed zoning ordinance for the city council's consideration, all with public notice and comment. In addition to the *uses* permitted in each zoning district, the ordinance would contain *bulk* or *dimensional requirements* governing such things as building height, number of stories per building, size, and percentage of lot covered. Second, the *board of adjustment* (sometimes called the board of zoning appeals) would interject flexibility into the system in selected cases by considering applications for variances and special exceptions (considered in section A.3, below). Today, almost all cities and counties follow the basic pattern set forth in the SZEA, albeit with additional and more complicated provisions. For example, some jurisdictions add an additional *overlay zone* to existing districts, to promote such things as historic preservation and protection of environmentally sensitive lands (we will see examples of overlay zones in section D's skills exercise), or provide for *transferable development rights* (which we will consider in *Penn Central Transportation Co. v. New York*, Chapter 13).

1. The Constitutionality of Zoning

The Village of Euclid, Ohio first adopted its zoning ordinance in 1922. Zoning had come into fashion and about half of the states had authorized their municipalities to adopt such ordinances. By the time a challenge to Euclid's ordinance reached the U.S. Supreme Court, more than 500 cities and towns had passed zoning ordinances, and several state courts had upheld the constitutionality of zoning under the states' police power authority.

In this important test case, Cleveland attorney James Metzenbaum defended Euclid. Metzenbaum had participated in the development of Euclid's zoning ordinance, and later wrote a treatise on the law of zoning. As Metzenbaum recalled in his treatise, the stakes of the Euclid litigation were high:

> It was recognized from coast to coast, that a defeat in this case, would cause all zoning ordinances in successive order throughout the land to fall, like a row of dominoes stood end to end.

James Metzenbaum, The Law of Zoning 111 (1955), *quoted in* David Callies, *Village of Euclid v. Ambler Realty Co.*, *in* Property Stories 406 (Gerald L. Korngold & Andrew P. Morriss, eds. 2nd ed. 2009).

Euclid v. Ambler Realty Co.

272 U.S. 365 (1926)

Reading Guide

The federal district court declared Euclid's ordinance "wholly null and void" and explained: "The plain truth is that the true object of the ordinance in question is to place all the property in an undeveloped area of 16 square miles in a strait-jacket. The purpose to be accomplished is really to regulate the mode of living of persons who may hereafter inhabit it. In the last analysis, the result to be accomplished is to classify the population and segregate them according to their income or situation in life." *Ambler Realty Co. v. Village of Euclid*, 297 F. 307, 316 (N.D. Ohio 1924).

It appeared that the nation's zoning ordinances would indeed "fall like a row of dominoes," as Euclid's attorney James Metzenbaum had feared. But the following decision proved that fear to be misplaced.

SUTHERLAND, J. [joined by TAFT, C.J., HOLMES, BRANDEIS, SANFORD, and STONE, JJ.]

The village of Euclid is an Ohio municipal corporation. It adjoins and practically is a suburb of the city of Cleveland. . . . East and west it is traversed by three principal highways: Euclid avenue, through the southerly border, St. Clair avenue, through the central portion, and Lake Shore boulevard, through the northerly border, in close proximity to the shore of Lake Erie. . . .

Appellee is the owner of a tract of land containing 68 acres, situated in the westerly end of the village, abutting on Euclid avenue to the south and the Nickel Plate Railroad to the north. Adjoining this tract, both on the east and on the west, there have been laid out restricted residential plats upon which residences have been erected.

On November 13, 1922, an ordinance was adopted by the village council, establishing a comprehensive zoning plan for regulating and restricting the location of trades, industries, apartment houses, two-family houses, single family houses, etc., the lot area to be built upon, the size and height of buildings, etc.

The entire area of the village is divided by the ordinance into six classes of use districts, denominated U-1 to U-6, inclusive; three classes of height districts, denominated H-1 to H-3, inclusive; and four classes of area districts, denominated A-1 to A-4, inclusive. The use districts are classified in respect of the buildings which may be erected within their respective limits, as follows: U-1 is restricted to single family dwellings . . . ; U-2 is extended to include two-family dwellings; U-3 is further extended to include apartment houses, hotels, churches, schools . . . ; U-4 is further extended to include banks, offices, studios, telephone exchanges, fire and police stations . . . ; U-5 is further extended to include . . . warehouses . . . ; U-6 is further extended to include . . .

manufacturing and industrial operations. . . . There is a seventh class of uses which is prohibited altogether.

Class U-1 is the only district in which buildings are restricted to those enumerated. In the other classes the uses are cumulative—that is to say, uses in class U-2 include those enumerated in the preceding class U-1; class U-3 includes uses enumerated in the preceding classes, U-2, and U-1; and so on. . . .

Appellee's tract of land comes under U-2, U-3 and U-6. The first strip of 620 feet immediately north of Euclid avenue falls in class U-2, the next 130 feet to the north, in U-3, and the remainder in U-6. The uses of the first 620 feet, therefore, do not include apartment houses, hotels, churches, schools, or other public and semipublic buildings, or other uses enumerated in respect of U-3 to U-6, inclusive. The uses of the next 130 feet include all of these, but exclude industries, theaters, banks, shops, and the various other uses set forth in respect of U-4 to U-6, inclusive. . . .

The enforcement of the ordinance is intrusted to the inspector of buildings, under rules and regulations of the board of zoning appeals. It is authorized to adopt rules and regulations to carry into effect provisions of the ordinance. Decisions of the inspector of buildings may be appealed to the board by any person claiming to be adversely affected by any such decision. The board is given power in specific cases of practical difficulty or unnecessary hardship to interpret the ordinance in harmony with its general purpose and intent, so that the public health, safety and general welfare may be secure and substantial justice done. . . .

The ordinance is assailed on the grounds that it is in derogation of section 1 of the Fourteenth Amendment to the federal Constitution in that it deprives appellee of liberty and property without due process of law and denies it the equal protection of the law, and that it offends against certain provisions of the Constitution of the state of Ohio. The prayer of the bill is for an injunction restraining the enforcement of the ordinance and all attempts to impose or maintain as to appellee's property any of the restrictions, limitations or conditions. The court below held the ordinance to be unconstitutional and void, and enjoined its enforcement. . . .

Before proceeding to a consideration of the case, it is necessary to determine the scope of the inquiry. The bill alleges that the tract of land in question is vacant and has been held for years for the purpose of selling and developing it for industrial uses, for which it is especially adapted, being immediately in the path or progressive industrial development; that for such uses it has a market value of about $10,000 per acre, but if the use be limited to residential purposes the market value is not in excess of $2,500 per acre; that the first 200 feet of the parcel back from Euclid avenue, if unrestricted in respect of use, has a value of $150 per front foot, but if limited to residential uses, and ordinary mercantile business be excluded therefrom, its value is not in excess of $50 per front foot.

It is specifically averred that the ordinance attempts to restrict and control the lawful uses of appellee's land, so as to confiscate and destroy a great part of its value. . . .

The record goes no farther than to show, as the lower court found, that the normal and reasonably to be expected use and development of that part of appellee's land adjoining Euclid avenue is for general trade and commercial purposes, particularly retail stores and like establishments, and that the normal and reasonably to be expected use and development of the residue of the land is for industrial and trade purposes. Whatever injury is inflicted by the mere existence and threatened enforcement of the ordinance is due to restrictions in respect of these and similar uses, to which perhaps should be added—if not included in the foregoing—restrictions in respect of apartment houses. Specifically there is nothing in the record to suggest that any damage results from the presence in the ordinance of those restrictions relating to churches, schools, libraries, and other public and semipublic buildings. It is neither alleged nor proved that there is or may be a demand for any part of appellee's land for any of the last-named uses, and we cannot assume the existence of facts which would justify an injunction upon this record in respect to this class of restrictions. . . .

Building zone laws are of modern origin. They began in this country about 25 years ago. Until recent years, urban life was comparatively simple; but, with the great increase and concentration of population, problems have developed, and constantly are developing, which require, and will continue to require, additional restrictions in respect of the use and occupation of private lands in urban communities. Regulations, the wisdom, necessity, and validity of which, as applied to existing conditions, are so apparent that they are now uniformly sustained, a century ago, or even half a century ago, probably would have been rejected as arbitrary and oppressive. Such regulations are sustained, under the complex conditions of our day, for reasons analogous to those which justify traffic regulations, which, before the advent of automobiles and rapid transit street railways, would have been condemned as fatally arbitrary and unreasonable. And in this there is no inconsistency, for, while the meaning of constitutional guaranties never varies, the scope of their application must expand or contract to meet the new and different conditions which are constantly coming within the field of their operation. In a changing world it is impossible that it should be otherwise. . . .

The ordinance now under review, and all similar laws and regulations, must find their justification in some aspect of the police power, asserted for the public welfare. The line which in this field separates the legitimate from the illegitimate assumption of power is not capable of precise delimitation. It varies with circumstances and conditions. A regulatory zoning ordinance, which would be clearly valid as applied to the great cities, might be clearly invalid as applied to rural communities. In solving doubts, the maxim "sic utere tuo ut alienum non laedas," which lies at the foundation of so much of the common low of nuisances, ordinarily will furnish a fairly helpful clew. And the law of nuisances, likewise, may be consulted, not for the purpose of controlling, but for the helpful aid of its analogies in the process of ascertaining the scope of, the power. Thus the question whether the power exists to forbid the erection of a building of a particular kind or for a particular use, like the question whether a particular thing is a nuisance, is to be determined, not by an abstract consideration of the building or of the thing considered apart, but by considering it in connection with the circumstances and the locality. . . . A nuisance may be merely a right thing in the wrong place, like a pig in the parlor instead of the barnyard. If the validity of the legislative classification for zoning purposes be fairly debatable, the legislative judgment must be allowed to control. . . .

We find no difficulty in sustaining restrictions of the kind thus far reviewed. The serious question in the case arises over the provisions of the ordinance excluding from residential districts apartment houses, business houses, retail stores and shops, and other like establishments. This question involves the validity of what is really the crux of the more recent zoning legislation, namely, the creation and maintenance of residential districts, from which business and trade of every sort, including hotels and apartment houses, are excluded. Upon that question this court has not thus far spoken. The decisions of the state courts are numerous and conflicting; but those which broadly sustain the power greatly outnumber those which deny it altogether or narrowly limit it, and it is very apparent that there is a constantly increasing tendency in the direction of the broader view. . . .

The matter of zoning has received much attention at the hands of commissions and experts, and the results of their investigations have been set forth in comprehensive reports. These reports which bear every evidence of painstaking consideration, concur in the view that the segregation of residential, business and industrial buildings will make it easier to provide fire apparatus suitable for the character and intensity of the development in each section; that it will increase the safety and security of home life, greatly tend to prevent street accidents, especially to children, by reducing the traffic and resulting confusion in residential sections, decrease noise and other conditions which produce or intensify nervous disorders, preserve a more favorable environment in which to rear children, etc. With particular reference to apartment houses, it is pointed out that the development of detached house sections is greatly retarded by the coming of apartment houses, which has sometimes resulted in destroying the entire section for private house purposes; that in such sections very often the apartment house is a mere parasite, constructed in order to take advantage of the open spaces and attractive surroundings created by the residential character of the district. Moreover, the coming of one apartment house is followed by others, interfering by their height and bulk with the free circulation of air and monopolizing the rays of the sun which otherwise would fall upon the smaller homes, and bringing, as their necessary

accompaniments, the disturbing noises incident to increased traffic and business, and the occupation, by means of moving and parked automobiles, of
larger portions of the streets, thus detracting from their safety and depriving
children of the privilege of quiet and open spaces for play, enjoyed by those in
more favored localities—until, finally, the residential character of the neighborhood and its desirability as a place of detached residences are utterly destroyed.
Under these circumstances, apartment houses, which in a different environment would be not only entirely unobjectionable but highly desirable, come
very near to being nuisances.

If these reasons, thus summarized, do not demonstrate the wisdom or
sound policy in all respects of those restrictions which we have indicated as
pertinent to the inquiry, at least, the reasons are sufficiently cogent to preclude
us from saying, as it must be said before the ordinance can be declared unconstitutional, that such provisions are clearly arbitrary and unreasonable, having
no substantial relation to the public health, safety, morals, or general
welfare. . . . Decree reversed.

VAN DEVANTER, MCREYNOLDS, and BUTLER, JJ., dissenting.

Notes

1. *Euclidean zoning—separation of uses:* After this decision established
the constitutionality of zoning, countless additional jurisdictions enacted *Euclidean zoning* ordinances of their own. The label has a dual meaning—it refers to
a zoning scheme similar to that adopted by the Village of Euclid, and it also
suggests a system that divides the land into geometric use districts (thereby
invoking the name of the Greek mathematician and geometer, Euclid). Notice
here that Euclid followed a *cumulative zoning* approach. The first district (U-1)
was reserved primarily for the most protected use—single-family residences.
The next district (U-2) allowed single-family uses, and also added slightly
more intensive uses, such as duplexes. The third district (U-2) allowed both
of those uses, and added several more intensive uses, including apartment
houses. The cumulative approach culminated in a sixth district (U-6), which
allowed a wide variety of uses, ranging from single-family homes to manufacturing and industrial operations.

2. *Substantive due process:* In *Euclid*, the plaintiff claimed that the challenged ordinance violated the federal and state constitutions because it
"deprives appellee of liberty and property without due process of law and
denies it the equal protection of the law." As you may have learned in your
Constitutional Law class, this is a type of *substantive due process* challenge
(as compared to procedural due process actions). The general test for such
claims, as articulated by the Court in *Euclid*, is whether the ordinance bears
a "substantial relation to the public health, safety, morals, or general welfare."

Just four years earlier, the Court had established the foundation of a related, but distinct, doctrine—the regulatory takings doctrine—in *Pennsylvania Coal v. Mahon* (which we will study in Chapter 13). Under that doctrine, assuming a regulation's constitutional validity, the court considers whether the Fifth and Fourteenth Amendments to the U.S. Constitution require the government to pay "just compensation" to those whose property has been "taken" by the regulation. Interestingly, Justice Oliver Wendell Holmes, Jr. had authored the *Pennsylvania Coal* opinion that *invalidated* a state law that purported to regulate the use of property. Just four years later, Justice Holmes joined in *Euclid*'s support for comprehensive land use regulation through zoning. For a while, the Court itself confused the regulatory takings doctrine with substantive due process analysis, but corrected its mistake in the unanimous decision *Lingle v. Chevron U.S.A. Inc.*, 544 U.S. 528 (2005).

3. *Practice pointer—selecting a litigation strategy:*   In *Euclid*, the plaintiff challenged the "mere existence and threatened enforcement" of the ordinance. Under such *facial challenges*, plaintiffs claim that a law is unconstitutional on its face and should be declared invalid. As an alternative, plaintiffs can bring *as-applied challenges*, under which they claim that a law is unconstitutional as applied to the particular facts of their situation. Successful as-applied challenges prevent enforcement against the plaintiff, but leave the law intact for potential application to others.

As a matter of litigation strategy, facial challenges are risky. Although they can strike an offending statute once and for all, the plaintiffs have a more difficult case to make than under narrower as-applied challenges. In fact, just two years later, Justice Sutherland wrote an opinion invalidating a Cambridge, Massachusetts zoning ordinance as applied to one particular landowner. *Nectow v. City of Cambridge*, 277 U.S. 183 (1928) (concluding that restricting a portion of Nectow's land to residential uses did not satisfy the "substantial relation" test). If you had represented the Ambler Realty Company in *Euclid*, would you have recommended that it bring a facial or an as-applied challenge, and why?

4. *A pig in the parlor—the role of nuisance:*   Notice Justice Sutherland's colorful and often-quoted statement, "A nuisance may be merely a right thing in the wrong place, like a pig in the parlor instead of the barnyard." Recall our discussion of nuisance law from Chapter 11. Would nuisance law be an adequate substitute for the zoning ordinance enacted by Euclid? If so, who would be the likely plaintiff(s)? What is the relationship between nuisance law and the state's police power? We will return to the latter question in *Lucas v. S. Carolina Coastal Council* (Chapter 13).

5. *Apartments as parasites:*   Notice the Court's harsh words with respect to apartment houses. Did the appellee want to develop its land into such housing? If not, why did the Court focus on the perceived evils of apartment houses? Multi-family housing has attracted considerable animosity, as we will see in section B, below.

6. *The importance of place—the family home and the American dream:* In contrast to the Court's discussion of apartments, notice its favorable view of quiet residential neighborhoods—a theme that recurs with some regularity in zoning cases. For example, the year before *Euclid* was decided, the California Supreme Court extolled the virtues of single-family neighborhoods:

> . . . [J]ustification for residential zoning may . . . be rested upon the protection of the civic and social values of the American home. . . . It is axiomatic that the welfare, and indeed the very existence, of a nation depends upon the character and caliber of its citizenry. The character and quality of manhood and womanhood are in a large measure the result of home environment. The home and its intrinsic influences are the very foundation of good citizenship . . . and the fostering of home life doubtless tends to the enhancement, not only of community life, but of the life of the nation as a whole.

Miller v. Board of Public Works, 234 P. 381 (Cal. 1925). Benign rhetoric aside, can you imagine circumstances under which Euclidean *segregation* of uses can produce undesirable consequences? We will return to this question in section B, below.

7. *More to the story:* As the Court explained, the Village of Euclid "adjoins and practically is a suburb of the city of Cleveland." Euclid Avenue, which runs through both the city and the village, was home to wealthy industrialists including John D. Rockefeller, whose ornate mansions graced the segment known as *Millionaire's Row*. Euclid likely hoped that similar prosperity would extend to its undeveloped lands just east of Cleveland.

Worthy Streator Mansion (1874), Euclid Avenue, Cleveland, Ohio
Photograph by Simmons and Titus
Source: Atlas of Cuyahoga County, Ohio, downloaded from Wikimedia Commons

By the 1920s, however, industrial development had claimed some of Cleveland's elegant mansions near downtown, and Euclid's ordinance reflected a fear that similar industrialization would destroy its residential neighborhoods. *See* The Cleveland Historical Team, *Millionaire's Row*, http://clevelandhistorical .org/ (visited Nov. 25, 2015); David Callies, *Village of Euclid v. Ambler Realty Co.*, in Property Stories 409-10 (Gerald L. Korngold & Andrew P. Morriss, eds. 2nd ed. 2009). After the Court's decision, Euclid developed into a thriving community for many years. During World War II, General Motors constructed a massive war plant on the Ambler property (after the village rezoned accordingly), which was later converted to automotive purposes until the plant's closure in 1994. Today, the Ambler property has been put to industrial use—just the type of use that the Euclid ordinance originally sought to preclude. For a complete account of the story behind *Euclid, See* Michael Allan Wolf, The Zoning of America: Euclid v. Ambler (Univ. Press of Kansas 2008).

A portion of the Ambler property today
Photograph courtesy of Michael Allan Wolf

2. The Nonconforming Use

Bd. of Supervisors of Cerro Gordo Cnty. v. Miller

170 N.W.2d 358 (Iowa 1969)

Reading Guide

When a community enacts or amends its zoning ordinance, lawfully existing uses not permitted by the new ordinance are said to be *nonconforming uses.*

> Should the owners of such properties be required to terminate the nonconforming uses immediately, be allowed to continue them indefinitely, or be given some reasonable period of time during which to phase them out?

RAWLINGS, J.

This appeal involves the constitutionality of certain provisions of a county zoning ordinance requiring discontinued nonconforming use of property within five years after its enactment.

By action in equity plaintiff board of supervisors sought to enjoin defendants' continued use of their land as an automobile wrecking establishment after expiration of prescribed amortization period. Defendants resisted contending the ordinance, as applied to them, constituted deprivation of property without due process of law. . . .

Prior to adoption of the challenged ordinance defendants were engaged in the operation of [a business known as Chazen's Auto Parts], and intentionally continued operations more than five years after enactment of the ordinance.

Under the terms thereof defendants' property is located in what is described as Zone A-Agricultural District. In material part the ordinance, Section XVI, provides:

> The lawful use of any building or land existing at the time of the enactment of this Ordinance may be continued although such use does not conform with the provisions of this Ordinance. . . .
>
> Notwithstanding any other provisions of this Ordinance: . . . Any automobile wrecking or junk yard in existence in a district in which it is a non-conforming use, prior to the effective date of this Ordinance, shall within five (5) years from such date become a prohibited and unlawful use and shall be discontinued; . . .

Despite the fact defendants assert 17 propositions relied upon for reversal, their argument is confined to claimed deprivation of property without due process of law. . . .

> The term "nonconforming use" is employed in the law of zoning, for the most part, to refer to a use which not only does not conform to the general regulation or restriction governing a zoned area but which lawfully existed at the time that the regulation or restriction went into effect and has continued to exist without legal abandonment since that time. . . .

McQuillin, Municipal Corporations, 1965 Rev. Vol. 8A, section 25.185, page 21. . . .

So it is apparent we are here confronted with a nonconformity under the controverted county plan, and the constitutional right of a municipality to amortize or phase it out of existence within a fixed period of time.

A brief survey of the cases and authorities in this area disclose nonconforming uses have been a problem since the inception of zoning. It was originally thought such uses would be few, and would naturally eliminate themselves through the passage of time, with restrictions on their expansion. But during the past two decades it has become increasingly evident pre-existing nonconformities have no natural tendency to fade away. On the contrary it appears they tend to continue and prosper because of the artificial monopoly accorded them by the law. However, it still remains, the basic aim and ultimate purpose of zoning is to confine certain classes of buildings and uses to specified localities. Nonconforming uses are inconsistent with that objective. In an effort to change nonconformance to conformance as speedily as possible, with due regard for the legitimate interests of the private property owner and the general public, legislative bodies have attempted different means to eradicate undesired uses.

The methods so employed include, (1) condemnation by use of eminent domain; (2) invoking the law of nuisance; (3) forbidding resumption of nonconforming uses after a period of nonuse or abandonment; (4) prohibiting or limiting extensions or repairs; and (5) amortizing the nonconformity over a reasonable period of time. . . .

. . . [A]s disclosed in *City of Los Angeles v. Gage*, [274 P.2d 34, 41 (Cal. Ct. App. 1954)], it has been reasonably determined the only effective method of eliminating nonconforming uses yet devised is to amortize the offending building, structure or business operation, and prohibit the owner or operator from maintaining it after expiration of a designated period or date. . . .

R]ecent judicial decisions reveal the pronounced trend is toward elimination of nonconformities by the amortization process. And the test most commonly employed by courts in determining reasonableness of the liquidation period is based upon a balancing of public good against private loss. This unavoidably necessitates an examination of the factual situation presented in each case. . . .

Here again we refer to *City of Los Angeles v. Gage, supra*. There, as in the case at bar, certain nonconforming uses were to be discontinued within five years after adoption of the zoning ordinance. Upholding the validity of this legislative proviso the court said, loc. cit., 274 P.2d 44:

> The distinction between an ordinance restricting future uses and one requiring the termination of present uses within a reasonable period of time is merely one of degree, and constitutionality depends on the relative importance to be given to the public gain and to the private loss. . . . The elimination of existing uses within a reasonable time does not amount to a taking of property nor does it necessarily restrict the use of property so that it cannot be used for any reasonable purpose. Use of a reasonable amortization scheme provides an equitable means of reconciliation of the conflicting interests in satisfaction of due process requirements. As a method of eliminating existing nonconforming uses it allows the owner of the nonconforming use, by affording an opportunity to make new plans, at least partially to offset any loss he might suffer. The loss he suffers, if any is spread out over a period of years, and he enjoys a monopolistic position by virtue of the zoning ordinance as long as he remains. If the amortization period is reasonable

the loss to the owner may be small when compared with the benefit to the public. Nonconforming uses will eventually be eliminated. A legislative body may well conclude that the beneficial effect on the community of the eventual elimination of all nonconforming uses by a reasonable amortization plan more than offsets individual losses.

In *Lachapelle v. Town of Goffstown*, [225 A.2d 624 (N.H. 1967)], an ordinance permitting the nonconforming use of land as a motor vehicle junk yard for only one year after its enactment was upheld. There, after an exhaustive review of zoning and the elimination of nonconformities, the court said at 225 A.2d 627:

> Junked automobiles are considered a health and safety hazard for numerous reasons. They tend to become homes for rats and vermin, children are attracted to them and most junked cars still have gas tanks with gasoline in them. They have trunk lids which may fall shut, or the car may be ready to fall if disturbed. However, another and more subtle criticism of junked autos is that they tend to create neighborhood blight. The presence of old cars on the streets (highways) gives the neighborhood a shabby and rundown appearance. This, in turn, creates secondary reactions regarding the cleanliness and care given the neighborhood by its residents. . . .

. . . Defendants have intentionally continued their wrecking operations beyond the fixed limitation period. The only evidence regarding their enterprise is that it is a substantial business operation. No showing is made relative to defendants' business investment, value of any improvements on their land, or extent of hardship, if any, in complying with the disputed ordinance.

Upon the basis of this record we are called upon to determine whether defendants adequately met and sustained the burden they assumed in challenging reasonableness of the ordinance as it applies to them. It is argued by defendants they did so.

In support of that position they cite and lean rather heavily on *Stoner McCray System v. City of Des Moines*, [78 N.W.2d 843 (Iowa 1956)]. But we find that case neither factually comparable nor here controlling. In *Stoner McCray* this court held unreasonable, a zoning ordinance which, in effect, provided for elimination of certain billboards within two years after the enactment. However, the record there disclosed the sign company, relying on permits issued by the municipality, had promptly made substantial investments in the construction of new and costly advertising boards.

The matter of monetary expenditures, though not alone necessarily determinative, is one element to be considered whenever relevant or possible, with regard to any zoning amortization program, in the weighing of private hardship against public health, safety, morals and welfare. . . .

. . . [T]he record is devoid of any informative showing as to other possible material elements or factors manifesting unreasonableness of the subject ordinance as applied to these defendants. . . .

It is to us evident defendants have failed to show, with sufficient certainty, the amortization provision of the contested ordinance, as applied to them, is unconstitutional. Also, the ordinance being facially valid and its reasonableness fairly debatable, it must accordingly be upheld.

Resultantly we now hold the challenged amortization provision of the Cerro Gordo County Zoning Ordinance, as it applies to defendants in this case, is not unreasonable and does not constitute an unconstitutional exercise of the police power delegated by our state legislature. . . . Affirmed.

STUART, LARSON, MOORE, and BECKER, JJ., dissenting.

. . . [W]e are now confronted for the first time with a zoning law which eliminates a lawful nonconforming use after a fixed period of time under the police power. In my opinion such legislation takes property without due process of law and just compensation. . . .

. . . I will do no more than point out in passing that almost all of the legislation which has come before the courts has not been within the definition of amortization. No effort has been made to provide a method by which the amortization period could be correlated to the actual remaining life of a particular type of structure or the particular use being eliminated. Fixed periods have been provided which have varied from one to thirty or more years. . . . Courts, without tests or guidelines, have held these periods reasonable or unreasonable on an ad hoc basis. It would be difficult, if not impossible, to explain why the useful economic life of an operating automobile salvage yard is limited to five years. . . .

There is a vast difference in kind between the unexercised right to use real estate for some purpose in the future, which right may or may not ever be invoked and the exercised right to devote real estate to a lawful purpose, which right has been invoked at the expenditure of time and money by the owner. The implications and effects are not similar and the losses sustained by the respective owners are far different. Limitations on future uses deprives the owner of some prospective advantage only. The termination of an existing use necessarily results in an out-of-pocket loss to the owner. . . .

Problem

Live from New Hampshire: Andrew owns the Empire Theater in Manchester, New Hampshire, which was built in 1912 to serve as a movie theater. The theater is located in what is now a B-1 zoning district. In 1990, the city granted a building permit for interior renovations of the theater, recognizing that, although the use of property as a movie theater was not allowed in a B-1 zoning district, the use of the Empire Theater to show movies was a preexisting, nonconforming use. Following the 1990 renovations, Andrew's tenant began arranging for live concerts at the theater. Dozens of live shows, mostly rock concerts, were performed at the theater until the city notified Andrew that the use of the theater as a live entertainment venue violated the zoning ordinance. Assume that you represent the city. What arguments will you make that the concerts should be discontinued? What arguments do you anticipate that Andrew will make in response? As a matter of public policy, *should* the concerts be allowed to continue? If so, for how long? *See Conforti v. City of Manchester*, 677 A.2d 147 (N.H. 1996).

3. Flexibility Mechanisms

Although zoning aims for a certain degree of uniformity, flexibility is also needed in a number of situations. The *A Place to Start* box introduces you to some of the most common flexibility devices.

A Place to Start | **Flexibility Mechanisms**

- *The variance:* If a literal application of the zoning ordinance would cause *unnecessary hardship* to the landowner (and the hardship was not self-imposed), the board of adjustment can authorize a variance from the ordinance, if not contrary to the public interest.

- *The special exception (also called* conditional use *or* special use*):* Zoning ordinances often list specific uses that may be permitted within a particular zone, but only after further review by the board of adjustment. The legislative authority has determined that such uses are generally compatible with the uses within a particular zone, but that they require additional case-by-case analysis to protect the public health, safety, and welfare.

- *The zoning amendment and spot zoning:* Municipalities periodically update their zoning ordinances. But if amendments impact the permitted uses within only a "spot" on the zoning map, courts will scrutinize carefully the proffered justifications for the amendment to make sure it advances public, not private, interests. If not, it may be struck as illegal *spot zoning*.

DIGGING DEEPER: What is the proper balance between uniformity and flexibility? What competing policy concerns are at stake?

The variance: Under the Standard Zoning Enabling Act (SZEA), the board of adjustment has the power to grant *variances* from the strict terms of the zoning ordinance. That includes the power,

> To authorize upon appeal in specific cases such variance from the terms of the ordinance as will not be conrary to the public interest, where, owing to special conditions, a literal enforcement of the provisions of the ordinance will result in unnecessary hardship, and so that the spirit of the ordinance shall be observed and substantial justice done.

SZEA, § 7, ¶3. There are two types of variance. First, under the *use variance*, applicants seek permission to use their property for a purpose not permitted within their zoning district. For example, if the Ambler Realty Company had wanted to build an apartment house or an industrial facility on a portion of its land located within the U-2 district of the Village of Euclid, it could have applied for a variance. Second, applicants can seek a *bulk variance* (also called a *dimensional variance*) if they want a waiver of a setback requirement, height restriction, or the like.

To prevail, the applicant must prove that a literal application of the zoning ordinance would cause it *unnecessary hardship.* Importantly, the applicant's inability to comply with the ordinance must be due to some special conditions, such as an irregularly configured building lot, and not result from some action of the applicant itself (such as selling off a portion of the lot, leaving the remaining portion too narrow to comply with setback requirements).

Like the allowance of *nonconforming uses* for reasonable amortization periods, the variance can preserve the constitutionality of the jurisdiction's zoning ordinance. As the Virginia Supreme Court explained,

> Zoning ordinances, of necessity, regulate land use uniformly within large districts. It is impracticable to tailor such ordinances to meet the condition of each individual parcel within the district. The size, shape, topography or other conditions affecting such a parcel may, if the zoning ordinance is applied to it as written, render it relatively useless. Thus, a zoning ordinance, valid on its face, might be unconstitutional as applied to an individual parcel, in violation of [the federal or state constitution].

> Because a facially valid zoning ordinance may prove unconstitutional in application to a particular landowner, some device is needed to protect landowners' rights without destroying the viability of zoning ordinances. The variance traditionally has been designed to serve this function. In this role, the variance aptly has been called an "escape hatch" or "escape valve." A statute may, of course, authorize variances in cases where an ordinance's application to particular property is not unconstitutional.

Cochran v. Fairfax County Bd. of Zoning Appeals, 594 S.E.2d 571 (Va. 2004).

The special exception (or, the conditional use or special use): Under the SZEA, the board of adjustment,

> . . . may, in appropriate cases and subject to appropriate conditions and safeguards, make special exceptions to the terms of the [zoning] ordinance in harmony with its general purpose and intent and in accordance with general or specific rules therein contained.

SZEA, § 7. As we have seen, within a particular zone, the local ordinance allows certain uses as of right, and might also prohibit certain uses. As an intermediate category, ordinances often list certain specific uses that *may be permitted* within the zone, but only after further review by the board of adjustment, and the potential imposition of conditions to minimize the impact of the special use within the district.

It is important to note the distinction between the variance and the special exception. The variance grants a *waiver* from the requirements of the zoning ordinance. The factors triggering the need for such relief would be difficult for the local legislative body to anticipate in advance and to write into the ordinance. In contrast, the special exception *implements* the terms of the zoning ordinance itself. It is relatively easy to anticipate the kinds of uses that should be permitted within a district, but only upon closer examination of the individual project itself. These types of uses include hospitals, schools, churches, and others.

As the Minnesota Supreme Court explained,

> [Special exceptions] were introduced into zoning ordinances as flexibility devices. They are designed to meet the problem which arises where certain uses, although generally compatible with the basic use classification of a particular zone, should not be permitted to be located as a matter of right in every area included within the zone because of hazards inherent in the use itself or special problems which its proposed location may present. By this device, certain uses (e.g., gasoline service stations, electric substations, hospitals, schools, churches, country clubs, and the like) which may be considered essentially desirable to the community, but which should not be authorized generally in a particular zone because of considerations such as current and anticipated trafffic congestion, population density, noise, effect on adjoining land values, or other considerations involving public health, safety, or general welfare, may be permitted upon a proposed site depending upon the facts and circumstances of the particular case.

Zylka v. City of Crystal, 167 N.W.2d 45, 48-49 (Minn. 1969).

The zoning amendment: As a third flexibility device, landowners sometimes seek to have the zoning ordinance itself amended to rezone their property to a more favorable use classification. Notice that this falls within the province of the local legislative body itself, such as the city or county council. In contrast, one of the legislature's agents (usually, the board of adjustment) resolves applications for variances or special exceptions. In theory, such legislative amendments should be subject to strict democratic safeguards. As the SZEA provides,

> The legislative body of such municipality shall provide for the manner in which ... [the boundaries of zoning districts] shall be determined, ... and from time to time amended, supplemented, or changed. However, no such ... boundary shall become effective until after a public hearing in relation thereto, at which parties in interest and citizens shall have an opportunity to be heard. ...
>
> ... In case, however, of a protest against such change, signed by the owners of 20 per cent or more either of the area of the lots included in such proposed change, or of those immediately adjacent ... , such amendment shall not

ecome effective except by the favorable vote of three-fourths of all the members
of the legislative body of such municipality. . . .

SZEA, §§ 4-5.

What happens if the legislative body rezones only a *spot* on its zoning map?
In such cases, it might appear that the legislature is affording special treatment
to a relatively small group of landowners (sometimes, only a single landowner),
rather than exercising its duty to advance the general public interest. Some
courts strike down such efforts as illegal *spot zoning* if the rezoning does not
conform to a broader plan or is not justified by special circumstances. "Spot
zoning" has no precise legal meaning, but is simply a shorthand characterization of rezoning exercises that do not bear a substantial relation to the general
welfare.

Problems

To gain some familiarity with zoning's flexibility mechanisms, work through
the following problems that focus on the *variance*. Courts apply a range of tests
to determine whether a variance should have been granted. The following are
representative:

- *Test 1:* The board of adjustment has no authority to grant a variance
  unless the effect of the zoning ordinance, as applied to the piece of
  property under consideration, would, in the absence of a variance,
  interfere with all reasonable beneficial uses of the property, taken as a
  whole. *See Cochran v. Fairfax County Bd. of Zoning Appeals*, 594 S.E.2d
  571 (Va. 2004).

- *Test 2:* To justify the grant of a dimensional variance, courts may consider
  multiple factors, including the economic detriment to the applicant if the
  variance was denied, the financial hardship created by any work
  necessary to bring the building into strict compliance with the zoning
  requirements and the characteristics of the surrounding neighborhood.
  To hold otherwise would prohibit the rehabilitation of neighborhoods by
  precluding an applicant who wishes to renovate a building in a blighted
  area from obtaining the necessary variances. *See Hertzberg v. Zoning Bd.
  of Adjustment*, 721 A.2d 43 (Pa. 1998).

Consider the factual scenarios below. Is the applicant entitled to a variance
under Test 1 or Test 2, respectively? Does the applicant seek a *use* variance
or a *dimensional* variance, and should that matter? What do you think is the
correct outcome, and why?

1. *The side-load garage:*   Michael R. Bratti was the owner of a tract of land
approximately 20,470 square feet in area. The property was zoned R-2, a

residential classification permitting two dwelling units per acre, and was improved by a home in which Bratti had resided for eight years. The zoning ordinance required side yard setbacks of at least 15 feet from the property lines. Bratti's existing home fit well within the setbacks.

Bratti filed an application with the board of zoning adjustment for variances. He proposed to demolish his existing home and erect a much larger house on the site. The proposed structure would come within 13 feet of the northerly property line, rather than the 15 feet required by the ordinance, and would be further extended into the setback area by three exterior chimneys which would extend beyond the northerly wall of the house. The proposed house would be 71 feet wide and 76 feet from front to back. The proposed encroachment into the side yard setback would extend the entire 76-foot depth of the house.

It was undisputed that Bratti's proposed house could be built upon the existing lot without any need for a variance by simply moving it two feet to the south, plus the additional distance required by the chimneys. Bratti explained to the Board, however, that he desired to have a "side-load" garage on the south side of his house and that a reduction of two feet of open space on the south side would make it inconvenient for vehicles to turn into the garage. The present house had a "front-load" garage that opened directly toward the street. When it was pointed out to Bratti that he could avoid this problem by reconfiguring his proposed house to contain a "front-load" garage, he responded that such a house would have less "curb appeal" than the design he proposed.

If the house were built in its proposed location, but reduced in size by two feet to comply with the zoning ordinance, there would be a resulting loss of 152 square feet of living space. The topography of the lot was such that it rose 42 feet vertically throughout its 198-foot depth from the street to the rear property line. However, there were two relatively level areas shown on the plans for the proposed dwelling, one in front of the house and one in the rear. It was conceded that an additional 152 square feet of living space could have been constructed in either of these areas, but Bratti explained that he wanted to use the level area in front of the house as a play area for children and for additional parking, and that he was unwilling to encroach upon the level area in the rear because he desired to use it as a large outdoor courtyard which he said was "the central idea in the house."

The proposed dwelling had two stories. A third story could have been added as a matter of right, without variances. Bratti conceded that this could easily be done and would more than accommodate the 152 square feet lost by compliance with the zoning ordinance, but that it would be aesthetically undesirable, causing the house to appear to be a "towering structure" as seen from the street. *See Cochran v. Fairfax County Bd. of Zoning Appeals*, 594 S.E.2d 571 (Va. 2004).

2. *Living on the corner:*   Jack D. Nunley and Diana M. Nunley owned a corner lot in the Town of Pulaski that contained .6248 acre. The lot was bounded by public streets on three sides. A street 40 feet wide ran along the front of the property and the intersection of that street with a street approximately 30 feet wide formed the southeastern corner of the lot. The 30-foot street ran northward from the intersection, forming the eastern boundary of the lot, and then curved to the west to form the lot's northern boundary. The curvature was gradual, having a radius of 34.53 feet. This curve formed the northeasterly corner of the lot.

The property was zoned R-1, a residential classification that contained a special provision relating to corner lots: "The side yard on the side facing the side street shall be at least 15 feet from both main and accessory structures."

The Nunleys petitioned the board of zoning adjustment for a variance from the required 15-foot setback to zero feet, in order to construct a garage at the northeast corner of the lot, the northeast corner of which would be placed tangent to the curving property line. There was no existing garage on the property, and the Nunleys explained that placing a garage in this location would provide the easiest access to the street. The topography of the lot was difficult, the curve along the 30-foot street lying at a considerable elevation above the floor level of the existing house. The garage could be constructed closer to the house without the need for a variance, but this would require construction of a ramp that would add considerably to the expense of the project. Also, the Nunleys explained, there was a stone retaining wall, five feet in height, behind the house that would be weakened or destroyed if the garage were to be built closer to the house.

Neighbors objected, pointing out to the board of zoning appeals that the construction of the garage so close to the corner would create a blind area that would be dangerous for traffic coming around the curve on the 30-foot street. They also complained that it would be an "eyesore" and would destroy existing vegetation. *See Cochran v. Fairfax County Bd. of Zoning Appeals,* 594 S.E.2d 571 (Va. 2004).

3. *Give me shelter:*   Miryam's is a nonprofit social service agency that provides shelter and services to homeless women. Miryam's sought zoning approval to convert a vacant four-story building into office space, counseling rooms and a reception area on the first floor, a living room, dining room and kitchen on the second floor, and 10 bedrooms with two beds in each on the top two floors to house 20 women. The building was formerly occupied by a bank and 12 apartment units, but has stood vacant for many years. It is located in a C-4 commercial zoning district that permits lodging houses but not group care facilities or institutional facilities.

Miryam's applied for the zoning permit characterizing its intended use of the building as a "lodging house." The City of Pittsburgh zoning ordinance requires that a lodging house contain 5,000 square feet, plus an additional 300 square feet for each sleeping room in excess of three. The ordinance requires a lodging house to provide one parking stall for each of the first 20 sleeping rooms, and one parking stall for every two sleeping rooms in excess of 20 rooms. Thus, under these requirements, Miryam's was required to have 7,100 square feet of space and 10 parking stalls in order to be approved as a lodging house. The property contains only 3,409 square feet and contains no parking stalls.

Miryam's clients would likely not be driving or parking motor vehicles; the clients and some of the employees would either be using public transportation or walking. Public parking lots were located nearby and a neighbor had offered to lease parking spaces to the employees. *See Hertzberg v. Zoning Bd. of Adjustment of Pittsburgh*, 721 A.2d 43 (Pa. 1998).

B. WHAT CAN BE REGULATED?

In *Euclid v. Ambler*, the U.S. Supreme Court championed the protection of the single-family neighborhood as it upheld the constitutional validity of zoning. Among other things, the Court believed that the exclusion of apartment houses, industry, and other more intensive uses would "increase the safety and security of home life" and "preserve a more favorable environment in which to rear children." But the district court had painted a far darker picture, asserting:

> The purpose to be accomplished is really to regulate the mode of living of persons who may hereafter inhabit it. In the last analysis, the result to be accomplished is to classify the population and segregate them according to their income or situation in life.

Ambler Realty Co. v. Village of Euclid, 297 F. 307, 316 (N.D. Ohio 1924).

Zoning today is ubiquitous, but the central tension highlighted in the *Euclid* litigation remains. Inevitably, zoning involves some degree of *exclusion* and *segregation* as it determines the compatibility of uses and assigns them to particular areas within the jurisdiction. Also inevitably, at some point the regulation of *uses* spills over into the regulation of *people*. Where should courts draw line between permissible (and generally, desirable) and impermissible zoning regulations? Constitutional and statutory provisions provide guidance, as explained in the *A Place to Start* box below.

A Place to Start | **Challenging Zoning Ordinances**

- *Equal protection clause of the U.S. Constitution:*
  - *Rational basis test:* The rational basis standard is the default test. Under it, courts ask whether the challenged law bears a *rational* relationship to a *permissible* (or legitimate) state objective. If not, then the court will strike the

law as an arbitrary exercise of the police power (or declare it unconstitutional as applied to the plaintiff).

■ *Strict scrutiny:* If the challenged law involves a *suspect class* (such as race, national origin, religious affiliation, or alienage) or a *fundamental right* (such as the right to vote or the freedoms of speech, religion, and association), then the government must demonstrate that the challenged law is *necessary* to further a *compelling* governmental interest.

■ *The federal Fair Housing Act:* We have already studied the FHA in connection with landlord-tenant law (Chapter 4) and with real estate transactions (Chapter 7).

■ *42 U.S.C. § 3604(a):* Recall that this section makes it unlawful, "To refuse to sell or rent . . . , *or otherwise make unavailable* or deny, a dwelling to any person because of race, color, religion, sex, familial status, or national origin" (emphasis added). The U.S. Supreme Court has held that this section is broad enough to reach discriminatory zoning ordinances.

■ *Disparate impact liability:* Plaintiffs need not demonstrate that the defendant acted with a discriminatory *intent*. Instead, they can prevail if they can adequately prove that the challenged law had a discriminatory *effect* upon a group protected under the Fair Housing Act.

DIGGING DEEPER: As a matter of litigation strategy, how should zoning challengers decide whether to bring their claims under federal or state constitutional law, or under the Fair Housing Act? From the perspective of local governments, how can officials craft ordinances that fit comfortably within the permissible statutory and constitutional framework?

In this section, we will look at three areas of tension. First, we will explore the meaning of *single family*, as defined by many zoning ordinances. Next, we will examine the benefits and challenges of *aesthetic regulation*. Finally, we will look at the problem of *exclusionary zoning* and housing that is not widely affordable.

1. Regulating "Family" Composition

Village of Belle Terre v. Boraas

416 U.S. 1 (1974)

Reading Guide

Can a group of students make up a "family"? If not, can students be excluded from single-family zoning districts? Do you agree with the majority or with the dissenting opinion?

DOUGLAS, J. [joined by BURGER, C.J. and STEWART, WHITE, BLACKMUN, POWELL, and REHNQUIST, JJ.]

Belle Terre is a village on Long Island's north shore of about 220 homes inhabited by 700 people. Its total land area is less than one square mile. It has restricted land use to one-family dwellings excluding lodging houses, boarding houses, fraternity houses, or multiple-dwelling houses. The word "family" as used in the ordinance means,

> (o)ne or more persons related by blood, adoption, or marriage, living and cook-ing together as a single housekeeping unit, exclusive of household servants. A number of persons but not exceeding two (2) living and cooking together as a single housekeeping unit through not related by blood, adoption, or marriage shall be deemed to constitute a family.

Appellees, the Dickmans, are owners of a house in the village and leased it in December 1971 for a term of 18 months to Michael Truman. Later Bruce Boraas became a colessee. Then Anne Parish moved into the house along with three others. These six are students at nearby State University at Stony Brook and none is related to the other by blood, adoption, or marriage. When the village served the Dickmans with an "Order to Remedy Violations" of the ordinance, the owners plus three tenants thereupon brought this action under 42 U.S.C. s 1983 for an injunction and a judgment declaring the ordinance unconstitu-tional. The District Court held the ordinance constitutional, . . . and the Court of Appeals reversed, one judge dissenting. . . .

This case brings to this Court a different phase of local zoning regulations from those we have previously reviewed. . . .

Our decision in *Berman v. Parker*, 348 U.S. 26 [(1954)], sustained a land use project in the District of Columbia against a landowner's claim that the taking violated the Due Process Clause and the Just Compensation Clause of the Fifth Amendment. The essence of the argument against the law was, while taking prop-erty for ridding an area of slums was permissible, taking it "merely to develop a better balanced, more attractive community" was not . . . . We refused to limit the concept of public welfare that may be enhanced by zoning regulations. We said:

> Miserable and disreputable housing conditions may do more than spread disease and crime and immorality. They may also suffocate the spirit by reducing the people who live there to the status of cattle. They may indeed make living an almost insufferable burden. They may also be an ugly sore, a blight on the com-munity which robs it of charm, which makes it a place from which men turn. The misery of housing may despoil a community as an open sewer may ruin a river.

> We do not sit to determine whether a particular housing project is or is not desirable. The concept of the public welfare is broad and inclusive. . . . The values it represents are spiritual as well as physical, aesthetic as well as monetary. It is within the power of the legislature to determine that the community should be beautiful as well as healthy, spacious as well as clean, well-balanced as well as carefully patrolled.

Id., at 32-33.

The present ordinance is challenged on several grounds: that it interferes with a person's right to travel; that it interferes with the right to migrate to and settle within a State; that it bars people who are uncongenial to the present residents; that it expresses the social preferences of the residents for groups that will be congenial to them; that social homogeneity is not a legitimate interest of government; that the restriction of those whom the neighbors do not like trenches on the newcomers' rights of privacy; that it is of no rightful concern to villagers whether the residents are married or unmarried; that the ordinance is antithetical to the Nation's experience, ideology, and self-perception as an open, egalitarian, and integrated society.

We find none of these reasons in the record before us. It is not aimed at transients. . . . It involves no procedural disparity inflicted on some but not on others. . . . It involves no "fundamental" right guaranteed by the Constitution, such as voting, *Harper v. Virginia State Board*, 383 U.S. 663; the right of association, *NAACP v. Alabama ex rel. Patterson*, 357 U.S. 449; the right of access to the courts, *NAACP v. Button*, 371 U.S. 415; or any rights of privacy, cf. *Griswold v. Connecticut*, 381 U.S. 479. . . . We deal with economic and social legislation where legislatures have historically drawn lines which we respect against the charge of violation of the Equal Protection Clause if the law be "reasonable, not arbitrary" (quoting *F. S. Royster Guano Co. v. Virginia*, 253 U.S. 412, 415) and bears "a rational relationship to a (permissible) state objective." *Reed v. Reed*, 404 U.S. 71, 76.

It is said, however, that if two unmarried people can constitute a "family," there is no reason why three or four may not. But every line drawn by a legislature leaves some out that might well have been included. . . . That exercise of discretion, however, is a legislative, not a judicial, function. . . .

The ordinance places no ban on other forms of association, for a "family" may, so far as the ordinance is concerned, entertain whomever it likes.

The regimes of boarding houses, fraternity houses, and the like present urban problems. More people occupy a given space; more cars rather continuously pass by; more cars are parked; noise travels with crowds.

A quiet place where yards are wide, people few, and motor vehicles restricted are legitimate guidelines in a land-use project addressed to family needs. This goal is a permissible one within *Berman v. Parker, supra*. The police power is not confined to elimination of filth, stench, and unhealthy places. It is ample to lay out zones where family values, youth values, and the blessings of quiet seclusion and clean air make the area a sanctuary for people. . . . Reversed.

Brennan, J., dissenting [omitted].

Marshall, J., dissenting.

In my view, the disputed classification burdens the students' fundamental rights of association and privacy guaranteed by the First and Fourteenth

Amendments. Because the application of strict equal protection scrutiny is therefore required, I am at odds with my Brethren's conclusion that the ordinance may be sustained on a showing that it bears a rational relationship to the accomplishment of legitimate governmental objectives. . . .

Had the owners alone brought this suit alleging that the restrictive ordinance deprived them of their property or was an irrational legislative classification, I would agree that the ordinance would have to be sustained. Our role is not and should not be to sit as a zoning board of appeals.

I would also agree with the majority that local zoning authorities may properly act in furtherance of the objectives asserted to be served by the ordinance at issue here: restricting uncontrolled growth, solving traffic problems, keeping rental costs at a reasonable level, and making the community attractive to families. . . . And, it is appropriate that we afford zoning authorities considerable latitude in choosing the means by which to implement such purposes. But deference does not mean abdication. This Court has an obligation to ensure that zoning ordinances, even when adopted in furtherance of such legitimate aims, do not infringe upon fundamental constitutional rights. . . .

. . . Zoning officials properly concern themselves with the uses of land— with, for example, the number and kind of dwellings to be constructed in a certain neighborhood or the number of persons who can reside in those dwellings. But zoning authorities cannot validly consider who those persons are, what they believe, or how they choose to live, whether they are Negro or white, Catholic or Jew, Republican or Democrat, married or unmarried.

My disagreement with the Court today is based upon my view that the ordinance in this case unnecessarily burdens appellees' First Amendment freedom of association and their constitutionally guaranteed right to privacy. Our decisions establish that the First and Fourteenth Amendments protect the freedom to choose one's associates. . . . Constitutional protection is extended, not only to modes of association that are political in the usual sense, but also to those that pertain to the social and economic benefit of the members. . . . The selection of one's living companions involves similar choices as to the emotional, social, or economic benefits to be derived from alternative living arrangements.

The freedom of association is often inextricably entwined with the constitutionally guaranteed right of privacy. The right to "establish a home" is an essential part of the liberty guaranteed by the Fourteenth Amendment. . . . And the Constitution secures to an individual a freedom "to satisfy his intellectual and emotional needs in the privacy of his own home." *Stanley v. Georgia*, 394 U.S. 557, 565 (1969). . . . Constitutionally protected privacy is, in Mr. Justice Brandeis' words, "as against the Government, the right to be let alone . . . the right most valued by civilized man." *Olmstead v. United States*, 277 U.S. 438, 478 (1928) (dissenting opinion). The choice of household companions—of whether a person's "intellectual and emotional needs" are best met by living with family, friends, professional associates, or others—involves deeply personal considerations as to the kind and quality of intimate relationships within the home. That decision surely falls within the ambit of the right to privacy protected by the Constitution. *See Roe v. Wade*, 410 U.S. 113, 153 (1973). . . .

The instant ordinance discriminates on the basis of just such a personal lifestyle choice as to household companions. It permits any number of persons related by blood or marriage, be it two or twenty, to live in a single household, but it limits to two the number of unrelated persons bound by profession, love, friendship, religious or political affiliation, or mere economics who can occupy a single home. . . . Belle Terre imposes upon those who deviate from the community norm in their choice of living companions significantly greater restrictions than are applied to residential groups who are related by blood or marriage, and compose the established order within the community. . . . The village has, in effect, acted to fence out those individuals whose choice of lifestyle differs from that of its current residents. . . .

This is not a case where the Court is being asked to nullify a township's sincere efforts to maintain its residential character by preventing the operation of rooming houses, fraternity houses, or other commercial or high-density residential uses. Unquestionably, a town is free to restrict such uses. Moreover, as a general proposition, I see no constitutional infirmity in a town's limiting the density of use in residential areas by zoning regulations which do not discriminate on the basis of constitutionally suspect criteria. This ordinance, however, limits the density of occupancy of only those homes occupied by unrelated persons. It thus reaches beyond control of the use of land or the density of population, and undertakes to regulate the way people choose to associate with each other within the privacy of their own homes.

Because I believe that this zoning ordinance creates a classification which impinges upon fundamental personal rights, it can withstand constitutional scrutiny only upon a clear showing that the burden imposed is necessary to protect a compelling and substantial governmental interest. . . . And, once it be determined that a burden has been placed upon a constitutional right, the onus of demonstrating that no less intrusive means will adequately protect the compelling state interest and that the challenged statute is sufficiently narrowly drawn, is upon the party seeking to justify the burden. . . .

A variety of justifications have been proffered in support of the village's ordinance. It is claimed that the ordinance controls population density, prevents noise, traffic and parking problems, and preserves the rent structure of the community and its attractiveness to families. As I noted earlier, these are all legitimate and substantial interests of government. But I think it clear that the means chosen to accomplish these purposes are both overinclusive and underinclusive, and that the asserted goals could be as effectively achieved by means of an ordinance that did not discriminate on the basis of constitutionally protected choices of lifestyle. The ordinance imposes no restriction whatsoever on the number of persons who may live in a house, as long as they are related by marital or sanguinary bonds—presumably no matter how distant their relationship. Nor does the ordinance restrict the number of income earners who may contribute to rent in such a household, or the number of automobiles that may be maintained by its occupants. In that sense the ordinance is underinclusive. On the other hand, the statute restricts the number of unrelated persons who may live in a home to no more than two. It would therefore prevent three unrelated people from occupying a dwelling even if among them they had but one income and no vehicles. While an extended family of a dozen or more might live in a small bungalow, three elderly and retired persons could not occupy the large manor house next door. Thus the statute is also grossly overinclusive to accomplish its intended purposes. . . .

Notes

1. *The legal claim:* Did the plaintiffs bring a statutory or constitutional challenge? If the latter, was it brought under federal and/or state law? Was it a facial or as-applied challenge? Can you articulate the plaintiffs' precise claim? It does not appear in its entirety in this opinion, but you should be able to piece it together from the analysis of the majority and the dissent.

2. *The legal test:* What test did the Court apply to determine the validity of Belle Terre's zoning ordinance?

3. *Policy:* In your opinion, should communities reserve certain districts for single-family use? If so, how should the zoning ordinance define single-family use? Be specific.

4. *The status of the law today:* Despite its more than 40-year-old conception of "family," *Belle Terre* remains good law today. *See, e.g., Ames Rental Property Ass'n v. City of Ames*, 736 N.W.2d 255 (Iowa 2007), *cert. denied*, 552 U.S. 1099 (2008) (upholding zoning ordinance that defines "family" as any number of related persons, or as no more than three unrelated persons). However, if the definition impinges on the ability of blood relatives to live together (particularly those with custody of minor children), then the ordinance might be found to lack a rational basis. *See, e.g., Moore v. City of East Cleveland*, 431 U.S. 494 (1977) (striking restriction of housing code limiting occupants of residences to specified degrees of relationship, which prevented a grandmother and two grandsons of different parentage from living together). In contrast, some state constitutions provide broader protection for various living arrangements. *See, e.g., McMinn v. Oyster Bay*, 488 N.E.2d 1240 (N.Y. 1985) (holding invalid under state constitution zoning ordinance's definition of "family" as any number of persons related by blood, marriage, or adoption, or as two persons not so related but both of whom are 62 years of age or older).

5. *Group homes for those needing supervision or assistance:* Many communities have supervised homes for persons with disabilities, the elderly, recovering addicts, troubled teenagers, and other groups that might not fit the

zoning ordinance's definition of "family." In *City of Cleburne v. Cleburne Living Center,* 473 U.S. 432 (1985), the Supreme Court struck under the equal protection clause a special permit requirement imposed on group homes for persons with mental disabilities, but not imposed on other group homes including fraternities. The Court purported to apply the deferential rational basis test, but Justice Marshall's concurring opinion argued that the majority had subjected the ordinance to a heightened level of scrutiny.

2. Regulating Aesthetics

State ex rel. Stoyanoff v. Berkeley

458 S.W.2d 305 (Mo. 1970)

Reading Guide

Ladue is a wealthy suburb of St. Louis, with a population of about 8,500. Its residents enjoy one of the highest median household income levels in the nation. The plaintiffs wanted to build an ultra-modern house in a traditional, well-established neighborhood. Should the city be allowed to prevent the plaintiffs from erecting a pyramid-shaped structure with triangular windows and doors?

PRITCHARD, COMMISSIONER.

Upon summary judgment the trial court issued a peremptory writ of mandamus to compel appellant [Berkeley, Building Commissioner for the City of Ladue,] to issue a residential building permit to respondents [Dimiter and Joan Stoyanoff]. The trial court's judgment is that the below-mentioned ordinances are violative of Section 10, Article I of the Constitution of Missouri, 1945 . . . in that restrictions placed by the ordinances on the use of property deprive the owners of their property without due process of law. Relators' petition pleads that they applied to appellant Building Commissioner for a building permit to allow them to construct a single family residence in the City of Ladue, and that plans and specifications were submitted for the proposed residence, which was unusual in design, "but complied with all existing building and zoning regulations and ordinances of the City of Ladue, Missouri."

It is further pleaded that relators were refused a building permit for the construction of their proposed residence upon the ground that the permit was not approved by the Architectural Board of the City of Ladue. Ordinance 131, as amended by Ordinance 281 of that city, purports to set up an Architectural Board to approve plans and specifications for buildings and structures erected within the city and in a preamble to,

> conform to certain minimum architectural standards of appearance and conformity with surrounding structures, and that unsightly, grotesque and unsuitable

structures, detrimental to the stability of value and the welfare of surrounding property, structures and residents, and to the general welfare and happiness of the community, be avoided, and that appropriate standards of beauty and conformity be fostered and encouraged.

It is asserted in the petition that the ordinances are invalid, illegal and void, "are unconstitutional in that they are vague and provide no standard nor uniform rule by which to guide the architectural board," that the city acted in excess of statutory powers . . . in enacting the ordinance, which "attempt to allow respondent to impose aesthetic standards for buildings in the City of Ladue, and are in excess of the powers granted the City of Ladue by said statute."

. . . Richard D. Shelton, Mayor of the City of Ladue, deponed . . . that the City of Ladue constitutes one of the finer suburban residential areas of Metropolitan St. Louis, the homes therein are considerably more expensive than in cities of comparable size, being homes on lots from three fourths of an acre to three or more acres each; that a zoning ordinance was enacted by the city regulating the height, number of stories, size of buildings, percentage of lot occupancy, yard sizes, and the location and use of buildings and land for trade, industry, residence and other purposes; that the zoning regulations were made in accordance with a comprehensive plan "designed to promote the health and general welfare of the residents of the City of Ladue," which in furtherance of said objectives duly enacted said Ordinances numbered 131 and 281. . . . It is then pleaded that relators' description of their proposed residence as "'unusual in design' is the understatement of the year. It is in fact a monstrosity of grotesque design, which would seriously impair the value of property in the neighborhood."

The affidavit of Harold C. Simon, a developer of residential subdivisions in St. Louis County, is that he is familiar with relators' lot upon which they seek to build a house, and with the surrounding houses in the neighborhood; that the houses therein existent are virtually all two-story houses of conventional architectural design, such as Colonial, French Provincial or English; and that the house which relators propose to construct is of ultramodern design which would clash with and not be in conformity with any other house in the entire neighborhood. It is Mr. Simon's opinion that the design and appearance of relators' proposed residence would have a substantial adverse effect upon the market values of other residential property in the neighborhood, such average market value ranging from $60,000 to $85,000 each.

. . . [Russell H. Riley, consultant for the city, stated that the] . . . ordinance which has been adopted by the City of Ladue is typical of those which have been adopted by a number of suburban cities in St. Louis County and in similar cities throughout the United States, the need therefor being based upon the protection of existing property values by preventing the construction of houses that are in complete conflict with the general type of houses in a given area. The intrusion into this neighborhood of relators' unusual, grotesque and nonconforming structure would have a substantial adverse effect on market values of other homes in the immediate area. According to Mr. Riley the standards of Ordinance 131, as amended by Ordinance 281, are usually and customarily applied in city planning work and are:

> (1) whether the proposed house meets the customary architectural requirements in appearance and design for a house of the particular type which is proposed (whether it be Colonial, Tudor English, French Provincial, or Modern),

> (2) whether the proposed house is in general conformity with the style and design of surrounding structures, and

> (3) whether the proposed house lends itself to the proper architectural development of the City; and that in applying said standards the Architectural Board and its Chairman are to determine whether the proposed house will have an adverse affect on the stability of values in the surrounding area.

Photographic exhibits of relators' proposed residence were also attached to Mr. Riley's affidavit. They show the residence to be of a pyramid shape, with a flat top, and with triangular shaped windows or doors at one or more corners.

[R]elators' position is that "the creation by the City of Ladue of an architectural board for the purpose of promoting and maintaining 'general conformity with the style and design of surrounding structures' is totally unauthorized by our Enabling Statute." (ss 89.020, 89.040, RSMo 1959, V.A.M.S.) It is further contended by relators that Ordinances 131 and 281 are invalid and unconstitutional as being an unreasonable and arbitrary exercise of the police power (as based entirely on aesthetic values); and that the same are invalid as an unlawful delegation of legislative powers (to the Architectural Board).

Section 89.020 provides:

> For the purpose of promoting health, safety, morals or the general welfare of the community, the legislative body of all cities, towns, and villages is hereby empowered to regulate and restrict the height, number of stories, and size of buildings and other structures, the percentage of lot that may be occupied, the size of yards, courts, and other open spaces, the density of population, the preservation of features of historical significance, and the location and use of buildings, structures and land for trade, industry, residence or other purposes.

Section 89.040 provides:

> Such regulations shall be made in accordance with a comprehensive plan and designed to lessen congestion in the streets; to secure safety from fire, panic and other dangers; to promote health and the general welfare; to provide adequate light and air; to prevent the overcrowding of land; to avoid undue concentration of population; to preserve features of historical significance; to facilitate the adequate provision of transportation, water, sewerage, schools, parks, and other public requirements. *Such regulations shall be made with reasonable consideration, among other things, to the character of the district and its peculiar suitability for particular uses, and with a view to conserving the values of buildings*

and encouraging the most appropriate use of land throughout such municipality.
(Italics added.)

Relators say that "Neither Sections 89.020 or 89.040 nor any other provision of Chapter 89 mentions or gives a city the authority to regulate architectural design and appearance. There exists no provision providing for an architectural board and no entity even remotely resembling such a board is mentioned under the enabling legislation." Relators conclude that the City of Ladue lacked any power to adopt Ordinance 131 as amended by Ordinance 281. . . . As to this aspect of the appeal relators rely upon the 1961 decision of *State ex rel. Magidson v. Henze*, 342 S.W.2d 261. That case had the identical question presented. . . . The court held that s 89.020, RSMo 1949, V.A.M.S., does not grant to the city the right to impose upon the landowner aesthetic standards for the buildings he chooses to erect.

As is clear from the affidavits and attached exhibits, the City of Ladue is an area composed principally of residences of the general types of Colonial, French Provincial and English Tudor. The city has a comprehensive plan of zoning to maintain the general character of buildings therein. The *Magidson* case, supra, did not consider the effect of s 89.040, supra, and the italicized portion relating to the character of the district, its suitability for particular uses, and the conservation of the values of buildings therein. These considerations, sanctioned by statute, are directly related to the general welfare of the community. . . . In *Marrs v. City of Oxford* (D.C.D. Kan.) 24 F.2d 541, 548, it was said, "The stabilizing of property values, and giving some assurance to the public that, if property is purchased in a residential district, its value as such will be preserved, is probably the most cogent reason back of zoning ordinances." The preamble to Ordinance 131 . . . demonstrates that its purpose is to conform to the dictates of s 89.040, with reference to preserving values of property by zoning procedure and restrictions on the use of property. . . . [In *Deimeke v. State Highway Commission*, Mo., 444 S.W.2d 480, 484] it is said, "Property use which offends sensibilities and debases property values affects not only the adjoining property owners in that vicinity but the general public as well because when such property values are destroyed or seriously impaired, the tax base of the community is affected and the public suffers economically as a result."

Relators say further that Ordinances 131 and 281 are invalid and unconstitutional as being an unreasonable and arbitrary exercise of the police power. It is argued that a mere reading of these ordinances shows that they are based entirely on aesthetic factors. . . . The argument ignores the further provisos in the ordinance: ". . . and that unsightly, grotesque and unsuitable structures, *detrimental to the stability of value and the welfare of surrounding property, structures, and residents, and to the general welfare and happiness of the community*, be avoided, and that appropriate standards of beauty and conformity be fostered and encouraged." (Italics added.) . . . [T]he aesthetic factor to be taken into account by the Architectural Board is not to be considered alone. Along with that inherent factor is the effect that the proposed residence would have upon the property values in the area. . . . The area under consideration is clearly, from the record, a fashionable one. In *State ex rel. Civello v. City of New Orleans*, 97 So. 440, 444, the court said,

> If by the term "aesthetic considerations" is meant a regard merely for outward appearances, for good taste in the matter of the beauty of the neighborhood itself, we do not observe any substantial reason for saying that such a consideration is not a matter of general welfare. The beauty of a fashionable residence neighborhood in a city is for the comfort and happiness of the residents, and it sustains in a general way the value of property in the neighborhood.

. . . The denial by appellant of a building permit for relators' highly modernistic residence in this area where traditional Colonial, French Provincial and English Tudor styles of architecture are erected does not appear to be arbitrary and unreasonable when the basic purpose to be served is that of the general welfare of persons in the entire community.

In addition to the above-stated purpose in the preamble to Ordinance 131, it establishes an Architectural Board of three members, all of whom must be architects. Meetings of the Board are to be open to the public. . . . The Board shall disapprove the application if it determines the proposed structure will constitute an unsightly, grotesque or unsuitable structure in appearance, detrimental to the welfare of surrounding property or residents. . . . If the Board's disapproval is given and the applicant refuses to comply with recommendations, the Building Commissioner shall refuse the permit. Thereafter provisions are made for an appeal to the Council of the city for review of the decision of the Architectural Board. . . .

Relators claim that the above provisions of the ordinance amount to an unconstitutional delegation of power by the city to the Architectural Board. It is argued that the Board cannot be given the power to determine what is unsightly   and   grotesque   and   that   the   standards . . . are inadequate. . . . Ordinances 131 and 281 are sufficient in their general standards calling for a factual determination of the suitability of any proposed structure with reference to the character of the surrounding neighborhood and to the determination of any adverse effect on the general welfare and preservation of property values of the community. . . .

The judgment is reversed. . . .

Notes

1. *Regulating architectural design:*   The property owners wanted to construct what the court described as a "highly modernistic" residence in a wealthy, traditional neighborhood. The proposed design featured a pyramid-

shaped house, with triangular windows or doors, and with a flat top. Should the owners have been allowed to build such a house? Who should be authorized to make such a decision?

2. *Aesthetics alone?*   In *Berman v. Parker*, 348 U.S. 26 (1954), the Supreme Court stated in dictum that aesthetics alone provided a sufficient basis for police power regulation: "It is within the power of the legislature to determine that the community should be beautiful as well as healthy, spacious as well as clean, well-balanced as well as carefully patrolled." By the end of the 20th century, a majority of decided opinions held that aesthetic concerns alone supplied a sufficient police power rationale for regulation. Today, most communities incorporate some aesthetic elements into their zoning ordinances, such as the regulation of historic preservation and advertising signs. However, such regulations generally do not rely solely on aesthetic justifications (except perhaps in some wealthy suburban areas and vacation communities). Powell on Real Property § 79D.02(2) (Michael Allan Wolf, gen. ed. 2015). The issue had not been well settled by the time of the *Stoyanoff* decision. Did Ladue base its ordinance solely on aesthetic considerations, or did it rely on additional concerns?

3. *Architecture as speech?*   Do architectural controls impinge on the right of free speech? If so, what would be the appropriate test under substantive due process? Who would be the proper plaintiff—the architect, the landowners, and/or the construction company? Although some commentators believe that architecture constitutes speech and that architectural regulations impermissibly purport to regulate the content of that speech, the U.S. Supreme Court has not so held. Daniel R. Mandelker, Land Use Law § 11.01 (5th ed. 2003, LexisNexis).

Problem

No shiny mobile homes: The zoning ordinance of Catawba County, North Carolina, contained the following provisions related to single-wide mobile homes:

> (A) Exterior finish. The exterior siding shall consist predominantly of vinyl or aluminum lap siding (whose reflectivity does not exceed that of flat white paint), wood or hardboard comparable in composition, appearance and durability to the exterior siding commonly used in standard residential construction.

> (B) Roof construction and pitch. The roof shall be designed to have a minimum rise of $2\frac{1}{2}$ feet for each 12 feet of horizontal run and finished with a type of shingle that is commonly used in standard residential construction.

Before amending its ordinance to include the above provisions, the county had received numerous citizen petitions to rezone portions of the county to exclude or restrict single-wide mobile homes. A group of mobile home manufacturers and building material suppliers brought suit, claiming, among other things, that the ordinance violated the due process or equal protection clauses of the U.S. Constitution.

Assuming *Stoyanoff* is binding precedent in the jurisdiction, should the court uphold the ordinance? Precedent aside, in your opinion should the court uphold the ordinance as a matter of public policy? Do you think the county designed the ordinance to protect property values or to accomplish some other purpose? What effect do you think the ordinance might have? *See CMH Mfg., Inc. v. Catawba Cnty.*, 994 F. Supp. 697 (W.D.N.C. 1998).

3. Exclusionary Zoning

In *Village of Belle Terre v. Boraas*, the Supreme Court upheld the village's restrictive definition of "family," even though the definition limited the number of students or other unrelated people who could live in single-family zones within the village. But can zoning go even farther, and incorporate measures with the purpose or effect of excluding people on the basis of socio-economic status, race, or some other factor?

Such practices—known as *exclusionary zoning*—have been the subject of equal protection challenges under the federal and state constitutions. But they can also be challenged under the federal Fair Housing Act (FHA) of 1968. Recall from Chapter 4 (section C.3) that the act makes it unlawful,

> To refuse to sell or rent after the making of a bona fide offer, or to refuse to negotiate for the sale or rental of, *or otherwise make unavailable* or deny, a dwelling to any person because of race, color, religion, sex, familial status, or national origin.

FHA, 42 U.S.C. § 3604(a) (emphasis added).

The FHA is broad enough to reach discriminatory zoning ordinances. But how could plaintiffs ever prove that a discriminatory intent motivated the passage of an exclusionary zoning ordinance? Such "smoking gun" evidence is notoriously difficult to acquire. As the Supreme Court has made clear, FHA plaintiffs need not prove discriminatory intent, but can instead make out a case under the so-called *disparate impact* theory of liability:

> . . . [T]he phrase "otherwise make unavailable" [in 42 U.S.C. § 3604(a)] is of central importance. . . . Congress' use of the phrase "otherwise make unavailable" refers to the consequences of an action rather than the actor's intent . . . This results-oriented language counsels in favor of recognizing disparate-impact liability. . . . Recognition of disparate-impact claims is consistent with the FHA's central purpose. The FHA . . . was enacted to eradicate discriminatory practices within [the housing] sector of our Nation's economy. . . . These unlawful practices include zoning laws and other housing restrictions that function unfairly to exclude minorities from certain neighborhoods without any sufficient justification.

Suits targeting such practices reside at the heartland of disparate-impact liability. . . . The availability of disparate-impact liability, furthermore, has allowed private developers . . . to protect their property rights by stopping municipalities from enforcing arbitrary and, in practice, discriminatory ordinances barring the construction of certain types of housing units. . . . Recognition of disparate-impact liability under the FHA also plays a role in uncovering discriminatory intent: It permits plaintiffs to counteract unconscious prejudices and disguised animus that escape easy classification as disparate treatment. In this way disparate-impact liability may prevent segregated housing patterns that might otherwise result from covert and illicit stereotyping.

Texas Dep't of Housing & Cmty. Affairs v. Inclusive Communities Project, Inc., 135 S. Ct. 2507, 2521-22 (2015). In clarifying that courts have long recognized disparate impact liability under the FHA, the Court cited to several cases, including the *City of Black Jack* case that follows.

United States v. City of Black Jack, Missouri

508 F.2d 1179 (8th Cir. 1974), *cert. denied,* 422 U.S. 1042 (1975)

Reading Guide

The previous case, *Stoyanoff v. Berkeley*, took place in Ladue, a wealthy inner-ring suburb of St. Louis. Just four years later and 17 miles away, the St. Louis community of Black Jack would become embroiled in its own litigation over a restrictive zoning ordinance.

In 1969, a non-profit Methodist organization developed a proposal for federally subsidized, racially integrated, moderate and low-income housing in Black Jack, a St. Louis suburb with an almost entirely white population. In response, Black Jack adopted a low-density zoning ordinance that would preclude development of multiple-family housing. The following litigation ensued.

HEANEY, C.J.

This action was brought by the United States against the City of Black Jack, Missouri, under Title VIII (Fair Housing) of the Civil Rights Act of 1968. 42 U.S.C. 3601 et seq. The complaint alleged that the City had denied persons housing on the basis of race, in violation of 3604(a), and had interfered with the exercise of the right to equal housing opportunity, in violation of 3617,[1] by adopting a zoning ordinance which prohibited the construction of any new multiple-family dwellings. In particular, it alleged that the ordinance operated

---

1. [Section 3617 makes it unlawful "to coerce, intimidate, threaten, or interfere with any person in the exercise or enjoyment of . . . any right granted or protected by [42 U.S.C. §§ 3603 through 3606]."—Eds.]

to preclude construction of a low to moderate income integrated townhouse development known as Park View Heights. . . .

. . . In 1970, the Black Jack area was unincorporated and was governed locally by St. Louis County. The county had adopted a master plan in 1965 which embraced the 1,700 acres which were later to become the City of Black Jack. That plan designated sixty-seven acres for multiple-family construction. In 1970, 15.2 of those acres were occupied by 321 apartments, 483.1 acres were occupied by single-family dwellings, and the rest of the land was undeveloped.

In 1969, the Inter Religious Center for Urban Affairs (ICUA) began planning Park View Heights to create alternative housing opportunities for persons of low and moderate income living in the ghetto areas of St. Louis. After a search for an appropriate site, ICUA settled on 11.9 acres on Old Jamestown Road, then in an unincorporated area, but now within the City of Black Jack. The site was designated for multiple-family structures. An option was obtained on the land, and in March, 1970, the sponsors filed a preliminary application with the Federal Housing Administration for initial approval of a proposed 236 [unit] development. The original plans envisioned 108 units comprised of two-story townhouses. Within a month, the proposal became a matter of public knowledge, and public opposition was swift and active.

On June 5, 1970, HUD issued a "feasibility letter," which amounted to a green light for federal funding, and which was accompanied by a reservation of federal funds for the development. As stated in *Park View Heights Corp. v. City of Black Jack*, 467 F.2d 1208, 1211 (8th Cir. 1972):

> Upon learning of the "feasibility letter," area residents began a drive to incorporate the area including the site of the proposed Park View Heights apartments. On June 26, 1970, the Citizens for the Incorporation of Black Jack presented two petitions requesting incorporation with 1,425 signatures to the St. Louis County Council. . . . [T]he St. Louis County Council incorporated the City of Black Jack, Missouri, on August 6, 1970.
>
> Between the date of the municipal incorporation and September 15, 1970, the municipal authority of the City of Black Jack was suspended by a Writ of Prohibition issued by a state court. Within six days after the writ was dissolved, the city Zoning Commission issued notices of hearings on a zoning ordinance. . . .
>
> The ordinance was enacted by the City Council on October 20, 1970. It prohibited the construction of any new multiple-family dwellings and made present ones nonconforming uses.

The racial composition of Black Jack and the surrounding area was set forth by the District Court in its opinion, and is not contested by the parties:

> Statistical information submitted shows that at the relevant time the area which is now the City of Black Jack was virtually all white, with a black population of between 1% and 2%. . . .

The virtually all-white character of Black Jack was in marked contrast to the racial composition of other parts of the St. Louis area. . . . In 1970, the pupil population of the City of St. Louis School District was 65.6% Black. . . . In 1970, the Kinloch School District, which is only two miles from the nearest boundary of the Hazelwood School District (of which Black Jack is a part), had 1,245 students, all of whom were black.

The percentage of blacks in St. Louis County has increased only slightly overall from 4.1% in 1950 to 4.8% in 1970. During the same period, the percentage of blacks in the City of St. Louis more than doubled from 17.9% to 40.9%.

Between 1950 and 1970, the population of the city declined . . . (by) 27%, while the population of the county more than doubled. . . . From 1960 to 1970, there were approximately 102,298 new housing starts in the county, and 15,348 in the city, a ratio of almost 7 to 1. During the same period, the city had a net decrease of 24,548 housing units, while the county had a net increase of 84,169. . . .

The concentration of blacks in the city and in pockets in the county is accompanied by the confinement of a disproportionate number of them in overcrowded or substandard accommodations. The 1970 census reveals that in St. Louis city and county approximately 40% of the black families, as compared with 14% of the white families, lived in overcrowded units. . . .

United States v. City of Black Jack, Missouri, 372 F. Supp. 319, 325 (E.D. Mo. 1974).

The District Court further found that the average cost of a home in the City of Black Jack in 1970 was approximately $30,000, and that the average income of Black Jack families is approximately $15,000 per year. It found that Park View Heights was designed to meet the housing needs of families making between $5,528 and $10,143 per year. . . .

. . . Congress has declared that the purpose of the Fair Housing Act of 1968 is "to provide, within constitutional limitations, for fair housing throughout the United States." 42 U.S.C. 3601. The Act was passed pursuant to congressional power under the Thirteenth Amendment to eliminate the badges and incidents of slavery. In construing the Civil Rights Act of 1866, also founded on that power, the Supreme Court has declared that . . . "When racial discrimination herds men into ghettos and makes their ability to buy property turn on the color of their skin, then it too is a relic of slavery." *Jones v. Mayer Co.*, 392 U.S. 409, 442-443 (1968). . . .

. . . The discretion of local zoning officials, recently recognized in *Village of Belle Terre v. Boraas*, 416 U.S. 1 (1974), must be curbed where "the clear result of such discretion is the segregation of low-income Blacks from all White neighborhoods." *Banks v. Perk*, 341 F. Supp. 1175, 1180 (N.D. Ohio 1972), *aff'd in part & rev'd in part without opinion*, 473 F.2d 910 (6th Cir. 1973).

The Burden of proof in Title VIII cases is governed by the concept of the "prima facie case." . . . To establish a prima facie case of racial discrimination, the plaintiff need prove no more than that the conduct of the defendant actually or predictably results in racial discrimination; in other words, that it has a discriminatory effect. . . . The plaintiff need make no showing whatsoever that the action resulting in racial discrimination in housing was racially motivated.[2] Effect, and not motivation, is the touchstone, in part because clever men may easily conceal their motivations, but more importantly, because, "whatever our law was once, . . . we now firmly recognize that the arbitrary quality of thoughtlessness can be as disastrous and unfair to private rights and the public interest as the perversity of a willful scheme." *Hobson v. Hansen*, 269 F. Supp. 401, 497 (D.D.C.1967), *aff'd* . . . 408 F.2d 175 (1969) (en banc).

Once the plaintiff has established a prima facie case by demonstrating racially discriminatory effect, the burden shifts to the governmental defendant to demonstrate that its conduct was necessary to promote a compelling governmental interest.[3] . . .

The District Court concluded that the ordinance had no discriminatory effect. It based this conclusion on its finding that, because Park View Heights was designed to meet the needs of families earning between $5,000 and $10,000 per year—a class including 32 percent of the black population in the metropolitan area and 29 percent of the white population—the ordinance had no measurably greater effect on blacks than on whites. The court's conclusion was in error. It failed to take into account either the "ultimate effect" or the "historical context" of the City's action. *See United Farmworkers of Florida Housing Project, Inc. v. City of Delray Beach*, 493 F.2d at 810. . . . The ultimate effect of the ordinance was to foreclose 85 percent of the blacks living in the metropolitan area from obtaining housing in Black Jack, and to foreclose them at a time when 40 percent of them were living in substandard or overcrowded units.

The discriminatory effect of the ordinance is more onerous when assessed in light of the fact that segregated housing in the St. Louis metropolitan area was, "in large measure the result of deliberate racial discrimination in the housing market by the real estate industry and by agencies of the federal, state, and

---

2. [FN 3] The United States contends that the ordinance ought also be enjoined because it was enacted for the purpose of excluding blacks. There is evidence in the record to support that contention. Opposition to Park View Heights was repeatedly expressed in racial terms by persons whom the District Court found to be the leaders of the incorporation movement, by individuals circulating petitions, and by zoning commissioners themselves. Racial criticism of Park View Heights was made and cheered at public meetings. The uncontradicted evidence indicates that, at all levels of opposition, race played a significant role, both in the drive to incorporate and the decision to rezone. . . . Nevertheless, we do not base our conclusion that the Black Jack ordinance violates Title VIII on a finding that there was an improper purpose.

3. [FN 4] The requirement that a governmental defendant demonstrate that its conduct is necessary to further a compelling governmental interest is most often expressed in cases involving equal protection challenges to statutes or ordinances creating "suspect classifications," . . . or impinging on "fundamental rights." . . . Even though this case is based on a federal statute, rather than on the Fourteenth Amendment, we believe that, once the United States established a prima facie case of racial discrimination, it became proper to apply the compelling governmental interest requirement of the equal protection cases.

local governments." *United States v. City of Black Jack, Missouri, supra,* 372 F. Supp. at 326.

Black Jack's action is but one more factor confining blacks to low-income housing in the center city, confirming the inexorable process whereby the St. Louis metropolitan area becomes one that "has the racial shape of a donut, with the Negroes in the hole and with mostly Whites occupying the ring." *Mahaley v. Cuyahoga Metropolitan Housing Authority,* 355 F. Supp. 1257, 1260 (N.D. Ohio 1973), *rev'd,* 500 F.2d 1087 (6th Cir. 1974). . . . Park View Heights was particularly designed to contribute to the prevention of this prospect so antithetical to the Fair Housing Act. . . . There was ample proof that many blacks would live in the development, and that the exclusion of the townhouses would contribute to the perpetuation of segregation in a community which was 99 percent white.

It having been established that the ordinance had a discriminatory effect, it follows that the United States had made out a prima facie case under Title VIII, and the burden shifted to the City to demonstrate that a compelling governmental interest was furthered by that ordinance. We turn to that question. The City asserted primarily the following governmental interests to justify the ban on further apartments: (1) Road and traffic control; (2) Prevention of overcrowding of schools; (3) Prevention of devaluation of adjacent single-family homes. . . .

In determining whether any of these rise to the level of a compelling governmental interest, we must examine: first, whether the ordinance in fact furthers the governmental interest asserted; second, whether the public interest served by the ordinance is constitutionally permissible and is substantial enough to outweigh the private detriment caused by it; and third, whether less drastic means are available whereby the stated governmental interest may be attained. *See Shapiro v. Thompson,* 394 U.S. 618, 637 (1969). . . .

We need not go beyond the first step in the inquiry, for we find that there is no factual basis for the assertion that any one of the three primary interests asserted by the City is in fact furthered by the zoning ordinance, and we find that the other asserted interests—at least on the facts of this case—are clearly not substantial in relation to the housing opportunities foreclosed. . . . [W]e conclude that the City does not use and has no need to use the ordinance for the governmental purposes suggested.

On the subject of roads and traffic, Mr. Barbero, the City's former mayor and lead witness, conceded on cross-examination that his opposition to Park View Heights on the basis of its impact on traffic and roads was based on incorrect information and was, therefore, wrong. The evidence amply supports his concession. . . .

The asserted community interest in preventing overcrowding of the schools also was not furthered by the ordinance. The St. Louis County Planning Department had determined that, in the school district which embraced Black Jack, apartments produced approximately one schoolchild for every five families, while single-family houses produced almost three schoolchildren, or fifteen times as many. In the light of that evidence, several defense witnesses conceded that the desire to prevent overcrowding of the school system could not supply a rational basis for the ordinance, and defense counsel stated at one point in the trial that school impaction was not an issue in the case. Moreover, there was nothing in the record to indicate that the school facilities were already overcrowded.

The third asserted justification of preventing devaluation of adjoining single family homes was also not furthered by the ordinance. The St. Louis Planning Department, after conducting a study, concluded that apartment complexes in the St. Louis metropolitan area had not had such an effect on property values. This conclusion was buttressed by the testimony of expert witnesses, and was not contradicted by any competent evidence. . . .

We hold that Zoning Ordinance No. 12 of the City of Black Jack violates Title VIII, because it denies persons housing on the basis of race, in violation of 3604(a), and interferes with the exercise of the right to equal housing opportunity, in violation of 3617. . . .

We, therefore, reverse and remand with instructions to the District Court to enter a permanent injunction upon receipt of this Court's order, enjoining the enforcement of the ordinance. . . .

Notes

1. *Limits on disparate impact liability:*   As we saw, the U.S. Supreme Court validated the use of disparate impact theory for Fair Housing Act claims. In so doing, however, the Court was careful to set forth limits to plaintiffs' reliance on proof of discriminatory *effect*, rather than discriminatory *intent*. Among other things, plaintiffs cannot rely "solely on a showing of a statistical disparity." Instead, they must satisfy a "robust causality requirement" by "point[ing] to a defendant's policy or policies causing that disparity" in order to "protect[ ] defendants from being held liable for racial disparities they did not create." In addition, defendants must be provided "leeway to state and explain the valid interest served by their policies." *Texas Dep't of Housing & Cmty. Affairs*, 135 S. Ct. at 2522-523. In contrast to claims brought under the Fair Housing Act, claims brought under the equal protection clause of the federal constitution require proof of discriminatory purpose or intent, not mere disparate impact. *See Village of Arlington Heights v. Metropolitan Housing Dev. Corp.*, 429 U.S. 252 (1977).

2. *The place—St. Louis and the struggle for integration:*   As suggested by *United States v. City of Black Jack*, St. Louis city and county have had a long and uneasy struggle over integration. The 1969 Park View Heights proposal for integrated moderate- and low-income housing developed just as the city was ending its failed experiment with high-density public housing segregated by race

into "ghettos." Just two years before the Eighth Circuit issued its opinion, the failure was made spectacularly visible by the demolition of the Pruitt-Igoe public housing towers—an iconic symbol of failed public housing policies that segregated low-income people of color into dense, crime-ridden facilities. *See* Richard Rothstein, *The Making of Ferguson: Public Policies at the Root of its Troubles,* Economic Policy Institute, Oct. 15, 2014.

Pruitt-Igoe collapses, with the St. Louis Arch in the background (1972)
Source: U.S. Dept. of Housing and Urban Development
Downloaded from Wikimedia Commons

The Park View Heights project was never constructed. Nevertheless, a variety of social and economic factors created a shift in Black Jack's demographic composition, and by 2000, Black Jack's population was 71% African American. As one writer explained, "[a]s African American occupancy increased in the inner north County suburbs, the logic and pattern of exclusive zoning simply drifted west. . . ." Colin Gordon, Mapping Decline: St. Louis and the Fate of the American City 150 (2008).

3. *State law and exclusionary zoning—the Mt. Laurel saga:* Mount Laurel, New Jersey, sought to exclude *all* low- and moderate-income housing from its jurisdiction by permitting only low-density, single-family housing

within residential districts. That is, because homes had to be situated on large lots, they tended to be more expensive, and thereby to exclude low-income people from the community. In a landmark decision, the state supreme court invalidated portions of the township's ordinance under the state constitution, and ordered the township to take additional action necessary to achieve "the fulfillment of its fair share of the regional need for low and moderate income housing." *Southern Burlington County NAACP v. Township of Mount Laurel*, 336 A.2d 713 (N.J. 1975), *cert. denied*, 423 U.S. 808 (1975). Mount Laurel failed to vigorously implement the court's instructions. Eight years later, the New Jersey Supreme Court found the township's ordinance remained "blatantly exclusionary," and therefore the court imposed more specific requirements on the township. *Mount Laurel II*, 456 A.2d 390 (N.J. 1983). Subsequently, the state legislature took additional action to promote affordable housing by passing the N.J. Fair Housing Act of 1985.

Although the Mount Laurel "fair share" doctrine has received considerable attention, it remains a minority view. Still, judicial mandate aside, numerous communities throughout the country have undertaken voluntary initiatives to promote affordable housing. *See, e.g.,* Tim Iglesias, *Maximizing Inclusionary Zoning's Contributions to Both Affordable Housing and Residential Integration*, 54 Washburn L.J. 585 (2015); J. Peter Byrne & Michael Diamond, *Affordable Housing, Land Tenure, and Urban Policy: The Matrix Revealed*, 34 Fordham Urb. L.J. 527 (2007).

C. BEYOND THE BLACK LETTER: URBAN AGRICULTURE

Under strict Euclidean zoning, agricultural and residential uses would be deemed incompatible and segregated from one another. Likewise, under traditional nuisance law, some agricultural operations constitute nuisances as to nearby residential areas. (Recall, for example, *Spur Industries v. Del Webb Development* from Chapter 11). Today, however, many communities are reversing course and exploring whether certain types of farming and urban life might be compatible after all.

Urban agriculture can take many forms, including small home vegetable or flower gardens, windowsill planters, rooftop gardens, greenhouse production, farm stands selling to the public, community gardens, and commercial flower operations. In a parallel development, some urban residents are interested in "micro-livestock" activities, including the raising of chickens, goats, and bees to produce fresh eggs, milk, and honey under humane conditions.

Urban agriculture offers many benefits. To some, it provides an opportunity to raise healthy, affordable food for one's own family and to teach children about how food is grown or raised. Financially struggling cities like Detroit and Buffalo see urban agriculture as a beneficial use for vacant, weed-filled lots and abandoned properties, and an activity that can bring communities together. Urban farming can also provide environmental benefits for those who wish to limit the use of pesticides and fertilizers in the production of their food. Urban agriculture even has an historical, patriotic component: During World Wars I and II, with canned goods in short supply, the federal government urged people to plant "war gardens" or "victory gardens" to feed themselves, so that farm commodities could be sent abroad to feed the troops.

Uncle Sam Says, Garden to Cut Food Costs (ca. 1917)
Source: National Archives (#5711623)

Today, a number of cities and states are revising their zoning ordinances to become more amenable to urban agriculture and community gardens. For example, the California Neighborhood Food Act of 2014 prevents landlords and homeowners associations from imposing certain barriers on those who wish to grow food at home for personal consumption. Detroit adopted a comprehensive urban agriculture ordinance that has paved the way for the city to turn some of its 200,000 vacant properties into an estimated 1,350 community gardens, farmer's markets, food trucks, and similar entrepreneurial efforts.[4]

---

4. Trish Popovitch, *10 American Cities Lead the Way with Urban Agriculture Ordinances*, Seedstock, May 27, 2014.

Other cities, including Austin, Chicago, and Portland have all added permissive urban agriculture provisions to their zoning ordinances.

Discussion Questions

1. *The idea of urban agriculture:* What do you think of allowing some gardening and animal-raising activities within cities? What are the potential positive and negative impacts of such activities? Do you know anyone who raises a garden, chickens, goats, or bees?

2. *Zoning and urban agriculture:*   What is the best way for municipalities to incorporate urban agriculture into their zoning ordinances? Consider the following questions, among others:

- Should the community recognize *use* rights for specific activities? What should those uses include? Should the uses be permitted *as of right* or should they be treated as *special exceptions* that require conditional use permits? As an alternative to use rights, should the community establish separate garden *zoning districts*?
- Where should such activities be allowed on a particular property—in the back yard, front yard, and/or side yard? Should tenants be allowed to engage in such activities? Should residents of common interest communities be allowed to engage in such activities, and does it matter whether the common interest community is made up of freestanding residences or multi-unit buildings?
- Should the size of gardens or number of animals be limited? If so, how?
- Should community gardeners be allowed to sell their products to others? Give them away?
- Apart from zoning considerations, should cities offer community education and garden training? What broad topics should such courses cover?

3. *Sources:*   For more information, *see, e.g.,* Jessica Owley & Tonya Lewis, *From Vacant Lots to Full Pantries: Urban Agriculture Programs and the American City*, 91 U. Det. Mercy L. Rev. 101 (2015); Jaime M. Bouvier, *How Cities Are Responding to the Urban Agriculture Movement with Micro-Livestock Ordinances*, 47 Urban Lawyer 85 (Oct. 27, 2015); Sarah B. Schindler, *Of Backyard Chickens and Front Yard Gardens: The Conflict Between Local Governments and Locavores*, 87 Tul. L. Rev. 231 (2012).

D. SKILLS PRACTICE: DRAFTING ZONING REGULATIONS

Increasingly, municipalities are addressing new areas of concern in their zoning ordinances. Such topics include affordable housing, energy conservation, sustainable development, biodiversity protection, and many others. Consider the four examples below, and then perform the listed tasks.

The Philadelphia Code
Neighborhood Conservation

§ 14-501. Overlay Zoning Districts

(2)(a): Overlay zoning district regulations apply in combination with underlying base zoning district regulations. . . . All applicable zoning code regulations apply in overlay districts, except that when overlay district standards conflict with standards that would otherwise apply . . . , the regulations of the overlay zoning district govern. . . .

§ 14-504. Neighborhood Conservation Overlay District

(1) Purposes. The NCO . . . district is intended to:

  (a) Promote the public welfare of the City by encouraging conservation and preservation through the revitalization of the physical environment that is unique to a specific neighborhood;
  (b) Provide a reasonable degree of control over the alteration and improvement of the exterior facades of existing buildings and the design of new construction to preserve the aesthetic fabric of these areas, without modifying the availability of permitted and special exception uses in the neighborhood . . . .
  (c) Enhance the City's attractiveness as a place to live, work, and enjoy its cultural, social, and historical opportunities and also to foster a renewed feeling of pride in one's neighborhood . . . .

(2) Planning Commission Review.

  (a) No building permit shall be issued to construct a building or alter the exterior of a building that is visible from a public street until the Commission has reviewed the application and confirmed that it complies with all regulations applicable to the applicable NCO area. . . .

The Portland, Oregon Code
Environmental Zones

§ 33.430.010. Purpose. Environmental zones protect resources and functional values that have been identified by the City as providing benefits to the public. The environmental regulations encourage flexibility and innovation in site planning and provide for development that is carefully designed to be sensitive to the site's protected resources. . . . The environmental regulations also carry out Comprehensive Plan policies and objectives.

33.430.015. Purpose of the Environmental Protection Zone. The Environmental *Protection* zone provides the highest level of protection to the most important resources and functional values. . . . Development will be approved in the environmental protection zone only in rare and unusual circumstances.

33.430.017. Purpose of the Environmental Conservation Zone. The Environmental *Conservation* zone conserves important resources and functional values in areas where the resources and functional values can be protected while allowing environmentally sensitive urban development. [Protections include standards for the maximum land area that can be disturbed, setback requirements to separate the disturbance area from the resource, and tree removal and replacement requirements. *See* 33.430.140.]

The Austin, Texas Code
Design Standards and Mixed Use
Chapter 25-2, Subchapter E

§ 1.1. General Intent. This Subchapter generally addresses the physical relationship between commercial and other nonresidential development and adjacent properties, public streets, neighborhoods, and the natural environment, in order to implement the City Council's vision for a more attractive, efficient, and livable community. The general purposes of this Subchapter include:

§ 1.1.1. To provide appropriate standards to ensure a high quality appearance for Austin and promote pedestrian-friendly design while also allowing flexibility, individuality, creativity, and artistic expression;

§ 1.1.2. To strengthen and protect the image, identity, and unique character of Austin and thereby to enhance its business economy; . . .

§ 1.1.5. To provide for and encourage development and redevelopment that contains a compatible mix of residential and nonresidential uses within close proximity to each other, rather than separating uses.

The Boulder, Colorado Code
Green Building Program

§ 10-7.5-1. Legislative Intent and Purpose. The purpose of this chapter is to protect the public health, safety, and welfare by regulating residential construction with the intent to conserve energy, water, and other natural resources, and preserve the health of our environment through optional and mandatory requirements related to design, construction, operations, recycling, and deconstruction. This chapter has the following additional purposes: . . .

(a) It includes mandatory green building requirements to ensure that construction waste and deconstruction materials are recycled, reused, or otherwise diverted from land fills, and minimum requirements to ensure that dwellings are constructed in an efficient manner; . . .

§ 10-7.5-3. Mandatory Green Building Requirements.

(a) Energy Efficiency—New Dwelling Units. An applicant for a building permit for each new dwelling shall demonstrate that the building is more efficient than a building that meets the minimum requirements of Chapter 10-7, "Energy Conservation Code." . . . Table 1A lists the minimum energy efficiency requirements. [For example, new construction of up to 3,000 square feet must be 14 percent more efficient than the specified standard; new construction of 3,001-5,000 square feet must be 43 percent more efficient than the standard; and new construction greater than 5,000 square feet must be 64 percent more efficient than the standard.]

Tasks

1. *The examples:* What approach did each of the sample zoning ordinances take? In particular, note the use of *overlay zones.* From the brief excerpts you reviewed, can you derive a general explanation of how overlay zones work?

2. *Evaluate your community:* Think about the community in which your law school is located. From a zoning perspective, what are the strengths of your community? What aspects could be improved? List three topics of regulation that you think would be suitable for additional consideration.

3. *Statement of purpose:* Choose one of the topics that you identified above. What substantive changes would be beneficial? Draft a one-paragraph statement of purpose for your proposed zoning amendment. What mechanisms could best achieve those changes? Develop a bullet list of potential implementing mechanisms.

E. CHAPTER REVIEW

1. Practice Questions[5]

1. *Apartments not welcome:* A city enacted a zoning ordinance that prohibited the construction of any new multiple-family dwellings in any zoning district, and made present ones nonconforming uses. Plaintiffs challenge the ordinance as violating the equal protection clause of the U.S. Constitution.

---

5. Answers appear in the Appendix to this casebook.

What test should the court apply in determining whether or not to uphold the ordinance?

    A. The ordinance must be a rational means of achieving a permissible governmental purpose.

    B. If plaintiffs can demonstrate that the ordinance primarily excludes persons of a certain economic status, then the city must prove the ordinance is necessary to achieve a compelling goal of the city.

    C. The ordinance must be necessary to achieve a permissible state objective.

    D. A and B above.

    2. *Give me space:*   A city enacted a zoning ordinance that required all single-family homes to be built on lots no smaller than three acres, which caused the homes to be more expensive than comparable homes on smaller lots in neighboring municipalities. If the plaintiff can demonstrate that people of color make up only .0004% of the city's population, then which statement is most accurate?

    A. The ordinance violates the equal protection clause of the U.S. Constitution.

    B. The ordinance violates the Fair Housing Act.

    C. The ordinance violates the equal protection clause of the majority of state constitutions.

    D. The ordinance violates the equal protection clause of some state constitutions.

    3. *The variance:*   If an applicant wants to receive a variance from a zoning requirement, which of the following is *not* an element that the party must prove?

    A. It is unnecessary for the landowner to suffer hardship because granting the variance will prevent the hardship.

    B. The applicant seeks a waiver of the ordinance's use restrictions, but not of its setback or other bulk restrictions.

    C. Granting the variance would not be contrary to the public interest.

    D. The affected lot is subject to special conditions.

2. Bringing It Home

Research your local community's zoning ordinance and find its relevant provisions on the issues listed below. It might be helpful to go to your community's Internet home page, and then look for links to *government, municipal code, land use, planning department,* or something similar.

    1. *Use districts:* What use districts does your community recognize? In which district do you live?

2. *Family:*   How does your community define "family" for purposes of the single-family use district? <u>Hint:</u> If "family" is not defined within the single-family use district provision, then search for a separate "definitions" section.

3. *Urban agriculture:*   Does your community have any regulations that apply to urban agriculture? <u>Hint:</u> It might appear in a grouping labeled "overlay districts" or something similar.

Constitutional Limits: Eminent Domain and Regulatory Takings

A. Eminent Domain
B. Regulatory Takings
C. Beyond the Black Letter: Eminent Domain Legislation
D. Skills Practice: Formulating a Discovery Plan
E. Chapter Review

Chapter 13-Cases

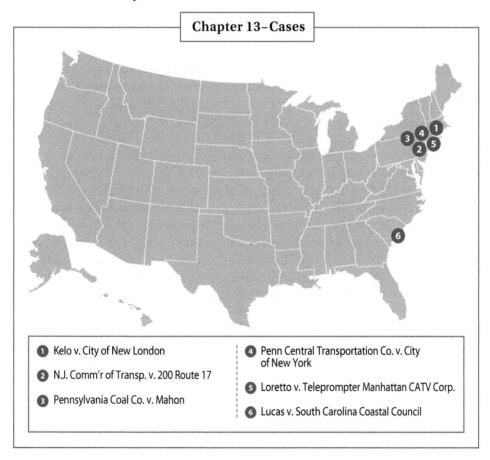

1. Kelo v. City of New London

2. N.J. Comm'r of Transp. v. 200 Route 17

3. Pennsylvania Coal Co. v. Mahon

4. Penn Central Transportation Co. v. City of New York

5. Loretto v. Teleprompter Manhattan CATV Corp.

6. Lucas v. South Carolina Coastal Council

As we have seen, a variety of legal mechanisms and institutions shape the scope of real property rights and the use of land. Private agreements can control land use far into the future through easements and running covenants, as we saw in Chapters 9 and 10. Likewise, the common law of trespass and nuisance addresses interferences with the possession and use of land, as covered in Chapter 11. Statutory limits, too, play a role, as through state and local zoning and land use planning, which we took up in the previous chapter. Finally, in this chapter, we turn our attention to two constitutional provisions that shape property rights and land use: the power of eminent domain and the regulatory takings doctrine.

A. EMINENT DOMAIN

[N]or shall private property be taken for public use, without just compensation.

—U.S. Constitution, Amendment V (1791)

Property can be condemned through the power of eminent domain. Such condemnations resemble forced sales by which property title actually passes to the government. The eminent domain *authority* has deep roots, extending back to ancient Rome, England, and American colonial times. Beyond the question of governmental authority, there is a question of whether the sovereign must pay *compensation* for condemned properties. The historical record indicates that Roman authorities provided such compensation. Likewise, the payment of compensation was routine in England, even though the sovereign was generally not required to do so. In colonial and post-revolutionary America, according to Professor William M. Treanor, the "decision whether or not to provide compensation was left entirely to the political process." William Michael Treanor, *The Original Understanding of the Takings Clause and the Political Process*, 95 Colum. L. Rev. 782, 783 (1995). In practice, compensation was often provided, and the practice continued to become more widespread over time. By the late 18th century when the Fifth Amendment was ratified, many state common law, statutory, and constitutional provisions required compensation.

As set forth above, the Fifth Amendment to the U.S. Constitution requires compensation when the federal government takes private property for a public use. The Fourteenth Amendment makes that clause applicable to the states. *See Chicago, B. & Q.R. Co. v. Chicago*, 166 U.S. 226 (1897). As a result, you will notice that parties in eminent domain cases (and regulatory takings cases, as considered in section B) include federal, state, and local units of government.

Note carefully what the Fifth Amendment does and does not do. It clearly requires "just compensation" when property is taken for "public use." However, it *does not establish* the power of eminent domain, but rather *limits* its exercise. In fact, because the Bill of Rights (of which the Fifth Amendment is a part) is concerned with the protection of individual liberties and the limitation of governmental power, it would be odd if the amendment authorized, rather than limited, such power. The body of the Constitution, too, is silent as to the basis of the eminent domain authority. Then, where can we find support for the power of eminent domain?

A variety of rationales have been suggested. In 1875, the U.S. Supreme Court articulated, "The right [of eminent domain] is the offspring of political necessity; and it is inseparable from sovereignty, unless denied to [the government] by its fundamental law." *Kohl v. United States*, 91 U.S. 367 (1875); *see also United States v. Carmack*, 329 U.S. 230, 241-42 (1946) (asserting that the Fifth Amendment contains "a tacit recognition of a preexisting power to take private property for public use, rather than a grant of a new power"). As *Kohl* explained,

> It has not been seriously contended . . . that the United States government is without power to appropriate lands or other property . . . for its own uses, and to enable it to perform its proper functions. Such authority is essential to its independent existence and perpetuity. These cannot be preserved if the obstinacy of a private person . . . can prevent the acquisition of the means or instruments by which alone governmental functions can be performed. The powers vested by the Constitution in the general government demand for their exercise the acquisition of lands. . . . These are needed for forts, armories, and arsenals, for navy-yards and light-houses, for custom-houses, post-offices, and courthouses, and for other *public uses.* If the right to acquire property for such uses may be made a barren right by the unwillingness of property-holders to sell . . . the constitutional grants of power may be rendered nugatory, and the government is dependent for its practical existence upon the will of a State, or even upon that of a private citizen. This cannot be.

91 U.S. at 371 (emphasis added). Notice *Kohl*'s reference to "public uses."

In section A, we begin by considering the scope of "public use," and then proceed to examine the requirement of "just compensation." The following *A Place to Start* box introduces you to some basic concepts and terminology that will be useful throughout this section.

A Place to Start: Eminent Domain

■ *Public use:* As state and federal courts work out the meaning of *public use*, they have tended to follow one of the following views. The U.S. Supreme Court's interpretation of the Fifth Amendment sets the baseline requirements that must be satisfied before condemnation is warranted; however, the states are free to set stricter standards that provide additional safeguards for property owners.

  ■ *The narrow view:* Under the narrow view, property can be taken by condemnation only in those situations in which the public actually and physically *uses*, or has the opportunity to use, the land that has been condemned.

  ■ *The broad view:* Under the broad view, a public use is any use that "manifestly contributes to the general welfare and prosperity of the whole community." Powell on Real Property §79F.03(a) (Michael Allan Wolf gen. ed. 2015), citing 2A Nichols on Eminent Domain, ch. 7, §7.02(1) (Matthew Bender).

■ *Just compensation:* Property can be condemned in whole and in part. Section A.2 will provide an overview of how the condemnation award is calculated in each of the following cases:

  ■ Complete condemnation

  ■ Partial condemnation

  ■ Property damage without condemnation

DIGGING DEEPER: As you learn more about eminent domain, think about what policies (legal and otherwise) the narrow and broad views of "public use" advance, respectively. Which view has the modern Supreme Court adopted as a matter of federal constitutional interpretation? Should the states take a narrower view, and if so, why?

Test Your Understanding

In each of the following situations, decide whether the proposed taking by eminent domain would satisfy the narrow and/or broad definitions of "public use." Consider further whether eminent domain *should be* broad enough to permit the proposed taking. If so, why? If not, why not, and can you think of any alternatives to condemnation through eminent domain?

1. *The busy highway:*   The main state highway between City *A* and City *B* is heavily traveled. During about four hours each day, drivers experience "stop and go" traffic, and average only 20 miles per hour (even though the speed limit is 40 miles per hour). The state plans to condemn a strip of land 12-feet wide on either side of the alignment to permit the construction of two additional travel lanes (one in each direction).

2. *Football mania:*   A major city identified a downtown location where it wanted to build a stadium complex to house a professional football team. Seventeen private landowners held title to the various tracts of land the city wanted to acquire. The city attempted to negotiate the purchase of the identified properties from those 17 private owners. Many negotiations were successful, but 6 landowners would not agree to sell to the city. When those negotiations broke down, the city took the remaining 6 properties by eminent domain. (For the purposes of this problem, you can assume that the state constitution delegated eminent domain authority to the city.) The city agreed to lease the stadium property to the professional football team for 30 years, to commence as soon as construction of the stadium project had been completed. *See generally Cascott, L.L.C. v. City of Arlington*, 278 S.W.3d 523 (Tex. App. 2009); *City of Oakland v. Oakland Raiders*, 646 P.2d 835 (Cal. 1982).

3. *Back to feudalism:*   By the mid-20th century, land ownership in Hawaii had been concentrated into the hands of only a few owners. In particular, 47% of the state's land was held by only 72 private landowners. In one portion of the state, a mere 22 landowners owned 72.5% of the fee simple titles. The state

legislature concluded that the oligopoly in land ownership was "skewing the state's residential fee simple market, inflating land prices, and injuring the public tranquility and welfare," and therefore enacted a condemnation scheme for redistributing title. The state proposed to condemn the title of numerous landowner/lessors and transfer it to the lessees currently residing on the properties. *See Hawaii Housing Authority v. Midkiff,* 467 U.S. 229 (1984).

4. *The depressed economy:* One neighborhood within a major city had become blighted. The city determined that the neighborhood had so deteriorated that 64.3% of its dwellings were beyond repair; housing conditions were overcrowded; there was a lack of adequate streets and alleys; and there was a lack of light and air. The city determined that the neighborhood had become "injurious to the public health, safety, morals, and welfare" and that it was necessary to "eliminate all such injurious conditions by employing all means necessary and appropriate for the purpose," including eminent domain. The city developed a scheme to condemn most of the properties within that blighted neighborhood, including a department store that was not itself blighted. *See Berman v. Parker,* 348 U.S. 26 (1954).

1. Public Use

Kelo v. City of New London

545 U.S. 469 (2005) *rehearing denied,* 545 U.S. 1158 (2005)

Reading Guide

- The validity of the eminent domain authority is a matter of little doubt today. But, the scope of "public use" that justifies its exercise is still a matter of great debate. In *Kelo,* the Court addressed a critical question: whether an economically distressed city can promote economic development by taking property from one private party and giving it to another private party—here, the Pfizer Corporation.

- Public use or public purpose? As you read this case, consider the difference in meaning, if any, between *public use* and *public purpose,* according to the majority and dissenting opinions. Which approach is best, and why? Does the Court adopt a narrow or broad view of the public use requirement?

STEVENS, J., joined by KENNEDY, SOUTER, GINSBURG, and BREYER, JJ.

In 2000, the city of New London approved a development plan that, in the words of the Supreme Court of Connecticut, was "projected to create in excess of 1,000 jobs, to increase tax and other revenues, and to revitalize an economically distressed city, including its downtown and waterfront areas." 843 A.2d 500, 507 (2004). In assembling the land needed for this project, the city's development agent has purchased property from willing sellers and proposes to use the power of eminent domain to acquire the remainder of the property from unwilling owners in exchange for just compensation. The question presented is whether the city's proposed disposition of this property qualifies as a "public use" within the meaning of the Takings Clause of the Fifth Amendment to the Constitution.

I

. . . Decades of economic decline led a state agency in 1990 to designate the City a "distressed municipality." In 1996, the Federal Government closed the Naval Undersea Warfare Center, which had been located in the Fort Trumbull area of the City and had employed over 1,500 people. In 1998, the City's unemployment rate was nearly double that of the State, and its population of just under 24,000 residents was at its lowest since 1920.

These conditions prompted state and local officials to target New London, and particularly its Fort Trumbull area, for economic revitalization. To this end, respondent New London Development Corporation (NLDC), a private nonprofit entity established some years earlier to assist the City in planning economic development, was reactivated. In January 1998, the State authorized a $5.35 million bond issue to support the NLDC's planning activities and a $10 million bond issue toward the creation of a Fort Trumbull State Park. In February, the pharmaceutical company Pfizer Inc. announced that it would build a $300 million research facility on a site immediately adjacent to Fort Trumbull; local planners hoped that Pfizer would draw new business to the area, thereby serving as a catalyst to the area's rejuvenation. After receiving initial approval from the city council, the NLDC continued its planning activities and held a series of neighborhood meetings to educate the public about the process. In May, the city council authorized the NLDC to formally submit its plans to the relevant state agencies for review.[1] Upon obtaining state-level approval, the NLDC finalized an integrated development plan focused on 90 acres of the Fort Trumbull area.

. . . The area comprises approximately 115 privately owned properties, as well as the 32 acres of land formerly occupied by the naval facility (Trumbull State Park now occupies 18 of those 32 acres). The development plan encompasses seven parcels. Parcel 1 is designated for a waterfront conference hotel at the center of a "small urban village" that will include restaurants and shopping. This parcel will also have marinas for both recreational and commercial uses. A pedestrian "riverwalk" will originate here and continue down the coast, connecting the waterfront areas of the development. Parcel 2 will be the site of approximately 80 new residences organized into an urban neighborhood and linked by public walkway to the remainder of the development, including the state park. This parcel also includes space reserved for a new U.S. Coast Guard Museum. Parcel 3, which is located immediately north of the Pfizer facility, will

---

1. [FN 2] Various state agencies studied the project's economic, environmental, and social ramifications. As part of this process, a team of consultants evaluated six alternative development proposals for the area, which varied in extensiveness and emphasis. The Office of Policy and Management, one of the primary state agencies undertaking the review, made findings that the project was consistent with relevant state and municipal development policies. . . .

contain at least 90,000 square feet of research and development office space. Parcel 4A is a 2.4–acre site that will be used either to support the adjacent state park, by providing parking or retail services for visitors, or to support the nearby marina. Parcel 4B will include a renovated marina, as well as the final stretch of the riverwalk. Parcels 5, 6, and 7 will provide land for office and retail space, parking, and water-dependent commercial uses. . . .

The city council approved the plan in January 2000, and designated the NLDC as its development agent in charge of implementation. . . . The city council also authorized the NLDC to purchase property or to acquire property by exercising eminent domain in the City's name. The NLDC successfully negotiated the purchase of most of the real estate in the 90–acre area, but its negotiations with petitioners failed. As a consequence, in November 2000, the NLDC initiated the condemnation proceedings that gave rise to this case.

II

Petitioner Susette Kelo has lived in the Fort Trumbull area since 1997. She has made extensive improvements to her house, which she prizes for its water view. Petitioner Wilhelmina Dery was born in her Fort Trumbull house in 1918 and has lived there her entire life. Her husband Charles (also a petitioner) has lived in the house since they married some 60 years ago. In all, the nine petitioners own 15 properties in Fort Trumbull. In all, the nine petitioners own 15 properties in Fort Trumbull—4 in parcel 3 of the development plan and 11 in parcel 4A. Ten of the parcels are occupied by the owner or a family member; the other five are held as investment properties. There is no allegation that any of these properties is blighted or otherwise in poor condition; rather, they were condemned only because they happen to be located in the development area. . . .

[The owners of the condemned property challenged the city's exercise of eminent domain power on the ground that the taking was not for a public use. After a 7-day bench trial, the Connecticut Superior Court granted relief for the owners with respect to parcel 4A, but not parcel 3, and cross-appeals were taken. The Connecticut Supreme Court affirmed in part and reversed in part, upholding the city's exercise of eminent domain over both parcels.]

III

Two polar propositions are perfectly clear. On the one hand, it has long been accepted that the sovereign may not take the property of *A* for the sole purpose of transferring it to another private party *B*, even though *A* is paid just compensation. On the other hand, it is equally clear that a State may transfer property from one private party to another if future "use by the public" is the purpose of the taking; the condemnation of land for a railroad with common-carrier duties is a familiar example. Neither of these propositions, however, determines the disposition of this case.

As for the first proposition, the City would no doubt be forbidden from taking petitioners' land for the purpose of conferring a private benefit on a particular private party. *See Hawaii Housing Authority v. Midkiff*, 467 U.S.

229 (1984) ("A purely private taking could not withstand the scrutiny of the public use requirement; it would serve no legitimate purpose of government and would thus be void"). . . . Nor would the City be allowed to take property under the mere pretext of a public purpose, when its actual purpose was to bestow a private benefit. The takings before us, however, would be executed pursuant to a "carefully considered" development plan. 843 A.2d. at 536. The trial judge and all the members of the Supreme Court of Connecticut agreed that there was no evidence of an illegitimate purpose in this case. . . .

On the other hand, this is not a case in which the City is planning to open the condemned land—at least not in its entirety—to use by the general public . . . But although such a projected use would be sufficient to satisfy the public use requirement, this "Court long ago rejected any literal requirement that condemned property be put into use for the general public." *Midkiff*, 467 U.S. at 244. Indeed, while many state courts in the mid–19th century endorsed "use by the public" as the proper definition of public use, that narrow view steadily eroded over time. Not only was the "use by the public" test difficult to administer (*e.g.*, what proportion of the public need have access to the property? at what price?), but it proved to be impractical given the diverse and always evolving needs of society. Accordingly, when this Court began applying the Fifth Amendment to the States at the close of the 19th century, it embraced the broader and more natural interpretation of public use as "public purpose." . . . We have repeatedly and consistently rejected that narrow test ever since. . . .

In *Berman v. Parker*, 348 U.S. 26 (1954), this Court upheld a redevelopment plan targeting a blighted area of Washington, D. C., in which most of the housing for the area's 5,000 inhabitants was beyond repair. Under the plan, the area would be condemned and part of it utilized for the construction of streets, schools, and other public facilities. The remainder of the land would be leased or sold to private parties for the purpose of redevelopment, including the construction of low-cost housing.

The owner of a department store located in the area challenged the condemnation, pointing out that his store was not itself blighted and arguing that the creation of a "better balanced, more attractive community" was not a valid public use. Writing for a unanimous Court, Justice Douglas refused to evaluate this claim in isolation, deferring instead to the legislative and agency judgment that the area "must be planned as a whole" for the plan to be successful. The Court explained that "community redevelopment programs need not, by force of the Constitution, be on a piecemeal basis—lot by lot, building by building." The public use underlying the taking was unequivocally affirmed:

> We do not sit to determine whether a particular housing project is or is not desirable. The concept of the public welfare is broad and inclusive. . . . The values it represents are spiritual as well as physical, aesthetic as well as monetary. It is within the power of the legislature to determine that the community should be beautiful as well as healthy, spacious as well as clean, well-balanced as well as carefully patrolled. In the present case, the Congress and its authorized agencies have made determinations that take into account a wide variety of values. It is

not for us to reappraise them. If those who govern the District of Columbia decide that the Nation's Capital should be beautiful as well as sanitary, there is nothing in the Fifth Amendment that stands in the way. *Id.* at 33.

In *Midkiff,* the Court considered a Hawaii statute whereby fee title was taken from lessors and transferred to lessees (for just compensation) in order to reduce the concentration of land ownership. We unanimously upheld the statute and rejected the Ninth Circuit's view that it was "a naked attempt on the part of the state of Hawaii to take the property of A and transfer it to B solely for B's private use and benefit." Reaffirming *Berman's* deferential approach to legislative judgments in this field, we concluded that the State's purpose of eliminating the "social and economic evils of a land oligopoly" qualified as a valid public use. Our opinion also rejected the contention that the mere fact that the State immediately transferred the properties to private individuals upon condemnation somehow diminished the public character of the taking. "[I]t is only the taking's purpose, and not its mechanics," we explained, that matters in determining public use. 467 U.S. at 244. . . .

Viewed as a whole, our jurisprudence has recognized that the needs of society have varied between different parts of the Nation, just as they have evolved over time in response to changed circumstances. Our earliest cases in particular embodied a strong theme of federalism, emphasizing the "great respect" that we owe to state legislatures and state courts in discerning local public needs. . . . For more than a century, our public use jurisprudence has wisely eschewed rigid formulas and intrusive scrutiny in favor of affording legislatures broad latitude in determining what public needs justify the use of the takings power.

IV . . .

. . . [P]etitioners maintain that for takings of this kind we should require a "reasonable certainty" that the expected public benefits will actually accrue. Such a rule, however, would represent an even greater departure from our precedent. "When the legislature's purpose is legitimate and its means are not irrational, our cases make clear that empirical debates over the wisdom of takings—no less than debates over the wisdom of other kinds of socioeconomic legislation—are not to be carried out in the federal courts." *Midkiff,* 467 U.S., at 242–243. . . .

In affirming the City's authority to take petitioners' properties, we do not minimize the hardship that condemnations may entail, notwithstanding the payment of just compensation. We emphasize that nothing in our opinion precludes any State from placing further restrictions on its exercise of the takings power. Indeed, many States already impose "public use" requirements that are stricter than the federal baseline. . . .[2] This Court's authority, however, extends

---

2. [FN 24] . . . [S]ome argue that the need for eminent domain has been greatly exaggerated because private developers can use numerous techniques, including secret negotiations or precommitment strategies, to overcome holdout problems and assemble lands for genuinely profitable projects. . . . Others argue to the contrary, urging that the need

only to determining whether the City's proposed condemnations are for a "public use" within the meaning of the Fifth Amendment to the Federal Constitution. Because over a century of our case law interpreting that provision dictates an affirmative answer to that question, we may not grant petitioners the relief that they seek. The judgment of the Supreme Court of Connecticut is affirmed.

KENNEDY, J., concurring. . . .

This Court has declared that a taking should be upheld as consistent with the Public Use Clause . . . as long as it is "rationally related to a conceivable public purpose." . . . This deferential standard of review echoes the rational-basis test used to review economic regulation under the Due Process and Equal Protection Clauses . . . The determination that a rational-basis standard of review is appropriate does not . . . alter the fact that transfers intended to confer benefits on particular, favored private entities, and with only incidental or pretextual public benefits, are forbidden by the Public Use Clause. . . .

Petitioners . . . argue that any taking justified by the promotion of economic development must be treated by the courts as *per se* invalid, or at least presumptively invalid. Petitioners overstate the need for such a rule, however, by making the incorrect assumption that review under *Berman* and *Midkiff* imposes no meaningful judicial limits on the government's power to condemn any property it likes. A broad *per se* rule or a strong presumption of invalidity, furthermore, would prohibit a large number of government takings that have the purpose and expected effect of conferring substantial benefits on the public at large and so do not offend the Public Use Clause. . . .

This is not the occasion for conjecture as to what sort of cases might justify a more demanding standard, but it is appropriate to underscore aspects of the instant case that convince me no departure from *Berman* and *Midkiff* is appropriate here. This taking occurred in the context of a comprehensive development plan meant to address a serious citywide depression, and the projected economic benefits of the project cannot be characterized as *de minimis.* The identities of most of the private beneficiaries were unknown at the time the city formulated its plans. The city complied with elaborate procedural requirements that facilitate review of the record and inquiry into the city's purposes. In sum, while there may be categories of cases in which the transfers are so suspicious, or the procedures employed so prone to abuse, or the purported benefits are so trivial or implausible, that courts should presume an impermissible private purpose, no such circumstances are present in this case. . . .

O'CONNOR, J., joined by REHNQUIST, C.J., and SCALIA and THOMAS, JJ., dissenting. . . .

. . . Under the banner of economic development, all private property is now vulnerable to being taken and transferred to another private owner, so long as it

---

for eminent domain is especially great with regard to older, small cities like New London, where centuries of development have created an extreme overdivision of land and thus a real market impediment to land assembly. . . .

might be upgraded—*i.e.,* given to an owner who will use it in a way that the legislature deems more beneficial to the public—in the process. To reason, as the Court does, that the incidental public benefits resulting from the subsequent ordinary use of private property render economic development takings "for public use" is to wash out any distinction between private and public use of property—and thereby effectively to delete the words "for public use" from the Takings Clause of the Fifth Amendment. . . .

Petitioners are not holdouts; they do not seek increased compensation, and none is opposed to new development in the area. Theirs is an objection in principle: They claim that the NLDC's proposed use for their confiscated property is not a "public" one for purposes of the Fifth Amendment. While the government may take their homes to build a road or a railroad or to eliminate a property use that harms the public, say petitioners, it cannot take their property for the private use of other owners simply because the new owners may make more productive use of the property. . . .

. . . We give considerable deference to legislatures' determinations about what governmental activities will advantage the public. But were the political branches the sole arbiters of the public-private distinction, the Public Use Clause would amount to little more than hortatory fluff. An external, judicial check on how the public use requirement is interpreted, however limited, is necessary if this constraint on government power is to retain any meaning. . . .

Our cases have generally identified three categories of takings that comply with the public use requirement, though it is in the nature of things that the boundaries between these categories are not always firm. Two are relatively straightforward and uncontroversial. First, the sovereign may transfer private property to public ownership—such as for a road, a hospital, or a military base. Second, the sovereign may transfer private property to private parties, often common carriers, who make the property available for the public's use—such as with a railroad, a public utility, or a stadium. But "public ownership" and "use-by-the-public" are sometimes too constricting and impractical ways to define the scope of the Public Use Clause. Thus we have allowed that, in certain circumstances and to meet certain exigencies, takings that serve a public purpose also satisfy the Constitution even if the property is destined for subsequent private use. . . .

. . . [This case] presents an issue of first impression: Are economic development takings constitutional? I would hold that they are not. . . . In *Berman,* we upheld takings within a blighted neighborhood of Washington, D.C. The neighborhood had so deteriorated that, for example, 64.3% of its dwellings were beyond repair. It had become burdened with "overcrowding of dwellings," "lack of adequate streets and alleys," and "lack of light and air." 348 U.S. at 34. Congress had determined that the neighborhood had become "injurious to the public health, safety, morals, and welfare" and that it was necessary to "eliminat[e] all such injurious conditions by employing all means necessary and appropriate for the purpose," including eminent domain. Mr. Berman's department store was not itself blighted. Having approved of Congress' decision to eliminate the harm to the public emanating from the blighted neighborhood, however, we did not second-guess its decision to treat the neighborhood as a whole rather than lot-by-lot. *See . . . Midkiff*, 467 U.S., at 244, ("[I]t is only the taking's purpose, and not its mechanics, that must pass scrutiny").

In *Midkiff*, we upheld a land condemnation scheme in Hawaii whereby title in real property was taken from lessors and transferred to lessees. At that time, the State and Federal Governments owned nearly 49% of the State's land, and another 47% was in the hands of only 72 private landowners. Concentration of land ownership was so dramatic that on the State's most urbanized island, Oahu, 22 landowners owned 72.5% of the fee simple titles. The Hawaii Legislature had concluded that the oligopoly in land ownership was "skewing the State's residential fee simple market, inflating land prices, and injuring the public tranquility and welfare," and therefore enacted a condemnation scheme for redistributing title. 467 U.S. at 232. . . .

Yet for all the emphasis on deference, *Berman* and *Midkiff* hewed to a bedrock principle without which our public use jurisprudence would collapse: "A purely private taking could not withstand the scrutiny of the public use requirement; it would serve no legitimate purpose of government and would thus be void." *Midkiff*, 467 U.S., at 245. . . .

The Court's holdings in *Berman* and *Midkiff* were true to the principle underlying the Public Use Clause. In both those cases, the extraordinary, pre-condemnation use of the targeted property inflicted affirmative harm on society—in *Berman* through blight resulting from extreme poverty and in *Midkiff* through oligopoly resulting from extreme wealth. And in both cases, the relevant legislative body had found that eliminating the existing property use was necessary to remedy the harm. Thus a public purpose was realized when the harmful use was eliminated. Because each taking *directly* achieved a public benefit, it did not matter that the property was turned over to private use. Here, in contrast, New London does not claim that Susette Kelo's and Wilhelmina Dery's well-maintained homes are the source of any social harm. Indeed, it could not so claim without adopting the absurd argument that any single-family home that might be razed to make way for an apartment building, or any church that might be replaced with a retail store, or any small business that might be more lucrative if it were instead part of a national franchise, is inherently harmful to society and thus within the government's power to condemn. . . .

The Court also puts special emphasis on facts peculiar to this case: The NLDC's plan is the product of a relatively careful deliberative process; it proposes to use eminent domain for a multipart, integrated plan rather than for isolated property transfer; it promises an array of incidental benefits (even esthetic ones), not just increased tax revenue; it comes on the heels of a legislative determination that New London is a depressed municipality. . . . But none has legal significance to blunt the force of today's holding. If legislative prognostications about the secondary public benefits of a new use can legitimate a taking, there is nothing in the Court's rule or in Justice Kennedy's gloss on that rule to prohibit property transfers generated with less care, that are less comprehensive, that happen to result from less elaborate process, whose only projected advantage is the incidence of higher taxes, or that hope to transform an already prosperous city into an even more prosperous one. . . .

Any property may now be taken for the benefit of another private party, but the fallout from this decision will not be random. The beneficiaries are likely to be those citizens with disproportionate influence and power in the political process, including large corporations and development firms. As for the victims, the government now has license to transfer property from those with fewer resources to those with more. . . .

THOMAS, J., dissenting.

Long ago, William Blackstone wrote that "the law of the land . . . postpone[s] even public necessity to the sacred and inviolable rights of private property." 1 Commentaries on the Laws of England 134–135 (1765). The Framers embodied that principle in the Constitution, allowing the government to take property not for "public necessity," but instead for "public use." . . . Defying this understanding, the Court replaces the Public Use Clause with a "[P]ublic [P]urpose" Clause . . . . This deferential shift in phraseology enables the Court to hold, against all common sense, that a costly urban-renewal project whose stated purpose is a vague promise of new jobs and increased tax revenue, but which is also suspiciously agreeable to the Pfizer Corporation, is for a "public use." . . .

Notes

1. *How much deference?*   The majority opinion, Justice Kennedy's concurrence, and Justice O'Connor's dissent disagree as to the amount of deference that the Court should give to New London's formulation of its development plan. Explain the differing perspectives.

2. *The place—New London, Connecticut:*   What is the relevant geographic scope for the "public use" determination—the city as a whole, the entire area condemned by the NLDC, each of the seven parcels included in the development plan, the individual lot of each petitioner, or something else? How, if at all, would your answer influence the outcome of this case? We have considered the relationship between geographic scale and legal outcome in several other contexts, including the "changed conditions" doctrine for covenant termination and the "reasonableness" rule for enforcement (or nonenforcement) of common interest community rules. Can you think of any other examples? How, if at all, are those examples relevant here?

3. *More to the story—the best laid plans . . .*   Under the NLDC's development plan, Pfizer would buy land in Fort Trumbull for an office and research facility, as well as housing for its future employees. With Pfizer's commitment, it seemed like Fort Trumbull would become a thriving neighborhood, complete with research facilities, attractive housing, shops, and beautiful parks. But none of this ever materialized. Instead, in 2009, after the onset of the great recession, Pfizer announced that it would leave New London to cut costs—taking 1,400 jobs with it—and consolidate its operation with an already existing Pfizer campus in neighboring Groton. Today, the Fort Trumbull neighborhood is virtually deserted. The houses of the *Kelo* petitioners were demolished, and all that remains is the abandoned Pfizer research buildings. Preservationist Avner Gregory purchased Suzette Kelo's "little pink house," dismantled it, and reassembled the structure in a neighborhood several miles away.

The home of Susette Kelo, June 27, 2005
Source: Spencer Platt / Staff / Getty Images

Kelo had originally purchased her home for $53,000 in about 1997. She had long wished to live by the beach, and after refurbishing the structure she selected the exterior paint color "Odessa Rose"—giving rise to the moniker, "the little pink house." After her home was condemned, she received $400,000 in compensation, but remained bitter toward those who had sanctioned what she viewed as the "stealing" of her home. In 2006, Kelo sent a holiday card to the 30 or so officials who had been active in the condemnation lawsuit, featuring a charming, snow-covered image of her little pink house. The message inside proclaimed,

> Here is the house that you did take.
> From me to you, this spell I make.
> Your houses, your homes, your family, your friends.
> May they live in misery that never ends.
> I curse you all. May you rot in hell. To each of you I send this spell.
> For the rest of your lives I wish you ill. I send this now by the power of will.

See Patrick McGeehan, *Pfizer to Leave City that Won Land-Use Case*, The New York Times, Nov. 12, 2009; George Lefcoe, Book Review, *Jeff Benedict's Little Pink House: The Back Story of the* Kelo *Case*, 42 Conn. L. Rev. 925 (2010).

4. *State legislative reactions:* *Kelo* was not alone in her outrage. After the Court's decision (and its invitation to states to strengthen their protections against eminent domain, if they so desired), many states in fact placed tougher restrictions on the condemnation power. *See* National Conference of State Legislatures, *Eminent Domain Overview*, http://www.ncsl.org/research/environment-and-natural-resources/eminent-domain-overview.aspx (visited July 16, 2015) (calculating that between 2005-2011, 42 states passed legislation or ballot measures responding to *Kelo*, and providing summary of reforms by state). Do such reforms suggest that *Kelo* was a good or a bad decision? Challenge yourself to articulate arguments on both sides of that question. We will look at some of the state legislative responses in the *Beyond the Black Letter* discussion problem in section C, below.

Problems

1. *A Polish community:* In 1980, the General Motors Corporation informed the city of Detroit that it would close its Cadillac and Fisher Body plants, but offered to build an assembly complex in the city if a suitable site could be found. Undisputed evidence cited by the Michigan Supreme Court (dissenting opinion) showed that unemployment was of "calamitous" proportions throughout the state of Michigan, and particularly in Detroit (up to 18%), whose "economic lifeblood" was the floundering automobile industry. Detroit identified a 465-acre site acceptable to GM, acquired the property by eminent domain, and then resold the property to GM. Detroit's asserted purpose for the condemnation and resale was to promote industry and commerce, thereby adding jobs and taxes to the economic base of the municipality and the state. The condemned properties were within an area the dissent described as "a tightly-knit residential enclave of first- and second-generation [Polish-Americans], for many of whom their home was their single most valuable and cherished asset and their stable ethnic neighborhood the unchanging symbol of the security and quality of their lives." Would Detroit's exercise of

eminent domain be valid under federal law after *Kelo*? As a matter of policy, *should* the city have been allowed to condemn private property in an attempt to save the city from economic ruin? *See Poletown Neighborhood Council v. City of Detroit*, 304 N.W.2d 455, 470 (Mich. 1981), *overruled, City of Wayne v. Hathcock*, 684 N.W.2d 765 (Mich. 2004).

2. *Parking at the airport:*   The Rhode Island Economic Development Corporation (EDC) filed an action to condemn a parking garage owned by a private operator adjacent to a public airport managed by the EDC (through its subsidiary). The EDC had been engaged in negotiations with the private garage operator over the future of potentially lucrative parking facilities at the airport. When the negotiations stalled, the EDC initiated an action to condemn the garage. The EDC acted under the state's "quick-take statute" that gave the EDC authority to condemn property under expedited procedures designed to avoid delaying the completion of public projects while the parties wrangled over various issues. The condemnation action was undertaken, in part, to enhance the EDC's negotiating position with the garage operator with respect to future parking facilities. Was EDC's exercise of eminent domain valid under post-*Kelo* federal law? Are the facts of this case analogous to those of *Kelo* or can they be distinguished? As a matter of policy, *should* the EDC have been allowed to condemn the private parking garage? *See Rhode Island Economic Development Corp. v. Parking Co., L.P.*, 892 A.2d 87 (R.I. 2006).

3. *Skills review—argument based on precedent:*   Recall the skills exercise of Chapter 1, which covered the development of precedent-based arguments. You represent the *Kelo* petitioners. How would you distinguish *Berman* and *Midkiff* and argue that they should not control the outcome in this case? Justice O'Connor's dissent should help you reconstruct the petitioners' argument. What are the weaknesses of that argument, and can they be overcome given the facts of the case? Conversely, reconstruct the respondents' counterargument that the facts of *Kelo* are analogous to those of *Berman* and *Midkiff* and, therefore, those cases are controlling. When articulating both petitioners' and respondents' arguments, be sure to clearly articulate the relevant rule, highlight how the facts of *Kelo* are similar (or different) from those cases, and explain why those similarities (or differences) should matter.

2. Just Compensation

Even when the issue of "public use" is not in dispute, the calculation of "just compensation" must be resolved in every eminent domain case. This is a highly fact-dependent inquiry that generates considerable litigation. We will undertake but a brief summary of the law here, followed by one case that gives you a flavor of the types of arguments landowners and government condemnation authorities make in just compensation litigation.

Complete condemnation—fair market value: In some cases, the government condemns a property owner's entire tract of land. In such cases, just compensation requires the payment of the land's *fair market value* at the time of the condemnation, measured as the sales price the property could command on the open market in a transaction between a willing buyer and a willing seller. Because a hypothetical *willing seller* is the benchmark for the calculation, the condemnation award generally excludes subjective or emotional value. Likewise, the condemnation award usually excludes lost profits, moving expenses, and the like. On the other hand, cutting in favor of the landowner, courts typically set the fair market value of the property as its value if put to its reasonably imagined *highest and best use.* Thus, a modest single-family home retained by an aging landowner in an increasingly commercialized neighborhood might be valued at the price the property would be worth if put to a commercial use consistent with local zoning. Courts generally decline to adjust the property value (upward or downward) to reflect the positive or negative impacts the government's proposed project will have on neighborhood property values.

Partial condemnation—severance damages: In some situations, the government might take only a portion of a landowner's property. For a road-widening project, for example, the government might take only a strip of land from each owner along the roadway corridor. In that case, the law uniformly requires payment of *severance damages* to make up for the reduced value of the landowner's remaining property. The total award can be calculated in one of two ways. First, the award can be calculated as the fair market value of the segment taken plus the difference in the remaining property's fair market value (before and after the condemnation). Alternatively, compensation can be calculated as the difference between the entire property's fair market value before the condemnation and the remaining land's value after the condemnation. Under either formula, if the remaining property increases due to *special benefits* accruing from the condemnation, then the award will be reduced by the amount of the special benefits. In general, special benefits are those that directly and proximately affect the property remaining, as distinguished from *general benefits*, which are incidental and shared by the general public within the area of the taking.

Property damage without condemnation—special damages: About half the states recognize that private property can be damaged by neighboring public improvements, even if the land has not been taken by eminent domain. Public improvements can include such things as airport runway use and changes in road access. In those cases, some states require the payment of damages for the diminution in value of the adjoining property, provided that the complaining landowner has sustained *special damages* distinct from those suffered by the general public.

N.J. Comm'r of Transp. v. 200 Route 17, L.L.C.

22 A.3d 1012 (N.J. Super. App. Div.), *cert. denied,* 34 A.3d 782 (N.J. 2011)

┌───┐
│   **Reading Guide**   │

The New Jersey Department of Transportation condemned 1.65 acres of the defendant's property, leaving it with 1.21 acres of vacant land. In such cases of *partial condemnation,* the state must award *severance damages*—here under New Jersey law, the fair market value of the 1.65 acres as of the date of the taking, based on the property's "highest and best use," plus an award for damages to the remaining 1.21 acres. But what does that mean? Is fair market value limited to the value of the property in its present condition, or can it also include projected future improvements?

└───┘

CARCHMAN, P.J.A.D.

This appeal by the State from a condemnation award, requires us to consider whether an appraiser, in opining as to the highest and best use of condemned property, may consider hypothetical costs of improvements and renovations to the property in determining its fair market value. We hold that the State is required to compensate a property owner for the land and improvements in their present condition, and the trier of fact may consider the reasonable probability of future renovations and approvals required to improve the property to its highest and best use, discounted by the value of the risks and costs of making such improvements. . . .

. . . On May 23, 2005, the State filed a verified complaint and declaration of taking seeking to acquire approximately 1.65 acres of defendant's 2.86 acre property. The property is located on Route 17 southbound in Maywood and Rochelle Park and is improved by a one-story 31,775–square–foot building, which was directly accessible from Route 17 southbound. The building was rented by Sears and contained a merchandise and service center, parts counter, warehouse and offices. The site is also improved with a blacktop parking lot, which provided parking for 112 cars. The building and improvements were included in the taking. The property remaining in defendant's possession after the taking was reduced to 1.21 acres of vacant land without direct access to Route 17.

At the time of the State's acquisition, the land use ordinance in Maywood permitted industrial uses only; the existing mixed use was a grandfathered, non-conforming use. . . .

At trial, the jury was charged with deciding the amount of just compensation defendant was owed for the property interests acquired by the State and damages to the remainder. . . . The State presented Norman Goldberg as a valuation expert. . . .

Goldberg valued the property in its actual physical condition as of May 23, 2005. . . . In forming his opinion as to value, he recognized the reasonable probability that the owner could obtain land use approvals to renovate the building for its highest and best use as a commercial property. Ultimately, Goldberg appraised the property at $5,637,000. . . .

Brody [defendant's expert] concluded that the "highest and best use" of the property would be as a commercial or retail building. Brody testified that to achieve that use, the property would require $1,589,000 in renovations to create an appropriate interior for the property. That cost included removing some of the interior and installing partitions and tiling. After considering all three of the above approaches, and deducting the $1,589,000 of improvement costs, Brody concluded that the fair market value of the property and damage to the remainder was $8,727,000. The jury returned a verdict of $8,096,140. . . .

We first set forth basic principles that inform our analysis. When the State exercises its power to take private property under the Eminent Domain Act, *N.J.S.A.* 20:3-1 to –50, the State must pay to the property owner an amount representing just compensation for the property taken. *N.J. Const.* art. I, ¶20; *State, by Comm'r of Transp. v. Caoili,* . . . 639 A.2d 275 (1994). Just compensation is "the fair market value of the property as of the date of the taking, determined by what a willing buyer and a willing seller would agree to, neither being under any compulsion to act." *Ibid.* . . . It is the "value that would be assigned to the acquired property by knowledgeable parties freely negotiating for its sale under normal market conditions based on all surrounding circumstances at the time of the taking." *Ibid.*

When calculating value in any condemnation case, the "inquiry is not limited to the actual use of the property on the date of taking but is, rather, based on [the property's] highest and best use." *Cnty. of Monmouth v. Hilton,* 760 A.2d 786 ([N.J. Super.] 2000). . . . Highest and best use has been defined as, "the use that at the time of the appraisal is the most profitable, likely use or alternatively, the available use and program of future utilization that produces the highest present land value provided that use has as a prerequisite a probability of achievement." *Ibid.*

Here, the parties do not dispute that the highest and best use of this particular property is as a commercial retail property. . . .

On appeal, the State asserts that the trial court erred in refusing to bar Brody's testimony as to the value of the property as if it had already been renovated. The State argues that it is too speculative to appraise the property using the value as if the property contained a commercial building, when currently, the property contains a service area as well as warehouse, office and retail space. Modifications would be required, and ascribing certain monetary amounts to those modifications is speculative.

The State further contends that the basis of the trial court's decision was the judge's "belief that it was not only reasonably probable that the necessary legal approvals would be granted to renovate the subject completely as a commercial property, but also that it was reasonably probable that a buyer on May 23, 2005, would in fact renovate the property completely as a commercial retail property at a substantial cost."

The distinction between enhancing market value and constituting the basis of market value is, in our view, critical, and it is this distinction that renders defendant's appraisal methodology legally defective. . . .

Ultimately, the issue can be restated as follows: What would a willing buyer pay a willing seller, without compulsion, for a substandard building, knowing that the buyer would be obligated to obtain appropriate land use and building approvals, as well as spend 1.5 million dollars for the property to achieve its highest and best use? This is different from defendant's expert's approach, which entailed simply assuming that the building was already improved and then deducting the costs of improvement.

To suggest that the two values are the same fails to account for the issues and costs involved in such a venture. Perhaps a buyer might pay a premium if it knew that such an investment would result in the property's highest and best use, but to suggest that the buyer would pay "full value" is speculative at best. To analogize, this is similar to predicting what a willing buyer would pay a willing seller for a "fixer-upper" knowing that an additional 1.5 million dollars would be necessary to achieve the highest and best use and increase the value of the property. There are uses and costs involved, beyond improvement costs, that must be considered. . . .

Defendant primarily relied on *Hilton*. In *Hilton*, the property contained a large Victorian house, which housed five families. Defendant's expert testified that the highest and best use would be as a mid-rise building with ninety-two units on a hypothetical four-lot assemblage. No permit had been applied for and no site-plan approval sought.

We explained, "[i]n sum, we are persuaded that appraising the value of defendant's property as if a four-lot assemblage had already taken place as of the date of taking and then basing highest and best use on such an assemblage constituted a fundamentally untenable and legally unsupportable approach." *Hilton, supra,* 760 A.2d 786. However, we also observed that these potential changes are relevant factors in calculating what a buyer might pay for the property. . . . Essentially in *Hilton* we . . . analogized the situation to zoning cases.

The State cites a number of cases for the proposition that in New Jersey, "appraisals based on speculative improvements that do not exist on the valuation date cannot be considered in valuing a property." Specifically, the State relies on . . . *Port Authority of New York v. Howell,* . . . 173 A.2d 310 (App. Div.), *certif. denied,* . . . 174 A.2d 927 (1961). . . .

Howell involved the taking of two properties. One included a two-and-a-half story house and garage on the lot. The other property contained a "shanty" and was operated as a used car lot. Defendant argued that the trial court should have admitted evidence of a hypothetical office building which conceivably could be erected on one of the lots. The trial court characterized this suggested testimony as "pure conjecture." *Howell, supra,* 173 A.2d 310. On appeal . . . we affirmed, holding that "[t]he trial court's rejection of appellants' proposed proofs based on a calculation of profits and costs arising from such a theoretical undertaking was fully justified." *Howell, supra,* . . . 173 A.2d 310. . . .

Here, defendant argues that the building should be valued as a renovated commercial structure, even though it is not renovated. This approach is too simplistic. Defendant extrapolates language from the cited cases to argue that the value of the property on the date of the taking is not determinative, and that "highest and best use" is a hypothetical concept which requires an assumption that all of the improvements and renovations an owner may have made to a property are in place. This is not the case here.

This property has a structure on it. Speculative improvements to the property, that do not exist on the valuation date, cannot be considered in valuing this property. Prior to this taking, there is no indication that defendant planned to make any of these improvements. It is illogical to suggest that the State is responsible for hypothetical improvements defendant could have made to its property, and then required to pay for the property, as if defendant had made them. This provides a windfall to the owner, who has not improved the property, but would be paid as if he had. Rather, the State is required to pay for the building "as is," considering the reasonable probability of future renovations and approvals required to improve the property to its highest and best use, discounted by the risks and costs of such venture, just as a buyer would pay for the building in its current condition, then make any improvements necessary to bring the building to the buyer's desired use.

We conclude that the State is entitled to a new trial on the issue of the fair market value of this property. Accordingly, we vacate the jury award and remand for a new trial as to just compensation for the taking of defendant's property. . . .

Notes

1. *Highest and best use:*   Reading between the lines, can you articulate the precise rules advocated for by the defendant landowner and the New Jersey DOT, respectively? What rule did the court apply?

2. *Not now, but soon:*   The analysis undertaken by the New Jersey Superior Court is representative. As one source explains, the highest and best use generally means "the *reasonably probable* and legal use . . . which is physically possible, appropriately supported, financially feasible, and that results in the

highest value." Did the defendant show that use of the property as a commercial or retail building was "reasonably probable"? What additional evidence could the defendant have supplied to strengthen its case, if any? *See* Harry J. Riskin & Cory K. Kestner, *Not Now, But Soon: Lessons in Making a Reasonable Probability Case for Rezoning, Assemblage, Lease Renewals and Other Value Enhancements*, ST030 ALI-ABA 473, 476 (Jan. 2012).

Although such value enhancement is warranted in some cases, courts are careful to screen from the jury evidence that is unreliable and speculative. As Riskin and Kestner explain,

> By valuing properties based upon uses that do not presently exist and are not currently legally permitted, there is a potential that property owners will seek compensation in excess of their property's fair market value. There is also a risk that values will be based upon uses that are only possible or speculative. The courts address these concerns in two ways. First, the court should perform a "gatekeeper" function and preview the evidence to ensure that it is sufficiently supported and that it is not merely an invitation for the jury to speculate. Second, where there is sufficient evidence that the proposed change is "reasonably probable," the value conclusion must reflect the fact that the change has not happened. A discount to a value based upon the proposed change will account for the uncertainty and risk that the change may not occur. In effect, when evidence of a different potential future use is admitted, it is for the purpose of showing an enhancement to value under the current conditions and not to prove a value as if the change had already occurred.

Id. at 477-78. Did the New Jersey Superior Court take one or both of those approaches? Did it reach a result likely to provide "just" compensation?

B. REGULATORY TAKINGS

There is general agreement that the drafters of the Fifth Amendment intended for the government to pay compensation when it physically appropriates or seizes private property. But what about those cases in which the government *regulates* property under its police power, but does not acquire title or otherwise physically take over the property? Should compensation be required, at least if the economic impact on the landowner is so severe that it is the functional equivalent of a physical appropriation of property? The regulatory takings doctrine posits an affirmative response to that question.

The controversial doctrine began to crystalize in 1922, when Justices Holmes and Brandeis staked out the parameters of the debate in *Pennsylvania Coal v. Mahon* (the first case in this section). Later in the 20th century, the Court showed a renewed interest in the doctrine. At the same time, a growing social movement of the 1980s and beyond was fueled by antipathy toward government regulation, and meshed with the legal idea that governments should compensate landowners when regulations "go too far" (in Justice Holmes' words in *Pennsylvania Coal v. Mahon*).

Supporters of the doctrine believe that it forces governments to act efficiently and fairly. A change brought about by regulation is efficient, advocates explain, if it "can improve the situations of some people without damaging the situations of any."[3] Frank I. Michelman, *Property, Utility, and Fairness: Comments on the Ethical Foundations of "Just Compensation" Law*, 80 Harv. L. Rev. 1165, 1175 (1967). To accomplish this, the government might be required to compensate those who would otherwise be worse off after regulation. The regulatory takings doctrine is also said to promote fairness, according to the Supreme Court, because it "bar[s] Government from forcing some people alone to bear public burdens which, in all fairness and justice, should be borne by the public as a whole." *Armstrong v. United States*, 364 U.S. 40, 49 (1960). *See generally*, Richard A. Epstein, *The Spurious Constitutional Distinction Between Takings and Regulation*, 11 Engage: J. Federalist Society Prac. Groups 11 (2010).

But others believe the doctrine is unsupported by constitutional text or the intent of the framers. The text of the Fifth Amendment, critics point out, contemplates the taking of property by the government, and says nothing about the *regulation* of property. Likewise, they continue, early sources reflect two primary rationales for the amendment, both of which concern physical seizure, and not regulation. First, reacting against Revolutionary war practices, the clause was designed to prohibit the military from seizing private goods during wartime without compensation. Additionally, letters written by James Madison suggest that he intended for the clause to require compensation to slave owners if slavery were abolished. As a consequence, critics conclude, the doctrine serves primarily to chill important regulation, and it allows the judiciary to intrude on the sphere of the political branches of government. *See generally*, William M. Treanor, *Regulatory Takings*, 12 Engage: J. Federalist Society Prac. Groups 4 (2011); John D. Echeverria, *The Death of Regulatory Takings*, 34 Ecology L.Q. 291 (2007); J. Peter Byrne, *Ten Arguments for the Abolition of the Regulatory Takings Doctrine*, 22 Ecol. L.Q. 89 (1995).

The debate continues about the doctrine's application and validity. As evidence of the continuing disagreement, you will notice that most of the cases in this section were decided by a slim majority of the Supreme Court, each over vigorous dissent. The following *A Place to Start* box introduces you to the tests and other considerations relied upon by the courts when resolving regulatory takings challenges.

---

3. "This principle is known to the initiated as the Pareto Rule and changes which conform to it are called Pareto-optimal." Michelman, 80 Harv. L. Rev. at 1175 fn. 24.

A Place to Start | Regulatory Takings

■ *Inverse condemnation:* When a regulation reduces the value of a landowner's property and the landowner sues to recover compensation, this is sometimes called an *inverse condemnation* action. Essentially, the landowner is claiming that the regulation went so far that it worked the functional equivalent of a condemnation of property by eminent domain, and therefore the government should be required to pay compensation. Whereas the government initiates *condemnation* actions, private property owners initiate *inverse condemnation* actions.

■ *The legal tests:* We will consider landmark cases in chronological order. Notice how various takings tests emerged over time:

  ▪ *Multi-factor approach:* The Supreme Court generally engages in an *ad hoc* evaluation, under which it weighs a number of factors to determine whether government action rises to the level of a compensable taking. *Penn Central* embodies this approach.

  ▪ *Categorical rules:* The Court has also developed two purportedly bright-line categorical rules that generally confine the analysis to a single factor that can override other countervailing considerations. *Loretto* and *Lucas* represent this approach.

■ *Two evolving issues:* Many commentators complain that the development of the regulatory takings doctrine has been muddled, inconsistent, and incoherent. To impose a bit of order on your study, it might be helpful to focus especially on a pair of issues:

  ▪ *The denominator question:* As you read the following cases, trace the Court's evolving position on how to measure the economic impact of a challenged regulation with reference to a fraction: The *numerator* represents the value of the property taken by regulation, and the *denominator* represents the property interest against which the loss in value is to be measured. As you will see, the proper measure of the denominator has been the subject of considerable confusion and disagreement; the issue is variously referred to as the *denominator question*, the *parcel as a whole* issue, and *conceptual severance*.

  ▪ *Average reciprocity of advantage:* This is a rough fairness consideration. Try to discern its precise meaning, as well as how it influences the outcome of either the multi-factor test or the categorical rules.

DIGGING DEEPER:

  ▪ As you read the material in this section, pay attention to the precise distinction between eminent domain and regulatory takings. Is one the natural outgrowth of the other, or not?

  ▪ Be sure to notice that the question of whether a particular regulation requires *compensation* is an issue distinct from the question of whether a particular regulation is *constitutionally valid*.

  ▪ Focus on litigation strategy. That is, which of the legal tests do property owners and government regulators, respectively, prefer, and why?

1. The Multi-Factor Approach

Pennsylvania Coal Co. v. Mahon

260 U.S. 393 (1922)

┌─────────────────── **Reading Guide** ───────────────────┐

This case is often said to be the foundation of the regulatory takings doctrine. To what extent is the doctrine a logical extension of the law of eminent domain, and to what extent is it a novel judicial invention? To understand the facts of this case, it is important to know that Pennsylvania law recognized three distinct legal estates in land: the *surface estate*, subsurface *mineral rights*, and the *support estate* (necessary to keep the surface from collapsing when the underlying minerals are removed). Each could be conveyed separately from the other.

└──┘

HOLMES, J.

This is a bill in equity brought by the defendants in error to prevent the Pennsylvania Coal Company from mining under their property in such way as to remove the supports and cause a subsidence of the surface and of their house. The bill sets out a deed executed by the Coal Company in 1878, under which the plaintiffs claim. The deed conveys the surface but in express terms reserves the right to remove all the coal under the same and the grantee takes the premises with the risk and waives all claim for damages that may arise from mining out the coal. But the plaintiffs say that whatever may have been the Coal Company's rights, they were taken away by an Act of Pennsylvania, approved May 27, 1921 (P. L. 1198), commonly known there as the Kohler Act. . . .

The statute forbids the mining of anthracite coal in such way as to cause the subsidence of, among other things, any structure used as a human habitation, with certain exceptions. . . . As applied to this case the statute is admitted to destroy previously existing rights of property and contract. The question is whether the police power can be stretched so far.

Government hardly could go on if to some extent values incident to property could not be diminished without paying for every such change in the general law. As long recognized some values are enjoyed under an implied limitation and must yield to the police power. But obviously the implied limitation must have its limits or the contract and due process clauses are gone. One fact for consideration in determining such limits is the extent of the diminution. When it reaches a certain magnitude, in most if not in all cases there must be an exercise of eminent domain and compensation to sustain the act. . . .

This is the case of a single private house. No doubt there is a public interest even in this, as there is in every purchase and sale and in all that happens within the commonwealth. Some existing rights may be modified even in such a case. . . . But usually in ordinary private affairs the public interest does not warrant much of this kind of interference. A source of damage to such a house is not a public nuisance even if similar damage is inflicted on others in different places. The damage is not common or public. . . . The extent of the public interest is shown by the statute to be limited, since the statute ordinarily does not apply to land when the surface is owned by the owner of the coal. Furthermore, it is not justified as a protection of personal safety. That could be provided for by notice. Indeed the very foundation of this bill is that the defendant gave timely notice of its intent to mine under the house. On the other hand the extent of the taking is great. It purports to abolish what is recognized in Pennsylvania as an estate in land—a very valuable estate—and what is declared by the Court below to be a contract hitherto binding the plaintiffs. If we were called upon to deal with the plaintiffs' position alone we should think it clear that the statute does not disclose a public interest sufficient to warrant so extensive a destruction of the defendant's constitutionally protected rights.[4]

But the case has been treated as one in which the general validity of the act should be discussed. The Attorney General of the State, the City of Scranton and the representatives of other extensive interests were allowed to take part in the argument below and have submitted their contentions here. It seems, therefore, to be our duty to go farther in the statement of our opinion, in order that it may be known at once, and that further suits should not be brought in vain.

It is our opinion that the act cannot be sustained as an exercise of the police power, so far as it affects the mining of coal under streets or cities in places where the right to mine such coal has been reserved. . . . What makes the right to mine coal valuable is that it can be exercised with profit. To make it commercially impracticable to mine certain coal has very nearly the same effect for constitutional purposes as appropriating or destroying it. This we think that we are warranted in assuming that the statute does.

It is true that in *Plymouth Coal Co. v. Pennsylvania*, 232 U. S. 531, it was held competent for the legislature to require a pillar of coal to the left along the line of adjoining property, that with the pillar on the other side of the line would be a barrier sufficient for the safety of the employees of either mine in case the other should be abandoned and allowed to fill with water. But that was a requirement for the safety of employees invited into the mine, and secured an average reciprocity of advantage that has been recognized as a justification of various laws.

. . . The protection of private property in the Fifth Amendment presupposes that it is wanted for public use, but provides that it shall not be taken for such

---

4. [Justice Holmes' first draft ended here. Can you discern a change in analysis for the remaining portion of his opinion? *See* Joseph F. DiMento, *Mining the Archives of Pennsylvania Coal: Heaps of Constitutional Mischief*, 11 J. Legal Hist. 396, 406 (1990).—Eds.]

use without compensation. . . . When this seemingly absolute protection is found to be qualified by the police power, the natural tendency of human nature is to extend the qualification more and more until at last private property disappears. But that cannot be accomplished in this way under the Constitution of the United States.

The general rule at least is that while property may be regulated to a certain extent, if regulation goes too far it will be recognized as a taking. . . . In general it is not plain that a man's misfortunes or necessities will justify his shifting the damages to his neighbor's shoulders. . . . We are in danger of forgetting that a strong public desire to improve the public condition is not enough to warrant achieving the desire by a shorter cut than the constitutional way of paying for the change. As we already have said this is a question of degree-and therefore cannot be disposed of by general propositions. . . .

We assume, of course, that the statute was passed upon the conviction that an exigency existed that would warrant it, and we assume that an exigency exists that would warrant the exercise of eminent domain. But the question at bottom is upon whom the loss of the changes desired should fall. So far as private persons or communities have seen fit to take the risk of acquiring only surface rights, we cannot see that the fact that their risk has become a danger warrants the giving to them greater rights than they bought. Decree reversed.

BRANDEIS, J., dissenting.

. . . Coal in place is land, and the right of the owner to use his land is not absolute. He may not so use it as to create a public nuisance, and uses, once harmless, may, owing to changed conditions, seriously threaten the public welfare. Whenever they do, the Legislature has power to prohibit such uses without paying compensation; and the power to prohibit extends alike to the manner, the character and the purpose of the use. . . .

Every restriction upon the use of property imposed in the exercise of the police power deprives the owner of some right theretofore enjoyed, and is, in that sense, an abridgment by the state of rights in property without making compensation. But restriction imposed to protect the public health, safety or morals from dangers threatened is not a taking. The restriction here in question is merely the prohibition of a noxious use. The property so restricted remains in the possession of its owner. The state does not appropriate it or make any use of it. The state merely prevents the owner from making a use which interferes with paramount rights of the public. Whenever the use prohibited ceases to be noxious—as it may because of further change in local or social conditions—the restriction will have to be removed and the owner will again be free to enjoy his property as heretofore.

The restriction upon the use of this property cannot, of course, be lawfully imposed, unless its purpose is to protect the public. But the purpose of a restriction does not cease to be public, because incidentally some private persons may thereby receive gratuitously valuable special benefits. Thus, owners of low buildings may obtain, through statutory restrictions upon the height of neighboring structures, benefits equivalent to an easement of light and air. *Welch v. Swasey,* 214 U.S. 91. . . . Further, a restriction, though imposed for a public purpose, will not be lawful, unless the restriction is an appropriate means to the public end. But to keep coal in place is surely an appropriate means of preventing subsidence of the surface; and ordinarily it is the only available means. Restriction upon use does not become inappropriate as a means, merely because it deprives the owner of the only use to which the property can then be profitably put. The liquor and the oleomargine cases settled that. *Mugler v. Kansas,* 123 U.S. 623, 668; *Powell v. Pennsylvania,* 127 U.S. 678, 682. *See also Hadacheck v. Los Angeles,* 239 U.S. 394. . . . Nor is a restriction imposed through exercise of the police power inappropriate as a means, merely because the same end might be effected through exercise of the power of eminent domain, or otherwise at public expense. Every restriction upon the height of buildings might be secured through acquiring by eminent domain the right of each owner to build above the limiting height; but it is settled that the state need not resort to that power. Compare *Laurel Hill Cemetery v. San Francisco,* 216 U.S. 358; *Missouri Pacific Railway Co. v. Omaha,* 235 U.S. 121. If by mining anthracite coal the owner would necessarily unloose poisonous gases, I suppose no one would doubt the power of the state to prevent the mining, without buying his coal fields. And why may not the state, likewise, without paying compensation, prohibit one from digging so deep or excavating so near the surface, as to expose the community to like dangers? In the latter case, as in the former, carrying on the business would be a public nuisance.

It is said that one fact for consideration in determining whether the limits of the police power have been exceeded is the extent of the resulting diminution in value, and that here the restriction destroys existing rights of property and contract. But values are relative. If we are to consider the value of the coal kept in place by the restriction, we should compare it with the value of all other parts of the land. That is, with the value not of the coal alone, but with the value of the whole property. The rights of an owner as against the public are not increased by dividing the interests in his property into surface and subsoil. The sum of the rights in the parts cannot be greater than the rights in the whole. The estate of an owner in land is grandiloquently described as extending *ab orco usque ad coelum.* But I suppose no one would contend that by selling his interest above 100 feet from the surface he could prevent the state from limiting, by the police power, the height of structures in a city. And why should a sale of underground rights bar the state's power? For aught that appears the value of the coal kept in place by the restriction may be negligible as compared with the value of the whole property, or even as compared with that part of it which is represented by the coal remaining in place and which may be extracted despite the statute. . . .

A prohibition of mining which causes subsidence of such structures and facilities is obviously enacted for a public purpose; and it seems, likewise, clear that mere notice of intention to mine would not in this connection secure the public safety. Yet it is said that these provisions of the act cannot be sustained as an exercise of the police power where the right to mine such coal has been reserved. The conclusion seems to rest upon the assumption that in order to justify such exercise of the police power there must be "an average reciprocity of advantage" as between the owner of the property restricted and the rest of the community; and that here such reciprocity is absent. Reciprocity of advantage is an important consideration, and may even be an essential, where the state's power is exercised for the purpose of conferring benefits upon the property of a neighborhood, as in drainage projects . . . , or upon adjoining owners, as by party wall provisions. . . . But where the police power is exercised, not to confer benefits upon property owners but to protect the public from detriment and danger, there is in my opinion, no room for considering reciprocity of advantage. There was no reciprocal advantage to the owner prohibited from using his [property] . . . unless it be the advantage of living and doing business in a civilized community. That reciprocal advantage is given by the act to the coal operators.

Notes

1. *A private dispute?* This case was decided during the so-called *Lochner* era, when an early version of *substantive due process* flourished (as distinguished from procedural due process). Under that view, federal courts protected certain fundamental rights from governmental interference under the due process clauses of the Fifth and Fourteenth Amendments, which prohibit federal and state governments from depriving persons of "life, liberty, or property, without due process of law." From the late 1800s to 1937, substantive due process analysis was used to strike down well over 100 economic and other regulations—including minimum wage laws and labor laws—in the name of *freedom of contract.* You have probably studied a number of those cases in your Constitutional Law class. *See, e.g., Lochner v. New York,* 198 U.S. 45 (1905) (striking a New York statute limiting the number of hours bakers could work as a violation of the bakers' freedom of contract). Is *Pennsylvania Coal v. Mahon* merely a private dispute that involves a single private house? What arguments does Justice Holmes make to that effect, particularly in the first portion of his opinion? Does he refer to freedom of contract? What does that mean under the facts of this case? Recall *Euclid v. Ambler Realty Company* from Chapter 12, decided just four years after *Pennsylvania Coal.* In that case, Justice Holmes joined the majority opinion in upholding the constitutionality of land use regulation through zoning. Can you reconcile Justice Holmes' two positions with respect to land use regulation in *Pennsylvania Coal* and in *Euclid*?

2. *The public interest?*   On the other hand, does *Pennsylvania Coal* raise broad public interest concerns, rather than simply implicating a private dispute? What arguments does dissenting Justice Brandeis make in support of that view? How does Justice Holmes respond? As Justice Holmes indicated, the City of Scranton and the Pennsylvania Attorney General contended that the dispute raised broad public interest concerns. Scranton's brief provides a dramatic description of the wide-ranging impacts resulting from mining-induced collapse of the land surface:

> Broken brick and rubble [cover] great areas formerly improved with handsome business blocks but now permitted, in the words of Governor Sproul, "to revert to the wilderness of abandon." Our once level streets are in humps and sags, our gas mains have broken, our water mains threatened to fail us in time of conflagration, our sewers spread their pestilential contents into the soil, our buildings have collapsed under their occupants or fallen into the streets, our people have been swallowed up in suddenly yawning chasms, blown up by gas explosions or asphyxiated in their sleep, our cemeteries have opened and the bodies of our dead have been torn from their caskets.

Brief for the City of Scranton, Intervenor, *Pennsylvania Coal Co. v. Mahon*, 260 U.S. 393 (1922), *quoted in* J. Peter Byrne, *Ten Arguments for the Abolition of the Regulatory Takings Doctrine*, 22 Ecol. L.Q. 89, 99-100 n.72 (1995).

3. *Too far?—the denominator question:*   Both majority and dissent compare the property interest purportedly taken by the Kohler Act to the property interest remaining in the coal company. Suppose that a total of 50 tons of coal lay beneath the Mahon property and that application of the Kohler Act required the coal company to leave 25 tons of that coal in place as the "support estate" to prevent subsidence of the surface. What percentage of the coal has been taken? Answer this question by constructing a fraction X/Y in which X represents the property interest taken from the coal company, and Y represents the property interest against which the loss in value is to be measured. Construct two different fractions, one from the perspective of the coal company and another from the perspective of the Mahons. From each perspective, does the Kohler Act go "too far"? Explain.

4. *Average reciprocity of advantage:*   What is the meaning of *average reciprocity of advantage*? Do the majority and dissent agree? This concept is a recurring theme in the Court's takings jurisprudence.

5. *A changing world—from* Pennsylvania Coal *to* Keystone Bituminous Coal: Sixty-five years after *Pennsylvania Coal*, the Supreme Court upheld the constitutionality of the Pennsylvania Subsidence Act, which required miners to leave 50% of coal deposits in place to prevent the collapse of the overlying land at the surface. *Keystone Bituminous Coal Ass'n v. DeBenedictis*, 480 U.S. 470 (1987). The five-justice majority in *Keystone Bituminous Coal*

purported to distinguish the challenged statute from the earlier Kohler Act whose application had been declared unconstitutional in *Pennsylvania Coal.* But in dissent, Chief Justice Rehnquist opined that the challenged statute affected coal mining interests "in a strikingly similar manner" as the Kohler Act. 480 U.S. at 506. Commentators, too, have noticed the similarity of the two laws, despite the differing outcomes of the cases, and have suggested that *Keystone Bituminous Coal* is a functional overruling of *Pennsylvania Coal.* As one scholar observed, the Court in *Keystone* skirted the obvious explanation that "in the intervening forty years, attitudes had changed and environmental awareness had increased such that—in this situation—public interests now outweighed private ones." Laura S. Underkuffler, *Property and Change: The Constitutional Conundrum*, 91 Texas L. Rev. 2015, 2022-2023 (2013) (describing *Keystone Bituminous Coal* as "essentially *Pennsylvania Coal* redux"). Despite the Court's retreat from (if not functional overruling of) *Pennsylvania Coal*, it remains an important cornerstone of the modern regulatory takings doctrine.

Pennsylvania house damaged by subsidence
Source: Pennsylvania Department of Environmental Protection

6. *The place—Pennsylvania coal country:*   According to the Pennsylvania Department of Environmental Protection, "[u]nderground coal mining creates mine voids that can collapse and cause the earth's surface to subside." In Pennsylvania, abandoned mines lie beneath more than a million homes, bearing witness to more than two centuries of coal mining in the state. Those properties are at risk of subsidence, the damage from which is generally not covered by homeowner insurance policies. Pennsylvania DEP, *What Is Mine Subsidence?, available at* http://www.dep.state.pa.us/msihomeowners/What IsMS.html (visited July 20, 2015).

Penn Central Transportation Co. v. City of New York

438 U.S. 104 (1978)

Reading Guide

♦ *The test: Penn Central* sets forth a test for regulatory takings that is still the dominant test today. How does the *Penn Central* test compare to the rule announced in *Pennsylvania Coal Co. v. Mahon*?

♦ *The denominator question:* As you read the case, notice the parties' opposing arguments as to how much property has been taken by the challenged law. Which view does the Court accept, and why?

♦ *Average reciprocity of advantage:* Does New York City's challenged law provide for an "average reciprocity of advantage," as considered in *Pennsylvania Coal*?

BRENNAN, J., joined by STEWART, WHITE, MARSHALL, BLACKMUN, & POWELL, JJ.

The question presented is whether a city may, as part of a comprehensive program to preserve historic landmarks and historic districts, place restrictions on the development of individual historic landmarks—in addition to those imposed by applicable zoning ordinances—without effecting a "taking" requiring the payment of "just compensation." Specifically, we must decide whether the application of New York City's Landmarks Preservation Law to the parcel of land occupied by Grand Central Terminal has taken its owners' property in violation of the Fifth and Fourteenth Amendments.

Over the past 50 years, all 50 States and over 500 municipalities have enacted laws to encourage or require the preservation of buildings and areas with historic or aesthetic importance. These nationwide legislative efforts have been precipitated by . . . a widely shared belief that structures with special historic, cultural, or architectural significance enhance the quality of life for all. Not only do these buildings and their workmanship represent the lessons of the past and embody precious features of our heritage, they serve as examples of quality for today. . . .

New York City, responding to similar concerns . . . , adopted its Landmarks Preservation Law in 1965. . . . The city acted from the conviction that "the standing of [New York City] as a world-wide tourist center and world capital of business, culture and government" would be threatened if legislation were not enacted to protect historic landmarks and neighborhoods from precipitate decisions to destroy or fundamentally alter their character. . . .

The New York City law is typical of many urban landmark laws in that its primary method of achieving its goals is not by acquisitions of historic properties, but rather by involving public entities in land-use decisions affecting these properties and providing services, standards, controls, and incentives that will encourage preservation by private owners and users. While the law does place special restrictions on landmark properties as a necessary feature to the attainment of its larger objectives, the major theme of the law is to ensure the owners of any such properties both a "reasonable return" on their investments and maximum latitude to use their parcels for purposes not inconsistent with the preservation goals. . . .

Although the designation of a landmark and landmark site restricts the owner's control over the parcel, designation also enhances the economic position of the landmark owner in one significant respect. Under New York City's zoning laws, owners of real property who have not developed their property to the full extent permitted by the applicable zoning laws are allowed to transfer development rights to contiguous parcels on the same city block. . . .

This case involves . . . New York City's . . . Grand Central Terminal (Terminal). The Terminal, which is owned by the Penn Central Transportation Co. and its affiliates (Penn Central), is one of New York City's most famous buildings. Opened in 1913, it is regarded not only as providing an ingenious engineering solution to the problems presented by urban railroad stations, but also as a magnificent example of the French beaux-arts style. . . .

On August 2, 1967, following a public hearing, the [Landmarks Preservation] Commission designated the Terminal a "landmark" and designated the "city tax block" it occupies a "landmark site." . . . Although appellant Penn Central had opposed the designation before the Commission, it did not seek judicial review of the final designation decision. . . .

On January 22, 1968, appellant Penn Central, to increase its income, entered into a renewable 50-year lease and sublease agreement with appellant UGP Properties, Inc. (UGP). . . . Under the terms of the agreement, UGP was to construct a multistory office building above the Terminal. UGP promised to pay Penn Central $1 million annually during construction and at least $3 million annually thereafter. The rentals would be offset in part by a loss of some $700,000 to $1 million in net rentals presently received from concessionaires displaced by the new building.

Appellants UGP and Penn Central then applied to the Commission for permission to construct an office building atop the Terminal. Two separate plans, both designed by architect Marcel Breuer and both apparently satisfying the terms of the applicable zoning ordinance, were submitted to the Commission for approval. The first, Breuer I, provided for the construction of a 55-story office building, to be cantilevered above the existing facade and to rest on the roof of the Terminal. The second, Breuer II Revised, called for tearing down a portion of the Terminal that included the 42d Street facade, stripping off some of the remaining features of the Terminal's facade, and constructing a 53-story office building. . . . After four days of hearings at which over 80 witnesses testified, the Commission denied this application as to both proposals. . . .

The Commission's reasons . . . are summarized in the following statement: "To protect a Landmark, one does not tear it down. To perpetuate its architectural features, one does not strip them off." . . . In conclusion, the Commission stated:

> [We have] no fixed rule against making additions to designated buildings—it all depends on how they are done. . . . But to balance a 55-story office tower above a flamboyant Beaux-Arts façade seems nothing more than an aesthetic joke. Quite simply, the tower would overwhelm the Terminal by its sheer mass. The "addition" would be four times as high as the existing structure and would reduce the Landmark itself to the status of a curiosity. . . .

. . . [A]ppellants filed suit . . . claiming, *inter alia*, that the application of the Landmarks Preservation Law had "taken" their property without just compensation in violation of the Fifth and Fourteenth Amendments. . . .

Before considering appellants' specific contentions, it will be useful to review the factors that have shaped the jurisprudence of the Fifth Amendment injunction "nor shall private property be taken for public use, without just compensation." The question of what constitutes a "taking" for purposes of the Fifth Amendment has proved to be a problem of considerable difficulty. While this Court has recognized that the "Fifth Amendment's guarantee . . . [is] designed to bar Government from forcing some people alone to bear public burdens which, in all fairness and justice, should be borne by the public as a whole," *Armstrong v. United States*, 364 U.S. 40, 49 (1960), this Court, quite simply, has been unable to develop any "set formula" for determining when "justice and fairness" require that economic injuries caused by public action be compensated by the government, rather than remain disproportionately concentrated on a few persons. Indeed, we have frequently observed that whether a particular restriction will be rendered invalid by the government's failure to pay for any losses proximately caused by it depends largely "upon the particular circumstances [in that] case."

In engaging in these essentially ad hoc, factual inquiries, the Court's decisions have identified several factors that have particular significance. The economic impact of the regulation on the claimant and, particularly, the extent to which the regulation has interfered with distinct investment-backed expectations are, of course, relevant considerations. So, too, is the character of the governmental action. A taking may more readily be found when the interference with property can be characterized as a physical invasion by government, *see, e.g. United States v. Causby*, 328 U.S. 256 (1946), than when interference arises from some public program adjusting the benefits and burdens of economic life to promote the common good.

"Government hardly could go on if to some extent values incident to property could not be diminished without paying for every such change in the general law," *Pennsylvania Coal Co. v. Mahon*, 260 U.S. 393 (1922), and this Court has accordingly recognized, in a wide variety of contexts, that government may execute laws or programs that adversely affect recognized economic values. . . .

More importantly for the present case, in instances in which a state tribunal reasonably concluded that "the health, safety, morals, or general welfare" would be promoted by prohibiting particular contemplated uses of land, this Court has upheld land-use regulations that destroyed or adversely affected recognized real property interests. . . .

[However,] government actions that may be characterized as acquisitions of resources to permit or facilitate uniquely public functions have often been held to constitute "takings." *United States v. Causby* . . . is illustrative. In holding that direct overflights above the claimant's land, that destroyed the present use of the land as a chicken farm, constituted a "taking," *Causby* emphasized that Government had not "merely destroyed property [but was] using a part of it for the flight of its planes." 328 U.S. at 262-263. . . .

[Appellants] . . . observe that the airspace above the Terminal is a valuable property interest. . . . They urge that the Landmarks Law has deprived them of any gainful use of their "air rights" above the Terminal and that, irrespective of the value of the remainder of their parcel, the city has "taken" their right to this superadjacent airspace, thus entitling them to "just compensation" measured by the fair market value of these air rights.

Apart from our own disagreement with appellants' characterization of the effect of the New York City law, the submission that appellants may establish a "taking" simply by showing that they have been denied the ability to exploit a property interest that they heretofore had believed was available for development is quite simply untenable. . . . "Taking" jurisprudence does not divide a single parcel into discrete segments and attempt to determine whether rights in a particular segment have been entirely abrogated. In deciding whether a particular governmental action has effected a taking, this Court focuses rather both on the character of the action and on the nature and extent of the interference with rights in the parcel as a whole—here, the city tax block designated as the "landmark site." . . .

Stated baldly, appellants' position appears to be that the only means of ensuring that selected owners are not singled out to endure financial hardship for no reason is to hold that any restriction imposed on individual landmarks pursuant to the New York City scheme is a "taking" requiring the payment of "just compensation." Agreement with this argument would, of course, invalidate not just New York City's law, but all comparable landmark legislation in the Nation. We find no merit in it. . . .

[T]o the extent appellants have been denied the right to build above the Terminal, it is not literally accurate to say that they have been denied *all* use of even those pre-existing air rights. Their ability to use these rights has not been abrogated; they are made transferable to at least eight parcels in the vicinity of the Terminal, one or two of which have been found suitable for the construction of new office buildings. Although appellants and others have argued that New York City's transferable development-rights program is far from ideal, the New York courts here supportably found that, at least in the case of the Terminal, the rights afforded are valuable. While these rights may well not have constituted "just compensation" if a "taking" had occurred, the rights nevertheless undoubtedly mitigate whatever financial burdens the law has imposed on appellants and, for that reason, are to be taken into account in considering the impact of regulation.

On this record, we conclude that the application of New York City's Landmarks Law has not effected a taking of appellants' property. The restrictions imposed . . . not only permit reasonable beneficial use of the landmark site but also afford appellants opportunities further to enhance not only the Terminal site proper but also other properties. Affirmed.

REHNQUIST, J., joined by BURGER, C.J. and STEVENS, J., dissenting.

Of the over one million buildings and structures in the city of New York, appellees have singled out 400 for designation as official landmarks. The owner of a building might initially be pleased that his property has been chosen by a distinguished committee of architects, historians, and city planners for such a singular distinction. But he may well discover, as appellant Penn Central Transportation Co. did here, that the landmark designation imposes upon him a substantial cost, with little or no offsetting benefit except for the honor of the designation. The question in this case is whether the cost associated with the city of New York's desire to preserve a limited number of "landmarks" within its borders must be borne by all of its taxpayers or whether it can instead be imposed entirely on the owners of the individual properties. . . .

Notes

1. *Applying the law to the facts:* Clearly articulate the rule announced by the Court. Suppose you represented the Penn Central Transportation Company. Make an argument that the facts of the case satisfy each prong of the Court's test. If you need additional facts, identify such missing facts and how they would affect your argument. Now, take the other side. If you represented New York City, what arguments would you make that the facts do *not* support a claim for compensation for a regulatory taking?

2. *The denominator question:*   Carefully articulate the scope of the relevant property interest to be measured under the regulatory takings test, according to Penn Central and the city, respectively. Which position did the Court adopt, and why? How does the *Penn Central* Court's position compare to that articulated in *Pennsylvania Coal*? In the cases that follow in this chapter, we will see that the Court's position on the denominator question continues to evolve. In large measure, the Court's position on that issue reflects its stance on the proper balance between private property rights and the public interest. Can you explain why?

3. *Average reciprocity of advantage:*   Is the issue of "average reciprocity of advantage" (as discussed by both majority and dissent in *Pennsylvania Coal*) relevant to the *Penn Central* test? If so, under which prong does it fit best? Was there an average reciprocity of advantage here? Should the answer to that question control the outcome of the case?

4. *A web of interests—revisiting the right to destroy:*   In *Eyerman v. Mercantile Trust Co.* (Chapter 1), we thought about whether property owners should have an unfettered right to destroy their own property, or whether there should be limits on that right under some circumstances. How did you come out on that question? Here, the Court asserted that historic preservation laws encourage or require the preservation of some buildings, in part because of "a widely shared belief that structures with special historic, cultural, or architectural significance enhance the quality of life for all." Do you agree with that view? Would you treat both properties the same—the Kingsbury Place home at issue in *Eyerman* and *Grand Central Terminal*? If not, how would you distinguish one case from the other?

5. *Transferable development rights:*   Notice the Court's treatment of transferable development rights and its statement that they "undoubtedly mitigate whatever financial burdens the law has imposed on appellants." To which prong of the *Penn Central* test does the question of transferable development rights apply, if any?

6. *The place—Grand Central Terminal:*   Grand Central Terminal originally served as an important gateway to New York City and as one endpoint of a transcontinental railroad line. First opened in 1913, the Beaux-Arts structure includes such architectural gems as a 50-foot gabled entrance with statues of Roman gods and goddesses Hercules, Minerva, and Mercury, and a 125-foot vaulted ceiling using gilded paint to depict the constellations of the evening sky. Although grand, the celestial map unfortunately transposed east and west. This was due, apparently, to the artist's error of placing his official star diagram on the floor as he projected it onto the ceiling, rather than holding it overhead. To make matters worse, a railroad company brochure bragged that the ceiling would teach astronomy to generations of school

children, and that they could rely on its accuracy because the "highest authorities" had developed the map after consulting treatises dating back to the Middle Ages. A commuter soon discovered the mistake, but authorities shrugged it off. According to a March 1913 report in the *New York Times*, "Officials at the Grand Central Station . . . didn't deny the charge that things were a bit mixed, but held that it was a pretty good ceiling for all that." The error was never corrected. Time took its toll on the terminal building, and it was repeatedly targeted for demolition. In fact, Grand Central Terminal's former counterpart—the neoclassical Pennsylvania Station of 1910—was demolished in 1964. New York City reacted in part by passing the Landmarks Preservation Law that was challenged in the case above. Today, Grand Central Terminal serves as a suburban commuter station. An extensive renovation was substantially completed by 1998. *See* New York Transit Museum, *Grand by Design*, http://www.gcthistory.com (visited Oct. 28, 2015).

Grand Central Terminal (1913) (photographer unknown)
Source: Library of Congress, American Landscape and Architectural Design, 1850-1920 Images of America: Lantern Slide Collection

7. *Just passing through—in the eye of the beholder:* Compare the architectural design of the 1913 Grand Central Terminal to Marcel Breuer's proposed design. Whether the city accepted or rejected the design plan would likely influence both the market value of Penn Central's property and the broader New York City streetscape for many generations to come. Recalling our

discussion of dead hand control, how should this decision be made to achieve what you think is the proper balance between the desires of present and future owners of that property, and between present and future residents of the city?

Marcel Breuer's Grand Central Tower (proposed)
Source: Benjamin Waldman, The New York City that Never Was: Grand Central Terminal Towers

2. The Categorical Approach

Loretto v. Teleprompter Manhattan CATV Corp.

458 U.S. 419 (1982)

Reading Guide

The Court has recognized two primary categorical tests for determining whether a regulatory taking has occurred. Why, in the Court's view, do cases like *Loretto* merit their own narrow rule, without room for consideration of a range of factors? As you read this excerpt, search for a clear articulation of the rule of the case.

MARSHALL, J., joined by BURGER, C.J. and POWELL, REHNQUIST, STEVENS, and O'CONNOR, JJ.

I

Appellant Jean Loretto purchased a five-story apartment building located at 303 West 105th Street, New York City, in 1971. The previous owner had granted appellees Teleprompter Corp. and Teleprompter Manhattan CATV (collectively Teleprompter) permission to install a cable on the building and the exclusive privilege of furnishing cable television (CATV) services to the tenants. The New York Court of Appeals described the installation as follows:

> ... TelePrompter installed a cable slightly less than one-half inch in diameter and of approximately 30 feet in length along the length of the building about 18 inches above the roof top, and directional taps, approximately 4 inches by 4 inches by 4 inches, on the front and rear of the roof. By June 8, 1970 the cable had been extended another 4 to 6 feet and cable had been run from the directional taps to the adjoining building at 305 West 105th Street.

... Teleprompter also installed two large silver boxes [approximately 18 inches by 12 inches by 6 inches] along the roof cables. The cables are attached by screws or nails penetrating the masonry at approximately two-foot intervals, and other equipment is installed by bolts. ...

Prior to 1973, Teleprompter routinely obtained authorization for its installations from property owners along the cable's route, compensating the owners at the standard rate of 5% of the gross revenues that Teleprompter realized from the particular property. To facilitate tenant access to CATV, the State of New York enacted § 828 of the Executive Law, effective January 1, 1973. Section 828 provides that a landlord may not "interfere with the installation of cable television facilities upon his property or premises," and may not demand payment from any tenant for permitting CATV, or demand payment from any CATV company "in excess of any amount which the [State Commission on

Cable Television] shall, by regulation, determine to be reasonable." The land-lord may, however, require the CATV company or the tenant to bear the cost of installation and to indemnify for any damage caused by the installation . . . [T]he State Commission has ruled that a one-time $1 payment is the normal fee to which a landlord is entitled. . . .

Appellant did not discover the existence of the cable until after she had purchased the building. She brought a class action against Teleprompter in 1976 on behalf of all owners of real property in the State on which Teleprompter has placed CATV components, alleging that Teleprompter's installation was . . . a taking without just compensation. . . . The Supreme Court, Special Term, granted summary judgment to Teleprompter and the city, upholding the constitutionality of § 828. . . . The Appellate Division affirmed without opinion. . . . [On appeal, the Court of Appeals, over dissent, upheld the statute. . . .

II

The Court of Appeals determined that § 828 serves the legitimate public purpose of "rapid development of and maximum penetration by a means of communication which has important educational and community aspects. 423 N.E.2d, at 329, and thus is within the State's police power. We have no reason to question that determination. It is a separate question, however, whether an otherwise valid regulation so frustrates property rights that compensation must be paid. We conclude that a permanent physical occupation authorized by government is a taking without regard to the public interests that it may serve. Our constitutional history confirms the rule, recent cases do not question it, and the purposes of the Takings Clause compel its retention.

A . . .

As *Penn Central* affirms, the Court has often upheld substantial regulation of an owner's use of his own property where deemed necessary to promote the public interest. At the same time, we have long considered a physical intrusion by government to be a property restriction of an unusually serious character for purposes of the Takings Clause. Our cases further establish that when the physical intrusion reaches the extreme form of a permanent physical occupation, a taking has occurred. In such a case, "the character of the government action" not only is an important factor in resolving whether the action works a taking but also is determinative.

When faced with a constitutional challenge to a permanent physical occupation of real property, this Court has invariably found a taking. . . .

[In *St. Louis v. Western Union Telegraph Co.*, 148 U.S. 92 (1893)] . . . the Court held that the city of St. Louis could exact reasonable compensation for a telegraph company's placement of telegraph poles on the city's public streets. The Court reasoned:

> The use which the [company] makes of the streets is an exclusive and permanent one, and not one temporary, shifting and in common with the general public. . . . *[T]he use made by the telegraph company is, in respect to so much of the space as it occupies with its poles, permanent and exclusive.* It as effectually and permanently dispossesses the general public as if it had destroyed that amount of ground. Whatever benefit the public may receive in the way of transportation of messages, that space is, so far as respects its actual use for purposes of highway and personal travel, wholly lost to the public. . . . *Id.* at 98-99, 101-102 (emphasis added). . . .

. . . Later cases, relying on the character of a physical occupation, clearly establish that permanent occupations of land by such installations as telegraph and telephone lines, rails, and underground pipes or wires are takings even if they occupy only relatively insubstantial amounts of space and do not seriously interfere with the landowner's use of the rest of his land. . . .[5]

More recent cases confirm the distinction between a permanent physical occupation, a physical invasion short of an occupation, and a regulation that merely restricts the use of property. In *United States v. Causby*, 328 U.S. 256 (1946), the Court ruled that frequent [military] flights immediately above a landowner's property constituted a taking, comparing such overflights to the quintessential form of a taking:

> If, by reason of the frequency and altitude of the flights, respondents could not use this land for any purpose, their loss would be complete. It would be as complete as if the United States had entered upon the surface of the land and taken exclusive possession of it. *Id.*, at 261. . . .

Although this Court's most recent cases have not addressed the precise issue before us, they have emphasized that physical *invasion* cases are special and have not repudiated the rule that any permanent physical *occupation* is a taking. The cases state or imply that a physical invasion is subject to a balancing process, but they do not suggest that a permanent physical occupation would ever be exempt from the Takings Clause.

Penn Central Transportation Co. v. New York City . . . contains one of the most complete discussions of the Takings Clause. The Court explained that resolving whether public action works a taking is ordinarily an *ad hoc inquiry* in which several factors are particularly significant—the economic impact of the regulation, the extent to which it interferes with investment-backed expectations, and the character of the governmental action. . . . The opinion does not repudiate the rule that a permanent physical occupation is a government

---

5. [FN 9] Early commentators viewed a physical occupation of real property as the quintessential deprivation of property. See, e.g., 1 W. Blackstone, Commentaries *139. . . .

action of such a unique character that it is a taking without regard to other factors that a court might ordinarily examine.[6] . . .

In short, when the "character of the governmental action," *Penn Central*, 438 U.S., at 124, is a permanent physical occupation of property, our cases uniformly have found a taking to the extent of the occupation, without regard to whether the action achieves an important public benefit or has only minimal economic impact on the owner.

B

The historical rule that a permanent physical occupation of another's property is a taking has more than tradition to commend it. Such an appropriation is perhaps the most serious form of invasion of an owner's property interests. To borrow a metaphor, *cf. Andrus v. Allard*, 444 U.S. 51, 65–66 (1979), the government does not simply take a single "strand" from the "bundle" of property rights: it chops through the bundle, taking a slice of every strand.

Property rights in a physical thing have been described as the rights "to possess, use and dispose of it." . . . To the extent that the government permanently occupies physical property, it effectively destroys *each* of these rights. First, the owner has no right to possess the occupied space himself, and also has no power to exclude the occupier from possession and use of the space. The power to exclude has traditionally been considered one of the most treasured strands in an owner's bundle of property rights. . . . Second, the permanent physical occupation of property forever denies the owner any power to control the use of the property. . . . Although deprivation of the right to use and obtain a profit from property is not, in every case, independently sufficient to establish a taking, . . . it is clearly relevant. Finally, even though the owner may retain the bare legal right to dispose of the occupied space by transfer or sale, the permanent occupation of that space by a stranger will ordinarily empty the right of any value, since the purchaser will also be unable to make any use of the property.

Moreover, an owner suffers a special kind of injury when a *stranger* directly invades and occupies the owner's property. . . . [P]roperty law has long protected an owner's expectation that he will be relatively undisturbed at least in the possession of his property. To require, as well, that the owner permit another to exercise complete dominion literally adds insult to injury. *See* Michelman, *Property, Utility, and Fairness: Comments on the Ethical Foundations of "Just Compensation" Law*, 80 Harv. L. Rev. 1165, 1228, and n. 110 (1967). . . .

The traditional rule also avoids otherwise difficult line-drawing problems. Few would disagree that if the State required landlords to permit third parties

---

6. [FN 11] The City of New York and the opinion of the Court of Appeals . . . argue that a similar invasion by a private party should be treated differently. We disagree. A permanent physical occupation authorized by state law is a taking without regard to whether the State, or instead a party authorized by the State, is the occupant. . . .

to install swimming pools on the landlords' rooftops for the convenience of the tenants, the requirement would be a taking. If the cable installation here occupied as much space, again, few would disagree that the occupation would be a taking. But constitutional protection for the rights of private property cannot be made to depend on the size of the area permanently occupied. . . .

Finally, whether a permanent physical occupation has occurred presents relatively few problems of proof. The placement of a fixed structure on land or real property is an obvious fact that will rarely be subject to dispute. Once the fact of occupation is shown, of course, a court should consider the *extent* of the occupation as one relevant factor in determining the compensation due.[7] For that reason, moreover, there is less need to consider the extent of the occupation in determining whether there is a taking in the first instance. . . .

C . . .

[W]e do not agree with appellees that application of the physical occupation rule will have dire consequences for the government's power to adjust landlord-tenant relationships. This Court has consistently affirmed that States have broad power to regulate housing conditions in general and the landlord-tenant relationship in particular without paying compensation for all economic injuries that such regulation entails. . . .

Our holding today is very narrow. We affirm the traditional rule that a permanent physical occupation of property is a taking. . . . We do not, however, question the equally substantial authority upholding a State's broad power to impose appropriate restrictions upon an owner's *use* of his property.

. . . The issue of the amount of compensation that is due, on which we express no opinion, is a matter for the state courts to consider on remand. . . .

BLACKMUN, J., joined by BRENNAN and WHITE, JJ., dissenting . . .

In a curiously anachronistic decision, the Court today acknowledges its historical disavowal of set formulae in almost the same breath as it constructs a rigid *per se* takings rule: "a permanent physical occupation authorized by government is a taking without regard to the public interests that it may serve." To sustain its rule against our recent precedents, the Court erects a strained and untenable distinction between "temporary physical invasions," whose constitutionality concededly "is subject to a balancing process," and "permanent physical occupations," which are "taking[s] without regard to other factors that a court might ordinarily examine."

---

7. [FN 15] . . . A number of the dissent's arguments—that § 828 "likely increases both the building's resale value and its attractiveness on the rental market" . . . and that appellant might have no alternative use for the cable-occupied space . . . —may also be relevant to the amount of compensation due. It should be noted, however, that the first argument is speculative and is contradicted by appellant's testimony that she and "the whole block" would be able to sell their buildings for a higher price absent the installation. . . .

... The Court's application of its formula to the facts of this case vividly illustrates that its approach is potentially dangerous as well as misguided. Despite its concession that "States have broad power to regulate ... the land-lord-tenant relationship ... without paying compensation for all economic injuries that such regulation entails," *ante*, at 3178, the Court uses its rule to undercut a carefully considered legislative judgment concerning landlord-tenant relationships. ...

I

Before examining the Court's new takings rule, it is worth reviewing what was "taken" in this case. At issue are about 36 feet of cable one-half inch in diameter and two 4 inch x 4 inch x 4 inch metal boxes. Jointly, the cable and boxes occupy only about one-eighth of a cubic foot of space on the roof of appellant's Manhattan apartment building. When appellant purchased that building in 1971, the "physical invasion" she now challenges had already occurred. Appellant did not bring this action until about five years later, demanding 5% of appellee Teleprompter's gross revenues from her building, and claiming that the operation of N.Y.Exec.Law § 828 ... "took" her property. The New York Supreme Court, the Appellate Division, and the New York Court of Appeals all rejected that claim. ...

The Court of Appeals found ... that § 828 represented a reasoned legislative effort to arbitrate between the interests of tenants and landlords and to encourage development of an important educational and communications medium.[8] ...

II

Given that the New York Court of Appeals' straightforward application of this Court's balancing test yielded a finding of no taking, it becomes clear why the Court now constructs a *per se* rule to reverse. The Court can escape the result dictated by our recent takings cases only by resorting to bygone precedents and arguing that "permanent physical occupations" somehow differ qualitatively from all other forms of government regulation. ...

... I find logically untenable the Court's assertion that § 828 must be analyzed under a *per se* rule because it "effectively destroys" three of "the most treasured strands in an owner's bundle of property rights."

A

The Court's recent Takings Clause decisions teach that *nonphysical* government intrusions on private property, such as zoning ordinances and other land-

---

8. [FN 25] The court found that the state legislature had enacted § 828 to "prohibit gouging and arbitrary action" by "landlords [who] in many instances have imposed extremely onerous fees and conditions on cable access to their buildings." 423 N.E.2d, at 328. ...

use restrictions, have become the rule rather than the exception. Modern government regulation exudes intangible "externalities" that may diminish the value of private property far more than minor physical touchings. Nevertheless, as the Court recognizes, it has "often upheld substantial regulation of an owner's use of his own property where deemed necessary to promote the public interest." *Ante*, at 3171. . . .

Precisely because the extent to which the government may injure private interests now depends so little on whether or not it has authorized a "physical contact," the Court has avoided *per se* takings rules resting on outmoded distinctions between physical and nonphysical intrusions. As one commentator has observed, a takings rule based on such a distinction is inherently suspect because "its capacity to distinguish, even crudely, between significant and insignificant losses is too puny to be taken seriously." Michelman, *Property, Utility, and Fairness: Comments on the Ethical Foundations of "Just Compensation" Law*, 80 Harv. L. Rev. 1165, 1227 (1967).

Surprisingly, the Court draws an even finer distinction today—between "temporary physical invasions" and "permanent physical occupations." When the government authorizes the latter type of intrusion, the Court would find "a taking without regard to the public interests" the regulation may serve. Yet an examination of each of the three words in the Court's "permanent physical occupation" formula illustrates that the newly-created distinction is even less substantial than the distinction between physical and nonphysical intrusions that the Court already has rejected. . . .

In sum, history teaches that takings claims are properly evaluated under a multifactor balancing test. By directing that all "permanent physical occupations" automatically are compensable, "without regard to whether the action achieves an important public benefit or has only minimal economic impact on the owner," . . . the Court does not further equity so much as it encourages litigants to manipulate their factual allegations to gain the benefit of its *per se* rule. . . . I do not relish the prospect of distinguishing the inevitable flow of certiorari petitions attempting to shoehorn insubstantial takings claims into today's "set formula." . . .

B

. . . [Section] 828 does not render the cable-occupied space valueless. As a practical matter, the regulation ensures that tenants living in the building will have access to cable television for as long as that building is used for rental purposes, and thereby likely increases both the building's resale value and its attractiveness on the rental market.[9] . . .

---

9. [FN 9] In her pretrial deposition, appellant conceded not only that owners of other apartment buildings thought that the cable's presence had enhanced the market value of their buildings, App. 102–103, but also that her own tenants would have been upset if the cable connection had been removed. *Id.*, at 107, 108, 110.

III

In the end, what troubles me most about today's decision is that it represents an archaic judicial response to a modern social problem. Cable television is a new and growing, but somewhat controversial, communications medium. *See* Brief for New York State Cable Television Association as *Amicus Curiae* 6–7 (about 25% of American homes with televisions—approximately 20 million families—currently subscribe to cable television, with the penetration rate expected to double by 1990). The New York Legislature not only recognized, but also responded to, this technological advance by enacting a statute that sought carefully to balance the interests of all private parties. New York's courts in this litigation, with only one jurist in dissent, unanimously upheld the constitutionality of that considered legislative judgment.

This Court now reaches back in time for a *per se* rule that disrupts that legislative determination.[10] Like Justice Black, I believe that "the solution of the problems precipitated by . . . technological advances and new ways of living cannot come about through the application of rigid constitutional restraints formulated and enforced by the courts." *United States v. Causby*, 328 U.S., at 274 (dissenting opinion). . . .

Notes

1. *The rule of the case:*   Clearly articulate the rule announced by the Court, and the facts that support each element of the rule. Then, construct the argument that Teleprompter would make that the rule does not apply to the facts of this case. Finally, determine how this case would come out under the rule of *Penn Central.* Is the result the same? If not, which rule comes to a better result, and why?

2. *Categorical vs. multi-factor rules:*   Can you think of any other categorical rules that you have encountered in law school (not necessarily in your Property course)? What are the strengths and weaknesses of each type of rule? In *Loretto*, what policies would the majority (and Mrs. Loretto) argue that the rule advances? How would Teleprompter respond?

3. *More to the story:*   On remand, the Court of Appeals of New York upheld the validity of the State Commission's finding that one dollar ordinarily constituted just compensation to landlords required to allow the installation of cable television facilities on their buildings. *Loretto v. Teleprompter Manhattan CATV Corp.*, 446 N.E.2d 428 (1983). However, neither Mrs. Loretto nor any other

---

10. [FN 12] . . . If, after the remand following today's decision, this minor physical invasion is declared to be a taking deserving little or no compensation, the net result will have been a large expenditure of judicial resources on a constitutional claim of little moment.

landlord in the certified class applied to the Cable Commission for an individualized determination of the amount of compensation owed them under § 828. Instead, the plaintiff filed a motion to recover more than half a million dollars in attorneys' fees on the ground that she was the prevailing party. That motion was denied. *Loretto v. Group W. Cable*, 522 N.Y.S.2d 453 (N.Y. App. Div. 1987). Do these facts suggest, as the dissent feared, that the net result of *Loretto* is "a large expenditure of judicial resources on a constitutional claim of little moment"? So it seemed, at least for almost 30 years following the *Loretto* decision.

4. *From cable television to raisins:*   But in 2015, in an opinion that may have broad consequences, the U.S. Supreme Court applied the holding of *Loretto* to personal property and also made clear that the takings clause affords no less protection to personal than to real property. The case involved the U.S. Department of Agriculture's "California Raisin Marketing Order," one of many marketing orders authorized by the Agricultural Marketing Agreement Act of 1937. The purpose of such orders is to help maintain stable markets for particular products (that is, to support prices by limiting supply) by requiring producers to turn over a specified percentage of their crop to the government. The required allocation is determined by a government entity composed largely of those in the business of growing the particular crop to be allocated. In 2002, the Hornes—a family involved in raisin growing—refused to give up some $480,000 worth of raisins, as required by the relevant raisin marketing order. When the government assessed a fine against them equal to the market value of the withheld raisins (as well as a civil penalty for noncompliance), the Hornes sued, claiming that the raisin "reserve requirement" was an unconstitutional taking of their property. The U.S. Supreme Court held in favor of the Hornes, citing to *Loretto* and explaining that "[*Loretto*'s] reasoning—both with respect to history and logic—is equally applicable to a physical appropriation of personal property." *Horne v. Dept. of Agriculture*, 135 S. Ct. 2419, 2427 (2015). Should the regulatory takings doctrine be extended to personal property? Why or why not?

Problems

Consider the following factual scenarios. For each one, determine whether it constitutes a taking under the *Loretto* rule. What arguments would the landowner and the government, respectively, make? What factors should be important to the court's resolution of the dispute?

1. *Free speech at the shopping center:*   A group of high school students set up a card table at a shopping center open to the public, distributed pamphlets, and asked passersby to sign petitions to be sent to members of Congress.

In keeping with shopping center policy, a security guard escorted them from the premises. The students sued to enjoin the shopping center from denying them access for the purpose of circulating their petitions. A state constitutional provision requires shopping center owners to permit individuals to exercise free speech and petition rights on their property to which they had already invited the general public. *See PruneYard Shopping Center v. Robins*, 447 U.S. 74 (1980).

2. *From cable television to wireless internet:* A state law requires all landlords to provide high-speed internet service in their buildings. The landlords must install all necessary equipment at their own expense.

3. *Rent control:* A local ordinance prohibits landlords from raising the rent owed by current tenants until the tenants decide to move out. In one unit of landlord's building, a tenant has rented a one-bedroom apartment for the past 30 years at a monthly rent of $250. At current market rates, the landlord leases a comparable unit for $900 per month.

Lucas v. S.C. Coastal Council

505 U.S. 1003 (1992)

┌─────────────────── **Reading Guide** ───────────────────┐

The rule enunciated in this case has been dubbed the "total takings" rule. This lawsuit concerns the fate of two vacant beachfront lots on the Isle of Palms, a barrier island off the coast of South Carolina. The area is prone to hurricane activity, with an overall historic average of one serious storm striking land every 21 years. As a natural protection against such storms, the barrier islands shelter the mainland from ocean waves and flooding. This buffering action takes its toll on the barrier islands, making them unstable areas for human development and triggering erosion, accretion, and sand movement. In 1988, South Carolina enacted the Beachfront Management Act. The parties agreed that the statute was designed, among other things, to protect life and property by maintaining the beach/dune system to serve as a storm barrier by dissipating wave energy. However, under the Act, the plaintiff was precluded from building on his two beachfront lots. How should the Court reconcile the property rights of the landowner with the protection of the public?

└──┘

Scalia, J., joined by Rehnquist, C.J., White, O'Connor, and Thomas, JJ.

In 1986, petitioner David H. Lucas paid $975,000 for two residential lots on the Isle of Palms in Charleston County, South Carolina, on which he intended to build single-family homes. In 1988, however, the South Carolina Legislature enacted the Beachfront Management Act, which had the direct effect of barring petitioner from erecting any permanent habitable structures on his two parcels. A state trial court found that this prohibition rendered Lucas's parcels value-less. This case requires us to decide whether the Act's dramatic effect on the economic value of Lucas's lots accomplished a taking of private property under the Fifth and Fourteenth Amendments requiring the payment of just compensation....

Prior to Justice Holmes's exposition in *Pennsylvania Coal Co. v. Mahon*, 260 U.S. 393 (1922), it was generally thought that the Takings Clause reached only a "direct appropriation" of property, or the functional equivalent of a "practical ouster of [the owner's] possession."... [The considerations discussed in that case] gave birth ... to the oft-cited maxim that, "while property may be regu-lated to a certain extent, if regulation goes too far it will be recognized as a taking."

Nevertheless, our decision in Mahon offered little insight into when, and under what circumstances, a given regulation would be seen as going too far for purposes of the Fifth Amendment.... We have, however, described at least two discrete categories of regulatory action as compensable without case-specific inquiry into the public interest advanced in support of the restraint. The first encompasses regulations that compel the property owner to suffer a physical invasion of his property. In general (at least with regard to permanent invasions), no matter how minute the intrusion, and no matter how weighty the public purpose behind it, we have required compensation....

The second situation in which we have found categorical treatment appro-priate is where regulation denies all economically beneficial or productive use of land.[11] ...

We have never set forth the justification for this rule. Perhaps it is simply, as Justice Brennan suggested, that total deprivation of beneficial use is, from the

---

11. [FN 7] Regrettably, the rhetorical force of our "deprivation of all economically feasible use" rule is greater than its precision, since the rule does not make clear the "property interest" against which the loss of value is to be measured. When, for example, a regulation requires a developer to leave 90% of a rural tract in its natural state, it is unclear whether we would analyze the situation as one in which the owner has been deprived of all economically beneficial use of the burdened portion of the tract, or as one in which the owner has suffered a mere diminution in value of the tract as a whole. (For an extreme—and, we think, unsupportable—view of the relevant calculus, see *Penn Central Transportation Co. v. New York City*, 438 U.S. 104 (1978), where the state court examined the diminution in a particular parcel's value produced by a municipal ordinance in light of total value of the takings claimant's other holdings in the vicinity.) Unsurprisingly, this uncertainty regarding the composition of the denominator in our "deprivation" fraction has produced inconsistent pronouncements by the Court. Compare *Pennsylvania Coal Co. v. Mahon*, 260 U.S. 393 (1922) (law restricting subsurface extraction of coal held to effect a taking), with *Keystone Bituminous Coal Assn. v. DeBenedictis*, 480 U.S. 470, 497-502 (nearly identical law held not to effect a taking). ...

landowner's point of view, the equivalent of a physical appropriation. . . . And the functional basis for permitting the government, by regulation, to affect property values without compensation—that "Government hardly could go on if to some extent values incident to property could not be diminished without paying for every such change in the general law"—does not apply to the relatively rare situations where the government has deprived a landowner of all economically beneficial uses.

On the other side of the balance, affirmatively supporting a compensation requirement, is the fact that regulations that leave the owner of land without economically beneficial or productive options for its use—as here, by requiring land to be left substantially in its natural state—carry with them a heightened risk that private property is being pressed into some form of public service under the guise of mitigating serious public harm. . . .

The trial court found Lucas's two beachfront lots to have been rendered valueless by respondent's enforcement of the coastal-zone construction ban. Under Lucas's theory of the case, which rested upon our "no economically viable use" statements, that finding entitled him to compensation. Lucas believed it unnecessary to take issue with either the purposes behind the Beachfront Management Act, or the means chosen by the South Carolina Legislature to effectuate those purposes. . . . By neglecting to dispute the findings enumerated in the Act or otherwise to challenge the legislature's purposes, petitioner "concede[d] that the beach/dune area of South Carolina's shores is an extremely valuable public resource; that the erection of new construction contributes to the erosion and destruction of this public resource; and that discouraging new construction in close proximity to the beach/dune area is necessary to prevent a great public harm.". . .

It is correct that many of our prior opinions have suggested that "harmful or noxious uses" of property may be proscribed by government regulation without the requirement of compensation. For a number of reasons, however, we think the South Carolina Supreme Court was too quick to conclude that that principle decides the present case. . . .

The transition from our early focus on control of noxious uses to our contemporary understanding of the broad realm within which government may regulate without compensation was an easy one, since the distinction between harm-preventing and benefit-conferring regulation is often in the eye of the beholder. It is quite possible, for example, to describe in either fashion the ecological, economic, and esthetic concerns that inspired the South Carolina Legislature in the present case. One could say that imposing a servitude on Lucas's land is necessary in order to prevent his use of it from harming South Carolina's ecological resources; or, instead, in order to achieve the benefits of an ecological preserve. . . . Whether Lucas's construction of single-family residences on his parcels should be described as bringing harm to South Carolina's adjacent ecological resources thus depends principally upon whether the describer believes that the State's use interest in nurturing those resources is so important that any competing adjacent use must yield.[12]

When it is understood that "prevention of harmful use" was merely our early formulation of the police power justification necessary to sustain (without compensation) any regulatory diminution in value; and that the distinction between regulation that "prevents harmful use" and that which "confers benefits" is difficult, if not impossible, to discern on an objective, value-free basis; it becomes self-evident that noxious-use logic cannot serve as a touchstone to distinguish regulatory takings—which require compensation—from regulatory deprivations that do not require compensation. A fortiori the legislature's recitation of a noxious-use justification cannot be the basis for departing from our categorical rule that total regulatory takings must be compensated. . . .

Where the State seeks to sustain regulation that deprives land of all economically beneficial use, we think it may resist compensation only if the logically antecedent inquiry into the nature of the owner's estate shows that the proscribed use interests were not part of his title to begin with. This accords, we think, with our takings jurisprudence, which has traditionally been guided by the understandings of our citizens regarding the content of, and the State's power over, the bundle of rights that they acquire when they obtain title to property. It seems to us that the property owner necessarily expects the uses of his property to be restricted, from time to time, by various measures newly enacted by the State in legitimate exercises of its police powers. . . . And in the case of personal property, by reason of the State's traditionally high degree of control over commercial dealings, he ought to be aware of the possibility that new regulation might even render his property economically worthless (at least if the property's only economically productive use is sale or manufacture for sale). . . .

Where "permanent physical occupation" of land is concerned, we have refused to allow the government to decree it anew (without compensation), no matter how weighty the asserted "public interests" involved, *Loretto v. Teleprompter Manhattan CATV Corp.,* 458 U.S. 419 (1982)—though we assuredly would permit the government to assert a permanent easement that was a pre-existing limitation upon the landowner's title. We believe similar treatment must be accorded confiscatory regulations, *i.e.,* regulations that prohibit all economically beneficial use of land: Any limitation so severe cannot be newly legislated or decreed (without compensation), but must inhere in the title itself, in the restrictions that background principles of the State's law of property and nuisance already place upon land ownership. A law or decree with

---

12. [FN 12] In Justice Blackmun's view, even with respect to regulations that deprive an owner of all developmental or economically beneficial land uses, the test for required compensation is whether the legislature has recited a harm-preventing justification for its action. Since such a justification can be formulated in practically every case, this amounts to a test of whether the legislature has a stupid staff. We think the Takings Clause requires courts to do more than insist upon artful harm-preventing characterizations.

such an effect must, in other words, do no more than duplicate the result that could have been achieved in the courts—by adjacent landowners (or other uniquely affected persons) under the State's law of private nuisance, or by the State under its complementary power to abate nuisances that affect the public generally, or otherwise. . . .[13]

It seems unlikely that common-law principles would have prevented the erection of any habitable or productive improvements on petitioner's land; they rarely support prohibition of the essential use of land. The question, however, is one of state law to be dealt with on remand. We emphasize that to win its case South Carolina must do more than proffer the legislature's declaration that the uses Lucas desires are inconsistent with the public interest, or the conclusory assertion that they violate a common-law maxim such as *sic utere tuo ut alienum non laedas.* As we have said, a "State, by *ipse dixit*, may not transform private property into public property without compensation. . . ." Instead, as it would be required to do if it sought to restrain Lucas in a common-law action for public nuisance, South Carolina must identify background principles of nuisance and property law that prohibit the uses he now intends in the circumstances in which the property is presently found. Only on this showing can the State fairly claim that, in proscribing all such beneficial uses, the Beachfront Management Act is taking nothing.

The judgment is reversed, and the case is remanded for proceedings not inconsistent with this opinion.

KENNEDY, J., concurring.

The South Carolina Court of Common Pleas found that petitioner's real property has been rendered valueless by the State's regulation. The finding appears to presume that the property has no significant market value or resale potential. This is a curious finding, and I share the reservations of some of my colleagues about a finding that a beachfront lot loses all value because of a development restriction. While the Supreme Court of South Carolina on remand need not consider the case subject to this constraint, we must accept the finding as entered below. Accepting the finding as entered, it follows that petitioner is entitled to invoke the line of cases discussing regulations that deprive real property of all economic value. . . .

In my view, reasonable expectations must be understood in light of the whole of our legal tradition. The common law of nuisance is too narrow a confine for the exercise of regulatory power in a complex and interdependent society. The State should not be prevented from enacting new regulatory initiatives in response to changing conditions, and courts must consider all

---

13. [FN 16] The principal *otherwise* that we have in mind is litigation absolving the State (or private parties) of liability for the destruction of "real and personal property, in cases of actual necessity, to prevent the spreading of a fire" or to forestall other grave threats to the lives and property of others.

reasonable expectations whatever their source. The Takings Clause does not require a static body of state property law; it protects private expectations to ensure private investment. I agree with the Court that nuisance prevention accords with the most common expectations of property owners who face regulation, but I do not believe this can be the sole source of state authority to impose severe restrictions. Coastal property may present such unique concerns for a fragile land system that the State can go further in regulating its development and use than the common law of nuisance might otherwise permit. . . .

BLACKMUN, J., dissenting.

Today the Court launches a missile to kill a mouse.

The State of South Carolina prohibited petitioner Lucas from building a permanent structure on his property from 1988 to 1990. Relying on an unreviewed (and implausible) state trial court finding that this restriction left Lucas' property valueless, this Court granted review to determine whether compensation must be paid in cases where the State prohibits all economic use of real estate. According to the Court, such an occasion never has arisen in any of our prior cases, and the Court imagines that it will arise "relatively rarely" or only in "extraordinary circumstances." Almost certainly it did not happen in this case.

Nonetheless, the Court presses on to decide the issue, and as it does, it ignores its jurisdictional limits, remakes its traditional rules of review, and creates simultaneously a new categorical rule and an exception (neither of which is rooted in our prior case law, common law, or common sense). I protest not only the Court's decision, but each step taken to reach it. More fundamentally, I question the Court's wisdom in issuing sweeping new rules to decide such a narrow case. Surely, as Justice Kennedy demonstrates, the Court could have reached the result it wanted without inflicting this damage upon our Takings Clause jurisprudence.

My fear is that the Court's new policies will spread beyond the narrow confines of the present case. For that reason, I, like the Court, will give far greater attention to this case than its narrow scope suggests—not because I can intercept the Court's missile, or save the targeted mouse, but because I hope perhaps to limit the collateral damage. . . .

Petitioner Lucas is a contractor, manager, and part owner of the Wild Dune development on the Isle of Palms. He has lived there since 1978. In December 1986, he purchased two of the last four pieces of vacant property in the development.[14] The area is notoriously unstable. In roughly half of the last 40 years,

---

14. [FN 3] The properties were sold frequently at rapidly escalating prices before Lucas purchased them. Lot 22 was first sold in 1979 for $96,660, sold in 1984 for $187,500, then in 1985 for $260,000, and finally, to Lucas in 1986 for $475,000. He estimated its worth in 1991 at $650,000. Lot 24 had a similar past. The record does not indicate who purchased the properties prior to Lucas, or why none of the purchasers held on to the lots and built on them. . . .

all or part of petitioner's property was part of the beach or flooded twice daily by the ebb and flow of the tide. Between 1957 and 1963, petitioner's property was under water. Between 1963 and 1973 the shoreline was 100 to 150 feet onto petitioner's property. In 1973 the first line of stable vegetation was about half-way through the property. Between 1981 and 1983, the Isle of Palms issued 12 emergency orders for sandbagging to protect property in the Wild Dune development. Determining that local habitable structures were in imminent danger of collapse, the Council issued permits for two rock revetments to protect condominium developments near petitioner's property from erosion; one of the revetments extends more than halfway onto one of his lots. . . .

STEVENS, J., dissenting.

Today the Court restricts one judge-made rule and expands another. In my opinion it errs on both counts. . . .

As the Court recognizes, *Pennsylvania Coal Co. v. Mahon* provides no support for its . . . categorical rule.

Nor does the Court's new categorical rule find support in decisions following *Mahon*. Although in dicta we have sometimes recited that a law "effects a taking if [it] . . . denies an owner economically viable use of his land," . . . our *rulings* have rejected such an absolute position. We have frequently—and recently—held that, in some circumstances, a law that renders property valueless may nonetheless not constitute a taking. . . .

In addition to lacking support in past decisions, the Court's new rule is wholly arbitrary A landowner whose property is diminished in value 95% recovers nothing, while an owner whose property is diminished 100% recover's the land's full value. . . .

The Court's categorical approach rule will, I fear, greatly hamper the efforts of local officials and planners who must deal with increasingly complex problems in land-use and environmental regulation. As this case—in which the claims of an *individual* property owner exceed $1 million—well demonstrates, these officials face both substantial uncertainty because of the ad hoc nature of takings law and unacceptable penalties if they guess incorrectly about that law. . . .

Notes

1. *The* Lucas *rule:* Carefully articulate the rule announced in *Lucas*. This categorical rule (the second we have seen, counting the rule of *Loretto*) has been dubbed the "total takings" rule. Note carefully the contours of this rule. Suppose that the value of Mr. Lucas' lots had been reduced by 99%, rather than rendered valueless. Would the *total takings* rule still apply? If not, what other rule could the Court use, and how would the case be decided?

2. *The* Lucas *defense:*   Clearly articulate the defense to the rule, and notice its reference to "background principles of the State's law of property and nuisance." From our study of property law, can you think of at least one such background principle other than nuisance law? Must the defense be rooted in common law, or can statutory law also supply background principles?

3. *The denominator issue:*   The Court has been troubled by the range of possibilities available for determining just how much property value has been lost as a result of governmental regulation. As the Court admits, "this uncertainty regarding the composition of the denominator in our 'deprivation' fraction has produced inconsistent pronouncements by the Court" (*see* the Court's footnote 7 in the excerpt above). What position does the *Lucas* Court take on this issue?

Ten years after the *Lucas* decision, the Court appeared to modify its position again in a case challenging a 32-month moratorium on development surrounding Lake Tahoe—the third deepest lake in North America, which straddles the border between California and Nevada. Faced with an upsurge of development pressures, regional authorities imposed a building moratorium while they devised a comprehensive land-use plan and studied the impact of development on Lake Tahoe's renowned clarity. A group of landowners claimed that the temporary moratorium constituted a categorical taking under *Lucas* during the period the moratorium was in effect. In rejecting that claim, the Court explained,

> Petitioners seek to bring this case under the rule announced in *Lucas* by arguing that we can effectively sever a 32–month segment from the remainder of each landowner's fee simple estate, and then ask whether that segment has been taken in its entirety by the moratoria. Of course, defining the property interest taken in terms of the very regulation being challenged is circular. With property so divided, every delay would become a total ban; the moratorium and the normal permit process alike would constitute categorical takings. Petitioners' "conceptual severance" argument is unavailing because it ignores *Penn Central's* admonition that in regulatory takings cases we must focus on "the parcel as a whole." . . . Thus, the District Court erred when it disaggregated petitioners' property into temporal segments corresponding to the regulations at issue and then analyzed whether petitioners were deprived of all economically viable use during each period. . . .
>
> An interest in real property is defined by the metes and bounds that describe its geographic dimensions and the term of years that describes the temporal aspect of the owner's interest. . . . Hence, a permanent deprivation of the owner's use of the entire area is a taking of "the parcel as a whole," whereas a temporary restriction that merely causes a diminution in value is not. Logically, a fee simple estate cannot be rendered valueless by a temporary prohibition on economic use, because the property will recover value as soon as the prohibition is lifted.

Tahoe-Sierra Preservation Council, Inc. v. Tahoe Regional Planning Agency, 535 U.S. 302, 330-31 (2002).

4. *More to the story—the Isle of Palms:* The Isle of Palms, where this dispute took place, is a very wealthy community. At the time of the Court's opinion, the area's median household income was about 81% above the national average. As Professor Vicki Been explains:

> In 1984, Lucas headed up a development partnership that purchased the Wild Dunes Beach and Racquet Club on the Isle of Palms for $25 million. The partnership . . . developed an exclusive 1500-acre gated community that included 2500 residences and vacation homes, two golf courses, and a large marina. The project made Lucas a wealthy man, generating $100 million in sales by its second year. In 1986, Lucas sold off his interest in the partnership. Just two months later, he repurchased for himself two of the last undeveloped beachfront lots for the sum of $975,000. The fate of these two lots—severed from some 2500 other lots in the resort—would become the limited focus of the Supreme Court litigation.

Vicki Been, *Lucas v. The Green Machine: Using the Takings Clause to Promote More Efficient Regulation?*, in Property Stories 221, 225 (G. Korngold & A. Morriss eds., 2004).

Isle of Palms waterfront luxury homes
Source: Photo by David Oppenheimer — Performance Impressions LLC

During the course of the litigation, the 1988 statute was amended to allow construction seaward of the baseline pursuant to special permits issued by the Coastal Council. On remand, the South Carolina Supreme Court stated that the Coastal Council "has not persuaded us that any common law basis exists by which it could restrain Lucas' desired use of his land; nor has our research uncovered any such common law principle." *Lucas v. South Carolina Coastal Council*, 424 S.E.2d 484, 486 (S.C. 1992). The parties ultimately resolved the lawsuit through a negotiated settlement under which South Carolina purchased the two lots owned by Mr. Lucas. In an ironic twist, the state subsequently sold the lots to a developer to recoup some of its costs, and the developer built houses on those two lots.

Problems

Based on the *Lucas* rule and its defense, would the government be required to provide compensation in the following instances?

1. *The faulty nuclear plant:*   A nuclear generating plant was built astride an earthquake fault. When the regulating agency discovered this fact, it ordered the corporate owner of the plant to remove all improvements from its land. As a result, the corporation's land has no other economically productive use.

2. *The seawall:*   The owners of oceanfront lots submitted a permit application to the City for permission to build a seawall along their property. The landowners believe the wall is essential to their future plans to build a motel on their lots. The city denied the permit because the sea wall would prevent the public from using a portion of the wet sand beach that runs along the property. *See Stevens v. City of Cannon Beach*, 854 P.2d 449 (Or. 1993).

3. The Give-and-Take of Regulation

As we have seen, in a number of cases the Court considered whether regulation can *increase*, as well as decrease, the value of regulated properties. How, if at all, did this observation affect the outcome of the cases? To provide a broader perspective on this question, consider the following scholarly commentary.

Givings

Abraham Bell & Gideon Parchomovsky, 111 Yale L.J. 547 (2001)

Eclipsed by their celebrated twin, takings, givings occupy a crucial yet barely visible role in the universe of constitutional property law. While takings—government seizures of property—have been the subject of an elaborate body of scholarship, givings—government distributions of property—have been largely overlooked by the legal academy. Givings are ever-present and yet not discussed. They can be found in almost every field of government endeavor related to property. . . . [For example], when the government relaxes environmental regulations, a giving occurs. The same occurs when the government grants a license to engage in a certain business or transfers title to land or a lesser property interest to a private actor. Other examples are legion.

Like a reflection in a mirror, the massive universe of takings is everywhere accompanied by givings. For every type of taking, there exists a corresponding type of giving. . . . [G]ivings come in three varieties. A physical giving occurs when the state grants a property interest to a private actor, such as when it grants broadcasting rights or easements to cable and cellular phone companies. In a regulatory giving, the state uses its regulatory power to enhance the value of certain private properties. This occurs, for instance, when the state eliminates development restrictions in wetlands. Finally, a derivative giving is present whenever the state indirectly increases the value of property by engaging in a physical or regulatory giving or taking. Instances of derivative givings include the building of a park or the shutting down of a power plant in a residential area. In both of these cases, the value of nearby property increases as a result of the government action, even though the government action had no direct physical or regulatory effect on the nearby property. . . .

. . . [T]akings and givings are so inextricably related that one cannot have a coherent takings jurisprudence without an attendant givings jurisprudence. . . .

. . . [O]nce one recognizes that relative wealth is a potentially relevant baseline for examining state actions vis-à-vis property, one realizes that the barrier between givings and takings is far from clear. When the state takes from Jane Smith, it has made her poorer relative to the rest of the world. When the state gives to everyone but Jane Smith, it has similarly made Jane Smith poorer. Yet, current takings jurisprudence is predicated on the assumption that the relevant baseline against which the government action is measured is absolute wealth rather than relative wealth; only diminutions in property value in absolute terms trigger compensation. Once relative wealth is considered, there is no longer any justification for continuing to ignore givings. . . .

. . . [T]he same vices of the political system that give rise to constitutional protection for property in the Takings Clause also require protection against unfettered givings. The Takings Clause is meant, at least in part, to ensure that an organized "faction," in the Madisonian sense, does not use its power to enrich itself at the expense of the unorganized public. In the context of takings, the principal concern is that the faction will enrich itself by converting the private property of unorganized property owners and bringing it into the public domain. In the context of givings, the major concern is that the faction will enrich itself from the public purse at the expense of the unorganized public. Whether the faction organizes a taking or a giving, there is reason to worry about the public's ability to defend itself from the faction's predations.

Finally, fairness and efficiency, the concerns animating takings jurisprudence, mandate a givings jurisprudence as well. The efficiency rationale for the Takings Clause is to ensure that the state exercises its eminent domain power only when the aggregate benefit exceeds the aggregate cost. Compensation for takings, on this view, forces the state to take into account the cost of its actions. However, the efficiency rationale for takings compensation also dictates that the state properly measure the benefits of its actions. Just as the state's failure to internalize the cost of takings creates fiscal illusion and inefficiency, the state's failure to internalize the benefit of givings creates fiscal illusion and inefficiency. Takings, when uncompensated, generate negative externalities; givings, when unaccounted for, generate positive externalities. From an economic standpoint, neither type of externality should remain outside the state's calculus.

The fairness principle embodied in the Takings Clause is that it is inequitable to "forc[e] some people alone to bear public burdens which, in all fairness and justice, should be borne by the public as a whole." By the same token, it is inequitable to bestow a benefit upon some people that, in all fairness and justice, should be given to the public as a whole. In a giving, a small group is able to force the public as a whole to subsidize the group's preferential treatment. For example, when the state permits logging companies to chop down trees in national forests for lumber, it is forcing the public as a whole to surrender natural resources for the private profit of the logging companies.

Like current takings jurisprudence, a givings jurisprudence must focus primarily on two questions. First, when does a giving occur? And second, when must the state collect a "fair charge" in exchange for the giving? This two-step inquiry parallels the two cardinal questions of takings jurisprudence. Translating the concept of givings into a coherent law thus requires many of the same compromises as the law of takings. Just as not every "taking" in the broadest sense is legally cognizable as such, not every "giving" need enter the law of givings.

In this Article, we sketch out a framework for analyzing givings. . . .

First, policymakers must determine whether the government act that bestows a benefit (and potentially constitutes a giving) could be characterized as a taking were it reversed. For example, if a downzoning of a certain magnitude would not have been considered a regulatory taking, an upzoning of the same magnitude should not be seen as a giving. . . .

Second, policymakers must determine the extent to which the recipients of the giving constitute a readily identifiable group and the degree to which the giving is available to the public at large. Here, too, the givings analysis can echo the takings analysis. The provision of public land and subsidized use of a public arena to a professional sports franchise in a for-profit, oligopolistic sports league looks very much like a giving. The provision of public education to the public at large on equal terms looks much less like a giving.

Third, policymakers must determine whether the giving can be clearly associated with a taking. When . . . property is taken specifically for the purpose of executing a giving, the state should require the potential beneficiary of the giving to account for a "private taking," in which the beneficiary directly compensates the owners of property taken. This rule would lead to a modified application of a nineteenth-century takings rule called the "benefit-offset" principle. The analysis might also be tied to the infrequently invoked modern doctrine of average reciprocity of advantage.

Fourth, policymakers must determine whether the recipient of the giving can refuse the benefit bestowed upon her. For example, if the giving consists of an increase in the permissible floor-area ratio . . . the recipient property owner can refuse the benefit by refraining from building according to the new permissive zoning rules. On the other hand, where the state builds a park, individual owners lack the ability to refrain from enjoying the benefits of being in the proximity of the greenery. When owners have the option to refuse the benefit of the giving, the state should demand immediate payment of a charge for the giving. . . .

The relationship between takings and givings suggests two principles for determining charges. First, it implies consideration of the overall effect of government actions, *i.e.*, both harms and benefits. Second, it implies that when compensable takings are associated with chargeable givings, the recipients of the giving should compensate the victims of the taking.

A natural starting point for our discussion is the benefit-offset principle of the nineteenth century. Under this principle, the government (or private agents empowered to take by eminent domain) would reduce compensation paid for takings by the value of the benefits that accrued to the aggrieved homeowner as a consequence of the government action. For example, when a railroad laid track through farmland, the value of all surrounding farmland would rise. Using delegated powers to take through eminent domain and applying the benefit-offset principle, railroads would take farmland in order to lay track and then reduce the amount of compensation by the value of the benefit to the owner's remaining farmland.

The benefit-offset principle was a more sophisticated version of today's average reciprocity of advantage doctrine, incorporating several elements lost in the later doctrine. First, while not using the term givings, the benefit-offset principle aggregated the total value of the derivative giving and physical taking in order to determine the amount of compensation. By contrast, the average reciprocity of advantage doctrine is binary. It determines either that there is a rough reciprocity, negating the finding of a regulatory taking and eliminating the need for compensation, or that there is no such reciprocity, whereupon compensation will be based solely on the value of the taking, while the giving is ignored. . . .

Notes

1. *The idea of givings:*   Do you agree with the authors' analysis? How does their concept of *givings* relate to the average reciprocity of advantage doctrine? In this chapter, we have seen at least three examples where the law explicitly considers the benefits, as well as the costs, conferred by governmental action: (a) the calculation of just compensation in the case of partial takings (section A.2 above); (b) *Penn Central* (discussion of mitigation through transferable development rights); and (c) *Loretto* (majority footnote 15, and dissent footnote 9). How, if at all, did the notion of givings affect the outcome in those cases?

2. *From eminent domain to regulatory takings?*   In the context of *partial* condemnations under eminent domain, it is clear that courts should deduct from the value of the condemned property any enhancement to the value of the remaining property generated by the challenged governmental action (section A.2 above). Should this offset apply to all exercises of eminent domain? Likewise, should it extend to the context of regulatory takings (at least in the case of physical takings)? Should the consideration of benefits be limited to the compensation phase of litigation, or is it relevant also to the determination of whether or not a regulatory taking has occurred? The Court is divided on these issues. *See Horne v. Dept. of Agriculture*, 135 S. Ct. 2419, 2433-36 (2015) (Breyer, Ginsburg, Kagan, JJ., dissenting) (in a *Loretto*-type physical taking case, arguing that both general and special benefits should be deducted from the compensation award; if the benefit equals or exceeds the value of the property taken, then regulation has not effected a taking without just compensation). What do you think is the best approach in terms of efficiency, fairness, or some other policy?

4. Exactions and Impact Fees

Local governments use a range of techniques to force private developments to share in the costs that they impose on the community's infrastructure. Such techniques are generally called *exactions* because as a condition of approving the developer's permit applications city agencies sometimes *exact* concessions—such as impact fees to help pay for the costs of new roads, sewers, schools, and other infrastructure necessitated by the development. If proposed exactions do not satisfy standards articulated by the Supreme Court, then they can be treated as takings. Three modern cases are particularly relevant to this analysis:

The essential nexus test: The Nollans sought a local permit to demolish an existing beachfront bungalow and to replace it with a three-bedroom house. As a condition of permit approval, the California Coastal Commission required the Nollans to donate a public easement parallel to the coastline to connect two public beaches separated by the Nollan property. As a rationale for the imposition of this condition, the Commission asserted that the easement would promote the legitimate state interest of minimizing the new home's "blockage of the view of the ocean" of passersby. Doubting that a *lateral* easement would facilitate a view of the ocean along a line of sight *perpendicular* to the coastline, the U.S. Supreme Court held that the exaction was an unconstitutional taking because there was no *essential nexus* between the condition imposed and the protection of a legitimate governmental interest. *Nollan v. California Coastal Comm'n*, 483 U.S. 825 (1987).

The rough proportionality test: Petitioner Dolan applied for a building permit to increase the size of her plumbing supply store and to pave her adjoining parking lot, both of which sat in the floodplain directly next to Fanno Creek. The City of Tigard, Oregon, had drafted a comprehensive plan and a master drainage plan, which sought to minimize flood hazards by restricting construction in the floodplain (because such construction paves over lands that would otherwise absorb and slow down floodwaters). The city conditioned approval of Mrs. Dolan's building permit on the dedication of a portion of her property for flood control and traffic improvements. The Supreme Court held that this was a taking because there was no "rough proportionality" between the degree of the condition imposed and the impact of the proposed development: "[I]f we find that a nexus exists [under the rule of *Nollan*] we must then decide the required degree of connection between the exactions and the projected impact of the proposed development. . . . The city must make some sort of individualized determination that the required dedication is related both in nature and extent to the impact of the proposed development." *Dolan v. City of Tigard*, 512 U.S. 374 (1994).

From physical takings to impact fees: The Court has extended the *Dolan* and *Nollan* tests from their original context of physical takings (where exactions require the dedication of easements, for example) to the situation where permit issuance is conditioned on the payment of monetary fees. Although the Court acknowledged that "[i]nsisting that landowners internalize the negative externalities of their conduct is a hallmark of responsible land-use policy," it viewed monetary exactions as "functionally equivalent to other types of land use exactions" and therefore subject to the *Nollan* and *Dolan* tests. *Koontz v. St. Johns River Water Management District*, 133 S. Ct. 2586, 2595, 2599 (2013).

C. BEYOND THE BLACK LETTER: EMINENT DOMAIN LEGISLATION

As we noted in section A.1, above, most states amended their eminent domain statutes or constitutional provisions in the wake of *Kelo*. The amendments took a variety forms, as the following examples suggest:

Georgia
Ga. Code Ann. § 22-1-1(1) (2006)

"Blighted property" . . . means any urbanized or developed property which: (A) Presents two or more of the following conditions: (i) uninhabitable, unsafe, or abandoned structures; (ii) inadequate provisions for ventilation, light, air, or sanitation; (iii) an imminent harm to life or other property . . . ; (iv) a site identified by the federal [EPA] as a Superfund site . . . ; (v) repeated illegal activity on the individual property of which the property owner knew or should have known; or (vi) the maintenance of the property is below state, county, or municipal codes for at least one year after notice of the code violation; and (B) Is conducive to ill health, transmission of disease, infant mortality, or crime in the immediate proximity of the property.

Idaho
Idaho Code Ann. § 7-701-A(2) (2006 and 2015)

Eminent domain shall not be used to acquire private property: (a) For any alleged public use which is merely a pretext for the transfer of the condemned property . . . to a private party; (b) For the purpose of promoting or effectuating economic development . . . ; or (c) For trails, paths, greenways or other ways for walking, running, hiking, bicycling or equestrian use, unless adjacent to a highway, road or street.

Missouri
Mo. Rev. Stat. § 523.274(1) (2006)

Where eminent domain authority is based upon a determination that a defined area is blighted, the condemning authority shall individually consider each parcel of property in the defined area. . . . If the condemning authority finds a preponderance of the defined redevelopment area is blighted, it may proceed with condemnation of any parcels in such area.

Michigan
Michigan Constitution, art. 10, § 2 (2006)

If private property consisting of an individual's principal residence is taken for public use, the amount of compensation made . . . shall not be less than 125% of that property's fair market value.

Virginia
Va. Code Ann. § 1-219.1(D) (2007)

[Subject to specified exceptions] property can only be taken where: (a) the public interest dominates the private gain and (b) the primary purpose is not private financial gain, private benefit, an increase in tax base or tax revenues, an increase in employment, or economic development. . . .

Discussion Questions

Assume that your state is considering amendments to its statutory law of eminent domain. What changes do you think are desirable, if any? To guide your analysis, consider the following questions. As you answer each question, challenge yourself to draft a specific statutory provision that addresses the relevant issue.

1. *The purposes of eminent domain:*   What purposes justify an exercise of eminent domain? Should legislation articulate those purposes affirmatively (what types of condemnations are allowed), negatively (what practices are prohibited), or both? Should private-to-private transfers be allowed? Is economic development a valid purpose?

2. *Blight:*   Can eminent domain be used to eliminate blight? If so, should blight be determined with respect to an individual property, a group of properties, or by some other standard? How should "blight" be defined?

3. *Principal residences:*   Should the family home be treated differently than other properties subject to eminent domain? If so, how?

4. *Mortgages:*   Recall our study of mortgage foreclosure from Chapter 7. A few jurisdictions have considered condemning "underwater" mortgages (those at risk of foreclosure) by buying out the mortgage holder and then renegotiating more favorable terms with the property owner/borrower. Is that a good idea? Should foreclosed properties be treated as blighted? Is the buying out of such mortgages a type of *giving*? Who benefits? As one report explains,

> Even as home sales prices increase in some parts of New York City . . . , there continue to be over 60,000 homeowners in crisis. These families, concentrated in predominantly African-American and Latino low- and moderate-income neighborhoods, continue to live in a precarious world where the values of their homes are less than the outstanding balances on their mortgages. . . .

> . . . Because the banks and government have not effectively helped underwater homeowners, the city lost $1.9 billion in property taxes and other expenses associated with vacant properties from 2008-13.

> Over 24,000 of the underwater mortgages in New York are private-label securitized mortgages (PLS). These are primarily high-interest, subprime mortgages that investment banks bundled and sold on the secondary market to investors, leading to the economic collapse of 2008. . . .

> . . . New York City has the power to bring banks and investors to the table to negotiate the purchase of PLS mortgages. If lenders are not willing to engage

in this pragmatic, financially astute solution, the city has the power to use eminent domain to purchase the underwater mortgages at fair market value and provide the necessary principle reduction modifications that will help homeowners, lenders, and neighborhoods.

New York City Communities for Change, *Thousands of Homeowners Still Drowning in Underwater Mortgages: How Toxic Loans Keep Fueling Foreclosures and the Need for Eminent Domain*, at 2, *available at* http://nycommunities.org/sites/default/files/How%20Toxic%20Loans%20Keep%20Fueling%20Foreclosures%20and%20the%20Need%20for%20Eminent%20Domain%20(1).pdf (visited July 23, 2015). *See also* Shaila Dewan, *A City Invokes Seizure Laws to Save Homes*, New York Times, July 29, 2013 (discussing Richmond, California's tentative plan to "become the first city in the nation to try eminent domain as a way to stop foreclosures").

D. SKILLS PRACTICE: FORMULATING A DISCOVERY PLAN

In this exercise, we will formulate a discovery plan for potential litigation related to the regulatory takings doctrine. The plan allows you to systematically gather information, documents, and other evidence relevant to your client's case. There are many components to a discovery plan, but as a start, focus on the elements described below.

Advocacy   The Discovery Plan

- *Claims and defenses:* Review the claims and defenses of the case asserted by both parties.
- *Identify factual evidence:* Identify the factual evidence necessary to support *each* of your client's claims and/or defenses. This will require you to review the elements of the applicable law. Then, do the same for each of your opponent's claims and/or defenses. This will allow you to conceptualize the litigation broadly and to anticipate how you will respond to your opponent's evidence.
- *Identify sources of evidence:* For each piece of evidence your client will need, identify potential sources of that evidence, including witnesses (both lay and expert) and documents.
- *Prepare for client interview:* Prepare a list of questions you will ask your client to assist you in gathering information and documents, and in identifying potential witnesses.

Community Health Councils, Inc. (CHC), based in Los Angeles, describes itself as "a non-profit, community-based health promotion and policy organization" whose mission is "to promote social justice and achieve equity in community and environmental resources to improve the health of underserved populations."[15] According to the draft of CHC's *South L.A. Fast Food Health Impact Assessment*:

> Decades of research indicate that an individual's health is not solely impacted by [that person's] . . . biological predisposition or the events that occur in [the] doctor's office. Societal and environmental factors play a dominant role in the trajectory of an individual's health. A rich and diverse food resource environment provides individuals with greater opportunities to make choices that support healthy living. South Los Angeles (South LA) validates this research: it has both a high concentration of fast food restaurants and, unfortunately, equally high rates of obesity and chronic disease.
>
> In response to the inequities and impact of South LA's food resource environment, the City of Los Angeles instituted an Interim Control Ordinance that temporarily banned the development of new stand-alone fast food restaurants in South LA from 2007 to 2010. The ban was followed by a General Plan amendment limiting new stand-alone fast food restaurants from locating within a $\frac{1}{2}$-mile radius of an existing fast food establishment. The overarching goal of the ordinance was to promote greater commercial diversity by preserving South LA's limited land for healthier alternatives to fast food. . . .
>
> South Los Angeles is known as a "built out" community with limited parcels available for development. . . . Restricting fast food restaurant development to preserve South LA's limited land for healthier uses is a strategy that can have a positive impact on the community. Studies have shown that residents living in close proximity to grocery stores experience improved Body Mass index outcomes, a calculation of weight and height to assess obesity. Since the 2007 [Interim Control Ordinance], seven new grocery stores have developed in South LA.[16]

CHC has further observed that South Los Angeles has become an "icon for the plight and struggle of the inner city" that "encapsulates the health consequences resulting from the disturbing inequality of the distribution of power, income, goods, and services" in Los Angeles County.[17]

Assume that a property owner purchased a five-acre parcel of land in 2006 in the heart of South Los Angeles, with the intention of developing a fast-food restaurant. When the city denied the necessary building and other permit applications because they conflicted with the Interim Control Ordinance, the landowner brought a regulatory takings lawsuit against the city.

---

15. Community Health Councils, Inc., *Who We Are*, http://chc-inc.org/about-chc-1 (visited July 23, 2015).

16. *Available at* http://www.chc-inc.org/downloads/CHC_SLA_Health_Impact_Assessment.pdf (visited July 23, 2015).

17. Community Health Councils, Inc., *South Los Angeles Health Equity Scorecard*, at 3, Dec. 2008, *available at* http://chc-inc.org/downloads/South%20LA%20Scorecard.pdf (visited July 23, 2015).

You are a government attorney working for the city of Los Angeles. The city's senior attorney has instructed you to come up with a "discovery plan" for the city to use to build its defense. To do so, perform the following tasks:

Tasks

1. *Determine claims and defenses:*   The senior attorney has not yet told you whether the landowner seeks to invoke the rule of *Penn Central* or of *Lucas* (or the relevant scope of the parcel the landowner claims that the Interim Control Ordinance has taken). What do you think is most likely? In either case, what arguments should the city make and/or what defenses should the city assert?

2. *Identify factual evidence supporting claims and defenses:*   Identify the evidence necessary to support all elements of each claim and defense. Evaluate the evidence from the perspective of both plaintiff and defendant.

3. *Identify sources of evidence:*   For each piece of the city's required evidence, what types of information, documents, and/or witness testimony (lay and expert) will you need? What sources will you explore to gather that evidence?

4. *Prepare for client interview:*   Prepare a list of questions that you will ask your client at your initial interview to identify knowledge of relevant evidence, witnesses, and location of required documents.

E. CHAPTER REVIEW

1. Practice Questions[18]

1. *The condemned restaurant:*   After graduating from the Culinary Institute, Gabby dreamed of operating her own restaurant. She purchased a suitable commercial building downtown that was the perfect place for her new restaurant. The building was in a somewhat run-down part of town, but the building itself was in great shape. Moreover, the area's affordable real estate was attracting a steady stream of young entrepreneurs and new businesses. After the restaurant had been successfully operating for about a year, Gabby received a certified letter from the City, which stated in part:

> The City has learned that Research & Development of America (RDA) would like to open a new $300 million research facility in our City, which will employ about 90 local residents. At the last City Council meeting, after public notice and

---

18. Answers appear in the Appendix to this casebook.

comment, the Council approved RDA's plan to relocate here. Further, the Council authorized the City Development Corporation ("CDC") to purchase a suitable tract of property or to acquire property by exercise of eminent domain in the City's name. After searching for suitable property, we have identified the block on which your property is located as suitable for RDA's new facility. Please contact us so that we can discuss the purchase of your property.

After Gabby informed the City that she did not wish to sell her property, the City initiated an action of condemnation against her property. Assume that you represent Gabby. What arguments will you make on her behalf?

2. *Wetland, dry land:*   Randall owns a two-acre tract of land, the western half of which is covered by wetlands. He submitted a proposal to the appropriate city planning agency for a building permit to construct two homes on the property, one on the eastern half and one on the western half (after adding soil to fill in the wetland). The city denied the permit for the home on the western half on the basis that the wetlands were protected by city ordinance and could not be filled in. Randall sued the city, claiming that it had taken his property without just compensation. What is the most likely result?

   A. Randall will prevail if he can demonstrate that the city has denied him all economically beneficial use of the western acre.
   B. Randall will prevail, unless the city has an applicable transferable development rights program.
   C. The city will prevail because *Lucas* instructs courts to look at the parcel as a whole.
   D. The city will prevail if it can demonstrate that its regulation has not gone too far.

3. *To cut or not to cut?*   Suma has owned a plot of land containing an old-growth forest since 1990. Last year, the state passed a regulation that prevents the destruction of any old-growth forest. When Suma's application for a logging permit was denied, Suma sued the state, alleging that the regulation is an unconstitutional taking of private property without just compensation that interferes with her plans to develop the property. What is the most likely result?

   A. Suma will prevail because the regulation creates a permanent physical occupation of her property by requiring the trees to remain on her property.
   B. Assuming the regulation diminishes the property's value by 95%, the state will lose.
   C. Suma will prevail if she can show that the regulation destroys all economically viable uses of her property and that destruction of old growth forests is not a common law nuisance.
   D. The state will prevail because the government action is of a character that promotes a valid public "use" and not merely a valid public "purpose."

2. Bringing It Home

Research your state's statutory law, and find its relevant provisions on the issues listed below. Can you recommend any additions or changes to your state's statutory treatment of eminent domain?

1. *Eminent domain:*   Does your state statutorily define *public use, blight,* or specifically permit or prohibit takings for *economic development?*

2. *The timing of statutory reform:*   Was your state's law amended significantly after *Kelo* (2005)? <u>Hint</u>: If you are using an online research service such as Westlaw or Nexis, click on a particular section of your state's eminent domain law. At the end of the statutory language, you will see a section called "Credits" (Westlaw) or "History" (Lexis) which lists the year(s) in which that section was amended. Click on the hyperlink for a specific amendment and you will be able to see additions and deletions to the previous version of the statutory language.

Chapter Review Practice Questions
Suggested Responses

Chapter 1

Sunken treasure: Under the rule of *Popov*, the owner of an abandoned baseball is the first person to "acquire unequivocal dominion and control" over it. In the salvage hypothetical, Warner will want to *distinguish* the facts of his case from those of *Popov* because it is unlikely that he could satisfy the *Popov* test. Instead, Warner will argue that the court should adopt a different rule better tailored to the circumstances. For example, Warner might suggest a rule under which a cognizable property interest in an abandoned vessel is awarded to the first person that (1) discovers the vessel, *and* (2) demonstrates an intent to assert sole and exclusive possession over it (which he arguably demonstrated by publishing a legal notice in the local newspaper).

There are at least two grounds upon which Warner can distinguish *Popov*. First, he can note the physical distinction between an abandoned baseball and an abandoned ship: it is possible for a single person to acquire unequivocal dominion and control over the baseball, but not over a large and unwieldy vessel in dangerous waters. As *Popov* explained, "[i]t is impossible to wrap one's arms around a whale, a fleeing fox or a sunken ship" (unlike a baseball). Therefore, the *Popov* rule requiring unequivocal control over disputed property should not be applied to an abandoned vessel because the standard would be virtually impossible to satisfy.

Second, Warner will assert that the two situations are distinguishable based on custom. As *Popov* noted, rules are contextual in nature and "are influenced by the custom and practice of each industry." As *Popov* explained, it is customary in major league baseball to award possession of balls hit into the stands to the first person who achieves full control over such baseballs. Warner would argue that the salvage industry follows a different custom under which absolute dominion and control are not required in order to establish possession. We would need to know more about the customs of major league baseball and the salvage industry in order to make this argument.

Despite these attempts to distinguish *Popov*, Warner's position is weaker than that of Deir and Little. This hypothetical is adapted from *Brady v. S.S. African Queen*, 179 F. Supp. 321 (E.D. Va. 1960). In that case, the court held that Deir and Little were entitled to receive the entire proceeds from the salvaged property. Even though Warner first arrived on the scene, the court held that "[a] salvor cannot assert a claim merely by boarding a vessel and publishing a notice, unless such acts are coupled with a then present intention of conducting salvage operations, and he immediately thereafter proceeds with activity in the form of constructive steps to aid the distressed property."

Chapter 2

1. *The pocket watch at the farm:*   The central issue is whether the finder (April) or the owner of the locus in quo (Farmer Brown) has relatively better title to the pocket watch. First, April will argue that the pocket watch should be treated as "lost" property. The common law rule is that lost property goes to the first finder, and not to the owner of the locus in quo. *See Armory v. Delamirie* (holding that finder has better title against all the world except the true owner). Property is defined as lost when the owner unintentionally and involuntarily parts with its possession and does not know where it is. *See Benjamin v. Lindner Aviation* (defining four common law categories of found property). Under our facts, the watch was found on the ground underneath an old stump. The most logical explanation is that the true owner parted with it unintentionally and involuntarily while chopping wood, thus qualifying as lost property. April might argue that if the watch is not categorized as "lost," then it should be treated as "treasure trove," which the common law awards to the finder (here, April). "Treasure trove" refers to money, coins, gold, silver, or bullion long ago hidden in the ground. *See Benjamin v. Lindner Aviation* (defining treasure trove and explaining that it must have been hidden for such a length of time that the owner is probably dead or undiscoverable). This is a weak argument because a gold watch probably does not fit into a category including money, coins, gold, silver, or bullion. Further, because the watch appears to have been close to the surface of the earth (and not buried more deeply), it seems unlikely that anyone hid it beneath the stump long ago.

In response, Farmer Brown will likely argue that the watch was mislaid rather than lost. Under the common law, the right of possession of mislaid property belongs to the owner of the premises upon which the property is found, as against all persons other than the true owner. *See Benjamin* (defining mislaid property as that which is voluntarily put in a certain place by the owner who then overlooks or forgets where the property is). However, there is no logical reason why the true owner would voluntarily place his watch under an old stump in the middle of a farm, so Farmer Brown's attempted categorization of the property as mislaid is weak.

Under the common law, it appears that April has a better claim to possession. If the jurisdiction has enacted a finders statute, it is possible that the result might be different. For example, a statute might award title to found property to the owner of the locus in quo (which would favor Farmer Brown rather than April). This is not very likely, however, as most finders statutes tend to vest title to found property in honest finders who are unable to find the true owner within a reasonable period of time. *See, e.g., Benjamin v. Lindner Aviation* (considering state statute that awards title to lost property to first finder who fails to discover true owner within 12 months of publishing notice of found property).

2. *The neighbor's fence:*   You should convey the following information and advice to Nora: After at least 10 years have passed, Joseph *might* be able to claim title to the portion of your yard enclosed by the privacy fence under the doctrine of adverse

possession. However, from the information you provided, it's unlikely that will happen because you gave Joseph permission to use your land when you told Joseph you didn't object to the fence's placement on your property. That permission will probably prevent him from proving the element of *hostility*, which requires a showing that Joseph used your land without your permission.

To obtain title to the part of your land enclosed by his fence, Joseph will have to prove that he *actually* used the land in a way that *excluded* you. Joseph's construction of the privacy fence probably satisfied these two elements because it enabled him to use your land to park his new second car, and it appears that the fence kept you from using that portion of your own land. Joseph will also have to prove that he used your land *continuously* for 10 years, which is the length of your jurisdiction's statute of limitations for actions in ejectment. Again, the presence of the fence suggests that Joseph's use of your property is continuous, and not merely sporadic. Even if Joseph is transferred out of town, the new owner could also claim your land after 10 years by "tacking" or adding her period of possession to Joseph's possession. The law will allow this tacking as long as there is privity or some reasonable property relationship between Joseph and the new owner of his property. The transfer of a deed from Joseph to the new owner will likely establish sufficient privity to allow tacking. In addition, Joseph will have to show that his occupation of your land is *open and notorious*, such that you would notice his presence if you made a reasonable inspection. In this case, the facts suggest that you actually know of the fence and its encroachment, so it is very likely a court would deem Joseph's use of your property to be open and notorious. Finally, as discussed above, Joseph will have to prove hostility—that he used your land without your permission. Although his use is *permissive* at this point, if your friendly relationship with him should deteriorate over time, it is possible a court would find that you revoked your permission and that Joseph's use became hostile (without your permission). At that point, all elements of adverse possession would be satisfied and the 10-year statute of limitations would begin to run.

The facts indicate that Joseph may have suffered some sort of mental breakdown a little while ago. That fact is irrelevant to the adverse possession determination. Certain disabilities suffered by the true owner (you), such as minority (being under your jurisdiction's age of minority), incarceration, mental incapacitation, and the like, might toll the statute of limitations and give you an extended period of time during which to bring an action in ejectment against Joseph. However, any disability suffered by the trespasser (Joseph) is irrelevant.

Perhaps your safest course of action would be to sign a document with Joseph indicating that his use of your land is *permissive* (not hostile), and that you can revoke your permission at any time. The agreement should also specify that it remains in effect if either of you sells your property or dies (and your property passes to your successors). Such a document would protect you from future claims of adverse possession by Joseph or by his successor if he should move out of town.

3. *The bracelet at the coffee shop:*   The correct answer is **C**. The bracelet was lost, rather than mislaid, because its owner apparently parted with it *involuntarily* by dropping it on the public sidewalk. The finder of a lost article acquires rights superior to those of everyone except the true owner. The finder holds the lost property in trust or as bailee for the true owner, but may enforce her rights against everyone else. Choices **A** and **B** are

incorrect because the finder of lost property does not have rights superior to the true owner. Choice **D** is incorrect because the bracelet was found outside the premises on the sidewalk and was not under the control of the coffeehouse or its owner, nor can it be characterized as "mislaid."

Chapter 3

1.   *A* takes a life estate, *B* takes a vested remainder in fee tail, and *D* takes a vested remainder in fee simple subject to open. There is no reversion remaining in *O* because *D* holds a vested interest in fee simple that is ready to take immediately if B's blood line should die out. *C*'s unborn children hold an executory interest that will partially divest *D*'s interest upon their birth.

2.   *A* takes a fee tail and *O* holds a reversion in FSA.

3.   *A* takes a fee simple subject to executory limitation and *B* takes a shifting executory interest in fee simple. There is no reversion left in *O*.

4.   *A* takes a life estate, *B* takes a vested remainder in fee simple subject to divestment, and *C* takes a shifting executory interest in fee simple. There is no reversion left in *O*.

5.   *A* takes a life estate, *B*'s children take a contingent remainder in fee simple, and *O* holds a reversion in fee simple absolute. It doesn't matter that *C* is currently living in Wyoming, because the condition precedent concerns the circumstances "at the time of *A*'s death." *C* also holds a contingent remainder that is contingent on living in Wyoming at the time of *A*'s death.

6.   *A* takes a fee simple subject to condition subsequent and *O* holds a right of entry.

7.   Under the original conveyance, *A* takes a life estate, *O* holds a reversion in fee simple subject to executory limitation, and *B* takes a springing executory interest. When *A* dies, *O*'s reversion becomes a present fee simple subject to executory limitation, and *B* continues to hold a springing executory interest. One day later, *B* has a fee simple absolute and *O* has nothing.

8.   *A* takes a life estate, *B*'s children take a contingent remainder in fee simple (because they are unascertained), and *O* retains a reversion in FSA.

9.   The conveyance creates a life estate in *A*, a contingent remainder in a life estate in *B*, and a vested remainder in *A* in fee simple absolute. *O* does not retain a reversion. None of the five common law rules apply yet. The doctrine of merger does not apply because all three interests were created by the same instrument.

10.   After *A* conveys "all my interest" to *C*, the life estate and next vested interest (a vested remainder in fee simple) have "come into the hands" of the same person—*C*. Under the doctrine of merger, the lesser estate merges into the larger and destroys any intervening contingent remainders. Therefore, after applying the common law rules, *A* holds a fee simple absolute and *B* holds nothing. The exception to merger does not apply here—the intervening contingent remainder would have been saved if all three interests had been created by the same instrument.

11.   The conveyance creates a life estate in *A*, a contingent remainder in fee simple in *B*'s children, and leaves a reversion in fee simple absolute in *O*. Upon *A*'s death, if the five common law rules apply, *C*'s contingent remainder will be destroyed because it has not vested at or before the termination of *A*'s life estate (because *C* is still 15 years old, the condition precedent has not been satisfied). *O*'s reversion will become a possessory

fee simple absolute. Alternatively, if the destructibility rule did not apply, then at A's death, O would hold a fee simple subject to executory limitation, and C would hold a springing executory interest in fee simple subject to partial divestment (sometimes called a fee simple subject to open) by any later-born children of B. Would the RAP also destroy this interest ab initio (if we have assumed that the destructibility rule will not later destroy the contingent remainder)? No—the condition requires the children to be 21 "at A's death." Thus, the interest is certain to vest or fail at that time, which is within the span of a life in being (A) at the time the interest was created.

12.   The conveyance creates a life estate in A, a contingent remainder in fee simple in O's heirs (who are unascertained until O's death), and a reversion in fee simple absolute in O. If the five common law rules apply, then under the Doctrine of Worthier Title, O holds a reversion in fee simple absolute and the heirs take nothing.

13.   The conveyance creates a life estate in A and a vested remainder in fee simple absolute in Harry. The language "A's heir" is mere surplusage, and Harry's remainder is vested because he is an ascertained person and there is no condition precedent. At A's death, Harry holds a fee simple absolute. The result does not change under the five common law rules. The Rule in Shelley's case might seem to apply, but the conveyance does not use the exact "magic words" necessary to trigger application of that rule ("to A's heirs" or "to the heirs of A's body"). Moreover, the conveyance applies to an identified person (Harry) and not to heirs ascertainable only at A's death.

14.   The conveyance creates a life estate in A, a contingent remainder in fee simple in A's children, and a reversion in fee simple absolute in O. If A has children at the time of the conveyance, the remainder is contingent because of the condition precedent; if A has no children, the remainder is contingent because of the condition precedent and because the children have not yet been ascertained. If the rule against perpetuities applies, then the gift to "A's children" is invalid. Contingent remainders are vulnerable under the rule. A could have an after-born child, X, who was not a life in being when the interest was created. Then all lives in being could die (A and any of A's children alive when the interest was created). Then, wait for 21 years. At that time, the interest in X might still be contingent (if X has not become a comedian). Therefore, the conveyance to "A's children" is void ab initio.

If the jurisdiction follows the destructibility of contingent remainders rule, then the result would be different. Under the destructibility rule, the interest in A's children would be destroyed if not ready to vest at or before the termination of A's life estate. Therefore, the gift to A's children must either vest or fail (under the destructibility rule) at A's death. Because A was a life in being at the time the interest was created, A serves as the validating life for the interest in A's children.

Chapter 4

Trading tenants: Ava and Braydon should win the lawsuit. Together they hold a term of years in the commercial building. The initial 1/1/2016 conveyance from Liam to Alice and Bob created a term of years because it has a specific beginning calendar date (it was effective immediately) and a specific ending date or formula (the facts state that the lease was to terminate 10 years after January 1, 2010, which would cause it to terminate on January 1, 2020). In addition, the lease complied with the statute of frauds (the facts state that the agreement was duly signed and dated by the parties). As a matter of terminology, Bob's transfer of his interest to Braydon was likely an assignment (rather than a sublease) because Bob conveyed his entire interest to Braydon (both assignment and original lease terminated on 1/1/2020). Further, the facts state that Braydon paid rent directly to Liam (Alice and Braydon "continued to pay $5,000 to Liam on the first day of each month"). Although Bob remained in privity of contract with Liam, Braydon entered into privity of estate with Liam.

Liam will argue that the tenants breached the lease when Bob purported to "sublease" his share of the tenancy to Braydon. He will point to his letter to Bob in which he specifically withheld his consent to the transfer to Braydon and terminated the tenancy. He will argue that such breach terminated the tenancy, thereby giving him the right to retake possession through his action for eviction. Liam's arguments are weak, and he will likely not prevail.

Braydon will first argue that the "sublease" by Bob was valid. The facts do not give any indication that the original lease contained a non-assignment clause prohibiting assignments without Liam's consent. In the absence of such language, periodic tenancies and terms of years are freely transferable by sublease or assignment unless the lease states otherwise. Even if the lease did contain such a provision, such restraints on alienation are disfavored and strictly construed against the landlord. Further, under the modern trend, landlords may not unreasonably withhold consent for subleases and assignments of commercial leases, such as the one initially conveyed to Alice and Bob (the facts state that Liam conveyed a leasehold "in a commercial building"). Further, Braydon will argue that Liam impliedly consented to the assignment (or waived his right to object) because he accepted rent directly from Braydon and cashed the checks.

Ava will argue that her leasehold interest is valid because death has no effect upon a term of years. The facts state that the conveyance to her was valid (Alice's "valid will duly conveyed her entire estate to her daughter Ava). Therefore, Ava simply took her mother's place as Bob (or Braydon's) cotenant.

Chapter 5

1. *Changes over time:*   Initially, Aiden, Brittany, and Cody each have an undivided 1/3 interest in the property as joint tenants. The conveyance by Cody severed the joint tenancy, but only as to Cody's interest. Thereafter, Darren held an undivided 1/3 interest as tenants in common with Aiden and Brittany. Aiden and Brittany held an undivided 2/3 interest as joint tenants with one another, and as tenants in common with Darren. After Aiden died, Brittany's right of survivorship took over the entire 2/3 interest. Thereafter, Brittany held an undivided 2/3 interest as tenant in common with Darren (who held an undivided 1/3 interest in the property).

2. *The sisters and the townhouse:*   *Who owns the townhouse?* Bella owns the townhouse in fee simple absolute because the grantor's intent was to create a joint tenancy with a right of survivorship. At Ava's death, her share of the cotenancy ceased, leaving nothing that could pass to the Humane Society by will. Therefore, Bella's right of survivorship took effect, giving her ownership of the entire property in fee simple absolute.

The grant here puts two property maxims at odds: the modern trend of favoring tenancy in common to promote free alienability against abiding by the grantor's intent.

The grant expressly used the words "tenants in common," but with a prefatory clause "jointly" and a modifier creating a right of survivorship. Tenancies in common do not have a right of survivorship. Accordingly the prefatory clause, plus the intent to create the right of survivorship is probably sufficient to make it clear that their aunt intended to create a joint tenancy with right of survivorship, and not a tenancy in common. The four unities (time, title, interest, possession) were present, so the grantor's intent was not defeated by a lacking unity. Ava and Bella acquired their property interests at the same time (at their aunt's death), by the same instrument (their aunt's will), received the same interest ("with equal rights and interests"), and held under a unity of possession ("with equal rights and interests"). Accordingly, the grant satisfied the four unities.

It is unlikely that the lease between Ava and Connor severed the joint tenancy. First, without more, there does not seem to be sufficient evidence that Ava intended to sever the joint tenancy. *See In re Estate of Johnson* (under intent-based test, requiring evidence that joint tenant intended to sever the joint tenancy into a tenancy in common, rather than to terminate the cotenancy altogether and assert sole ownership). Moreover, in jurisdictions following the four unities rule, it does not appear that the conveyance of a lease is sufficient to destroy any of the unities. *See Tenhet v. Boswell* (note following *In re Estate of Johnson*). Unlike a mortgage in a title theory state (*see Harms v. Sprague*, note case following *Johnson*), a leasehold is a nonfreehold estate and its conveyance is unlikely to destroy the unity of title.

Is the estate liable to Bella for one-half the rental value of the townhouse for the period Ava was in possession? No. Under the majority rule, one cotenant in exclusive possession does not owe rent to the others unless there has been an ouster. Under our facts, there is no indication that Ava ousted Bella from the townhouse or that Bella was refused entry upon demand. Instead, it appears that Ava was simply exercising her right to occupy the entire premises under the unity of possession. *See Parker v. Shecut* (requiring unequivocal actions to establish an ouster).

Is the estate liable to Bella for one-half of any rent Ava collected from Connor? Yes, Ava's estate is liable for rent collected from Connor. If one cotenant leases a portion of the premises to an outside party, then the cotenant is liable to the others for their share of the rents received, under the theory that the lessor is acting as agent for all cotenants.

Chapter 6

1. *Drilling for oil:* The correct answer is **B**. Under the common law rule, the first to capture a "fugitive resource" acquires title to it. Choice **A** is not correct because the *ad coelum* doctrine would seem to support Sarah's claim (not Jayden's), at least for the portion of the oil that originated from beneath her land. In any case, the *ad coelum* doctrine is not a good fit for fugitive resources that do not consistently remain beneath one particular landowner's surface property. Choice **C** is incorrect because the discovery doctrine applies to real property and has not been extended beyond the context of *Johnson v. M'Intosh*. Choice **D** is also incorrect. Literally, *Ghen* awarded the whale to the person who first kills it, but more broadly, it is simply a rule of first possession.

2. *Owning a condominium:* The correct answer is **D**. Condominiums are a type of liberal commons that are a private/commons hybrid. Recall that condominiums involve private ownership of the interior of each unit (often, in fee simple absolute), and that the

exterior of the buildings and any common areas are owned as tenants in common by all residents. As such, they are not purely private property because one owner lacks the ability to exclude all other owners. But neither are they purely commons property, because each owner retains the right to exclude non-owners. Answer **A** is incorrect because condominiums are not purely private property. With respect to the common areas, no owner has a right to exclude the others. Answer **B** is incorrect. Condominiums are not public property because they typically are not owned by governmental entities. Finally, answer **C** is incorrect. Condominiums are not commons property because each owner has a right to exclude non-owners.

3. *The Raging River and the power company:*   The correct answer is **A.** Under the *Illinois Central* exception, the state can grant its submerged lands into private ownership if such conveyance is not contrary to the public trust interest in the remaining lands and waters. Choice **B** is incorrect because *Illinois Central* makes clear that the states cannot abdicate their duty to hold submerged lands in trust for the benefit of the people. Choice **C** is incorrect because the public trust doctrine does allow for a narrow exception, as set forth in *Illinois Central.* Choice **D** is incorrect because navigable watercourses are not a commons over which states retain no authority. This problem is based on a real case, *PPL Montana, LLC v. Montana,* 132 S. Ct. 12115 (2012) (determining relevant segments of rivers to be nonnavigable and therefore rejecting Montana's claim that the utility owed the state compensation for its use of the riverbeds over which Montana unsuccessfully claimed ownership). This problem, of course, is oversimplified. In actual practice, the federal government would also have something to say about this because it has a "navigation servitude" to keep the nation's navigable watercourses open for unobstructed navigation for use in commerce and other purposes. And as you might imagine, Congress has passed statutes regulating power generation.

Chapter 7

1. *The one-car Tudor:*   The correct answer is **B** because the existance or violation of private restrictions (such as restrictive covenants) makes title unmarketable. Although Barbara agreed through the contract to accept restrictions and easements of record, she did not waive her right to object to *violations* of such restrictions (here, the existence of a one-car garage violates the convenant's requirement that all houses must have at least a two-car garage). Answer **A** is incorrect. It states a proposition that is true in jurisdictions that follow the *Lohmeyer v. Bower* approach to marketability, but the contract waived Barbara's right to object to recorded covenants and other encumbrances. Answer **C** misstates the facts of this hypothetical. Answer **D** is not correct in jurisdictions that follow *Lohmeyer* (where the mere existence of a restrictive covenant did render title unmarketable).

2. *Murder on the premises:*   The correct answer is **B** because courts typically require sellers to disclose defects that are material, latent, and known/should be known to the seller (*see* notes following *Stambovsky v. Ackley*). The facts make clear that the defect is latent or hidden (because the prior murder would not be apparent from an inspection of the premises) and known to Sofia. Answer **A** is incorrect because sellers do not clearly have a duty to disclose past murders to sellers. Answer **C** is incorrect because the past murder can better be described as latent (hidden) and not apparent to potential buyers. Answer **D** is incorrect because caveat emptor is no longer the majority rule.

3. *Backing out of his promise:*   The correct answer is **D**. The check does not qualify as a writing that complies with the statute of frauds because it does not contain the signature of the party to be bound (seller Sergio). Answer **A** is true, but incomplete (the signed writing must also contain Sergio's signature). Answer **B** is incorrect because the stringent "unequivocally referable" standard cannot be satisfied simply by the filing of a lawsuit. Answer **C** is incorrect because inadequate restitution would help to make the case for contract enforcement (not for nonenforcement, as the response suggests).

4. *Adverse possession:*   The correct response is **D.** Although title by adverse possession can be "marketable title" (but not marketable *record* title until it has been adjudicated and recorded), Sapphire must make the case before a court or other appropriate tribunal. Response **A** is true but incomplete Answer **B** is an incorrect statement of the law. Answer **C** is incorrect. Although the absence of a "time is of the essence" would assist Sapphire by potentially allowing her time to prove her case, it is not enough for Sapphire to prevail.

Chapter 8

1.   The correct response is **C.** The jurisdiction has a notice statute (the phrase "unless such conveyance is duly recorded" refers to a conveyance in COT #1 unrecorded *at the time* of a subsequent conveyance). Under that statute, Carlos will prevail if the conveyance to Bianca was unrecorded at the time he received his deed (Bianca's later recording doesn't count) and if he took without notice of Bianca's prior interest. The facts indicate that both requirements were satisfied. First, Bianca did not record until after Carlos accepted his deed. Second, Carlos lacked notice of Bianca's prior interest. Carlos lacked actual notice (he "had no notice of the deed to Bianca"), record notice (Bianca's deed was not recorded until later), and inquiry notice (Bianca was not in possession so as to prompt further inquiry).

2.   The correct response is **A.** There is a prior unrecorded conveyance in COT #1 because Aaron's deed was unrecorded at the moment *Bianca* took title. Because Bianca took without notice and recorded first, her title is superior to Aaron's title under any type of recording act. Therefore, the shelter rule protects her interest and allows her to pass good title to Carlos, even though Carlos took *with* notice of the prior conveyance to Aaron, and Carlos recorded after Aaron. Any other result would penalize Bianca, who was "rescued" under all three types of recording acts from the common law default rule that would otherwise favor Aaron's prior interest in the property.

3.   The correct response is **A.** In a notice jurisdiction, Bianca's title is superior to that of Aaron's because she took title without notice of Aaron's prior interest (he did not record until later). However, because Bianca did not promptly record her title, she failed to give notice to subsequent purchasers such as Carlos. At the time he took title, Carlos had no notice of the prior conveyance to Bianca (because she did not record until later). Therefore, Carlos' interest is superior to Bianca's interest.

4.   Under any type of recording act, Bianca holds better title than Aaron because she took without notice of Aaron's prior interest and recorded first. Therefore, under the shelter rule, Bianca can pass good title to Carlos, even though he was not a BFP (he did not pay value and he took *with* notice of the prior conveyance to Aaron).

5.   Bianca prevails under any type of recording act. At the moment Bianca took title, she was a BFP (she had not yet received notice of the prior conveyance to Aaron and she paid value). She also won the race to the courthouse and recorded first.

Chapter 9

1. *The buried utility cable:*   The correct response is **A.** Laura has an easement implied from prior use. The requirements include proof of unity of title during the time of prior use and prior use (apparent, continuous, and necessary). Response **C** is incorrect. Although courts will closely scrutinize claimed reservations, there is sufficient evidence here to prove Laura's implied easement. Response **D** is incorrect. Although she might also be able to prove an easement implied from necessity, we would need more evidence as to whether she has strict necessity (the mere fact that her parcel is landlocked does not necessarily mean that there is no other path for an underground utility cable to follow).

2. *Driving through the neighbor's property:*   The correct response is **D.** If the jurisdiction follows the "stranger to the deed" rule, then it will not recognize easements reserved in favor of third parties such as Brian. Brian has not acquired an easement by prescription (response **A**) because he used the road with the permission of Amy and therefore his use was not hostile. Although Brian's easement might have terminated upon sale (response **B**), it would continue in jurisdictions that reject the "stranger" to the deed rule. Although Brian may have an express easement across Anita's property (response **C**), he will have nothing if the jurisdiction follows the old common law "stranger to the deed" rule.

3. *A lakefront resort:*   The correct response is **B.** Most courts today hold that commercial easements in gross are both divisible and transferable (including assignments), provided that the burden is not increased. Easements are not required to "touch and concern" land (as suggested by response **A**).

4. *A change of plans:*   The correct response is **D.** Under the majority rule, an easement appurtenant must be used only for the benefit of the dominant parcel (here, Steve's Lot #2). As long as the easement is used for the benefit of Lot #2, however, the burden may expand to allow for reasonable, foreseeable expansion of the uses on Lot #2. Answer **C** is incorrect. The common law rigidly insists on confining the benefit to the dominant parcel, even if there is no increased burden on the servient tract (here, Charlotte's Lot #1).

Chapter 10

1. *Good fences make good neighbors:*   Abu's promise creates an affirmative covenant (response **C**). It is affirmative because he promised to perform a specific act (maintain his fence), and it is a covenant (rather than an easement) because it promises to perform an act and does not grant him the right to use the land of another (as would an easement).

2. *The deteriorating fence:*   The correct response is **C.** Because Mia seeks money damages, the agreement must satisfy the requirements of real covenants running at law. Here, there is no horizontal privity of estate between the original promising parties (Abu

and Martha). They were simply neighbors, and there is no evidence that they were in a landlord-tenant relationship, shared simultaneous privity, or successive privity. Although the Restatement (Third) of Property, Servitudes, calls for an abandonment of the horizontal privity requirement, there is no evidence that this jurisdiction has adopted the minority Restatement approach.

3. *Fix that fence!*   The correct response is **A**. In this case, the problem must be analyzed as an equitable servitude because Mia is seeking injunctive relief. In equity, no horizontal privity is required (response **C**). Although equity does require vertical privity (response **D**), that requirement is satisfied here by Martha's conveyance of her full property interest to Mia.

4. *No fences make good neighbors?*   Zelda's negative promise (to never erect a fence) created either a negative easement or a negative covenant. Because the promise does not fit easily into one of the four negative *easement* categories recognized at common law (involving light, air, artificial stream flow, and building support), the promise is a negative *covenant* (response **A**).

5. *The buried wetland:*   The correct response is **D**. If Micah seeks damages, he generally must satisfy the requirements of real covenants running at law, including horizontal privity (satisfied by the conveyance of Tract #2 by Sophia to Mason), relaxed vertical privity on the benefit side (satisfied by the lease from Mason to Micah), and strict vertical privity on the burden side (***not satisfied*** by Sophia's conveyance of a 99-year lease to Sara).

Chapter 11

1. *The siren and the birds:*   *Trespass:* It is unlikely that Abigail can bring a trespass action. To do so, she would have to prove that an intentional act of the county (testing its emergency alert siren system) caused a physical invasion of her property. The plaintiff would not be able to prove a physical invasion unless the jurisdiction recognizes sound as a tangible thing.

Private nuisance: Abigail can probably bring a valid claim for private nuisance. To do so, she must prove that the county engaged in a volitional act that caused an unreasonable and substantial interference with her use and enjoyment of her property. Under our facts, the county affirmatively undertook to lease space on the tower for an emergency alert system and also intended to test the system regularly. Therefore the county's conduct was intentional. Second, Abigail must prove that she has an interest in the land affected. This element is satisfied because the facts state that she owned a cabin on a secluded mountain property. Third, Abigail must prove that the county's testing of the siren caused a nontrespassory interference with her use and enjoyment of the land. If the court treats sound as something other than a tangible, physical invasion, then she will be able to show that the county interfered with her use and enjoyment of the land. Fourth, Abigail must prove that the siren's interference rose to a level that was substantial and unreasonable to a plaintiff of average sensitivity. The facts state that the emergency tests caused her to go inside and close her windows, and that they might have interfered with her birdwatching activities. We would need more facts to decide if this element is satisfied. However, if the court follows the utilitarian balancing test of the Restatement (Second) of Torts, Nuisance, §§ 826-828, then Abigail may have difficulty proving that the gravity of the harm outweighs the utility of the actor's conduct. Here, that would mean that Abigail would have to show that the weekly interferences (for 15 minutes) with her outdoor activities outweighed the utility of the county's testing of its safety system. This would be the biggest hurdle that Abigail would have to overcome in bringing a private nuisance action.

Public nuisance: To bring a public nuisance action, Abigail must show that the county's intentional act (testing its siren) caused an unreasonable interference with the public health, safety, morals, comfort, or convenience. As described above, she would have to demonstrate that the interference was substantial and unreasonable. In addition, public nuisance actions are generally brought by public officials. If a private plaintiff such as Abigail wants to bring such an action, then she must prove that she suffered harm distinct in kind (and not merely degree) from that suffered by the general public. Abigail will argue that the harm she suffered was different than that suffered by the general public because she enjoyed birdwatching and because her home was located in close proximity to the siren testing equipment. We would need more facts to determine whether others also lived nearby and/or enjoyed birdwatching in the area.

2. *The elements of private nuisance:*   To establish a private nuisance, the plaintiff must prove that the defendant caused a nontrespassory, substantial and unreasonable interference with the plaintiff's use and enjoyment of land. Therefore, answers **A** and **D** are *not* elements that the plaintiff must prove. The essence of a nuisance claim is that the defendant's conduct *interferes* with the plaintiff's use and enjoyment, not that the defendant's conduct is unlawful (as answer **A** incorrectly suggests). The interference must be indirect in the sense that it is nontrespassory (answer **B**). The level of the interference must be unreasonable and substantial (answer **C**). Although the defendant must have intended to take action, it is not necessary that the defendant intended to interfere with the plaintiff's land use and enjoyment (as answer **D** incorrectly suggests).

3. *The plaintiff:*   The correct response is **B**. In a public nuisance action, the plaintiff is usually a public official bringing an action on behalf of the general public. In some cases, private individuals can also bring public nuisance actions if they suffer harm distinct in kind and not merely degree from that suffered by the general public (therefore response **D** describes a likely plaintiff). In a public nuisance action, the plaintiff must have some sort of an interest in the land purportedly affected by the nuisance, including such things as a life estate, or perhaps even an adverse possessory interest in some cases (therefore responses **A** and **C** describe potential plaintiffs). Only response **B** describes someone who has no possessory interest in the affected land, and therefore the party least likely to be able to bring a nuisance action.

Chapter 12

1. *Apartments not welcome:*   The correct response is **A**. The ordinance must be a rational means of achieving a permissible governmental purpose. Answer **B** is incorrect because economic status is not a protected class. Answer **C** is incorrect because it incorrectly pairs a *necessary* means with a *permissible* governmental purpose (the rational basis test simply requires a rational means/permissible governmental purpose, whereas the strict scrutiny test requires a necessary means/compelling governmental purpose).

This hypothetical is from the *Black Jack* case, which was brought under the FHA, not under the equal protection clause. *Black Jack* was likely brought under the FHA so that the plaintiffs could take advantage of the disparate impact theory. Under the equal protection clause, plaintiffs must instead bear the more onerous burden of proving a discriminatory intent or purpose (rather than a discriminatory effect). *See Village of Arlington Heights v. Metropolitan Housing Development Corp.,* 429 U.S. 252 (1977).

2. *Give me space:* The correct response is **D.** This hypothetical is modeled after the *Mount Laurel* case (note 3 following *United States v. City of Black Jack*). Some state constitutions, like New Jersey's, have been interpreted to require each jurisdiction to provide for its "fair share" of affordable housing, but this is a minority view. Under the equal protection clause, mere statistical disparity is not enough. Instead, as *Black Jack* shows, the plaintiff must establish robust causality—the ordinance *caused* the municipality's racial imbalance, not that it was a pre-existing situation.

3. *The variance:* The correct response is **B**, which is the only answer that does not set forth a required element for obtaining a variance. Both use and bulk restrictions can be the proper subject of a variance.

Chapter 13

1. *The condemned restaurant:* Gabby will have a difficult time making arguments in opposition to the city's eminent domain action. Nevertheless, she will draw on some of the limitations in *Kelo v. City of New London* when formulating her arguments. First, she will argue that "the sovereign may not take the property of *A* for the sole purpose of transferring it to another private party *B*, even though *A* is paid just compensation" unless the transfer serves some legitimate public purpose, as stated by the *Kelo* majority. The city plans to transfer Gabby's private property to Research & Development of America, presumably a private corporation. The city has not articulated a clear public purpose for the transfer, but has only asserted that RDA will employ about 90 local residents. Although economic redevelopment can be a valid public purpose, the city cannot assert such purpose as a mere pretext for a private-to-private transfer. Here, the transfer will create only 90 jobs, and it is not clear that the city is in need of economic redevelopment (the facts state that Gabby's building is in a somewhat run-down part of town, but also that the area was attracting a steady stream of young entrepreneurs and new businesses). In contrast to the stronger public purposes served by the condemnations in *Kelo* (1,000 jobs and increased tax revenues), *Berman* (redevelopment in a blighted neighborhood where housing for about 5,000 people "was beyond repair"), and *Hawaii Midkiff* (eliminating the "social and economic evils of a land oligopoly"), the public purpose rationale in the hypothetical case seems thin (although we would need more facts, such as the population of the city and the current number of available jobs).

Second, although the Supreme Court has upheld condemnations for private-to-private transfers, it has done so in cases where the taking "would be executed pursuant to a carefully considered development plan" (*Kelo*, Justice Kennedy concurring). Here, the city asserted that it provided public notice and received public comment on its RDA relocation plan, but it is not clear that such efforts rise to the level of the carefully considered plan sustained in *Kelo*.

Finally, as Justice Kennedy noted in his *Kelo* concurrence, a heightened standard of review might be appropriate in some cases where "the transfers are so suspicious, or the procedures employed so prone to abuse, or the purported benefits are so trival . . . that courts should presume an impermissible private purpose." Here, in contrast to the cases noted by Justice Kennedy, the private beneficiary is known in advance, the projected economic benefits can conceivably be cast as *de minimis*, and there is no evidence that the city is suffering from a serious citywide depression that will be addressed by a comprehensive development plan. Under such circumstances, Gabby will argue that the city must show more than its RDA relocation plan is rationally related to a conceivable public purpose.

In addition to those two arguments under federal constitutional law, Gabby will research whether the relevant state has enacted legislation (possibly in the wake of *Kelo*) imposing additional limitations on the power of eminent domain.

2. *Wetland, dry land:*   The correct response is **D** (drawing on the broad test from *Pennsylvania Coal Co. v. Mahon*). Answer **A** is not the best answer because the Supreme Court now seems to focus on the "parcel as a whole" when determining whether or not a total taking has occurred. *See Tahoe-Sierra Preservation Council, Inc. v. Tahoe Regional Planning Agency* (note case after *Lucas v. S.C. Coastal Council*). Answer **B** is not correct because the mere existence of a transferable development rights program is not sufficient to provide a defense to the city. Answer **C** is incorrect because *Lucas* did not look at the parcel as a whole (although the Supreme Court later did so in *Tahoe-Sierra Preservation Council*).

3. *To cut or not to cut:*   The correct response is **C**, which is drawn from the *Lucas* test (the total takings test) and defense (drawing on background principles of state law). Answer **A** does not follow logically from *Loretto*'s permanent physical invasion test. Answer **B** is incorrect because anything short of a 100% diminution in value requires consideration of the three *Penn Central* factors. Answer **D** is incorrect because this goes to the question of whether or not the state can condemn property under its eminent domain authority, not whether a state regulation works a regulatory taking.

TABLE OF CASES

Italics indicate principal cases.

INDEX